WASHINGTON BOATING AND WATER SPORTS

WASHINGTON BOATING AND WATER SPORTS

FIRST EDITION

Terry Rudnick

FOGHORN ✺ OUTDOORS

WASHINGTON BOATING AND WATER SPORTS
FIRST EDITION

Printing History
1st edition—April 2000

5 4 3 2 1 0

All photographs by Terry Rudnick,
except where otherwise noted.

Front cover photo: © Index Stock Imagery

Editors: Jean-Vi Lenthe, Carolyn Perkins, Jeannie Trizzino, Marisa Solís
Design and Production: David Hurst, Aaron Cruse
Cartography: Mark Aver, Mike Morgenfeld, Chris Alvarez
Index: Erin Van Rheenen

ISBN: 1-57354-071-4
Library of Congress
Cataloging-in-Publication Data
has been applied for.

Published by
Avalon Travel Publishing
5855 Beaudry St.
Emeryville, CA 94608 USA

Printed in the United States of America

Please send all comments, corrections,
additions, amendments, and critiques to:
Foghorn Outdoors
WASHINGTON BOATING
AND WATER SPORTS
First Edition
Avalon Travel Publishing
5855 Beaudry St.
Emeryville, CA 94608 USA
email: info@travelmatters.com
website: www.travelmatters.com

Distributed in the United States and Canada
by Publishers Group West.

*This book is for Adam,
the light of my life for the past 17 years.*

TABLE OF CONTENTS

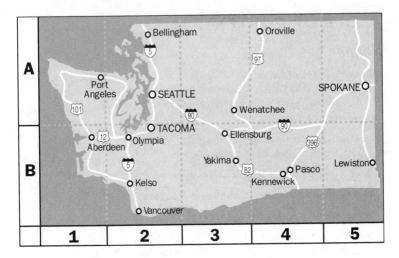

MAPS

HOW TO USE THIS BOOK

One challenge that comes from creating a comprehensive guide to the state's 1,000+ boating spots is the task of how best to present all the information. We started by dividing Washington into 10 sections using a standard grid format. Each of the 10 sections represents a chapter, which is composed of all boating spots found in that area. Reference maps showing the 10 divisions of Washington state can be found on the opposite page and on the last page of this book. Detailed maps of each section are located at the beginning of each chapter. Unless otherwise noted, on all maps one inch equals approximately 20 miles.

Here are two approaches to using this book:

1. If you know the name of the lake, creek, reservoir, pond, river, or coastal area you want to go to, or the corresponding geographical area (a town or national park, for example), turn to the index beginning on page 409 to locate it.

2. If you want to boat in a particular part of the state, turn to the Washington state map on the opposite page or on the last page of this book. Locate the area you're interested in and turn to the corresponding chapter, which opens with a map on which every boating spot is clearly numbered. On this map you can locate individual boating or water sport destinations and then turn to those numbered sites in the chapter.

Acknowledgments

Thanks to the many people who helped in many ways as I researched and wrote this book. Those who helped with it included Kendra Bartlett, Adam Rudnick, Amy Jackson, Jessica Eklund, and Roxie Stancil. Thanks to all of you for a job well-done. Mark Kenny also deserves my thanks for the advice he offered and the research materials he loaned. Thanks to James Horan, who gladly allowed me to take time off when I had to write. Thanks to my son, Adam, for his patience and understanding as his dad waded through another book project. And thanks especially to Roberta Garrett, who knew I could do it and who understands why I do it.

Research Assistant: Kendra Bartlett

Our Commitment

We are committed to making *Washington Boating and Water Sports* the most accurate, thorough, and enjoyable guide to pleasure boating facilities in the state. You can rest assured that every boating spot in this book has been carefully reviewed and double-checked. However, with the change of seasons, you can bet that some of the fees listed herein have gone up and that some boating destinations may have opened, closed, or changed hands. If you would like to comment on the book, whether it's to suggest a location that's been overlooked or to let us know about any noteworthy experience—good or bad—that occurred while using *Washington Boating and Water Sports* as your guide, we would appreciate hearing from you. Please address all correspondence to:

Foghorn Outdoors:
Washington Boating and Water Sports
First Edition
Avalon Travel Publishing
5855 Beaudry Street
Emeryville, CA 94608
U.S.A.

email: info@travelmatters.com

BOATING TIPS

Boating Safety Equipment

One of the first things I did when I bought my first boat was to ask around about what equipment I was required to have onboard. I was surprised at the wide range of answers I got, most of them at least partly incorrect. Somebody told me a paddle was required equipment, in case my motor broke down. It's a good idea, and I do carry one, but it's not required by state or federal law. Someone else said I had to have a spotlight if I was going to run at night. Again, nice to have, but not required. On the other hand, no one told me about needing a sound-making device, which is required, and only one out of the four or five people I talked to mentioned the requirement to carry flares and other visual distress equipment.

So, what *do* you need on your boat? For safety's sake, I'd say load 'er down with all the equipment you can get onboard. Legally, though, there are just a few basics that you must have.

Horn, Whistle, Bell If your boat is under 12 meters (mine sure as hell is, way under) all you need in Washington is some means of making an efficient sound signal. "Efficient," of course, means more than a grunt or a short shriek: that's no way to get someone's attention. An efficient sound comes from a whistle or horn capable of producing a blast of two seconds or more. The device can be mouth-, hand-, or power-operated, but it must be audible for at least one-half mile. Handheld air horns work very well, as do some whistles, so I carry an air horn under my boat seat and have a whistle on my key ring. In addition, all my life jackets are equipped with whistles.

Boats 12 meters (39.4 feet) or more in length must be equipped with a whistle and a bell. The whistle must be audible for at least one mile, and the mouth of the bell has to be at least 200 millimeters (nearly eight inches) in diameter.

Life Jackets Since 1995 both state and federal law have required that all recreational boats, of any length, with or without motors of any kind, must carry U.S. Coast Guard-approved Type I, Type II, or Type III life jackets in good condition and the right sizes for everyone on board. In addition, all Class I, Class 2, and Class 3 boats (16 feet and over) must carry at least one Class IV (throwable) flotation device. Canoes and kayaks 16 feet and over are exempted from this second requirement.

Fire Extinguishers Boat owners need to consider both the number and type of extinguishers they should have onboard. Fire extinguishers are rated by their ability to put out fires of different kinds and sizes, and there are minimum requirements depending on the size and design of your boat. For starters, all inboard boats and all outboard boats 26 feet and longer must have approved fire extinguishers. In addition, outboards under 26 feet must carry extinguishers if they have any of the following:

- Closed compartments under seats and thwarts where portable fuel tanks may be stored

- Double bottoms that are not sealed to the hull or that are not completely filled with flotation material

- Closed living spaces

- Closed storage compartments where combustible or flammable materials are stowed

- Permanently installed fuel tanks

- As for how many and what kind of extinguishers are required, boats under 26 feet need one B-I or equivalent, boats 26 to 40 feet must have two B-I or equivalent, and boats 40 to 65 feet must have three B-I or equivalent extinguishers. B-type extinguishers are rated for flammable liquids, and include carbon dioxide, Halon/Freon, dry chemical, and foam types.

And even if it's not required on your outboard, you'll probably feel better if you have one anyway. I've never used mine, but I sure like looking down and seeing it there.

Visual Distress Equipment

All recreational boats must be equipped with visual distress signals (flares and such) when the boat is used on coastal waters and the ocean. Some boats are exempt from the requirements for day signals but must carry night signals when operating at night. Those exemptions include

- Recreational boats less than 16 feet long

- Open sailboats less than 26 feet long that are not equipped with propulsion machinery

- Manually propelled boats

Pyrotechnic visual distress signals must be U.S. Coast Guard-approved, in serviceable condition, and readily accessible. They're marked with a date showing their serviceable life and do not meet legal requirements after that date. (Expired signals may, however, be carried as extras.)

If you carry pyrotechnic devices (flares), a minimum of three must be carried. Any combination can be carried as long as they add up to three signals for day use and three signals for night use. Three day/night signaling devices meet both requirements.

U.S. Coast Guard-approved pyrotechnic visual distress signals and associated devices meet both requirements. They include the following:

- Pyrotechnic red flares, either handheld or aerial
- Pyrotechnic orange smoke, handheld or floating
- Launchers for aerial red meteors or parachute flares

Non-pyrotechnic visual distress signaling devices must carry the manufacturer's certification that they meet Coast Guard requirements. Like the others, they must be in serviceable condition and readily accessible. This group includes orange distress flags and electric distress signals. If you're smart, you'll carry a selection of distress signals. No one device is perfect for all situations.

Backfire *Flame* *Arresters* To safeguard against fire, all inboard, gasoline-burning motorboats must have a U.S. Coast Guard-approved backfire flame arrester on each carburetor.

Ventilation *System* Boat manufacturers install exhaust blowers in engine compartments so gasoline fumes can be eliminated before the engines are started. State and federal rules require ventilation of all enclosed engine and fuel tank compartments on gasoline-powered boats. These regulations are very specific about details of boat ventilation systems. For example, ventilation ducts have to be at least two inches in diameter, and exhaust ducts must extend from the lower bilge to cowls in the open air.

Boater's Pre-Season Checklist

There's not really a start or an end to the boating season here in the Evergreen State, but most of us have times when we're less active on the water than other times. Those lulls are great times to take care of all the little things that will help make life on the water (or getting to the water) more pleasant next time around. A pre-season checklist is one way to help remind yourself of what needs to be done between seasons or at least once a year. Here's a list that works for me:

Boat • Check and repair all lights. These are among the most common victims of corrosion and vibration. Keeping your running lights and other boat lights working properly requires continuous attention, regular cleaning, and frequent repair.

- Check and maintain batteries. Check water levels and add water as needed, disconnect and clean terminals, lubricate terminals to reduce corrosion, and be sure to tighten cable connections when you're done.

- Check and repair all wiring, electrical connections, and switches, and replace bad or old fuses.

- Clean the bilge and check the bilge pump. Don't wait until you're on the water to find out it doesn't work. Fishing line, sand, gravel, and everything else you can think of ends up in the bilge, clogging and damaging the pump.

- Check the horn, whistle, or other sound device. This is required equipment, yet many don't have one that works. It's not a bad idea to have two or three noisemakers onboard in case of emergency.

- Inspect all hoses and fittings, paying special attention to fuel lines and connections. One problem here and you could lose power or become the victim of a serious fire or explosion. Plastic fitting and rubber fuel lines have fairly short life expectancies, especially those exposed to heat, cold, and bright sun. Be sure fuel line clamps are snug but not cutting into the tubing.

- Test steering, throttle, and shift systems, which have the nasty habit of sticking or freezing up when they're not used regularly and kept lubricated.

- Check and repair seals around deck hatches, portals, and windshield, as well as all through-hull fittings. These are often the culprits when leaks begin to develop.

- Repair and lubricate snaps and zippers on those soft tops.

- Check all instruments and gauges, and fix the ones that aren't working.

- Replace zinc anodes.

- Check, clean, and repair deck drains and strainers.

- Pick up and clean, repair, replace, or discard all the loose ends from previous seasons. In my case these include knives with broken blades, rusty fishing lures, short bits of nylon and poly line, miscellaneous sinkers, and a plastic container with a large glob of unidentifiable items stuck together with rust.

- Straighten, clean, and repair dock lines and anchor lines.

- Stock up on spare parts, like an extra set of spark plugs, extra fuel filter, back-up gas line and bulb for portable tanks, spare fuses, hose clamps, and electrical fittings

- Replace windshield wiper blades at least every couple of years.

- Do a thorough cleaning inside and out, polish the metal and wood, maybe add a little touch-up paint, and give the bottom a good scrub-down. Then as the season progresses, at least you know that any dents, dings, and dirt are new dents, dings, and dirt.

- If your boat is registered, be sure your tabs are current. You have to renew them every year, remember?

Motor

- Inspect fuel fittings and hoses, and replace if they show signs of cracks, weakness, or wear. I know-I mentioned this earlier, but it's important.

- Check drive oil (and engine oil as appropriate). If it looks like coffee with cream, you have a problem. Creamy brown or gray oil has water in it and means you have a leak somewhere that should be repaired immediately.

- Clean or replace spark plugs. They're cheap but absolutely necessary, so don't skimp. Bad or dirty plugs can conk out with little or no warning, and they're much easier to change at the dock or on the trailer than on open water.
- Test trim and tilt; lubricate steering arm.
- Fill portable fuel tanks with fresh mix.
- Fill engine oil reservoir, if appropriate.
- Remove engine cover and check out all lines, wiring, and other obvious sources of potential problems. Clean up any grease, oil, or other messes and determine their source. Make repairs as needed.

Trailer
- Check tail lights, brake, and signal lights, replace bulbs, clean connections, or repair wiring as needed. This is a continuous job and almost always necessary at the beginning of the season.
- Inspect trailer tires for wear, weathering, and inflation. If you don't have a spare, get one now.
- Check wheel bearings and repack them regularly. They work hard on those little trailer wheels and take a beating from regular immersion in salt and fresh water. Of course you should always keep them well greased.
- Check the trailer frame for rust or damage and make repairs before they become problems.
- Be sure your license tabs are current.

Tool Kit Check your boat's tool kit. Clean and repair any tools that need it. What's that you say, you don't even *have* a tool kit? Here are some things to include:

Wrenches
- Open and box wrenches
- Socket set, 3/8-inch drive
- Adjustable wrenches, at least two, six to 12 inches
- Allen wrenches, assorted sizes
- Small pipe wrench
- Spark plug wrench (be sure it's the right size for your plugs)

Other Tools
- Screwdriver sets, including both slotted and Phillips
- Pliers (regular and needlenose)

- Hammer
- Knife
- Channel locks
- Wire cutters/strippers

Odds and Ends

- DC test light
- Duct tape
- Short lengths of assorted wire
- Replace old, damaged lifejackets with new, Coast Guard-approved ones, and be sure to have enough of them, the right size for anyone who'll be on board.
- Test all accessories, such as depthsounders, radios, VHF, Loran and/or GPS units, flashlights, and spotlights. Clean electrical connections and replace batteries as needed.
- Check fire extinguisher(s) and recharge if necessary.
- Check expiration dates on flare kits and replace missing or expired flares.
- Go through your boat's first-aid kit and replace any missing items or expired medications.
- Buy new tide and current tables and update charts and other navigation guides.
- Get the latest copy of the *Washington Boater's Guide,* which is free from the Washington State Parks and Recreation Commission's Boating Programs Office, tel. (360) 902-8551. If you aren't familiar with it, this 80-page guide contains information on boat registration, rules of the road, required equipment, fire prevention, accident reporting, a list of boat-sewage pump-outs and dump stations, and other useful information. It's updated every year or two.
- Take a boating course from the United State Power Squadrons or U.S. Coast Guard Auxiliary. It's inexpensive and very informative. If you took a course years ago, consider taking a refresher; you'll probably be surprised at how much you've forgotten. To find out about classes, call (800) 336-BOAT. A home-study boating course is also available from the Washington State Parks and Recreation Commission Boating Programs office, tel. (360) 902-8551.

Miscellaneous

This list works for me. It includes the basics, because my boat is your basic, no-nonsense boat with relatively few bells and whistles (in fact, no bells at all and only three whistles). Anyway, if your boat is bigger and better, which many are, your checklist needs to be bigger and better as well. It might include, but, as they say, isn't limited to the following tasks:

- Check bilge blowers.

- Clean shore power and water hose connections.
- Check trim tabs.
- Flush the water tank and purge lines.
- Check, polish, and, if necessary, repair plumbing.
- Clean refrigerators, ice boxes, and coolers.
- Clean and reorganize drawers and cupboards; lubricate hinges and rollers.
- Check and test live wells and wash-down systems.
- Clean and check stoves, ovens, and other appliances.
- Check exhaust fittings.
- Check and test the charging system.
- Check all belts and replace worn ones.
- Check all fluids and refill as necessary.
- Service and test the generator.

Boat Ramp Basics

How many times have you backed your boat trailer up to a ramp first thing in the morning or motored into the loading float at the end of a day on the water and then had to wait 10, 15, 20 minutes or more while some jackass pulled in diagonally across two lanes, fiddled around in the ramp, either not knowing or not caring that everyone else in the world was trying to get on with their lives? Or perhaps an even more important question: How often have *you* been that jackass?

It's true that some people just don't care about anyone else and think that every boat ramp in the world was built for their personal convenience. That's the only possible explanation for people going off and leaving their cars and trailers parked in the middle of a ramp, or washing down in the middle of a ramp, or taking up both lanes of a two-lane ramp with their race boats while other cars and trailers stack up behind them, or leaving their boats nosed up on a ramp while they wander off to find their car. I've seen all these things, and I'm sure you have, too.

But more often than not the slow-downs at ramps are caused by people who don't really know what they're doing, not those who couldn't care less. Spend an hour or two at a boat ramp watching the goings-on and it becomes pretty clear that many boaters don't have a clue. It's a great spectator sport if you don't happen to be waiting to get your boat in or out of the water.

Whether you don't know or don't care, try to remind yourself that boat ramps are busy places, often with large crowds waiting to get out and have a good time. There's often a long line even when things are going smoothly, so don't make the lines even longer by being inconsiderate or incompetent. That's a very good way to make enemies.

If you're one of those folks who feel really lucky every time they pull off a successful launch or retrieval of their boats in less than 15 minutes, you need to take some steps to improve your time. Here are some tips:

- Take some time to practice backing your trailer. A large parking lot or quiet cul de sac is a good place to practice. Get used to using your mirrors and turning the rear of the car in the opposite direction that you want the trailer to go. It's amazing how quickly you'll get the hang of it when there aren't a lot of others waiting for you to get it right.

- Load your boat before you leave home, or at least in the parking lot prior to actually backing into the ramp. The ramp is for launching and retrieving, not for loading and rearranging all your equipment.

- If you have some kind of problem and can't get running right away, take the boat over to a nearby beach, float, or somewhere else away from the traffic.

- Pull the boat out of traffic areas to wipe it down, unload, clean fish, change your shoes, comb your hair, shave, make cell-phone calls, and some of the other stupid things I've seen people do while six other boat owners waited.

- And remind your non-boat-owning friends not to park in boat trailer parking spaces or, worse, in the middle of the ramps themselves.

Don't Drink and Drive: It Applies to Boaters, Too

We hear the "Don't drink and drive" message almost every day. Unfortunately, too many boaters fail to realize that it applies to boats just as it applies to cars. Death by drowning isn't any prettier than dying by the side of the road, and alcohol increases the odds, whether you're in a car or a boat. The message is especially relevant during the warm days, long weekends, and holidays of summer when tens of thousands of Washingtonians turn to the water for rest, relaxation, and recreation. Too often, water recreation and alcohol consumption go hand in hand, sometimes with tragic results. No one has a problem with boaters having a beer or two, or even a cold mixed drink at the end of the day, but anyone who boats and drinks should understand that the consequences can be severe.

Washington automobile drivers with a blood-alcohol content of 0.08% or higher are considered legally drunk, and the same standard applies to boat operators. The effects of alcohol, in fact, may be greater on the water, where wind, wave action, and bright sunlight tend to increase its impact. Only a drink or two may impair a boater's vision, hearing, balance, and especially judgment.

According to the Boat Owners Association of the United States, a boat operator with a blood alcohol content above 0.10% is 10 times more likely to be killed in a boating accident than a boater who hasn't taken a drink.

While operating a boat under the influence of alcohol is a sure recipe for disaster, boat passengers aren't immune to the hazards of boating and drinking. The loss of balance and lack of concentration resulting from drinking a couple of beers or a cocktail can easily lead to passengers falling overboard and drowning or suffering serious injuries.

Like automobile drivers, boat owners should appoint a qualified "designated skipper," someone not drinking alcohol, who can run the boat and keep a watchful eye on passengers.

A Few Words about Life Jackets

There's a common misconception among boaters and others who spend a lot of time around the water that life vests, float coats, and other so-called personal flotation devices (PFDs) are only for people who can't swim. Maybe a better way to look at life jackets and other flotation equipment is that they're for people who might possibly find themselves in the water at one time or another-that's most of us. One reason people don't wear them is that they know how to swim. That's great if you fall overboard a few yards from the beach or if you don't hit your head as you fall out of the boat or if you don't suffer any other kind of injuries that might hamper your ability to swim or if the water temperature is 80 or 90 degrees so that you don't begin almost immediately suffering the effects of hypothermia. Unfortunately, it's not a perfect world out there on the water, and the list of anglers, paddlers, tubers, and others who have drowned in Washington waters over the years includes dozens who would have called themselves strong swimmers.

State and federal law require that all boats carry a Coast Guard-approved life jacket for everyone onboard, and those life jackets have to be in good condition and have to be the right size for the boat operator and his or her passengers. Four torn and tattered child-size life jackets for four adults on a boat won't do the trick. It will also draw a hefty fine for the boat owner if the boat is stopped by a marine enforcement officer.

Just carrying legal life jackets for everyone onboard is one thing, but wearing the things is even better. Many of us make sure our kids are wearing life jackets, never giving a thought to the fact that they might save *our* lives as well. Collisions, capsizings, swampings, and other boating mishaps usually happen quickly and without warning,

Types of PFDs

Type I Offshore life jackets have at least 22 pounds of buoyancy, will turn most unconscious wearers face up in the water, and are best for rough, open waters. They're somewhat bulky and restrictive, but they'll float you best.

Type II Near-shore vests provide at least 15 pounds of buoyancy and are considered adequate for calm waters where the chances of rescue are good.

Type III "Flotation aids" have 15 pounds of buoyancy and are good for calm waters where fast rescue is likely. They're available in the widest range of sizes and widest range of styles and are usually the most comfortable of all PFDs. The main disadvantage of these popular vests is that they may not float you head-back if you're unconscious.

Type IV Throwable devices such as cushions, rings and horseshoe buoys are not meant to be worn but tossed to someone in trouble, generally for situations where a person will be rescued in a short time. The problem with these, of course, is that a person must hang on to them.

Type V These PFDs are special-use items made for special and specific uses on the water. Their labels state what those uses are—work vests, sailboarding, etc.—and they're legal PFDs only when worn for those uses.

which means there isn't time to don PFDs when they're suddenly needed. And what if you get knocked out of the boat or simply lose your balance and fall overboard while you're changing seats, standing to net a fish, or emptying your bladder of that beer you had for lunch? You're in the water without a lifejacket.

Okay, I'm done preaching. Here are some basics facts about life jackets and life jacket laws in the state of Washington:

- As of July 1999, children 12 years and younger must wear a U.S. Coast Guard-approved life jacket on boats shorter than 19 feet whenever the vessel is underway and when the child is on an open deck or open cockpit.

- State and federal law dictate that PFDs be "readily accessible," which means the plastic wrappers need to be off, and the PFDs shouldn't be buried under everything else you own down in the bottom of a bow compartment. This regulation applies to all vessels from canoes, kayaks, and cartop rowboats to the biggest yacht on Puget Sound.

- If your boat is 16 feet or longer, you also must carry at least one throwable device, such as a life ring or float cushion.

- Shop around the for the right kind of PFD for your needs. If you don't know the difference between Type I (offshore), Type II (near-shore), Type III (flotation aid), Type IV (throwable), and Type V (special use) PFDs, it's time to learn. There are jackets, vests, suspenders, and other flotation equipment out there now to suit every boating or water sport situation. Some are big, warm, and waterproof, while others are small, flexible, and unobtrusive so that you can paddle, cast, or do whatever you need to do without even noticing that you have on a life jacket.

- Check to see that all your PFDs carry the Coast Guard approval tag. If they meet the requirements, it says so on a tag inside the jacket. It's perfectly legal to manufacture and sell PFDs that aren't Coast Guard approved. These jackets still float and may save your life, but they don't meet the federal and state PFD requirements.

- Okay, here's the information about the various types of PFDs, even though I hinted you'd have to find out for yourself.

- Try it on. A life jacket that's too small or too big may not save your life. If it's too small and you can't even get it zipped, tied, or buttoned, you could easily fall out of it in the water. If it's too big, the same thing can happen. Many small children have drowned after slipping out the bottom of a life jacket that was too big for them. Life jackets should fit comfortably and snugly under or over whatever clothing you have on.

- Take special care in picking life jackets for infants and toddlers. Select the kind of PFDs that will roll the kids onto their backs and keep their chins above water. That's something they're usually incapable of doing on their own when they go into the water. A crotch strap will keep the PFD from riding up too high or slipping off.

- Never substitute flotation toys, such as air mattresses, water wings, or plastic rings, for Coast Guard-approved PFDs.

- Try it out. The best way to be sure that a PFD will be there for you when you need it is to wade out into a swimming pool or lake until the water is to the bottom of your life jacket; then lie back in the water and see what happens. If it doesn't have enough flotation or fits you wrong, that's a good place to find out, not when you've just fallen out of your sailboat in the middle of Puget Sound or Lake Chelan. If it's an inflatable, give the cord a pull to be sure everything works properly; those cartridges aren't that expensive. Take the whole family along on these test missions and help children get used to their life jackets. Show them how to relax, lie on their backs, and allow the life jackets to do their stuff.

- Speaking of inflatables, while they're wonderful for their versatility (some are merely suspenders until you inflate them, while others have pockets for fishing tackle), they're only going to save your life if they inflate. That sounds simple, but if you get hurt before or as you go into the water, you may be unable to inflate the jacket. That's why they aren't recommended for waterskiing, PWC riding, and other sports where you may hit the water at a high rate of speed and have no chance to inflate the PFD.

- Take good care of your life jacket and it will take good care of you. Dry it in the sun or a dry room after each use to keep the material from becoming rotten and weak. Don't put it on or near a stove or heater. Be careful with knives, fish hooks, and other sharp objects that could put a hole in your PFD and allow water to leak into the fabric or flotation material. Don't cut any straps or otherwise alter a PFD so that it fits you or someone else a little better; if it doesn't fit the wearer, get one that does. Be careful about piling other equipment on your PFD. That could damage it and reduce its flotation capability.

- And here's one you may never have thought of unless it's happened to you: Consider wearing a life jacket or some kind of flotation device whenever you're around the water, not just in a boat. I've fallen into ice cold rivers from high banks; I've stepped into deep holes where I suddenly found myself in over my head; and I've seen lots of people fall off docks, piers, and gangways. I know steelhead anglers who have replaced their standard fishing vests with float vests after close calls on the river. Think about it.

Hypothermia—Always a Threat

Hypothermia is a constant possibility for Northwest boaters, and it takes the lives of several Washingtonians each year. Our marine waters and most of the state's lakes and streams remain cold throughout the year, so hypothermia is a danger that knows no season. A boater who ends up in the water may begin falling victim to hypothermia in a matter of only a few minutes, so quick action is often the key to survival. Understanding and avoiding hypothermia can mean the difference between being alive or dead when help arrives.

What Is Hypothermia? Hypothermia is subnormal temperature within the central body. When a person is immersed in cold water, the skin and nearby tissues cool very fast, although it may take 10 to 15 minutes before the temperature of the heart and brain starts to drop. When the core temperature drops below 90 degrees Fahrenheit, serious complications begin to develop. Death may occur at about 80 degrees Fahrenheit; however, a person may drown at a higher temperature due to loss of consciousness or inability to use the arms and legs.

How Long Can You Survive in Cold Water? Survival in cold water depends on many factors. The temperature of the water is only one. Others include body size, fat, and activity in the water. Large people cool more slowly than small people. Fat people cool more slowly than thin people. Children cool faster than adults.

By swimming or treading water, a person will cool about 35% faster than if remaining still. Drown-proofing—the technique of staying afloat, face-down, with lungs full of air, and raising the head every 10 to 15 seconds for a breath—conserves energy, but also results in rapid heat loss through the head and neck. This technique reduces survival time by nearly half in cold water. An average person, wearing light clothing and a life jacket, may survive two to three hours in 50 degree Fahrenheit water by remaining still. This survival time can be increased considerably by getting as far out of the water as possible and covering the head. Getting into or onto anything that floats can save your life.

What Do You Do if an Accident Occurs? If you fall into cold water, remember that water conducts heat many times faster than air. Most boats will float even when capsized or swamped, so get into or on the boat to get as far out of the water as possible. Wearing a lifejacket is a must. It will keep you afloat even if you are unconscious. Remaining still and, if possible, assuming the fetal posture (or Heat Escape Lessening Posture—HELP) will increase your survival time. About 50% of the body's heat is lost from the head. It's therefore important to keep your head out of the water. Other areas of high heat loss are the neck, the sides, and the groin. You should note that it's impossible to assume the HELP position while wearing some PFDs. However, even a partial HELP position gives some protection to the high heat-loss areas, thus increasing survival time.

If there are several people in the water, huddling close, side by side in a circle, will help preserve body heat. Placing children in the middle of the circle will lend them some of the adult body heat and extend their survival time.

Whether or not to try swimming to shore after an accident is a most difficult decision. It depends on many things. Some good swimmers have been able to swim nearly a mile in 50-degree water before being overcome by hypothermia. Others have not been able to swim 100 yards. And distances on the water are very deceptive. Staying with the boat is usually the best thing to do. This will make it easier for rescuers to spot you. Even a capsized boat is easier to see than a person in the water. *Do not swim* unless there is absolutely no chance of rescue and you are certain you can make it. If you do swim, use a lifejacket or some other flotation aid.

First Aid for Hypothermia Victims **Dos:**

• Make sure the victim has an open airway and is able to breathe. Then check for respiration and pulse. Respiration may be slow and shallow, and the pulse may be very weak. So check these vital signs very carefully. If there is no pulse or respiration, CPR must be started immediately.

• Prevent further heat loss:

1. Gently move the victim to shelter and warmth as rapidly as possible.

2. Gently remove all wet clothing; cut it away if necessary. The small amount of heat energy the victim has left must not be expended on warming and drying wet clothing.

3. Wrap the victim in blankets or a sleeping bag. If available, place warm water bottles or other gentle sources of heat under the blanket on the victim's neck, groin, and on the sides of the chest.

- Transport the victim to a hospital as soon as possible. Only a physician should determine when the patient should be released. Incorrect treatment of hypothermia victims may induce a condition known as after-drop. After-drop is a continued fall in the victim's core temperature even after he has been rescued. This is caused by improper rewarming, which allows cold, stagnant blood from the extremities to return to the core of the body. When this cold blood returns to the core of the body it may drop the core temperature below a level that will sustain life. For the same reason, hypothermia victims must be handled gently and should not be allowed to walk.

Don'ts:

- Don't place an unconscious victim in a bath tub.

- Don't give a victim anything to drink, not even hot liquids, and especially not alcohol.

- Don't rub the victim's skin, especially not with snow.

Because most boaters who die in water-related accidents had no intention of going in the water, the obvious answer is to avoid those behaviors that cause accidental immersion. Therefore,

How Can You Avoid Hypothermia?

- Do not stand or move around in a small boat.

- Do not overload your boat or distribute the load unevenly.

- Do not decelerate suddenly, allowing the stern wake to overtake and swamp the boat by washing over the transom.

Finally, always wear a lifejacket on the water.

File a Float Plan

No one expects trouble on the water, but any number of things can turn a pleasant day of cruising, sailing, or paddling into a misadventure, an inconvenience, or even a life-threatening ordeal. One way to help ensure a safe return is to file a float plan before you go. If you get into trouble and don't return from your trip on time, authorities can start a search sooner and begin looking in the right places if you leave a few tidbits of accurate information to use as a starting point.

A float plan should include the name and description of your boat, including registration numbers, color, length, style, and other information that would make it easier to spot and identify. Information about radio equipment onboard and frequencies used is also helpful. If you're towing or carrying your boat to your trip's starting point, include a vehicle description and license number along with details of where you'll be launching. Include the number and names of all persons onboard, time and date you're leaving, your destination, and when you're planning to return.

Be sure to include the name and phone number of the state or local law enforcement agency with jurisdiction in the area you plan to boat. They're the ones who should get the first call if you're overdue.

File your float plan with a reliable friend or relative who will notify authorities if necessary. And be sure to contact that person immediately upon your return or if during your trip you change your plans in a way that may alter your return time.

Boat Theft

Yes, I know, this is going to be a bummer just when you were getting ready to get out on the water and enjoy yourself, but I've read more than once that thieves steal something like 1,000 boats a month in this country. We're talking entire boats, not to mention the hundreds of thousands of dollars' worth of outboard motors, depthsounders, GPS units, fishing tackle, and other equipment they take from boats when owners aren't looking. The way I see it, we can continue to let these lowlifes steal us blind, forcing us to work harder so can afford to replace what was stolen and leaving us less time to spend on the water, or we can fight back. I'm not talking about vigilante justice here (though I'm not necessarily against that option), but I am proposing that we simply take a few precautions to make it harder for thieves.

Actually, foiling these bums is pretty easy; just a little time and effort on our parts can make their jobs more difficult. Here are some tips that will help protect your boats, motors, and equipment:

1. Engrave your name and driver license number on everything. It takes a while the first time around, but then you can simply mark new things as you get them. Be sure to include the two-letter state prefix before or after the number so they know it's a Washington number (or whatever state you might live in). Thieves have a tougher time selling it if it's engraved, and you stand a much better chance of getting it back should authorities find it in a thief's stash. What's more, the police have a better chance of prosecuting if the property can be identified as yours.

2. Keep records of your valuables. Again, if you have serial numbers, model numbers, and other details recorded, you stand a better chance of getting it back should the culprit be arrested. Such

details are also helpful when you file an insurance claim to replace your loss. But remember to keep these records in a secure place like a safe or deposit box. Don't do as a friend of mine did and keep the records of all his boating equipment in (you guessed it) the boat that was stolen from him.

3. Take record keeping a step further and photograph it, too. Photos will often turn up items you didn't record or forgot about. Again, keep the photos in a safe place. Date the photos and add details on the back to help identify items in the photo.

4. Since small, easy-to-carry items are the things most often stolen, don't leave them on your boat when you're not using it, or at least don't leave them right out in the open. The harder you can make it for thieves, the less chance they'll hit you, so lock equipment away, or better yet, remove it from the boat when trailering, parked on the street, or any time your boat is left unattended. When securing your boat, take home as much gear as you can, including your VHF, cell phone, CB, outboard engines, and fishing tackle. If it is not practical to take it with you, store it onboard in a cabinet or locker with a good quality lock. Make sure you remove the key code or combination code from any lock you use. Chain dinghies or outboards left on board.

5. You're better off mooring your boat or parking your boat trailer out in the open, where passersby might spot thieves in action. Dark, out-of-the-way places, as they say about germs, are breeding grounds for boat thieves.

6. Always use a hitch lock, whether your trailer is hitched to your rig or sitting unused. Locks aren't a great deterrent for experienced boat thieves, but they would prefer not to deal with them if they have a choice. If your hitch is locked and the one next to it isn't, you may be the lucky one.

7. Use wheel locks or remove a wheel from boat trailers that aren't being used. Someone is bound to notice if a thief starts dragging your boat trailer down the highway with sparks or fire flying from one wheel, so the thieves probably won't chance it.

8. Use alarms and warning decals. Dishonest folks will think twice about crawling into a boat with stickers all over it warning about alarms, horns, and other loud noises. Sometimes all you need are the decals, but having the real alarm to back them up also helps.

9. Help the police help you by reporting theft quickly and accurately. Some boats have been recovered a few miles from the crime scene because the victims acted quickly, called 911 to report a crime that just took place, and got immediate response. As they say, a warm trail is easier to follow.

Personal Watercraft: They're Boats, Too

The latest estimates I've heard put the total number of personal watercraft (PWC—also commonly referred to as Jet Skis, which is a brand name) in this country at over one million. About 24,000 of those PWC are registered in Washington, so they're now a major part of the boating scene here as well as everywhere else.

What many operators of these fast, maneuverable little craft don't know is that they have to obey the same rules as all other boaters plus a few special ones of their own. Personal watercraft are boats, and their operators are the skippers of those boats. Boat skippers are responsible for knowing and abiding by all the local, state, and federal boating laws on the waters they use.

Like all boaters, PWC riders are responsible for their own wakes and the damage those wakes might do. Like all boaters, PWC riders must stay reasonable distances from other boats, docks, piers, swimmers, wildlife, and the shoreline, a basic boating rule that's broken dozens of times daily by PWC riders on some waters.

Like most other powerboats, PWC must be registered and display legal boat numbers and current tabs on their hulls. Speed limits and other rules of the road apply to PWC just as they do to other boats.

In addition, Washington has some rules on the books that apply specifically to personal watercraft:

- Everyone operating or riding on PWC must wear a Coast Guard-approved Type I, Type II, or Type III life jacket in good condition and the right size for the person wearing it.

- PWC aren't equipped with lights, so it's legal to ride them only from sunrise to sunset, no exceptions.

- Anyone operating PWC must be at least 14 years of age.

- It's unlawful for anyone to rent, lease, or hire out a personal watercraft to kids under the age of 16 years.

- Anyone riding PWC equipped by the manufacturer with a lanyard-type engine cutoff switch must attach the lanyard to his or her body, clothing, or PFD. It's illegal to remove or disable a cutoff switch installed by the PWC manufacturer.

In addition to these regulations, it's also a very good idea to wear goggles, sunglasses, or some other kind of eye protection, since these water buggies often scoot along at speeds of 30 miles an hour or more. Some kind of footwear is also helpful. If you're lending your PWC to someone with little or no experience, spend time teaching them not only all the details of how the thing works, but familiarizing them with the rules as well. As the owner of the boat, you're responsible for their actions. If you're new to the sport yourself, you might want to enroll in a boating course yourself to learn your responsibilities and maybe enjoy the sport a little more.

Safety Tips for River Runners

You won't have to look far in this book to find a long list of rivers offering great paddling and whitewater opportunities. Moving-water sports are among the fastest-growing boating activities in the Northwest, where there are inviting rivers and creeks almost everywhere you turn. While river running is a great sport, it also has some inherent dangers that you don't find in other boating and water activities. People who play on and in the rivers of Washington have to be more alert, more observant, and more capable of making quick decisions than most of their still-water counterparts.

As the sport has grown, so has the number of boating accidents on whitewater streams. The potential dangers became painfully evident in 1997 and 1999, years of heavy snowmelt in which many of Washington's rivers ran bank to bank for long periods during the spring and early summer. Both years saw unusually high numbers of boating fatalities associated with river-running sports. Although some of these mishaps involved commercial rafting companies, the majority were in private boats—just folks out on their own to have a good time on the river.

While huge river flows can add a great deal of excitement to a whitewater trip, such flows also can increase the dangers, especially for inexperienced boaters. Heavy flows can dramatically change a river's personality, forming channels where they don't exist in normal flows and depositing stumps, logs, and other debris in the river. During high flows, there may be no beach or quiet water where a boater can pull over to rest or to avoid obstacles farther downstream. Higher flows also mean more powerful flows, where a boat and boater may be at the mercy of pounding water. If you make a mistake, the river may take you where it wants; if you capsize, you're swept away like a stick in the current. What's more, high water usually means cold water, making hypothermia a much greater risk.

Even with these potential dangers, whitewater rafting, kayaking, and even tubing can be safe and enjoyable if you take a few simple precautions. Following are a few basic rules for moving-water safety.

- Ask around before you go. This book is loaded with names and phone numbers of rafting companies and other businesses you can call to get a river report. You can also call a friend who has been there recently. Find out about flow levels, new surprises in the river, changes in the status of put-ins/take-outs, and other pertinent information. You can also check the on-line river-flow information provided by the National Oceanic and Atmospheric Administration (NOAA). The web page address is www.nwrfc.noaa.gov/data/streamflow/streamflow.shtml.

- Don't assume anything. Just when you think you know a river like the back of your hand, it will surprise you. Treat every run on a river as if it's your first and you'll be ready for changes.

- Scout ahead. If you don't know what's around the next bend in the river, get out, walk around, and see for yourself. Scouting is also a very good idea when running new rapids for the first time. You can often tell much more about a stretch of river from the bank above than you can from the surface of the river. Plan your line through the rough spots before you're in the middle of it.

- Don't be too proud to portage. If scouting shows you water that you consider dangerous, walk around it. It's better to be safe and have the chance to come again some other time than gamble and lose.

- Don't paddle alone. Always run rivers using the buddy system, and two buddies in two other boats are better than one. That way there's always plenty of help should it be needed.

- Just because the pros can do it . . . . Commercial river-running companies are in business because they know the rivers and how to run them. They're on the same river for days at a time, so they get to know every wave, every hole, every eddy. They can make it look easier than it really is, and they're equipped for everything. Don't assume that just because they can do it, you can pull it off on your own.

- Secure all equipment in the boat so there's less danger of becoming tangled in gear or having to grab something that flies out.

- Carry a throw-bag and a length of safety rope.

- ALWAYS wear a Coast Guard-approved life jacket and, in most rivers, a helmet. The latter might be left behind if you're on very calm streams, but it's good insurance.

- Wear a wet suit or dry suit. Even on warm days the constant soaking and chilly water can get to you in a hurry. A suit will protect against hypothermia and make for a more pleasant day on the river.

- If you fall into the water, keep your feet downstream and near the surface. Don't stand unless the water is too shallow to swim in.

Washington's Boat Registration Requirements

Some states require that all recreational boats be registered, while others have no vessel-registration requirements at all. Washington is among the majority of states that fall somewhere between those two extremes. Here in the Evergreen State, whether or not you must register your boat depends on the boat's length, how it's powered, and where you operate it.

According to state law, a vessel under 16 feet long, with a motor of 10 horsepower or less, and used solely on nonfederal waters is not required to be titled or registered.

The part about boat length and motor size is pretty easy to understand, but what's this stuff about nonfederal waters? It's easier to explain "federal" waters than "nonfederal" waters, so here goes: Federal waters include Puget Sound, Hood Canal, Lake Washington, Lake Union, Lake Sammamish, the Columbia and Snake Rivers, the Lake Washington Ship Canal, Capitol Lake, the Pend Oreille River, Walla Walla River, Yakima River, and "other bodies of water affected by the ebb and flow of the tide and on or bordering federal land." If you have questions about any of that last part, even state authorities suggest that you contact the nearest local marine law enforcement office. In almost all cases, that means the sheriff's office in the county where the body of water in question happens to be located.

If your boat is 16 feet or longer and your motor over 10 horsepower, it doesn't matter where you use it—it must be registered. So the first thing you need to know is that the Washington State Department of Licensing oversees the titling and registration of boats as well as motor vehicles. They're the ones who send out the vessel-registration renewal notices every spring, but you don't have to visit their office in Olympia or send your money to Olympia; you may register at your county auditor's office or at local licensing sub-agents scattered throughout every county. Boat registration tabs are valid from July 1 through June 30, and once your boat is registered, every year you'll receive a renewal notice several months before the June 30 expiration date.

To register your boat, you must provide the model year and make of the vessel, purchase price and purchase year, overall length, hull identification number (if any), and Coast Guard number or document number (if applicable). You'll have to submit the ownership documents such as certificate of title, and all owners (if more than one) must sign the paperwork.

First-time registration charges in Washington are $20.50 for vessels under 16 feet and all vessels exempt from excise tax (those used for commercial fishing, owned by nonprofit organizations, or held for sale by a dealer). Boats 16 feet and over are subject to excise tax based on 0.5% of the fair market value.

If you have questions about vessel registration, contact the Washington State Department of Licensing, Vessel Licensing Section, P.O. Box 9909, Olympia, WA 98507-8500; tel. (360) 902-4089.

Additional Information

Even a book as comprehensive as *Washington Boating and Water Sports* can't list every important fact a boater or water enthusiast may want to know. We cannot, for example, predict the weather, and weather can play a big part in the success or failure of an aquatic adventure in the Pacific Northwest. Boating regulations change, sometimes on short notice, and even those that have been in place for some time can seem complicated to novice boaters or newcomers to the Evergreen State, requiring further explanation or interpretation. For readers who may want further information on a wide range of boating-related subjects, we have compiled a list of agencies and organizations that have something to offer Washington boaters.

- **Washington State Parks and Recreation Commission:** Every state has an agency that's responsible for administering its boating laws, and in Washington that agency is State Parks. If you have a question about statewide boating rules and regulations, contact the State Parks Boating Programs office at P.O. Box 42650, Olympia, WA 98504-2650; tel. (360) 902-8551.

- **Washington State Department of Licensing:** This agency oversees titling and registration of boats as well as motor vehicles. If you have questions about registering your boat, renewing your annual boat tabs, or related topics, they're the ones to talk to. Contact the Department of Licensing at P.O. Box 9909, Olympia, WA 98507-8500; tel. (360) 902-4089; email: webmaster@dol.wa.gov.

- **Interagency Committee for Outdoor Recreation:** Better known as IAC, it assists state and federal agencies and nonprofit organizations in planning, acquiring, and developing recreational resources, including boating facilities. Most public boat ramps are developed and maintained with funds administered by IAC. Contact it at P.O. Box 40917, Olympia, WA 98504-0917; tel. (360) 902-3000; email: info@iac.wa.gov.

- **Washington Department of Fish and Wildlife:** Anglers, crabbers, clam diggers, and wildlife enthusiasts of many kinds may want information from WDFW about regulations, seasons, licenses, and other subjects. Contact the agency at 600 Capitol Way North, Olympia, WA 98501-1091; tel. (360) 902-2200; website: www.wa.gov/wdfw.

- **United States Coast Guard:** The Coast Guard has an obvious presence in Washington, especially along our marine waterways. The telephone number for the 13th District Office in Seattle is tel. (206) 220-7000. The Coast Guard also operates a toll-free information number, tel. (800) 368-5647 (8 a.m. to 4 p.m., weekdays). Its website is at www.uscgboating.org. For Coast Guard emergencies, call (206) 217-6000 or use VHF channel 16.

Local Marine Patrol Agencies: The State Parks Boating Programs office contracts with local law enforcement agencies, mostly county sheriff and city police departments, to carry out marine enforcement and boater education throughout Washington. Counties and cities set speed limits and other boating regulations for specific waters in their jurisdiction, so local sheriff and police departments enforce these and statewide boating regulations. County sheriff's offices are good places to start looking if you need information about boating rules on a specific body of water.

- **U.S. Power Squadrons/U.S. Coast Guard Auxiliary:** These volunteer boating organizations offer a wide range of boating classes and educational courses. For information on Power Squadron classes, call (800) 367-8777 or visit their website at www.usps.org. Coast Guard Auxiliary course information is available at tel. (800) 982-8813.

- **National Oceanic & Atmospheric Administration (NOAA):** This is perhaps the most important agency of all to Northwest boaters because it's the one that produces nautical charts and also includes the National Weather Service. For information on charts and other helpful publications, call (206) 553-7656.

One inch equals approximately 20 miles.

MAP A1

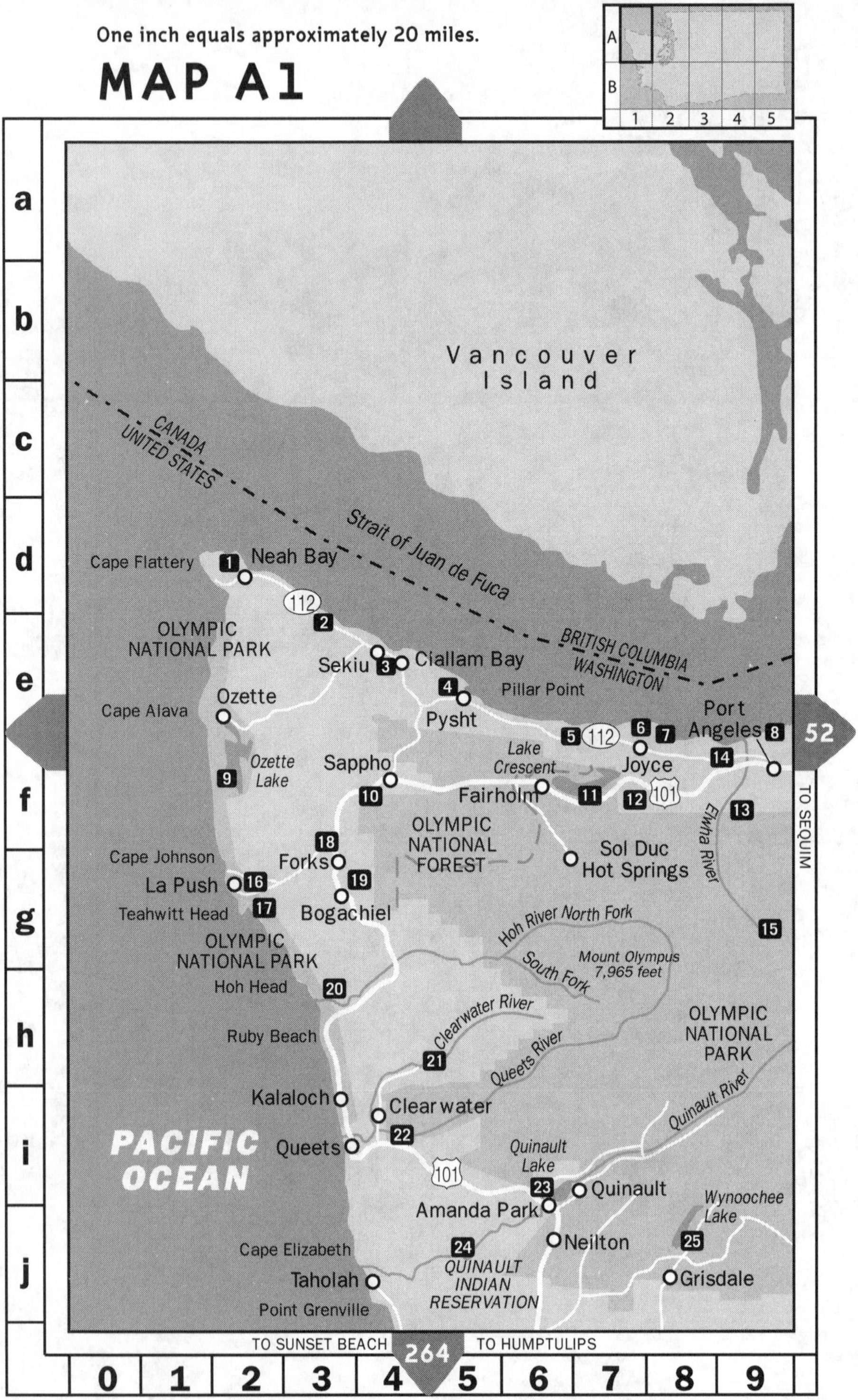

CHAPTER A1

❶ Neah Bay

Rating: 7

The natural beauty of the rocky, forested shoreline, the abundance of wildlife, and the clean, cold water at this edge of the continent might prompt you to look skyward and say thanks. The town itself, on the other hand, is a bit dismal, so you may not want to spend much time ashore there. Highlights include the Makah Museum and a chance to see the cedar canoe *Hummingbird* moored at the Makah Marina. It's the craft that tribal members used during the controversial "hunt" that resulted in the killing of a gray whale in the spring of 1999. Maybe you can even score a package of whale meat; I hear there's plenty that's gone uneaten. If you prefer live marine mammals to dead ones, you might want to paddle, sail, or power your way slowly along the beach in either direction from Neah Bay. Depending on the time of year, you may spot seals, sea lions, porpoise, and whales of several sizes, shapes, and colors. Bald eagles are everywhere, as are a striking variety of waterfowl and shorebirds. Otters are common, and you may spot a black-tailed deer or black bear along the beach.

The harbor at Neah Bay is protected by a rock jetty that extends several hundred yards out to Waadah Island, making this one of the most well-sheltered harbors on the Strait of Juan de Fuca. Once you round the island, it's a six-mile run to Tatoosh Island and the open waters of the Pacific. There are several small bays, many of them partially clogged with kelp, to explore along the way if you're making the run in a small powerboat or paddle craft. Large boulders and fully or partially submerged rock piles along the way call out for investigation if you're a diver or angler. This entire area boasts large schools of black rockfish, lots of kelp greenling, lingcod, and other tasty bottomfish. Tatoosh Island and the rocky reef connecting it to the mainland are especially productive fishing and diving spots, as is Duncan Rock to the north of Tatoosh. If you visit either spot, do it when the tide is slack. The water gets moving around both of these big rocks, producing some nasty currents at Tatoosh and some big rollers and waves around Duncan. Spend some time prowling along the east side of the island and find the spot where you can look through the rocks at open water on the other side.

Boaters who round Cape Flattery and head south down the rocky coast are treated to some of the most spectacular shoreline this country has to offer. The place names along here are well known by anglers because the sites have traditionally provided some of the best salmon and bottomfish action found anywhere in Washington; they include Hole in the Wall, Skagway Rocks, Spike Rocks, Father and Son Rocks, and Point of the Arches. While they're all beautiful, they offer little or nothing in the way of protection should the ocean decide to kick up, fog in, or otherwise turn nasty. This is a place where every boater should pay close attention to the weather and be prepared for any situation; help may be some distance away.

If you're planning a trip to the Neah Bay area, you'll need NOAA's nautical charts 18484, 18485, or 18460 to help you get around better and more safely and also to help you locate the many submerged rock piles, reefs, holes, and other structures that provide great fishing and diving.

Location: At Neah Bay, northwest tip of the Olympic Peninsula; map A1, grid d2.

How to get there: Follow U.S. 101 north from Hoquiam or west from Port Angeles to the town of Sappho and turn north on Highway 113, which meets Highway 112 about 11 miles north of Sappho and continues on as Highway 112 about 26 miles to Neah Bay. Just past Sekiu the road becomes narrow and has some tight turns in spots.

Boat ramp: There's one located immediately west of Big Salmon Fishing Resort. It's wide enough for launching two boats at the same time, provided both operators realize they're not alone in the world. The ramp also has a short moorage float for lunch traffic. Cost is $7 in and out.

Facilities: The new (1997) Makah Marina gets a lot of publicity, and it's adequate if you come here by water, but it seems to say "Keep Out" to folks who trailer their boats to Neah Bay. The marina itself doesn't have a launch ramp or sling, and the paved parking lot has only car parking—NO trailer parking. Signs in the lot warn of a four-hour parking limit. Apparently the facility is for tribal and local use but not for the rest of us. Neah Bay has cabins, motels, RV parks, and fishing resorts, none of them fancy. Boat rentals are available from spring to fall, and there are two public fuel docks. A grocery/dry goods store carries everything from rubber boots to peanut butter, and there's one cafe near the east end of town.

Water sports/restrictions: All water sports are permitted.

Contact: Big Salmon Fishing Resort, tel. (360) 645-2374 (April to October only) (VHF ch. 68); Makah Marina, tel. (360) 645-3015 (VHF ch. 66); Cape Motel and RV Park, tel. (360) 645-2250. For nautical charts of the Neah Bay area, contact Captain's Nautical Supply, tel. (206) 283-7242.

❷ Snow Creek

Rating: 6

Like most of the Strait of Juan de Fuca, salmon fishing has long been the mainstay of boating activity here, but bottomfishing, diving, and paddling are enjoying increased popularity; and most cruisers and sailors who happen onto this little corner of the Evergreen State quickly add it to their list of favorite destinations. Snow Creek is often overlooked by weekenders in a hurry to get to the more well-known facilities and fishing grounds of Neah Bay. The beauty of Snow Creek is that it has most of the things boaters need, without the distractions sometimes associated with Neah Bay. But if you do need something that Snow Creek doesn't have, such as a few days' worth of groceries, it's only a five-minute drive or a 10-minute run by boat to the "big city." It's also an easy run to the west to reach the fishing grounds or the fantastic coastal scenery available to Neah Bay visitors. And if you decide to head east rather than west out of Snow Creek, you're likely to have miles of rocky shoreline, forested hillsides, and fishy-looking kelp beds to yourself. Divers, paddlers, and anglers are usually drawn to nearby Sail and Seal Rocks, just to the northwest of Snow Creek.

The scenery overall may not be quite so dramatic here as it is west of Neah Bay, but the wind, tides, and currents are a lot more gentle, which the small-boat traveler is likely to appreciate. Remember, though, that the submerged rock piles, boulders, rocky shoreline, and massive kelp beds that make this such a haven for photographers, anglers, and wildlife enthusiasts also make it hazardous for boaters asleep at the switch. Even with a good chart and good depthsounder I've come closer to some prop-mangling obstacles than I'd like to admit.

Get a copy of NOAA nautical chart 18484 for good detail of the Snow Creek/Neah Bay area, chart 18485 to cover all of Cape Flattery, or chart 18460 for the entire western half of the Strait of Juan de Fuca.

Location: East of Neah Bay, near northwest tip of the Olympic Peninsula; map A1, grid d3.

How to get there: Follow U.S. 101 north from Hoquiam or west from Port Angeles to the town of Sappho and turn north on Highway 113, which meets Highway 112 about 11 miles north of Sappho and continues on as Highway 112. Drive about 24 miles to mile marker 1, where signs point to the right turn into the resort.

Boat ramp: There's a rail launch at the resort.

Facilities: Snow Creek Resort is open from spring to fall and has over 350 feet of moorage floats, three dozen moorage buoys, rest rooms and showers, tent and RV sites, boat rentals, and a small store that carries fishing tackle and air for divers. It also has a rail launch and haul-out facilities.

Water sports/restrictions: Cruising, fishing, crabbing, diving, and paddling are the main attractions, and visitors without boats find excellent tide pooling. Always watch for submerged rocks and reefs when boating here, and keep your tide book handy.

Contact: Snow Creek Resort, tel. (360) 645-2284 (April to October only). For nautical charts of this area, contact Captain's Nautical Supply, tel. (206) 283-7242.

3 Sekiu/Clallam Bay

Rating: 8

Every year a few more cruisers, paddlers, and divers discover what Northwest anglers have known for decades: Clallam Bay is a water lover's dream. It's relatively protected from all but the nastiest nor'westers, so you can usually find a place to do whatever it is you enjoy doing on the water. Upon spending a June day here recently, a friend of mine asked, "When are people going to discover this place and take advantage of all it has to offer? It's a paradise and there's nobody here." That wasn't the case on a summer day 15 or 20 years ago, when hundreds of anglers crowded onto the water and into the motels, restaurants, and RV parks of Sekiu and Clallam Bay to get a shot at some of the best salmon fishing the Northwest had to offer. Salmon seasons are now short, and most of the facilities are still here, but nonanglers have been slow to fill the void. One problem is that the somewhat Spartan motel rooms, stick-to-your-ribs restaurant meals, and other amenities here are anglers' fare, and anglers are easy to please as long as the fish are biting. Some nonfishing boaters may want a little more luxury than Sekiu has to offer.

But if you don't need "fancy" to enjoy life, you'll love Sekiu/Clallam Bay. There are still halibut and other bottomfish to catch, salmon to catch at certain times of year, excellent diving opportunities, wide-open spaces for powerboaters and sailors, shoreline nooks and crannies for paddlers to explore, and lots of shoreside recreation for good measure. Wildlife is abundant both above and below the water's surface. Divers are discovering Sekiu a little faster than other water enthusiasts, thanks at least in part to Jerry Scott, owner of Curley's Resort in the middle of Sekiu. He sells equipment, fills air tanks, and offers printed directions to some of the area's top diving locations, including a great spot right at the Sekiu jetty at the northwest corner of town.

The NOAA nautical chart for this western end of the Strait of Juan de Fuca is chart 18460. Because of its scale, it's a little light on detail, so it shouldn't replace common sense and regular use of your depthsounder. If you don't have a boat but still want to enjoy Clallam Bay, wait for the tide to ebb, park along the street in Sekiu, hit the beach, and head east toward the far side of the bay. Despite the nearby highway, it's one of the Northwest's most pleasant beach-combing spots.

Location: At Sekiu, north side of Olympic Peninsula; map A1, grid e4.

How to get there: Drive west from Port Angeles on U.S. 101 and either exit onto Highway 112 and continue west or stay on U.S. 101 to the town of Sappho and turn north on Highway 113. Where Highways 112 and 113 meet, continue northwest on Highway 112 to Clallam Bay and then to nearby Sekiu.

Boat ramp: There's a boat ramp at the Coho Resort, another off Highway 112 just before you turn right to drop down into Sekiu, a third at Van Riper's Resort, and a fourth at Olson's Resort. Launch fee is $5 at each of the four.

Facilities: Food, lodging, boat rentals, moorage, air for scuba tanks, bait, tackle, fuel, and other needs all are available in Sekiu and nearby Clallam Bay.

Water sports/restrictions: Fishing, sailing, cruising, paddling, diving, and crabbing are available, but don't forget the tides and their influence on all water sports here. Swimming's a possibility but only if you're damn tough.

Contact: Curley's Resort and Dive Center, tel. (360) 963-2281; Olson's Resort, tel. (360) 963-2311; Van Riper's Resort, tel. (360) 963-2334; Coho Resort, tel. (360) 963-2333(April through September only); Straitside Resort, tel. (360) 963-2100. For charts of the Sekiu/Clallam Bay area, contact Captain's Nautical Supply, tel. (206) 283-7242.

4 Pillar Point

Rating: 6

Long a favorite haunt of summer and fall salmon anglers, the waters around Pillar Point see relatively little boating traffic these days, thanks to major fishing restrictions. Silver King Resort, which for many years provided most of the facilities for anglers and other boaters in this area, has closed, reducing boat traffic even further. Passing cruisers and sailors will find limited anchorage possibilities in the sheltered shallow bay at the mouth of the Pysht River, where shorebirds, waterfowl, marine mammals, and other wildlife provide plenty of good viewing and photographic possibilities. The Pysht estuary is immediately south of the tall rock spire that gives the area its name. It's well protected from a southerly or westerly wind, but when the breeze comes out of the north or east, it's time to go somewhere else.

The small Clallam County Parks boat ramp southeast of the point is a good place to launch kayaks, canoes, cartoppers, and small trailer boats, but not for anything over about 18 feet. There are no floats, and launched boats must be pulled onto the beach or held out in the water while you're preparing to get under way. Several large boulders near the end of the ramp don't help at all. And if a stiff northerly or easterly is blowing, launching even a small boat can be difficult and dangerous.

However, when the weather is decent, this is a beautiful place to paddle, cruise, sail, and explore. Even when salmon, halibut, and lingcod seasons are closed, there are greenling, rockfish, sole, perch, and other smallish fish to catch; and crabbing can be good near the mouth of the Pysht. Paddlers can get several hundred yards up into the river on a high tide.

NOAA's nautical chart 18460 provides the best picture of this western end of the Strait of Juan de Fuca.

Location: At Pysht, east of Clallam Bay, on Strait of Juan de Fuca; map A1, grid e5.

How to get there: Drive west out of Port Angeles on U.S. 101 or north from Forks and turn north at the town of Sappho onto Highway 113 (also known as Burnt Mountain Road). Drive 13 miles to the intersection of Highway 112, turn east (right), and drive six miles to Pillar Point Road, which is marked by a large sign reading "Pillar Point Recreation Area." Turn north (left) onto Pillar Point Road and follow it 0.2 mile down the hill to the Clallam County park called Pillar Point Fishing Camp.

Boat Ramp: There's a single-lane paved ramp at the park, but if there's much of a wind, it's a nasty place to launch a boat of any size.

Facilities: Besides the boat ramp, the four-acre park has 37 campsites, rest rooms, picnic tables, and a picnic shelter. The main camping area is open from May 15 through September, with a $9 camping fee (Clallam County residents pay only $7). From October through mid-May the main camping area is closed, but some tent and RV campers set up temporary residence in the gravel parking lot next to the boat ramp, and nobody seems to mind. There is no dock or float, and there are no moorage buoys.

Water sports/restrictions: Fishing is the main attraction, but cruising, crabbing, and diving are great options along this scenic stretch of the Strait of Juan de Fuca.

Contact: Clallam County Parks and Fair Department, tel. (360) 417-2291. For charts of the Pillar Point area, contact Captain's Nautical Supply, tel. (206) 283-7242.

5 Whiskey Creek

Rating: 6

When it comes to water sports, there's a little bit of everything but not too much of anything going on here. Used primarily by summer visitors, the Whiskey Creek stretch of the Strait of Juan de Fuca is somewhat a victim of its own location. Folks from the Sequim-Port Angeles area know about it, but most boaters from other parts of the Northwest pass it up on their way to more remote but better-known destinations farther west. However, trailer boaters looking for a new spot to explore should consider a two- or three-day visit to Whiskey Creek. The fact that it offers the only publicly available boat ramp on the Strait of Juan de Fuca between Freshwater Bay and Pillar Point is reason enough to give Whiskey Creek a look.

Location: Northwest of Joyce; map A1, grid e7.

How to get there: Drive west from Port Angeles on U.S. 101 about three mils to the junction of Highway 112; turn right on Highway 112 and follow it 13 miles to the sign reading "Whiskey Creek Recreation Area." Turn right at the sign onto Whiskey Creek Beach Road and drive 1.4 miles to Whiskey Creek Beach.

Boat Ramp: There's a protected boat ramp at Whiskey Creek Beach that's open from May through September.

Launch fee is $3 round-trip.

Facilities: The privately owned resort at Whiskey Creek Beach has rental cabins near the beach, and tent and RV sites are available by the day, week, or month. The nearest food and fuel are in Joyce, four miles away. Other amenities are in Port Angeles.

Water sports/restrictions: All water sports are permitted, but fishing, crabbing, and diving draw most of the visitors.

Contact: Whisky Creek Beach, tel. (360) 928-3483 (rings at a home number during the off-season, fall to spring).

6 Salt Creek Recreation Area

Rating: 6

The rocky cliffs overlooking the Strait of Juan de Fuca here afford such a great view that it was a harbor-defense site during World War II. You can still prowl through some of the old bunkers at the west end of the recreation area. But Salt Creek offers much more than nice scenery. The rocky shoreline directly in front of the recreation area and nearby Crescent Bay to the west provide a haven for divers almost any time of year and for paddlers and small-boat explorers when wind and water conditions allow. Some even launch kayaks and canoes right off the rocky shelf at the foot of the recreation area's walkway, but it's a tricky spot to launch and shouldn't be attempted unless the water is calm. The rewards of a visit to Salt Creek are many, from catching greenling right off the rocks to exploring one of the most wildlife-rich stretches of shoreline you'll find anywhere in the Northwest.

Location: On the Strait of Juan de Fuca at east end of Crescent Bay, northeast of Joyce; map A1, grid e8.

How to get there: Take Highway 112 off U.S. 101 about three miles west of Port Angeles and drive west seven miles to Camp Hayden Road. Turn north (right) and drive 3.5 miles to Salt Creek Recreation Area.

Boat ramp: There is no boat ramp here.

Facilities: Clallam County maintains 90 RV and tent sites, rest rooms and showers, an RV dump station, picnic tables, and playground equipment. Campsites are $8 a night for Clallam County residents, $10 for nonresidents. There are no docks or moorage facilities. Grocery stores are nearby in Joyce, and all other facilities can be found in Port Angeles.

Water sports/restrictions: Diving, kayaking, and tide-pool exploration are the top draws here.

Contact: Salt Creek Recreation Area, tel. (360) 928-3441; Clallam County Parks and Fair, tel. (360) 417-2291.

7 Freshwater Bay

Rating: 7

Most of my trips to Freshwater Bay have been in pursuit of chinook salmon, but I've enjoyed this place even when the fish weren't biting. The fact is that if you're in a boat or near the water here, you'll soon find something to capture your interest. Like many others who prowl this gorgeous section of the Strait of Juan de Fuca, I've spent hours poking around the edge of the kelp in search of assorted treasures; and it seemed that every time I looked up there was some kind of wildlife swimming past, flying over, or standing there looking at me. Anglers have always loved this place, paddlers are beginning to explore it more frequently, and it's a haven for divers. When boating here, though, remember that facilities are limited, rocks and floating logs are abundant, and when fishing is slow, there may be few other boaters around. This is a place to be on your best watch, to use your electronics, and to take nothing for granted. You don't want to spend an afternoon banging up against that beautiful, rocky shoreline. Oh, and one more thing. More than any other place I can think of, I've seen people launch their boats at the Freshwater Bay ramp, head out for the open waters of the Strait of Juan de Fuca, and leave their cars and trailers parked in the way of others trying to launch. The parking area here is big enough to hold half the boat trailers in Clallam County, so be sure to park yours more than 20 feet from the top of the ramp. Thanks. (There, I got that off my chest.)

Location: Strait of Juan de Fuca, between Port Angeles and Joyce; map A1, grid e8.

How to get there: Drive west from Port Angeles on U.S. 101 about three miles and turn (right) onto Highway 112, which continues west. Drive 4.3 miles on Highway 112 to Freshwater Bay Road and turn north (right). Continue 3.5 miles on Freshwater Bay Road to the bay.

Boat ramp: There's a paved boat ramp that reaches the water on tides of about five feet or higher. Below that, you're driving out onto hard-packed sand and gravel to launch. Since there's no float or dock at the ramp, launching in a northerly or northeasterly wind can make this a real crapshoot.

Facilities: There's a concrete boat ramp with lots of parking and a couple of rest rooms, as well as an overflow parking area on the hill immediately west of the main lot. There are no docks, no floats, and no moorage. The nearest grocery stores and restaurants are out on Highway 112, and Port Angeles has a full line of facilities.

Water sports/restrictions: The flat, shallow bay limits launching to boats of about 18 feet and under, but cruisers, anglers, and sailors in larger craft often make their way here from Port Angeles and points east. The waters immediately west of the bay are popular with salmon and halibut anglers, and the bay itself offers fair to good crabbing. The rocky structure and kelp beds from Observatory Point at the west end of Freshwater Bay all the way out to Salt Creek to the west provide a haven for divers. Kayakers and other paddlers can easily launch at Freshwater Bay to explore the shoreline in either direction.

Contact: Port Angeles Boat Haven Harbor Master, tel. (360) 457-4505. For nautical charts of this area, contact Captain's Nautical Supply, tel. (206) 283-7242.

8 Port Angeles

Rating: 8

This largest city on the Strait of Juan de Fuca is a haven for boaters of all kinds, whether they're out for a Sunday in the sun or embarking on a summer-long trip to British Columbia or Alaska. You can clear U.S. Customs at the Port Angeles City Pier if you're among the latter. Besides the obvious advantages of being located near the east end of the Strait of Juan de Fuca, Port Angeles is a favorite of boaters because it has both wide-open waters and a large, protected harbor. Cruisers, sailors, and anglers can make the short run from P.A. to the open waters of the strait in a few minutes, while kayakers and cartoppers in search of Dungeness crab can stay inside the harbor and be protected from all but a stiff east wind.

Nonboaters can also find plenty to see and do along the Port Angeles waterfront, especially around the city pier and municipal park located off Lincoln Street just east of the Victoria ferry terminal. The Feiro Marine Lab is worth visiting, or you can try your luck fishing for pile perch and striped seaperch around the pier pilings. You may want to perch a while yourself, maybe on one of the driftwood logs at Hollywood Beach, where the kids can roll up their pants and wade or play along the gravel beach. It's located between the marine lab and the nearby Red Lion Inn. When I'm in Port Angeles without a boat, though, I tend to head for Ediz Hook, where I bide my time talking to anglers returning to the city boat ramp or hiking along the beach on the inside of the hook. When tide and water conditions permit, I may even hike the outside of the hook. Either way, I see plenty of diving ducks, shorebirds, seals, and other wildlife, and usually can find any number of ways to shoot a couple rolls of film.

Nautical chart 18465, which covers the eastern end of the Strait of Juan de Fuca and Admiralty Inlet, will help you locate it and will provide insights into other worthwhile fishing spots throughout the area.

Location: Strait of Juan de Fuca from Angeles Point to Green Point; map A1, grid e9.

How to get there: Take U.S. 101 to Port Angeles and continue straight through to the west end of town rather than turning south (left) on Lincoln Street. This puts you on Front Street, which continues west to the Port Angeles Boat Haven and Ediz Hook, where the town's boat ramps are located. To reach the Port Angeles City Pier, turn north on Lincoln Street and drive one block to the water.

Boat ramp: There's a Port of Port Angeles boat ramp at the east end of the boat haven and a bigger, better one at the west end of the boat basin. The problem with the one at the west end is that in the fall the port pulls the moorage float and walkway at the west ramp and leaves the facility unmaintained until spring, so if you want to launch here during the winter, you have to use the east ramp. There's a $6 launch feet at both of these port-operated ramps, but Clallam County residents can buy an annual launch permit for $21. The third ramp is on Ediz Hook, which is reached by following Front Street past the port facilities and through the Diashawa Paper Mill. Continue 1.5 miles past the mill to the ramp, which is on the right just before you reach the Coast Guard gate. This ramp is free and has moorage floats and room for launching three boats at a time.

Facilities: Port Angeles Boat Haven has a year-round fuel dock, permanent and transient moorage, rest rooms, showers, bait, and ice. Besides the three paved ramps, there's a City of Port Angeles picnic and beach access area on Ediz Hook, 0.2 mile past the paper mill. Kayaks, sailboards, and small cartoppers can be launched on the beach at this access, which has parking for about 15 vehicles. The City Pier at the foot of Lincoln Street has some transient moorage for $8 per night. Port Angeles also has plenty of restaurants, motels, shops, galleries, bars, grocery stores, and other amenities.

Water sports/restrictions: All water sports are permitted in and around Port Angeles Harbor, but fishing, sailing, crabbing, kayaking, and cruising are the most popular.

Contact: Port Angeles Boat Haven Harbor Master, tel. (360) 457-4505; Port of Port Angeles, tel. (360) 457-8527. For nautical charts of this area, contact Captain's Nautical Supply, tel. (206) 283-7242.

9 Lake Ozette

Rating: 7

At 7,787 acres this is one of the largest natural lakes in the Northwest. And since it's within the boundaries of Olympic National Park, it's also one of the region's most pristine, with nary a sign of man and his propensity for clearing the land and building things. This is a place where you can get out on the water in the early morning mist or the fading light of evening and feel close to the natural beauty of the Olympic Peninsula. Oh sure, there are times, especially in July and August, when you'll see other boats on the lake, some of them fairly good-size powerboats, but on a lake this large and this pristine, you can find a place to call your own even during this busy time at Ozette. Visit in early April before fishing season starts or in September after the Labor Day crowds go home, and you're almost sure to have hundreds of acres of lake to yourself. Let's face it: 20 miles off the main drag is a long way, especially if you're trailering a boat; and a lake with no fast food, no laundry, no hot showers, and no latte stands doesn't qualify as a perfect destination for a lot of folks. As a result most boaters don't bother with Lake Ozette. Most boaters are missing a unique experience.

Ozette's forested, undeveloped shoreline is popular with paddlers, many of whom make multiday trips around the lake and stay in the various shoreline campsites. Because this lake is so large and so lightly used except during the busier times of late spring and summer, many canoe and kayak enthusiasts here are rewarded with uninterrupted hours —even days—of peace and quiet, not having to put up with the sounds of boaters in their gas-powered craft. Powerboats come and go here, but they're not all that common. Regulations banning the use of personal watercraft went into effect in Olympic National Park in October 1998, and it applies here. One word of warning, though: the wind can come up in a hurry out here at the extreme western edge of the Lower 48, and on a lake this large a little wind equals lots of big whitecaps in a few minutes. Be on your toes, especially when exploring Ozette in a small boat, and get off the water in a hurry if the weather begins to kick up.

Location: South of Ozette, west side of Olympic Peninsula; map A1, grid f2.

How to get there: Drive west out of Sekiu on Highway 112 and turn south (left) on Hoko-Ozette Road. Drive 17.4 miles and turn left on Swan Bay Road to reach the northeast corner of the lake or continue on another four miles to the Ozette Ranger Station at the north end of the lake.

Boat ramp: A gravel boat ramp is at Swan Bay, another along the lake shore about 2.4 miles past Swan Bay Road, and a third near the ranger station at the north end of the lake.

Facilities: The 18 drive-in campsites at the north end of the lake are available on a first-come, first-served basis, and usually fill up during the summer. Some of the sites are near the beach, within a few yards of the water. These sites are free and available year-round. There are also several primitive campsites scattered around the lake, most notably in Erickson Bay, near the lake's northwest corner. The Lost Resort General Store, located near the Ozette Ranger Station, offers groceries and has canoe rentals but is not open year-round, catering primarily to summer visitors from Memorial Day to Labor Day. The nearest fuel, motels, and restaurants are in Sekiu/Clallam Bay.

Water sports/restrictions: Fishing, paddling, and cruising are the main attractions, but all water sports except PWC riding are permitted.

Contact: Ozette Ranger Station, tel. (360) 963-2725; Lost Resort General Store, tel. (360) 963-2899, tel. (800) 950-2899.

10 Lake Pleasant

Rating: 6

Easy access from the highway makes this a popular lake on a warm summer day, but limited facilities and parking at the community beach take a little of the pleasure out of Lake Pleasant during those busy times. It sometimes gets downright crowded. But most people don't seem to mind, especially after the water warms into the comfortable range, which usually happens around the middle of July. The swim beach is one of the nicest in Clallam County.

Location: West of Sappho; map A1, grid f4.

How to get there: Take U.S. 101 north from Forks or west from Port Angeles to Beaver and turn north at Lake Pleasant Grocery onto West Lake Pleasant Road. Drive 0.3 mile to Lake Pleasant Community Beach on the right.

Boat ramp: There's a single-lane ramp at the community beach and moorage floats from spring to fall.

Facilities: Besides the ramp, Lake Pleasant Community Beach has toilets, kids' playground equipment, and a nice, gravel swim beach. Lake Pleasant Grocery has the minimum daily requirements; other facilities are in Forks.

Water sports/restrictions: All water sports are permitted.

Contact: Lake Pleasant Grocery, tel. (360) 327-3211; Clallam County Parks and Fair Department, tel. (360) 417-2291.

11 Lake Crescent

Rating: 8

The biggest news for boaters here in recent years was the ban on personal watercraft issued by the United States Park Service in the fall of 1998. This big, clear, cold lake is within the boundaries of Olympic National Park, one of several parks in the country to ban PWC because of their incompatibility with other recreational uses of the lakes. But this 5,000-acre lake alongside U.S. 101 at the rugged north end of the Olympic Peninsula is a near-perfect place for most other water sports. The exception might be swimming, unless you are without nerve endings throughout your body. If Crescent isn't the coldest lake in Washington during a typical summer, I don't what lake could be colder. I last took a dip here in the early '60s, and I still haven't fully recovered. Scuba divers, provided they're protected with adequate layers of Neoprene, find this a fascinating place to explore, thanks to the fact that Crescent is every bit as clear as it is cold.

If you're a boater, pay attention to weather and wind changes, especially if you're out in the open parts of this big lake. The wind can build here in a hurry, and the lake's surface can go from glass smooth to whitecaps before you can find cover if you're caught out in the middle in a paddle craft, rowboat, or small outboard.

Location: Midway between Port Angeles and Sappho; map A1, grid f7. (See Lake Crescent inset map.)

How to get there: Take U.S. 101 north from Forks 28 miles or west from Port Angeles 17 miles to reach the lake, which parallels the north side of Highway 101 for over 10 miles.

Boat ramp: The following boat ramps are listed on the Lake Crescent inset maps:

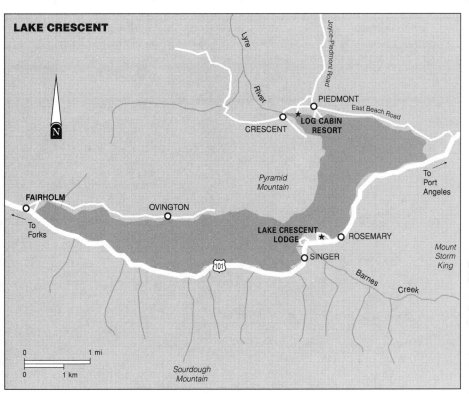

LAKE CRESCENT

- **Fairholm:** Located at the west end of the lake.
- **Lake Crescent Lodge:** Located on the south shore.
- **Log Cabin Resort:** Located at the northwest end of the lake.

Facilities: Log Cabin Resort on the north end of the lake has rental cabins, lodge rooms, RV sites, a restaurant, fishing dock, store, and boat rentals (canoes, rowboats, and paddle boats). Reach it by taking East Beach Road off U.S. 101 at the east end of the lake or by turning south off Highway 112 onto Joyce-Piedmont Road and driving 4.4 miles. Fairholm is at the west end, just off the highway, and offers a cafe, general store, fuel, and RV and tent sites. In the middle, just off U.S. 101, is Lake Crescent Lodge, with boat rentals, cabins, and a restaurant.

Water sports/restrictions: All water sports are popular here except PWC riding, which has been banned by the Park Service.

Contact: Log Cabin Resort, tel. (360) 928-3325 (April through October); Lake Crescent Lodge, tel. (360) 928-3211; Fairholm, tel. (360) 928-2141; Olympic National Park Headquarters, tel. (360) 452-0330.

12 Lake Sutherland
Rating: 6

Once a haven for slow-moving trollers in search of giant cutthroat trout, the pace has quickened a great deal at Sutherland in recent years. You're much more likely to find water-skiers and PWC riders than anglers now, especially after the lake begins to warm in late June. If you prefer your water sports to move at a fast clip, this is a good bet. As a reminder, however, the restricted-speed times and other boating regulations are posted at the public boat ramp, and the Clallam County Sheriff's Department does visit Sutherland now and then to make sure everyone's playing by the rules.

Location: East of Lake Crescent; map A1, grid f7.

How to get there: Take U.S. 101 west from Port Angeles and drive 12 miles to South Shore Road. Turn south (left) and follow South Shore Road 1.5 miles to the public access area.

Boat ramp: There's a single-wide, paved boat ramp at the public access area.

Facilities: The Department of Fish and Wildlife access area has pit toilets and parking for about a dozen cars. Shadow Mountain General Store and RV Park is on the north side of the highway, about midway along the lake's north shore. Motels, restaurants, and other amenities can be found in Port Angeles.

Water sports/restrictions: All water sports are permitted. There's a 40 mph speed limit on the lake, except 10 mph limit from sunset to sunrise. PWC riding and waterskiing are prohibited from sunset to sunrise.

Contact: Shadow Mountain General Store and RV Park, tel. (360) 928-3043.

13 Lake Aldwell

Rating: 6

Anglers and paddlers use this Elwha River reservoir more than anyone else, and it's well-suited to those activities. Most of the shoreline is natural, and it's a haven for birds and wildlife, including a large flock of swans that call the lake

home during part of the year. They stand out like icebergs against the dark water and green shoreline. They won't give you any trouble, so show them the same courtesy.

Location: Southwest of Port Angeles; map A1, grid f8.

How to get there: Drive west from Port Angeles on U.S. 101 about eight miles; cross the Elwha River bridge and turn north (right) onto Lake Aldwell Road, which is marked with a sign reading "Indian Creek Recreation Area." Drive 0.6 mile to the access area at the head of the lake.

Boat ramp: There's a boat ramp at the upper (south) end of the lake.

Facilities: Except for the access area, there are no facilities on the lake. Elwha River Resort and Cafe is nearby, and other amenities are in Port Angeles.

Water sports/restrictions: All water sports are permitted, but the small boat ramp and access area limit traffic here to mostly smaller trailer boats, cartoppers, canoes, and kayaks.

Contact: Shadow Mountain General Store and RV Park, tel. (360) 928-3043.

14 Elwha River

Rating: 6

This is a good place for the not-too-experienced kayaker or river rafter to learn what it's all about. With some fairly fast water, several good rock gardens, but no heavy-duty rapids that could beat you up, the Altaire-to-Aldwell run is a good Class II run. But at maybe 4.5 miles it's a short run that will take you only a couple of hours to complete. If you're not sure about your own capabilities but want to experience the Elwha, you might want to run the river with a guide, such as the one mentioned in the "Contact" section below.

Location: Flows into Strait of Juan de Fuca west of Port Angeles; map A1, grid f8.

How to get there: Take U.S. 101 west from Port Angeles and turn south (left) on Olympic Hot Springs Road, following it five miles to Altaire Campground.

Boat ramp: You can launch your kayak or raft at Altaire or drag it over the bank alongside Hot Springs Road a short distance downstream. The take-out point is at the upper end of Lake Aldwell, just downstream from the U.S. 101 bridge.

Facilities: There's a public access area and boat ramp with room for about eight cars on Lake Aldwell. Altaire Campground is open from spring to fall only and has 30 RV and tent sites. Elwha Campground is open year-round and has 41 RV and tent sites. The camping fee at both is $10 per night. Elwha Resort and Cafe is right off U.S. 101 and has cabins, RV spaces, tent sites, and a small store. Other campgrounds are nearby, and complete facilities are available in Port Angeles.

Water sports/restrictions: The Elwha offers fun and relatively safe paddling possibilities.

Contact: Olympic National Park, tel. (360) 452-0330; Olympic Raft & Guide Service, tel. (360) 452-1443.

15 Lake Mills

Rating: 6

If peace and solitude are high on your list, this Elwha River impoundment is a good bet, especially if you avoid the major holiday weekends. Mills is far enough off the beaten path that most boaters ignore it, and it's long enough to allow you to get away from those other boaters who do make the trip. A prohibition on PWC riding went into effect here in the fall of 1998 as part a regulation change throughout Olympic National Park. Paddling or cruising the lake's forested shoreline will give you a chance to spot deer, elk, eagles, and other wildlife without spotting a lot of other people.

If you explore the lake in a small boat, kayak, or canoe, take a few minutes to study the information posted at the boat launch. Among other things, it advises boaters to be alert for the afternoon winds that often kick up out of the south during the afternoon and early evening. That southerly breeze may produce three- to five-foot whitecaps on Lake Mills and will keep paddlers and small-boat operators from getting back to the boat ramp. Pay attention to the weather and head back early if the wind starts whistling up the Elwha River Canyon.

One disappointment here is that the dam and small parking area nearby were built without any consideration for public viewing, and little has been done over the years to remedy that problem. If you crowd right up to the chain-link fence and stand on your toes, you can get a partial view of the gorgeous canyon immediately below the dam, but it's not easy. The view of this entire canyon could change, though, if sentiment toward removing both Elwha dams continues to grow. Lake Mills could be gone in a few years, providing a look at what this river valley looked like before the dam was completed in 1920.

A special reward for boaters here is a side trip to nearby Olympic Hot Springs, a five-mile drive and 2.4-mile hike farther up the road. The hike is an easy one on an old roadbed, and there are several springs of varying temperature when you reach the end. There's considerable parking space near the gate at the end of the road, and during weekend and summer days there may be 15 or 20 cars parked there, many of them hot springs visitors. Some of them wear swimsuits; most don't. Just so you know.

Location: Southwest of Port Angeles; map A1, grid g9.

How to get there: Drive west on U.S. 101 out of Port Angeles about eight miles and turn south (left) on Olympic Hot Springs Road, following it 5.7 miles to Glines Canyon Dam and the lake behind it.

Boat ramp: There's a gravel ramp with a small float and limited parking about 300 yards up the beach from the dam.

Facilities: There's a toilet at the boat ramp and access area, but that's about it. Altaire Campground, which you'll pass on the way to the lake, is open from spring to fall and has 30 campsites. A little farther down Hot Springs Road is Elwha Campground, which has 41 campsites for tents and RVs. Camping fee is $10 per night at both campgrounds. The nearest groceries and beverages are back at Elwha River Resort and Cafe, where you turn off U.S. 101. All other facilities are in Port Angeles.

Water sports/restrictions: You can't water-ski or ride PWC here, but all other water sports are permitted. Swimming is a possibility near the ramp, but the water is cold, the bottom is littered with limbs and debris, and I wouldn't recommend it. The size and condition of the gravel boat ramp make it difficult to launch boats larger than about 16 feet.

Contact: Olympic National Park, tel. (360) 452-0330.

16 LaPush

Rating: 6

Once a thriving resort town catering to salmon anglers, LaPush for the past couple of decades has had little to offer visiting boaters. Amenities for tourists were all but nonexistent here on the Quillayute Indian Reservation. That's too bad, since this is perhaps the most beautiful spot on the entire Washington coast. The good news is that one of the state's newest marinas is now in operation here, once again making this reservation village at the mouth of the Quillayute River a viable destination for boaters and other water recreationists. If you've never visited this gorgeous part of the world, maybe the new facilities will prompt you to give it a look. It's worth what turns out to be a very long trip from anywhere else in the Northwest. Forests of Douglas fir, western red cedar, and hemlock extend right down to the rocky shoreline in many spots, and the edge of the Pacific here is a beachcomber's dream. Like much of the Washington coast, it's also a place where a growing number of surfers gather to catch a wave. This also may be the most beautiful place in the Evergreen State to surf, with long expanses of clean beaches, but the nearby rock spires serve as a reminder to stay in control.

Wind and weather conditions (and boating experience) permitting, cruisers, sailors, anglers, divers, and even paddlers can find water and adventure the like of which they may not have realized existed here in the Evergreen State. But don't take the water here for granted, or you can find yourself in trouble quickly. With the combination of tides, fast-changing weather blowing in off the Pacific, and the somewhat unpredictable influence of the Quillayute River, just getting in and out of LaPush by water can be quite tricky. You may recall that this is where three U.S. Coast Guardsmen lost their lives on a stormy night in 1997, so it's not a place for novice boaters to try their hand at "this boating thing." Pay attention to what you're doing, especially in a paddle craft or small powerboat.

Along with Neah Bay to the north, La-Push is one of two jumping-off points for boaters wanting to explore the wild and woolly expanses of the northwest Washington coast. But LaPush is a long way from most anywhere, whether you're boating or trailering there, so few people make the trip. If you do, you'll need at least one of the following nautical charts: 18485, 18460, or 18480.

Location: West of Forks; map A1, grid g2.

How to get there: Take U.S. 101 to La-Push Road, about two miles north of Forks, and turn west. Follow LaPush Road about 14 miles to LaPush.

Boat ramp: There are now two boat ramps in LaPush, both located near Quileute Marina.

Facilities: LaPush now has two boat ramps, a new marina with nearly 100 slips, fuel, sewage pump-out service, and waste-oil tank. Food, lodging, and campgrounds are available a short distance from the marina. All amenities are available in Forks, about 18 miles away.

Water sports/restrictions: Cruising, paddling, surfing, diving, and fishing are possibilities. But don't do any of them unless you understand the dangers of the open Pacific Ocean and are equipped to deal with them.

Contact: Quileute Marina, tel. (360) 374-5392 (VHF ch. 80); Olympic Sporting Goods, tel. (360) 374-6330. For nautical charts of the Northwest Coast contact Captain's Nautical Supply, tel. (206) 283-7242.

17 Quillayute River

Rating: 6

If you're looking for a slow, gentle river to spend a half day of gentle paddling, this could be the spot for you. Unlike the smaller, faster Bogachiel and Sol Duc Rivers farther upstream, the Quillayute is a gentle giant, very suitable to novice kayakers and rafters looking to get their feet wet. Maybe that was a bad choice of words, but you get the picture. The five-mile paddle from Lyendecker Park to the Dickey River is scenic but safe. But remember that this entire stretch is influenced by the tide, and on a flood tide you may have to keep paddling to continue downstream.

Although generally avoidable, sweeper alders and cedars may hang off the bank into the river, especially after any period of heavy rain that causes flooding conditions. You may also encounter a logjam or two here, so pay attention. Also keep in mind that paddlers here often have to share the river with anglers and tribal gillnetters, especially in spring and fall when the salmon are running, and during the winter when steelhead season is in full swing. Always be on the lookout for nets and flying lures.

Location: Enters Pacific Ocean at La-Push, west side of Olympic Peninsula; map A1, grid g2.

How to get there: Take U.S. 101 to the town of Forks and turn west on LaPush Road about two miles north of town. Turn right on Mora Road, which parallels the north side of the Quillayute.

Boat ramp: You'll find a boat ramp at Lyendecker County Park, where the Bogachiel and Sol Duc Rivers meet to form the Quillayute, and a rough take-out spot at the mouth of the Dickey River, which enters the Quillayute about a mile above LaPush.

Facilities: Mora Campground, at the confluence of the Quillayute and Dickey Rivers, has 94 RV and tent sites, available at $10 per night. Three Rivers Resort offers cabins, RV and tent sites, hot showers, a small store with groceries and tackle, laundry facilities, and a guide service. Food, gas, lodging, tackle, and fishing guides are available in Forks.

Water sports/restrictions: Fishing and paddling are the main attractions on the Quillayute.

Contact: Olympic Sporting Goods, tel. (360) 374-6330; Three Rivers Resort, tel. (360) 374-5300.

18 Sol Duc River

Rating: 7

There was a time not all that many years ago when the Sol Duc was largely the sole domain of salmon and steelhead anglers, but not so any more. Lots of whitewater enthusiasts have come to realize that this main tributary of the Quillayute River system is one of the Olympic Peninsula's best streams for whitewater thrills, so rain-gear-clad anglers often find themselves sharing the Sol Duc with paddlers in brightly colored nylon and poly fibers. They may not always enjoy the company, but they generally accept it. The wildest and most exciting stretch of the river is the long run from Forest Service Road 2918 down to the Sol Duc Hatchery, a distance of about 24 miles. There's some Class III water along this stretch, so don't attempt it if you don't know what you're doing. The lower stretch from the hatchery down to the U.S. 101 bridge near Forks is much shorter and much gentler, topping out at Class II. If you want an even easier paddle, launch at the U.S. 101 bridge and take all day to float clear down to Lyendecker County Park at the confluence of the Sol Duc and Bogachiel Rivers. It's about a 14-mile float.

Location: North and west of Forks, flowing into Quillayute River; map A1, grid f3.

How to get there: Drive west from Port Angeles or north from Hoquiam on U.S. 101, which parallels much of the river and crosses it just north of the town of Forks. Turn south (left) on Forest Service Road 2918 to reach upper portions of the main Sol Duc and the South Fork Sol Duc or continue west toward Forks to reach lower sections of the river. To get to the lower Sol Duc, turn west off U.S. 101 north of Forks onto LaPush Road.

Boat ramp: There are several places along Forest Road 2918 where a small boat or kayak can be launched over the bank, with developed boat ramps at Klahowya Campground and the Sol Duc Salmon Hatchery near the town of Sappho. Another is located just upstream of the U.S. 101 bridge over the Sol Duc about three miles north of Forks off Salmon Drive. Another well-used access area is off Mora Road on the lower river at Lyendecker County Park.

Facilities: Three Rivers Resort has cabins, RV and tent sites, a grocery store with tackle and fishing licenses, a restaurant that serves lunch and dinner, hot showers, a coin laundry, and guide service. Other river guides and outfitters, motels, bed-and-breakfasts, groceries, gas, restaurants, and other services are available in Forks.

Water sports/restrictions: Fishing and whitewater paddling are the main draws here, but a few hardy souls also run the Sol Duc in inner tubes.

Contact: Three Rivers Resort, tel. (360) 374-5300, Olympic Sporting Goods, tel. (360) 374-6330; Forks Chamber of Commerce, tel. (360) 374-2531.

19 Bogachiel River

Rating: 6

The 15-mile stretch of river from Bogachiel State Park down to Lyendecker

County Park is a fairly easy run, with a few of Class II rapids providing the greatest excitement. Most of the run, though, is through moderately gentle rapids and winding turns that give plenty of opportunity to take in the view of nearby mountains, forests and a good mix of agricultural lowlands. Like the Sol Duc, the Bogachiel is very popular with salmon and steelhead anglers, so paddlers can expect company during much of the year. Give them plenty of room to fish; if they're anchored and casting toward deep water, take the shallow-water route behind them wherever possible. Like most other Olympic Peninsula rivers, the Bogachiel offers the opportunity to see and photograph lots of wildlife, including elk, deer, eagles, osprey, and even an occasional black bear.

Location: Follows Clallam-Jefferson county line to join the Sol Duc River west of Forks; map A1, grids g4.

How to get there: Take U.S. 101 north from Hoquiam or west from Port Angeles and drive to Forks. Turn west at the south end of town to reach Bogachiel Road, which goes to the Bogachiel Rearing Ponds. Turn west on LaPush Road about two miles north of town to reach the lower end of the river. To reach upper portions of the river, drive east off U.S. 101 on South Bogachiel Road or turn off the highway at Bogachiel State Park, which is well marked.

Boat ramp: A good put-in spot is at Bogachiel State Park and another at Lyendecker County Park, where the Bogachiel meets the Sol Duc to form the Quillayute River.

Facilities: Bogachiel State Park has a few tent and RV sites, rest rooms, showers, and a boat ramp. Forks has motels, restaurants, grocery stores, gas stations, some rough-and-tumble bars and taverns, and several river-guide businesses.

Water sports/restrictions: Fishing and paddling are both popular here, and some of the local kids like to swim and inner tube parts of the river.

Contact: Olympic Sporting Goods, tel. (360) 374-6330; Bogachiel State Park, tel. (360) 374-6356; Forks Chamber of Commerce, tel. (360) 374-2531.

20 Hoh River

Rating: 7

Anglers have been running McKenzie-style drift boats down this big glacial river for over 30 years, and they still are the most common craft you'll see on the Hoh, especially during the winter steelhead season that runs from December through March. During the spring and summer months, on the other hand, there are at least as many paddlers as anglers here.

The most exciting water is on the upper river from the ranger station at the end of Upper Hoh Road down to the Oxbow access, and it's a stretch of river where you have to be on the alert for sweepers, especially if you're floating the river after a heavy rain that may have dislodged trees from the bank. The canyon section, just above Oxbow, is perhaps the prettiest part of the entire river. The lower river is more gentle and a little less scenic, but you still stand a good chance of coming around a corner to the sight of several Roosevelt elk standing at river's edge or perhaps a bald eagle snatching a cutthroat trout from the shallows or working over the carcass of a salmon that has washed up onto the beach. There are a few Class II rapids scattered along the length of the Hoh, most of them on the upper stretch above Oxbow.

Location: Flows into Pacific Ocean north of Kalaloch; map A1, grid h4.

How to get there: Take U.S. 101 north from Hoquiam or west from Port Angeles. The highway parallels the south side of the river downstream from the bridge, or turn west on Lower Hoh Road just north of the bridge to drive down the north side of the river. To reach the upper Hoh, turn east on Upper Hoh Road about two miles north of the bridge.

Boat ramp: Full-fledged boat ramps are at the Washington Department of Natural Resources' access areas at Oxbow (just above the U.S. 101 bridge) and at Cottonwood (off Lower Road about 3.5 miles downstream of the bridge). At other places you can drive out onto a gravel bar or launch a boat off the side of the road.

Facilities: You'll find a store and campground on the south side of the river just south of the bridge and another on the upper river. Both have cabins for rent. Motels and other facilities are available in Forks. Several Department of Natural Resources campgrounds are scattered along the river, including Cottonwood Campground on the lower Hoh, Willoughby, Morgan's Crossing, Spruce Creek, Huelsdonk and Hoh Rain Forest campgrounds on the upper river.

Water sports/restrictions: Kayaking, rafting, and fishing are the main attractions.

Contact: Westward Hoh River Resort, tel. (360) 374-6657, Olympic Sporting Goods, tel. (360) 374-6330; Forks Chamber of Commerce, tel. (360) 374-2531.

21 Clearwater River

Rating: 6

This is not a difficult or hazardous stream for paddlers with any experience at all, but you may get a workout ducking overhanging limbs and trees or even getting out to drag through a few extremely shallow flats and tiny channels. Even the named rapids—Skookumchuck, Barker, and Preacher's—are barely Class II water, so you can enjoy them right along with the rest of this easy float through typical Olympic Peninsula countryside.

Location: Flows into the Queets River, east of Queets, west side of Olympic Peninsula; Map A1, grid h4.

How to get there: Drive north from Hoquiam on U.S. 101 about 62 miles and turn north (right) on Clearwater Road, which parallels the river for more than 12 miles. (If you come to the Queets River Bridge on U.S. 101, you've gone past the Clearwater Road about 4.5 miles back.)

Boat ramp: There's a take-out spot three-quarters of a mile above the confluence of the Clearwater and Queets Rivers, and a rough put-in another eight miles upstream where Clearwater Road crosses the river.

Facilities: There's nothing along the river, but gas, food, and lodging are available at Kalaloch, 10 miles to the north on U.S. 101.

Water sports/restrictions: Fishing and whitewater paddling are the main attractions.

Contact: Clearwater Ranger Station, tel. (360) 962-2283; Olympic National Park, tel. (360) 452-4501.

22 Queets River

Rating: 7

I chose the Queets for my maiden voyage when I bought my used drift boat back in 1977. I spent the first hour on the river roping the boat, my passenger, and my German short-haired pointer through the long rock garden that lies a few hundred feet downstream of the campground at Sam's Rapid. I was sweaty, tired, mad, and still within sight of the put-in, and quickly decided that if I was going to be a river boater, I'd better learn how to row the damn thing in a hurry. The rest of the float down to wherever I ended that trip was a joy, and I think we even put a summer-run steelhead in the boat at some point during that first float. The moral of the story is that the Queets does offer some challenge, especially for the novice river runner, but the rewards are well worth the effort.

This is a beautiful stream, with enough Class II+ water to keep you thinking but also lots of places where you can let the oars or paddles drag, kick back, and enjoy the true essence of the Olympic Peninsula. There's a good chance you'll see Roosevelt elk along the way, and there are also black-tailed deer, river otter, eagles, osprey, beaver, mink, and a variety of waterfowl along the river. Whitewater enthusiasts tend to prefer the float from Sam's Rapid down to Hartzell Creek, while anglers like to launch at Streater Bar or Hartzell Creek and float down to the mouth of the Clearwater, especially during the winter steelhead season. The reason they like this lower run is that it provides a better shot at the large run of hatchery steelhead returning to the Salmon River, which enters the Queets about two miles up the Queets Valley Road.

I don't know anyone who does so, but adventurous paddlers could take inflatables or other light craft up the trail that heads upstream from the campground at Sam's Rapid and spend a very pleasant few hours working their way down through the moderate rapids and small rock gardens scattered along the upper Queets.

Location: Enters Pacific Ocean at Queets, near Jefferson-Grays Harbor county line; map A1, grid i4.

How to get there: Take U.S. 101 north from Hoquiam and turn north (right) on Queets River Road, right at the Grays Harbor-Jefferson county line. Follow the road upstream as far as 14 miles.

Boat ramp: There are put-in/take-out spots at the Queets River Campground (also called Sam's Rapid, Sam's River, Sam's River Campground, and Sam's Campground, depending on whom you ask), Streater Bar, River View, Hartzell Creek, and at the confluence of the Queets and Clearwater Rivers.

Facilities: Queets River Campground is at the end of the road and has tent spaces with no hookups of any kind. The nearest restaurant, gas, lodging, and groceries are at Kalaloch, about 10 miles north of the entrance to Queets River Road.

Water sports/restrictions: Fishing and whitewater paddling draw most visitors to the Queets.

Contact: Clearwater Ranger Station, tel. (360) 962-2283 (daytime hours only).

23 Lake Quinault

Rating: 7

The speed limit, the limited number of launch ramps and facilities, the location so many miles from any major population center, and perhaps the natural serenity of the Olympic Peninsula keep this 3,700-acre gem of a lake from becoming a mob scene. If it were located a few miles from Seattle, it would be crowded and crazy, but lucky for all of us, it's nestled in the forested hills of the peninsula, so it's a place where boaters can get away, soak in the natural beauty, and take things at a slow, enjoyable pace.

There are, unfortunately, two problems here. One is that the limited open season doesn't allow for escaping to Lake Quinault if the urge should strike you on a warm March weekend or a calm day in November. Oh yes, the lodges and resorts are open and running at full speed, but the boating season is closed. The second problem is the wind, which can come up with no warning and whip the big lake to a froth in a matter of minutes. You don't want to be in the middle of Lake Quinault when that happens, no matter what size your boat.

Location: At Amanda Park; map A1, grid i6.

How to get there: Take U.S. 101 north from Hoquiam about 38 miles and turn east (right) onto well-marked South Shore Road before you cross the river at Amanda Park, or continue on U.S. 101 and turn right on North Shore Road about three miles past Amanda Park.

Boat ramp: There are single-lane boat ramps at Willaby and Falls Creek Campgrounds, both of which are on South Shore Road. The ramps are available only when the campgrounds are open, which is from April through October.

Facilities: Lake Quinault Lodge, Rain Forest Resort Village, Willaby Campground, and Falls Creek Campground are all within a mile and a half of each other on South Shore Road. Canoes, paddle boats, and rowboats are available for rent by the hour at Lake Quinault Lodge, and canoe rentals are available at Rain Forest Resort Village. Rain Forest has a limited number of RV sites with hookups, available on a first-come, first-served basis. Lake Quinault Resort Motel and July Creek Campground (walk-in sites only) are on the north side of the lake, off North Shore Road. Food, gas, and tackle are available in nearby Amanda Park.

Water sports/restrictions: The lake is within the boundaries of the Quinault Indian reservation, so fishing and boating are managed by the Quinaults. They open the lake to boating and fishing early April (usually the first weekend) and close it at the end of October. Speed limits of 5 mph within 100 yards of shore and 24 mph elsewhere on the lake are enforced by tribal police. Waterskiing and PWC riding are prohibited. Fishing, sailing, canoeing, and cruising all are popular during the season. The gravel beaches at the three resorts offer good swimming opportunities, although the lake is chilly except during a few weeks in July and August.

Contact: Lake Quinault Resort, tel. (800) 650-2362; Lake Quinault Lodge, tel. (800) 562-6672; Lakeside Retreat, tel. (360) 288-2633; Olympic National Park, Quinault Area, tel. (360) 288-2444; Quinault Indian Nation tel. (360) 276-8211.

24 Upper Quinault River

Rating: 6

Although most visitors come here to hike the trails or simply take in the incredible rain forest, a few visit the Quinault Valley to spend time on the river. Most are anglers in search of trophy-class wild steelhead, but a few are paddlers looking for a little whitewater and a chance to float one of the clearest streams on the Peninsula. The upper Quinault isn't big, isn't bad, isn't particularly dangerous, and therefore isn't high on any list of Washington's whitewater streams. In fact, most of the paddling books I've read fail to mention the Quinault at all. But it's a fun little river, with enough small boulder patches, fast-water chutes, sweepers stretching across all or part of its width to give paddlers a challenge and a long look at some exceptional scenery. You're more likely than not to see at least one herd of elk if you make the trip from the bridge all the way down to the lake, and lots of other wildlife to boot.

Location: Flows into Lake Quinault; map A1, grid j5.

How to get there: Drive north from Hoquiam on U.S. 101 and turn west on South Shore Road, passing Lake Quinault and continuing about four miles past the end of the lake to where the road begins to parallel the south side of the river.

Boat ramp: There's a good spot to launch a boat beneath the Quinault Loop bridge, about eight miles above the lake, and another about three miles downstream from the bridge.

Facilities: Lake Quinault Lodge, Rain Forest Resort Village, Willaby Campground, and Falls Creek Campground are all within a mile and a half of each other on South Shore Road. Rain Forest has a limited number of RV sites with hookups, available on a first-come, first-served basis. Lake Quinault Resort Motel and July Creek Campground (walk-in sites only) are off North Shore Road on the north side of the lake. Food, gas, and tackle are available in nearby Amanda Park, and a grocery store/cafe is on South Shore Road, across the road from Lake Quinault Lodge.

Water sports/restrictions: The upper Quinault offers some fishing and paddling opportunities.

Contact: Lake Quinault Lodge, tel. (800) 562-6672; Rain Forest Resort Village, tel. (800) 255-6936; Lake Quinault Resort Motel, tel. (800) 650-2362; Olympic National Park, Quinault Area, tel. (360) 288-2444.

25 Wynoochee Lake

Rating: 6

This four-mile-long impoundment, created with the completion of Wynoochee Dam in 1972, is a little too far off the main highway to attract huge crowds, and that's just fine with the folks who are willing to spend the time and drive the extra miles to get here. You can usually find plenty of room to paddle, sail, or motor in solitude, especially if you head up the lake toward the north end, away from the boat ramp and campgrounds down near the dam.

The lake is at its best and prettiest in the spring and early summer, when the water level is right up near the Douglas fir and hemlock trees that line its shoreline. In September and early October, when western Washington often sees some of its most pleasant weather, Coho Campground and Wynoochee Lake are virtually uninhabited, and that's the time of year some people prefer to visit this high-country reservoir. The bank is quite steep along much of the shoreline, so swimming access is a bit of a problem except at the day-use area near the dam, where a large, roped swimming area has been created over a large shoal. The beach here is gradual, and the water warms much faster than the rest of the lake. The only problem with the swimming area is that it gets steadily smaller as the summer progresses and the water level drops.

One word of warning: The view down into the river from the visitor center or from the top of the dam will give you the willies; at least it always has that effect on me.

Location: Olympic National Forest, north of Grisdale; map A1, grid j8.

How to get there: Take Highway 8 and U.S. 12 west from Olympia, turning north (right) at the Devonshire Road/Wynoochee Dam exit a mile west of Montesano. Look straight across Devonshire Road when you reach the end of the exit and you'll see the sign pointing the way to Wynoochee Lake. From there it's a 35-mile drive up the Wynoochee River

Valley. The road is paved for the first 17 miles, but it's gravel from there to the lake. At the 33.5-mile mark you'll come to a left turn with a sign pointing to Wynoochee Dam and Coho Campground. Take that left and drive 0.3 mile to a Y, where you'll go right. From there it's 0.9 mile to the Wynoochee Dam Visitor Center, 1.2 miles to the road leading to the day-use swim area and road crossing the top of the dam, and 1.4 miles to Coho Campground, all on the right side of the road.

Boat ramp: There's a good paved ramp at Coho Campground near the southwest corner of the lake. The ramp is wide enough for two boats to launch at the same time, and it extends more than 50 yards down the hill, to accommodate launching even during the low water levels of late summer and fall.

Facilities: Coho Campground has 58 camping sites, about half of which are wide, paved RV spaces that will accommodate rigs up to 36 feet long. All have picnic tables and barbecue pits. The drive-in spaces go for $10 a night, walk-in tent sites for $7 a night. All sites are first-come, first served. Launching is free. Just up the west side of the lake from Coho Campground is Chetwoot Campground, which is walk-in or boat-in only. The eight primitive campsites at Chetwoot are no-fee sites. There are no stores, gas stations, or lodging facilities near the lake, so bring everything you may need.

Water sports/restrictions: Anglers, paddlers, sailors, powerboaters, and PWC riders share this lake in relative harmony, and the day-use access near the dam has plenty of room for swimmers and picnickers. A buoy line near the south end of the lake keeps boats away from the dam and the swimming area. Other than that, the only restrictions are good boating sense and the possibility of hitting a floating log or other debris that occasionally washes into the lake from the Wynoochee River.

Contact: Olympic National Forest, Hood Canal Ranger District, tel. (360) 877-5254.

JONES ISLAND

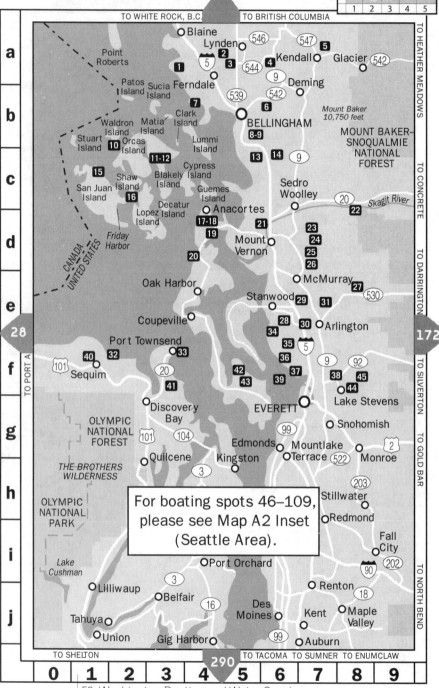

For boating spots 46–109, please see Map A2 Inset (Seattle Area).

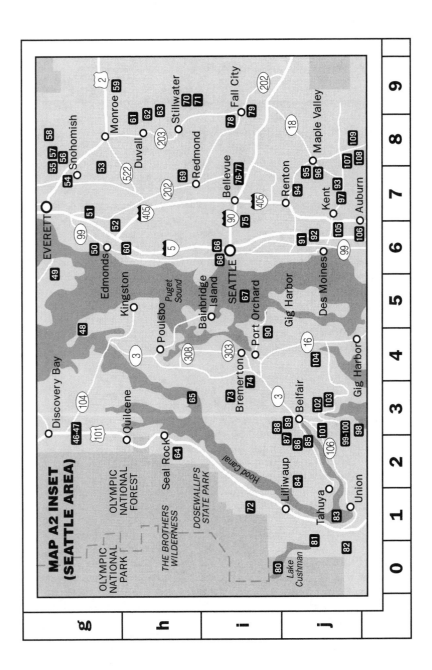

MAP A2 INSET (SEATTLE AREA)

CHAPTER A2

1 Lake Terrell

Rating: 7

At 440 acres, Terrell is a large lake by western Washington standards, but you'll have trouble finding any water deeper than about 10 feet, so it's also shallow by western Washington standards. Put all this together and you end up with a big lake that warms very quickly with a few days of sunny spring weather. By mid-summer it offers some of the warmest water in northwestern Washington, and many of the usual warm-water recreational activities kick into gear. This is as great place for early morning and evening paddling around water's edge, and with several miles of shoreline, there are plenty of places to investigate and things to see.

Location: West of Ferndale; map A2, grid a3.

How to get there: Take Interstate 5 to Ferndale and drive west about four miles on Mountain View Road to Lake Terrell Road. Turn right and drive about three-quarters of a mile to the lake.

Boat ramp: There's a Department of Fish and Wildlife access area with a concrete-plank boat ramp and loading float on the west side of the lake. The boat ramp is closed in conjunction with the boat-fishing closure from October to mid-January. A $10 WDFW access decal is required to use the public launch area.

Contact: Lake Terrell Wildlife Area, tel. (360) 384-4723.

Facilities: Ferndale has restaurants, motels, gas, tackle, and other necessities.

Water sports/restrictions: All water sports are allowed, but fishing from boats is forbidden from early October until January 15. Read the current fishing regulations for details on that one.

2 Nooksack River

Rating: 8

Rafters and kayakers from all over the Pacific Northwest come to the Nooksack to test their skills, some in their own craft and others aboard guided rafts that run the river under the names of several commercial operations.

Whitewater enthusiasts favor the Nooksack's two main tributaries, the North Fork and South Fork, both of which offer good stretches of Class III water and, depending on the height of the flow and where you launch, the potential for more challenging and technical Class IV and even Class V water that shouldn't be attempted by any but the most experienced and fearless of river runners. Perhaps the best run on the North Fork is the 7.5-mile stretch from Douglas Fir Campground down to Maple Falls. Kayakers can boat this part of the river in most conditions, but rafters will want moderate to high flows of about 1,000 cfs or more. Most of the Class III water on this stretch is found along the first two miles or so, but the lower section's Class II water does include enough snags, sweepers, and other potential hazards to merit a warning that boaters have to pay attention.

A 10-mile float down to Saxon Road on the South Fork Nooksack also contains a short stretch of Class III water but is generally much more gentle and relaxing than the North Fork run just described. The South Fork above Saxon Road is well suited to kayaks, rafts, and even canoes, but rafters will probably want at least a moderate flow and water level for optimum floating. Below Saxon Road the river slows considerably and provides a very good run for canoes and inner tubing. On a clear day this stretch provides some great views of the snow-covered Twin Sisters, so don't be in a hurry to get downstream and off the river; scenery like this isn't available just anywhere.

The main Nooksack, downstream from the confluence of the North and South Forks near the town of Deming, doesn't contain any particularly notorious rapids, but that doesn't mean it should be taken for granted. Although snags, sweepers, and rapids are easy to spot if you're paying attention, the main Nooksack is cold, and its surprisingly strong current moves along at a fast enough clip to catch the inattentive river-runner off-guard. Boaters have gotten into trouble in many places here, and the docile looking Nooksack has claimed the lives of several people over the years. If you want to, though, you can paddle and float the entire main Nooksack from Deming downstream to Ferndale.

Location: Flows into Bellingham Bay, northwest of Bellingham; map A2, grid a4.

How to get there: To reach the South Fork Nooksack, exit Interstate 5 onto Highway 20 at Burlington and drive east to Sedro Woolley, then north on Highway 9 to the river. Upper portions of the South Fork may also be reached by driving east from Sedro Woolley on Highway 20 and turning north (left) on Ensley Road. To reach the North Fork and Middle Fork Nooksack, turn east off Highway 9 near Deming onto Highway 542. Turn south (right) onto Mosquito Lake Road to reach the Middle Fork, but stay on Highway 542 to reach several good stretches of the North Fork.

Some popular stretches of the main Nooksack are within easy driving range of Highway 9 west of Deming. Turn west off Highway 9 at Everson to drive downstream to Lynden and then continue downstream toward Ferndale. Along the way, about a dozen roads extend to or near the river. Reach the south side of the main river between Ferndale and Everson by driving east out of Ferndale on Paradise Road and turning north on Northwest Drive. Again, several intersecting roads reach the river.

Boat ramp: Kayaks can launch or take out on the South Fork from Ensley Road, from Saxon Road just above where it crosses the river, at the end of Strand Road (off Highway 9 between Van Zandt and Acme), or off Highway 9 near the confluence of the South and North Forks. North Fork put-in spots include Highway 542 at Douglas Fir Campground, Maple Falls, and just downstream from the Nooksack Fish Hatchery. The best place to launch or take out on the main Nooksack is beneath the Highway 542 bridge over the river at Cedarville. There's a concrete-plank ramp here, but it was in bad condition at last check. Downstream is a public access area off Highway 539 (Meridian Road) a short distance southwest of Lynden where boats can be dragged or carried to the water. There's also a Department of Fish and Wildlife boat ramp and access area south of Ferndale at about river mile six. Located at the north end of Hovander County Park, this ramp sometimes becomes difficult or impossible to use because of silt buildup. A $10 Washington Department of Fish and Wildlife access decal is required to use the public launch areas maintained by the WDFW.

Facilities: Ferndale RV/Campground, about a mile and a half north of town just off Interstate 5, has tent and RV sites and other camping facilities. Other options include the Cedars RV Resort and Mountain View RV Park. Scottish Lodge Motel, the Best Western Voyagers' Landing, and several bed-and-breakfasts are also available in Ferndale. Dutch Village Inn, Windmill Inn Motel, and Hidden Village RV Park are among the possibilities in Lynden. Sedro Woolley offers the Skagit Motel, Riverfront RV Park, and Wildwood Resort. Several commercial rafting companies offer trips on the Nooksack.

Water sports/restrictions: Kayaking and rafting are popular on the upper portions of the North and South Forks, with some tubing and canoeing getting popular farther downstream on the lower stretches of the forks and on the main river.

Contact: Pacific Water Sports, tel. (206) 246-9385; Ferndale RV/Campground, tel. (360) 384-2622; The Cedars RV Resort, tel. (360) 384-2622; Best Western Voyagers' Landing, tel. (360) 380-4600; Mountain View Bed & Breakfast, tel. (360) 384-3693; River Riders, Inc., tel. (800) 448-RAFT; Alpine Adventures, tel. (800) 926-7238; River Recreation, Inc., tel. (800) 464-5899.

3 Wiser Lake

Rating: 7

At just over 120 acres, this lake is big enough to provide something for virtually every kind of water enthusiast, but far enough off the beaten path to keep the crowds relatively small. Its biggest claim to fame might be the fact that it's a two-part lake, divided near its west end by the highway. The boat ramp is on the larger, eastern portion of the lake. Known mostly for its bass fishing, it's also popular with paddlers, especially in the spring and fall. During the warmer months the lake is big enough for waterskiing and other faster-moving activities. Most of that occurs on the bigger part of the lake, from the highway east.

Location: Southwest of Lynden, Whatcom County; map A2, grid a5.

How to get there: Take Interstate 5 to Ferndale and go east on Axton Road about four miles to Highway 539 (Guide Meridian Road). Turn north (left) on SR 539 and follow it 10 miles to Wiser Lake Road. Turn right and drive 100 feet to the public access area on the right.

Boat ramp: There's a concrete-plank Department of Fish and Wildlife boat ramp on the north side of the lake, but like many, it was in fairly sad shape the last time I was there (early 1999). A $10 Washington Department of Fish and Wildlife access decal is required to use the public launch areas maintained by the WDFW.

Facilities: Hidden Village RV Park is just south of the lake and has both tent and RV spaces, a laundry, dump station, and other facilities.

Water sports/restrictions: All water sports are permitted, but this lake has a lot of regulations to help keep law and order. Here goes: First, motors of all kinds are prohibited on the lake from October 15 to March 1. When the lake is open to motor use, there's a no-wake regulation from 8 p.m. to noon, so skiing and other fast-water sports are allowed only from noon to 8 p.m. A maximum of six ski boats at a time is permitted on the lake, and they have to follow the standard counterclockwise traffic pattern. Waterskiing is prohibited from the dock at the public access area. And the smaller part of the lake, west of the bridge, has a no-wake regulation at all times. Whew, that's a lot of specific regulations for such a small lake.

Contact: Hidden Village RV Park, tel. (360) 398-1041; Priced Less Sporting Goods, tel. (360) 855-0895.

4 Fazon Lake

Rating: 5

At only about 30 acres, this isn't a big boating/water sports destination, except with anglers. But if you're looking for a quiet place to paddle or maybe play with your cartopper sailboat, Fazon might fit the bill nicely. Its location, about 10 miles from Bellingham, helps to keep the lake peaceful and quiet most of the time.

Location: South of Everson, Whatcom County; map A2, grid a6.

How to get there: Take Highway 542 northeast from Bellingham about four miles to Everson-Goshen Road, turn north (left), and drive four miles to Hemmi Road. Turn right on Hemmi, go one-quarter mile, and turn left to the lake.

Boat ramp: A paved access area, boat ramp, and rest rooms, managed by the Department of Fish and Wildlife, are on the south side of the lake. The ramp is a typical concrete-plank type, but it was in fairly tough shape in the spring of 1999, with some of the metal plank fasteners sticking up where they could cause tire damage. Check before launching just to be safe. A $10 WDFW access decal is required to use the public launch area.

Facilities: The nearest fuel, groceries, motels, and RV parks are in and around Bellingham, Ferndale, and to a lesser extent Lynden, all about 10 miles from the lake.

Water sports/restrictions: Except for restrictions on boat fishing in the fall and early winter, the only limiting factor here is the size of the lake.

Contact: Lake Terrell Wildlife Area, tel. (360) 384-4723; Priced Less Sporting Goods, tel. (360) 855-0895.

5 Silver Lake

Rating: 7

This 175-acre lake near the British Columbia border in northern Whatcom County is a long way from any of Washington's population centers, but it offers a little bit of everything for water lovers during the summer months. The best swimming beach is at the county park near the south end, but boaters or skiers looking to launch will find less congestion on summer weekends at the WDFW ramp at the north end. Things may get a little busy on a particularly nice summer weekend or major holiday, but usually there's plenty of room for everyone to enjoy his or her sport without getting in each other's way.

Location: North of Maple Falls, Whatcom County; map A2, grid a7.

How to get there: Take Interstate 5 to Bellingham and turn east on Highway 542, following it about 32 miles to Maple Falls. Turn north on Silver Lake Road and drive about four miles to the lake.

Boat ramp: There's a single-lane Department of Fish and Wildlife boat ramp at the north end of the lake with enough room to park about a dozen trailers, and a county park with a ramp near the south end. A $10 WDFW access decal is required to use the public launch area at the north end of the lake.

Facilities: Silver Lake Park has decent swim beach, boat rentals, rental cabins, campsites with and without hookups, play equipment, a bathhouse with showers, a picnic shelter, and barbecue grills. It also has lots of wide-open lawn space for lounging around on warm summer days. There isn't much in the way of other facilities in this part of Whatcom County.

Water sports/restrictions: All water sports are permitted. No-wake regulations are in effect from opening day of the general fishing season (late April) until May 20 each year. From May 20 to June 30, no-wake rules are in effect from 7 p.m. until 10 a.m.

Contact: Silver Lake Park, tel. (360) 599-2776.

6 Squalicum Lake

Rating: 6

Its small size (about 30 acres), gravel ramp, relatively out-of-the-way location, and most of all, its no-gas-motors regulation make this a great place for the canoeist or kayaker to get away from the crowds and noise of the bigger, busier lakes of northwest Washington. Chances are your only company will be the handful of fly-fishing enthusiasts who work the lake throughout its year-round angling season.

Location: Northeast of Bellingham; map A2, grid b6.

How to get there: Take Interstate 5 to Bellingham and follow Highway 542 northeast out of town. About six miles from Bellingham you'll come to the end of a two-mile straightaway, and as the highway turns left, you'll take the gravel road to the right. If you miss it and go straight, you'll quickly come to Squalicum Lake Road, but it doesn't go to Squalicum Lake.

Boat ramp: There's a WDFW access area and gravel ramp at the northeast corner of the lake. A $10 WDFW access decal is required to use the public launch area.

Facilities: Bellingham, about six miles to the southwest, has fuel, accommodations, boat repair shops, groceries, and everything else you'll need.

Water sports/restrictions: Gas-powered motors are prohibited here.

Contact: Priced Less Sporting Goods, tel. (360) 855-0895.

7 Strait of Georgia/ Rosario Strait

Rating: 9

Considered by some to be more of a jumping-off spot to places in British Columbia or the San Juan Islands, this northernmost part of Puget Sound is an absolutely fascinating boating destination in its own right. In fact, you can stay in the area featured in this listing and *still* boat in Canada (sort of) or enjoy an island experience. It's all here.

The Canadian adventure part of the story is Point Roberts, a big sand spit that originates in British Columbia but is actually part of Whatcom County, Washington, U.S. of A. The good ol' longitudinal line at 49°00' and some change that divides our state from their province cuts right across Point Roberts, leaving it hanging in Washington waters. On a map that includes only the Evergreen State and none of the attached Canadian countryside, it looks like an island with a squared-off top. Those limited to land travel can get to Point Roberts only by actually passing through Canadian customs, driving across part of southern British Columbia, and then passing back through U.S. customs; but boaters can simply make the short run from Blaine or a longer trip from Bellingham or the San Juans and pull into Point Roberts without leaving the comfort of their own country. Now you're starting to fully appreciate the advantages of water travel, right? No matter how you go there, you'll probably enjoy the waterfront feel of the place, not to mention the views across Georgia Strait to the Gulf Island and San Juans or eastward to the Washington mainland.

But Point Roberts is only a small part of the story for boaters and water enthusiasts on this upper end of the Puget Sound system. Venture (carefully) through the entrance to Drayton Harbor and the border town of Blaine for a closer look, and you'll find plenty of places to paddle, swim, wind surf, or do just about anything else you like to do on the water. Or round Birch Point and cruise into shallow Birch Bay with its large state park and plenty of shoreline to investigate by boat.

If paddling or small-boating in and around a wildlife-rich estuary is your idea of a good time, you can get your fill along the vast flats at the northeast corner of Lummi Bay or around the corner to the west, where the Nooksack River enters the north side of Bellingham Bay. The city of Bellingham itself is worth exploring in virtually any kind of boat; there are a number of restaurants, shops, and other businesses within easy reach of the docks at any of the city's marinas or moorages.

A short distance south of Bellingham is one of the prettiest spots in Washington, Chuckanut Bay. The steep tree-lined banks and large boulders scattered everywhere make this place a fascinatingly beautiful destination for boaters and shore-based travelers alike, but boaters get to see it all, from every angle. Powerboaters have to be careful around all those boulders and rocky reefs, especially around the entrance to the bay, but paddlers can get around safely to explore it all.

Just south of the bay is Larrabee State Park, the oldest and one of the most beautiful in the Washington State Parks system. Like the entrance to Chuckanut Bay, large boulders just offshore at the park enhance the view across toward Lummi Island and add to the possibilities for boaters, divers, and anglers at Larrabee.

South of Larrabee is Samish Bay, well protected from southerlies by Samish Island, which stretches about four miles along the bay's southwest side. With nothing in the way of boating facilities, it gets little attention as a cruising or paddling destination. As for the islands offshore, Lummi is the largest and, with its 1,400-foot Lummi Peak, the most easily identifiable of the bunch. There's a ferry from the mainland to the island's northeast corner. Much of it is Indian reservation land, but there are limited facilities, mostly on the east side. This east side of the island also provides several decent anchorages for larger boats. The more exposed west side of the island, including Lummi Rocks and the steep cliffs along the southwest side, provide good diving opportunities.

Eliza Island to the east and Sinclair and Vendovi islands to the south also are worthwhile diving and boating destinations, but they have nothing in the way of facilities for visiting boaters. Eliza and Vendovi are privately owned. Much larger Guemes Island is also short on facilities, but Anacortes is nearby, so most boaters can visit it easily on a day trip. Saddlebag Island, just east of Guemes, is a State Marine Park with primitive campsites that are part of the Cascadia Marine Trail, where paddlers can spend the night as they make their way through Puget Sound and the San Juans. Cypress Island, just west of Guemes, is another big island and has a great deal of public land and access. There are several trails leading from the beach where boaters can get out and do some serious exploring, but finding a place to anchor can be somewhat of a problem. Eagle Harbor, near the island's northeast corner, is relatively shallow, and there are fish pens scattered throughout Deepwater Bay to the south. Anacortes is the gateway to these southern islands as well as the San

Juans to the west and the north end of Swinomish Channel to the southeast. It has boating facilities of all kinds, some good restaurants, bed-and-breakfast facilities, rentals and charters, and some very impressive scenery of its own to draw boaters of all kinds.

Location: From Point Roberts south to Anacortes; map A2, grid b4

How to get there: Highways running west off Interstate 5 between Mount Vernon and Blaine provide most of the access to these waters.

Boat ramp: There are 15 boat ramp/hoist facilities available to boaters in this area:

- **Point Roberts:** There are two places to launch at Point Roberts, one at Lighthouse County Park and the other at Point Roberts Marina Resort. The County Parks ramp has one lane with a concrete surface and loading floats. There's room nearby to park about 30 cars and trailers. The marina has both a fixed hoist and a portable hoist. The launch fee for smaller boats using the fixed hoist is $12. Boats over 20 feet using the larger hoist pay by the foot.

- **Blaine:** The Port of Bellingham maintains a two-lane concrete-plank ramp off Marine Drive in Blaine. The launch fee is $3 round-trip, and the ramp has loading floats and a large parking area.

- **Birch Bay:** There's a one-lane, gravel ramp at Birch Bay State Park, with a gravel parking area for about two dozen cars and trailers. There's a $3 launch fee, with a $40 annual launch permit available from Washington State Parks.

- **Gooseberry Point:** There are two fixed hoists near the Lummi Island ferry at Gooseberry Point, with a launch fee charged on a per-foot basis.

- **Bellingham:** The Glenn Street ramp

in Bellingham's Squalicum Harbor is a four-lane, hard-surface launch site with two large loading floats and lots of parking on a paved lot. The launch fee is $3. A short distance south is the Port of Bellingham's Sixth Street ramp, with two concrete lanes and a loading float. A nearby gravel parking area has room for about a dozen cars and trailers. South of Bellingham, along Chuckanut Drive, is Larrabee State Park, with a one-lane concrete ramp and a small gravel parking area. Like other state park ramps with no special facilities, there's a $3 launch fee here.

- **Anacortes:** There's a fixed hoist with a loading float at Cap Sante Marina in Anacortes. To the west of town is Washington Park's two-lane concrete boat ramp and good-sized loading float, a popular launch site among boaters heading for the San Juans. The gravel/grass parking area has enough room for 100 cars and trailers (80 for overnight parking and 20 marked for day-use only). There's a $5 round-trip launch fee and a $5 per night parking fee. South of the park is Skyline Marina, where there are a fixed hoist and a portable hoist to accommodate boats of all sizes. There's a by-the-foot launch fee here.

- **Fidalgo Bay:** Southeast of Anacortes, in Fidalgo Bay, there's a one-lane concrete ramp at Fidalgo Bay Resort, but it's for guests of the resort and nearby RV park only.

- **March Point:** A one-lane, gravel ramp at March Point, between Fidalgo Bay and Padilla Bay, is on Shell Oil Company property off March Point Road. I wouldn't recommend it for large boats, but launching is free.

- **Swinomish Channel (north end):** There's a Skagit County Parks boat ramp at the east end of the Highway 20 bridge over Swinomish Channel, about five miles southeast of Anacortes. It's a two-lane concrete ramp with a loading float and parking for about 20 cars and trailers.

- **Padilla Bay:** Along the east side of Padilla Bay, south of Bayview State Park, is a one-lane concrete ramp managed by the Washington Department of Ecology. Parking is limited, and I would recommend this ramp only to those pulling smaller boats. Launching at low tide is difficult or impossible.

Facilities: The big circular boat harbor at Point Roberts Marina has gas and diesel, open moorage, power and water to the docks, rest rooms with showers, a restaurant and bar, laundry, and boat-sewage pump-out facilities. Lighthouse County Park at Point Roberts has RV and tent sites, picnic tables and kitchen shelters, rest rooms, and a clean, gravel beach for swimming and beachcombing. Blaine Harbor Marina has a fuel dock, visitor moorage, portable sewage pump-out facility, laundry, rest rooms with showers, open moorage for over 700 boats, a restaurant, and laundry. Westman Marine in Blaine Harbor has haul-out facilities.

Semiahmoo Marina has fuel docks, some 500 feet of open moorage, power and water to the docks, rest rooms with showers, boat-sewage pump-out and dump stations, laundry facilities, and marine supplies. Birch Bay State Park has over 160 RV and tent sites, rest rooms with showers, a large picnic area, and saltwater beach. Fisherman's Cove Marina has fuel docks (gas only), boat repairs, and haul-out facilities. Squalicum Harbor offers about 1,5000 feet of moorage floats, fuel docks, power and water to the floats, marine repairs, laundry facilities, several restaurants nearby, power and sailboat charters, rest rooms with showers, and other amenities. Fairhaven Marina has moorage available from spring to fall only, with water and portable boat-sewage pump-out facilities.

Fuel docks are also available in Bellingham at Hawley's and Harbor Marine Fuel. Larrabee State Park has 77 RV and tent sites, beach access, picnic areas, and rest rooms with showers. Bayview State Park has 76 RV and tent sites, picnic tables, cooking shelters, a swim beach, rest rooms and showers. Cap Sante Boat Haven in Anacortes is a Port of Anacortes facility with fuel docks, open moorage, rest rooms with showers, laundry facilities, boat repairs, power to the docks, and boat-sewage facilities. Groceries, marine supplies, and other amenities are within walking distance. Cap Sante Marine has fuel docks, marine supplies, repairs and haul-out facilities. Dive shops are located in Anacortes and Bellingham.

Water sports/restrictions: All water sports are permitted. NOAA chart 18421 covers the entire area included in this listing. Other useful charts include 18423 (Bellingham to Everett), 18424 (Bellingham Bay), and 18430 (Northern Rosario Strait).

Contact: Point Roberts Marina Resort, tel. (360) 945-0927; Blaine Harbor Marina, tel. (360) 332-8037; Semiahmoo Marina, tel. (360) 371-5700 (VHF ch. 68); Westman Marine, tel. (360) 332-5051; Fisherman's Cove Marina, tel. (360) 758-7050; Squalicum Harbor (Port of Bellingham), tel. (360) 676-2542 (VHF ch. 16); Fairhaven Marina, tel. (360) 647-2469; Harbor Marine Fuel (Bellingham), tel. (360) 734-1710; Bellingham Dive & Travel, tel. (360) 734-1770; Washington Divers (Bellingham), tel. (360) 676-8029; Cap Sante Boat Haven (Anacortes), tel. (360) 293-0694 (VHF ch. 66); Skyline Marina, tel. (800) 828-7337; Anacortes Diving & Supply, tel. (360) 293-2070; Washington

State Parks, tel. (800) 233-0321 (information), tel. (800) 452-5687 (reservations); Blaine Visitor Information Center, tel. (800) 624-3555; Bellingham/Whatcom County Convention and Visitor Bureau, tel. (800) 487-2032; Birch Bay Chamber of Commerce, tel. (360) 371-5004; Anacortes Chamber of Commerce Visitor Information Center, tel. (360) 293-3832. For nautical charts of this area, contact Captain's Nautical Supply, tel. (206) 283-7242.

8 Lake Padden

Rating: 7

One of Whatcom County's favorite swimming, wading, splashing-around, and cooling-off spots, Padden is within easy driving, pedaling, even walking range of most folks in the Bellingham area. The city park has an excellent swim beach, and there's plenty of shoreline access for folks who want to wade, fish, or goof around in the shallow water. Thanks to the prohibition on gas-powered motors, paddlers and anglers are the fastest-moving folks on Padden, so it's much more of a mellow, laid-back, take-the-kids-out-for-a-pleasant-afternoon-in-the-sun kind of place than larger and livelier Lake Whatcom to the north. Its fairly large size (150 acres) and relatively deep waters (50 feet in spots) make it a rather slow-warming lake, though, so it's often well into June before local water lovers really converge on this suburban gem of a lake.

Location: South of Bellingham; map A2, grid b5.

How to get there: Take the North Samish Way exit off Interstate 5 at Bellingham and follow the road to the north end of Lake Padden.

Boat ramp: There's a good ramp on the north side of the lake. A $10 WDFW access decal is required to use the public launch area maintained by the Washington Department of Fish and Wildlife.

Facilities: Besides the boat ramp, a city park provides lots of shoreline access for swimming. Food, gas, lodging, and other facilities are nearby in Bellingham.

Water sports/restrictions: Internal combustion engines are prohibited on the lake. Paddling, swimming, and fishing are the big draws.

Contact: Priced Less Sporting Goods, tel. (360) 855-0895; Yeager's Sporting Goods & Marine, tel. (360) 384-1212; H&H Outdoor Sports, tel. (360) 733-2050.

9 Lake Whatcom

Rating: 9

This is Whatcom County's biggest and best water playground, and there's activity of all kinds here on a warm summer evening or weekend. With over 5,000 surface acres, there's room for everyone to do their thing and not really be in each other's way. The main reason is that public access is limited to the park at the north end and the public access at the south end, with lots of open water between them. The gravel and sand swim beach at Bloedel Donavan Park is one of the best in this part of western Washington, and it's not unusual to see a couple of hundred people using it on a warm day.

Although a warm Saturday in July probably wouldn't be the best time for it, Whatcom's partially undeveloped shoreline is a great place for near-shore paddling in a canoe or kayak. There's an abundance of wildlife, especially around the southeast corner of the lake, which is the least developed. Whatcom happens to be one of Washington's top smallmouth bass lakes, by the way, and there are often anglers working its docks and floats in search of fish. Give them a break and try not to get in their way as they poke along the shoreline.

Location: Southeast of Bellingham; map A2, grid b6. (See the Lake Whatcom inset map.)

How to get there: Take Interstate 5 to Bellingham and take Exit 253, turning east on Lakeway Drive and following it two miles to Electric Avenue. Turn left (north) on Electric Avenue and drive one mile to Bloedel Donavan Park on the right. To reach the public access area and boat ramp near the south end of the lake, stay on Lakeway Drive (past Electric Avenue) to Lale Louis Road, turning right and following Lale Louis to Lake Whatcom Boulevard. Turn left on South Bay Drive and left again into the access area.

Boat Ramp: The following boat ramps are listed on the Lake Sammamish inset map:

- **Bloedel Donavan Park:** There's a three-lane boat ramp with two large floats at Bloedel Donavan Park near the north end of the lake.

- **Lake Whatcom Public Access Area:** This access area is in South Bay, at the south end of the lake. The ramp is a gravel one laner, with a rock wall along one side to protect it from weather and rough water, so it's usually a good place to launch while avoiding the crowds at the bigger launch to the north. A $10 WDFW access decal is required to use the public launch area maintained by the Washington Department of Fish and Wildlife.

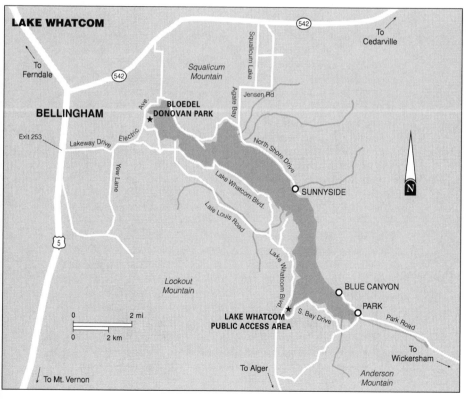

Facilities: Bloedel Donavan Park has a swim beach, picnic area, playground, dressing room, and lots of parking. There's even a putt-putt golf course if you should want more dry-land fun. All amenities are available in Bellingham.

Water sports/restrictions: All water sports are permitted.

Contact: Bellingham Parks and Recreation Department, tel. (360) 676-2093; Priced Less Sporting Goods, tel. (360) 855-0895; Yeager's Sporting Goods & Marine, tel. (360) 384-1212; H&H Outdoor Sports, tel. (360) 733-2050; Sudden Valley RV Park and Campground, tel. (360)734-6430.

10 Northern San Juan Islands

Rating: 10

Where do I start when trying to describe what many consider the Pacific Northwest's top boating destination? The term "boater's paradise" finds its way into print way too often, but in the case of these magnificent islands and the maze of gorgeous waterways surrounding them, just calling them paradise isn't enough. And the northern islands, with lots of state parks and few towns, are the best of the bunch. They contain more wildlife, fewer people, more interesting and intriguing places to explore, and are more laid back than the "civilized" southern islands.

Rather than lumping the northern islands together and trying to capsulize the boating and water recreation opportunities available throughout, let's take a quick look at each:

Orcas Island: Just barely the largest island in the entire chain, Orcas would be a boater's/tourist's destination extraordinaire even if it sat out there all by itself. The view from Mount Constitution, highest point in the islands, is worth the entire trip, and Orcas is also home to huge Moran State Park, with not one, but two large lakes that offer excellent boating and fishing in their own right. Both lakes, Cascade and Mountain, are listed elsewhere in this section. East Sound, which divides the island roughly in half, is a protected, seven-mile-long waterway that leads to the doorstep of Eastsound, which some consider the cultural center of the island. There's a day-use float for boaters who want to spend some time prowling around the nearby shops and eateries. If there's no room on the float, you can usually beach skiffs on the smooth gravel beach, but be aware of the changing tides. About halfway up the east side of East Sound is Rosario Resort, a world-class boaters' destination that features the Moran Mansion, a nationally recognized historic site. The resort's outdoor pool with its fantastic view of East Sound isn't bad, either.

If I had to pick, though, I would rather spend my time exploring the island's other two major harbors, West Sound and Deer Harbor. Both are lightly developed and offer lots of rocky shoreline to investigate from either a motor or paddle craft. Divers like them, too, and both have marinas with moorage, fuel, and groceries. The facilities at Deer Harbor were almost completely rebuilt in 1998. President Channel, the waterway directly west of Orcas, offers excellent fishing at times, especially for winter blackmouth chinook salmon. The island's rocky, boulder-strewn western shoreline is also a great place to explore in a small motor craft or kayak, and divers like to prowl it, too. Doe Island, which hugs the southeast side of Orcas, is also a popular dive location. The entire six-acre island is a marine state park with a dock and summertime moorage floats.

Waldron Island: I can't think of Waldron without remembering a September morning in the early '80s when I was fishing near the shoreline boulders along the island's east side, south of Mail Bay. As I looked up from tying a hook or something, there stood the goofiest looking goat I've ever seen! The thing had long horns that curled out from its head about two feet on each side, and it was covered with dirty hair that hung nearly to the ground. And as if its wild appearance weren't enough, it was standing atop a slick rock, nibbling happily on rockweed and other treasures from the sea. It looked like some kind of sea goat from hell, unlike anything you'd ever see in Farmer Brown's barnyard. I don't know exactly what it was, how it got there, or anything else about it, but I've often wondered how many other folks it startled during its life on Waldron Island. Maybe you'll see one of its descendants while you prowl the edges of Waldron; then again maybe you'll decide that I hallucinated the whole incident. Anyway, there's plenty of shoreline to explore here, but don't plan on going ashore; there are no public facilities here.

The east side of the island is a good place to do some light-tackle fishing for greenling, rockfish, and small lingcod, and salmon anglers sometimes do well off Sandy Point and Point Disney on the west side. North Bay and Cowlitz Bay, located on either side of Sandy Point, offer good anchorage when the weather is calm, but strong winds that often howl up and down Boundary Pass will send you searching for more protected water. Immediately north of Waldron is Skipjack Island, and to the east of it tiny Bare Island; both are wildlife preserves where landing your boat is prohibited. That prohibition, however, shouldn't stop you from wetting a line or diving in the area, because there's plenty to see, spear, and catch here. Midway between Skipjack and Bare is a reef with plenty of rockfish, greenling, cabezon, small lingcod, and other bottomfish to keep you busy.

Two miles north of Bare Island is a buoy right on the U.S./Canada border, marking the shallow north end of Boundary Reef, another popular destination of both bottomfish anglers and divers. Timing your fishing trip or your dive for slack tide periods, of course, is very important here because the water does snort through Boundary Pass when the tide is ebbing and flooding.

Stuart Island: One of the most popular spots in the San Juans, Stuart is home to a state marine park where boaters may choose to moor in either of two large, protected harbors. Reid Harbor, whose entrance is at the southeast corner of the island, is over a mile and a half long and is extremely well protected from a wind in any direction. There's a State Parks float with over 600 feet of moorage space at the head of the harbor, with 15 moorage floats scattered around nearby. (See "Facilities," below, for moorage fees at all state marine parks.) The parks has a marine pump station, and there are tent sites, fire pits, fresh water, pit toilets, and picnic tables on shore.

Prevost Harbor, on the north side of the island, also offers protected moorage on seven buoys and 257 feet of moorage float space. These are also Washington State Parks facilities, and boaters here have access to those same tent sites, water, picnic tables, pit toilets, and fire pits. It's only a couple of hundred feet over a steep rise to the Reid Harbor side of the island.

If you spend any time here, give yourself an extra two hours to hike westward from either side of the island to the lighthouse on Turn Point. The rocky point affords a great view up Boundary Pass to the northeast, down Haro Strait to the south. Immediately north and northwest are the Canadian Gulf Islands, and to the west is Vancouver Island. It's well worth the two-mile hike. Boating into Reid Harbor, by the way, is routine, but if you're entering Prevost Harbor for the first time, be advised that most boaters favor coming in around the west end of Satellite Island, with lies immediately north of the harbor. Small boats can get around the east end of Satellite on most tides, but the many rocks and shoals make it a tricky entry for larger boats on anything but a high flood tide. Like virtually all of the San Juans, Stuart has a fascinating shoreline that screams out for exploration by boaters of all kinds.

I happen to favor the rugged cliffs and steep drop-offs along the island's northwest end and southern midsection, while many paddlers gravitate more toward the usually tranquil waters on the north side, especially around Satellite Island and the many large boulders, reefs, and kelp patches at its east end. These rocky areas offer excellent light-tackle angling possibilities for kelp greenling and smallish rockfish of several kinds, as well as a chance to snorkel or scuba dive during calm tides. Johns Island, immediately east of Stuart, is privately owned and has no public access or public facilities.

Sucia, Patos and Matia Islands: To many Washingtonians, these most northerly islands in the San Juans represent the region's ultimate boating destination. Small, distant, and relatively unprotected on three sides, they're as much a challenge as they are a place to go, at least in the minds of many boaters whose time on the water may be limited to a week or two every summer. Sucia, the largest of the three, is a state marine park, with State Parks moorage buoys located in Echo Bay (14 buoys), Fox Cove (4), Shallow Bay (8), Ewing Cove (4), and Snoring Bay (2).

Fossil Bay, at the south end of Sucia, has 16 moorage buoys and nearly 800 feet of moorage on a State Parks float. Campsites on the island are popular with small-boat visitors, and there's also a fairly extensive trail system around the island. Ewing Cove, on the north side of Echo Bay, offers an underwater park where divers can investigate the wonders of the islands without venturing more than a few yards offshore, and the pock-marked limestone provides thousands of tide pools where beachcombers can check out crabs, starfish, anemones, and other shallow-water creatures. The island is very popular with kayakers, most of whom make the two-mile paddle from the north end of Orcas; and the reefs surrounding the island also make it very popular with divers and bottomfish anglers in search of quillback rockfish, lingcod, cabezon, and other species.

Alden Bank, another popular and productive bottomfish spot, is located four miles northeast of Sucia. Patos Island, about half the size of Sucia, is the northernmost of Washington's San Juans. It's also a state marine park and has two moorage buoys, a couple of primitive campsites and a fantastic view up the Strait of Georgia to the northwest. The light at Alden Point, at the west end of the island, is worth visiting and is one of the most popular photographers' subjects in the San Juans. Matia Island, to the southeast of Sucia, is even smaller than Patos, but has a moorage float (summers only) that provides over 140 feet of space for boats, with a couple of buoys anchored nearby. All these facilities and several campsites are located at the island's west end. The rest of the island is a wildlife preserve with no camping allowed. The rocks and kelp beds around Puffin Island immediately east of Matia are worth checking out if you're looking for a place to do a little shallow-water snorkeling or a spot to catch a couple of foot-long greenling for the evening feast. There's also a lot of bird life to photograph or just enjoy.

Spieden Island: Cruising or paddling completely around this long, tall, thin island directly north of San Juan Island is a real eye-opener for anyone doing it the first time. The south side of Spieden looks so different from the north side that you'd think they were at widely differing latitudes or maybe even on different planets. Both sides are steep, but there's hardly a tree on the grassy south side, while the north side looks something like a second-growth conifer forest in the foothills of the Cascades or Olympics. It's a real lesson in Northwest geography and weather.

As if this vast difference between the two sides of Spieden weren't shocker enough for island newcomers, what about those of us who saw it for the first time during the '70s and '80s, when strange creatures of all kinds roamed the island in nightmare-inducing hordes? The first time I spotted a small herd of dark-brown forms about two-thirds of the way up the slope on the island's open south side, I blamed it on something I ate—or more likely drank—beside the campfire the evening before. But when other members of the group confirmed the sighting and helped eliminate the likelihood of any alcohol-related hallucination, I remembered Spieden's history, which included its use as a private hunting preserve, where exotic critters from faraway places were released and then pursued by hunters who presumably were bored with the usual fare of blacktail deer, Roosevelt elk, black bear, Rocky Mountain goat, and other species native to this neck of the woods. Some of the imported goats, sheep, and other exotics managed to outlast the supply of human hunters, and for years after you never really knew what you might see grazing on Spieden's high ridges or nibbling on shoreline greenery. I haven't seen any of the island's unusual beasts during more recent trips, so maybe they've died off or been eliminated. Then again . . . . So don't be surprised if you round Green Point and come face-to-muzzle with something that looks as if it came from another continent; it probably did. While you're looking for exotics, take some time to look at the native species as well, such as all the birds and seals that frequent Sentinel Island in Spieden's south side and the bald eagles keeping watch over the island's shore. If you're lucky, you may even have dolphins ride your bow wake through Spieden Channel, as I did one sunny July afternoon several years ago.

Jones Island: If I had to pick a favorite spot from among the hundreds of good ones in the San Juans, I might have to go with Jones Island. Maybe that's because I spent my first-ever night in the islands camped near the edge of the peaceful bay on Jones' north side, or maybe because it's where I was camping when I caught the largest lingcod of my life, or because it was always one of my son Adam's favorite places to visit on our early boat-camping adventures. Or maybe it's just because Jones is a beautiful little island with lots of wildlife, a great view up President Channel to Sucia and Patos Islands and the Strait of

Georgia, and enough trees to make you feel as if you're out in the wilderness even when there are dozens of other campers in boats and tents all around.

This entire island near the southwest corner of Orcas is a state park, with a moorage float, five buoys, and fresh water on the north side, along with several choice spots to pitch a tent. The much skinnier bay on the south side offers a couple of moorage buoys and a large, grassy hillside where it's easy to find a tent site. If you're in any shape at all, you can walk from one end of Jones to the other in a few minutes. Along the way you'll probably pass some of the island's resident black-tailed deer, most about the size of a Labrador retriever, thanks to generations of not-too-selective breeding with members of their immediate families. What they lack in size, they make up in aggressive feeding habits, and they'll munch virtually everything you leave scattered around your campsite. And the raccoons are downright assertive to the point of making many park visitors wish it were OK to carry—and use—firearms in Washington's state parks. The critters not only have learned how to open latched coolers, raid open boats, gnaw their way into unguarded tents, and perform other cute raccoon tricks, but in some cases have bitten and scratched campers who weren't quick enough in their responses to requests for handouts. Lock everything up, DON'T FEED THE ANIMALS, make the four-legged marauders feel unwelcome when you visit Jones, and you'll probably get along with them just great.

But don't spend all your time on shore. The island's rocky shore is a joy to explore from the water, no matter what kind of boat you're in, and there are other fascinating places to visit in any direction you want to go. If you don't feel like exploring, simply throw a blanket on the north side's gravel beach and enjoy the sun for a while, or if it's a really nice July afternoon, go for a dip in the clear waters at the edge of that beach; it's one of the best swimming spots in the islands.

Doe Island: This tiny island near the southeast corner of Orcas is often overlooked by boaters rushing across Rosario Strait on their way from the mainland to more well-known San Juans destinations. Although much of it is private, it features a state marine park with a 30-foot float (60 feet of moorage space) that's in place during the summer months. If you're looking for a place to get away close, you might try its primitive campsites for a night or two. The only other public amenities on the island itself are picnic tables and a pit toilet (no fresh water), but other facilities not far away on Orcas. The small float and park may get crowded on nice weekends or during the summer, so don't be surprised if all moorage space is taken. Ask other boaters about rafting alongside them, but don't be tempted to use any of the nearby moorage floats; they're all private. Although the float is gone during the colder months, Doe Island is a worthwhile stop for day visit at that time, especially if you want to get away from people.

Clark Island: Like others scattered throughout the San Juans, this entire island is a marine state park, but one that tends to get less traffic than many of the others. That's too bad, because this 55-acre island is a terrific place to stop and play for a few hours or even a couple of days. There are nine moorage buoys along the west side of the island, with tent sites and a pit toilet on the island. Several areas near the buoys offer gravel beaches where skiffs or smaller trailer boats can be beached. Even a little swimming and wading go on here during the warmest days of summer. The island has lots of tide pools, plenty of wildlife and other attractions, and the cluster of small islands and reefs near its south end are great for snorkeling or scuba diving, as well as prospecting with a fishing rod for small rockfish and other species. Barnes Island, immediately west of Clark, is private and has no public facilities or access.

Location: Marine waters immediately surrounding Patos, Sucia, Matia, Waldron, Stuart, Orcas, Spieden, Jones, Crane, Obstruction, and the smaller islands comprising the northern half of the San Juan Island group; map A2, grid b2.

How to get there: Ferry from Anacortes to Orcas Island or launch at Anacortes and run west, across Rosario Strait. From the south, run north across the Strait of Juan de Fuca from Sequim or Port Angeles.

Boat Ramp: There are paved launch ramps and hoists at six locations on Orcas Island:

• **Bartwood Lodge:** The ramp at Bartwood Lodge is near the northernmost tip of the island. It's a concrete, one-lane ramp with a summertime loading float. Drive north out of Eastsound on Horseshoe Highway and go right on Mount Baker Road, following it a quarter mile to North Beach Road. Turn left on North Beach Road and drive half a mile to Anderson Road, turning right and driving three-quarters of a mile to the resort sign.

• **Smuggler's Resort:** Follow the above directions out of Eastsound. Smuggler's is immediately east of Bartwood at the northern tip of the island. This is another one-lane concrete ramp.

• **West Beach Resort:** From the Orcas Island ferry landing, drive north on Horseshoe Highway past Eastsound and turn west (left) on Enchanted Forest Road, following it just under three miles to the resort. The single-lane concrete ramp has a loading float. It's available to resort guests and by appointment to non-guests. Round-trip launching and parking costs $10 per day.

• **West Sound Marina:** There's a portable hoist with a loading float at the marina, which is located on Deer Harbor Road, about 2.5 miles northwest of the Orcas Island ferry landing. The launch fee increases with the size of your boat.

• **Obstruction Pass:** The fifth ramp on the island, managed by San Juan County Parks, is near the south tip of the island, on Obstruction Pass. To reach it, follow Point Lawrence Road east from Olga for three-quarters of a mile and turn south (right) on Obstruction Pass Road, following it a mile and a half to the ramp. This is a one-lane concrete ramp with a loading float that comes out of the water in winter.

• **Rosario Resort:** A sixth ramp, located near Rosario Resort on the east side of East Sound, has parking for registered resort guests only. It's a one-lane concrete ramp. To reach it, drive just over 13 miles east from the Orcas ferry landing on Horseshoe Highway, then right on Rosario Road to the resort.

Ramps on the mainland that provide the nearest departure points to the northern San Juans include those at Washington Park and Cap Sante Marine in Anacortes, the four-lane Washington State Parks ramp at Cornet Bay, the one lane at Bowman Bay, the small ramp at Larrabee State Park a few miles south of Bellingham, and Squalicum Harbor and Fairhaven Marinas in Bellingham. Skyline Marina, southwest of Anacortes, doesn't have a ramp, but many boaters use its 50-ton sling to launch for their runs to the San Juans.

Facilities: You can chose anything from lounging around a luxury resort to roughing it in a tent or living aboard at one of the several state park islands. Marine state parks in the northern San Juans include those at Clark, Doe, Jones, Matia, Patos, Posey, Stuart, and Sucia Islands. Stuart Island has both floats and buoys in two locations, Reid Harbor and Prevost Harbor. Sucia Island marine campers may choose moorage buoys from among those in Echo Bay, Fox Cove, Shallow Bay, Ewing Cove, Snoring Bay, and Fossil Bay. Fossil Bay also offers nearly 800 feet of moorage float space. Marine park float and dock space costs $8 per night for boats under 26 feet, $11 per night for boats 26 feet and over; moorage buoys cost $5 per night. Annual moorage permits also are available and are valid at all marine parks. They cost $50 for boats under 26 feet, $80 for larger boats.

Moorage, fuel, and other boaters' necessities also are available at Bartwood Lodge, Deer Harbor Marina, West Sound Marina, West Beach Resort, and Rosario Resort. There are several good restaurants and places to shop in Eastsound and Orcas, located on opposite ends of Orcas Island. Marine assistance is available from Tim's Marine/ACATeam, tel. (360) 378-9636 (VHF ch. 16).

Water sports/restrictions: All water sports are popular here, except PWC riding, which has been banned by the San Juan County Board of Commissioners.

Contact: Washington State Parks and Recreation Commission, tel. (800) 233-0321; Deer Harbor Marina, tel. (360) 376-3037 (VHF ch. 78); Port of Friday Harbor, tel. (360) 378-2688 (VHF ch. 66); West Sound Marina, tel. (360) 376-2314 (VHF ch. 16); Rosario Resort, tel. (360) 376-2222

(VHF ch. 78); Bartwood Lodge, tel. (360) 376-224; Tim's Marine/ACATeam, tel. (360) 378-9636 (VHF ch. 16); Washington State Ferries, tel. (800) 843-3779. For information about sea kayaking trips in the San Juans, contact Pacific Water Sports, tel. (206) 246-9385. For nautical charts of this area (NOAA charts 18421, 18423, 18430, 18431), contact Captain's Nautical Supply, tel. (206) 283-7242.

11 Cascade Lake

Rating: 8

As if all the saltwater recreation throughout the San Juans weren't enough, Cascade Lake and nearby Mountain Lake stand out as freshwater boating and playing destinations in their own right. Cascade covers 170 acres and offers a number of accessible beaches for swimming, wading, even trout fishing from the bank. Although it's quite large, it's also very shallow, with a maximum depth of about 15 feet, so it warms very quickly in the summer and is warm enough for swimming and other water sports before many other lakes its size. That's part of the reason why it's such a popular destination for vacationing campers, especially those with kids. That's a good thing to know if you're thinking about visiting Moran State Park but can't decide whether you want to spend your time at Cascade or at Mountain Lake to the east. Mountain is much deeper and much cooler, at least during the early part of the summer.

Location: Just east of East Sound on Orcas Island; map A2, grid c3.

How to get there: Take the ferry from Anacortes to Orcas Island and drive north to Eastsound. From there drive southeast on Orcas-Olga Road to the lake, on the left.

Boat ramp: There's a State Parks boat ramp at the north end of the lake.

Facilities: Moran State Park offers good bank access with picnic tables at the day-use park on the lake's north end, as well as a number of tent sites at campgrounds on the north end, east side, and south end of the lake. All other amenities are available in Eastsound, including some interesting shops and restaurants.

Water sports/restrictions: All water sports are permitted.

Contact: Moran State Park, tel. (360) 376-2326; Washington State Parks and Recreation Commission, tel. (800) 233-0321 (information), tel. (800) 452-5687 (reservations).

🔢 Mountain Lake

Rating: 8

Although it's only two miles from Cascade Lake and within the confines of the same Moran State Park, Mountain Lake has an entirely different personality from the slightly smaller lake just to the west. It covers over 190 acres, making it the biggest lake in the entire island chain At over 100 feet deep, it's also the deepest and coolest, so swimmers tend to get a late start here unless we have a very early warm streak here in the Northwest. While swimming action gets going as early as Memorial Day weekend at Cascade Lake, it may be the Fourth of July before many folks get brave enough to swim seriously in Mountain Lake. Because of its large size, this gem of the San Juans has plenty of room for all kinds of boating activities, and its deep, cool waters also hold an attraction for summertime anglers and divers s well.

Location: Eastern Orcas Island; map A2, grid c3.

How to get there: Take the ferry from Anacortes to Orcas Island and drive north, through Eastsound, and then southeast on Orcas-Olga Road. Continue past Cascade Lake and drive two miles to Mountain Lake.

Boat ramp: There's a State Parks boat ramp on the west side of the lake, at the campground.

Facilities: Moran State Park provides public access and tent sites for campers. Other amenities are available in Eastsound.

Water sports/restrictions: All water sports are permitted.

Contact: Moran State Park, tel. (360) 376-2326.

🔢 Lake Samish

Rating: 8

This 815-acre lake within easy view of freeway drivers is actually two distinctly different lakes connected by a narrow neck of shallow water. Both sections play host to large numbers of swimmers, skiers, PWC riders, knee-boarders, and other water lovers, especially from Memorial Day to Labor Day. Samish Park, located near the bridge that crosses over the narrow isthmus connecting the two parts of the lake, has an excellent swim beach and a large, roped swimming area, but it can get crowded on a warm summer afternoon. The park may have as many as 300 cars a day coming and going through its narrow entrance on a weekend, and it's not unusual for the parking lot to fill and for cars to line up and wait for an empty space to develop. Paddleboats, available for rent during the summer, are a popular attraction, but using them can be a little treacherous if the PWC jockeys get out of hand. PWC riders have plenty of room to maneuver on the two main parts of the lake, but sometimes they get carried away and zoom through the pilings beneath the bridge. That's dangerous, illegal, and stupid, and the culprit usually gets reported in short order.

If you're into calmer aquatic pursuits, you might visit the lake late in the evening after things calm down a bit or during the off-season of spring or fall. The western end of the lake, which rests in a deep bowl overlooked by steep hills, is a great place to prowl in a kayak or canoe early or late in the day. A bald eagle, osprey, or any of several waterfowl species could make the trip especially rewarding. If you're a diver, Samish offers a couple of widely varying kinds of water to explore. The larger main lake to the south is shallow and somewhat weedy, offering divers a good look at a large but typical western Washington lowland lake. The smaller, northern part of the lake, on the other hand, drops off quickly into deep cold water, where you can explore depths as great as 150 feet, unusual for a lake in the Puget Sound basin. While you're down there, you might catch a glimpse of a large salmonid or two, more than likely the large cutthroat trout for which Samish has a reputation among local anglers.

Location: Southeast of Bellingham; map A2, grid c5.

How to get there: Take Interstate 5 to about six miles south of Bellingham, where the freeway parallels the east side of the lake for about two miles.

Boat ramp: A public access area and boat ramp on the east side of the lake and a Whatcom County Parks launch at the northwest corner are both suitable for launching smaller boats, but check out the public access ramp before using it. At last look it was in rough shape. A $10 Washington Department of Fish and Wildlife access decal is required to use the public launch areas maintained by the WDFW.

Facilities: Samish Park, a part of the Whatcom County Parks system, is open for day use until 9 p.m. in the summer,

with a $3 fee to nonresidents of the county. It has a large, roped swim area and paddleboat rentals. Food, gas, RV parks and other amenities are readily available in Bellingham, and there are plenty of accommodations nearby, including bed-and-breakfasts and motels.

Water sports/restrictions: All water sports are permitted.

Contact: Priced Less Sporting Goods, tel. (360) 855-0895.

14 Cain Lake

Rating: 6

If you're looking for peace and quiet on a smallish lake that's within easy reach of the interstate, this may be your little slice of heaven. Cain covers just 70 acres, and even though there are quite a few private homes around its shores, it remains peaceful because of tight regulations and the limiting nature of its public access area. Big motors and speed are big no-nos here, so trolling is as fast paced as it gets. Electric motors are the most powerful gizmos you can hang on the back of your boat. All this makes Cain a great place to haul your canoe or kayak for a quiet evening of paddling and cogitating, or if you prefer, just paddling. The trout fishing's some of the best in Whatcom County, by the way, so take your favorite fly rod or spinning outfit along and you may enjoy the trip even more.

Location: South of Lake Whatcom, on Whatcom-Skagit county line; map A2, grid c6.

How to get there: Take the Alger exit off Interstate 5 and drive through "town" on Cain Lake Road, following it north 3.7 miles to Camp 2 Road, on the left. Follow Camp 2 Road 0.3 mile to the public access area, which is nestled in a grove of fir and cedar trees on the right-hand side of the road to the lake.

Boat ramp: The Department of Fish and Wildlife maintains a small, single-lane gravel ramp with room for only about 10 cars in its lot. A $10 Washington Department of Fish and Wildlife access decal is required to use the public launch areas maintained by the WDFW.

Facilities: Bellingham, about 10 miles to the northeast, offers the nearest lodging and choices of restaurants.

Water sports/restrictions: Fishing and paddling are the main events here. The lake has a no-wake speed limit, and gas-powered motors are prohibited.

Contact: Glenhaven Country Store, tel. (360) 595-9114; Priced Less Sporting Goods, tel. (360) 855-0895.

15 Sportsman's Lake

Rating: 6

This 65-acre lake is only about 10 feet deep at its deepest point and has lots of brushy cover and weeds around its edges. It might be possible to swim at or near the access area, but I wouldn't because of the weeds, fish guts, and chance of getting a hook stuck in my foot. This is a nice place to paddle or motor around in a small boat. Most of the lake's surface is open early in the summer, but it can get thick by August.

Location: Northwest of Friday Harbor, San Juan Island; map A2, grid c1.

How to get there: Take the Anacortes ferry to Friday Harbor (San Juan Island) and drive northwest on Tucker Road, which becomes Roche Harbor Road. Check your odometer at Friday Harbor High School and drive 3.5 miles to an unmarked gravel road on the left. Follow that gravel road about 200 feet to the lake.

Boat ramp: There's a State Department of Wildlife ramp (single-lane, sand and gravel) on the lake, with a small gravel parking area and pit toilets. A $10 Washington Department of Fish and Wildlife access decal is required to use the public launch areas maintained by the WDFW.

Facilities: All amenities are available in Friday Harbor and Roche Harbor. Prices, however, will be on the high side.

Water sports/restrictions: All water sports are permitted, but limited from mid- to late summer by the lake's excessive weed growth.

Contact: Friday Harbor Hardware, tel. (360) 378-4622; San Juan Island Chamber of Commerce, tel. (360) 378-5240.

16 Southern San Juan Islands

Rating: 10

Once you visit this place, you just want to keep coming back for more because you can't ever see it all. This southern portion of Washington's most intriguing boating destination is a little closer to the populated mainland, offers more amenities, and is therefore a little busier than the northern islands, but there are still lots of uncrowded places to visit and more than enough to see and do. Although the year-round human population here has jumped considerably in the past two decades, San Juan County remains one of Washington's least populated, so it never really gets too crowded. You might not believe that if you try catching a ferry from Anacortes to the islands on the Friday afternoon before a long summer weekend and find yourself at the back of what seems to be a never-ending line of RV and boat-trailer traffic, but it's true.

There's no doubt that the San Juans have been discovered, so try to avoid the busiest vacation times if you can. If you can run across to this watery paradise in your own boat rather than riding a

Washington State Ferry, you'll do less waiting, and if you visit before mid-June or after Labor Day, all the better. Of course, summer in the San Juans is phenomenal, so you may just decide to join the crowds in the southern islands and not worry about the fact that you aren't alone. Once you're on, in, or around the water here, it doesn't seem to matter much what everyone else is doing.

Here are some of the highlights of the southern San Juans:

San Juan Island: Although slightly smaller than Orcas Island to the north, this is the most populated island in the group, and Friday Harbor, on its east side, is the closest thing to a city in all the San Juans. Friday Harbor is the social and commercial center of the islands, and in some ways it's the recreational center as well. This is the place where British and American troops gathered during the 1860s, set to square off over ownership of the islands after an American farmer shot a British pig that was raiding his garden. That set off the so-called Pig War, which was really more of a 12-year camping trip in the San Juans than a real war, but of some historical significance nonetheless.

One of two U.S. Customs offices in the islands is located in Friday Harbor, and the other is at the north end of the island in Roche Harbor, so there are times in the summer when there are nearly as many boats flying the Canadian maple leaf as there are flying the Stars and Stripes. Both are places where on a sunny summer day or warm weekend you'll find luxurious 80-footers sharing moorage space with a small fleet of sea kayaks or several 16- to 18-foot outboards sporting rod holders, buckets of herring, and fish boxes filled with lingcod, rockfish, and halibut. People-watching here can be every bit as much fun as boat watching. And then there's whale watching, best practiced from a rocky bluff near Lime Kiln Point, about halfway down the west side of the island. It's now a state park and a great place to spot one of the area's several resident pods of orcas. Minke whales and several species of porpoise also show themselves here regularly. If you're into knowing more about whales and other marine mammals, you might also want to visit the whale museum in Friday Harbor.

Although exploring the dry parts of San Juan Island is interesting and fun, it's even better on the water, and there's no shortage of ways to get wet around this big island. If you aren't stuck on shore, for example, you may get an even better view of those orcas and other marine mammals from the friendly confines of your own boat. Lots of folks make a weekend or even an entire vacation out of exploring the west side of San Juan Island in search of that once-in-a-lifetime view or perfect picture of a whale. If you do it, remember that there's sometimes a fine line between whale watching and whale harassment, with the major difference being that the latter can result in prison time and a whopping fine, not to mention injury to you and/or the whale you're watching.

To avoid the risk of going $20,000 in debt and having several tons of whale come crashing across your bow, don't approach moving or resting whales head-on; don't approach within 100 feet of any whale; if whales come within 100 feet of your boat, put your engine in neutral and do not engage props until whales are at the surface and clear of the boat; parallel the course and speed of moving whales; when less than 600 feet from whales, approach still whales at idle or no-wake speed; when in sight of any whales (1,500 feet) avoid excessive speed or sudden changes in speed or direction.

Besides offering the opportunity to spot whales, the west side of San Juan Island also happens to be one of the prettiest and most inviting places in the Pacific Northwest to explore by boat. The protected waters between Henry Island and the northwest corner of San Juan—including Roche Harbor and Westcott, Nelson, and Garrison Bays—usually are flat enough even in brisk weather conditions that they can be explored by kayak or skiff. Things may quickly get noticeably rougher as you head south out of Mosquito Pass and into the open waters of Haro Strait, so there will be days when you won't want to see the island's western shoreline from the friendly confines of your sea kayak—or even your 20-foot outboard. On a calm day, though, take your time paddling or motoring your way along this stretch of rocky shore, because it's all spectacular. The lighthouse at Lime Kiln Point is worth photographing, and wildlife of all kinds is abundant.

Cruisers, sailors, and paddlers working their way down the west side of the island will eventually round Pile Point and if the tide is high, notice what looks like an inviting, protected bay. But take a closer look at a chart or island map, and you'll discover that it's aptly named False Bay, which has the nasty habit of going virtually dry as the tide ebbs. Stay out unless you have the time to stay several hours. Cattle Point and the southern tip of San Juan Island are spectacularly beautiful, but watch the tides and currents here, as some impressive rips occur. Conditions get a lot friendlier after you pass the Cattle Point light and turn north past Goose Island and into San Juan Channel. Now you're in Griffin Bay, where the water is typically calm

and where there are several good places to anchor a large boat or beach a smaller one and explore. There are also lots of small reefs and rock piles to explore if you're carrying your tanks or fishing rods.

To the north just east of Friday Harbor's southern entrance is Turn Island, another great place to explore by water or land. Its rather limited camping and mooring facilities are open all year, and there are lots of trails leading all over the island. Take a camera and a long lens along, because there's lots of wildlife to see and photograph.

Lopez Island: If San Juan is the busiest and most heavily populated of the islands, then Lopez is the most mellow and pastoral, a perfect destination for boaters who want to get back to simpler times and a slower pace. In some ways it's also one of the most unusual islands in the groups, unless you see nothing unusual about cactus growing near the beach in typically rainy northwestern Washington. Located at the edge of the Olympic Mountains' rain shadow, the south end of Lopez gets very little precipitation. If you plan to boat camp or stay on the island, take your bicycle along; this is one of Washington's best biking destinations.

If there's such a thing as a busy place on Lopez, it's Fisherman Bay, about one-third of the way down the island's west side. Facilities here include Islands Marine Center and the Lopez Islander Resort and Marina, which between the two of them have everything a person could expect to need for a San Juans visit of a week, a month, or an entire summer. This large protected bay has no-wake regulations throughout, so it's a great place for kayaking and canoeing in calm protected waters. The challenge for big-boat enthusiasts here is in entering and leaving the narrow entrance, which bottlenecks down to a few yards in spots. It also has a nasty reef on the outside and another well inside the bay that cause problems for inattentive boaters every year. Follow the markers carefully and keep an eye on your depthsounder all the way in and out of the bay.

Davis Bay, Mackaye Harbor, Outer Bay, Hughes Bay, and the many small islands and rocks along the southwest corner of Lopez are paradise for the boater who likes to explore shallow-water nooks and crannies, and there are numerous places here to dive and fish for greenling, lingcod, and rockfish. Lopez Sound, on the east side of the island, offers protection in most weather conditions and has a number of popular anchorages for larger boats. Near the northeast corner of the island is Spencer Spit State Park, which is popular with campers who arrive by boat and by land via the Washington State ferry that lands at Upright Head at the extreme northern tip of the Island.

Shaw Island: With much larger islands all around it, Shaw goes unnoticed by many visitors to the San Juans, and that seems to be just fine with most of the folks who live on this island near the center of the San Juan archipelago. If you're looking for night life or streets filled with tourist attractions, don't go to Shaw, but don't overlook it if you're in search of quiet waters to explore. You'll probably begin to realize that Shaw isn't Party Central USA as soon as you arrive, especially if you arrive from the north, as most visitors do. The first person you spot at the ferry landing or the one who greets you at the little store near the ferry landing is likely to be a Franciscan nun. The Franciscans have been running the ferry landing and the store for years. Just as there is little excitement on the island, there is also little in the way of facilities for boaters.

Blind Island Marine State Park is located at the northwest entrance to Blind Bay, and it's one of the Cascadia Marine Trail sites where all camping spots are set aside for paddlers. There's plenty of room to anchor right there in Blind Bay. Besides the limited facilities at the north end of Shaw, there's a small county campground on 30 acres in Indian Cove near the south end. It has a dozen campsites, a rather rough boat ramp and one of the nicest swimming beaches in the islands.

If you're into fresh sea food that you catch yourself (and who isn't?), you might drop a crab pot or two around Shaw, especially near the entrance to Blind Bay and shallow-water areas of Indian Cove. Crabbing also is a possibility in Parks Bay on the island's west side, but crabs are about all you can harvest there; both Parks and nearby Hicks Bay are part of the San Juan Islands Marine preserve system, so you can't harvest other shellfish or marine bottomfish. The many small islands off the northwest corner of Shaw—Crane, Cliff, Yellow, McConnell, Wasp and the others—don't offer much in the way of facilities or even public access, but the maze of waterways and shorelines they offer the exploring boater are enough to keep you busy for a long time.

Blakely Island: Most of this large island is private, so the main attraction for boaters is Blakely Island General Store and Marina, located in a sheltered cove at the north end of the island. The moorage floats offer complete protection from every direction, and it has a fuel dock with room for several large boats at a time. The park area at the marina is a good place for picnics and barbecues. Peavine Pass runs right by, and Obstruction Pass lies just beyond to the north. Both are popular routes into the islands from the east, so this marina can get busy during the summer and on long weekends. Thatcher Pass, to the south of Blakely, also is a major boat-traffic route in and out of the San Juans and provides a view of the island's sparsely populated west side. Every time I pass by Thatcher Bay, I wish I lived in the house that sits on the low-bank hillside at the end of the bay.

Location: Marine waters immediately surrounding San Juan, Lopez, Shaw, Decatur, Blakely, and the smaller islands that comprise the southern half of the San Juan Island group; map A2, grid c2.

How to get there: Ferry from Anacortes to Lopez Island, Shaw Island, or San Juan Island, or launch at Anacortes and run west across Rosario Strait. From the south, run north across the Strait of Juan de Fuca from Sequim or Port Angeles.

Boat ramp: Nine boat ramps are located in the southern islands, four of them on San Juan Island, four on Lopez Island, and one on Shaw Island:

San Juan Island:

- **Roche Harbor Resort:** The single-lane concrete ramp at the resort will accommodate boats of almost any size, and there's room to park about 50 cars and trailers nearby. This is a gated ramp with a $14 round-trip launch fee. To reach it, drive north out of Friday Harbor on Tucker Road, stay left at the Y to hit Roche Harbor Road, and drive 10 miles to the end of the county road. Turn left to drop down the hill into the resort.

- **Snug Harbor Resort:** Drive from the ferry terminal at Friday Harbor on Spring Street, go two blocks and turn right on Second Street. Drive seven miles to Mitchell Bay Road, turn left, and drive 2.5 miles to the resort. The ramp has one lane, and the concrete slab is in good shape.

- **San Juan County Park:** Located in Smallpox Bay, halfway down the west side of the island, the park features a new concrete ramp (built in 1997). Launching is free at this one-lane ramp. To reach it, drive from the Friday Harbor ferry landing on Spring Street, going two blocks to Second Street. Turn right and drive seven miles, turning left on Mitchell Bay Road. Mitchell Bay Road becomes Westside Road, which leads two miles to the park and its boat ramp.

- **Jackson Beach:** This Port of Friday Harbor park is located in Griffin Bay, southeast of Friday Harbor, and has a one-lane concrete ramp that's seen better days. To reach it, leave the Friday Harbor ferry landing on Spring Street, turn left on Argyle Avenue and follow it three-quarters of a mile, turning left on Pear Point Road. Follow Pear Point Road half a mile to Jackson Beach Road, turn right, and drive about 300 yards to the ramp.

Lopez Island:

- **Odlin County Park:** The one-lane concrete ramp at this San Juan County Parks facility sometimes collects sand and debris that make launching tough, especially early in the spring. It's located about a mile southwest of the Lopez Island ferry ramp, on Port Stanley Road.

- **Islands Marine Center:** This facility on the west side of Lopez Island in Fisherman Bay has both a single-lane concrete ramp and a portable hoist for launching. Fees are charged for both, and an appointment is required to use the hoist. To reach Islands Marine, drive south on Ferry Road about three miles from the Lopez ferry landing.

- **Hunter Bay Ramp:** This one-lane concrete ramp near the southeast corner of Lopez Island is a little hard to find, but is a good small-boat ramp. To reach it, drive south from the Lopez ferry landing on Ferry Road, turning east (left) on Center Road about two miles from the ferry. Drive 5.8 miles on Center Road to where it becomes Mud Bay Road. Follow Mud Bay another 2.2 miles to Island Road. Go left on Island Road a mile and a half to its end at the Hunter Bay ramp.

- **MacKaye Harbor Ramp:** This is another decent small-boat ramp, located at the southwest corner of Lopez Island. To get there, take Ferry Road south from the Lopez ferry 2.1 miles and turn left on Center Road. Go 5.8 miles on Center to where it becomes Mud Bay Road, and continue three miles to Mackaye Harbor Road. Turn right and go one block to an unmarked road that leads to the ramp.

Shaw Island:

- **South Beach Park Ramp:** Shaw Island's only boat ramp is in Indian Cove, near South Beach on the southeast side of the island. It's a natural sand ramp, suitable to smaller trailer boats. Launching is free, but there's a $4 daily fee for parking more than one day. Drive 1.2 miles on Blind Bay Road from the Shaw Island ferry ramp and turn left on Squaw Bay Road, following it three-quarters of a mile to the sign pointing the way to the park.

Ramps on the mainland that provide the nearest departure points to the southern San Juans include those at Washington Park and Cap Sante Marine in Anacortes, the four-lane Washington State Parks ramp at Cornet Bay, the one-lane ramp at Bowman Bay, the small ramp at Larrabee State Park a few miles south of Bellingham, and Squalicum Harbor and Fairhaven Marinas in Bellingham. Skyline Marina southwest of Anacortes doesn't have a ramp, but many boaters use its 50-ton sling to launch for their runs to the San Juans.

Facilities: The state marine park on James Island (immediately east of Decatur Island) offers 134 feet of float space and five moorage buoys, as well as primitive campsites and pit toilets. Moorage fees are $8 a night for boats under 26 feet, $11 for boats 26 feet and over.

Spencer Spit Marine State Park, at the northeast corner of Lopez Island, has 16 moorage buoys, primitive campsites, rest rooms, and picnic tables. There are four moorage buoys and four campsites on Blind Island, another state marine park located near the entrance to Blind Bay on the north side of Shaw Island. A fourth marine state park is located on Turn Island, just east of Friday Harbor in San Juan Channel. It has three moorage buoys, primitive campsites, and picnic tables. The fee for moorage buoys at all marine state parks is $5 per night. Odlin County Park on Lopez Island has 30 campsites with a low beach and small dock for loading and unloading only, pit toilets, and fresh water.

James Island, Blind Island, and Spencer Spit State Marine Parks have Cascadia Marine Trail tent sites for paddlers, and there are other Marine Trail sites on Posey Island (north end of San Juan Island) and Griffin Bay (managed by the State Department of Natural Resources, located near the southeast corner of San Juan Island). Washington State Parks charges $7 per night to use its Marine Trail sites. More plush accommodations, from rustic cabins to comfortable suites and bed-and-breakfast units, are available in Friday Harbor, Roche Harbor, Lopez (Fisherman Bay), and Snug Harbor. Hotel de Haro, more than 100 years old and one of the prettiest places in the islands, is in the heart of Roche Harbor and has over 50 units of various kinds. Moorage, fuel, power, showers, pump-out facilities, groceries, and other amenities for boaters can be found at the Port of Friday Harbor, Roche Harbor Resort, and Snug Harbor Resort, all on San Juan Island; Lopez Islander and Islands Marine Center on Lopez Island; Blakely Island General Store and Marina on Blakely Island; and Little Portion Store (limited guest moorage) on Shaw Island. Marine assistance is available from Tim's Marine/ACATeam in Friday Harbor.

Water sports/restrictions: All water sports are popular here except PWC riding, which has been banned by the San Juan County Board of Commissioners.

Contact: San Juan Island Chamber of Commerce, tel. (360) 378-5240; Port of Friday Harbor, tel. (360) 378-4477; Roche Harbor Resort, tel. (360) 378-2155 (VHF ch. 16, 9); Snug Harbor Resort, tel. (360) 378-4762; Lopez Islander, tel. (360) 468-2233 (VHF ch. 78); Island Marine Center, tel. (360) 468-3377 (VHF ch. 69); Shipyard Cove Marina, tel. (360) 378-5101; Blakely Island General Store and Marina, tel. (360) 375-6121; Little Portion Store, tel. (360) 468-2288; Tim's Marine/ACATeam, tel. (360) 378-9636 (VHF ch. 16); Washington State Parks and Recreation Commission, tel. (800) 233-0321; Washington State Ferries, tel. (800) 843-3779. For information about sea kayaking trips in the San Juans, contact Pacific Water Sports, tel. (206) 246-9385. For nautical charts of this area (NOAA charts 18421, 18423, 18429, 18430, 18433, 18434), contact Captain's Nautical Supply, tel. (206) 283-7242.

🔟7 Heart Lake

Rating: 6

The folks from nearby Anacortes and Mount Vernon come here to paddle, water-ski, fish, ride PWC, and take part in other freshwater pursuits, but there's nothing special about Heart to prompt a visit from folks who live all over western Washington. In fact, most visitors to this area are headed elsewhere, especially to the San Juan Islands or perhaps to the Mount Vernon area for the spring flower extravaganza.

Location: Southwest of Anacortes, map A2, grid d4.

How to get there: Take Interstate 5 to Burlington, turn west on Highway 20 and drive to Anacortes. Drive west through town to H Avenue and turn south (left). Follow H until it becomes Heart Lake Road, which continues south to the lake, which will be on the right.

Boat ramp: There's an adequate boat ramp at the public access area. A $10 Washington Department of Fish and Wildlife access decal is required to use the public launch areas maintained by the WDFW.

Facilities: Anacortes has all the needed amenities.

Water sports/restrictions: All water sports are permitted.

Contact: Ace in the Hole Tackle, tel. (360) 293-1125.

🔟8 Lake Erie

Rating: 7

This lake has a little bit of everything, from fishing and swimming to paddling, skiing, and boarding. It covers well over 100 acres, so there's plenty of room for all activities without anyone getting in anyone else's way.

Location: Southwest of Anacortes, Fidalgo Island; map A2, grid d4.

How to get there: Take Highway 20 west from Interstate 5 and drive about 13 miles to Dean's Corner. Turn south (left) and drive two miles to Campbell Lake Road. Turn right and drive about a mile and a half to Rosario Road and turn left to the lake.

Boat ramp: The public access area is at the west end of the lake and has a concrete ramp and a gravel ramp side by side. The gravel ramp might be the safer of the two, since last time I was there the concrete ramp was a little banged up, and the metal spikes were starting to show. A $10 Washington Department of Fish and Wildlife access decal is required to use the public launch areas maintained by the WDFW.

Facilities: Lake Erie Resort, Grocery and Trailer Park is nearby, providing most of the necessities for a weekend stay in the area. Other amenities are available in Anacortes.

Water sports/restrictions: All water sports are permitted.

Contact: Lake Erie Resort, Grocery and Trailer Park, tel. (360) 293-2772.

19 Campbell Lake

Rating: 7

This big lake (over 400 acres) is very shallow, so it warms quickly with a few days of nice weather in the spring. This makes it a popular lake with bass anglers and other warm water fishermen, but also with folks who just like warm water for their various boating and splashing activities (and who doesn't?). The good thing about Campbell is that there's plenty of room for everybody to do their thing without getting in each other's way too badly. That still doesn't mean that the bass anglers will appreciate it if you try to jump their bow with your PWC or pass between them and the end of their line on water skis, but everyone can peacefully coexist if they work at it just a little. If you're a speedster, stay away from the bass boats and the paddlers.

By July, when the water has warmed considerably, this is a great swimming lake, but there's no gravel beach or public access where swimming is a good idea. Some folks use their boats as swimming and diving platforms and aquatic home bases. The big, rocky island in the middle of the lake draws some swimmers, but it also draws bass anglers, so use good judgment before deciding to call it your own personal swim beach.

Location: South of Anacortes, Fidalgo Island; map A2, grid d4.

How to get there: Take Highway 20 south from Anacortes or north across Deception Pass from Whidbey Island and you'll see the lake right along the west side of the road.

Boat ramp: There's a Washington Department of Fish and Wildlife ramp and access area on the lake. A $10 Washington Department of Fish and Wildlife access decal is required to use the public launch areas maintained by the WDFW.

Facilities: Lake Campbell Motel is located on the east side of Highway 20, right across from the lake. Other amenities are available in Anacortes, about four miles to the north. Deception Pass State Park, four miles to the south, has over 240 tent and RV sites, showers, and other camping facilities.

Water sports/restrictions: All water sports are permitted.

Contact: Lake Campbell Motel, tel. (360) 293-5314; Washington State Parks and Recreation Commission, tel. (800) 233-0321 for information, tel. (800) 833-6388 for reservations.

20 Cranberry Lake

Rating: 7

Like most waters in and around state parks, Cranberry hosts a lot of people during the summer, but at nearly 150 acres, there's room here for the anglers, canoeists, swimmers, and others to sort of separate and stay out of each other's way. On days when human activity is on the low side, this a good place to paddle the shoreline and enjoy the unspoiled, natural shoreline that surrounds most of the lake. Wildlife viewing is a possibility. But when you consider the fact that Deception Pass State Park has more visitors each year than Yellowstone, you'll realize that days with light human activity aren't very common. Most visitors come here to take in the inspiring scenery or see how badly they can scare themselves by looking into the depths from the Deception Pass bridge, but the lake also gets lots of use.

Location: Near the northwest tip of Whidbey Island; map A2, grid d4.

How to get there: Take Interstate 5 to Burlington and turn west on Highway 20, following it about 20 miles to Deception Pass State Park. Cross the Deception Pass bridge, drive about half a mile, and turn west (right) to the lake.

Boat ramp: There's a small, gravel boat ramp at the north end of the lake.

Facilities: State Parks maintains a boat ramp on the north end of the lake and a fishing pier on the east side. The state park has about 60 tent sites, which are available on a first-come, first-served basis.

Water sports/restrictions: Paddling, fishing, and swimming are the best bets. Gasoline engines are prohibited here.

Contact: Deception Pass State Park, tel. (360) 675-2417.

21 Lower Skagit River

Rating: 7

Besides being the biggest river in the Puget Sound region, the Skagit boasts another interesting claim to fame; as rivers go, it's put together backwards. Rather than converging forks somewhere along the upper end of the watershed flowing together to form a main stream, the Skagit has its forks at the lower end, near its mouth. Kinda strange, huh? The North Fork and South Fork Skagit split and go their separate ways about six miles upstream from their respective mouths, with each fork also splitting off into a myriad of sloughs and channels that could keep an adventurous boater busy for days. The delta between the two forks is known as Fir Island, and it's one of western Washington's richest wildlife areas, so there's always something flying over, running from, swimming through, or skittering across the water. Snow geese, bald eagles, great blue herons, and great horned owls are among the common sights.

For all the natural beauty and inviting waterways, however, the Skagit delta is a place where powerboaters, paddlers, and rowers have to stay on their toes. The sloughs and channels that comprise the lower Skagit estuary rise and fall, disappear and reappear with the tide. A spot where the water was 10 feet deep in the morning may be dry in the early afternoon, so keep your tide book in your pocket and pay constant attention to water levels as you explore. Failure to do so can leave you high and dry or worse, and you don't want to become a Skagit River statistic.

The North and South Forks themselves, as well as the main Skagit up past Mount Vernon to Sedro Woolley, are large rivers, offering a wide range of moving-water boating possibilities. In most places there's plenty of depth for propeller-powered boats, and those are still more common here than the jet-powered craft used farther upriver and on many of western Washington's smaller, shallower streams. This is big enough water to allow plenty of room for gas-powered craft and arm-powered craft alike, so there's little conflict between the two even on a warm summer weekend.

It's always a little touchy recommending swimming on a big, chilly river that's capable of sweeping away a double-wide mobile home if it wanted to, but a few folks do cool their toes and more on the lower Skagit on a hot summer day. Edgewater Park in Mount Vernon is one place where you can do that, but always remember that this is a deep, cold river with current and everything.

Location: From Skagit Bay northeast to Sedro Woolley; map A2, grid d6.

How to get there: Take Interstate 5 to Highway 534 and drive west through Conway. Turn north (right) on Dike Road or Mann Road to reach the South Fork Skagit, or continue west on Fir Island Road to Moore Road and turn north to get to the North Fork. Exit Interstate 5 at Mount Vernon and drive west on Penn Road or Highway 536 to reach the main stem Skagit from the forks upstream to the Interstate 5 bridge. To reach the river upstream of Interstate 5, drive east on Highway 20 from Burlington and turn south onto various roads in and around Sedro Woolley.

Boat ramp: There are many boat ramps along this stretch of river, including:

- **The Skagit Wildlife Area** off Mann Road (South Fork)

- **Conway Park** (South Fork)

- **Blake's Skagit Resort & Marina** (North Fork)

- **Off Moore Road** (North Fork)

- **The Spudhouse launch, Young's Bar** and **Edgewater Park** in Mount Vernon

- **Near Burlington**

- **Sedro Woolley**

Many, if not all, of these launches sometimes become clogged with sand and debris, especially after a period of high water. A $10 Washington Department of Fish and Wildlife access decal is required to use the public launch areas maintained by the WDFW.

Facilities: Riverbend RV Park near Mount Vernon, Riverfront RV Park at Sedro Woolley, and Creekside Camping near Concrete all have both tent and RV sites. Mount Vernon, Sedro Woolley, and Concrete all offer motel and bed-and-breakfast accommodations. Food and gas are available in all three towns.

Water sports/restrictions: Both powerboat enthusiasts and paddlers can find plenty to see and do along the Skagit, but you must always keep in mind that this is moving water, with its share of submerged stumps and other obstacles that come and go with changing water levels. The North and South Forks are greatly influenced by changing tides.

Contact: Priced Less Sporting Goods, tel. (360) 855-0895; Sedro Woolley Chamber of Commerce, tel. (360) 855-1841; Creekside Camping, tel. (360) 826-3566.

22 Middle Skagit River

Rating: 5

This 30-miles stretch of the Skagit, or at least much of it, is used primarily by steelhead and salmon anglers, but boaters of all kinds use it to some degree. It's big water, a river that's nearly as deep and wide up around Hamilton as it is down along its lower reaches near

Mount Vernon, but for my money it doesn't offer the boating variety and scenery that are available on the lower Skagit. Maybe that's because I enjoy the wildlife variety to be found in estuaries such as the Skagit Flats. This middle portion of the Skagit also has little in the way of whitewater or even what anyone would call fast water, so you won't find the pools, riffles, and gravel bars that are abundant farther upstream. Most rafters, kayakers, and canoeists drive past this middle part of the river on their way upstream to Rockport, Marblemount, and other upper river destinations.

Location: From Sedro Woolley upstream (east) to Concrete; map A2, grid c8.

How to get there: Take Interstate 5 to Burlington and turn east on Highway 20, which parallels the north side of the river to Concrete and beyond. Several roads leading south (right) from Highway 20, including Highway 9 at Sedro Woolley, Cockerham Road east of Lyman, and Russell Road at Birdsview, lead to the river.

Boat ramp: There are concrete-plank ramps just upstream from Sedro Woolley, off McDonald Avenue, off the South Skagit Highway at the mouth of Gilligan Creek, and off Shangri-La Road near Hamilton. You'll also find a couple of rough launches at the mouth of Pressentin Creek, a mile east of Birdsview. All of these ramps are managed and maintained (sort of) by the Department of Fish and Wildlife. A $10 Washington Department of Fish and Wildlife access decal is required to use the public launch areas maintained by the WDFW.

Facilities: Sedro Woolley is your best bet for food, gas, lodging, boating supplies, and other necessities.

Water sports/restrictions: Power-boating, drift boating, rafting, canoeing, and kayaking all are popular here.

Contact: Pacific Water Sports, tel. (206) 246-9385; Priced Less Sporting Goods, tel. (360) 855-0895; Sedro Woolley Chamber of Commerce, tel. (360) 855-1841.

23 Clear Lake

Rating: 9

Easy access and a nice county park right along Highway 9 help to make this 223-acre lake very popular with boaters and water lovers around the Sedro Woolley-Mount Vernon area. The big swim beach at the county park sees plenty of action on a warm summer afternoon, and there's so much traffic on the park's water slide that it probably should have a speed limit and crossing guard on duty, but it's all good, clean fun for Skagit County kids. Though it has the facilities for access and a broad range of water sports, Clear Lake is lightly developed, so it's also a good place for contemplative paddlers to patrol the shoreline in quest of calm waters and wildlife of all kinds. The 25 mph speed limit—and a homemade-looking sign reading "No Jet Skis" (i.e., PWC) posted at the public boat ramp—seem to help keep the powerboat traffic from getting too crazy here, and even those who do go wild have enough room on this big lake to keep from doing much damage to themselves or anyone else. Add it all up and Clear Lake is one of western Washington's most versatile water sports destinations.

Location: South of Sedro Woolley; map A2, grid d7.

How to get there: Exit Interstate 5 just north of Mount Vernon on College Way, which becomes Highway 538, and drive four miles east to Highway 9. Turn north (left) and drive just over three miles to the lake. The poorly marked public ac-

cess area is reached by turning east off Highway 9 onto Day Creek Road, following it half a mile to C Street, and turning right down the newly paved road, which ends at the water.

Boat ramp: There's a newly renovated concrete-slab ramp at the public access area as of spring 1999. A $10 Washington Department of Fish and Wildlife access decal is required to use the public launch areas maintained by the WDFW.

Facilities: Besides the public access area and ramp, there's a Skagit County Parks and Recreation park on the west side of the lake with a large swim beach, water slides, moorage, a play area, and picnic tables.

Water sports/restrictions: Most water sports are permitted, but the lake has a 25 mph speed limit.

Contact: Lake McMurray Store, tel. (360) 445-3565.

24 Beaver Lake

Rating: 6

This lake is also known by some of the locals as Mud Lake, which may not attract tourists, but perhaps that's the whole idea. At 73 acres, it often gets overlooked by boaters, especially those looking for enough room to really get up and go. The lake also is quite shallow, which means it warms up quickly after a few days of nice weather. That warm water will tempt you to get in and take a dip, but there isn't anything here that would qualify as a public swim beach, and I wouldn't recommend swimming at the public access/boat ramp. Making it worse is that, judging by what I saw last time I was there, some of the local party animals must spend some time here. There was a lot of broken glass and other junk scattered around, and I was wondering if I was going to get out with

my tires fully inflated. I sure wouldn't think about swimming in a place where I'm almost afraid to drive.

Location: South of Sedro Woolley; map A2, grid d7.

How to get there: Take Interstate 5 to just north of Mount Vernon and turn east on College Way (Highway 538). Drive to Highway 9, turn north, and drive to the Walker Valley Road; turn right and drive about a mile and a half to the lake.

Boat ramp: The Department of Fish and Wildlife maintains a public access area with a two-lane gravel boat ramp and toilets on the lake's west side. A $10 Washington Department of Fish and Wildlife access decal is required to use the public launch areas maintained by the WDFW.

Facilities: Food, gas, lodging, and other facilities are located nearby in Sedro Woolley and Mount Vernon.

Water sports/restrictions: Paddling, fishing, and other small boat activities are popular here.

Contact: Lake McMurray Store, tel. (360) 445-3565.

25 Big Lake

Rating: 9

If I had been running things back when, I would have tried to get a little more creative in naming this large Skagit County lake. Then again, maybe the folks who went around naming things in the old days did a fair job of describing what you get here. It's a, well, big lake, at over 545 acres. On a summer weekend when the mercury climbs into the high 80s, it could also be named Busy Lake, maybe even Crazy Lake if you don't happen to like swimmers, skiers, PWC riders, and powerboats of all description zooming and zinging around in every direction. Things have been known to get a just a little out of hand here.

Unless you get invited to one of the private beaches in front of the many homes that dot the Big Lake shoreline, your best swimming beach is at Big Lake Resort, and it also gets a little busy on a warm day. In case you head for the water without a boat, never fear; the resort also has rentals, but I'd call ahead to see about reservations if I was interested in renting one on a summer weekend.

Location: Southeast of Mount Vernon; map A2, grid d7.

How to get there: Take Interstate 5 to Conway and turn east on Highway 534, then north on Highway 9 to the lake; or exit Interstate 5 just north of Mount Vernon on College Way (Highway 538) and turn south (right) on Highway 9 to the lake.

Boat ramp: You'll find a single-lane boat ramp and large, gravel parking lot at the Department of Fish and Wildlife access area on the west side of the lake, and another ramp at Big Lake Resort, also on the west side. The WDFW ramp was showing serious signs of wear last time I was there (1998), and I haven't heard anything about its being replaced or repaired yet, so check it out before you back in. A $10 Washington Department of Fish and Wildlife access decal is required to use the public launch areas maintained by the WDFW.

Facilities: Food, gas, lodging and other amenities are available in Sedro Woolley and Mount Vernon.

Water sports/restrictions: All water sports are permitted.

Contact: Big Lake Grocery, tel. (360) 422-5253.

26 Lake McMurray

Rating: 6

This is one of Skagit County's most popular trout-fishing lakes, but other boating/water sports activities are limited primarily to the folks who own homes around the lake's shoreline. The public access area isn't marked out on Highway 9, so newcomers have a hell of a time even finding the public access area, and when they do finally make it to the water, they find a small ramp, tiny parking lot and a generally not-too-user-friendly facility unless they have a small boat and an urge to go fishing.

Location: Southeast of Conway, Skagit County; map A2, grid d7.

How to get there: Drive to Conway on Interstate 5 and turn east on Highway 534, which meets Highway 9 on the west side of the lake.

Boat ramp: There's a public access area with boat ramp and limited parking at the southeast corner of the lake. A $10 Washington Department of Fish and Wildlife access decal is required to use the public launch areas maintained by the WDFW.

Facilities: Nearby is Lake McMurray Store, which carries food and beverages, bait, tackle, and other goodies. The nearest town with a complete line of restaurants, motels, and other amenities is Mount Vernon, about 10 miles to the northwest.

Water sports/restrictions: Fishing and paddling are the main draws here. The lake has a 5 mph speed limit.

Contact: Lake McMurray Store, tel. (360) 445-3565.

27 Lake Cavanaugh

Rating: 8

This big Skagit County lake offers over 800 acres in which to romp, stomp, and do your thing; but because of its size and depth, it's slow to warm in the summer. It's popular with anglers in the spring, but fishing activity tends to taper off as the summertime boating folks begin to show up, usually around the end of June. The lake's large size and relative distance from, well, almost anywhere keep Cavanaugh from ever getting really crowded, so there's room to pursue more casual boating pastimes even while the PWC set enjoy the lake.

Location: Northwest of Oso, just north of Skagit-Snohomish county line; map A2, grid e8.

How to get there: Drive northeast from Arlington on Highway 530 and turn north (left) at Oso onto Lake Cavanaugh Road, or take the College Way (Highway 538) exit off Interstate 5 near Mount Vernon and drive east to Highway 9. Turn south, drive past Big Lake, and turn east (left) on Lake Cavanaugh Road, following it about 10 miles to the lake.

Boat ramp: The Department of Fish and Wildlife maintains a gravel boat ramp and access area near the east end of the lake. At last report the rocky parking area and road in to it were very rough, so be careful when trailering a boat. A $10 Washington Department of Fish and Wildlife access decal is required to use the public launch areas maintained by the WDFW.

Facilities: The nearest food, gas, lodging, and other amenities are in Arlington, about 10 miles to the southwest.

Water sports/restrictions: All water sports are permitted.

Contact: Lake McMurray Store, tel. (360) 445-3565.

28 Sunday Lake

Rating: 7

Its small size (37 acres) and the unfinished nature of its boat ramp just about limit the use of this lake to paddlers and anglers using small cartopper boats.

That's fine, of course, if you're looking for a quiet place to spend a couple of hours on a calm Saturday morning or a warm evening after work. The lake's proximity to Interstate 5 makes it easy to reach, even for boaters from the Seattle area to the south. Keep it in mind if you're looking for a place to stretch your arms and ease your mind. And despite its name, feel free to visit the lake seven days a week.

Location: East of Stanwood, map A2, grid e6.

How to get there: Take Interstate 5 to Highway 532 and drive west to 28th Avenue NW. Turn south (left) and drive less than a mile to the lake.

Boat ramp: The lake has an undeveloped access area with a rough boat ramp that's suited only to smaller boats. A $10 Washington Department of Fish and Wildlife access decal is required to use the public launch areas maintained by the WDFW.

Facilities: Food, gas, lodging, and other amenities are most readily available in Marysville, about 14 miles to the south.

Water sports/restrictions: Paddling and fishing are the main attractions.

Contact: John's Sporting Goods, tel. (425) 259-3056.

29 Pilchuck Creek

Rating: 6

This little Stillaguamish River tributary offers some thrilling whitewater, including some Class IV and Class V rapids that should be run only by experienced boaters. The stretch above Pilchuck Creek Campground is only a trickle during dry periods and considered a boating possibility only during very high water in fall and winter, and then only by kayakers. The five-mile run from the campground down to Highway

9 is mostly Class III and not too tough, except that there's a huge drop near the start of the run that merits as Class V rating. Don't go near it unless you're a real hotshot and have plenty of backup around in case of a problem. The six-mile float from Highway 9 down is a more gentle one, topped by a couple of Class III rapids, but there are sweepers and log jams appearing and disappearing along this stretch constantly, so pay attention. More than one boater has gotten into serious trouble here, and this part of the creek has taken some lives.

Location: Flows into the Stillaguamish River near Sylvana; map A2, grid e7.

How to get there: To reach the lower section of the creek, exit Interstate 5 onto Highway 530 and drive west, through Sylvana, to Norman Road, which parallels about two miles of Pilchuck Creek. Some of the middle portion of the creek is accessible by taking the Highway 532 exit off Interstate 5 and driving east toward Highway 9. To reach upper portions of Pilchuck Creek, take Highway 9 north from Arlington and turn east on Grandstrom Road, which parallels the west side of the creek for several miles.

Boat ramp: There's a rough launch for kayaks where Lake Cavanaugh Road meets the river a couple of miles upstream from Pilchuck Creek Campground, another at the campground itself, a third at the Highway 9 bridge over the creek, and a fourth a mile downstream from the Interstate 5 bridge on 236th Avenue (off Interstate 5 Exit 210).

Facilities: There are small grocery stores and a few gas stations around, but little else.

Water sports/restrictions: Because of its small size and abundance of log jams, this primarily a kayaker's stream, with some rafting and drift boating on the lower section below Highway 9.

Contact: John's Sporting Goods, tel. (425) 259-3056.

30 Stillaguamish River

Rating: 8

If you're looking for a river with multiple personalities, the Stillaguamish system is the Sybil of Northwest streams. Depending on where you might be along the length of the "Stilly," you could find yourself drifting lazily through meandering estuaries bordered by lowland pastures or fighting for your life on some of the most challenging Class V+ whitewater you would ever want to see. The main Stillaguamish and its two major branches, the North and South Forks, come about as close as any river system in Washington to having something for every river enthusiast.

If it's pray-out-loud-and-hang-on-for-all-you're-worth water that turns you on—and if you're a very accomplished paddler—you might want to investigate the possibility of running Robe Canyon, which is on the South Fork Stilly above Granite Falls. This three-mile-long series of steep drops, car-size boulders, nasty ledges, and 10-foot haystack waves was considered impassable by boaters 15 or 20 years ago, but these days a few really good kayakers with really good equipment—and perhaps a death wish—run it on a fairly regular basis. Even a few rafters have dared to drop into the foaming jaws of this beast, and some have made it through relatively unbruised. I can't overstate the fact that this is a stretch of river for experienced veterans only, and even then it should be run only by teams of boaters who can help each other out when the nearly inevitable happens.

If you're a boater who has plans for the

rest of his or her life, you might want to stick with the more civilized stretches of the Stillaguamish, such as the stretch from Big Four Campground down to Verlot, more than a dozen miles of Class II to Class IV water that can be run in a single day but which is more often split into two separate runs. Those wanting to make their way through Class II dodge-and-dart water in a kayak may prefer the upper run from Big Four down to River Bar Campground. From River Bar down to Verlot you'll see a few more rafts entering the river along with the smaller boats, and you'll find several exhilarating runs of Class III and even Class IV rapids and boulder patches.

The 12-mile stretch of the South Fork Stilly from the Granite Falls bridge down to River Meadows County Park near Arlington includes some interesting Class II water near its upper end, but it mellows out above the access point at Jordan to become mostly a flat-water float the rest of the way. Often traveled by steelhead anglers in drift boats, it's also a popular summer float among canoeists and can even be recommended as a safe section of river for inner tubers and other splash-and-slap water lovers. The county park at River Meadows is also a possibility for close-to-shore swimming and wading.

The North Fork Stillaguamish, more famous for its steelhead fishing than its boating, is a much more subdued stream than its sister fork to the south. There are some fun stretches of Class II rapids above Swede Heaven and a few more between Swede Heaven and Cicero, but for the most part the North Stilly is a mellow, friendly river that can be paddled in rafts or canoes quite easily. It's also popular with drift boaters, most of whom are in search of steelhead, salmon, and sea-run cutthroat trout.

The main Stillaguamish, below the confluence of the North and South Forks near Arlington, is a slow, wide, meandering river with only a few mild rapids and an occasional sweeper or small log jam to keep in mind, but there is one notable obstruction. About a quarter mile downstream from Interstate 5, there's a low-head dam across the river that canoeists and other leisurely boaters will want either to portage around or line over. People have gone over it in kayaks and other craft, but it does create a reversal current under moderate and high flow conditions, so it's safer to avoid it. Below the dam, the main Stilly soon becomes an estuary and a series of connecting sloughs. These are great for prospecting and exploring in a paddle or motor craft, but be aware of the tides and the impact they have on water levels.

Location: Flows into Port Susan west of Arlington, Snohomish County; map A2, grid e7.

How to get there: Take Interstate 5 to Highway 530 and turn west toward the lower river or east toward Arlington to reach upstream stretches of the river. Highway 530 parallels the North Fork Stillaguamish. To reach the South Fork, drive east on Highway 530 out of Arlington, turn south on Arlington Heights Road and south again on Jordan Road.

Boat ramp/put-in: There's an access area on Hat Slough, just west of Marine Drive on the lower Stillaguamish and two places to launch paddle craft and other small boats near the confluence of the North and South Forks at Arlington. One is a Department of Fish and Wildlife launch just upstream from Interstate 5 and the other is Haller City Park just north of Arlington. The North Fork Stillaguamish has a Department of Fish and Wildlife access area at Cicero and another good access site at Haltereman, as well as many spots along Highway 530 where over-the-bank launching of small boats is possible. The South Fork Stillaguamish has places to launch small boats at Jordan, Riverside County Park, and at the Mountain Loop Highway bridge two miles north of Granite Falls, as well as farther upriver at Verlot, River Bar, and Big Four campgrounds. A $10 Washington Department of Fish and Wildlife access decal is required to use the public launch areas maintained by the WDFW.

Facilities: Food, gas, and one motel (Arlington Motor Inn) are available in Arlington.

Water sports/restrictions: Kayaking and rafting are popular throughout the main river and both forks, and drift boating, canoeing, and tubing on the lower North and South Forks and main Stillaguamish.

Contact: Pacific Water Sports, tel. (206) 246-9385.

31 Lake Armstrong

Rating: 6

At only 30 acres, Armstrong is too small to interest powerboaters, so it's largely the stomping grounds of anglers and paddlers. A few local kids from Arlington visit the public access area for a summertime swim now and then, but swimming in one of these access sites usually isn't a very good idea because of the likelihood of getting fish hook stuck in a big toe or some other sensitive part of the anatomy. Like it or not, some anglers become slobs at the end of a day's fishing, and they may throw old hooks, pull tabs from cans, and other nasty little trinkets into the water as they load up to go home.

Location: North of Arlington; map A2, grid e7.

How to get there: Take Interstate 5 to Highway 530 and drive east to Arlington. Drive north out of town on Highway 9 and turn east (right) on Armstrong Road. Drive about half a mile to the first left and follow the road to the lake.

Boat ramp: The lake has a small access area and boat ramp. A $10 Washington Department of Fish and Wildlife access decal is required to use the public launch areas maintained by the WDFW.

Facilities: Food, gas, and fishing tackle are available in Arlington.

Water sports/restrictions: Paddling and fishing are the main activities here.

Contact: Lake McMurray Store, tel. (360) 445-3565.

32 Dungeness Spit/Sequim and Discovery Bays

Rating: 9

The description "something for everyone" gets used a lot, but it applies to the boating opportunities here about as well as anywhere in the Pacific Northwest. While providing access for big-boat enthusiasts to the wide-open Strait of Juan de Fuca and waters beyond in virtually every direction, the protected nooks and crannies here at the eastern end of the Strait also offer excellent places for small-boat enthusiasts to paddle, row, sail, motor, swim, wade, or use just about any means of locomotion they may prefer. And the location—right around the corner from Admiralty Inlet and Puget Sound—makes this a great jumping-off point to more distant spots or a close-to-home destination for boaters leaving the Puget Sound population centers by water or land.

Although Discovery Bay, Sequim Bay, and Dungeness Spit are all within only a

few minutes of each other by boat, they offer enough variety of things to see and do to keep a visitor exploring and enjoying for days. The area's salmon and bottom-fish action is enough to draw some folks here year-in and year-out, and these protected waters also offer excellent crabbing for both Dungeness and red rock crab. It's probably not common knowledge, but Discovery Bay also provides good shrimping—in season, of course.

Discovery Bay is over eight miles long and fairly protected from all winds except northerlies, so kayakers find it a worthwhile day trip. Protection Island, about two miles north of the bay entrance and very obvious to boaters coming from any direction, is a wildlife refuge that offers boaters a wide array of sight-seeing and photography possibilities, but you have to do it all from the water because the island is closed to public access.

Sequim Bay is only about one-third as large, but Travis Spit extends most of the way across its entrance, so it's extremely well-protected from the weather. While the entrance is narrow, it's well-marked, so boaters who follow the markers in and out will find at least 10 feet of water beneath them. Many folks will tell you Sequim Bay is even prettier and more interesting than Discovery Bay and is worth exploring in whatever kind of boat you operate. The clam digging also is excellent, and folks come here from all over western Washington to dig steamers and other varieties. The state park is also a popular diving destination. And yes, John Wayne Marina really is named after the Duke. He used to visit this area in his boat named *Wild Goose* and liked it so well that he donated over 20 acres, with specific instructions that a marina be built there. Who could say no to Rooster Cogburn?

Like Protection Island, Dungeness Spit is a wildlife refuge, but the public is allowed to hike its length (for a $2 entry fee) or beach a small boat on its shores. If the latter appeals to you, you'll need to call ahead to the U.S. Fish and Wildlife Service several days in advance for a landing permit. The number to call is (360) 457-8451. If you're going to hike the spit, by the way, you'd be better off doing it sooner rather than later: sand deposits continue to add to its length, and it grows 25 to 30 feet longer each year (a little bit of trivia I just couldn't help but pass along). A large parking lot and trailhead provide access for shore-bound visitors. Besides the wildlife and gorgeous views of the Strait and south end of Vancouver Island on a clear day, the world's longest natural sand spit offers visitors a chance to see and explore one of the Northwest's oldest lighthouses, which is located near the end of the spit. It's a special reward for those who have the endurance to hike the entire spit, but boaters can get close enough for a peak with much less effort.

Exploring this area in any boat larger than a paddle craft requires that you pay close attention to your depth sounder and to the tides. Sequim Bay, Dungeness Bay, and much of the near-shore water between the two is an ever-changing seascape of sand and gravel, with plenty of spots to run aground. Nautical chart 1471 has all the details, and you'll want it close by as you prowl these inviting waters.

Location: Strait of Juan de Fuca, north and east of Sequim; map A2, grid f2.

How to get there: Drive east from Port Angeles or north from Olympia on U.S. 101. The highway runs alongside parts of the Discovery Bay and Sequim Bay shorelines. To reach Dungeness Spit, drive to the town of Sequim and turn north on Sequim-Dungeness Way, following it north 11 miles to the water.

Boat ramp: Cline Spit and Dungeness boat ramps are both located inside Dungeness Bay, between the spit and the mainland. Inside Sequim Bay, there are ramps at the county park (off Port Williams Road), at John Wayne Marina, and at Sequim Bay State Park. The John Wayne ramp is the best of the bunch and has facilities for boaters that the others don't offer. It also has the most parking. There's a $4 launch fee at the state park, with an annual launch permit available for $40 (good at all state parks ramps).

Facilities: John Wayne Marina has moorage, fuel, a marine store, restaurant, and other necessities. Sequim Bay State Park has over 400 feet of moorage dock space, half a dozen moorage floats, tent and RV sites, rest rooms with showers and picnic tables, not to mention about 1,000 feet of saltwater beach to explore and dig clams. If you're interested in letting someone else run the boat while you gawk, Sequim Bay Tours and Charters operates out of Sequim. If you need motel accommodations, the Best Western Sequim Bay Lodge is located nearby along U.S. 101. If you get hungry while you're boating on Discovery Bay, don't worry; the Original Oyster House has good food, good service, big-screen TVs, and cold beer and is accessible from the water, with lots of moorage-float space. Another popular restaurant close to the water is the Three Crabs, north of Sequim. Anyone in town can tell you how to get there, but you'll probably need reservations.

Water sports/restrictions: All water sports are permitted. Personal watercraft use is prohibited near Dungeness Spit, and beaching a boat there requires a permit.

Contact: John Wayne Marina, tel. (360) 417-3440 (harbormaster), marina and fuel dock tel. (360) 683-9898; Sequim Bay State Park, tel. (360) 683-4235; Washington State Parks and Recreation Commission, tel. (800) 233-0321 (information), tel. (800) 452-5687 (reservations); Sequim Bay Lodge, tel. (800) 622-0691; Sequim Visitor Center tel. (360) 683-6197; Three Crabs Restaurant, tel. (360) 683-4264.

33 Port Townsend/Admiralty Inlet

Rating: 10

I don't think it's possible to love the water and not fall in love with Port Townsend the first time you see it. Almost everything about the place is water-oriented, and you can be happy here whether you're on shore looking out across the water or on the water looking back toward shore. The scenery is grand, the water is usually calm, and there are hundreds of interesting places to explore and things to do. You could probably spend the whole summer cruising, sailing, or paddling around the north end of the Quimper Peninsula and still feel as though you didn't get to do it all.

Fort Worden State Park, whose boat ramp offers easy access to the salmon grounds at Midchannel Bank as well as the kelp beds west of Point Wilson, has long been one of my favorite places in Washington. It also has a great gravel/sand beach for swimming, wading, or just beachcombing; an extensive trail system; old military bunkers to explore on the beach; and the spiffy old barracks and parade grounds (where much of the movie *An Officer and a Gentleman* was filmed) up on the hill. When it's open, the Marine Science Center on the old pier near the boat ramp is worth visiting.

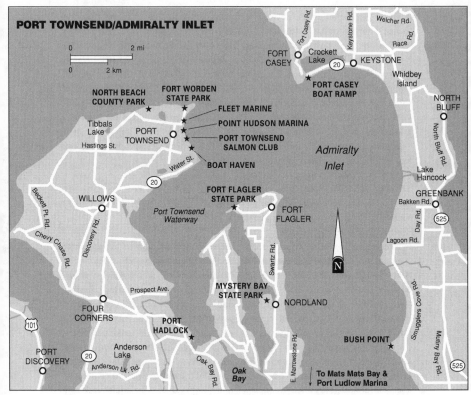

PORT TOWNSEND/ADMIRALTY INLET

0   2 mi

0   2 km

Fort Casey Rd.

Keystone Rd.

Welcher Rd.

Race Rd.

FORT CASEY

Crockett Lake

20

KEYSTONE

Whidbey Island

NORTH BLUFF

FORT CASEY BOAT RAMP

North Bluff Rd.

NORTH BEACH COUNTY PARK

FORT WORDEN STATE PARK

FLEET MARINE

POINT HUDSON MARINA

Tibbals Lake

PORT TOWNSEND

PORT TOWNSEND SALMON CLUB

Admiralty Inlet

Hastings St.

Water St.

BOAT HAVEN

Lake Hancock

20

GREENBANK

Bakken Rd.

WILLOWS

FORT FLAGLER STATE PARK

Port Townsend Waterway

FORT FLAGLER

Day Rd.

525

Beckett Pt. Rd.

Discovery Rd.

Lagoon Rd.

Chevy Chase Rd.

Swartz Rd.

N

Prospect Ave.

MYSTERY BAY STATE PARK

NORDLAND

Smugglers Cove Rd.

Mutiny Bay Rd.

FOUR CORNERS

PORT HADLOCK

101

PORT DISCOVERY

20

Anderson Lake

BUSH POINT

525

Anderson Lk. Rd.

Oak Bay Rd.

Oak Bay

E. Marrowstone Rd.

To Mats Mats Bay & Port Ludlow Marina

Another state park about three miles southeast of town has, over the past few years, stolen some of my affection from the bigger Fort Worden. Fort Flagler State Park, located on the north tip of Marrowstone Island, is far off the well-traveled path, so the mood is peaceful and laid-back. If you arrive by land, you'll enjoy the large campsites, many of them separated by thick groves of small trees and bushes for added privacy. If you come by water, you'll find a large moorage float near one of the two boat ramps, offering easy access to the park's many miles of hiking trails and bicycle paths. Salmon fishing can be very good right out in front of the park during the summer, and when the coho are in, it's sometimes possible to entice them with a long cast from the beach. If not, they're certainly within reach of paddlers and small-boat operators only a few hundred feet from the water's edge. This area also offers excellent crabbing, with both Dungeness and red rock crab available in many areas throughout Kilisut Harbor. Sometimes the best catches are made right along the west side of the park, near the harbor's north entrance, but if you place crab pots here, remember to leave the main channel open.

The beach on the park's Kilisut Harbor side, by the way, is well protected from the wind, and is a good place to lounge around the driftwood to catch a few summertime rays or have a picnic on the gravel beach. Paddlers and power-boaters alike enjoy the protected waters of Kilisut Harbor, but much of it is fairly shallow. Use chart 18471 and pay attention to your depthsounder. The main ramp at Fort Flagler and the ramp at Mystery Bay, about halfway down the harbor, provide easy access for the trailer-boater. The route into the harbor, by the way, is around the west end of the sand spit that juts out from Fort Flagler across the north harbor entrance. I've eased my 17-foot center-console through the gap near the spit's east end a couple of times during high tide, but following the markers around the end is certainly a smarter way to do it.

If you round Marrowstone Point at the northeast corner of the island, you can either turn south toward Puget Sound or cross Admiralty Inlet to explore the west side of Whidbey Island with its many state parks on old military sites. If you go south along Marrowstone, you'll rewarded with a great view of expansive gravel beaches and breathtaking high banks along much of the island's east side. Oak Bay, which separates the south end of Marrowstone from the mainland, is a peaceful and scenic waterway with lots of sandy shores, rows of driftwood, and great potential for seeing birds and wildlife. Farther south is Port Ludlow, one of the most well-protected bays in the entire Puget Sound area and a year-round destination for boaters and people who just want to get away. Boats of all kinds prowl Ludlow all year, some heading into or out of Hood Canal, others coming and going from the Strait of Juan de Fuca and San Juan Islands to the north or Puget Sound to the south.

It's rare to visit Port Townsend when there isn't some kind of festival, fair, or show going on, most of them having something to do with music, art, or boating. Among the bigger water-related activities here every year are the Shipwright's Regatta (late January), Sea Kayaking Symposium (late September), and, of course, the Wooden Boat Festival (early September). If you're a boater and haven't been to the Wooden Boat Festival, you can't imagine what you're missing. The town also has a summertime farmers market, which, like most of its major events, is easily accessible from the water. And speaking of water accessible, the town's new Union Wharf, just north of the ferry landing at the foot of Taylor Street, offers guest moorage for several visiting boats and provides some interesting interpretive information about the town. To go with all kinds of boating, Port Townsend also offers very good diving opportunities. Besides the natural wonders of bull kelp forests, lots of reefs and boulders to poke around, plenty of octopus, bottomfish, and other creatures you may want to get to know personally, the area's rich nautical history provides the opportunity to find all kinds of artifacts along the city's waterfront. The area is influenced by some stiff tides, so be sure to consult tide and current guides before entering the water.

If you paddle, sail, or motor south from town toward the south end of Port Townsend, there are a couple more local landmarks you may want to be aware of, one to avoid and one to visit if you can find the time. The first is the big naval reservation on Indian Island, between Port Townsend and Marrowstone Island. There's a big sign on the Navy pier warning boaters to stay away, and judging by the amount of attention I got when I cruised by a little closer than I should have one summer day a few years ago, they mean it! If you don't want to draw mortar fire across your bow, steer clear. The second point of interest—the one you should get close to—is the Ajax Cafe, located near Port Hadlock at the south end of Port Townsend. You'll need reservations because the place is always packed for dinner, but it's one of the most fun places I've ever eaten, and the food is as wonderful as the atmosphere. It's funky and it's loud, but it's a place you can take the kids and everyone will have a good time.

Location: North end of Quimper Peninsula, west of Whidbey Island; map A2, grid f3. (See Port Townsend/Admiralty Inlet inset map.)

How to get there: Take U.S. 101 to Discovery Bay and turn north on Highway 20, following it to Port Townsend, where several boat ramps are available. Or from the east, launch at any of several ramps on the west side of Whidbey Island to reach the area.

Port Townsend/Admiralty Inlet boat ramps: The following boat ramps, except for those at Mats Mats Bay and Port Ludlow Marina, are listed on the Port Townsend/Admiralty Inlet inset map:

- **North Beach County Park:** On the Port Townsend side of Admiralty Inlet, immediately west of the Fort Worden park boundary, this single-lane ramp sometimes gets clogged with sand and driftwood. But a worse problem is that inconsiderate hikers using the nearby trail sometimes park in the middle of the ramp, and they may not come back for hours.

- **Fort Worden State Park:** This park has a two-lane concrete ramp with a loading float and lots of nearby parking. It also has rest rooms, RV sites, and other amenities nearby.

- **Fleet Marine:** This is one of three launching possibilities near the north end of Port Townsend's business district. Fleet Marine has a portable hoist and lots of parking.

- **Point Hudson Marina:** Also near the north end of the business district, the Port of Port Townsend ramp at Point Hudson is a single-lane concrete ramp that's a little steep but plenty adequate for most trailer boats.

- **Port Townsend Salmon Club:** This ramp is at the end of Water Street and sometimes fills with sand and driftwood, but is now open to public use. Only club members may park in the ramp area, but there's some street parking when the downtown district isn't too busy.

- **Boat Haven:** The Port Townsend Boat Haven at the south end of town has both a portable hoist and a fairly new boat ramp, with a large paved parking area.

- **Fort Flagler State Park:** Across Port Townsend (the waterway), at the north end of Marrowstone Island, is Fort Flagler State Park, which has two boat ramps. One is inside the spit at the north end of Kilisut Harbor, the other on the open beach about 200 yards to the northeast. Sand and debris sometimes collect on the second ramp, but even then it's usually possible to launch a small boat with a four-wheel drive vehicle and save some running time out of the harbor. Both of these ramps are open during the summer months only.

- **Mystery Bay State Park:** South of Fort Flager, about halfway down the east side of Kilisut Harbor, Mystery Bay State Park has a single-lane concrete ramp and a small, gravel parking area. Remember that there's a $3 or $4 launch fee at all state park facilities (unless you're camping there), and a $40 annual permit is available that allows launching at all of them.

- **Port Hadlock:** At the south end of Port Townsend (the waterway), at the end of Lower Hadlock Road, Port Hadlock offers a single-lane ramp with loading float.

- **Oak Bay:** Near the northeast corner of Oak Bay is a Jefferson County Parks boat ramp that's suitable for smaller trailer boats. It's a mile southeast of Port Hadlock, off Portage Way.

- **Mats Mats Bay:** To the south (not visible on the inset map) is the Port of Port Townsend's boat ramp in Mats Mats Bay. It's a concrete-plank ramp that was in a fairly bad state of disrepair in the fall of 1998.

- **Port Ludlow Marina:** Farther south (also not visible on the inset map) is Port Ludlow Marina, where there's a fixed hoist ($3 each way; bring your own sling).

- **Fort Casey State Park:** This ramp is located across Admiralty Inlet from Port Townsend on Whidbey Island.

- **Bush Point:** This ramp is also on Whidbey Island, but farther south down Admiralty Inlet.

Facilities: Fort Worden and Fort Flagler State Parks have RV hookups, tent sites, and picnic areas and provide access to several miles of inviting beaches. Fort Casey, Fort Ebey, and Fort Worden State Parks all have tent sites. Port Townsend is a popular tourist town with all amenities and more than enough little shops for you to spend all your money in a single day. The many Victorian bed-and-breakfasts are not only pleasant places to stay but are gorgeous works of architectural art. All marine services are available in Port Townsend, including boat rentals, charters, and a dive shop. Port Ludlow Marina, tucked away in a protected bay near the entrance to Hood Canal, has nearly 100 guest slips, a fuel dock, pump-out facilities, a small store, two restaurants, and a nearby inn and RV park.

Water sports/restrictions: All water sports are permitted.

Contact: Port Townsend Chamber of Commerce Visitor Information Center tel. (888) 365-6978; Port of Port Townsend, tel. (360) 385-2355 (VHF ch. 9); Fleet Marine, Inc., tel. (800) 952-6962; Port Townsend Dive Shop, tel. (360) 379-3635; Kayak Port Townsend, tel. (360) 385-6240; Fort Worden State Park, 385-4730; Fort Flagler State Park, tel. (360) 385-1259; Fort Ebey State Park, tel. (360) 678-4636; Washington State Parks and Recreation Commission, tel. (800) 233-0321 (information), tel. (800) 452-5687 (reservations); Port Ludlow Marina, tel. (800) 308-7991; Port Ludlow Resort, tel. (800) 732-1239; Port Ludlow RV Park, tel. (360) 437-9110. This boat-oriented town and the county around it also have their own marine trades directory, published by the Jefferson County Economic Development Council. To get a copy, write the council at P.O. Box 877, Port Townsend, WA 98368. For nautical charts of this area, contact Captain's Nautical Supply, tel. (206) 283-7242.

34 Martha Lake

Rating: 8

I've always thought it was interesting that there are four lakes named Martha in the state of Washington, and that three of them are within a few miles of each other in Snohomish County. What's more, the two most popular Martha Lakes are almost identical in size, within one acre. Now, is that fascinating trivia or what? No? OK then, this lake used to be popular with anglers, but bird predation and other problems have greatly diminished the fishing opportunities, so swimmers, skiers, and others have the lake almost to themselves. The lake warms quickly in the summer, and by July it's a hot spot for most water sports. The resort has a decent swim beach, so

don't use the public access area for that.
Location: Northwest of Marysville, near Warm Beach; map A2, grid e6.

How to get there: Take the Smokey Point exit off Interstate 5 north of Marysville and drive west seven miles on Highway 531. Bear right to Lakewood Road, which runs along the south side of the lake.

Boat ramp: The lake has a public access area and boat ramp at its north end. A $10 Washington Department of Fish and Wildlife access decal is required to use the public launch areas maintained by the WDFW.

Facilities: There's a resort on the lake with a swim beach and other amenities.

Water sports/restrictions: All water sports are permitted.

Contact: Martha Lake Resort, tel. (360) 652-8412; Lake Goodwin Resort, tel. (360) 652-8169 (just in case no one answers at Martha Lake Resort).

35 Lake Ki

Rating: 7

The third-largest of seven popular lakes within a couple miles of each other, Ki has a major highway running right alongside its shore to provide easy access. At nearly 100 acres, it's big enough to offer something for everyone, but if you don't feel that you have room to do your thing here, you can drive a few minutes south to Lake Goodwin or Shoecraft Lake and start over. There are places to swim along the highway on the north side of the lake, but be alert for glass and other litter that may have been thrown by two-legged pigs from passing cars.

Location: Northwest of Marysville; map A2, grid f6.

How to get there: Take Interstate 5 to Smokey Point and turn west on Highway 531, which runs right alongside the north

end of the lake about three miles from the freeway.

Boat ramp: The lake has a two-lane, gravel Washington Department of Fish and Wildlife boat ramp. A $10 Washington Department of Fish and Wildlife access decal is required to use the public launch areas maintained by the WDFW.

Facilities: Wenberg State Park is on nearby Lake Goodwin, as are Lake Goodwin Resort and Cedar Grove Resort (see below). Lake Ki has a public access area with boat ramp and toilets.

Water sports/restrictions: All water sports are permitted.

Contact: Lake Goodwin Resort, tel. (360) 652-8169; Wenberg State Park, tel. (360) 652-7417.

36 Lake Goodwin

Rating: 8

With both a state park and two private resorts on its shores, this 550-acre lake has lots of access and lots of possibilities when it comes to water-related activities. This would have to qualify as one of Snohomish County's top waterskiing lakes, provided you get out on the water early enough to take advantage of calm water before the PWC and other power-boats begin to kick up a lot of chop. Swimming, waterskiing, and PWC riding all are popular, and the big lake can get a little crowded during the summer. While summer is the busiest time here, spring can also see a lot of activity here, thanks to the lake's reputation for good fishing. If you want peace and quiet, wait until after Labor Day to visit.

Location: Northwest of Marysville; map A2, grid f6.

How to get there: Take the Smokey Point exit off Interstate 5 and drive west on Highway 531; turn south on Lake

Goodwin Road to reach the east side of the lake. The highway becomes Lakewood Road at that point, and if you drive past Lake Goodwin Road on Lakewood, you soon come to the north end of the lake. To reach the west side of Goodwin, continue on to 52nd Avenue and turn south (left).

Boat ramp: There's a boat ramp at Wenberg State Park. The launch fee is $3; an annual launch permit is available from State Parks for $40.

Facilities: Wenberg State Park is on the east side of the lake and has rest rooms and showers, tent and RV spaces. Lake Goodwin Resort, at the north end of the lake, also has tent and RV sites, as well as a small store with tackle and licenses, propane, laundry, and an RV dump station. Cedar Grove Resort, on the west side of the lake, has tent and RV spaces and an RV dump station.

Water sports/restrictions: All water sports are permitted.

Contact: Wenberg State Park, tel. (360) 652-7417; Washington State Parks and Recreation Commission, tel. (800) 233-0321 (information), or tel. (800) 452-5687 (reservations); Lake Goodwin Resort, tel. (360) 652-8169; Cedar Grove Resort, tel. (360) 652-7083.

Location: Northwest of Marysville; map A2, grid f7.

How to get there: Exit Interstate 5 at Smokey Point and drive west on Highway 531, which becomes Lakewood Road near the north end of Lake Goodwin. Turn south (left) on 52nd Avenue NW and follow it about a mile and a half to the lake.

Boat ramp: The lake has a State Department of Fish and Wildlife boat ramp near its southwest corner. A $10 Washington Department of Fish and Wildlife access decal is required to use the public launch areas maintained by the WDFW.

Facilities: Cedar Grove Resort is only a mile away on the west side of Lake Goodwin. Lake Goodwin Resort and Wenberg State Park are also nearby on Lake Goodwin. Shoecraft has a public access area, boat ramp, and pit toilets near its southwest corner.

Water sports/restrictions: All water sports are permitted.

Contact: Cedar Grove Resort tel. (360) 652-7083; Lake Goodwin Resort, tel. (360) 652-8169; Washington State Parks and Recreation Commission, tel. (800) 233-0321 (information), or tel. (800) 452-5687 (reservations).

₃₇ Shoecraft Lake

Rating: 7

This 135-acre lake located almost at the corner of Lake Goodwin sometimes gets forgotten because of the bigger lake nearby, but it offers all the same recreational possibilities in a smaller package. It doesn't have the access that Goodwin has, since it has no state park or private resort on its shores, so it's harder to find a swimming spot here, but all the boating activities are available here.

₃₈ Lake Cassidy

Rating: 7

This 125-acre lake a few miles east of Marysville is about as close to a typical western Washington lake as you'll find anywhere. Large enough to ski and ride PWC on, yet with some nice shoreline scenery and enough places for a paddler or angler to get away from most of the more extreme activities, it's easy to understand the lake's popularity. But for all it has to offer, Cassidy is small enough and far enough off the main traffic flow to maintain a sense of law and order (at least most of the time). Lake Stevens is much larger and only about two miles away, so it gets much more attention from boaters and helps to keep things more sane at Cassidy. If there's a down side, it might be that some of the locals come here to party. Judging by the amount of litter and broken glass I saw in and around the public access area last time I was there, this might be one of the Marysville area's Friday or Saturday night hot spots.

Location: East of Marysville; map A2, grid f8.

How to get there: Take Interstate 5 to Everett and turn east on U.S. 2, then north on Highway 204. Turn north again on Highway 9 and drive just over three miles to the sign pointing right to Lake Cassidy.

Boat ramp: There's a Department of Fish and Wildlife access area with a boat ramp on the west side of the lake. It's a four-lane gravel ramp with a large gravel parking area that will hold a couple dozen cars with boat trailers. A $10 Washington Department of Fish and Wildlife access decal is required to use the public launch areas maintained by the WDFW.

Facilities: All other facilities are available in nearby Lake Stevens and Marysville.

Water sports/restrictions: All water sports are permitted.

Contact: John's Sporting Goods, tel. (425) 259-3056.

39 Northern Puget Sound to Deception Pass

Rating: 10

With a place like Deception Pass, how could this part of Puget Sound be anything but a boater's magnet? There are lots of reasons why Deception Pass State Park has more visitors each year than Yellowstone National Park and several other world-famous landmarks. Sure, many of those gawkers and gaspers come to the pass by land, but water is the big draw, specifically the water that surges through the narrow, rocky channel separating the north end of Whidbey Island from the southwest corner of Fidalgo Island/Deception Pass. There are few places more beautiful, and when the tide is surging, there are few places more awe inspiring. If you want a first-hand look at the power of nature, this is as good a place as any.

If you're looking for a place to learn the basics of boating or to try scuba diving for the first time, this is NOT a good place. There's a name for those who have failed to fully understand or respect the power of the water that churns back and forth between Rosario Strait and the north end of Skagit Bay: casualties. Currents through Deception Pass sometimes reach seven or eight knots, creating dangerous eddies and huge waves, especially when a strong ebb meets stiff westerly winds near the west entrance to the pass. The steep rock walls on both sides offer no escape for boaters who run into difficulty. Boaters who do travel through the pass—at least the smart ones—time their passage to coincide with slack tides. During the slack, in fact, even paddlers make their way in and out of Deception Pass, and a few expert divers have been known to explore its rocky depths. Those who have emerged from the pass tell tales of large lingcod and other impressive denizens of the deep.

The long, gravel beach at West Point, on the south side of the west entrance to the pass, is popular with swimmers, beachcombers, sun bathers, and in the late summer and fall, salmon anglers who catch coho and pink salmon from the beach. Just east of the pass, fall fishing for pink salon is sometimes red hot in and around Cornet Bay. Farther east, near the north end of Skagit Bay, are a couple of beautiful state marine parks. Skagit Island State Park, the smaller and more northerly of the two, has only two moorage buoys to offer as facilities for boaters, while Hope Island, about a mile south, has five buoys and several primitive campsites. Both are well protected from wind and weather, but boat traffic can be fairly constant during the summer, especially along the west end of Hope Island. A few miles to the east, seven-mile-long Swinomish Channel runs north and south, connecting Skagit Bay on the south to Padilla Bay on the north, but separating Fidalgo Island from the mainland in the process.

The north end of the channel presents little problem for boaters, but be careful to follow the channel markers in and out of the south entrance. More than one boater trying to take the shortest line between two points has found himself perched atop the riprap that extends along the south side of the channel some distance into Skagit Bay. Once in the channel itself, maintain a slow speed, not only because there's a good chance of meeting a boat bigger than yours anywhere along the way, but also to give yourself plenty of time to see and admire the gorgeous homes on the rocky, forested hillsides south of LaConner. There's also a lot of wildlife to see, including probably the most great blue herons you've ever seen. And keep your eye peeled for at least one bald eagle, one that hasn't moved for a while. (No more hints.)

Just south of LaConner is the Rainbow Bridge, which is worth a photo or two when the lighting is right. LaConner itself is a great place to visit, either by land or water. Many of the waterfront restaurants, bars, motels, bed-and-breakfast facilities, and other businesses have floats and piers to help draw boaters in for a closer look. Always plan on spending at least a couple of hours in LaConner before moving on. Much of Skagit Bay's east side is one big estuary, where the North Fork Skagit and South Fork Skagit split into dozens of smaller channels and sloughs before ending their journey to the saltchuck. (See listing 21, Lower Skagit River, in this chapter).

Crescent Harbor, Oak Harbor, and Penn Cove, on the east side of Whidbey Island, offer enough square miles of interesting waterways to keep a boater busy for days. The inner harbor at Oak Harbor is especially well protected from the wind, and a large marina complex there provides anything a visiting boater might need. Penn Cove may be best known to many as the home of Penn Cove mussels, but it's also a worthwhile place for boat exploration. Penn Cove leads to one of Washington's most quaint and interesting little towns, Coupeville. Waterfront shops and stores, easily accessible by water, thanks to the long wharf that runs well out into Penn Cove, are worth exploring, as are the historic displays and museums, turn-of-the-century homes, bed-and-breakfasts, and restaurants. An early March visit to the Coupeville area will put you there during the Penn Cove Mussel Festival, an opportunity to gorge on the delectable bivalves with hundreds of other seafood enthusiasts and maybe even take part in some of the other fun activities. If you're in or near town around early evening at any other time of year, call for a reservation at Rosi's Garden Restaurant, where the mussels are always fresh and everything else on the menu is outstanding.

To the south, Holmes Harbor is worth investigating when you're on the east side of Whidbey, and it has a nice county park at its south end, but it's not as protected from the wind as it might appear on a map or chart. Although perhaps not much of a boating destination itself, Saratoga Passage, between the east side of Whidbey and the west side of Camano Island, certainly can make life more pleasant for boaters traveling north from Seattle or Everett toward the San Juans, Bellingham, or Canadian destinations or returning from those spots to the population centers of central Puget Sound. Saratoga Passage is often much flatter than Admiralty Inlet when the weather's nasty, so traveling up the east side of Whidbey Island instead of the west side will often make the difference between continuing the voyage and staying put for a day or two.

There are, of course, places along the way that are well worth spending some time, including Camano Island State Park. Besides its standard tent and RV sites, the park is part of the Cascadia Marine Trail system and has primitive tent sides for paddlers who arrive by water. It's also a popular dive spot with plenty of worthwhile underwater structure to investigate. Port Susan and the Stillaguamish River estuary at its northeast corner are also worthy of investigation, whether you're in a powerboat or paddle craft. Powerboaters might want to wait for a high tide to explore the upper end of this waterway.

If you're really adventurous, you might even make your way up through Devil's Slough, passing beneath the Highway 532 bridge and emerging at the south end of Skagit Bay. After all, who wouldn't want to tempt fate by running a boat through a spot called Devil's Slough? What a great story for your grandchildren. Depending on the size of your boat, this is another passage that probably should be reserved for times of relatively high tide. Kayak Point County Park, about halfway up the east side of Port Susan, is a nice place to stop for a picnic lunch, but the pier there is for fishing, not mooring. Don't pass through Saratoga Passage in any kind of boat without stopping at Langley, just north of Whidbey Island's Sandy Point. Although often crowded during the summer and on nice weekends at other times of year, all the little shops, restaurants, and other attractions are worth the trouble of finding a place to moor.

Gedney Island, in the middle of Possession Sound about midway between Everett and Langley, was once a place where anglers could expect to find good fishing for big chinook salmon throughout much of the year. The fishing isn't as good as it used to be, but the island—also known by the locals as Hat Island—does draw boaters in for a closer look, and the surrounding shoals are popular with divers. Don't go ashore, though, since the island is privately owned.

About three miles to the east is an island you can visit, and many boaters do. It's Jetty Island, the long spit formed by decades of Snohomish River sediment that stretches north to south and shields the Everett waterfront. The entire island is a wildlife sanctuary and a great place to see and photograph a wide range of shore birds and waterfowl. There's a small dock for visiting boats, and the City of Everett even offers boat tours to the island.

Just north of Everett is the sprawling Snohomish River estuary, with three main channels and several smaller sloughs to explore. It's possible to run upstream for miles in Ebey Slough, Steamboat Slough, and the main river channel. The main channel is the waterway between Jetty Island and the city waterfront. Some of the smaller sloughs and bays may be navigated in a paddle craft during moderately high tides. Everett attractions include the Port of Everett's sprawling marina, the biggest such facility in the Pacific Northwest. Besides all marine services, the marina has restaurants, shops, and other businesses. That's good, because Everett's main business district is some distance away and difficult to reach on foot from the marina. Southwest of Everett, down Possession Sound past the interesting waterfront town of Mukilteo, is the south end of Whidbey Island and the large shoal south of Possession Point. Long a hot spot for salmon fishing, it also offers excellent diving opportunities (watch the tides and always use your diver-down flag).

The outside (western) shores of Whidbey are exposed to the strong southerlies and westerlies that can ruin a boater's day, but also offer a wide variety of places to see and things to do. The view to the west includes an unobstructed look right down the Strait of Juan de Fuca, and places like Fort Ebey and Fort Casey State Parks are well worth some time. The fishing also can be very good here, especially during the height of the coho runs in early fall. Keystone is a staging area for several good dives along the west side of the island. The only problem is one of access since there's just one public boat ramp along the entire west side of the island north of Mutiny Bay. Fuel docks and other boating facilities are just about as scarce as launch ramps. Ramps and marine services in Port Townsend are the closest available for many boaters.

Near the south end of Admiralty Inlet, on the Kitsap Peninsula's northeast corner, is Point No Point, with its long gravel beach and excellent view across Puget Sound to the mainland and the Cascades. This was the focal point of activity when salmon fishing was a year-round activity throughout Puget Sound, but it's still worth a visit today. The point still looks like the old days to me, whether I'm seeing it from the water or from the shore. On a calm sunny day it's a great place to be whether you're sailing, paddling, cruising, or walking the beach. A resort and a county park provide access to this part of Puget Sound.

Appletree Cove and the town of Kingston are farther south along the Kitsap Peninsula shoreline. The cove itself is well protected from the wind, so some paddlers and other small-boat operators can be found playing here, but don't forget that it's also a ferry terminal and you have to be heads-up when boating here. Across the sound to the east is Edmonds, a waterfront town with all the boating amenities, including a full-service marina. With its long fishing pier, artificial and natural reefs for divers to explore, and easy access to waterways in three directions, Edmonds is a hub of water sports activity. And if you're not on the water, this is also a good place to be stuck on shore, with plenty of things to see and do and at least as many places to spend some of your money.

Location: Marine waters of Puget Sound from Deception Pass southward to Kingston, on the east side of the Kitsap Peninsula; map A2, grid f6.

How to get there: Take Highway 20 west from Burlington to Deception Pass and south down the north end of Whidbey Island. Highway 525 becomes the main north-south travel route on the island south of Keystone. Turn west off Interstate 5 at Conway to reach LaConner and Swinomish Channel. Take Highway 532 west from Interstate 5 to reach Camano Island, Saratoga Passage, Port Susan, and the south end of Skagit Bay. Various roads and streets leading west of Interstate 5 and U.S. 99 from Edmonds to Everett provide access to Puget Sound near the southern end of this area. Take Highway 307 to Highway 104 and turn west to reach Kingston, on the west side of Puget Sound.

Boat ramp:

- **Bowman Bay Ramp:** One of two ramps at Deception Pass State Park, this one is west of the Deception Pass Bridge in Bowman Bay. The ramp is a one laner with a concrete surface and small, gravel parking area. To reach it, take Highway 20 and turn west on Rosario Road just north of the Deception Pass Bridge and then turn left immediately to Bowman Bay. There's a $3 round-trip launch fee, with an annual permit available for $40 from the State Parks and Recreation Commission.

- **Cornet Bay:** Also a State Parks facility, this site is four lanes wide, all paved, with loading floats. Because it has loading floats and other facilities, it costs $4 to launch at this State Parks ramp. The $40 annual permit from State Parks is valid here. To reach it, turn east of Highway 20 just south of the Deception Pass State Park entrance and follow Cornet Bay Road about a mile to the ramp.

- **LaConner:** There are two ramps in this little town near the south end of Swinomish Channel. The Port of Skagit County's LaConner Marina has a fixed hoist where you pay by the foot to launch. To reach it, follow Third Street north out of the downtown area for one mile and you'll see the sling on your left. To the south a short distance is the Sherman Street ramp, managed by the City of LaConner. It's a one-lane concrete ramp with a loading float and small parking area. To get there, turn south on Second Street to its end, where it becomes Caldonia Street. Continue south on Caldonia one block and turn right on Third Street, following it to Sherman, where you turn right and go 200 yards to the ramp.

- **Oak Harbor Marina:** From Highway 20 in Oak Harbor, turn east on Pioneer Way and go one mile, through the large parking area, to the ramp. It's a six-lane concrete ramp with a fixed hoist nearby. There's one loading float and a large, gravel parking area.

- **Beach Park Ramp:** Just west of Oak Harbor Marina there's a one-lane concrete ramp and free launching. Reach it by taking Pioneer Way off Highway 20 and turning south on Baywatch, following it a quarter of a mile to the ramp.

- **Penn Cove County Park:** South of Oak Harbor is Penn Cove, where there's an Island County Parks and Recreation Department ramp on the north side. It's a one-lane concrete ramp with a gravel parking area big enough for about a dozen cars and trailers. Drive south from Oak Harbor on Highway 20 about two miles to Monroe Landing Road and follow it to the end, a distance of about a mile and a half.

- **Captain Coupe Park:** On the south side of Penn Cove, at the east end of Coupeville, is Captain Coupe Park, where there's another one-lane concrete ramp with a gravel parking area. Take Main Street in Coupeville to N.E. Ninth Street and turn right, following it a quarter of a mile to the park and ramp.

- **Fort Casey State Park:** The only boat ramp north of Mutiny Bay on the west side of Whidbey Island is the one next to the Port Townsend ferry dock near Fort Casey State Park. It's actually a State Parks launch and is a steep two-lane concrete ramp with a large, gravel parking area. Launching here can be a little tricky on a low tide, thanks to algae and gravel on the ramp. There's a $4 launch fee.

- **Maple Grove Ramp:** Located at the north end of Camano Island, this ramp is managed by Island County Parks and Recreation. It's a one-lane concrete ramp that has a small, gravel parking area and limited boat storage at its upper end. To get there, drive west from Stanwood on Highway 532 about four miles, then northwest on North Camano Drive for another 2.5 miles. Turn right on Maple Grove Street and follow it just under half a mile to the ramp, at the bottom of the hill.

- **Cavalero Beach County Park:** There's an Island County Parks ramp at this popular park on the east side of Camano. Reach it by taking Highway 532 west from Stanwood for four miles. Turn south on East Camano Drive and go five miles, turning east on Cavalero Road to the park. This ramp is a one-lane concrete facility that's seen better days. It's best for smaller trailer boats and paddle craft.

- **Camano Island State Park:** This park on the west side of Camano Island has a two-lane concrete ramp that's in good shape, with room for about three dozen cars and trailers in the nearby gravel parking area. There's a $3 round-trip launch fee, with an annual launch permit available for $40. To reach it, take Highway 532 west from Stanwood about four miles, turning south on East Camano Drive and continuing another six miles. Turn west on Monticello Drive, go two miles, and turn south on West Camano Drive, following it 1.2 miles to Lowell Point Road, where you turn right and drive to the park.

- **Kayak Point Ramp:** On the mainland side of the water, Snohomish County Parks and Recreation maintains a one-lane concrete ramp at Kayak Point County Park, off Kayak Point Road and Marine Drive. It has room to park about 20 cars and trailers, and there's a $3 launch fee.

- **Langley Ramp:** On Whidbey Island just north of Langley is a single-lane concrete boat ramp managed by the City of Langley. All you have to do to find it is follow the main drag from downtown Langley toward the water.

- **Langley Marina:** This facility has a fixed hoist that can handle boats under 24 feet and four tons. There's a $30 round-trip charge for the hoist. Reach it by driving west from Clinton on Highway 525 about three miles and turning right on Langley Road. Go 3.2 miles to the town of Langley and go right at the stop sign toward the water.

- **Bush Point Resort:** This facility on the west side of Whidbey Island has a fixed hoist and a gravel parking area with enough room for about two dozen cars and trailers. From Clinton, go west on Highway 525 to mile post 19 and turn left on Bush Point Road, following it three miles to a Y, where you'll bear left on Scurlock Road. Continue three-quarters of a mile on Scurlock, turning left on Main Street and following it to the bottom of the hill.

- **Mutiny Bay Ramp:** Farther south along the west side of the island is the one-lane concrete ramp at Mutiny Bay. Managed by Island County Parks and Recreation, it has parking for about two dozen cars and trailers. From Highway 525 turn west on Fish Road, following it one mile to Mutiny Bay Road, where you turn left and go a quarter mile to Robinson Road.

Turn right on Robinson and follow it 100 yards to the water.

- **Freeland Park Ramp:** Holmes Harbor, on the east side of Whidbey, has a one-lane hard-surface ramp at Freeland County Park. The ramp has a loading float, but the gravel parking area appears large enough for only eight or nine cars and trailers. It's located right in the small town of Freeland.

- **Dave Mackie Park:** There's a good single-lane ramp at this Island County Parks and Recreation facility, located just north of Indian Point at the south end of Whidbey. It has parking for about two dozen cars and trailers.

- **Waterfront Park Ramp:** Just north of Possession Point at the southeast corner of the island is a one-lane concrete ramp at Possession Beach Waterfront Park. It has one loading float and parking for about 15 cars and trailers. To get there, drive west from Clinton for three miles on Highway 525 and turn south on Cultus Bay Road, following it five miles. Turn east on Possession Road and follow it to the park and ramp.

- **Everett Marine Park:** The biggest boat ramp in Washington is located at the marine park in Everett. It has 13 paved lanes and seven loading floats for your boating pleasure, and on a busy weekend every lane is full. Protected from the worst of the wind and weather by Jetty Island, it's as good a place to launch a boat as you could ask. As you might guess, it also has a huge parking lot. Maintained by the Everett Parks and Recreation Department, it has a $5 launch fee. To reach it, take Exit 195 off Interstate 5 and go west 3.8 miles to 10th Street, where you turn right and go 100 yards to the park.

- **Everett Marina:** This Port of Everett facility has a fixed hoist and a portable hoist for launching boats at its facility off Marine View Drive. The site also has a loading/boarding float. Take Exit 195 off Interstate 5, go west on Marine View Drive four miles. and turn right on 14th Street.

- **Waterfront Park:** This park and ramp are on the north side of the Snohomish River mouth immediately north of Everett, and it provides access to Possession Sound and Puget Sound. It has a two-lane concrete ramp with loading floats and parking for about 40 cars and trailers. Get there by taking Exit 195 off Interstate 5 and driving west on Marine View Drive for 2.3 miles, where you turn north on Highway 529. Cross the Snohomish River and turn right on 28th Place NE (the first right after the river).

- **Mukilteo State Park:** Located just south of the Mukilteo-Clinton ferry dock, this park has a four-lane concrete ramp that's open during daylight hours only, but it has overnight parking for cars and trailers at $5 per night. The launch fee is $4 round-trip. From Interstate 5 at Everett, take Exit 189 and go west on Highway 526 about five miles to its end. Turn right on Highway 525, go two miles to the Mukilteo Ferry and turn left on Front Street to the park.

- **Edmonds Marina:** One of the most popular marinas on Puget Sound, Edmonds has two hoists for launching, with a per-foot launch fee. To get there, take Interstate 5 to Exit 177 and go west on Highway 104 about five miles to the ferry terminal. Turn left just before your reach the ferry toll booth and follow Dayton Street across the railroad track to the stop sight. Turn right and you'll see the slings straight ahead.

- **Point No Point Resort:** This once-bustling resort has a hoist that will handle boats up to 16 feet long for a $12 launch fee. Get to it by driving north from Poulsbo on Highway 307 to Highway 104, following it north. SR 104 becomes Hansville Road, which continues north. Turn right on Point No Point Road and go one mile to the resort, which is on the left.

- **Eglon Ramp:** There's a bruised and battered little concrete boat ramp at Eglon about midway between Point No Point and Kingston. This one is recommended for smaller trailer boats and cartoppers only.
- **Kingston Cove Marina:** This Port of Kingston facility has a two-lane concrete ramp and a fixed hoist for launching. There's a loading float at both launch sites, and parking for about 50 cars and trailers. To reach it, drive north from Poulsbo on Bond Road (Highway 307) for nine miles to Kingston, staying in the far right lane marked "Local," as opposed to the ferry traffic lane. Go right on Washington Boulevard, following it to the marina lot. The ramp is at the far corner of the parking area.

Facilities: Deception Pass State Park is one of the largest state parks in Washington and one of the most popular visitor destinations in the country. It has over 240 campsites, access to saltwater beaches, a freshwater lake, picnic areas and cooking shelters, an RV dump station, concession stands, and other amenities. This is also a state marine park, and there are five moorage buoys and nearly 130 feet of float space on the Bowman Bay end of the pass and over 1,100 feet of moorage float space in Cornet Bay. There are a boat-sewage dump station in Bowman Bay and both a dump station and a pump-out facility at Cornet Bay. Deception Pass Marina in Cornet Bay has open moorage, fuel docks, and a small grocery/tackle store.

LaConner Marina has guest moorage, power and water to the docks, fuel docks, rest rooms with showers, laundry facilities, marine repairs, and boat storage. LaConner Landing offers fuel docks, sewage pump-out facilities, and a small store. Among the great La-Conner eateries within walking distance of the water is Palmer's Restaurant and Pub, where the food is so good that it's even worth putting up with the smoke in the bar if you don't have restaurant reservations. (Does that sound like personal experience or what?) Oak Harbor Marina has lots of guest moorage (open), fuel docks, power to the docks, rest rooms with showers, boat-sewage pump-out facilities, a laundry, and boat haul out.

Coupeville Wharf, a Port of Coupeville facility, provides lots of moorage, fuel, rest rooms with showers, and access to several businesses. Beach Park has a large saltwater beach, picnic and play areas, a kitchen shelter, RV sites, and rest rooms and showers. Fort Casey State Park has three dozen tent sites, picnic areas, kitchen shelters, and rest rooms with showers. Camano Island State Park has 87 tent sites, picnic tables, rest rooms with showers, and a large day-use area with beach access and picnic tables. Facilities at Langley Boat Harbor on Whidbey Island include open moorage, power to the docks, and rest rooms with showers. Langley Marina has marine repairs and hardware, a dive shop, boat-sewage dump, and rest rooms with showers.

Tulalip Marina, north of Everett, has fuel docks, open moorage, power to the docks, rest rooms, boat-sewage pump-out facilities, and a small store and cafe. Everett Marine Park has a ramp for launching sailboards, picnic areas and tables, and fishing dock. Everett Marina has fuel docks, open moorage on over 1,800 feet of float space, water and power to the floats, rest rooms and showers, laundry facilities, and boat-sewage pump-out and dump station facilities.

Edmonds Marina (Port of Edmonds) has a fuel dock with gas and diesel, covered and open moorage, power and water to the docks, rest rooms with showers and boat-sewage pump-out facilities. Maybe the best thing about the marina is that there's an Anthony's restaurant right next door. Point No Point Resort has RV sites, rental cabins, rental boats, laundry facilities, picnic tables, and rest rooms. Port of Kingston Marina has open moorage, gas and diesel, power and water to the docks, rest rooms with showers, boat-swage pump-out and dump station, and laundry.

Water sports/restrictions: All water sports are permitted. Most of this area is covered by NOAA chart 18441, but others, including charts 18424 (Bellingham to Everett), 18427 (Anacortes to Skagit Bay), and 18444 (Everett Harbor), are also valuable.

Contact: Washington State Parks and Recreation Commission, tel. (800) 233-0321 (information), tel. (800) 452-5687 (reservations); Anacortes Diving and Supply, tel. (360) 293-2070; Deception Pass Marina, tel. (360) 675-5411 (VHF ch. 16); LaConner Marina, tel. (360) 466-3118 (VHF ch. 68); LaConner Landing Marine Services, tel. (360) 466-4478; Oak Harbor Marina, tel. (360) 679-2628 (VHF ch. 16); Whidbey Island Dive Center, tel. (360) 675-1112; Langley Boat Harbor, tel. (360) 221-4246; Langley Marina, tel. (360) 221-1771; Tulalip Marina, tel. (360) 651-4999; Everett Marina, tel. (425) 259-6001 (VHF ch. 16); Edmonds Marina, tel. (425) 774-0549; Greater Oak Harbor Chamber of Commerce Visitor Information Center, tel. (360) 675-3535; Camano Island Chamber of Commerce Visitor Information Center, tel. (800) 910-2256; Snohomish County Tourism Bureau, tel. (888) 338-0976; Everett Area Chamber of Commerce, tel. (425) 252-5181; Kingston Area Chamber of Commerce, tel. (360) 297-3813. For nautical charts of this area, contact Captain's Nautical Supply, tel. (206) 283-7242.

40 Dungeness River

Rating: 5

Some parts of this little Clallam County river stand as a tribute to man's stupidity in dealing with a once-natural stream, but it does offer some challenging little rapids, boulder patches, and slots for people in the right kind of boats. It's small for a drift boat, too technical for a canoe, and there are too many tough pockets, logjams, and tricky turns for safe tubing. But a good kayaker can run parts of it during periods of moderate flow when most of the boulders and logs have enough water running over them to allow passage. I wouldn't even think about running any of this one without a helmet; there are way too many rocks and very few soft spots should you find yourself upside-down.

Location: Enters Strait of Juan de Fuca north of Sequim; map A2, grid f1.

How to get there: Take U.S. 101 to Sequim and turn north on Sequim Avenue-Dungeness Way, which crosses the river near its mouth. Roads to the left near the river mouth provide access upstream. To reach the upper portion of the Dungeness, drive west from Sequim and turn south on River Road or Taylor Cutoff Road.

Boat ramp/take-out: It's possible to drop a small boat or kayak over the bank off River Road below the Dungeness Fish Hatchery and at the fishing access near Taylor Cutoff Road, both upstream of U.S. 101. Below U.S. 101 there are places to put a boat in the water near the Runion Road bridge and downstream off the Old Olympic Highway.

Facilities: Rainbow's End RV Park is about a mile and a half west of the river. Sequim Bay State Park, about six miles east, has about two dozen RV sites. Food, gas, and lodging are available in Sequim.

Water sports/restrictions: Kayaking is OK, but larger and smaller craft could have problems. Tubing or swimming is not recommended.

Contact: Rainbow's End RV Park, tel. (360) 683-3863; Sequim Bay State Park, tel. (360) 683-4235; Swain's tel. (360) 452-2357.

41 Anderson Lake

Rating: 9

This 70-acre lake is one of those peaceful, quiet, beautiful places that everyone should visit now and then just because. If you can enjoy it from the water, all the better. The serenity of this place is greatly enhanced by the prohibition on internal combustion engines with their smoke, noise, and the need for speed they seem to encourage. Fishing boats equipped with quiet electric motors are about as high tech as things seem to get around here, but oars and paddles are the most common mode of locomotion. The fishing here is what's known in piscatorial circles as quality angling, as opposed, I guess, to quantity angling, with catch-and-release regulations in effect during the last two months of the season. Anderson could accurately be described as a quality boating destination as well.

Location: Northwest of Chimacum on the Quimper Peninsula; map A2, grid f3.

How to get there: Take U.S. 101 to the south end of Discovery Bay, turn east on Highway 20, and drive about four miles to Anderson Lake Road. Follow Anderson Lake Road about a mile and a half to the lake.

Boat ramp: There's a boat ramp at the state park that is suitable for cartoppers and small trailer boats. The launch fee is $3; a $40 annual launch permit is available from the Washington State Parks and Recreation Commission.

Facilities: Anderson Lake State Park is a day-use park with no camping facilities, but it has rest rooms.

Water sports/restrictions: Swimming, paddling, and fishing are the main water sports here. Gasoline engines are prohibited on the lake.

Contact: Washington State Parks and Recreation Commission, tel. (800) 233-0321.

42 Goss Lake

Rating: 6

Covering only about 55 acres, Goss is too small for any real skiing or speedboating crowds, so it maintains a fairly quiet personality and slow pace throughout most of the year. It's a popular spring fishing spot, but you can nearly always find plenty of room to paddle or play wherever you want here during the warmer months. In the fall you'll probably have the whole lake to yourself if you should decide to pay a visit.

Location: Whidbey Island northeast of Freeland, map A2, grid f5.

How to get there: Take the ferry from Mukilteo to Clinton and drive northwest on Highway 525 about 10 miles to Freeland; turn north on East Harbor Road and right on Goss Lake Road. It's about a mile and half to the lake, on the right.

Boat ramp: There's a small Department of Fish and Wildlife access area with a single-lane boat ramp on the east side of the lake. A $10 Washington Department of Fish and Wildlife access decal is required to use the public launch areas maintained by the WDFW.

Facilities: The nearest food, gas, and lodging are in Langley, two miles to the east.

Water sports/restrictions: Canoeing, fishing, and small-boat operation are popular here.

Contact: John's Sporting Goods, tel. (425) 259-3056; Ted's Sports Center, tel. (425) 743-9505.

43 Lone Lake

Rating: 7

This 90-acre lake is very shallow and has few trees around it, so it heats up quickly after a few days of nice summer weather. You can comfortably swim here before most other lakes warm up into the comfortable range. A speed limit and noise restriction keep the fast-boat folks away from Lone, but there are other places around the island to go fast, so it's OK. The county park offers an adequate but not fancy place to swim and play around the water.

Location: Whidbey Island, east of Freeland; map A2, grid f5.

How to get there: Take the ferry from Mukilteo to Clinton and take Highway 525 about seven miles northwest to Bayview Road. Turn north on Bayview and drive just under two miles to Andreason Road, where you turn west and drive half a mile to Lone Lake Road, which leads to the access area.

Boat ramp: There's a large county access area, swim beach, and two-lane boat ramp on the north side of the lake. The two-lane ramp is the concrete-plank type, but it may not be in very good shape, so take it easy.

Facilities: The nearest amenities are in Langley, about two miles away.

Water sports/restrictions: Paddling, swimming, and fishing are the main attractions. The lake has a no-wake speed limit.

Contact: Island County Parks and Recreation Department, tel. (360) 679-7373; John's Sporting Goods, tel. (425) 259-3056; Ted's Sports Center, tel. (425) 743-9505.

44 Lake Stevens

Rating: 8

When a lake is big enough and popular enough to have a town spring up around it and even be named after it, well, it's gotta be a hot spot, and Lake Stevens is. The lake covers more than 1000 acres and has about eight miles of shoreline, and during summer—or any decent weekend in the spring or fall—the lake seems to be the recreational and social center of southern Snohomish County. Boating, fishing, PWC riding, tubing, swimming, and especially waterskiing are big draws here, and when the weather's nice there are thousands of people in, on and around this enormous and enormously popular body of water. Things really get hopping during the fourth weekend in July, when the Lake Stevens Aquafest is under way. This community festival, a celebration of water activities and great excuse for a good time, attracts visitors from as far away as Seattle to the south and Bellingham to the north, not to mention a few thousand local resident water lovers.

Location: At the town of Lake Stevens, east of Everett; map A2, grid f8.

How to get there: Take Interstate 5 to Everett and turn east on U.S. 2. Turn north on Highway 204 and follow it about three miles to the lake.

Boat ramp: There's a three-lane concrete-plank ramp near the south end of the lake at Wyatt Park (Snohomish County) and a single-lane ramp in the northeast corner of the lake at North Cove Park (City of Lake Stevens). There's a $3 launch fee at Wyatt Park.

Facilities: Wyatt Park has a large, sand-bottom swim area, a large dock, rest rooms, and picnic tables. Food, gas, lodging, and all other facilities are plentiful throughout the area.

Water sports/restrictions: All water sports are permitted. The lake has a long list of specific waterskiing regulations enacted and enforced by the City of Lake Stevens. Boaters and skiers should contact the city of they need specific details.

Contact: Snohomish County Parks Department, tel. (425) 339-1208; Lake Stevens Aquafest, tel. (425) 397-2344; Lake Connor Park, tel. (425) 334-5055; John's Sporting Goods, tel. (425) 259-3056.

Location: South of Granite Falls, Snohomish County; map A2, grid f8.

How to get there: Take Interstate 5 to Everett and exit east on U.S. 2; then turn north on Highway 204 and cross Highway 9 to Lake Stevens. Drive north from Lake Stevens to Granite Falls on Highway 92. Turn south through town and continue south on Robe-Menzel Road to Utley Road. Turn right and drive about a mile to the lake, which is on the right.

Boat ramp: a Department of Wildlife access area on the lake has a boat ramp and toilets. A $10 Washington Department of Fish and Wildlife access decal is required to use the public launch areas maintained by the WDFW.

Facilities: You'll find food, gas, and lodging in Granite Falls.

Water sports/restrictions: All water sports are permitted here.

Contact: John's Sporting Goods, tel. (425) 259-3056.

45 Bosworth Lake

Rating: 7

Most of the crowds appear on this 95-acre lake early in the spring when trout fishing is the draw for thousands of people around Snohomish County. After that, things calm down somewhat, at least when you compare the activity here to what goes on at Lake Stevens to the west. Bosworth isn't big enough or close enough to the major highway systems to draw outlandishly large mobs, so it's a place where some folks go on a hot summer weekend to enjoy the water without as much craziness as they might have to contend with elsewhere. This pretty lake is worth visiting on a weekday evening, early in the morning, or perhaps during an Indian summer September day, when you're likely to have the whole thing to yourself.

46 Lake Leland

Rating: 7

This 100-acre lake just off U.S. 101 is a busy place during the warm months of spring and summer, when anglers, swimmers, PWC riders, paddlers, and virtually every other kind of water user flock to its shores from all over eastern Jefferson County. About the only limiting factor is the size of the gravel parking area at the WDFW access area, because it's the only place where the public can get to Leland. If you like solitude, paddle the grassy shoreline or sail the open water at midlake during the week or on a weekend when the weather is a little short of perfect. Otherwise expect company.

Location: North of Quilcene, Jefferson County; map A2, grid g2.

How to get there: Drive north on U.S. 101 from Quilcene and turn left on Lake Leland Road. If you miss the first sign, just continue on and you'll get a second chance about a mile farther up the road. From the east take Highway 104 west from the Hood Canal Floating Bridge and turn south onto U.S. 101; drive about three miles to Lake Leland Road, on the right.

Boat ramp: There's a Department of Fish and Wildlife access area with a two-lane gravel boat ramp, fishing dock, and toilets on the east side of the lake.

Facilities: There's a county park with tent and RV sites across the gravel road from the access area. The nearest food and gas are in Discovery Bay and Quilcene, the nearest lodging in Quilcene.

Water sports/restrictions: Paddling, powerboating, sailing, skiing, swimming, and PWC riding are all popular here. A $10 WDFW access decal is required to use the public launch area at the north end of the lake.

Contact: The Fish In Hole, tel. (360) 385-7031; Quilcene Hotel, tel. (360) 765-3447.

47 Crocker Lake

Rating: 7

Nearby Leland Lake gets most of the swimmers and speedboaters, so this 65-acre lake right along U.S. 101 seems reserved for more casual pursuits, especially fishing and canoeing. It's a nice place to spend a summer evening patrolling the shoreline in search of birds and other critters or trolling a fly along the surface for rainbow trout. Things are laid back here, even though cars are zooming by only a few yards away.

Location: South of Discovery Bay, Jefferson County; map A2, grid g3.

How to get there: Drive north on U.S. 101 from Quilcene and you'll see the lake

on the right about three miles north of Lake Leland. From the east take Highway 104 west from the Hood Canal Floating Bridge and turn south onto U.S. 101; drive about a mile, and you'll see the lake on the left.

Boat ramp: The lake has a rather rough boat ramp on its west side right along the highway, so be careful when backing your trailer in and unloading. A $10 Washington Department of Fish and Wildlife access decal is required to use the public launch areas maintained by the WDFW.

Facilities: There are limited facilities available to the north in Discovery Bay. Quilcene, to the south, has one hotel and one motel, as well as food, gas, and other supplies.

Water sports/restrictions: Paddling and fishing are the primary activities.

Contact: The Fish In Hole, tel. (360) 385-7031; Maple Grove Motel, tel. (360) 765-3410; Quilcene Hotel, tel. (360) 765-3447.

48 Buck Lake

Rating: 7

Except for the county park and two or three houses set back from the water, Buck Lake looks much the same now as it must have 50 years ago. There aren't any docks, piers, bulkheads, or closely cropped lawns, and a few hours here may give you the feeling that you're well off the beaten path. The brush, trees, and weeds surrounding most of the lake offer lots of opportunity to see and hear wildlife of many kinds, and there's a powerful feeling of peace and solitude most of the time. Exceptions are on weekends early in the spring fishing season and occasionally on summer evenings when teenagers and full-grown kids come to the small park to drink and/or play their music too damned loud. Luckily the lake's location some distance from the nearest town keeps such disruptions from occurring very often.

Location: North end of Kitsap Peninsula; map A2, grid g5.

How to get there: Take Highway 104 west from Kingston or Bond Road north from Poulsbo to Miller Bay Road. Drive north on Miller Bay Road just over seven miles. Immediately past the signs pointing right to Point No Point, turn left on Buck Lake Road, following it just over half a mile to the third 90-degree corner. Bear right at that third turn and follow the road down the hill a quarter of a mile to the lake.

Boat ramp: There's a county-maintained boat ramp on the lake.

Facilities: The county park provides some bank access, used mostly by anglers. Food and gas are available in Hansville.

Water sports/restrictions: Fishing and paddling are the primary attractions here.

Contact: Silverdale Chamber of Commerce Visitor Information Center, tel. (360) 692-6800

49 Deer Lake

Rating: 6

One of more than a half dozen Deer Lakes in Washington, this 80-acre lake that's only minutes from the Clinton ferry dock offers boaters a chance to pursue at least some of their favorite activities. A speed limit and noise restrictions limit the possibilities but don't affect anglers, paddlers, swimmers, and other more peaceful pastime seekers.

Location: West of Clinton, near southeast corner of Whidbey Island; map A2, grid g6.

How to get there: Take the Washington State Ferry from Mukilteo to Clinton, drive up the hill several blocks, and take Holst Road southwesterly from town. The lake is on the right, just over a mile from Clinton.

Boat ramp: The Island County Parks and Recreation Department maintains a one-lane concrete ramp on the lake, but it's not in very good shape, or at least it wasn't in the summer of 1998.

Facilities: Deer Lake Park has a halfway decent swim beach with a float and small picnic area. Food, gas, and several bed-and-breakfasts are available in Clinton.

Water sports/restrictions: All water sports are permitted here.

Contact: John's Sporting Goods, tel. (425) 259-3056; Ted's Sports Center, tel. (425) 743-9505.

50 Lake Serene

Rating: 5

This 42-acre lake near Everett is popular with urban folks, so it's not as serene as it must have been back when it was named. But then, lots of places around the Puget Sound region have changed a lot in the past 100 years or so, haven't they? Anyway, this is a nice little lake for paddling or getting wet in, at least after the wave of spring anglers has thinned out. That usually happens by Memorial Day because this small shallow lake warms quickly and trout fishing tapers off fast.

Location: Southwest of Everett, map A2, grid g6.

How to get there: Drive north from Lynnwood on Highway 99 to Shelby Road; turn west and drive to 43rd Avenue; turn north and you're there.

Boat ramp: There's a public access area with a boat ramp and toilets at the west end of the lake.

Facilities: Food, gas, lodging, and other amenities are available nearby.

Water sports/restrictions: Paddling, fishing, and some swimming occur here. **Contact:** Ted's Sports Center, tel. (425) 743-9505.

51 Silver Lake

Rating: 4

It's too bad that a lake this size so close to so many people in the Seattle-Everett area doesn't have better public access for boating and other water sports. It's one of the very few 100-acre lakes anywhere in the Northwest that don't have a public boat ramp of some kind. You can, of course, stay at the RV park and enjoy the lake, but only a relative few folks at a time can use it that way.

Location: South of Everett; map A2, grid g7.

How to get there: Southbound on Interstate 5, take Exit 189 and drive south on Highway 527 to 112th; turn west (right) and drive to Silver Lake Road; turn south (left) and drive to the lake. Northbound on Interstate 5, take Exit 186 and drive east to Highway 527; turn north (left) and drive to 112th; turn left, and then turn left again on Silver Lake Road.

Boat ramp: It's possible to carry a small boat from the street to the water near the lake's southeast corner, but the only boat ramp on the lake is for guests at the RV park.

Facilities: There's a city park with bank access and rest rooms on the west side of the lake, and it's possible to fish or swim from the bank at the park. Silver Lake RV Park is on the west side of the lake and has RV and tent sites, as well as a boat ramp and beach access for park guests only. The RV park is open year-round.

Water sports/restrictions: All water sports are permitted **Contact:** Silver Lake RV Park, tel. (800) 362-5762; John's Sporting Goods, tel. (425) 259-3056.

52 Martha Lake

Rating: 8

Yes, another Snohomish County Martha Lake, one of three within easy driving distance of each other. This one is probably the best of the bunch when it comes to water recreation. It has a nice swim beach at the county park, a fairly roomy public access area, quite a lot of parking at both sites, and the lake's a pretty one. Fishing can be good here, too, in case you happen to visit it in the spring or early summer when the trout are still biting. If not, just enjoy yourself with whatever kind of play you happen to prefer.

Location: Northeast of Alderwood Manor; map A2, grid g6.

How to get there: Drive north from Seattle or south from Everett on Interstate 5 and turn east on 164th Street SW (Exit 183 off the freeway). The lake is about half a mile off the freeway, on the north (left) side of the street.

Boat ramp: There's a Department of Fish and Wildlife boat ramp on the southeast corner of the lake. A $10 Washington Department of Fish and Wildlife access decal is required to use the public launch areas maintained by the WDFW.

Facilities: At the site of what for many years was a private resort on the lake, a new county park has a nice swim beach and play and picnic area. Small stores and gas stations are nearby. Lodging is available near the freeway exit.

Water sports/restrictions: All water sports are permitted.

Contact: Snohomish County Parks and Recreation Department, tel. (425) 339-1208.

53 Snohomish River

Rating: 7

If you're looking for a quiet, pristine stream or the challenge of roiling white water, go elsewhere; the Snohomish and its lower river sloughs are too close to Everett's industrial area, Interstate 5, and the general activity of Puget Sound's population centers to be pristine. And because it is mostly estuary, you're as likely to find yourself floating upstream as downstream throughout much of the river's length. Still, this is a big, wide river with many miles of tidewater sloughs to explore, lots of waterfowl and other wildlife, and plenty of elbow room where boaters of all kinds can enjoy the water without getting in each other's way too much.

Quite a few paddlers launch at the public fishing access about three miles up the Snoqualmie or its counterpart on the Skykomish just south of Monroe about four miles above the confluence, from where they can enjoy several miles of moving water down to Cady Park in Snohomish. Powerboaters, on the other hand, often work their way upstream from the saltwater ramp on the Everett waterfront or from the Langus ramp on Smith Island. Kayakers and canoeists also ply the lower reaches of the Snohomish, prowling the estuaries of the main river itself or the three big sloughs that crisscross several times before finally entering Possession Sound. Those sloughs, Ebey, Union, and Steamboat, are also very much influenced by the tides, so all boaters should consult a tide book before hitting the water. Tidal surprises can send you upriver when you want to go down, or leave you high and dry when you need water under your hull.

Location: Enters Puget Sound immediately north of Everett; map A2, grid g7.

How to get there: Take Interstate 405 to Highway 522 and turn east. Drive to the bridge that crosses the Snohomish just below the confluence of the Snoqualmie and Skykomish Rivers. Turn north (left) on Elliott Road and take side roads to the east to reach the river at various points. Another alternative is to take Interstate 5 to Everett and drive east on U.S. 2 to Snohomish, where two highway bridges cross the river. Turn west from there or cross the river and turn west to fish either side of the river between Snohomish and Everett. The lower river and its sloughs around Everett can be reached via Frontage Road and 24th Street NE to Smith Island Road and also from Waterfront Park off 10th Street in northwest Everett.

Boat ramp: Paddlers can launch at public access areas on the lower Snoqualmie or lower Skykomish Rivers a couple of miles from where they meet to form the Snohomish. Launching is also possible at Cady City Park in Snohomish. There's a good boat ramp at Langus Park on Smith Island, and boaters can easily get to the mouth of the Snohomish from the saltwater ramp in Possession Sound on the Everett waterfront.

Facilities: Food, gas and lodging are readily available in Snohomish and Everett.

Water sports/restrictions: Powerboating and paddling are popular. There is some tubing, drift boating, and swimming on the upper portions of the Snohomish.

Contact: John's Sporting Goods, tel. (425) 259-3056; Sky Valley Traders, tel. (360) 794-8818.

54 Blackman's Lake

Rating: 6

Located within the city limits of Snohomish, this 60-acre lake is popular from spring to fall, with swimmers and small-boat enthusiasts flocking here on warm summer weekends. The year-round fishing season helps to spread out angling activity. Used mostly by locals, it doesn't get much recreational use by folks from outside Snohomish County. Evening paddling and morning fishing will give you a chance to enjoy some tranquility before people begin to drop by for a few hours or for the day.

Location: At Snohomish; map A2, grid g7.

How to get there: Take Interstate 5 to U.S. 2 at Everett and head east toward Snohomish. Turn south on Highway 9 and follow it about a mile and a half to the lake, on the left.

Boat launch: There's a Department of Fish and Wildlife access area and boat ramp on the south end of the lake. A $10 Washington Department of Fish and Wildlife access decal is required to use the public launch areas maintained by the WDFW.

Facilities: Besides the public boat ramp there's a city park that provides access near the lake's northeast corner. A fishing pier located near the north end of the lake is wheelchair-accessible. Food, gas, lodging, and other facilities are nearby in Snohomish.

Water sports/restrictions: All water sports are permitted.

Contact: Snohomish County Parks and Recreation Department, tel. (425) 339-1208; Sky Valley Traders, tel. (360) 794-8818.

55 Flowing Lake

Rating: 7

If there's such a thing as a western Washington lake that's perfectly suited to both trout and bass fishing, it might be Flowing Lake. Its more than 130 acres can be roughly divided between the shallow east side and the deep west side, offering a wide range of boating and water sports possibilities. If you're looking for warm water early in the summer, head for the fast-warming shallows at the northeast or southeast corners of the lake in mid- to late June, before the rest of the lake has even started to warm. Much of the water in these areas is less than 20 feet deep, so it doesn't take many days of 80-degree weather to bring it up to human comfort range. The western third of the lake, on the other hand, has depths as great as 60 feet, so it warms more slowly. Much of the entire lake, however, is popular with water-skiers, PWC riders, and other top-of-the-water recreationists.

Location: North of Monroe; map A2, grid g8.

How to get there: Take U.S. 2 to Snohomish and turn east on Three Lake Road, driving about five miles to the lake.

Boat ramp: You'll find a boat ramp at the Department of Fish and Wildlife access area at the lake's southeast corner and another at the county park on the north side. Both are single-lane concrete-plank ramps and both have a loading float. There's a $3 launching fee at the county park. A $10 Washington Department of Fish and Wildlife access decal is required to use the public launch areas maintained by the WDFW.

Facilities: Besides a ramp, the lake has a good deal of bank access and a swim beach at the Snohomish County Park.

The park also has 10 tent sites and 32 drive-through sites for RVs up to 25 feet long, some with complete hookups. The park is open from the middle of May through September. Food, gas, tackle, lodging, and other amenities are available in Monroe.

Water sports/restrictions: All water sports are permitted here.

Contact: Flowing Lake County Park, tel. (360) 568-2274; Snohomish County Parks and Recreation Department, tel. (425) 339-1208; Sky Valley Traders, tel. (360) 794-8818.

56 Panther Lake

Rating: 6

This 45-acre lake near Snohomish isn't much of a draw for the big-boat or fast-boat crowd, with much larger lakes in the vicinity offering them a lot more room to practice their pursuits. Panther is much better suited to paddling a canoe around its edges or casting a line for its resident trout. It's peaceful here, and that's the way most of its visitors seem to like it.

Location: Northeast of Snohomish; map A2, grid g8.

How to get there: Take U.S. 2 to Snohomish and drive east on Three Lakes Road. About three miles east of Snohomish, turn north (left) at Jamison Corner onto Panther Lake Road, which leads to the west side of the lake.

Boat ramp: The lake has a Department of Fish and Wildlife boat ramp. A $10 Washington Department of Fish and Wildlife access decal is required to use the public launch areas maintained by the WDFW.

Facilities: Food, gas, lodging, and other amenities are available in Snohomish and Monroe.

Water sports/restrictions: Paddling, fishing, and small-boat use are the primary draws here.

Contact: Sky Valley Traders, tel. (360) 794-8818.

57 Storm Lake

Rating: 6

Part of Storm Lake's popularity is its proximity to Flowing Lake, which happens to be only a few hundred feet away to the west in the well-named Three Lakes country of Snohomish County. It also happens to be along the way (well, sort of) to much larger Lake Roesiger. Storm, though, has an identity all its own, and it also has some things going for it that the aforementioned Flowing and Roesiger don't. For one thing, Flowing Lake is smaller and shallower than the other two, so it warms a little more quickly after a few days of warm weather in the spring and early summer. That tends to make the swimming and other splash sports just a little more comfortable here early in the fun season. And once the warm weather finally comes to the Northwest for good, Storm may be somewhat overlooked by fun seekers in search of bigger bodies of water to conquer. Keep that in mind if you want a place with a bit more elbow room on a warm August day or if you want a solitary paddle on a balmy summer's eve. It may be only one of many lakes in the area, but Storm can hold its own among the competition, thank you.

Location: North of Monroe; map A2, grid g8.

How to get there: Take U.S. 2 to Snohomish and drive east on Three Lakes Road about five miles to the lake.

Boat ramp: There's a one-lane, gravel Department of Fish and Wildlife ramp with limited parking at the north end of the lake. A $10 Washington Department of Fish and Wildlife access decal is required to use the public launch areas maintained by the WDFW.

Facilities: Food, gas, and lodging are available in Snohomish and Monroe.

Water sports/restrictions: All water sports are permitted, but use by large boats is limited.

Contact: Sky Valley Traders, tel. (360) 794-8818.

58 Lake Roesiger

Rating: 8

This 350-acre lake north of Monroe is quite unusual in that it's more like three lakes in one: the largest and deepest northern section, where there are spots well over 100 feet deep; the shallow flats of the lake's wasp-like midsection, which warms much more quickly than the rest of the lake in summer; and the south end of the lake, much like the north end, but a little smaller and not quite so deep. Add them all together and you have a lake that offers something for virtually every kind of boater and water enthusiast. There's lots of room for the fast-moving folks to ski, run PWC, kneeboard, go tubing, or whatever they like without getting in each other's way. All the while, hardy swimmers can test the lake's cooler-than-most waters, anglers can pursue trout around the lake's edges, and divers can explore the chilly depths of the lake's two main sections. Talk about a lake with everything.

Location: Northeast of Monroe; map A2, grid g8.

How to get there: Take U.S. 2 to Monroe, turn north on Woods Creek Road, and drive about 12 miles to the lake.

Boat ramp: There's a Department of Fish and Wildlife access area with a single-lane boat ramp near the south end of the lake. A $10 Washington Department of Fish and Wildlife access decal is required to use the public launch areas maintained by the WDFW.

Facilities: A county park provides access and a swim beach on the east side. It has eight tent sites but no RV hookups, and it's during open summer months only. Food, gas, tackle, lodging, and other amenities are available in Monroe.

Water sports/restrictions: All water sports are permitted.

Contact: Lake Roesiger Park, tel. (360) 568-5836; Snohomish County Parks and Recreation Department, tel. (425) 339-1208; Sky Valley Traders, tel. (360) 794-8818.

59 Skykomish River

Rating: 8

Few western Washington rivers are any prettier or more famous for their whitewater than this one, known lovingly by rafters, kayakers, and steelhead anglers alike as the "Sky." Before it joins the Snoqualmie near the town of Monroe to form the Snohomish River, it offers more than 60 miles of clean, cool water for people to swim, wade, splash, paddle, row, motor, and smile in.

If any two words best sum up the Skykomish mystique, they have to be "Boulder Drop." Yeah, you've heard the words before, huh? If you've done much river running in the Northwest, there's a good chance you've even experienced Boulder Drop. It's the name of the river's best-known and perhaps most cantankerous piece of white water, and it's a dandy. Everyone who has run it remembers it, some with a fond smile, some with a groan of anguish, some with a shudder of terror, but isn't that what whitewater paddling is all about? Located a short distance downstream from the confluence of the North and South Forks, this Class IV/Class V (depending on the river level) boulder patch is the highlight of the Sky's most famous run, which starts at the small town of Index on the North Fork and usually ends at Gold Bar some seven miles downstream on the main river. Even without its main attraction, this would be a spectacular Class III run on Washington's first stream to be included among the nation's Wild and Scenic Rivers. Many folks make this trip with a commercial rafting company, but lots of freelancers run it too. Different water levels call for different plans of attack at Boulder Drop, especially if you don't want to find yourself just another casualty hanging from the Picket Fence, the formation of the half dozen pointed boulders in the middle of the mishmash; so always pull to the right and scout it carefully. If it all seems too intimidating, don't be too proud to take the chicken's path around it on the right shore. Lots of folks do, especially the first time through.

Another challenging run on the Skykomish system is down the North Fork from above Troublesome Creek to Index. There's some Class IV water here, so don't make it your first-ever river trip, but if you have some whitewater experience under your belt and feel up to it, this is a great run during periods of spring snow melt, when the North Fork is running about 2,000 to 3,000 cubic feet per second.

If you're not sure about Boulder Drop or even the Class IV water of the North Fork, you might try the Class II South Fork run downstream from where the Tye and Beckler Rivers meet or even the calm, Class I main river from Big Eddy downstream. This stretch runs some 22 miles and may be chewed off in bite-size pieces such as Big Eddy to Sultan, Sultan to Monroe, and Monroe to the confluence of the Sky and Snoqualmie or even farther downstream to Cady Park in Snohomish.

Location: Joins Snoqualmie River southwest of Monroe; map A2, grid g9. (Only the lower portion of the river is shown on this map.)

How to get there: Take U.S. 2 to Monroe and continue east along the north side of the main Skykomish and the South Fork to its source at the confluence of the Tye and Beckler Rivers. To reach the North Fork Skykomish, turn north off U.S. 2 to Index and follow Index-Galena Road up the North Fork.

Boat ramp/put-in: There are boat ramps just off Highway 203 (Lewis Street Bridge) at the south end of Monroe, at Ben Howard Road two miles east of Highway 203, at Sportsman Park near the mouth of the Sultan River in Sultan, at the fishing access just east of Gold Bar, at the bridge near Index on the North Fork, and below Sunset Falls on the South Fork. There are also rough launches and places to drop a kayak into the river at several gravel bars and wide spots along the road, especially on the upper reaches of the North Fork and South Fork.

Facilities: Several whitewater outfitters offer trips down the Skykomish, including Alpine Adventures, Chinook Expeditions, Downstream River Runners, Redline River Adventures, and Wave-Trek, Inc. Food, gas, and lodging are available in Monroe, Sultan, and other locations along U.S. 2.

Water sports/restrictions: Kayaking, rafting, tubing, and drift boating are popular, with some swimming in the slower stretches.

Contact: Pacific Water Sports, tel. (206) 246-9385; Alpine Adventures, (800-RAFT-FUN); Chinook Expeditions, tel. (800) 241-3451; Downstream River runners, tel. (360) 805-9899; Redline River Adventures, tel. (800) 290-4500; WaveTrek, Inc., tel. (800) 543-7971; Sky Valley Traders, tel. (360) 794-8818.

60 Lake Ballinger

Rating: 8

This 100-acre lake has a little something for every water lover, including good access and a year-round fishing season. Its shoreline is well developed, and lots of the use here is by shoreline residents. Still, the city park opens the way for boaters, skiers, swimmers, PWC riders, wind-surfers, and anglers from other parts of the county and the state, and the locals don't seem to mind. The lake is a little slow to warm, so I wouldn't recommend it as a swimming hole until about the first of July. If you're part polar bear, though, knock yourself out.

Location: West of Mountlake Terrace, just north of Snohomish-King county line; map A2, grid h6.

How to get there: Take Interstate 5 to the north end of Seattle and go west at Exit 177 on Highway 104 (also known as 205th Street at this point). The road runs along the south shore of the lake about half a mile off Interstate 5.

Boat ramp: There's a city park boat ramp and fishing pier near the north end of the lake.

Facilities: The 50-acre city park has a swim beach, rest rooms, picnic area, and lots of access to the lake. Food, gas, and lodging are all available within a few minutes' drive.

Water sports/restrictions: All water sports are permitted.

Contact: Snohomish County Parks and Recreation Department, tel. (425) 339-1208.

61 Lake Hannan

Rating: 7

It's a fair distance off the beaten path and has no formal facilities for boaters, but this small lake southeast of Monroe has a charm that draws anglers and paddlers from spring through fall. It's peaceful and quiet most of the time and a good place to visit if you like the idea of having an entire lake to yourself. Don't bother trying to drag your big bass boat or high-powered ski boat to Hannan; there's no place to launch it, and the lake's too small for that sort of thing anyway. Go to Fontal or one of the other large lakes in the area for those fast-boat kinds of recreation.

Location: Southeast of Monroe; map A2, grid h8.

How to get there: Take U.S. 2 to Monroe and turn south on Highway 203. Drive about two miles to High Rock Road and turn east. Turn east (left) on Lake Fontal Road and drive seven miles to the west side of the lake, on the right.

Boat ramp: There is no developed ramp, but it's possible to drag a cartopper or canoe into the lake.

Facilities: There are no facilities on the lake. The nearest food, gas, and lodging are in Monroe, about eight miles to the south.

Water sports/restrictions: Paddling, fishing and some swimming are the main activities.

Contact: Sky Valley Traders, tel. (360) 794-8818.

62 Lake Margaret

Rating: 7

It's a little small for skiing and other fast-boat recreation, so this 44-acre lake near Duvall is used mostly by canoeists and anglers. Some kids swim at the public access area, but I wouldn't. Back when I was a kid, we stopped here once on our way back from a junior high school track meet, and our coach/bus driver told us it was OK to jump in for a quick dip. Several of us did, and one of the kids went home with a big gash in his foot from a broken bottle. Unfortunately, such hazards are quite common at public access areas. Use the area for swimming at your own risk, and don't say you weren't warned.

Location: Northeast of Duvall, near the King-Snohomish county line; map A2, grid h9.

How to get there: Take Highway 203 to Duvall and follow Cherry Valley Road out of town to the east. Turn north (left) at the intersection of Kelly Road and drive about three miles to the lake.

Boat ramp: There's a Department of Fish and Wildlife boat ramp on the lake. A $10 Washington Department of Fish and Wildlife access decal is required to use the public launch areas maintained by the WDFW.

Facilities: The nearest food and gas are in Duvall.

Water sports/restrictions: Paddling and fishing are good here.

Contact: Sky Valley Traders, tel. (360) 794-8818.

63 Lake Joy

Rating: 5

Covering about 100 acres, this is one of the largest lakes in western Washington without a boat ramp or official public access area. I include it here only because it's possible to carry a small boat or canoe to the water and get away from almost all other boating activity. If you're a hermit-type boater, this may be the place for you. If you want more in the way of facilities and other human activity around you when you play, go elsewhere.

Location: Northeast of Stillwater; map A2, grid h9.

How to get there: Take Highway 203 south from Duvall or north from Carnation to Stillwater. Turn east on Kelly Road and drive about three miles to Lake Joy Road, which circles the lake.

Boat ramp: There is no ramp, but some boaters carry small craft to the water's edge for launching.

Facilities: The nearest food and gas are in Duvall and Carnation.

Water sports/restrictions: Paddling and fishing are the options.

Contact: Sky Valley Traders, tel. (360) 794-8818.

64 Dosewallips River

Rating: 6

I can remember standing on the Forest Service Bridge near the mouth of Wilson Creek about 25 years ago, peering down into the narrow canyon below and wondering whether I could squeeze through in a drift boat. Of course, getting a drift boat into the river somewhere upstream would have been the first challenge, if I had owned a drift boat at the time. I don't know anyone who has shoehorned a drift boat between those narrow canyon walls under that bridge, but quite a few folks have since run the Dosewallips Canyon in kayaks and other, skinnier craft.

The upper Dosey is one of the Olympic Peninsula's prettiest places, and it's also becoming a bit of a kayaker's destination. But it's not for the novice river runner, since the rocky ledges and narrow canyons are far too tight and technical for a casual first float. In fact, the upper Dosey is a Class IV+ stream where only experienced river folk should test their skills. Below the bridge near Wilson Creek, things get more tame and the river is a Class III down to the state park. There are, however, several places where sweepers, stumps, and submerged obstacles can reach out and grab you, so be on your toes anywhere on the Dosey.

Location: Enters Hood Canal at Brinnon; map A2, grid h2.

How to get there: Drive north from Shelton on U.S. 101 to Dosewallips State Park or continue past the park and turn west on Dosewallips Road to parallel the north side of the river for several miles.

Boat ramp/put-in: Kayaks and small rafts may be launched over the bank at Elkhorn Campground, at Dosewallips State Park near the mouth of the river, and at a few less-used spots along the Dosewallips River Road between the two.

Facilities: Dosewallips State Park is one of the newer, more modern facilities in the Washington State Parks system and offers 40 RV sites with complete hookups, rest rooms, and showers. It also offers several hundred yards of river access. Nearby Brinnon General Store has groceries, gas, and other supplies. The Bayshore Motel is nearby for folks who might want a permanent roof over their heads.

Water sports/restrictions: Kayaking is a possibility along much of the river, swimming and tubing down around the state park.

Contact: Dosewallips State Park, tel. (360) 796-4415; Washington State Parks and Recreation Commission, tel. (800) 233-0321 (information), tel. (800) 452-5687 (reservations); Pacific Water Sports, tel. (206) 246-9385; Brinnon General Store, tel. (360) 796-4400; Bayshore Motel, tel. (360) 796-4220.

65 Upper Hood Canal

Rating: 8

If you like to do your boating where there's plenty of room to maneuver and not much other human activity around, the upper half of Hood Canal just might be your idea of boaters' heaven. The biggest town actually on the water here is Quilcene, population: not many. It's a long way to any major population center, and in parts of the canal even road access is limited. In some stretches you can travel by boat for miles without finding anything in the way of boating facilities or access to the water. That's not to say that there aren't places where boaters may congregate to take in the sights find things to do ashore.

Near the west side of the canal's north entrance is Port Ludlow, a popular boating destination with all the amenities of a waterfront resort. Across the canal is Foulweather Bluff, which lives up to its name when tidal currents in and out of the canal meet the stronger currents of Admiralty Inlet and conflicting winds; it can get downright nasty, even on an otherwise pleasant day. To the south, on the east side of the canal, is Port Gamble, site of a clean little town with an interesting museum. The huge harbor is well protected and provides an excellent place to anchor and wait out rough weather. Suquamish Harbor, on the west side of the canal, isn't quite so boater friendly since it features several rocky reefs and is much more exposed.

The Hood Canal Floating Bridge spans the upper end of the canal between

Salsbury Point and Termination Point. The best place for sailboats to pass under the mile-and-a-half-long bridge is at the east end, where clearance is about 55 feet. Passing under the lower west end of the bridge is a little trickier, not only because the clearance is only 35 feet, but also because of Sisters, two large rock formations that poke their heads out of the water about half a mile southwest of the bridge. They're shown on chart 18441 and marked with buoy, but be alert anyway-they're two sisters you don't want to meet.

If you're around the bridge during the late summer or fall, don't be surprised to see anglers casting for salmon and other game fish. Some folks have figured out how to catch the abundant chum salmon that pass through the canal on their way to the Hoodsport Salmon Hatchery and tributary streams to the south, and the fishing can be hot at times. Divers also are attracted to the bridge and the nearby rock piles, which have lingcod, rockfish, wolf eels, and other attractions.

Farther down the east side is Kitsap Memorial State Park, which has no moorage facilities, but its gravel beach is a good place to dig clams or go beachcombing. The next several miles of the canal all the way down to Oak Head and beyond, while extremely beautiful, can also become quite nasty when a stout southerly or northerly comes barreling up or down between the steep hills on both sides of the water. There aren't too many good places to hide from the wind along this stretch, so be alert to changes in weather conditions and wind speed. Boaters passing through this section of the canal should also note that this is an operating and exercising area for the U.S. Navy. The submarine base at Bangor is on the east shore, just north of King Spit.

Almost due south of Oak Head and the south end of the Toandos Peninsula is Seabeck Bay, which is protected from southerly and westerly winds. Besides having a marina with fuel and some moorage, this is the home of world-famous (or, at least, locally famous) Seabeck Pizza. Nearby Misery Point has a boat ramp, and the artificial reef 200 yards north of the lighted buoy is a productive angling and diving spot. A short run out of Seabeck Bay, around Misery Point, and you're suddenly at Miami Beach, even though it may have seemed that you couldn't possibly have gone that far. Actually, it's not Florida's Miami Beach, but the Washington version, with its great view northward into Dabob Bay and northwest to the Olympics. Scenic Beach State Park is there, and it's easy to see how it got its name.

Turn north at Tskutko Point and you'll enter Dabob Bay, which extends about 12 miles off the main canal and branches off around the west side of the Bolton Peninsula to form Quilcene Bay. This is the home of those famous Quilcene oysters, but the restaurants and shops of town are some distance from the Port of Port Townsend marina on the west side of the bay. Dabob is another place where the Navy sometimes plays its rather serious war games, so if the warning lights are flashing or a Navy vessel tells you to clear out, do so before you become the object of torpedo target practice. The bay has a number of worthwhile dive spots, one of the best known of which is Pulalli Point, about halfway up Dabob's west side. The rocky walls and reefs there offer a wide range of aquatic life, including octopus and several species of rockfish.

Dosewallips State Park, on the west side of the canal at the entrance to Dabob Bay, doesn't have any boating facilities, but it's a great place to dig clams and gather oysters on a low tide during the shellfish season. The park, located right on the Dosewallips River, also has RV and tent sites and other amenities. Immediately north is Brinnon, which has lodging and a couple of small stores. Three miles south of Dosewallips State Park is Pleasant Harbor, one of the prettiest spots on the entire canal and one of the most popular with boaters. Besides offering good anchorage and moorage on private and State Parks floats and buoys, it's a great place to eat. Pizza and clam chowder are the two main courses, and both are excellent; take it from one who knows.

Farther south is Triton Cove, formerly a private resort but now a day-use Washington State Parks facility. If you're in the Triton Cove/Triton Head area to dive or fish for bottomfish, by the way, take a close look at your chart and you'll notice a spot to the northwest, near the middle of the canal, that's marked "rocky" and shows 18 fathoms of water surrounded by depths of 48 to nearly 100 fathoms. As you might guess, this rocky pinnacle is worth investigating on slack tide.

Location: Foulweather Bluff south to Triton Head, west side of Kitsap Peninsula; map A2, grid h3.

How to get there: Take U.S. 101 north from Shelton or south from Discovery Bay to reach much of the west side of the canal. To reach Dabob Bay and the west side of the canal along the Toandos Peninsula, take Highway 104 to the west side of the Hood Canal Floating Bridge and turn south on South Point Road. Among the routes to the east side of the canal, take Highway 3 or Highway 16 to Bremerton and drive north on Highway 3 to Seabeck Highway, which runs west to Warrenville and Seabeck. Another route is to continue north from Bre-

merton on Highway 3, which parallels the east shore of the canal from Kitsap Memorial State Park north to Port Gamble. Other roads off Highway 3 and Highway 104 provide further access to the canal's east side.

Boat ramp: There are seven boat ramps on the northern half of Hood Canal:

- **Termination Point Ramp:** Starting at the north end of the canal, just north of the west end of the Hood Canal Floating Bridge is a two-lane concrete ramp near Shine Tidelands State Park. The ramp is tucked away in Bywater Bay at the end of Termination Point Road. Wood and other debris sometimes collect on and around this ramp, which has a $3 launch fee. Turn north off Highway 104 at the west end of the Hood Canal Floating Bridge onto Paradise Bay Road; then take an immediate right onto Termination Point Road, following it to the end.

- **Hicks County Park Ramp:** This Jefferson County Parks ramp is near the entrance to Squamish Harbor, a mile and a half west of the Hood Canal Floating Bridge's west end, off Shine Road. It's a single-lane concrete ramp with a gravel parking area for about a dozen cars and trailers. Driftwood and sand also pile up in front of this ramp, sometimes making it difficult to launch. Traveling west on Highway 104, turn left at the west end of the Hood Canal floating Bridge onto Shine Road and drive a mile and a half to the ramp, on the left.

- **Salsbury Point Ramp:** Across the canal and immediately north of the floating bridge's east end is the three-lane concrete ramp at Salsbury Point County Park. This Kitsap County Parks and Recreation facility has loading floats, a large, paved parking area, and rest rooms. Turn off Highway 104 and onto Wheeler Road at the east end of the bridge; then go right on Whitfort Road to the ramp.

- **Quilcene Marina:** The marina is on the west side of Quilcene Bay. This Port of Port Townsend facility has a one-lane concrete ramp with a loading float and a large gravel parking area. It's well protected from rough water and provides easy access to Dabob Bay. Take U.S. 101 to Quilcene and turn southeast on Linger Longer Road, following it just under two miles to the marina and ramp.

- **Point Whitney Ramp:** South of the entrance to Quilcene Bay is Point Whitney, where there's a single-lane ramp near the WDFW's shellfish research facility. Although there's a concrete ramp down there somewhere, it was buried under sand and gravel in 1998 and 1999, making it usable only for cartoppers and small trailer boats towed by four-wheel-drive vehicles. The parking area is also gravel. A sign near this ramp reminds boaters that the U.S. Navy sometimes tests torpedoes and "other underwater weapons" in Dabob Bay, and when the red beacons light up, go elsewhere to launch. Turn east off U.S. 101 onto Bee Mill Road, about 7.5 miles south of Quilcene (near milepost 303) and wind your way about two miles to the end of the road. The shellfish laboratory is on the right, the boat ramp to your left.

- **Misery Point Ramp:** This Department of Fish and Wildlife ramp is a one laner with a concrete surface and large, gravel parking area. This is another ramp where sand and gravel often get in the way of launching, but nearby Scenic Beach State Park makes this a handy ramp for camper-boaters visiting the north end of the canal. A $10 Washington Department of Fish and Wildlife access decal is required to use the public launch areas maintained by the WDFW. It's reached by driving southwest from Seabeck on Seabeck-Holly Road just over half a mile and turning right on Miami Beach Road.

- **Triton Cove:** Formerly a private resort, Triton Cove is now a Washington State Parks facility. This single-lane concrete ramp has a loading float and dock, with room to park about two dozen cars and trailers. Watch for the large rock just out from the ramp, slightly to the south. There's a $3 launch fee, with an annual permit available for $40. The ramp is 19 miles south of Quilcene right alongside U.S. 101.

Facilities: Quilcene Marina has limited open moorage, power to the docks, fuel, boat repairs, rest rooms with showers, and boat-sewage pump-out facilities. Seabeck Marina offers open moorage, fuel docks (gas only), rest rooms, and restaurants. At Pleasant Harbor Marina you'll find guest and permanent moorage, power and water to the docks, fuel docks, a convenience store and deli, rest rooms with showers, and other facilities. Camping facilities on and around the northern half of the canal include Dosewallips State Park (off U.S. 101 near the mouth of the Dosewallips River), Scenic Beach State Park (near Seabeck), and Kitsap Memorial State Park (at Lofall, south of the Hood Canal Floating Bridge).

Water sports/restrictions: All water sports are permitted. The best NOAA nautical charts for this area are 18458 and 18476. Mason County boating regulations include a 6 mph speed limit within 100 feet of any swimmer, within 150 feet of any shoreline or nonmotorized vessel, and within 300 feet of any public boat ramp; an 8 mph speed limit on freshwater lakes from a half hour after sunset to a half hour before sunrise; and a 50 mph speed limit during daylight hours on all waters unless otherwise posted. Water-skiers must stay at least 300 feet from the shoreline on salt water and at least 150 feet from the shoreline on fresh water. All ski/tow traffic must go in a counterclockwise direction.

Contact: Quilcene Marina, tel. (360) 765-3131; Seabeck Marina, tel. (360) 830-5179; Dosewallips State Park, tel. (360) 796-4415; Cove Park, tel. (360) 796-4723; Scenic Beach State Park, tel. (360) 830-5079; Kitsap Memorial State Park, tel. (360) 779-3205; Washington State Parks and Recreation Commission, tel. (800) 233-0321 (information), tel. (800) 452-5687 (reservations). Hoodsport & Dive (Shelton), tel. (360) 877-6818; Mike's Diving Center (Shelton), tel. (360) 877-9568; IPort Townsend Dive Shop, tel. (360) 379-3635; For nautical charts of this area, contact Captain's Nautical Supply, tel. (206) 283-7242.

66 Green Lake

Rating: 8

Its location right in the middle of the Northwest's biggest city would make Green Lake a good candidate for Washington's busiest body of water even if it weren't such a nice recreation spot. This 255-acre lake almost in the heart of Seattle offers lots to do, and thousands of folks come here even without any intention of getting wet. Some hike, some ride, some roller-blade, some crash into others doing the same thing they're doing, some crash into others doing entirely different things. Those who actually make it to the water can add several other recreational activities to their menus, from rowing to paddling boating, canoeing, kayaking, sailing, sailboarding, fishing, swimming, and diving.

The lake's no-motors regulation extends to electrics as well as internal-combustion rigs, so your boat has to be powered by the wind or by your own body to be legal here. That helps to keep the lake a little quieter and adds some sense of nature to an otherwise very urban place. It also makes boating and swimming here a lot safer. The large swim beaches on each side of the lake, as you might guess, get very busy in the summer as swimmers of all ages come here by car, bus, bicycle, foot, and virtually every other means of locomotion imaginable to get into the water on a warm day. If you get tired of the water for some reason, Woodland Park Zoo is right across the street near the southwest corner of the lake.

Location: Within the City of Seattle; map A2, grid i6.

How to get there: Take Highway 99 north from Lake Union in Seattle, and at N.W. 65th Street watch for the lake on the east (right) side of the road.

Boat ramp: The lake doesn't have a boat ramp, but cartoppers and other small craft may be carried to the edge of the lake and launched.

Facilities: A concessionaire at the north end of the lake, Green Lake Boat Rental, has boats for rent. Rowboats, paddle boats, canoes, and kayaks rent for $10 an hour, small sailboats and sail boards for $14 an hour. It's open from 10 a.m. to dusk, weather permitting, from April 1 through September 30. The lake has two roped swim beaches, one on the east side and one on the west. There are several public fishing docks and piers around the lake, not to mention the world-famous trail around the lake that draws hikers, bikers, boarders, and other urbanites who like to stay on the move.

Water sports/restrictions: All wind-powered and people-powered water sports are permitted. Gas and electric motors are prohibited.

Contact: Green Lake Boat Rental, tel. (206) 526-8087 or tel. (206) 527-0171 (recording); Seattle Parks and Recreation Department, tel. (206) 684-4074.

67 South-Central Puget (including Seattle and Bremerton)

Rating: 10

This busiest section of Puget Sound is also perhaps the most fascinating, with attractions that range from the bustling Seattle waterfront to the wooded and lightly developed shorelines of Port Orchard. Cruise, paddle, or sail through Agate Passage between Bainbridge Island and the Kitsap Peninsula, and you've visited one of the most beautiful waterways in the Pacific Northwest. Sample an Indian-style salmon dinner on Blake Island, and you've tasted some of this region's finest seafood cuisine. It's all available in this part of Puget Sound, and there's a great deal more. Just visiting the area's state parks by water can keep most boaters busy for weeks. They include Fay Bainbridge, at the north end of Bainbridge Island; Fort Ward, at the island's south end; Illahee, on the west side of Port Orchard; Manchester, on the south shore of Rich Passage; Blake Island, near the north end of Vashon Island; Saltwater, south of Des Moines; and Dash Point, a few miles north of Tacoma.

Of these, Saltwater, Dash Point, and Illahee tend to be the most popular and busiest, while Manchester and Fort Ward offer the peace and slow pace you may be looking for when you hit the water. Blake Island is accessible only by water, but a special ferry from Seattle and the popularity of the alder-smoked salmon keep it hopping during the spring and summer months. Except for Manchester and Dash Point, all of these parks have at least some kind of moorage facilities to accommodate visitors who arrive by boat.

Taking a look at some of the high points of this area from north to south, one of the first places of interest, especially for anglers, is Point Jefferson, affectionately known to salmon fishermen as "Jeff Head." Fishing for winter chinook and summer coho salmon still can be good here, even during these times of not-so-hot salmon angling opportunities in the Northwest.

To the southwest is Port Madison, a large bay that separates the easternmost extension of the Kitsap Peninsula from Bainbridge Island to the south. Port Madison is somewhat protected from weather out of the south and southwest, which helps to make it a place where there's some kind of boating activity going on virtually every day of the year. At the southwest corner of Port Madison is Agate Passage, the narrow channel separating the Kitsap Peninsula from the northwest corner of Bainbridge Island. Whether you enter the passage from the north or south, you'll quickly spot the Agate Pass Bridge, an impressive span that's far enough in the air to give you a tingle in your gut whether you're passing under it on the water or across it on Highway 305. Agate Passage connects to the north end of Port Orchard, an exceptional boating spot in its own right.

Manzanita Bay at the northeast corner of Port Orchard is a popular little hideaway for boaters out of the Seattle area, although you realize that's not really hidden if you begin to count the Bainbridge Island waterfront homes looking down upon it. To the northwest are Liberty Bay and the waterfront town of Poulsbo. The bay is popular with paddlers, sailors, and cruisers alike, all of whom find something to see (and buy) in Poulsbo's downtown district. I've spent entire afternoons in the Marine Science Center alone; it's near the south end of town. Warning: Don't even step off your boat in Poulsbo if you have a weakness for candy and other treats or for art and antiques.

If you're traveling down the west side of Port Orchard around lunch- or dinnertime, you might pull into Burke Bay and check out Brownsville. Besides the excellent marina facilities, there's a waterfront walkway with lots of grass around for picnicking or just relaxing. The east side of Bainbridge Island is also worth exploring by water. Eagle Harbor at the town of Winslow is a great place to moor and hit the turf. Waterfront piers lead to several good restaurants, shops, galleries, watering holes, and historic points of interest; and the town's shaded waterfront park is also worth a visit anytime you're in the area. Follow the channel markers into Eagle Harbor to avoid shoals on both sides.

If you want less activity and fewer people, enter Blakely Harbor to the south, once a hub of logging and milling activity. Blakely Rock, just east of the harbor entrance, can get you in trouble if you're an absolutely oblivious boater, but it's worth exploring with fishing tackle or scuba gear if you go there on a flood tide. Unlike longer, narrower Eagle Harbor, the more open Blakely Harbor provides a panoramic view of the Seattle skyline, which is awesome on a clear night.

As for Seattle, where do I start in describing the many options a boater has here? Part of the attraction is that you don't have to stop at the shoreline if you come to the Emerald City by water, thanks to the Chittenden (Ballard) Locks and Lake Washington Ship Canal, which connects Puget Sound to Lake Washington and Lake Union. (More on them in their own listings elsewhere in this chapter.)

With places like the Pike Place Market, the Seattle Aquarium, and summertime concerts on the waterfront—not to mention hundreds of other possibilities on and near its shores—the Seattle waterfront on Elliott Bay has long been a popular destination of Northwest residents and tourists alike, but until recently a lack of facilities for boaters has made access by water difficult for most people. That has changed dramatically since the mid-'90s, with the addition of the Elliott Bay Marina, Bell Harbor Marina, and related facilities aimed specifically at serving boaters and enhancing the image of the city's waterfront. Boaters once had to land at Shilshole to the north, venture far south of the downtown waterfront into the south end of Elliott Bay, or take their chances on a not-very-boater-friendly maze of old piers and buildings if they wanted to enter Seattle from the water; but no more.

Seattle is now a great place to take a boat, and it's getting better all the time. You still have to pay attention to avoid the ferries and many commercial vessels entering this busy port at all times of the day and night, but now at least you have places to stay when you get there, ways to get from your boat to shore, and more to see and do within easy walking distance of your moorage. Seattle has a vast system of parks and playgrounds managed by the Seattle Parks and Recreation Department, including several on and near the waters of Puget Sound. They include, from north to south, Carkeek Park, near the city's north end; Golden Gardens Park, north of Shilshole; Discovery Park at West Point; Magnolia Park, near the north end of Elliott Bay; Myrtle Edwards Park, north of the downtown business district; the downtown area's Waterfront Park; Seacrest Park, on the west side of Elliott Bay; and Lincoln Park, near the city's southwest corner.

West of Seattle, across Puget Sound and through Rich Passage, are Sinclair and Dyes Inlets, better known to most folks as the Port Orchard and Bremerton areas. Rich Passage, which separates the south end of Bainbridge Island from Point Glover and the Kitsap Peninsula, is a narrow, picturesque waterway that illustrates as well as anyplace I can think of the beauty of boat travel on Puget Sound. There are a couple of homes on Point White at the southwest corner of Bainbridge where I'd live in a heartbeat if I had the money that I suspect they would cost.

To the southwest are Port Orchard and Bremerton, both worthwhile boating destinations, although I prefer the small-town feel of Port Orchard over the larger Bremerton. The two are only about a mile apart by water, but 12 miles separate them if you drive around Sinclair Inlet by car. Mooring at Port Orchard Marina will put you within easy walking distance of the town's cozy little business district, which has lots of little shops, stores, and restaurants. If you pass through Port Washington, the narrow waterway separating Bremerton and East Bremerton, the channel will eventually open into Dyes Inlet, with fast-growing Silverdale at its head end.

If you've ever tried driving through Silverdale, you'll appreciate the fact that you can get around its "old town" area much faster by water than by road. Waterfront Park provides good access to the inlet near the south end of town, and when the wind comes up, it's a popular spot for launching sailboards. The waters on both sides of Vashon Island are very popular with boaters, and it's interesting to note the difference between the two sides of the island. On the east side you can look to the east and see sprawling south King County, with homes and development almost everywhere you look. Cruise, paddle, or sail through Colvos Passage on the west side of Vashon, however, and things don't seem quite so civilized or quite so hectic. Paddlers who visit Vashon are especially fond of Quartermaster Harbor, the four-mile-long channel separating Vashon from Maury Island to the east. The lighthouse at Point Robinson at the east corner of Maury Island is a photographer's delight.

Divers enjoy prowling Quartermaster Harbor as well as the edges of both Vashon and Maury Islands. One of the most popular dive spots in central Puget Sound is the artificial reef off Point Heyer, about midway down Vashon's east side. Artificial reefs also provide excellent diving opportunities near the south end of Blake Island and just southwest of Alki Point. All of these reefs are in water 50 to 100 feet deep and should be marked with a pair of white WDFW buoys. Other good dive spots in the south central Puget Sound area include the offshore reef between President Point and Point Jefferson, the north and south entrances to Agate Passage, the rocky drop-off on Point Glover at Manchester State Park, the underwater park just across the channel at Fort Ward State Park, Blakely Rock at the entrance to Blakely Harbor, the piers and pilings along the Seattle waterfront, Seahurst Park and Three Tree Point near Burien, and the underwater park dive site just offshore at Saltwater State Park. If none of these sounds appealing, you won't have to study a chart very long to find lots more possibilities.

Location: From the King-Snohomish county line south to Browns Point, north of Tacoma, map A2, grid i5.

How to get there: Dozens of major roads leading west from Interstate 5 in the Seattle area lead to the water, depending on what part of the sound you want to reach. Highway 16, west from Tacoma, leads to the waterfront and also across the Narrows Bridge to Gig Harbor and the Bremerton area. From there, Highway 3 heads north to provide access to waters along the east side of the Kitsap Peninsula.

Boat ramp: More than two dozen boat ramps and hoist facilities are located on this part of Puget sound and its adjacent marine waters:

- **Miller Bay Ramp:** There's a privately owned boat ramp in Miller Bay, at the northwest corner of Port Madison, that's open to public use for a $4 fee. The single-lane concrete ramp has seen better days but is still a decent bet for smaller trailer boats. From Poulsbo go northeast on Bonds Road and turn right on Gunderson Road, then right again on Miller Bay Road. Follow Miller Bay Road 3.5 miles and turn left at the sign pointing to Bay Marina.

- **Charles Lawrence Ramp:** The next ramp to the south is at Suquamish. The Charles Lawrence Memorial Ramp is a one-lane concrete ramp managed by the Suquamish Indian Tribe. It has limited parking on a gravel lot. Drive east from Poulsbo on Highway 305 and turn left on Suquamish Road as you approach the Agate Pass Bridge. Follow Suquamish Road one mile to the town of Suquamish and go straight where the road turns sharply left. Watch for the ramp on the right, just past a big white building on the right.

- **Fay Bainbridge State Park:** Located at the northeast corner of Bainbridge Island, this popular state park has a one-lane concrete boat ramp. It's a good ramp when it's clear of debris, but there are times when logs and sand clog it and make it unusable. There's a $3 launch fee,

with a $40 annual permit available from the State Parks and Recreation Commission. Get there by taking turning east off Highway 305 on East Day Road and following it to Sunrise Drive. Turn north and go 1.7 miles to the park.

- **Waterfront Park:** On the east side of Bainbridge Island is the ramp at Waterfront Park in Eagle Harbor. This City of Bainbridge Island ramp is a one laner with a loading float. Unless you've used it before, it's perhaps the most well-hidden ramp on Puget sound. To reach it, take Winslow Way to Madison Avenue and turn toward the water. Go about half a block to Bjune Drive, turn left, and there's the ramp, on the right.

- **Fort Ward State Park:** Located near the south end of Bainbridge Island, it has a two-lane concrete ramp with a gravel parking lot big enough for about a dozen cars and trailers. The ramp is quite new and in good shape, but gravel sometimes collects near the bottom of it, hindering launching. There's a $3 launch fee here, with a $40 annual launch permit available from the Washington State Parks and Recreation Commission. To reach it from Highway 305, turn west on Sportsmen's Club Road and go south on Blakely Avenue to Pleasant Beach Road. Turn right on Pleasant Beach Road and follow the State Parks signs to the park and ramp.

- **Poulsbo Marina:** The Port of Poulsbo has a one-lane concrete ramp at Poulsbo Marina near the south end of town. The ramp is in good shape, and there are lots of restaurants and shops within walking distance. Check out the Marine Science Center while you're there, especially if you have kids along. The ramp is on Hostmark Street at the south end of Poulsbo's waterfront downtown district.

- **Keyport Ramp:** At Keyport, near the south entrance to Liberty Bay, there's a Port of Keyport ramp. It's a one laner with a loading/boarding float and a small parking area. To get there, go east on Highway 308 to Keyport. When the U.S. Naval Reservation is a block ahead, turn left on Washington Avenue and go two blocks to the ramp.

- **Eddie Vine Ramp:** On the King County (east) side of Puget Sound, one of the area's best ramps is located just north of Shilshole Bay Marina. This Seattle Parks and Recreation Department ramp has four lanes and three loading floats, with lots of paved parking nearby. A paved walkway connects the ramp area with the nearby marina and moorage facilities. To get there, take Aurora Avenue (Highway 99) to 46th Avenue (Market Street) and turn west. Bear left at Seaview Avenue NW and drive past Shileshole Bay Marina to the ramp, on the left.

- **14th Avenue Ramp:** South of Shilshole on 14th Avenue NW there's another Seattle Parks and Recreation Department launch site, this one with two concrete-plank ramps and two loading floats on the north side of the Fremont Canal, which leads through the Ballard Locks to Puget Sound. Take Aurora Avenue to 46th Avenue, which becomes Market Street as you go west. Turn south (left) on 14th Avenue NW and go just over a mile to the end of the street and the boat ramp.

- **Don Armeni Ramp:** On the west side of Seattle's Elliott Bay is the Don Armeni Boat Ramp with four concrete lanes and two loading floats. There's a $3 launch fee at this Seattle Parks and Recreation Department facility. To get there from Interstate 5, take Exit 163 and go west on the West Seattle Freeway for two miles to Harbor Avenue and go right. Follow Harbor Avenue about two miles to the ramp.

- **Brownsville Marina:** There's a good two-lane concrete ramp with a loading float at the Port of Brownsville Marina on the west side of Port Orchard. It has a $2 launch fee, and there are stores and other facilities within easy walking distance. To get there, drive north from Silverdale on Silverdale Way and turn right on Waga Way. Go left on Highway 303, right on Ogle Road, and follow it one block to the marina on the right.

- **Illahee State Park:** Located near the south entrance to Port Orchard, the park offers a one-lane concrete boat ramp with a loading float and parking for about 20 cars and trailers. The launch fee at this State Parks facility is $3 round-trip. To get there, drive north from Bremerton on Highway 303 and go east (right) on Highway 306, also known locally as Sylvan Way. Follow it to its end and turn left into the park entrance.

- **Evergreen Park:** Near the east end of Port Washington in Bremerton is Evergreen Park, a Bremerton Parks and Recreation Department site with a two-lane concrete ramp and one loading/boarding float. Lions Park is another Bremerton Parks and Recreation facility, and it has a three-lane hard-surface ramp with a loading float and parking for over 20 cars and trailers. To get there, drive north from East Bremerton on Highway 303; turn west on Sheridan Road, following it to Elm Street and turning left. Follow Elm to Lebo Street, turn right, and go two blocks to the park, which is on the left.

- **Tracyton Ramp:** To the northwest at the confluence of Port Washington with Dyes Inlet is the Tracyton ramp, a one-lane concrete-plank ramp with a small, gravel parking area. Reach it by driving out of East Bremerton on Highway 303 and turning west on Riddell Road, which becomes Tracyton Boulevard. Turn south (left) on Tracy

Avenue and drive about 200 yards to the boat ramp at the end of the street.

- **Waterfront Park:** There's another Waterfront Park (besides the one on Bainbridge Island, above) at the upper end of Dyes Inlet in Silverdale. It's managed by the Port of Silverdale and has a two-lane concrete ramp with a loading/boarding float and gravel parking area big enough to hold about 20 cars and trailers. Get there by taking Silverdale Way south from the main shopping area to Byron Street and turning east (left). Go to McConnell and turn right, following it to the end.

- **Chico Ramp:** Go south along the west side of Dyes Inlet on Chico Way to Meredith Street, and you'll come to the Chico Ramp, a Port of Bremerton facility with one concrete lane and only enough room to park three or four cars and trailers.

- **Water Street Ramp (Port Orchard):** At the town of Port Orchard across Sinclair Inlet from Bremerton are two ramps. The better of the two is the Water Street Ramp, managed by Port Orchard's Parks and Recreation Department. This two-lane concrete ramp has a loading/boarding float and large, gravel parking area. To reach it, drive east from Highway 16 on Highway 166 to Port Orchard. The boat ramp is on the left, right across the street from the large Port Orchard Municipal Building.

- **Retsil Boat Launch:** At the east end of Port Orchard is the Department of Fish and Wildlife's ramp near the soldiers' home facility at Retsil. This one-lane concrete ramp has parking for about half a dozen cars and trailers. It's on the north (left) side of Bay Street as you travel east out of town. A $10 Washington Department of Fish and Wildlife access decal is required to use the public launch areas maintained by the WDFW.

- **Pomeroy Ramp:** At Manchester south of the southern entrance to Rich Passage, there's a good ramp managed by the Port of Manchester. It's a two-lane concrete ramp with a loading float and limited parking. Next to it is Pomeroy Park, where there are limited picnic facilities. The ramp entrance is next to the Manchester Food Center off Main Street in Manchester.

- **Harper Ramp:** About three miles south of Manchester, at the north end of Southworth, is a natural, mostly gravel ramp in the sheltered bay at Harper. You can launch small trailer boats here, but it's a better bet for kayaks and other cartoppers. If you use this ramp in winter, you'll likely be greeted by a flock of several hundred American widgeon. To find it, drive east from Port Orchard on Highway 166 about 6.5 miles and turn left on Olympiad Drive. Take an immediate left again and you're there.

- **Olalla Ramp:** Olalla is halfway down the west side of Colvos Passage, near the boundary of King, Pierce, and Kitsap Counties. There's a boat ramp there, managed by the Port of Bremerton. It's a one-lane concrete ramp with a small, gravel parking area. The ramp is usable only at high tide, so plan your launching and boat retrieving accordingly. To get there, turn east from Highway 16 at milepost 20 onto Burley Olalla Road and drive 2.3 miles to Olalla Valley Road. Continue 1.6 miles on Olalla Valley Road to the ramp, on the right.

- **Burton Park Ramp:** One of two ramps in Quartermaster Harbor, between Vashon and Maury Islands, the Burton Park Ramp is a one-lane concrete ramp with limited parking. The adjacent park has picnic tables and rest rooms. To reach it, drive to the town of Burton near the southeast corner of Vashon Island, and go east on Burton Drive, following it half a mile to 97th Avenue. Go right on 97th Avenue, which becomes Bayview Drive, and drive three-quarters of a mile to the ramp.

- **Dockton Boat Launch:** The Dockton Park ramp is a two-lane concrete-plank facility with a loading float and paved parking area. Like the Burton ramp, it's maintained by the King County Parks and Recreation Department. From the Vashon Highway (the island's main north-south route), turn east on Quartermaster Drive and follow it to Dockton Road, turning right and following it to Dockton Park.

- **Des Moines Marina:** The town of Des Moines is on the east side of Puget Sound, between Seattle and Tacoma. Des Moines Marina has two fixed hoists for launching during daylight hours only. The launch fee is determined on a per-foot basis. To reach the marina, take Highway 516 to Des Moines and turn north on Highway 509. Almost immediately turn west (left) on 227th Street and drive two blocks to Dock Avenue and turn left to the marina.

- **Redondo Boat Launch:** To the south of Des Moines is the Redondo ramp, a two-lane concrete ramp with a loading float. This is a good ramp, despite being quite open to the wind and weather. Get there from Interstate 5 by taking the 272nd Street exit and driving west to the waterfront. Along the way, 272nd Street bears south and eventually becomes 281st Street, then makes a hard left to become Redondo Beach Drive. If you're pulling a boat trailer, slow down for the sharp left turn where 281st becomes Redondo Beach Drive. Watch for Salty's Restaurant and you're there.

Facilities: Fay Bainbridge State Park has 26 RV and tent sites, picnic areas and tables, kitchen shelters, rest rooms with showers, an RV dump station, and beach access. Eagle Harbor Marina on Bainbridge Island has some guest moorage, power to the docks, rest rooms with showers, and boat-sewage pump-out facilities. Winslow Wharf Marina has open moorage, power to the docks, rest rooms with showers, boat-sewage dump stations and pump-out facilities. Harbour Marina also has open moorage, power and water to the floats, rest rooms with showers, and pump-out facilities Eagle Harbor Waterfront Park has moorage, a swim beach, picnic areas, and a large lawn near the water.

Fort Ward Marine State Park at the southern tip of Bainbridge Island has two moorage buoys and several wooded tent sites near the water. Poulsbo Marina has moorage, gasoline and diesel, rest rooms with showers, power to the docks, pump-out and dump station for boat sewage, and a beach-front picnic area. It's within easy walking distance of Poulsbo's interesting waterfront business district. Silverdale Marina has moorage and rest rooms and is near a waterfront park with swimming and picnic areas.

Brownsville Marina has open and covered moorage ($8 minimum, $17 maximum), fuel docks, power to the docks, rest rooms and showers, boat-sewage pump-out and dump-station facilities, and a store with a deli, groceries, hardware, and other items. Illahee Marine State Park has 350 feet of moorage float space and five mooring buoys, a boat-sewage dump station, a gravel swim beach, rest rooms, picnic tables, and kitchen shelters.

Port Orchard Marina has open moorage (35 cents per foot, $7 minimum), fuel docks, power and water to the docks, rest rooms, showers, boat-sewage pump-out and dump facilities, a laundry and is within easy walking distance of downtown Port Orchard and its many stores, shops and restaurants. Bremerton Marina has been newly renovated and features open moorage (30 cents per foot, $6 minimum), water and power to the docks, sewage pump-out and dump station, rest rooms with showers, laundry facilities, and fuel docks.

Shilshole Bay Marina on the Seattle side of the sound is a Port of Seattle facility that has lots of open moorage, including about three dozen guest slips, power and water to the docks, rest rooms with showers, waste oil disposal station, and boat-sewage pump-out and dump station. There are boat haul-out and repair services at the south end of the marina and a Texaco fuel dock with gas and diesel at the north end.

Elliott Bay Marina has open moorage, a fuel dock and marine service center, power and water to the floats, rest rooms with showers, a boat-sewage pump-out and dump station, restaurants, and easy access to the Seattle waterfront and downtown Seattle.

Bell Harbor Marina, also on the Seattle waterfront, has open moorage, power and water to the docks, rest rooms and showers, a boat-sewage pump-out facility, and great access to the Seattle waterfront. The nearby Anthony's restaurant doesn't hurt its popularity, either.

Harbor Island Marina, at the mouth of the Duwamish River in the south end of Elliott Bay, has open moorage, showers and rest rooms, and a boat-sewage pump-out facility.

South of Seattle, Des Moines Marina, managed by the City of Des Moines, has open moorage, a fuel dock, power and water to the docks, rest rooms with showers, boat-sewage facilities and one of Puget Sound's most popular fishing piers right next door. Marine services, restaurants, and other amenities are within walking distance. On a clear day, the view across the water to the Olympics isn't bad either. Saltwater State Park, just south of Des Moines, has two moorage buoys, 50 RV and tent sites, rest rooms with showers, picnic tables, kitchen shelters, and a large, gravel beach. Dash Point State Park, farther south along the mainland side, offers over 100 RV tent sites, rest rooms with showers, picnic areas and kitchen shelters, rest rooms with showers, and saltwater beach.

Blake Island Marine State Park has two dozen moorage buoys and over 1,700 feet of moorage float space, a boat-sewage pump-out facility, primitive campsites, fresh water on the island, and a popular Indian longhouse restaurant that serves alder-cooked salmon (open during the summer only). Dockton Park on Vashon Island has open moorage, rest rooms with showers, boat-sewage pump-out and dump station, picnic tables and kitchen shelters, as well as a saltwater beach and a large play area with playground equipment. Dive shops and dive charters are available in Seattle, Bremerton, and on Bainbridge Island.

Water sports/restrictions: All water sports are permitted. NOAA charts covering this area include 18441 (Northern Puget Sound), 18448 (southern Puget Sound), 18474 (Shilshole Bay to Commencement Bay), 18449 (Seattle to Bremerton), and 18445 (Possession Sound to Olympia).

Contact: Washington State Parks and Recreation Commission, tel. (800) 233-0321 (information), tel. (800) 452-5687 (reservations); Eagle Harbor Marina, tel. (206) 842-4003; Winslow Wharf Marina, tel. (206) 842-4202; Harbour Marina, tel. (206) 842-6502; Eagle Harbor Waterfront Park, tel. (206) 842-1212; Spirit Diver (charter) and Exotic Aquatics (dive shop), tel. (206) 842-1980; Poulsbo Marina, tel. (360) 779-3505; Silverdale Marina, tel. (360) 698-4918; Brownsville Marina, tel. (360) 692-5498 (VHF ch. 16); Port Orchard Marina, tel. (206) 876-5535 (VHF ch. 16); Bremerton Marina, tel. (360) 373-1035 (VHF ch. 16); Puget Sound Dive Enterprises (Bremerton), tel. (360) 377-0554; Sound Dive Center (Bremerton), tel. (800) 392-3483); Shilshole Bay Marina, tel. (206) 728-3006 (VHF ch. 17); Elliott Bay Marina, tel. (206) 282-0626 (VHF ch. 78A); Bell Harbor Marina, tel. (206) 615-3965 (VHF ch. 66A); Harbor Island Marina, tel. (206) 624-5711; Underwater Sports, tel. (800) 252-7177; Starfire Charters (dive charter), tel. (206) 364-9858; Sound Waves Scuba (Vashon Island), tel. (206) 463-6152; Whitewater Sports (paddling equipment and sea kayak trips), tel. (206) 246-9385; Des Moines Marina, tel. (206) 824-5700 (VHF ch. 16); Dockton Park (King County Parks and Recreation Department), tel. (206) 463-2947; Bainbridge Island Chamber of Commerce, tel. (206) 842-3700; Bremerton Area Chamber of Commerce, tel. (360) 479-3579; Des Moines Chamber of Commerce Visitor Information Center, tel. (206) 878-7000; Port Orchard Chamber of Commerce Visitor Information Center, tel. (800) 982-8139; Seattle-King County Convention and Visitors Bureau, tel. (206) 461-5840; Silverdale Chamber of Commerce Visitor Information Center, tel. (360) 692-6800; Vashon-Maury Island Chamber of Commerce, tel. (206) 463-6217. For nautical charts of this area, contact Captain's Nautical Supply, tel. (206) 283-7242.

68 Lake Union (including the Lake Washington Ship Canal)

Rating: 7

Whoever coined the phrase "Getting there is half the fun" must have been thinking about Lake Union. That's because for most people, getting to Lake Union means getting there by way of the Lake Washington Ship Canal, a fascinating waterway that dissects the city of Seattle just north of its downtown business district. The two nearest boat ramps are on the north side of the canal, so even those who trailer their boats to the area technically come to Lake Union by water.

The lake itself is about as urban as can be, and serves as a home base for many people who work in the city. Chandler's Cove, at Lake Union's southeast corner, is a floating community of live-aboards and visiting vessels, and the lake is also the site of Seattle's largest concentration of houseboats. On a breezy afternoon the lake's surface may come to life with sailboats as urbanites sneak away from their offices early and head for the water.

One of the most prominent landmarks on the lake is Gas Works Park, where the City of Seattle has created a recreational haven at the site of the city's old natural gas plant. Adults can inspect the hulks of the old machinery while the kids clamber around the hulks of elaborate playground equipment. At the opposite (south) end of the lake is another must-see, the Center for Wooden Boats, a hands-on museum that contains one of the most impressive collections of wooden craft you'll ever see. It's even possible to take a ride on some of the exhibits. Pretty cool. The Lake Washington Ship Canal, though, is even more fascinating than Lake Union. Turn-of-the-century excavation of two canals, one between Portage Bay and Lake Washington's Union Bay and the other between Salmon Bay and the northwest corner of Lake Union, connected Lake Washington to Puget Sound. The so-called Montlake Cut and + linking the two lakes to salt water were, of course, constructed for the sake of commerce, but the canal's value to recreational boaters throughout the Puget Sound area is immeasurable.

A steady stream of motor yachts, sailboats, fishing boats, canoes, and kayaks make their way in and out of Puget Sound through the canal every day, and on weekends it can be one of the busiest waterways in western Washington. In fact, things can get downright crowded in the canal's two narrowest spots, the Montlake and Fremont cuts. A trip through the entire five-mile canal will take you under six highway bridges and a Burlington-Northern railway bridge, which range from 30 feet to well over 100 feet above the water. You don't have to worry about the Interstate 5 or Aurora bridges, but some of the others are worth thinking about if you take a sailboat through the canal. You may have to request the raising of several bridges along the way. You'd better know the height of your mast and understand the signaling system to get the bridges raised. The signal is one long blast followed by one short blast, and should be sounded at least 100 yards from the bridge you intend to pass under. The Ballard, Fremont, University, and Montlake bridges are closed from 7 to 9 a.m. and 4 to 6 p.m. weekdays to accommodate rush-hour highway traffic. Most of these are not tended during the night, from 11 p.m. to 7 a.m., so boaters need to call (206) 386-4251 or VHF channel 13 an hour before arrival to have bridges opened during the night.

And then there are the Hiram M. Chittenden Locks, the most fascinating part of the trip through the canal for the majority, the most terrifying boating experience ever for some. Although I can't document it with scientific proof, I think the people who dislike going through the locks are the same ones who have never learned how to launch their boats without tying up traffic at the ramp for an hour or more. Ill-prepared, inattentive, and drunken boaters are the ones who usually have problems at the locks, and they can also cause problems and delays for other boaters. Luckily, most other boaters are prepared to help out and deal with such situations. The lock attendants, who have seen and fixed about any kind of boating disaster imaginable, are usually right there to help get things squared away.

Besides all the usual required safety equipment, all boats passing through the locks have to be equipped with two 50-foot mooring lines, one at the bow and one at the stern, and fenders for both sides of the boat. Even though there are two locks, a large one and a small one, waiting lines often form at both ends, especially during weekends and summer evenings. Give yourself plenty of time, have something else to do on the boat while you wait (picnic baskets and anglers tying leaders for the next trip are common sights), and wait your turn. Remember that just because you're first in line, you may not be the first boat allowed into the locks. Government vessels have first priority, followed by commercial passenger vessels on scheduled trips, then freighters, fishing vessels and tow boats, followed by recreational vessels—that's you. Only the lowly log raft is lower on the locks' pecking order than pleasure craft, so deal with it.

Watch the traffic lights as you enter the locks and listen for instructions over the public address system from the lock attendants. Watch the attendants for mooring directions and be prepared to pass him or her a loop of line. If they put you in the large lock, you'll need someone on the bow and on the stern to pay out and take in line as the water drops and raises, but it's a good idea to keep someone near the lines even if you're put in the small lock. Although it has floating guide walls to which you'll be connected, they can stick on their way up or down, leaving you and your boat in the precarious positions of being lifted out of the water or taken down with the wall. You wouldn't like either one of those scenarios, so have someone paying close attention to the lines and ready to act in case of a problem.

There are lots of other dos and don'ts relating to the Chittenden Locks, and they're all covered in a brochure produced by the U.S. Army Corps of Engineers, which operates the locks. To get a copy of *Guidelines for Boaters,* write: Seattle District, U.S. Army Corps of Engineers, P.O. Box 3755, Seattle, WA 98124-2255. It also offers classes in boating through the locks. To reserve a spot, call the lockmaster at tel. (206) 783-7000.

Location: In Seattle, map A2, grid i6.

How to get there: Take Interstate 5 to Seattle and the Mercer Street exit (Exit 167). Bear right as you emerge from the tunnel and turn left onto Westlake Avenue or go right to Eastlake Avenue, both of which follow the lake's shoreline around to the north. Westlake Avenue becomes Nickerson and parallels part of the Lake Washington Ship Canal's south side. Nickerson also leads to 15th Avenue NW, which crosses the ship canal and leads to N.W. Market Street in Ballard. Turn west on Market and you're paralleling the north side of the ship canal to the Chittenden Locks.

Boat ramp: There's a Seattle Parks and Recreation Department ramp on the north side of the Lake Washington Ship Canal at the end of 14th Street. It's a two-lane concrete-plank ramp, with loading/boarding floats. There's another Seattle Parks and Recreation Department ramp on N.W. Northlake Way, near the end of Sunnyside Avenue, also on the north side of the ship canal. It's also a two-lane concrete-plank ramp, with one loading float.

Facilities: There are several fuel docks and other facilities on the north side of the Lake Washington Ship Canal, between the Ballard (15th Avenue NW) Bridge and the Chittenden Locks. Some cater mostly to commercial craft and carry diesel only. You'll find both gas and diesel at the Chevron dock. Ballard Mill Marina, in the same area (east of the locks) has open moorage, power to the docks, rest rooms and showers and boat-sewage pump-out facilities. One of Seattle's biggest marine stores, the Crow's Nest, is located on the north end of Lake Union, just west of Gas Works Park. Morrison's North Star Marina is on the west side of the lake, offering gas and diesel, rest rooms, and a boat-sewage pump-out facility. Henry Marina, at the south end of the lake, has open moorage, power to the docks, and boat-sewage pump-out facilities. Chandler's Cove, at the south end of the lake, is a permanent moorage that may have guest moorage space available; call ahead.

Water sports/restrictions: Except for a marked course in Lake Union, there's a seven-knot speed limit on the lake and along the entire length of the Lake Washington Ship Canal. Boats entering the Chittenden Locks are limited to two knots. Anchoring is prohibited in the lake.

Contact: Fremont Bridge (for nighttime bridge opening on the ship canal), tel. (206) 386-4251 (VHF ch. 13); Ballard Mill Marina, tel. (206) 789-4777; Morrison's North Star Marina, tel. (206) 284-6600.

69 Cottage Lake

Rating: 7

Once a favorite of King County water lovers, Cottage was tied up in private ownership for about 15 years, from the late '70s to the early '90s, but now it's open to the public again, complete with a county park that provides public access and small fishing dock. You can't get trailer boats to the water, so there's no big-boat activity, but this is a great place to paddle the shoreline or use a small powerboat to prowl around, fish, or just enjoy a quiet evening on the lake.

Location: East of Woodinville; map A2, grid h7.

How to get there: Take Interstate 405 to Highway 522 and turn east to Woodinville. Drive east from Woodinville on Woodinville-Duvall Road and watch for signs pointing south (right) to the lake. If you come to Avondale Road, you've gone about a quarter of a mile too far.

Boat ramp: There's a new King County park on the lake with a launch site where small boats can be launched.

Facilities: The county park has fishing piers and a swim beach. Food and gas are available in Woodinville, and there are numerous motels along Interstate 405.

Water sports/restrictions: Paddling, fishing, and swimming are the main draws here.

Contact: The Fishin' Tackle Store, tel. (425) 869-5117.

70 Tolt River

Rating: 7

It's about six miles from the end of Tolt River Road down to the mouth of the river, and most of it is an easy run through forest and farm country, a nice place to be on a sunny summer day. There are, however, quite a few logs, limbs, and other woody debris in the river, and in some places they make the Tolt seem a little too narrow for comfort, especially if you're aboard an inner tube or inflatable craft. And if you think there's more woody stuff in the Tolt than there was years ago, you're right. In an effort to re-create salmon habitat that has been systematically removed in past decades, some agencies are now going to some great lengths to put it back. That's happened on the Tolt, among other western Washington streams. What's good for salmon isn't necessarily good for river runners, but live with it; we gotta have fish. But don't take chances or push your luck, and you shouldn't have any problems. When the water level drops, this stretch of river gets shallow, so you may have to get out and drag your boat in a few places, especially at the upper end of the run.

Location: Flows into Snoqualmie River near Carnation; map A2, grid h9.

How to get there: Take Highway 203 to Carnation and turn east on Tolt River Road, which parallels the north side of the river.

Boat ramp: There's a place to drag a small boat to the river at the upper end of Tolt River Road and another at the mouth of the Tolt where it meets the Snoqualmie.

Facilities: Food and gas are available in Carnation.

Water sports/restrictions: Kayaking and tubing are popular, and small inflatables may also be used here when the river level is fairly high.

Contact: Pacific Water Sports, tel. (206) 246-9385.

7.1 Langlois Lake

Rating: 5

The lake's small size (40 acres), chilly water, and limited access restrict most activities to fishing and paddling. Except for the access area, the entire shoreline is privately owned, so water lovers don't come here in large numbers. Swimmers are especially scarce, and for good reason: this little lake is very deep, with some spots close to 100 feet, so it warms very slowly in the summer and would tend to freeze the you-know-whats off a brass you-know-what if they tried to swim here in any but the warmest days of late July or August. Even then, it's doubtful.

Location: Southeast of Carnation; map A2, grid h9.

How to get there: Take Highway 203 to Carnation. About a mile south of town, turn east on Lake Langlois Road, also known as N.E. 24th Street, which goes to the east side of the lake.

Boat ramp: The lake has a public access area and boat ramp. A $10 Washington Department of Fish and Wildlife access decal is required to use the public launch areas maintained by the WDFW.

Facilities: Food, gas, and tackle are available in Carnation.

Water sports/restrictions: Paddling and fishing are the main sports here.

Contact: Sky Valley Traders, tel. (360) 794-8818.

7.2 Hamma Hamma River

Rating: 4

Limited access and private property cause the same problems for boaters as they do for anglers on this small Hood Canal tributary, so most boating activity is limited to the estuary below U.S. 101. The area does, however, offer lots of opportunity to see and photograph a wide range of shore birds, waterfowl, raptors, deer, elk, otter, harbor seals, and other wildlife, so it's worth exploring. Salmon, mostly chums, also make their way up the river in large numbers from October through December, to provide lots of fish viewing (but not catching).

Location: Flows into west side of Hood Canal at Eldon; map A2, grid i1.

How to get there: Drive north from Shelton on U.S. 101 and turn west on Forest Road 24 (Jorsted Creek Road) or Forest Road 25 to reach upper sections of the river from the south or north side. If you take Forest Road 24, turn north on Forest Road 2480 to reach the river. A short section of the lower river is accessible from U.S. 101 near the highway bridges.

Boat ramp: It's possible to drag a small boat, kayak, or canoe over the bank near the U.S. 101 bridges near the mouth of the river.

Facilities: The Forest Service's Hamma Hamma Campground has 15 tent and RV sites, vault toilets, and drinking water. Food and gas are available at the tiny town of Eldon.

Water sports/restrictions: Kayaking, canoeing, and motorboating are possible in and around the mouth of the river.

Contact: Olympic National Forest, Hood Canal Ranger District, tel. (360) 877-5254; Eldon Store, tel. (360) 877-5374.

7.3 Wildcat Lake

Rating: 6

Access is limited here or this 110-acre lake near Bremerton would have a lot more activity every summer weekend.

As it is, fishing is the main draw, but there's also ample room for waterskiing, PWC riding, and other water sports. This is also a good place for some peaceful paddling, especially in the fall after the water begins to cool and those who do come here for warm-weather water sports disappear altogether.

Location: Northwest of Bremerton; map A2, grid i3.

How to get there: Drive north out of Bremerton on Highway 3 and turn west on the Seabeck Highway. Turn west again on Holly Road and drive to Lakeview Road; turn south (left) and drive to the north side of the lake.

Boat ramp: The lake has a large public access area with a concrete boat ramp and a gravel ramp alongside it. A $10 Washington Department of Fish and Wildlife access decal is required to use the public launch areas maintained by the WDFW.

Facilities: There are also pit toilets and plenty of room for bank anglers. Scenic Beach State Park is about 10 miles away to the northwest. Food, gas, and lodging are available in Bremerton.

Water sports/restrictions: All water sports are permitted.

Contact: Kitsap Sport Shop, Bremerton, tel. (360) 373-9589.

74 Kitsap Lake

Rating: 7

One of the biggest bodies of fresh water in the Bremerton-Kitsap County area, Kitsap Lake has something to offer just about anybody who likes to play on or in the water. Covering some 240 acres, it's big enough to accommodate skiers, swimmers, anglers, paddlers, PWC riders, wakeboarders, and everyone else, seemingly with room to spare. The swim beach at Kitsap Lake Park is big enough

for hundreds of people to cool off during the heat of summer. Both the public access area and the park are open all year, so boaters and anglers who want to escape the crowds of summer can use Kitsap at their leisure during the off-season.

Location: Immediately west of Bremerton; map A2, grid i4.

How to get there: Take the Seabeck Highway west out of Bremerton and turn south (left) on East Kitsap Lake Road or West Kitsap Lake Road.

Boat ramp: There's a blacktop two-lane public boat ramp at the southwest corner of the lake and another ramp at Kitsap Lake Park on the west side.

Facilities: Kitsap Lake Park has a nice swim beach, picnic area, playground toys, and rest rooms. All amenities are available within a few miles, in the Bremerton area.

Water sports/restrictions: All water sports are permitted.

Contact: Kitsap Sport Shop, Bremerton, tel. (360) 373-9589.

75 Lake Washington

Rating: 10

Not many cities can boast having a huge expanse of salt water at their front door and a sprawling body of fresh water 'round back; Seattle can make such a claim. Seattleites who don't want to play in Elliott Bay or Puget Sound need only turn east to find all the freshwater fun they can handle, in the form of 17-mile-long Lake Washington. Luckily for the rest of us, Seattle residents aren't the only ones who get to enjoy the lake. Folks in Renton, Bellevue, Mercer Island, Kirkland, and Kenmore also call Washington "their" lake, and the rest of us are free get there by land, sea, or air any time we feel the urge. At more than

22,000 surface acres, there's plenty of room here for everyone to have a good time. When it comes to water activities, you name it and someone's probably doing it on or in Lake Washington right now. If you think I'm exaggerating, you should know that there are people who swim here every day of the year. They may not be quite normal, but they help to prove my point.

Public swim beaches are found virtually around every corner at parks operated by the Seattle Parks and Recreation Department, King County Parks Department, and Kirkland, Bellevue, and Renton Parks and Recreation Departments. The possibilities on the east side of the lake include Juanita Beach Park in Juanita; Waverly, Marina, and Houghton Beach Parks in Kirkland; Enatai Beach Park in Bellevue; Luther Burbank Park at the north end of Mercer Island; Kennydale Beach Park north of Renton; and expansive Gene Coulon Park in Renton.

Public swim beaches on the Seattle side of the lake are even more numerous, and include Madison Park, Matthews Beach, Magnuson Park, Madrona Park, Seward Park, Pritchard Island Beach, and Mount Baker Park. And these are only the sites with official swimming areas and life guards.

As you may already have determined if you read the list of ramps and other facilities scattered around the lake, this also is a boater's lake, and we're talking craft of all kinds. Paddlers love Lake Washington because they can almost always find a place to hide from the worst of the wind and weather; it may take a little traveling, but it can be done. One favorite haunt of kayak and canoe enthusiasts is Union Bay, near the University of Washington just north of the Evergreen Point (Highway 520) Bridge. Well

protected from the wind, it also is bordered on the south side by the Washington Park Arboretum, where, except for the freeway noise from overhead, paddlers can pretend that they're nowhere near the largest metropolis in the Pacific Northwest. The UW's Waterfront Activities Center is near the west end of Union Bay, and you can rent canoes here if you don't have your own. Call (206) 543-2217 to see about canoe rentals.

Other popular paddling spots on the big lake include the three bays immediately northeast of the Evergreen Point Bridge—Fairweather Bay, Cozy Cove, and Yarrow Bay—as well as the Meydenbauer Bay area north of Mercer Island and the fairly well-protected water along the west side between Seward Park and the west end of the Mercer Island (Interstate 90) Floating Bridge. Incidentally, paddlers and all other boaters should note that the floating spans do a good job of blocking the wind. When a strong southerly is churning up four-foot whitecaps on most of the lake, things are calm on the north side of both bridges, at least for a few hundred yards. Oh yes, one more note about the bridges: you can pass under them near their east and west ends. Clearance is 35 feet under the Mercer Island span, 45 feet under the Evergreen Point Bridge.

While we're talking about taller boats, it's worth mentioning that owners of power- and sailboats like it here because they can enjoy big-water freedom without the headaches of saltwater corrosion and associated maintenance. That's not to say, of course, that people who use their boats on Lake Washington don't use them on Puget Sound. Thanks to the Lake Washington Ship Canal, the salty waters of the sound are less than a half dozen miles and a trip through the Ballard Locks away. Except for the extreme north end of the lake at Kenmore and the south end near Renton—where inlet rivers have deposited decades of silt and made for large, shallow flats— Lake Washington is very big-boat friendly. Sure, you have to pay attention to your depthsounder and should always have your chart (18447SC) nearby, but bigger boats can travel throughout much of the lake without worrying all the time about shallow water.

Even Union Bay at the entrance to the ship canal has a dredged channel that allows some deep-draft vessels to make their way in and out of the lake. There are plenty of hangouts on the lake for big-boat enthusiasts to congregate, too, the most popular of which is Andrews Bay, between the Bailey Peninsula and the mainland near the southwest corner of the lake. Although city and county officials in recent years considered putting the bay off-limits to the many boats that used it as an overnight anchorage, conditions were agreed to in 1998 that allowed boats to continue using the beautiful bay for overnight anchorage, at least on a year-by-year basis. A three-knot speed limit, 72-hour maximum stay, and other conditions are now in place, or at least they were at the end of summer, 1999. Fairweather Bay, Cozy Cove, and Yarrow Bay, located side by side just north of the Evergreen Point Bridge's east end, also offer decent anchorage, but the many private buoys in the area limit the possibilities.

While Lake Washington provides water recreation of all kinds throughout the calendar year, it's at its all-time busiest during one week in August: Seafair. The big event is the hydroplane race on Sunday, but time trials and other race-related activities start a week earlier.

Log booms placed around the race course start filling up with boats (reservations required) long before the opening gun for Sunday's first race, and a party atmosphere firmly engulfs the lake throughout race weekend. Most folks have a great time, but if you're looking for peace and quiet on the water, Lake Washington is the last place on earth you'll want to be that weekend. By the middle of the next week everything's back to normal.

Location: Immediately east of Seattle; map A2, grid i6. (See Lake Washington inset map.)

How to get there: There are so many ways to get to so many access points on this huge lake that it's impossible to list them all here. Just one way to get to good fishing is to take Interstate 405 to Kirkland and turn west on Central Way. Turn north on Market Street to reach some of the more northerly parts of the lake or turn south on Lake Washington Boulevard (which eventually becomes Bellevue Way) to reach fishing docks, parks, and boat ramps along the rest of the lake's east side.

Boat ramp: There are nine public boat ramps on the lake: These are listed on the Lake Washington inset map.

- **Kenmore Ramp:** The northernmost ramp on Lake Washington is in Kenmore, where the Sammamish River flows into the north end of Lake Washington. Managed by the Washington Department of Wildlife, it's a one-lane concrete-plank ramp that's in good shape and has a parking area large enough for about 40 cars and trailers. A $10 Washington Department of Fish and Wildlife access decal is required to use the public launch areas maintained by the WDFW. To get there, take the Woodinville exit off Highway 405 and drive east on Highway 522 four miles to

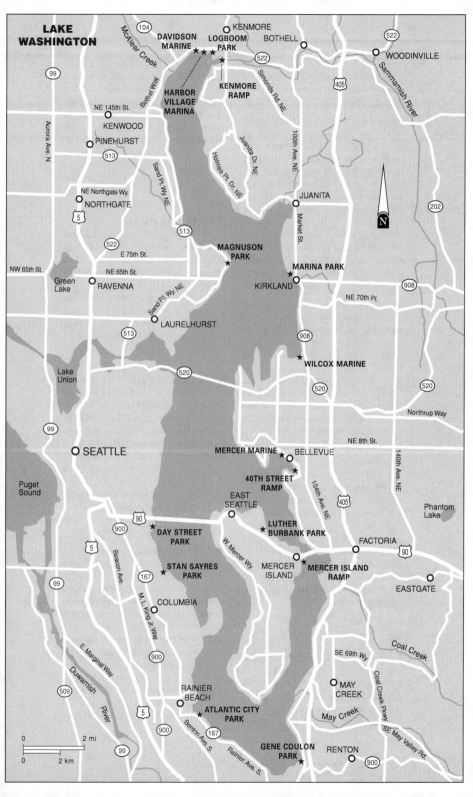

Juanita Drive. Turn south (left) on Juanita Drive and go a quarter of a mile, turning right immediately after crossing the bridge.

- **Marina Park:** The next ramp on the lake's east side is in Kirkland, at Marina Park. It's a good ramp, one lane wide, with a loading/boarding float. There's a $4 launch fee at this one. Parking for cars with boat trailers is limited, to say the least. Unless you launch early and park on the nearby street, you could have trouble finding a place to park. To reach this ramp, take Highway 405 to Kirkland and go west on N.E. 85th Street to Market Street. Turn left on Market and you'll see the ramp on the right.

- **Magnuson Park:** Straight across the lake from the Kirkland site is Seattle's Magnuson Park, with a four-lane concrete ramp near its south end. There are loading/boarding floats between the ramps, which are in excellent shape. There's a $3 launch fee here. To reach it, take Montlake Boulevard north. It will become Sand Point Way eventually, so stay on it to 65th Street NE and you'll be at the park entrance.

- **Day Street Park:** Seattle Parks and Rec's Day Street Park has a new (1999) one-lane concrete ramp for kayaks, canoes, sail boards, and other craft small enough to be hand carried. To find it, drive north from Seward Park on Lake Washington Boulevard until it becomes Lakeside Avenue South. Go a quarter of a mile on Lakeside and, right under the Interstate 90 Bridge, turn right at the park entrance.

- **Stan Sayres Park:** Also on the lake's west side a mile and a half to the south of Day Street, is Stan Sayres Park, another Seattle Parks and Recreation facility where there's an eight-lane hard-surface ramp with several loading floats. The paved parking area isn't large enough for all the cars and trailers on busy summer weekend or during those times when there's a sockeye salmon fishing season on the lake. The launch fee here is $3. To reach it from Interstate 90, take the Rainier Avenue exit and go south to Genesee Street, turning left and following Genesee half a mile. Turn right on 43rd Avenue South and go another half-mile to Lake Washington Boulevard. Turn right and drive one block to the park entrance on the left.

- **Atlantic City Park:** Another large ramp facility is located at Atlantic City Park, about two miles north of Renton. This Seattle Parks and Recreation site has eight concrete lanes and several loading/boarding floats. The standard $3 launch fee applies here. Take Rainier Avenue north out of Renton about two miles and turn east (right) on Seward Park Avenue, following it a quarter of a mile to the ramp.

- **Gene Coulon Park:** This popular waterfront park in Renton has an eight-lane concrete ramp with loading floats. The launch fee varies at this Renton City Parks launch site depending on the season. The most you'll pay is $10, during Seafair weekend. To get there, take Highway 405 to the Sunset Boulevard exit (Exit 5) and go west on Park Drive, turning right on Lake Washington Boulevard. Drive 100 yards to the stop sign and turn left into the park.

- **40th Street Ramp:** Farther up the east side of the lake is the Bellevue Parks Department's ramp on S.E. 40th Street. It's a two-lane concrete ramp with a loading float between the lanes. The launch fee here is $4. It's a little hard to find the first time. Take Exit 13A off Highway 405 and drive west one block on Eighth Street, turning left on 11th Avenue NE. Go half a mile on 11th Avenue and turn right on Main Street. Drive two blocks on Main and turn right again on 114th Avenue SE, which eventually becomes 118th Avenue as it winds toward the lake. Turn right again on S.E. 40th Street and follow it to the ramp.

- **Mercer Island Ramp:** Mercer Island Parks and Recreation manages a ramp on the lake located under the Interstate 90 bridge on the east side of the island. The fee to use this two-lane concrete ramp is $4 round-trip. To get there, take Interstate 90 east from Seattle, taking Exit 8 to Mercer Way. Go 100 yards on Mercer Way to the boat ramp sign on the left and turn down the hill to the ramp.

Facilities: Davidson Marine, at the north end of the lake, has a fuel dock, rest rooms, marine parts and service. Harbor Village Marina, at the north end of the lake in Kenmore, has open moorage, power to the docks, rest rooms with showers, and a boat-sewage pump-out facility. Logboom Park in Kenmore has moorage floats, a swim beach, rest rooms, a fishing pier, picnic tables, and kitchen shelters. Kirkland's Marina Park, just off Market Street, offers guest moorage, a fishing pier, a swim beach, picnic tables, and rest rooms. Carillon Point Marina has some guest moorage, power and water to the docks, rest rooms with showers, boat-sewage and dump-station facilities, and access to nearby restaurants and shopping.

Wilcox Marine, in Yarrow Bay south of Kirkland, has fuel docks, rest rooms, and boat-sewage pump-out facilities. Seattle's 190-acre Magnuson Park has a large swim beach, picnic tables, rest rooms, and lakeside hiking trails. Mercer Marine in Bellevue has fuel docks (gasoline only), rest rooms, marine service, and supplies. Stan Sayres Park has day-use moorage, beach frontage, rest rooms, and lots of lawn for picnicking and lounging around.

Luther Burbank Park, at the northeast corner of Mercer Island, has day-use moorage, rest rooms, a large swim area, and picnic tables. Renton's Gene Coulon Park has moorage floats, canoe, sailboat and sailboard rentals, rest rooms with showers, picnic tables, kitchen shelters, fishing pier, tennis courts, lots of grassy playground areas, and an on-site Ivar's seafood restaurant (in case you can't catch your own fish in the lake). And on the subject of food, hungry boaters around the north end of the lake can take advantage of several lakeside restaurants with private floats and docks that offer free moorage to customers while they dine.

Water sports/restrictions: All water sports are permitted. No-wake regulations are strictly enforced in and around shoreline/moorage/swim areas and the two floating bridges. The no-wake distance is generally 100 yards, but it's as much as 300 yards in some places.

Contact: Seattle Parks and Recreation Department, tel. (206) 684-4075 (parks information and boat ramp permits); Davidson Marine, tel. (425) 486-7141; Harbor Village Marina, tel. (425) 485-7557; Marina Park (City of Kirkland), tel. (425) 828-1220; Carillon Point Marina, tel. (425) 822-1700; Mercer Marina (Bellevue), tel. (425) 641-2090; Gene Coulon Park (Renton Parks and Recreation Department), tel. (425) 277-5541.

76 Lake Sammamish

Rating: 10

One of King County's most popular places, Sammamish offers nearly 5,000 acres of water to play on, in, and around. Since I have nothing better to do, I sometimes wonder if it would be so popular if it still went by the name it used to have, Squak Lake. Oh well, I guess it doesn't matter. Anyway, when it's really busy, which is fairly often, there are

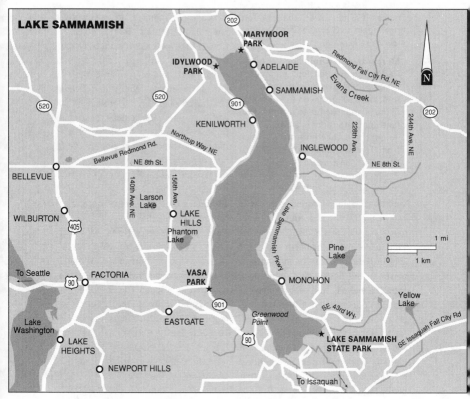

LAKE SAMMAMISH

thousands of people boating, skiing, boarding, paddling, swimming, diving, and wading here at once. So large and long that in the good old days before blacktop highways there were ferries hauling freight up and down it, Sammamish is one of those rare places where there really is something for everyone who enjoys the water. Three major swim beaches—Lake Sammamish State Park, Vasa Park (private), and Idylwood Park—offer enough shoreline to accommodate hundreds of swimmers and splashers. Vasa Park is one of the last lake resorts in Washington that still have a high dive, so there's a place for nonmotorized daredevils.

Some days it seems that there are as many boats on the lake as there are

swimmers, and a vast majority of them are personal watercraft and ski boats. High-speed sports of all kinds are big here, so big that water-related manufacturing businesses have sprung up around this part of King County in response to what has taken place on Sammamish.

It's generally considered the birthplace of wakeboarding, and on a warm weekend it's not uncommon to see dozens of boarders doing their double-bind 180s, Indy bones, front flips, and other stunts all over the lake. Unlike the skiers, these high jumpers prefer rough water, and when a few of them start doing their thing, it's not long before there's plenty of it. Add personal watercraft to the mix—and they are certainly a part of it here—and the surface of Sammamish gets frothy on a sunny afternoon. If you want to ski smooth waters on Sammamish, you'd better get up before the boarders emerge.

Even with all the motorized activity, this is a good place for paddlers, as long as they don't get too brave and try to get from one side of the lake to the other on a busy weekend. The weedy areas at the north and south ends of the lake are especially popular with canoe and kayak enthusiasts, and those who paddle the south end have the option of going some distance into Issaquah Creek, which enters the lake on state park property between the swim beach and the boat ramp.

Divers are also in love with Sammamish, not only because it drops to depths of greater than 100 feet in places, but because it has one very unusual attraction, its sunken forest. Along Greenwood Point, between the state park and Vasa Park at the lake's southwest corner, are some 70 submerged trees, part of an ancient forest that slipped into the lake, according to scientists, more than 1,000 years ago. It's an intriguing place.

Location: Northwest of Issaquah; map A2, grid i7. (See Lake Sammamish inset map.)

How to get there: Take Interstate 90 southeast from Bellevue or northwest from Issaquah and turn north into Lake Sammamish State Park.

Boat ramp: The following boat ramps are listed on the Lake Sammamish inset map:

• **Lake Sammamish State Park:** There's a 10-lane boat ramp with loading floats in Jensen's Cove, at the east end of the state park, which encompasses the lake's entire south end.

• **Vasa Park:** Located on the west side of the lake, near the south end, Vasa Park also has a boat ramp.

Facilities: One of the Seattle area's biggest and most popular swim beaches is at Lake Sammamish State Park, which would help to explain why its parking lot, which holds several hundred cars, is sometimes full when the weather is warm and sunny on a spring or summer weekend. There are also swim beaches, picnic tables and other amenities at county-run Idylwood Park, which is at the lake's north end, and at Vasa Park, near the south end. Vasa Park has 16 tent sites and five RV sites with hookups. Marymoor Park covers some 400 acres from the lake's north end to Highway 520. Boat and kayak rentals are available on and near the lake.

Water sports/restrictions: All water sports are permitted.

Contact: Lake Sammamish State Park, tel. (206) 455-7010; Washington State Parks and Recreation Commission, tel. (800) 233-0321 (information); Vasa Park, tel. (425) 746-3260; King County Parks and Recreation Department, tel. (206) 684-7050; Klub Kayak, tel. (206) 637-8838; Northwest Kayaks, tel. (425) 869-1107.

77 Pine Lake

Rating: 8

If it weren't for huge lake Sammamish just over the hill, a place like Pine Lake might be one of the most popular boating/ swimming/fishing spots in western Washington. But since it's only about 90 acres in size and a little out of the way for folks going to and from via Interstate 90, Pine Lake tends to get a little bit lost in the shuffle. That's good for the thousands of folks who have already discovered this little urban jewel of a lake and the even more gemlike park along its eastern shoreline. They have plenty of watery fun without having to compete with the large crowds and occasional weekend traffic jams at Sammamish. The county park swim beach, while not big, is well-maintained and safe, and the narrow boat ramp keeps boat traffic from getting out of hand. This is a great place to bring the family.

Location: North of Issaquah; map A2, grid i8.

How to get there: Take Exit 15 off Interstate 90 and turn north (over the freeway if you're headed east). Follow S.E. 56th Street one mile to East Lake Sammamish Parkway, turn north (left), and drive just over a mile to 43rd Way. Turn right on 43rd Way and follow it up the hill 2.5 miles to the Pile Lake County Park entrance on the left.

Boat ramp: There's a single-lane boat ramp at the county park.

Facilities: Pine Lake County Park on the east side of the lake also offers a gravel/sand swim beach, fishing pier, rest rooms, play area, and picnic tables. Food, gas, and lodging are available in Issaquah, three miles south.

Water sports/restrictions: All water sports are permitted.

Contact: King County Parks and Recreation Department, tel. (206) 684-7050.

78 Snoqualmie River

Rating: 8

Interstate 90 crosses the South Fork Snoqualmie near North Bend and parallels it much of the way to the Snoqualmie Pass summit. For many cross-state travelers on this major route through the Cascades, the clear, cold little stream alongside the highway is the high point of a trip through hills recently scalped and scarred by clear-cut logging. There are several wide spots off the highway to stop and walk over the bank to the river. But you'll quickly find that no matter the time of year, this isn't a great place to cool your toes, at least not unless you want to watch your entire leg turn purple from the cold in about three seconds. This is mountain water at its best, not well suited to swimming.

Boaters, on the other hand, find the South Fork a great place to stretch their arms and work their shoulders. The four-mile float from Olallie/Twin Falls State Park down to the 436th Avenue bridge in North Bend is a nice little Class II outing, great for kayaks and a possibility for rafters and even skilled canoeists when the water level is up a bit in early to midsummer. Just don't capsize or even hang your hands in the water for any length of time.

The Middle Fork Snoqualmie has even more to offer paddlers, although getting to the river at the various put-in and take-out points is somewhat more complicated. There are nearly 20 miles of Class II to Class III+ water for paddlers to enjoy between the mouth of the Taylor River and the town of North Bend, with a couple of bridges and roadside take-out sites along the way so that boaters can break this long stretch of river into two or three very manageable floats.

The middle part of this run, from the concrete bridge on Middle Fork Road down to Tanner, is the most exciting and most popular, with some impressive boulder runs and a couple of house-size rocks appropriately known as House Rocks. The mossy boulders and relative abundance of forest cover along this stretch of the Snoqualmie makes the entire Middle Fork a stream worth investigating, especially for kayakers. Rafters can use it, especially in the higher flows of spring and early summer, but at other times it's a tight squeeze for the fatter boats.

The upper North Fork Snoqualmie is another possibility for kayakers, but gate closures on the main logging road up the river often make access impossible. If you can get above the Spur Ten gate, the nearby bridge is a good take-out spot for floats on the upper reaches of this fork. If you do get on the North Fork, take out above the canyon at Ernie's Grove. A few daredevils have paddled the canyon and come out alive at the bottom end, but many boaters consider it the most dangerous, most challenging stretch of runnable river in western Washington. It's basically a series of small waterfalls ranging from three and four feet to more than 25 feet high. Even advanced paddlers have to portage in several places.

The main Snoqualmie is a piece of cake compared to the forks, except that you wouldn't want to launch anything at the town of Snoqualmie for a paddle down to Fall City. There's a little obstacle known as Snoqualmie Falls that would cause considerable damage to your boat and your body. The waterfall, though, is something you'll want to see if you're in the area. It's spectacular. Above the falls from where the North and Middle Forks meet down to either of two rough take-out sites along Mill Pond Road, the water is gentle and slow, excellent for leisurely paddling in a canoe or raft. Tubing is another good possibility here, as many local kids could testify, and there are also a couple of deep swimming holes, the best of which is about a quarter mile downstream of the confluence of the South Fork Snoqualmie and the main river.

From the rough boat launch near the mouth of Tokul Creek downstream, the Snoqualmie slows, tames, and soon starts to meander, so there's plenty of opportunity for a leisurely float through lowland fields and alder flats. After a few short riffles and some boulders to negotiate immediately below the public fishing area near the mouth of Tokul Creek, the river becomes a place where you won't even have to paddle for hundreds of yards at a time, except maybe to keep the boat pointed downstream. This also becomes the realm of tubers, drift boaters, and calm-water craft of various kinds. Kick back and enjoy, or wet a line if salmon or steelhead season happens to be open. If it's summer, you might even consider a little swimming from one of the low gravel beaches that show themselves every so often. If you're adventurous (and not too heavy), maybe you'll want to test one of the several rope swings you'll find overhanging the river on this lower stretch.

Location: Joins Skykomish River southwest of Monroe; map A2, grid i8.

How to get there: Take Interstate 90 to Preston and drive north to Fall City or take Highway 202 from Redmond to Fall City, cross the river, and either turn right and continue on Highway 202 upstream, or turn left and take Highway 203 downstream. The North Fork Snoqualmie is accessible via Weyerhaeuser Company roads out of Snoqualmie, while the Middle Fork is reached by logging roads running east from North Bend.

Boat Ramp: There are access points of various quality in several places along the river, including Duval, the mouth of the Tolt River, midway between Carnation and Fall City off Highway 202, the mouth of the Raging River, and just below the mouth of Tokul Creek, all on the main Snoqualmie. On the South Fork Snoqualmie are rough put-in spots for kayaks and other small boats at the 436th Avenue bridge in North Bend and at Olallie/Twin Falls State Park. Similar rough launches are available on the Middle Fork Snoqualmie at the concrete bridge on Middle Fork Road, at the end of Tanner Road SE, and at the bridge in North Bend where Ballarat Road crosses the river.

Water sports/restrictions: Kayaking, some rafting on the forks, drift boating, rafting, canoeing, tubing, and swimming are OK on the main river.

Contact: Pacific Water Sports, tel. (206) 246-9385.

79 Raging River

Rating: 4

For its size this is a challenging, even nasty, little river for paddlers. About the only time it's high enough to float is after a good rain from fall to spring, but it seems that every high water brings down new trees into the river and causes other changes that present a danger to boaters. A typical run down the Raging involves about equal doses of time in and out of the boat, so even serious boulder-dodgers tend to consider it more trouble than it's worth. A good rain may change the river considerably, so scouting and dragging around obstacles is a must. All that getting in and out, walking and dragging is tiresome, but if you get lazy and just go for it, this river can do you some serious harm. Unless you're in top shape and willing to work hard for a few good dashes around boulders and through medium-fast chutes, go elsewhere.

Location: Joins the Snoqualmie River at Fall City; map A2, grid i9

How to get there: Take Interstate 90 to Preston and turn north onto Preston-Fall City Road, which parallels the river.

Boat ramp: Kayaks may be dropped over the bank at the bridge on Upper Preston Road, and there's a rough boat launch at the mouth of the river in Fall City.

Facilities: Food, gas, lodging, and other amenities are available in Fall City and Snoqualmie, much more in North Bend.

Water sports/restrictions: Kayaking is the only real possibility.

Contact: Pacific Water Sports, tel. (206) 246-9385.

80 Lake Cushman

Rating: 8

Like many of Washington's biggest fresh-water recreation spots, Cushman is a reservoir that was created back in the good old days when people went around building dams across rivers wherever and whenever they felt like it. They didn't need any special licenses or permits, didn't have to make sure it was OK with the public to stop the water running through the river valley, and didn't worry that their actions were wiping out salmon, steelhead, and trout populations that had thrived in the river for thousands of years. Some heavy equipment, a few hungry workers, and an insatiable urge to harness Mother Nature for profit was about all that anyone needed to be a dam builder.

Now Cushman is one of those dams that some people, including the Skokomish Indians, who live on the Skokomish River downstream from Cushman and another dam below it, wouldn't mind seeing torn out in an effort to help rebuild salmon and steelhead runs. I don't know if that will ever happen, but there's little question that Cushman Dam has had a powerful impact on the Skokomish River system and its fish and wildlife populations.

The good news is that where once there was a river full of fish there is now a 4,000-acre reservoir where lots of water-related recreation flourishes today. And most of the big impoundment's shoreline remains undeveloped, so you don't feel as if you're playing in someone's front yard whenever you take to the water here. Fishing is still a possibility, but Cushman is, in most people's estimation, only a so-so bet when it comes to angling opportunities. Most folks come here to pursue other aquatic interests, and you can see or take part in just about every boating-related activity here on a warm summer day. It's a popular lake among water-skiers, especially early in the day before the usual afternoon breezes put a chop on the water and make for tougher skiing. Also putting a chop on the water are the many personal watercraft that gravitate to the big reservoir throughout the warmer months. Wakeboarding and tubing are enjoying increased popularity at Cushman, too, as might be expected. A reservoir this large also has room for some of the bigger, faster boats that are popular with people who have a lot more money than those of us in the writing business. Sailing, paddling, and the other more leisurely boaters also find plenty of room to practice their specialties, particularly in the spring and fall when other activities slow considerably.

Like other Northwest reservoirs, Cushman has its share of stumps, rocks, and other hazards that are submerged when the reservoir is full but not necessarily when water levels drop. They upper end of Cushman is full of such obstacles, so be aware of them and take the time to know what's beneath the surface wherever you play.

Location: Northwest of Hoodsport, Mason County; map A2, grid i0.

How to get there: Take U.S. 101 to Hoodsport and turn west on Highway 119 (Lake Cushman Road) and follow it about five miles to the lake.

Boat ramp: There are three boat ramps on the east side of the lake, one a Department of Wildlife ramp near the south end, one at Lake Cushman Resort a little farther north, and a third at the Lake Cushman State Park. A $10 Washington Department of Fish and Wildlife access decal is required to use the public launch areas maintained by the WDFW.

Facilities: Lake Cushman Resort has cabins, RV and tent sites, a grocery store, and moorage floats. Lake Cushman State Park offers about 60 tent sites and 30 RV sites with full hookups, as well as rest rooms with showers and an RV pump-out station. All other amenities are available in Hoodsport, a few miles away.

Water sports/restrictions: All water sports are permitted. Mason County boating regulations include a 6 mph speed limit within 100 feet of any swimmer, within 150 feet of any shoreline or nonmotorized vessel, and within 300 feet of any public boat ramp; an 8 mph speed limit on freshwater lakes from a half hour after sunset to a half hour before sunrise; and a 50 mph speed limit during daylight hours on all waters unless otherwise posted. Water-skiers must stay at least 300 feet from the shoreline on salt water and at least 150 feet from the shoreline on fresh water. All ski/tow traffic must go in a counterclockwise direction.

Contact: Lake Cushman Resort, tel. (360) 877-9630; Lake Cushman State Park, tel. (360) 877-5491; Washington State Parks and Recreation Commission, tel. (800) 233-03212 (information), tel. (800) 452-5687 (reservations).

81 Kokanee Lake

Rating: 7

Narrow and quite deep, this 150-acre reservoir, also known as Lower Cushman, looks a lot like a miniature version of the real Lake Cushman immediately upstream. The main difference is that due to its much smaller size Kokanee Lake has special restrictions that keep all the bigger, faster craft away. As noted above, motors larger than 7 hp aren't allowed on the lake. That in itself means water-skiers and PWC riders can't do their thing here, but the regs for Kokanee spell out very clearly that personal watercraft are a no-no, just in case any PWC jockeys aren't sure how big their engines might be. It's evident that reservoir has been set aside for the more peaceful and quiet. I remember dropping by Kokanee one Independence Day weekend a few years ago and being surprised to find only one boat trailer in the parking lot at the lake's public access area. That boater was fishing a few hundred feet away, and there was no other boating activity on the lake at all. Meanwhile, a couple of miles away, Lake Cushman was a frenzy of activity. That's the difference special boating regulations can make on a lake.

Location: West of Hoodsport, Mason County; map A2, grid j0.

How to get there: Take U.S. 101 to Hoodsport and turn west onto Highway 119 (Lake Cushman Road). Drive just under three miles to Cushman-Potlatch Road and turn left, go just under a mile to Lower Lake Road, turn right and drive down the hill to the boat ramp near the south end of the lake.

Boat ramp: There's a small boat ramp with limited bank access near the dam at the south end of the lake. A $10 Washington Department of Fish and Wildlife access decal is required to use the public launch areas maintained by the WDFW.

Facilities: Lake Cushman Resort is less than three miles to the north, and Lake Cushman State Park is about six miles away. Lake Cushman Grocery is right across Highway 119, a mile from the lake.

Water sports/restrictions: Fishing, paddling, and rowing are the main attractions. The lake has some special regulations that are unique within Mason County: internal combustion engines are limited to no more than 7 hp, and personal watercraft are specifically prohibited.

Contact: Lake Cushman Resort, tel. (360) 877-9630; Lake Cushman State Park, tel. (360) 877-5491; Washington State Parks and Recreation Commission, tel. (800) 233-0321 (information), tel. (800) 452-5687.

82 Skokomish River

Rating: 6

Most boaters pass over the Skokomish on their way to somewhere else, seldom giving the river a second glance as they head up U.S. 101 toward Hood Canal, the Strait of Juan de Fuca, the north end of the Olympic Peninsula, or even a ferry ride to Whidbey Island or some Canadian destination. But this gentle river, whose North Fork is harnessed behind not one but two hydroelectric dams, is worth investigating by paddlers who want to get away from the boating crowds in particular and most of the human population in general. I can say from painful firsthand experience that there are no places on the Skokomish upstream of U.S. 101 where you can trailer a drift boat to the water, having spent the better part of a rainy winter's night trying and failing on every road that offered even the suggestion of leading to the water. The one that held the most promise dead-ended at a huge blow-down that appeared to have been there a long time. After backing our pickup/camper rig and boat trailer over a quarter mile along the narrow winding road to the highway, my boating buddy and I concluded that we'd never try again, and I suggest that you don't either.

But if your boat is small enough to carry or drag a few hundred feet, you'll enjoy the Skokomish. It's always a good bet for spotting a wide variety of birds and other wildlife from the water, and in fall it has a large run of chum salmon. The only problem with all those salmon is that they draw tribal net fishermen and anglers in good numbers. This is the one time of year when the Skokomish gets a little busy.

Location: Flows into the south end of Hood Canal, Mason County; map A2, grid j0.

How to get there: Take U.S. 101 north from Shelton and turn west (left) on Skokomish Valley Road to drive upstream. To reach lower portions of the river, turn east off U.S. 101 onto Purdy Cutoff Road and follow the river downstream.

Boat ramp: It's possible to drag a small boat or kayak over the bank where the river flows next to Skokomish Valley Road, about three miles west of U.S. 101, and there's a second good hand-launch site at a point where the river runs close to Highway 106 about three-quarters of a mile from the mouth of the river.

Facilities: There's a Forest Service campground on the upper South Fork Skokomish, at the mouth of Brown Creek. Potlatch State Park, about five miles north of the river on U.S. 101, has 24 camping sites, some with RV hookups. Food, gas, and lodging are available in Shelton to the south and Hoodsport to the north.

Water sports/restrictions: Kayaking, canoeing, rafting, and tubing are the best possibilities.

Contact: Verle's Sport Center, tel. (360) 426-0933; Potlatch State Park, tel. (360) 877-5361; Olympic National Forest, Hood Canal Ranger District, tel. (360) 877-5254.

83 Lower Hood Canal (from Triton Head south)

Rating: 9

The lower end of this long, narrow waterway has about as much to do as any boater or water lover could ask. On a calm day it can be like one big mirror, the perfect place to water-ski until your arms, legs, and back simply give up the ghost. When the wind builds from the south, though, the canal can quickly become a wind-surfer's paradise. Divers love the canal because of its slow currents and clear water. It's a place where sleek 50-footers share the water with 18-foot fishing boats. Those fishing boats in turn share the canal with 10-foot skiffs out to set their crab pots or explore a clam beach.

You can also add canoes and kayaks to the mix, as they're often found paddling along the rocky shoreline, exploring the many shallow bays or trekking from one small town to the next. Dive boats, sailboats, PWC, low-profile duck boats and all the rest are also found here. During May you might encounter hundreds of boats equipped with shrimp-pot pullers, while in November the canal is clogged with tribal gill-net boats out to harvest chum salmon. While navigation can get a little tricky when those last two activities are going on, there's plenty of room for boaters to get away and find some solitude. That's because there are no large cities and only a few small towns scattered along the banks of this 55-mile-long ribbon of salt water.

Except for the obvious clearcuts, much of the canal's shoreline and the surrounding slopes look very much as they did 50 or 75 years ago. Views from the water can be breathtaking, especially toward the west, where the foothills of the Olympics rise almost vertically from the edge of the canal to several thousand feet above sea level. The contours beneath the surface are similar in many places to those above the water; there are many places where the canal is 400, 500, even 600 feet deep. By contrast, many of the bays where rivers and creeks enter the canal are quite shallow, filled with the sediment deposits from decades of fall floods and spring snowmelt. Boaters have to study their charts carefully and watch their depthsounders closely around all these estuaries. And don't forget that if you anchor in these shallow bays and stream mouths at high tide, your boat could be on solid ground at low tide.

However, low tide happens to be a great time to visit many of the canal's estuaries and public beaches in search of tasty table fare. Oysters, various hardshell clams, shrimp, and of course Dungeness and red rock crab are abundant throughout the canal. The State Parks beaches at Potlatch, Twanoh, and Belfair are obvious possibilities for oysters and clams. Other public beaches where clam digging and oyster gathering can be very productive are at Sisters Point, along the west side of Annas Bay, south of Musqueti Point, south of Hoodsport, on the south side of Dewatto Bay, in and north of Lilliwaup Bay, south of Eagle Creek, north of Anderson Cove, and a long stretch of beach south of Chinom Point. Crabbing is good along much of the canal's shoreline, but Annas Bay near the mouth of the Skokomish River and the waters from Union to Belfair are especially productive areas for crab.

Divers like Hood Canal almost as much as shellfish enthusiasts do because there's an almost endless variety of dive spots here. One of the best known is the Octopus Hole, a ledge right alongside U.S. 101 where the big, eight-armed mollusks are abundant. Wolf eels also are common at this popular shore-dive spot located 1.2 miles south of the Lilliwaup Bay bridge and 3.2 miles north of Hoodsport. Farther north is Mike's Beach, a popular destination with diving facilities and several small reefs just offshore. Farther south, a short distance north of Hoodsport, are Sund Rock and the North Wall, a couple of large reefs that offer great opportunities to see octopus, wolf eel, rockfish, and other species. South of that is the diving variety around the mouth of Jarsted Creek, where there are dozens of old pilings and a near-shore reef to investigate.

The Sunrise Beach area, at the north end of Hoodsport, has not only lots of worthwhile bottom structure to investigate but also shoreside diving facilities to make diving access easy. If you prefer to do your fishing from the surface while you're exploring the southern half of the canal, you'll find several good possibilities. Trolling along the shoreline for sea-run cutthroat trout can be very good throughout the canal, and during October and November it fills with chum salmon bound for area hatcheries and local rivers such as the Dosewallips, Duckabush, Hamma Hamma, Skokomish, Tahuya, and Dewatto. Although not well known for its bottomfishing, there are spots in Hood Canal where you can catch quillback, copper, and other rockfish species, along with some lingcod and other bottomfish. Use your chart and depthsounder to find the steep, rocky drop-offs that these species inhabit.

Whether you're digging clams, gathering oysters, sinking pots for crab, jigging for rockfish, trolling for trout, or diving for botttomfish, be sure to consult the Department of Fish and Wildlife's current regulations pamphlet, The rules, seasons, and limits change continually, and you want to be sure you're playing by the rules.

Location: Mason County; map A2, grid j1.

How to get there: Take U.S. 101 north from Shelton to reach the entire west side of the canal. To reach the south side from the Great Bend to the tip, take Highway 106 east from U.S. 101 or west from Belfair. To reach the north side of the canal from the tip to the Great Bend, take Highway 3 to Belfair and turn west on Highway 300.

Boat ramp: Eight boat ramps are available along the lower end of the Hood Canal:

- **Triton Cove State Park:** The northernmost ramp in this part of the canal (also mentioned in the Upper Hood Canal section) is on the west side of the canal, at Triton Cove, where there's a Washington State Parks ramp. This single-lane concrete ramp has a loading float and dock, with room to park about two dozen cars and trailers. Watch for the large rock just out from the ramp, slightly to the south. It's located right alongside U.S. 101 19 miles south of Quilcene. There's a $3 launch fee, with an annual permit available for $40.

- **Mike's Beach Resort:** Located near Lilliwaup, this facility has a launch that will handle boats up to about 22 feet. It's a one-lane concrete ramp with a loading float and limited parking. There's a launch fee depending on the size of the boat. To get there, drive north from Shelton or south from Quilcene to the resort, located between mileposts 317 and 318.

- **Menard's Landing:** There's a one-lane gravel ramp at Tahuya, on the north side of the canal's Great Bend. This Port of Tahuya ramp is best suited to small trailer boats and craft that can be carried to the water. Like the ramp's use, its gravel parking area is limited. Drive west from Belfair on Highway 300, which becomes North Shore Road. Turn north (right) on Belfair-Tahuya Road and go four miles to N.E. Dewatto Road, turning left and driving another quarter mile to Tee Lake Road. Turn right and drive a mile to the Public Fishing sign. You're there.

- **Hood Canal Park (Potlatch) Ramp:** Just south of Potlatch on the west side of the canal is a Tacoma Public Utilities ramp, a two-lane concrete launch with a large, gravel parking lot. It's right alongside the highway and easy to spot when you reach the hydro plant on the other side of the road. Launching is free here, but be very careful of fast-moving traffic from the north when you're turning south out of the lot.

- **Union Ramp:** There's a free ramp with limited parking in the town of Union. It's a two laner that would be very useful if it offered more parking. Take Highway 106 to Union and watch for the yellow storage building. The ramp is on the west side of the building.

- **Twanoh State Park:** The park has a good two-lane ramp with parking for about 20 cars and trailers. There's a $4 launch fee, but an annual permit is available from State Parks for $40. To get there, take Highway 106 west from Belfair or east from U.S. 101 near Shelton. The park and ramp are visible from the road.

- **Port of Allyn Ramp:** Located a mile west of Belfair State Park off Highway 300, this single-lane ramp has a gravel parking area with room for about half a dozen cars and trailers. Launching is free.

- **Summertide Resort:** This private resort and marina is open only from spring to fall. The ramp is adequate for most trailer boats. To reach it, drive 16 miles west from Belfair on Highway 300 and turn left into the resort.

Facilities: Mike's Beach Resort near Lilliwaup has boat and kayak rentals, RV and tent sites, cabins, dormitory-style rooms, and divers' air. Hoodsport & Dive has kayaks rentals, scuba equipment for rent, air fills and dive charters in Hoodsport. Rest-a-While Resort between Hoodsport and Lilliwaup has RV sites, a dry-storage boatyard, and a small store. Hoodsport Marina and Cafe has limited guest moorage and a waterfront restaurant.

A short distance south, on the north edge of Hoodsport, is Sunrise Motel and Restaurant, with nearby moorage facilities. South of Hoodsport is Potlatch State Park, which has RV and tent sites, five mooring buoys, rest rooms, and showers. Hood Canal Marina in Union has guest moorage, power to the docks, fuel (gasoline only), and marine repairs.

To the east is Alderbrook Inn, where you'll find over 2,000 feet of dock space, power to the docks, rest rooms with showers, boat-sewage facilities, boat rentals, a restaurant, swim beach, and other amenities. Farther east, Twanoh State Park has over 190 feet of moorage float space, seven moorage buoys, RV and tent sites, rest rooms with showers, a large, gravel swim beach, picnic tables and cooking shelters, and a small stream with large runs of chum salmon in it during the late fall.

Belfair State Park, about three miles west of Belfair on Highway 300, has over 180 tent and RV sites, but access by boat is limited by the shallow mud flats. To the west is Summertide Resort and Marina, with over 550 feet of moorage docks, rest rooms with showers, RV and tent sites, rental cabins, and a small store.

Water sports/restrictions: All water sports are permitted. Use NOAA nautical chart 18476 when boating on the south half of Hood Canal. Mason County boating regulations include a 6 mph speed limit within 100 feet of any swimmer, within 150 feet of any shoreline or nonmotorized vessel, and within 300 feet of any public boat ramp; an 8 mph speed limit on freshwater lakes from a half hour after sunset to a half hour before sunrise; and a 50 mph speed limit during daylight hours on all waters unless otherwise posted. Water-skiers must stay at least 300 feet from the shoreline on salt water and at least 150 feet from the shoreline on fresh water. All ski/tow traffic must go in a counterclockwise direction.

Contact: Mike's Beach Resort, tel. (360) 877-5324; Rest-a-While Resort, tel. (360) 877-9474; Summertide Resort, tel. (360) 275-2268; Potlatch State Park, tel. (360) 877-5361; Twanoh State Park, tel. (360) 275-2222; Belfair State Park, tel. (360) 275-0668; Washington State Parks and Recreation Commission, tel. (800) 233-0321 (information), tel. (800) 452-5687 (reservations). For nautical charts of this area, contact Captain's Nautical Supply, tel. (206) 283-7242.

84 Dewatto-Area Lakes
Rating: 6

Tee Lake, which covers 38 acres and has a fair amount of development around it, is popular with local water-skiers, PWC riders, and other thrill-seeking boaters, but most of the other lakes in this group are quite small and are most popular with anglers and paddlers. Access to some is so limited that it's difficult to launch anything more than a small rowboat or raft, canoe or kayak. Of the six lakes in this group, Cady happens to be my favorite. Development around its shores is all but nonexistent, and fly-fishing-only regulations help to keep the fishing crowds small. Don't be too surprised if you spot an eagle or two at Cady.

Location: Southwest of Belfair, east side of Hood Canal, Map A2, grid j2.

How to get there: Take Highway 3 to Belfair and turn west on Highway 300 (North Shore Road). Turn north on Belfair-Tahuya Road at the town of Tahuya and drive about four miles to Dewatto Road. Turn west (left) and watch for Tee Lake Road on the right. West of Tee Lake, roads to the left lead to Cady, Don, U, Robbins, and Aldrich Lakes. Watch closely for signs pointing to the respective lakes.

Boat ramp: Except for U Lake, all have small Department of Fish and Wildlife access areas with boat ramps suitable for cartoppers and other small boats.

Facilities: Small stores in the area have groceries and gas, and complete facilities are available in Belfair. Belfair State Park, between Belfair and the lakes on Highway 300, has 33 tent sites and 47 RV sites with water, electricity, and sewer hookups. Lakehaven Manor, a new and interesting bed-and-breakfast, is located on the shores of Cady Lake, and is the only development there.

Water sports/restrictions: All water sports are permitted on Tee Lake, but their small size, limited access, and prohibitions on internal combustion engines restrict activity on the other lakes. Mason County boating regulations include a 6 mph speed limit within 100 feet of any swimmer, within 150 feet of any shoreline or nonmotorized vessel, and

within 300 feet of any public boat ramp; an 8 mph speed limit on freshwater lakes from a half hour after sunset to a half hour before sunrise; and a 50 mph speed limit during daylight hours on all waters unless otherwise posted. Waterskiers must stay at least 300 feet from the shoreline on salt water and at least 150 feet from the shoreline on fresh water. All ski/tow traffic must go in a counterclockwise direction.

Contact: Belfair State Park, tel. (360) 275-0668.

85 Haven Lake

Rating: 7

This 70-acre lake has lots of homes around its shoreline, and like nearby Lake Wooten it gets to be a busy place every summer. Skiers, anglers, and paddlers are on the water early and late, with PWC, tubers, wakeboarders, and swimmers prevalent throughout the day. Everyone has a blast.

Location: Northwest of Belfair, Mason County; map A2, grid j2.

How to get there: Take Highway 3 to Belfair and turn west on Highway 300. Drive about half a mile past Belfair State Park and turn north (right) at the sign pointing the way to Haven and other area lakes. Drive about seven miles to the lake.

Boat ramp: The lake has a public access area with a boat ramp and toilets. A $10 Washington Department of Fish and Wildlife access decal is required to use the public launch areas maintained by the WDFW.

Facilities: The nearest gas, food, and tackle are in Belfair and vicinity. Belfair State Park has tent and RV sites, rest rooms, and showers.

Water sports/restrictions: All water sports are permitted. Mason County

boating regulations include a 6 mph speed limit within 100 feet of any swimmer, within 150 feet of any shoreline or nonmotorized vessel, and within 300 feet of any public boat ramp; an 8 mph speed limit on freshwater lakes from a half hour after sunset to a half hour before sunrise; and a 50 mph speed limit during daylight hours on all waters unless otherwise posted. Water-skiers must stay at least 300 feet from the shoreline on salt water and at least 150 feet from the shoreline on fresh water. All ski/tow traffic must go in a counterclockwise direction.

Contact: Belfair State Park, tel. (360) 275-0668; Washington State Parks and Recreation Commission, tel. (800) 233-0321 (information), tel. (800) 452-5687.

86 Lake Wooten

Rating: 7

From the time it opens to fishing in late April until the summertime sun chasers pack it up at the end of the long Labor Day weekend, there's a lot happening here on this 70-acre Mason County gem of a lake. Many of the folks having fun here are lakeside residents; there's a road all the way around the lake providing access to the dozens of home surrounding it. But that doesn't mean there's not room for you, too. The boat ramp is a good one for launching small to medium-size craft of all kinds, and Lake Wooten is all that far away from boaters throughout the south Puget Sound region.

Location: Northwest of Belfair, Mason County; map A2, grid j2.

How to get there: Take Highway 3 to Belfair and turn west on Highway 300. Drive about half a mile past Belfair State Park and turn north (right) at the sign pointing the way to Wooten and other area lakes. Drive about seven miles to

Haven Lake and continue along its east side another mile to Wooten Lake. The road runs completely around the lake.

Boat ramp: The lake has a boat ramp and access area. A $10 Washington Department of Fish and Wildlife access decal is required to use the public launch areas maintained by the WDFW.

Facilities: Belfair State Park, about a mile to the southeast, has 33 tent sites and 47 sites for RVs that are complete with water, electricity, and sewer hookups.

Water sports/restrictions: All water sports are permitted. Mason County boating regulations include a 6 mph speed limit within 100 feet of any swimmer, within 150 feet of any shoreline or nonmotorized vessel, and within 300 feet of any public boat ramp; an 8 mph speed limit on freshwater lakes from a half hour after sunset to a half hour before sunrise; and a 50 mph speed limit during daylight hours on all waters unless otherwise posted. Water-skiers must stay at least 300 feet from the shoreline on salt water and at least 150 feet from the shoreline on fresh water. All ski/tow traffic must go in a counterclockwise direction.

Contact: Belfair State Park, tel. (360) 275-0668; Washington State Parks and Recreation Commission, tel. (800) 233-0321 (information), tel. (800) 452-5687 (reservations).

87 Panther Lake

Rating: 6

This 100-acre lake was the focus of some heated discussions about personal watercraft a few years ago after some lakeside residents complained that they were getting tired of all the zigging and zagging that the PWC riders were doing here. The issue culminated in the Board of Mason County Commissioners prohibiting the use of PWC on the Mason County portion of the lake. The main complication is that only about one-third of the lake is in Mason County, while the rest of the lake, including the public access area, is in Kitsap County. One limiting factor here is the gravel boat ramp and the rather strange situation where the boat ramp's parking area is located across the road. This catches lots of first-time visitors more than a little off guard, but at least there is some public access.

Location: Kitsap-Mason county line, north of Belfair; map A2, grid j2.

How to get there: Take Highway 3 to Belfair and turn west on Highway 300. About a mile west of Belfair, turn north (right) on Sand Hill Road and drive about seven miles to Gold Creek Road. Turn left and almost instantly you're on Panther Lake Road, which encircles the lake.

Boat ramp: There's a gravel boat ramp on the south side of the lake (with its parking area and rest rooms across the road). A $10 Washington Department of Fish and Wildlife access decal is required to use the public launch areas maintained by the WDFW.

Facilities: Belfair offers the nearest selection of grocery stores, gas stations and other facilities. Belfair State Park, with tent and RV sites, is about eight miles south of the lake.

Water sports/restrictions: All water sports are permitted, EXCEPT that personal watercraft are prohibited on the Mason County portion of the lake. Mason County boating regulations also include a 6 mph speed limit within 100 feet of any swimmer, within 150 feet of any shoreline or nonmotorized vessel, and within 300 feet of any public boat ramp; an 8 mph speed limit on freshwater lakes from a half hour after sunset

to a half hour before sunrise; and a 50 mph speed limit during daylight hours on all waters unless otherwise posted. Water-skiers must stay at least 300 feet from the shoreline on salt water and at least 150 feet from the shoreline on fresh water. All ski/tow traffic must go in a counterclockwise direction.

Contact: Kitsap Sport Shop, Bremerton, tel. (360) 373-9589; Belfair State Park, tel. (360) 275-0668; Washington State Parks and Recreation Commission, tel. (800) 233-0321(information); tel. (800) 452-5687 (reservations).

88 Mission Lake

Rating: 7

The small gravel boat ramp and rather out-of-the-way location of this 88-acre lake near the Kitsap-Mason county border keep the crowds small here most of the time. It's a nice place to ski, fish, paddle, or do whatever it is you like to do on the water, but chances are there won't be many others on the lake doing it with you. For some folks, that's just fine.

Location: West of Gorst, Kitsap Peninsula; map A2, grid i3.

How to get there: Drive to Belfair on Highway 3, turn west on Highway 300, and drive about a mile to Sand Hill Road. Turn north (right) and drive about seven miles to Tiger Lake. Turn right to Tiger-Mission Road, turn north (left), and drive 1.5 miles to the south end of Mission Lake.

Boat ramp: There's a small gravel access area and boat ramp for cartoppers and small trailer boats at the southeast corner of the lake. A $10 Washington Department of Fish and Wildlife access decal is required to use the public launch areas maintained by the WDFW.

Facilities: Belfair has the nearest food, gas, and lodging.

Contact: Belfair State Park, tel. (360) 275-0668; Washington State Parks and Recreation Commission, tel. (800) 233-0321 (information); Kitsap Sport Shop, Bremerton, tel. (360) 373-9589.

89 Tiger Lake

Rating: 6

Like nearby Panther Lake, Tiger was the scene of some fairly wild PWC operation in the mid-'90s, so a group of lakeside residents presented a petition to the Mason County Board of Commissioners, and the board prohibited PWC use on the part of the lake within Mason County. The rule here has more teeth, though, than on Panther, since most of Tiger Lake is in Mason County. If you're a PWC rider, you can find lots of other larger lakes to pursue your sport, and if you happen to be on the anti-PWC side of the fence, this might be one of the lakes you visit just little more often. Take your pick.

Location: North of Belfair, Kitsap Peninsula; map A2, grid i3.

How to get there: Drive to Belfair on Highway 3, turn west on Highway 300, and drive about a mile to Sand Hill Road. Turn north (right) and drive seven miles to the lake, which has roads all the way around it.

Boat ramp: The large gravel access area at the north end of the lake offers room to launch at least three boats at a time. A $10 Washington Department of Fish and Wildlife access decal is required to use the public launch areas maintained by the WDFW.

Facilities: Belfair offers the nearest food, gas, and lodging. Belfair State Park is about seven miles south of the lake.

Water sports/restrictions: All water sports are permitted, EXCEPT that personal watercrafts are prohibited on the Mason County portion of the lake.

Mason County boating regulations also include a 6 mph speed limit within 100 feet of any swimmer, within 150 feet of any shoreline or nonmotorized vessel, and within 300 feet of any public boat ramp; an 8 mph speed limit on freshwater lakes from a half hour after sunset to a half hour before sunrise; and a 50 mph speed limit during daylight hours on all waters unless otherwise posted. Water-skiers must stay at least 300 feet from the shoreline on salt water and at least 150 feet from the shoreline on fresh water. All ski/tow traffic must go in a counterclockwise direction.

Contact: Kitsap Sport Shop, Bremerton, tel. (360) 373-9589; Belfair State Park, tel. (360) 275-0668.

90 Long Lake

Rating: 6

At well over 300 acres, Long has enough room for folks to do what they want, so boating activities of all kinds take place here. Facilities are limited, though, so the boating crowds never seem to get too big or too out of hand.

Location: South of Port Orchard, Kitsap County; map A2, grid i4.

How to get there: Take Highway 16 south from Port Orchard; turn east on Sedgewick Road and south on Long Lake Road, which parallels the east side of the lake.

Boat ramp: The lake has a public access area with boat ramp and toilets. A $10 Washington Department of Fish and Wildlife access decal is required to use the public launch areas maintained by the WDFW.

Facilities: Food, gas, and lodging are available in Port Orchard and a little farther north in Bremerton.

Water sports/restrictions: All water sports are permitted.

Contact: Kitsap Sport Shop, Bremerton, tel. (360) 373-9589.

91 Angle Lake

Rating: 7

This 102-acre lake is just south of Sea-Tac International Airport, with embarrassingly easy access right off bustling Pacific Highway South (Highway 99). It should come as no surprise, then, that it gets some impressive crowds of folks on a warm weekend or summertime afternoon. The county park on its west side has a nice swim beach with lots of grassy real estate where you can throw your towel or blanket between dips in the drink. Away from the swim beach, boat traffic on a sunny day tends to be inner tubes and air mattresses, but some anglers continue to troll and cast here throughout the season.

Location: Southeast of Seattle-Tacoma Airport; map A2, grid j6.

How to get there: Take the 200th Street exit off Interstate 5 near Des Moines and drive west on 200th to Pacific Highway South. Turn north (right) and drive about four blocks to the lake, which is visible on the right.

Boat ramp: There's a King County park with boat ramp on the west side of the lake.

Facilities: The county park has a good swim beach, play equipment, a large lawn area and rest rooms. Food, gas, lodging, and other facilities are available within a few blocks.

Water sports/restrictions: Swimming, paddling and fishing are permitted here. The lake has an 8 mph speed limit.

Contact: King County Parks and Recreation Department, tel. (206) 870-6527; Auburn Sports and Marine, tel. (253) 833-1440.

92 Green/Duwamish River

Rating: 8

Anyone visiting the lower reaches of this river system for the first time and then venturing 20 or 30 miles upstream and seeing it again would have trouble accepting the fact that the two could possibly be the same river. Maybe that's why we give it two names, the Green and the Duwamish. It's easier to accept the many faces of the Green if we call its lower part the Duwamish, so we don't have to think of them as one body of water.

The estuary portion of the Duwamish is deep, slow, and industrialized, so it melds well with Seattle's Elliott Bay, into which it empties. See Entry 67, "South-Central Puget."

As for the moving-water portion of the Green/Duwamish, it has plenty to offer boaters and water recreationists of many kinds. The most attractive part of the river is the well-known Green River Gorge, located some 15 miles east of Auburn not far from the Cascade foothills. Containing nearly three dozen spots offering Class III and even some Class IV rapids, it's a beautiful but challenging 12-mile run that shouldn't be taken lightly when it comes to safety. Very popular with kayakers and rafters, it also draws its share of tubers and others very likely to be underequipped for its big boulders, ledges, and bumpy chutes. It's really too much water for the casual joyriders who venture through it from time to time, often after one too many cold beers on a warm summer day. Places like the Class IV Ledge Drop and Nozzle tend to be unforgiving and unsympathetic in the way they treat boaters, so unprotected tubers may be gobbled up and spit out without ever having a fighting chance.

Most of the kick-back-and-enjoy water is downstream from Flaming Geyser State Park, and especially below the 212th Avenue (Whitney) bridge. This is one of few places along the Green where there's an official spot to launch a boat, complete with a paved parking lot and a flat spot to back a trailer in and slide a drift boat or raft into the river. There are a few sweepers, logjams, and partially submerged roots, stumps, and trees between Whitney and Highway 18, but nothing that a moderate amount of awareness and rowing or paddling ability wouldn't be able to avoid. Like the river above it, this stretch of the Green features a shoreline that is for the most part undeveloped. This is agricultural country, and you're much more likely to see Holsteins than houses along the bank. You will, however, encounter an occasional steelhead or salmon angler, and during the summer months a fair percentage of the anglers here will be fishing from drift boats.

Signs of human activity become more obvious below Highway 18, especially from Auburn downstream. The river doesn't really go downtown until it gets to South Center and Tukwilla, thanks to a lot of high clay banks and the fact that it skirts the edges of Auburn, Kent, and Renton, but you'll no longer have that wilderness feeling on the lower half of the Green/Duwamish.

This lower, urban and suburban section of the river is well channeled between high banks or rock bulkheads, but its meandering nature keeps the flow slow and steady, and there are lots of deep pools that are suitable for swimming and snorkeling. Be sure to do both, preferably where there's a low bank or a gravel bar on at least one side of the river, so there's a gentle slope to get out of the river in case you want or have to in a hurry.

Location: Flows into Elliott Bay and Puget Sound at Seattle; map A2, grid j6.

How to get there: Take Highway 167 to Highway 18 and drive east through Auburn to the Green Valley Road. Follow Green Valley Road east along the river. To fish lower portions of the Green, take Highway 167 between Auburn and Kent and take cross roads off the freeway to reach the river. The estuary portion of the Duwamish is accessible from Elliott Bay, on the Seattle waterfront.

Boat ramp/put-in: There's a four-lane launch ramp with floats at Don Armeni Park, on the west side of Elliott Bay, which provides access to the lower Duwamish. From there upstream there aren't any official boat ramps, but there are several places where river craft may be launched with varying degrees of effort. One such place is immediately upstream of the Highway 18 bridge, off lower Green Valley Road east of Auburn. Another is at the Whitney Bridge, where 212th Avenue SE crosses the river a mile and a half west of Flaming Geyser State Park. Boaters also launch and take out at Flaming Geyser, as well as several miles upstream at Green River Gorge Resort and Kanaskat-Palmer State Park. A $10 Washington Department of Fish and Wildlife access decal is required to use the public launch areas maintained by the WDFW.

Facilities: Boaters in Elliott Bay and the lower Duwamish will find a full array of amenities at Harbor Island Marina, Elliott Bay Marina, and, of course, throughout the Seattle area. Food, gas, lodging, and all other facilities are available in Auburn and Kent for those using upriver portions of the Green/ Duwamish.

Water sports/restrictions: Powerboating, rafting, kayaking, tubing, diving, and swimming all are available. Fishing from a boat is prohibited during the winter steelhead season from November 1 through March 15, but boating is OK during that period.

Contact: Auburn Sports and Marine, tel. (253) 833-1440; Pacific Water Sports, tel. (206) 246-9385.

93 Lake Wilderness

Rating: 7

The name's a little deceiving now because there isn't much wilderness left anywhere in south King County, but this 67-acre lake east of Kent is at least somewhat removed from the hustle and bustle of the big city. It is, that is, until a warm summer weekend, when lots of folks converge on Lake Wilderness and its little county park. The gradual depth increase at the swim beach provides lots of room to swim and wade, so plenty of kids can flock to the place and still leave elbow room for a few more. Anglers turn out here in good numbers during April and May, when Wilderness can be one of the better trout-fishing spots in southeastern King County. On a warm summer evening, it's a great place to launch a canoe or kayak and go for a peaceful paddle.

Location: East of Kent; map A2, grid j7.

How to get there: Take Highway 18 north from Auburn and turn east (right) on Highway 516 (Kent-Kangley Road). Drive about 3.6 miles and turn north (left) at the signs pointing the way to Lake Wilderness Park and Lake Wilderness Golf Course. Drive about a mile and a half to the lake, on the right.

Boat ramp: The lake has a two-lane concrete Washington Department of Fish and Wildlife access area and boat ramp that wasn't in very good shape last time I saw it, along with a King County park where cartoppers and paddle craft may be launched from the beach. A $10

WDFW access decal is required to use the public launch area.

Facilities: The county park has a swim beach and picnic area, as well as playground toys.

Water sports/restrictions: Paddling, swimming, and fishing are the main activities here.

Contact: Auburn Sports and Marine, tel. (253) 833-1440.

94 Lake Desire

Rating: 7

Its location near the population centers of southeastern King County and the fact that it's very shallow and warms quickly with a few summer days make this 70-acre lake near Renton a popular place with water enthusiasts of all kinds. Luckily, there are quite a few other small lakes in the neighborhood to keep Desire from being a total mob scene all summer.

Location: Southeast of Renton; map A2, grid j7.

How to get there: Drive east from Renton on Petrovitsky Road and turn north (left) on 184th Avenue SE and follow it about half a mile to Lake Desire Drive. Turn left and drive one mile to the lake.

Boat ramp: The lake has a public access with a new fishing dock and boat ramp at its north end. The water at the boat ramp is shallow, so be careful when launching a powerboat here. A $10 Washington Department of Fish and Wildlife access decal is required to use the public launch areas maintained by the WDFW.

Facilities: Other facilities are available in Renton.

Water sports/restrictions: All water sports are permitted.

Contact: Auburn Sports and Marine, tel. (253) 833-1440.

95 Spring (Otter) Lake

Rating: 7

The public access area here is on the small side, so there isn't much room for cars with boat trailers. What's more, the boat ramp is even more confining, so it keeps the big boys with their big boats from getting very interested in Spring Lake. That's OK with the folks who use the lake regularly, most of whom are out either for a little peaceful fishing action or a few quiet hours paddling the shoreline of this 67-acre lake between Kent and Renton. The lake is a change of pace from the usual hectic lifestyle in this busy part of King County. All that human activity is going on nearby, but you can get away from it here without having to go anywhere.

Location: Southeast of Renton; map A2, grid j7.

How to get there: Drive east from Renton on Petrovitsky Road and turn north (left) on 196th Avenue SE. Turn left again on S.E. 183rd Street and drive to Spring Lake Drive. The lake is on the left.

Boat ramp: A public access areas and boat ramp are located near the northeast corner of the lake. A $10 Washington Department of Fish and Wildlife access decal is required to use the public launch areas maintained by the WDFW.

Facilities: The nearest amenities are in Kent, Renton and Maple Valley.

Water sports/restrictions: Paddling and fishing are the primary water sports here.

Contact: Auburn Sports and Marine, tel. (253) 833-1440.

96 Shadow Lake

Rating: 6

The strangest thing about this 40-acre lake east of Renton is that you have to navigate a long, narrow canal between the boat ramp and the main body of the lake. Actually, "navigate" isn't an accurate description, since the canal is pretty much a straight shot, and there's no chance you could wander off course unless you were really screwed up in the head. Anyway, the short trip from access area to lake is part of the adventure in visiting this small King County lake, best known for the strings of panfish and occasional large bass it produces for persistent anglers. It's also a nice place to explore by canoe or kayak or if you're interested in a place where you can stretch your arms in a small rowboat.

Location: Northeast of Kent; map A2, grid j7.

How to get there: Drive east from Renton on Petrovitsky Road and turn south (right) on 196th Avenue SE then east (left) on 213th Street. The lake is on the left.

Boat ramp: There's a boat ramp at the north end of the lake. A $10 Washington Department of Fish and Wildlife access decal is required to use the public launch areas maintained by the WDFW.

Facilities: All other facilities are available in Renton.

Water sports/restrictions: Paddling and fishing are the best bets here.

Contact: Auburn Sports and Marine, tel. (253) 833-1440.

97 Lake Meridian

Rating: 7

This 150-acre lake near Kent became a part the city in 1996, and with that annexation came a little law and order that was welcomed by many lake residents. Things were, in the estimation of some, getting dangerously out of control before that. Lake regulations such as following a counterclockwise pattern when skiing or PWC riding on the lake are now generally followed. The 8 mph speed limit after 6 p.m., which used to be ignored by some, is also being more rigidly enforced, so it's once again safe to venture onto the lake in a canoe or small fishing boat during a warm summer evening without feeling that you might be putting your life on the line. The county swim beach is a good one and very popular with South King County swimmers and parents looking for a safe place to take the youngsters wading and splashing around.

Location: Southeast of Kent; map A2, grid j7.

How to get there: Take Kent-Kangley Road (Highway 516) east from Kent about three miles until to you see the lake right alongside the road on your left. Turn left into the county park at the lake's southeast corner or go a block past it to the light and turn left to reach the Department of Fish and Wildlife boat ramp on the east end of the lake.

Boat ramp: The county park has bank access and a boat ramp that closes at sunset, while the WDFW ramp is open 24 hours. A $10 WDFW access decal is required to use the public launch area.

Facilities: The county park has a large swim beach, fishing pier, picnic area, and playground toys.

Water sports/restrictions: All water sports are permitted. The speed limit drops to 8 mph at 6 p.m. daily.

Contact: Auburn Sports and Marine, tel. (253) 833-1440.

98 Benson Lake

Rating: 7

The main public access to this lake is via the Department of Fish and Wildlife access area on the east side, and it sometimes gets more than a little crowded. The gravel access site isn't very big to begin with, and the bank drops right off into deep water, so fishing can be good here. Sometimes boaters trying to launch and anglers trying to fish from shore get in each other's way, but the situation hasn't resulted in any knockdown, drag-out fist fights, at least not yet. Being considerate of others here will help to keep potential hostilities to a minimum. And if you do decide to launch here or use a corner of the access area for a quick dip, you'd best be sure to have one of those $10 access decals from the Department of Fish and Wildlife. They're now required of anyone using WDFW launch/access areas, and it won't go unnoticed here if you should try to sneak in without one.

Location: Southwest of Allyn in Mason County; map A2 inset, grid j2.

How to get there: Take Highway 3 north from Shelton or south from Belfair and turn west on Mason Lake County Park Road. Turn left on East Benson Road and almost immediately turn right into the public access area.

Boat ramp: The gravel access area on the east side of the lake has a gravel boat ramp and room for several cars and boat trailers. A $10 WDFW access decal is required to use the public launch area.

Facilities: Twanoh State Park to the north on Hood Canal offers tent and RV sites, rest rooms, and showers.

Water sports/restrictions: Paddling, rowing, and fishing are the main attractions. Since 1996 the lake has had a prohibition on internal combustion engines.

Contact: Verle's Sport Center, tel. (360) 426-0933; Twanoh State Park, tel. (360) 275-2222.

99 Mason Lake

Rating: 9

At nearly 1,000 acres, this is the largest body of fresh water for miles around, so it stands to reason that's it's also one of Shelton and Mason Counties most popular summertime water holes. There's room to ski, room to swim, room to fish, room to tube, room to ride PWC, and on a warm day all of these things are happening, and more. Even with all that room, though, the boats sometimes seem to get close together on holiday weekends and during other peak-use periods. Mason County authorities patrol the lake regularly and pay special attention to folks who forget or don't know about the counterclockwise ski pattern rule. Do it right and you won't be the one all the other skiers point to when the marine patrol guys show up. Oh yes, one more word of warning: you may have to wait in line to get in and out of the water here, especially on busy weekends. The boat ramp at the county park is the only public ramp on this huge lake, and it's sometimes a bottleneck. You may have to be patient in getting your boat in and out of the water, and you may also have trouble finding a place to park if you get there late in the day.

Location: Southwest of Allyn, Mason County; map A2, grid j2.

How to get there: Take U.S. 101 to Shelton and exit east onto Highway 3, through Shelton, and continue northeasterly on Highway 3 to Mason-Benson Road, about 11 miles out of Shelton. Turn left and drive about three miles to the lake.

Boat ramp: There's a two-lane concrete-plank boat ramp with a loading float at Mason Lake County Park near the north end of the lake. The ramp area has a large gravel parking area.

Facilities: The county park has a gravel swim beach, picnic area, and other amenities. Twanoh State Park is only a few miles to the north and has over 60 tent and RV sites.

Water sports/restrictions: All water sports are permitted here. Mason County boating regulations include a 6 mph speed limit within 100 feet of any swimmer, within 150 feet of any shoreline or nonmotorized vessel, and within 300 feet of any public boat ramp; an 8 mph speed limit on freshwater lakes from a half hour after sunset to a half hour before sunrise; and a 50 mph speed limit during daylight hours on all waters unless otherwise posted. Water-skiers must stay at least 300 feet from the shoreline on salt water and at least 150 feet from the shoreline on fresh water. All ski/tow traffic must go in a counterclockwise direction.

Contact: Verle's Sport Center, tel. (360) 426-0933; Twanoh State Park, tel. (360) 275-2222; Washington State Parks and Recreation Commission, tel. (800) 233-0321 (information), tel. (800) 452-5687 (reservations).

100 Trails End (Prickett) Lake

Rating: 6

Most of this somewhat hidden lake south of Hood Canal is no more than 20 feet deep, so it warms quickly with the summer sun. Unfortunately, it also fills up fairly fast with pads and other aquatic vegetation as it warms, so boating gets increasingly difficult as summer progresses. The vegetation problem and the small size of the boat ramp and parking lot keep most of the big boats off, so it's a decent place to find safe and quiet canoeing.

Location: West of Allyn, Mason County; map A2, grid j3.

How to get there: Drive south from Belfair or north from U.S. 101 near Shelton on Highway 106 and turn east on Trails Road (sign points the way to Mason Lake Road). Go a mile and a half, turn left on Trails End Road, and drive half a mile to the lake's access area on the left.

Boat ramp: There's a small gravel parking lot and gravel boat ramp at the access area. Both have very limited room, and the boat ramp tends to clog with dollar pads late in the summer. A $10 WDFW access decal is required to use the public launch area.

Facilities: Twanoh State Park, about six miles to the west on Highway 106, has 47 tent sites and 18 RV spaces with hookups, rest rooms and showers. Restaurants, fast food, lodging, and other facilities are available in Belfair.

Water sports/restrictions: All water sports are permitted. Mason County boating regulations include a 6 mph speed limit within 100 feet of any swimmer, within 150 feet of any shoreline or nonmotorized vessel, and within 300 feet of any public boat ramp; an 8 mph speed limit on freshwater lakes from a half hour after sunset to a half hour before sunrise; and a 50 mph speed limit during daylight hours on all waters unless otherwise posted. Water-skiers must stay at least 300 feet from the shoreline on salt water and at least 150 feet from the shoreline on fresh water. All ski/tow traffic must go in a counterclockwise direction.

Contact: Twanoh State Park, tel. (360) 275-2222.

101 Devereaux Lake

Rating: 7

I've described lots of spots as "nice places to visit, but wouldn't want to live there," but Devereaux isn't one of those places. In fact, I would like to live there. If I did, I'd be the only one living there because except for the public access area on the south side of the lake and the Girl Scout camp on the other side, there's no development on this 94-acre lake near Allyn. You can't say that about very many western Washington lakes, especially lakes this large that happen to be located a few yards from a major state highway. Yes, if I lived on the shores of Devereaux Lake, I'd have it much to myself throughout most of the year. Ah yes, what a pleasant thought . . . but back to reality.

The small, rough boat launch, tiny access area, and a restriction on gas-powered motors all help to keep larger craft off the lake, and there are only a couple of times when its surface gets what anyone would describe as busy. One is during the first few weeks of the general fishing season in late April and May because this is one of Mason County's better prospects for big rainbow trout. The second busy time is when all the kids from the scout camp take off across the lake on their traditional swim. The first time I witnessed it I wasn't sure what the heck was happening, but later I discovered that it's a kind of rite of passage for kids who are about to end their weekly stay at the camp. I guess the deal is that if you can make it through the swim alive, you get to go home; if you drown in the lake, you have to stay. Anyway, except for the possibility of being swamped by a school of young swimmers, Devereaux is a safe and relaxing place to paddle, row, troll, or whatever slow-moving activity you like to do on the water. But don't even think about building your dream home there; I've already staked out the prime spots for myself.

Location: North of Allyn, Mason County, map A2, grid j3.

How to get there: Take Highway 3 south from Belfair or north from Allyn and turn west onto Devereaux Road; drive about one-quarter mile to the lake on the left.

Boat ramp: The Department of Fish and Wildlife has a large access area with a concrete boat ramp near the north end of the lake. A $10 Washington Department of Fish and Wildlife access decal is required to use the public launch areas maintained by the WDFW.

Facilities: Both Belfair and Twanoh State Parks are within reasonable driving range, and both have tent and RV sites, rest rooms, and showers. Food, gas, and lodging are available both to the north and south on Highway 3.

Water sports/restrictions: Paddling, rowboating, and fishing are the main attractions. Gasoline engines are prohibited here as of 1997.

Contact: Belfair State Park, tel. (360) 275-0668; Twanoh State Park, tel. (360) 275-2222; Washington State Parks and Recreation Commission, tel. (800) 233-0321 (information), tel. (800) 452-5687 (reservations).

102 Wye Lake

Rating: 8

At only 38 acres, Wye Lake came very close to being left out of this book because of its small size and limited boating possibilities. What's more, it has houses and summer cottages around its entire shoreline, so you wouldn't think it's a very scenic place to visit. But there are things about this little lake in southern Kitsap County that just make it a place you should see at least once, and you should see it from the water. The folks who cleared their property and built their homes here seem to have gone out of their way to keep the place looking as natural as possible. It's also quiet here, thanks in part to the fact that internal combustion engines aren't allowed on the lake, so you have to get around by electric power, wind power, or muscle power. It's a nice place to fish and a great place to paddle on a calm summer evening. In case you wonder about the name, it used to be Y Lake, because the lake is shaped like the next-to-last letter of the alphabet. At the risk of sounding like Dr. Seuss, they changed the name from Y to Wye, I don't know why.

Location: Southwest corner of Kitsap County, southeast of Belfair; map A2, grid j3.

How to get there: From the east take Highway 16 to Bethel and turn west on Lider Road, drive about two miles to Lake Flora Road, and turn left. Drive about four miles to Dickenson Road and turn south (left), following it about three miles to where it makes a hard right and becomes Carney Lake Road. Another hard right in the road quickly follows, and at that point you turn right onto Wye Lake Boulevard. Take the first left and drive down the hill about 200 yards to the boat ramp on the right. From the west take Highway 3 south from Bremerton or north from Belfair and turn east onto Lake Flora Road. Turn south (right) onto Dickenson Road and follow it to Wye Lake Boulevard.

Boat ramp: There's a gravel access area and concrete boat ramp at the south end of the lake, with pit toilets and enough room to park maybe a dozen cars. A $10 Washington Department of Fish and Wildlife access decal is required to use the public launch areas maintained by the WDFW.

Facilities: The nearest food and gas are about four miles to the south.

Water sports/restrictions: Paddling, fishing, and swimming are the main activities here. Gas-powered engines are prohibited on the lake.

Contact: Kitsap Sport Shop, Bremerton, tel. (360) 373-9589.

103 Carney Lake

Rating: 6

Its small size (only 39 acres) almost kept this rural Pierce County lake from making the cut for this book, but then it occurred to me that some of its limitations are what make it just the kind of place that some boaters might seek out. Popular with anglers in the spring, it closes to fishing on the first of July and doesn't reopen until the first of September. That means if you want to visit it just for the sake of paddling around and enjoying the scenery and not be bothered by anglers, this is a good one to visit in the summer. What's more, there's a year-round prohibition on gas motors here, so you never have to see, hear, or smell an outboard if that kind of thing bothers you. Throw in the fact that Carney has only a few homes scattered along its shores, with lots of waterfowl and other wildlife in abundance, and you might just find this a very worthwhile destination for your next canoe or kayak trip.

Location: Kitsap-Pierce county line, southeast of Belfair; map A2, grid j3.

How to get there: Take Highway 16 to Purdy and turn west on Highway 302. Less than a mile after passing the sign pointing to the Minter Creek Salmon Hatchery, turn west (right) at the intersection where the sign points toward Shelton. Drive about three miles to Wright-Bliss Road and turn north (right). Go north on Wright-Bliss Road just over two miles to the lake.

Boat ramp: There's a rather rough gravel access area and boat ramp on the lake's west side. A $10 Washington Department of Fish and Wildlife access decal is required to use the public launch areas maintained by the WDFW.

Facilities: The nearest gas and groceries are at a BP station where you turn onto Wright-Bliss Road.

Water sports/restrictions: Paddling, fishing and other small-boat uses are the main draws. Internal combustion engines are prohibited on the lake.

Contact: Kitsap Sport Shop, Bremerton, tel. (360) 373-9589.

104 Horseshoe Lake

Rating: 6

I've raved about the big bed of water lilies here in a previous book, but it's worth mentioning again. If you decide to visit this lake in early summer, take a camera, because the pink and white lilies are absolutely gorgeous. You can row or paddle right up to them if you want, but try not to do any damage. The county park here is one of southern Kitsap County's favorite swimming spots, so keep it in mind on a warm summer weekend. At only 40 acres, Horseshoe doesn't get very much big-boat traffic, so it's also a nice place to paddle or fish from a small boat. It's well off the beaten path as far as car traffic is concerned, so even though it has a fair amount of development around it, it doesn't get too busy in the summer.

Location: Kitsap-Pierce county line, northwest of Purdy; map A2, grid j4.

How to get there: Take Highway 16 to Purdy and turn west on Highway 302. Cross the tip of Henderson Bay at Wauna and continue about two miles to 94th Avenue NW. Turn north (right) and drive 1.4 miles to the boat ramp, which is immediately past the county park, on the right.

Boat ramp: There's a large gravel access area and boat ramp at the southwest corner of the lake. A $10 Washington Department of Fish and Wildlife access decal is required to use the public launch areas maintained by the WDFW.

Facilities: Horseshoe Lake County Park offers a nice swim beach and picnic area, as well as rest rooms.

Water sports/restrictions: Paddling, swimming, and fishing are the primary activities.

Contact: Kitsap Sport Shop, Bremerton, tel. (360) 373-9589.

105 Lake Fenwick

Rating: 7

Located at the western edge of the Green River Valley between the sprawling cities of Kent and Federal Way, you might expect this little 18-acre lake to be a hellhole of noise and craziness on a pleasant summer weekend, but not so. With no real development on its shores and a prohibition against the use of gasoline motors on its waters, Fenwick remains a quiet little pond where you can get away for some aquatic R&R while enjoying a morning of casting for trout or paddling the shoreline to take in the natural sights. There's a lot of bird life here, so you can always find something to draw your attention. If there's any human noise or commotion, it will probably be coming from the fishing dock near the boat ramp.

Location: Southwest of Kent; map A2, grid j6.

How to get there: Take Interstate 5 to the South 272nd exit north of Federal way and drive east on 272nd. As you start down the hill look for the Lake Fen-

wick Road and turn north (left) and watch for the lake on the right.

Boat ramp: There's a small boat ramp, managed by the City of Kent, on the west side of the lake.

Facilities: All amenities are available to the east in Kent and to the southwest in Federal Way.

Water sports/restrictions: Paddling and fishing are the main draws here. Gas-powered motors are prohibited.

Contact: Auburn Sports and Marine, tel. (253) 833-1440.

106 North Lake

Rating: 8

This 55-acre south King County lake is one of the area's more popular, especially among early season trout anglers, so you might want to avoid it from late April to late May if you're looking for an uncrowded lake to do some peaceful paddling or a place to water-ski without wiping out several dozen of your fellow Homo sapiens. The two-lane boat ramp and parking area are completely blacktopped and have served the area well since being redesigned and rebuilt in the early '80s.

Location: West of Auburn; map A2, grid j6.

How to get there: Take Interstate 5 to the South 320th exit in Federal Way and turn east on 320th. Drive half a mile, turn south (right) on Weyerhaeuser Way, and go about half a mile to the access area on the left.

Boat ramp: There's a Department of Fish and Wildlife boat ramp with beach access for fishing and wading. A $10 WDFW access decal is required to use the public launch area.

Contact: Auburn Sports and Marine, tel. (253) 833-1440.

Facilities: Food, gas, lodging, and other

amenities nearby in Federal Way.

Water sports/restrictions: All water sports are permitted.

107 Lake Morton

Rating: 6

The lake's relatively small size (66 acres) and powerboat restriction keep things quiet and peaceful here, so it's a good place to paddle, row, fly-fish, and generally pursue life's more peaceful forms of water recreation. The lake's quiet nature is further enhanced by the fact that its fishing season runs year-round, eliminating some of the commotion that commonly occurs around the last Saturday in April, when the general fishing season opens on many waters. Things kick up a little in early May, when Morton gets its annual plant of hatchery rainbow trout, but after a few weeks things get back to normal, and peace once again reigns here.

Location: East of Auburn; map A2, grid j8.

How to get there: Drive east from Covington on Covington-Sawyer Road and take the second road to the south (right) to the lake.

Boat ramp: There's a good boat ramp with beach access on the northwest corner of the lake. A $10 WDFW access decal is required to use the public launch area.

Facilities: Auburn and Kent, a half dozen miles to the west, have a complete assortment of stores, accommodations, and other facilities.

Water sports/restrictions: Paddling, sailing, swimming, and fishing are the options. Gas motors are not allowed on the lake.

Contact: Auburn Sports and Marine, tel. (253) 833-1440.

108 Lake Sawyer

Rating: 8

With a year-round fishing season, a county park and private resort on its shores, and easy access from the population centers of south King County, it's easy to understand Lake Sawyer's popularity among water lovers. With swimming, skiing, fishing, boarding, PWC riding, and virtually everything else going on here, it gets hectic at times, especially on holiday weekends and during any extended period of nice weather from May to September. The swim beach at Sunrise Resort is a nice one and is especially busy at times. It's a large lake, covering nearly 280 acres, with plenty of open water for the big-boat folks, yet some reedy backwaters where paddlers and small-boat enthusiasts might want to explore and view wildlife.

Location: Northwest of Black Diamond; map A2, grid j8.

How to get there: Drive east from Kent on Kent-Kangley Road (Highway 516) and turn south (right) on 216th Avenue SE, which is about three miles east of Highway 18. Just over a mile down 216th, turn east (left) on Covington-Sawyer Road to the lake.

Boat ramp: There's a paved boat ramp at the northwest corner of the lake. A resort has rental cabins and trailers, RV sites, boat and canoe rentals, and a country store.

Facilities: Sunrise Resort on the lake's west side has cabins and trailers, RV and tent sites, boat and canoe rentals, and a small store. Lake Sawyer Store a short distance away has additional groceries, fishing tackle, and other supplies. Food, gas, lodging, and the rest of the requirements are a few miles to the west in Kent, Renton, and Auburn.

Water sports/restrictions: All water sports are permitted and popular here.

Contact: Sunrise Resort, tel. (253) 630-4890; Auburn Sports and Marine, tel. (253) 833-1440.

109 Lake Twelve

Rating: 5

Although well off the beaten path for most folks, this 45-acre lake near the small town of Black Diamond can be worth the drive if you're looking for a place that's peaceful and quiet. It's a nice place for a quiet paddle, and it might be a good idea to take a fishing rod along, since fishing for a variety of species here can be good. The down side here is that the lake is getting smaller lately, thanks to rampant weed growth around its shoreline. By late summer the weeds are thick and actually limit the boating opportunities quite substantially.

Location: Northeast of Black Diamond; map A2, grid j8

How to get there: Take Highway 169 north from Enumclaw to Black Diamond and turn east on Green River Gorge Road. Turn north (left) on Lake Twelve Road (270th Avenue SE) about a mile and a half out of Black Diamond.

Boat ramp: The lake has a boat ramp and toilets at its public access area. A $10 WDFW access decal is required to use the public launch area.

Facilities: Food and gas are available in and around Black Diamond. Kanaskat-Palmer State Park, about four miles to the east, has limited tent and RV sites, rest rooms and showers.

Water sports/restrictions: Paddling and fishing are the best bets.

Contact: Auburn Sports and Marine, tel. (253) 833-1440; Kanaskat-Palmer State Park, tel. (360) 886-0148.

LAKE CHELAN

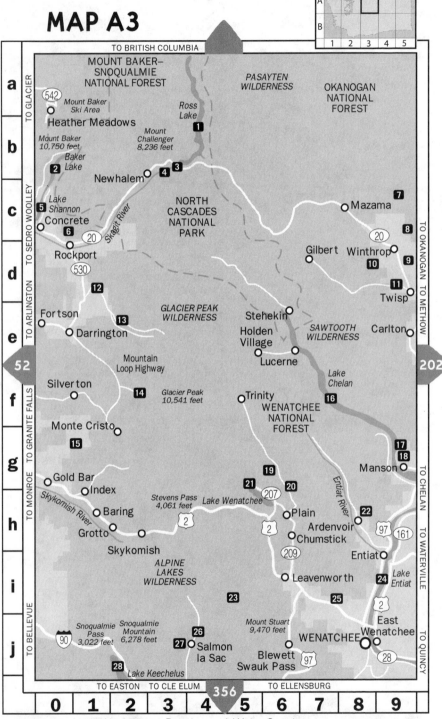

MAP A3

TO BRITISH COLUMBIA

MOUNT BAKER–
SNOQUALMIE
NATIONAL FOREST

PASAYTEN
WILDERNESS

OKANOGAN
NATIONAL
FOREST

a

542
Mount Baker
Ski Area

Heather Meadows

Ross
Lake
1

b

Mount Baker
10,750 feet
Baker
Lake

2

Mount
Challenger
8,236 feet
4 **3**

Newhalem

NORTH
CASCADES
NATIONAL
PARK

7

c

Lake
Shannon

5

Concrete
6

20

Skagit River

Mazama

8

20

Gilbert Winthrop

10

9

TO OKANOGAN   TO METHOW

d

Rockport

530

12

11

Twisp

e

Fortson

13

Darrington

GLACIER PEAK
WILDERNESS

Stehekin

Holden
Village

Lucerne

SAWTOOTH
WILDERNESS

Carlton

52

Mountain
Loop Highway

Lake
Chelan

202

f

Silverton

14

Glacier Peak
10,541 feet

Trinity

WENATCHEE
NATIONAL
FOREST

16

g

Monte Cristo

15

17

18

Manson

h

Gold Bar

Index

Skykomish River

Baring

Grotto

Skykomish

Stevens Pass
4,061 feet

2

Lake Wenatchee

21

207

19

20

Plain

2

Entiat River

Ardenvoir

Chumstick

209

22

97 161

TO CHELAN   TO WATERVILLE

Entiat

ALPINE
LAKES
WILDERNESS

Leavenworth

24

Lake
Entiat

i

23

25

j

90

Snoqualmie
Pass
3,022 feet

Snoqualmie
Mountain
6,278 feet

26

27 Salmon
la Sac

28 Lake Keechelus

Mount Stuart
9,470 feet

Blewett
Swauk Pass

97

WENATCHEE

East
Wenatchee

28

TO QUINCY

TO EASTON   TO CLE ELUM   **356**   TO ELLENSBURG

TO GLACIER   TO SEDRO WOOLLEY   TO ARLINGTON   TO GRANITE FALLS   TO MONROE   TO BELLEVUE

0 1 2 3 4 5 6 7 8 9

CHAPTER A3

◼ Ross Lake

Rating: 7

If I had to pick Washington's ultimate getaway boating spot, Ross Lake would certainly be among the finalists if not the hands-down winner. It's one of the state's biggest bodies of fresh water, yet there's virtually no development along its shores and almost nothing in the way of facilities for boaters and other visitors. Access by any means other than by foot is limited to the extreme north and south ends of the lake, and even at those locations there are limitations that keep many would-be visitors from bothering to try.

The reservoir created by the construction of Ross Dam on the Skagit River is over 20 miles long, extending across the border into British Columbia at its north end. If you want to use your own powerboat on the lake, that's where you have to go to launch it; the lake's only boat ramp (actually two of them a short distance apart) is at Hozomeen Campground, which is on the east side of the lake on the Washington side of the border, but you have to trailer up into Canada and turn back south into Washington to reach it. From there you're free to fish, explore the lake, or boat camp at any of the several lakeside campsites along both shores. This is true pioneer boating, since there are no fuel docks or other facilities except down at Ross Lake Resort at the south end. Paddlers have the same option of hauling their craft up to Hozomeen and paddling downlake, but they may also get to the lake from the south side, since Ross Lake Resort does offer a portage service around Ross Dam and onto the lake. The resort has several cabins and bunkhouses right on the water, with rental boats, canoes, and kayaks for the guests.

If all this sounds like too much hassle, that's what keeps Ross Lake the way it is. It's big, but it's desolate; it's near, but it's far away; it's there to be enjoyed, but not without considerable effort; it's a place where all boats are welcome, but boating traffic is light. As I said, it might be Washington's ultimate boating getaway.

Location: East end of Whatcom County; map A3, grids a4 and b4. (See Ross Lake inset map.)

How to get there: Take Exit 230 off Interstate 5 at Burlington and drive 68 miles east on Highway 20 to Diablo. Catch the Seattle City Light tugboat at 8:30 a.m. or 3 p.m. to the base of the dam, where you'll be picked up and ferried to the resort. Hikers may continue east on Highway 20, past Diablo to the trailhead east of the lake. Some 10 campsites are scattered along the trail to about two-thirds of the way up the lake. (A water taxi service from the resort is also available to take you to any of these campsites.) If trailering a boat to the north end, take Interstate 5 to Bellingham and turn east on Highway 539 to Sumas. Continue east on Canada Highway 401 to Silver Creek cutoff two miles west of Hope; then drive south, back across the border to Hozomeen on the east side of the lake.

Boat ramp and boaters' campgrounds: The boat ramp and these campgrounds are listed on the Ross Lake inset map:

- **Ross Lake Resort**
- **Green Point Campground**
- **Cougar Island Campgound**
- **Roland Point Campground**

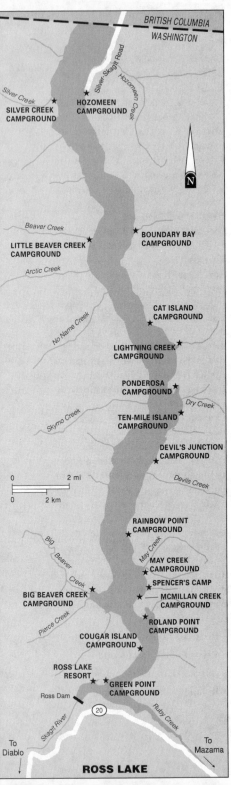

ROSS LAKE

- **McMillan Creek Campground**
- **Spencer's Camp**
- **May Creek Campground**
- **Big Beaver Creek Campground**
- **Rainbow Point Campground**
- **Devil's Junction Campground**
- **Ten-Mile Island Campground**
- **Ponderosa Campground**
- **Lightning Creek Campground**
- **Cat Island Campground**
- **Little Beaver Creek Campground**
- **Boundary Bay Campground**
- **Silver Creek Campground**
- **Hozomeen Campground:** The only boat ramp on the lake is at the north end at Hozomeen Campground.

Facilities: Ross Lake Resort, near the dam at the south end, has cabins and bunkhouse units for over 80 guests; boats (14-footers with 9.9 horsepower outboards), canoes, and kayaks for rent; and a water taxi for backpackers and hikers; but bring your own food. Hozomeen Campground, at the north end, has RV and tent sites, rest rooms, and drinking water.

Water sports/restrictions: All water sports are permitted.

Contact: Ross Lake Resort, tel. (206) 386-4437 (Seattle phone number); Ross Lake Ranger Station, North Cascades National Park, tel. (360) 873-4590.

2 Baker Lake

Rating: 8

At nearly 3,600 acres, this impoundment on the Baker River is a vast water resource that most Washingtonians never see or take advantage of. That's because it's so far from where most of us live. You don't stumble onto Baker Lake by accident when you're on your way to somewhere else; it *is* somewhere else. Because of its large size, high elevation, and the fact that it fills with chilly river water all spring, it's slow to warm in the summer. That keeps most boaters, swimmers, and skiers away until the Fourth of July holiday, but from then until Labor Day it gets steady use from folks who have discovered all it has to offer.

And it has a lot. Its immense size alone makes it a worthwhile destination for folks who like to get out and explore by water, and quite a few folks come here just to cruise and take in the mountain scenery. Many paddlers do the same, some of them launching at one campground ramp and making their way up or down the lake to another, perhaps camping at a spot in the middle to make it a multiday trip. Several small bays and stream mouths along the way add to the interesting possibilities. As the lake warms, the PWC riders, water-skiers, wakeboarders, and swimmers make their appearance, usually in that order. Although the water never gets what most of us would call warm, it is refreshing, and swimming is an option at all the lakeside campgrounds as well as Baker Lake Resort. Anglers in search of kokanee find good fishing from spring to early fall.

If there's a downside, it's that boaters have to keep an eye on the weather because it can affect the big lake in a hurry. The wind can come whistling up the lake, even during summer, so don't let it catch you off guard.

Location: North of Concrete in the Mount Baker National Forest; map A3, grid b0.

How to get there: Take Highway 20 east from Interstate 5. About five miles east of Hamilton, turn north (left) on Baker Lake Road and follow it about 17 miles to the first of several roads leading right toward the lake.

Boat ramp: The lake has no fewer than six boat ramps, four maintained by the U.S. Forest Service, one by Puget Sound Energy, and one by the Trillium Corporation. Five are along the lake's west side; the sixth is near the dam at the extreme south end.

Facilities: Baker Lake Resort, about two-thirds of the way up the west side of the lake, has boat moorage, boat rentals, a large swim beach, cabins, RV and tent sites, a picnic area, rest rooms, play equipment, and a convenience store. Forest Service campgrounds at Horseshoe Cove, Panorama Point, and Shannon Creek are on the lake, and Park Creek Campground is a short distance from the water. All have tent and RV sites and water. Other amenities are back on Highway 20 in Hamilton and Concrete.

Water sports/restrictions: All water sports are permitted.

Contact: Mount Baker-Snoqualmie National Forest, Mount Baker Ranger District, tel. (360) 856-5700.

3 Diablo Lake

Rating: 7

Although less than one-tenth the size of immense Ross Lake immediately to the north, Diablo holds its own when come to attracting boaters and other water lovers. That's probably because its location right along Highway 20 and the availability of two boat ramps make it much each easier to get to with a boat than the bigger Ross Lake. At nearly 1,000 acres, Diablo would be considered a large lake if were located anywhere but in the shadow of the huge impoundment immediately upstream. Like Ross on the upstream side and Gorge Lake just downstream, Diablo is the result of a dam on the upper Skagit River. The canyon it filled is a deep one, and there are places in the lake with depths of 300 feet, so the water stays cool even in summer. But it's a fascinating place to explore, with its canyon walls and nearby mountains in every direction. And because if its size, there's room for everyone to play without getting in each other's way. The campgrounds and resort all provide opportunities for swimming.

Location: On the Skagit River immediately south of Ross Lake, southeast corner of Whatcom County; map A3, grid b4.

How to get there: Exit Interstate 5 at Burlington and drive east about 68 miles on Highway 20.

Boat ramp: There's a two-lane concrete ramp with a loading float at Colonial Creek Campground near the south end of the lake. Diablo Lake Resort has a ramp for customer use.

Facilities: Diablo Lake Resort has tent and RV sites, rest rooms, and showers. Colonial Creek Campground offers more than 150 tent and RV sites, rest rooms with showers, moorage floats, and a picnic area. Buster Brown, Hidden Cove, and Thunder Point Campgrounds are also on the lake's shoreline.

Water sports/restrictions: All water sports are permitted.

Contact: Diablo Lake Resort, tel. (206) 386-4429 (Seattle number).

4 Gorge Lake

Rating: 6

Limited facilities and the fact that Diablo Lake is right next door and Ross Lake is only a few miles away keep the crowds small on this long, skinny reservoir. It's the farthest downstream and the smallest of three Skagit River impoundments. Long, thin, and deep, it covers just over 200 acres. As its name suggests, it has steep hillsides rising almost vertically from its shoreline to the sky, so the scenery is limited.

Location: On the Skagit River immediately downstream from Diablo Lake, southeastern Whatcom County; map A3, grid b3.

How to get there: Take Interstate 5 to Burlington and turn east on Highway 20, following it to the lake.

Boat ramp: There's a one-lane concrete-plank ramp at Gorge Lake Campground.

Facilities: Gorge Lake Campground has tent and RV sites, picnic tables, fire pits, and vault toilets.

Water sports/restrictions: All water sports are permitted. The upper (east) end of the lake often has a noticeable current that boaters should be aware of.

Contact: Mount Baker-Snoqualmie National Forest, Mount Baker Ranger District, tel. (360) 856-5700.

5 Lake Shannon

Rating: 6

The Baker River isn't very big, but it provides the water for both 2,100-acre Shannon and its younger, larger sibling, Baker Lake. Between the two of them they offer more than 5,600 acres for boaters to play on and explore. Shannon is within easier reach of folks from the Puget Sound population centers, but for my money it's not quite as interesting as the bigger reservoir immediately upstream. And its facilities for boaters, including boat ramps, are more limited. While Baker has four places to launch boats of various sizes,

Shannon has only one, near its south end about three-quarters of a mile above the dam. But Shannon does warm a little faster in the summer, so it might be a better bet for that first-of-the-year tubing trip or ski weekend. Watch out of the fishermen, though; Shannon is a favorite haunt of Whatcom and Skagit County kokanee anglers from spring through midsummer.

Location: Immediately north of Concrete, Skagit County; map A3, grid c0.

How to get there: Drive east from Interstate 5 on Highway 20 to the town of Concrete. Turn north on Baker River Road, which parallels the east side of Lake Shannon.

Boat ramp: There's a boat ramp maintained by Puget Sound Energy at the southeast corner of the lake, at the end of a gravel road to the left off Baker River Road. The single-lane gravel ramp has a large parking area with room for several dozen cars and trailers.

Facilities: There's a motel in Concrete and an RV park just off Highway 20 on Baker Lake Road.

Water sports/restrictions: All water sports are permitted.

Contact: North Cascade Inn, tel. (800) 251-3054; Creekside Camping, tel. (360) 826-3566.

6 Upper Skagit River

Rating: 8

Many folks who have seen and boated all or most of the Skagit will tell you that this upper portion, from the base of Gorge Dam downstream to Concrete and the mouth of the Baker River, is the best part, and I would have to agree. This is about as close to God's country as you can get on a river whose very flow is controlled by man and his machines. Even with a well-traveled highway along its northern bank and three dams immediately upstream determining what the river levels will be the day you're there, much of this stretch of river will give you the feeling that you're somewhere wild.

The river is gentle, except during periods when a lot of water is spilling over the dams and the flow balloons to 4,000 or 5,000 cubic feet per second. During the normal flow of 1,500 to 3,000 feet, it's mostly Class I water with a few Class II rapids and one stretch of Class III tumblers above the mouth of Copper Creek, visible from the highway as you go upstream to launch. Folks who like the thrill of this bumpy water usually launch at the Goodell Creek Campground and float down to the ramp at Copper Creek, a run of nearly 10 miles. Or by continuing on to Marblemount, they can add about six miles of Class I and Class II water to the trip. The trip from the Department of Fish and Wildlife's Marblemount boat ramp down to Howard Miller Steelhead Park at Rockport or on through to the Fabor's Ferry ramp east of Concrete is even more gentle and will take you through the famous Skagit River Bald Eagle Natural Area.

Making this trip from about Thanksgiving until the end of February will afford the opportunity to see dozens of bald eagles along the river. This stretch is the winter home to one of the largest eagle populations in the Lower 48. The birds congregate to feast on the carcasses of pink and chum salmon that wash up on the gravel and sand bars along several miles of river. Commercial eagle-watching trips are available from several companies named earlier in this listing.

Location: From Concrete upstream to Gorge Dam; map A2, grid c0.

How to get there: Take Interstate 5 to Burlington and turn east on Highway 20. The highway follows the Skagit upriver nearly 60 miles to Diablo Dam.

Boat ramp: There are six boat ramps along this stretch of the Skagit:

- **Fabor's Ferry Ramp:** The Washington Department of Fish and Wildlife's Fabor's Ferry ramp is a one-lane concrete launch located about five miles east of Concrete, off Highway 20. To reach it, drive east from concrete about five miles on Highway 20 and turn right onto an unmarked gravel road, following it to its end at the edge of the river. A $10 WDFW access decal is required to use the public launch areas maintained by the Washington Department of Fish and Wildlife.

- **Howard Miller Steelhead Park:** Farther upstream, near Rockport, is the Howard Miller Steelhead County Park, managed by Skagit County Parks and Recreation. Accumulations of sand sometimes clog this ramp. Drive nine miles east from Concrete on Highway 20 to Rockport, and turn right toward the river.

- **Skagit River Bald Eagle Natural Area Ramp:** This access area and ramp, which were all but washed out as of spring 1999, are located off Highway 20.

- **Marblemount Ramp:** WDFW-maintained, this ramp lies beneath the Cascade River bridge across from Marblemount. It's another one where large amounts of sand sometimes pile up and make launching difficult.

- **Copper Creek Ramp:** This ramp is located at the mouth of Copper Creek about five miles east of Marblemount.

- **Goodell Creek Campground:** Although this campground does not have a formal ramp, paddlers and steelhead anglers sometimes carry or drag their boats to the water here.

It's located right alongside Highway 20 a mile and a half west of Newhalem.

Facilities: Rockport State Park has about 50 RV sites and 10 tent sites, rest rooms and showers. There are also two private RV parks/resorts near Rockport. The Totem Trail Motel is also found in the same town. Rockport Country Store has groceries, tackle, and river information. Several rafting companies offer trips on the upper Skagit, especially for winter eagle-watching excursions.

Water sports/restrictions: All river sports are permitted.

Contact: Rockport Country Store, tel. (360) 853-8531; Rockport State Park, tel. (360) 853-8461; Washington State Parks and Recreation Commission, tel. (800) 233-0321 (information), tel. (800) 452-5687 (reservations); Alpine Adventures, tel. (800) 926-7238; Downstream River Runners, tel. (360) 805-9899; Redline River Adventures, tel. (800) 290-4500; River Recreation, Inc., tel. (800) 464-5899; Wild and Scenic River Tours, tel. (800) 413-6840.

◼ Chewack (Chewuch) River

Rating: 6

Depending on how long a run you make and what stretch of river you pick, you can just about make a trip down the Chewack as tough or as easy as you want. A run from Camp 4 Campground down to Falls Creek Campground or beyond to the mouth of Cub Creek would likely be the easiest, as there are no rapids tougher than Class III along this stretch. Upstream there's a Class IV section near the mouth of Lake Creek, and downstream there's a rock wall stretching across the entire river a short distance upstream from Winthrop.

Unless you're an experienced paddler, I wouldn't run that low rock dam. The rapids up at Falls Creek are rated Class IV. This is a small river that tends to move right along, so even seemingly docile rapids and holes can sneak up on you if you react and adjust too slowly. Another potential danger here comes from off the steep bank. It's not unusual to come around a tight corner or through a boulder garden and find yourself staring at all or part of a pine tree across the river. Always be on the lookout for such obstacles, both while you're paddling and where possible, as you're driving up the river to launch.

Location: Flows into Methow River at Winthrop; map A3, grid c9.

How to get there: Take Highway 20 to Winthrop and drive north up Chewack Road (Forest Service Road 51) or Eastside Chewack Road (Forest Road 5010).

Boat ramp: Calling them boat ramps might be a stretch, but there are places where you can drag/carry a kayak or small raft to the river with varying amounts of sweat involved. One is just below the mouth of Andrews Creek about 21 miles up Forest Service Road 51/5160; another is two miles downstream near the mouth of Lake Creek. It's easier at Camp 4, Chewack and Falls Creek Campgrounds, and some people also launch or take out along the road between Cub Creek and Eightmile Creek, a few miles upstream from Winthrop.

Facilities: There are five U.S. Forest Service campgrounds scattered along the river between Winthrop and Thirtymile Campground. There are several motels and a couple of RV parks in Winthrop, as well as food, gas, and other amenities.

Water sports/restrictions: Kayaking, rafting, fishing, and some tubing are the draws here.

Contact: Okanogan National Forest, tel. (509) 826-3275; Pine-Near Trailer Park, tel. (509) 996-2391; Methow Valley KOA Campground, tel. (509) 996-2258; Chewuch Inn, tel. (509) 996-3107.

8 Pearrygin Lake

Rating: 8

Long a favorite of Okanogan County trout anglers, Pearrygin over the past decade or so also has become a popular destination for skiers, PWC riders, and others who like their boating a little more fast paced. The slow trollers and the fast planers butted heads over use of the lake for a few years; then in 1995 Okanogan County's commissioners enacted what they thought was a workable compromise. Unlike most lakes in the county, which allow skiing and PWC riding until 9 p.m. on Wednesday, Friday, and Saturday during the summer, the cutoff for their use on Pearrygin is 6 p.m. throughout the fishing season. That season runs from the fourth Saturday in April through the end of October. Now the lake's anglers, paddlers and other flat-water enthusiasts can use the lake early in the morning and all evening without having to compete with the faster movers. Limiting them to only nine hours a day on the water doesn't seem to have bothered the lake's skiers and PWC operators very much, either; they still turn out at the state park and both private resorts in large numbers all summer. One thing you may notice if you're not a PWC enthusiast is that the noise from these zigzagging craft seems to be amplified at Pearrygin, thanks to the echoing effect of the nearby hills. It starts sounding as though you're in some kind of weird sound chamber when large numbers of the fast little craft get going in every direction.

Location: Northeast of Winthrop; map A3, grid c9.

How to get there: Take Highway 20 to Winthrop and drive northeasterly from town about two miles to the lake.

Boat ramp: There's a boat ramp at Pearrygin Lake State Park, another at Derry's Resort, one at Jeffrey's Silverline Resort, and a fourth at the Department of Fish and Wildlife's public access area. The state park ramp has one lane with a loading float and parking for about 30 cars with trailers. There's a $4 launch fee (and a $40 annual permit available) if you're not camping at the park. The ramp at Derry's Resort also is one lane, but it has no loading float. The ramp at Jeffrey's Resort is unpaved and has a couple of loading floats. A fee is charged to launch at both resorts. The Department of Wildlife boat ramp is gravel and has room for about two dozen cars and boat trailers. A $10 WDFW access decal is required to use the public launch areas maintained by the Washington Department of Fish and Wildlife.

Facilities: Derry's Resort has RV sites with full hookups, tent sites, rental cabins, motor boats, and paddle boats for rent, playground equipment, a large swimming area, convenience store, RV dump station and a large lawn area near the water. Jeffery's Resort has RV and tent sites, rest rooms with showers, a swim beach, and small store. Other amenities are available in Winthrop.

Water sports/restrictions: All water sports are permitted. Waterskiing and PWC riding are limited to the hours of 9 a.m. to 6 p.m. during fishing season, which runs from late April through October.

Contact: Pearrygin Lake State Park tel. (509) 996-2370 (April to November); Derry's Pearrygin Lake Resort, tel. (509) 996-2322.

9 Davis Lake

Rating: 4

It goes without saying that at only 40 acres, this isn't one of Washington's boating meccas, but like nearby Cougar and Campbell Lakes, it has an interesting fishing season that keeps the anglers and the nonanglers from ever having any reason for conflict. You see, when the weather is warm and the sun seekers want to use the lake, the anglers are gone, because the fishing season here opens September 1 and runs through the end of March. The lake freezes over in the winter when anglers are here, so most boaters aren't interested then anyway. Isn't it nice when things work out to everybody's advantage?

Location: Southeast of Winthrop; map A3, grid d9.

How to get there: Take Highway 20 to Winthrop and drive southeast out of town on the east side of the Methow River to Bear Creek Road. Drive east on Bear Creek Road to Davis Lake Road and turn south (right). Drive about a mile on Davis Lake Road to the lake on the right.

Boat ramp: On the east side of the lake is a single-lane gravel ramp managed by the Department of Fish and Wildlife. A $10 Washington Department of Fish and Wildlife access decal is required to use public launch areas maintained by the WDFW.

Facilities: Motels, RV parks, restaurants, grocery stores, and other facilities are nearby in Winthrop.

Water sports/restrictions: Paddling and fishing are permitted.

Contact: Pine-Near Trailer Park, tel. (509) 996-2391; Methow Valley KOA Campground, tel. (509) 996-2258; Chewuch Inn, tel. (509) 996-3107.

10 Patterson Lake

Rating: 7

While Pearrygin Lake anglers and paddlers are waiting patiently for 6 p.m. to roll around and spell the end of another day for skiers and PWC riders, those who pursue more casual boating pursuits at Patterson Lake already are going about their business of having fun on the water. That's because this lake has had a no-wake, 8 mph speed limit for years, so the speed lovers must go to Pearrygin and other places. That may limit the boating possibilities on this 130-acre Okanogan County lake, but it is kinda nice to have a place where peace and quiet rule. It seems that there are fewer and fewer of those places these days.

Location: Southwest of Winthrop; map A3, grid d9.

How to get there: Take Twin Lakes Road southwest from Winthrop, then west on Patterson Lake Road about four miles to the lake.

Boat ramp: There's a public access area with rest rooms and a boat ramp. A $10 Washington Department of Fish and Wildlife access decal is required to use public launch areas maintained by the WDFW.

Facilities: Patterson Lake Resort has boat rentals, tent and RV sites, cabins and other amenities. Other amenities are available in Winthrop, a few miles to the south.

Water sports/restrictions: Paddling and fishing are the main attractions here. The lake has an 8 mph speed limit.

Contact: Patterson Lake Resort, tel. (509) 996-2226.

11 Twisp River

Rating: 6

The same thing that makes this a difficult stream for anglers to fish makes it a challenging river for boaters to navigate, but a few do it every year during the high water of spring and early summer. There are no real eddies, no pools, none of the places where anglers like to cast for resting trout. Those are also the places where boaters like to stop to rest a bit on their way through a run, but the Twisp has almost none of them. The 1999 season here was a long one, thanks to the heavy snowpack of the previous winter, but usually we're talking about a window of perhaps six weeks when there's enough water in the Twisp to provide a safe but invigorating run. It's mostly Class II water, with a couple of Class III spots, but the whole thing is one long series of boulders and small chutes, so you have to work the entire time. Spring runs also mean the possibility of downed trees and other debris in the river, so be alert and stop to scout where you can; there won't be many opportunities.

Location: Joins the Methow River at the town of Twisp; map A3, grid d9.

How to get there: Take Highway 20 to Twisp and turn east on Twisp River Road, which follows the river upstream for miles.

Boat ramp: There are no official ramps on the river, but it's possible to carry a small boat to the river from Twisp River Road in several locations.

Facilities: U.S. Forest Service campgrounds at War Creek, Mystery, Poplar Flat, and South Creek offer about three dozen tent and trailer sites altogether, with the largest number available at War Creek and Poplar Flat. These two larger campgrounds also have drinking water, which isn't available at South Creek or Mystery. Food, gas, lodging, RV parks, and other facilities are available in and around Twisp, including Riverbend RV Park just north of town.

Water sports/restrictions: Kayaking and trout fishing are the main attractions.

Contact: Okanogan National Forest, Twisp Ranger District, tel. (509) 997-2131; Riverbend RV Park, tel. (509) 997-3500.

12 Sauk River

Rating: 8

From Darrington down it's clear sailing —er, paddling—over Class II water. The Sauk gets smaller as summer progresses, so most folks run it in the spring and early summer when snowmelt keeps it flowing at 4,000 to 6,000 cfs, enough to give a good ride and less contact with the river's resident boulders.

Location: Flows northward to join the Skagit River near Rockport; map A3, grid d1.

How to get there: Take Interstate 5 to Burlington and turn east on Highway 20, following it to Rockport. Turn south (right) on Highway 530 at Rockport and follow it up the Sauk River Valley to Darrington. An alternate route is to turn east off Interstate 5 on Highway 530 near Arlington and follow it to Darrington. The Mountain Loop Highway and Darrington-Clear Creek Road trace the east and west sides of the Sauk, re-

spectively, upstream from Darrington.

Boat ramp: The most commonly used put-in/take-out spots are at Bedal Campground, White Chuck Campground at the mouth of the White Chuck River, the Sauk Prairie bridge at Darrington, the mouth of the Suiattle River between Darrington and Rockport, and the Sauk Park access area about four miles downstream from the mouth of the Suiattle.

Facilities: Several whitewater outfitters offer guided trips on the Sauk, including Wild and Scenic River Tours, Downstream River Runners and Alpine Adventures. Rockport State Park, located near the mouth of the Sauk on the north bank of the Skagit River, has 50 RV sites with hookups and a limited number of tent sites, as well as rest rooms with showers. U.S. Forest Service campgrounds located at Clear Creek and Bedal also have tent and RV sites. Food, gas, tackle, and fishing licenses are available in Darrington.

Water sports/restrictions: Kayaking, rafting, and canoes are OK on some stretches.

Contact: Wild and Scenic River Tours, tel. (800) 413-6840; Downstream River Runners, tel. (360) 805-9899; Alpine Adventures, tel. (800) 926-7238; Sauk River Sporting Goods, tel. (360) 436-1500; Mount Baker-Snoqualmie National Forest, Darrington Ranger District, tel. (360) 436-1155; Rockport State Park, tel. (360) 853-8461; Washington State Parks and Recreation Commission, tel. (800) 233-0321 (information), tel. (800) 452-5687 (reservations).

13 Suiattle River

Rating: 8

Since it runs through a flatter, more gentle valley than some of the other rivers in the area, the Suiattle is a user-friendly stream, a favorite of intermediate-level paddlers on their own as well as people who prefer to book a commercial trip and let someone else do much of the thinking and make most of the arrangements. The 27-mile stretch of river from Sulphur Creek Campground down to the river mouth and beyond can be cut into two nearly equal parts at the Forest Service Road 25 bridge, so it's up to the paddler to decide whether to make the upper run or the lower one. The difference in terms of challenge is slight, but the upper run is rated Class III and the lower only a Class II. Both are lots of fun, with relatively little danger except for the possibility of getting wet from spray in a few places. The Suiattle usually has enough water in it to support year-round or nearly year-round floating, which also adds to its popularity. So does the mountainous scenery on a clear day.

Location: Joins the Sauk River north of Darrington; map A3, grid e2.

How to get there: Take Highway 530 east from Interstate 5, through Arlington, then through Darrington. Right after the highway crosses the Sauk River about seven miles north of Darrington, take the first right, on Forest Service Road 26, which follows the Suiattle upstream.

Boat ramp: The most commonly used launch sites are at Sulphur Creek Campground and the Forest Service Road 25 bridge just off Forest Service Road 25. Boaters who launch at the bridge usually float the entire lower Suiattle and into the Sauk, where they take out at the Highway 530 bridge, about a mile below the mouth of the Suiattle.

Facilities: There's a U.S. Forest Service campground with tent and RV sites, rest rooms, and picnic tables at

Buck Creek, about 16 miles upriver. Food and gas are available in Darrington. Some commercial rafting companies run the Suiattle, including Alpine Adventures, Redline River Adventures, and Wild and Scenic River Tours.

Water sports/restrictions: All river sports are permitted.

Contact: Alpine Adventures, tel. (800) 926-7238; Redline River Adventures, tel. (800) 290-4500; Wild and Scenic River Tours, tel. (800) 413-6840; Sauk River Sporting Goods, tel. (360) 436-1500; Mount Baker-Snoqualmie National Forest, Darrington Ranger District, tel. (360) 436-1155.

14 White Chuck River

Rating: 7

It's not very big, but it can be nasty, so it's recommended for serious paddlers only. There are a couple of steep drops that are quite challenging, and the appearance of logs and debris in the river after a period of flooding can make it downright dangerous. Ask around or follow someone who knows the river, and don't be too proud to portage.

Location: Flows into the Sauk River southeast of Darrington; map A3, grid f2.

How to get there: Take Highway 530 east from Interstate 5 to Darrington, cross the Sauk River just east of town and turn south on the Mountain Loop Highway (Forest Service Road 22). Cross the White Chuck River at its confluence with the Sauk River and turn east (left) upstream.

Boat ramp: It's possible to carry a boat to the water near the mouth of Crystal Creek about six miles above the mouth of the White Chuck, and you can take out at the confluence of the White Chuck and Sauk.

Facilities: There are U.S. Forest Service campgrounds with tent and trailer sites to the north at Clear Creek and to the south at Bedal, both on the Sauk River.

Water sports/restrictions: The river's size makes it mainly a kayaks-only stream.

Contact: Sauk River Sporting Goods, tel. (360) 436-1500; Mount Baker-Snoqualmie National Forest, Darrington Ranger District, tel. (360) 436-1155.

15 Spada Lake (Sultan Reservoir)

Rating: 7

If you're looking for a big lake in the mountains where you can get out and stretch your paddling muscles without having to buck the wakes or hear the sputtering of big gas-powered boats, Spada may be your dream come true. Many of the lakes with no-gas-motor regulations are smaller ones, but Spada covers nearly 1,900 acres, so you can paddle to your heart's content here. This Sultan River impoundment serves as a source of drinking water down in the lower country, so that's part of the reason for the special boating rules. Another reason is that the reservoir has a wild population of resident rainbow and cutthroat trout, with special fishing regulations in place to discourage anglers from hammering them too hard. Combine these restrictions with the fact that the lake is well off the main highway, and it's easy to understand why it's a good place to find peace, solitude, and quiet boating. Oh yes, and on a clear day it affords a magnificent view of surrounding mountains.

Location: Northeast of Startup, Snohomish County; map A3, grid g0.

How to get there: Take U.S. 2 to Sultan; about a mile east of town turn north on Sultan Basin Road, following it about 15 miles to the lake.

Boat ramp: There's a boat ramp near the east end of the lake.

Facilities: The nearest food, gas, lodging, and tackle are back on U.S. 2 in the towns of Sultan and Monroe.

Water sports/restrictions: Paddling, fishing, and sailing are the best possibilities. Internal combustion engines are prohibited, but it's one of the few lakes with selective fishing regulations where electric motors are allowed.

Contact: Sky Valley Traders, tel. (360) 794-8818; Mount Baker-Snoqualmie National Forest, Skykomish Ranger District, tel. (360) 677-2414.

16 Lake Chelan

Rating: 10

The rating system doesn't go any higher, so Chelan gets a 10. If ever there was a 10 among the hundreds of good ones in Washington, this has to be it. Period. Many of the premier destinations of the world fall victims to their own popularity, but it hasn't happened here; it's almost as though the more people who come here to enjoy it, the better it gets for everyone. Maybe that's because the lake is so big that it never gets crowded, a likely explanation when you consider the fact that it's 55 miles long. And it's not only long, but deep, too. Would you believe there's a place where the lake's bottom is 1,486 feet from its surface? In places the lake bottom is nearly 400 feet below sea level.

But as Al Bundy or someone once said, size isn't everything, and Chelan has a great deal going for it besides its impressive dimensions. The lakeside scenery isn't bad, either, especially a few miles up the lake where pine-covered slopes dominate the picture. And then there's the beautiful weather, which is about the best you could hope for when most folks come to visit—clear skies and warm temperatures. Drop a crystal-clear 55-mile-long lake into a setting like that and you have the recipe for a perfect boating and water sports destination. OK, I know I'm starting to sound like some TV commercial, but I can't help it. This place has everything a water enthusiast could want.

If you like, you need only hang around the warm, shallow flats near the bottom end of the lake. That's where most of the people and most of the facilities are, and it's a great place to play in the sun. This is the warmest part of the lake, so swimming and other nonmotorized fun are a big deal here. This is an especially good place to play if you like to spend part of your time on or in the water and part of it poking around stores, restaurants, and other places where you can spend your money. If you do your boating on this eastern end of the lake, though, be aware of the buoy line that marks the strict no-wake zone. The line is several hundred yards from the end of the lake, and marine enforcement patrols keep a close eye on it; if you get overanxious and hit the throttle before passing the buoys, you're setting yourself up for trouble. Many serious boaters, though, like to get away from town and venture up-lake, and you have over 50 miles of up-lake to venture in here. Off they go, big inboards, cigarette boats, sailboats, PWC, outboards with trolling motors and downriggers, ski boats, kayaks, canoes, and just about anything else that floats. They're all popular and part of the boating scene at Chelan.

Besides the obvious things to do on a boat on such a huge body of water, many boaters take advantage of all the side trips and other activities around the lake. Wildlife watching is a great option, since mule deer, black bear, mountain goats, and bighorn sheep may be visible along the water's edge or prowling the pine-covered hills that surround it. Boat camping is also big, and there are several places to camp. Besides Lake Chelan and 25-Mile Creek State Parks, the possibilities include Lake Shore Park, Mitchell Creek, Deer Point, Safety Harbor Creek, Big Creek, Corral Creek, Graham Harbor, Prince Creek, Domke Falls, Refrigerator Harbor, Lucerne, Moore Point, Flick Creek, Manly Wham Campground, Weaver Point, and Purple Point. Needless to say, many of these fill up early during long weekends and at the height of the summer. Domke Falls, on the south side of the lake about three-quarters of the way up, is a worthwhile destination, and you can even hit the nearby trail to Domke Lake if you feel particularly energetic.

At the upper end of the lake, Stehekin is a worthy boating destination on its own, even if it weren't located on the shores of Washington's most intriguing lake. You can tour the old town or take a bus tour up the Stehekin Valley. Trout fishing is good in the Stehekin River, and some adventurous paddlers even find ways to take their kayaks to the Stehekin and run the river. The fishing on Lake Chelan is some of the best in eastern Washington and includes the very real possibility of boating a trophy-class chinook salmon or lake trout. The big lake produced a new state-record laker in 1999. The big ones are caught by trolling in the deeper parts of the lake, but nearshore fishing produces good catches of plump rainbow trout and hard-fighting smallmouth bass.

I've really only scratched the surface (no pun intended) when it comes to boating and playing opportunities at Chelan, but you get the idea. Heck, I didn't even mention parasailing (until now) or some of the other options. The rest is up to you; trailer your boat to Chelan and discover some of the other possibilities on your own.

Location: Stretches from town of Chelan to Stehekin, Chelan County; map A3, grid f7.

How to get there: Take Interstate 97 north from Wenatchee all the way to the south end of the lake or turn north (left) on Navarre Canyon Road and follow it to Lake Chelan State Park, about a quarter of the way up the lake.

Boat ramp: The lake has five public boat ramps. The Chelan County PUD's Riverwalk Park ramp and the City of Chelan's Lakeshore Marina ramp are both in the town of Chelan. The Riverwalk ramp, a free two laner with a loading float and room for 14 cars with trailers, is reached by turning on Farnham Street next to Chelan High School and following it about 200 yards to Emerson Street, which leads down a short hill to the ramp. The Lakeshore Marina ramp is on the left side of Highway 150 as you drive north out of town. It's also a two laner with floats, and has a $3 launch fee and $2 parking fee. The Manson Parks and Recreation District manages the lake's biggest and best ramp, a spiffy, four-lane concrete job with three loading floats and room for well over 100 vehicles. It's located just off Highway 150 at Wapato Lake Road, across the road from Mill Bay Casino. There's no use fee. Lake Chelan State Park and 25-Mile Creek State Park also have ramps, both single laners with loading floats. The launch fee at both is $4 round-trip, with $40 annual permit available that lets the user launch at any Washington State Parks ramp. Launching is free at the state parks if you're camping there.

Facilities: The Caravel Resort is right on the lake and within walking distance of the Riverfront Park boat ramp and all the shops and restaurants in downtown Chelan. Many of its units have fully equipped kitchens, and all are a few steps from the lake. If you want to soak away the sore muscles after playing all those fish, try one of the Jacuzzi suites. Reservations are recommended for the summer months. RV and tent spaces are available at Lake Chelan State Park, but in summer most spaces are reserved far in advance. There are also private RV parks and campgrounds in and around Chelan. Moorage is available at Lakeshore Marina, Manson Bay Park, Mitchell Creek, Deer Point, Big Creek, Safety Harbor, Corral Creek, Graham Harbor, Prince Creek, Domke Falls, Refrigerator Harbor, Lucern, Holden Village, Moore's Point, and Stehekin Landing, not to mention several waterside motels that also have moorage slips. Boat fuel is available in six locations, including 25-Mile Creek (about one-third of the way up the lake) and Stehekin (at the extreme north end). Camping is available at 14 locations along the lake's shore, including two state parks and several Forest Service sites. There are four marine pump-out facilities on the lake. Several boat-rental offices have everything from sailboards and personal watercraft to sailboats and houseboats. Charters for fishing, touring, diving, and sightseeing are available in and around the town of Chelan. If you want to see all of Lake Chelan, including a short stay in Stehekin at the head of the lake, from a boat other than yours, the tour boats *Lady of the Lake II* and *Lady Express* make their runs from Chelan daily during the summer, and the faster *Lady Express* also makes several runs per week during the off-season. Round-trips run $22 per person on the slower boat, $41 per person on the *Express.*

Water sports/restrictions: All water sports are permitted.

Contact: The Chelan Chamber of Commerce, tel. (800) 4-CHELAN; Lake Chelan Boat Company (*Lady of the Lake* trips), tel. (509) 682-2224; Caravel Resort, tel. (509) 682-2582 or tel. (800) 962-8723; Washington State Parks and Recreation Commission, tel. (800) 233-0321 (information), tel. (800) 452-5687 (reservations); Stehekin Lodge, tel. (509) 682-4494.

17 Wapato Lake

Rating: 7

Those of us who live within the marine influence of western Washington are missing several things that eastern Washington residents may take for granted. Sure, you'll say, summertime sun is a good example. Yes, but I'm talking about something else; I'm talking about turtles. That's right, turtles-those strange reptiles that carry their campers on their backs. While they're relatively rare on the west side of Washington's Cascades, they're quite common on the east side, and perhaps nowhere are they more common than Wapato Lake. Paddle, row, or slowly motor along the lake's shoreline during the summer and you'll see lots of them. I get excited with every one I see, which may say something about how enter-taining my life is, but I think it's just because I don't get to see them that often in my own stomping grounds. Anyway, if you visit Wapato during any of the warmer months, you'll see turtles. You'll also see one of the prettiest lakes in Chelan County, as far as I'm concerned. Not too heavily developed, the lake looks much the same as it did when I first saw it some 40 years ago and probably the way it looked 40 years before that. At nearly 190 acres, it's big enough to allow folks to pursue their favorite boating activities, but small enough to have a friendly, cozy feel to it. If you're visiting nearby Lake Chelan and want a change of pace, Wapato may be worth a two-day side trip.

Location: North of Manson, east side of Lake Chelan; map A3, grid g9.

How to get there: Take Highway 150 from Chelan toward Manson and turn right on Swartout Road. Go two miles and turn right again on Wapato Lake Road, which parallels the entire southwest side of the lake. To reach the public access area and Paradise Resort, turn north on East Wapato Lake Road and drive 0.1 mile to both facilities on the left.

Boat ramp: There's a public access area and a boat ramp on the lake and three private campgrounds with boat ramps. A $10 WDFW access decal is required to use the public launch areas maintained by the Washington Department of Fish and Wildlife.

Facilities: Kamei Resort, Paradise Resort, and Wapato Lake Campground offer dozens of RV and tent sites, cabins, swim beaches, rest rooms with showers, boat rentals, convenience stores, and other amenities.

Water sports/restrictions: All water sports are permitted.

Contact: Kamei Resort, tel. (509) 687-

3690 (spring to fall); Paradise Resort, tel. (509) 687-3444; Wapato Lake Campground, tel. (509) 687-6037.

18 Roses Lake

Rating: 4

Its relatively small size (130 acres) and lack of scenery or facilities make Roses one of Chelan County's lightly used lakes, except by anglers. Long famous for its good trout fishing, the addition of several warm-water species in recent years keeps anglers coming back, but recreational boating isn't a big deal here. The restrictive speed limit early and late in the day during the summer may also be a factor. It's an OK place to ski during the day, but the boat ramp is in disrepair, and some folks with ski boats are likely scared away by the possibility of getting stuck or doing damage to their boats or trailers.

Location: North of Manson, east side of Lake Chelan; map A3, grid g9.

How to get there: Take Highway 150 from Chelan toward Manson; turn right on Swartout Road, right on Wapato Lake Road, and drive three miles to Roses Avenue. Turn left on Roses Avenue and drive three-quarters of a mile to Green Avenue, following it 0.4 mile to the boat ramp on the right.

Boat ramp: The southeast end of the lake has a single-lane ramp and a large dirt access area with room for at least a dozen cars and trailers. It's a Department of Wildlife access, and a $10 Washington Department of Fish and Wildlife access decal is required to use all public launch areas maintained by the WDFW.

Facilities: Everything you may need is available in Chelan, a few minutes away to the south.

Water sports/restrictions: The rules are posted on a large sign near the boat ramp, but for the record, there's a 3 mph speed limit on the lake at all times from November 1 through the end of March. During the rest of the year, that 3 mph limit is in effect from 6 p.m. to 7 a.m.

Contact: Kamei Resort, tel. (509) 687-3690; Paradise Resort, tel. (509) 687-3444; Wapato Lake Campground, tel. (509) 687-6037.

19 Chiwawa River

Rating: 6

Long the stomping grounds of trout anglers and hunters in search of grouse and mule deer, the pine flats east of Lake Wenatchee are seeing more and more cars with boat racks on top as larger numbers of paddlers from all over Washington learn about and converge on this little Wenatchee River tributary that provides an interesting change of pace from what most folks come to this part of the state to enjoy. Sure, the Wenatchee is perhaps the best boating river in the state, and the Chiwawa doesn't compare, but that's exactly what makes it worth a look. It's small water, best run when spring runoff brings it up to at least 1,000 cfs flow. That's when you'll find a lot of Class II and Class III rapids that require quick moves and fast thinking to keep you off the rocks. There's a manmade obstacle in the form of a wood-and-pipe weir across the river near Plain, so watch for the signs and be ready to portage on the right side of the river. Other than that, it's a good ride for paddlers of intermediate skills or better.

Location: Flows into the Wenatchee River southeast of Lake Wenatchee; map A3, grids g6 and h6.

How to get there: Drive east from Stevens Pass or west from Leavenworth on U.S. 2 and turn north on Highway 207 near Lake Wenatchee. At Nason Creek Campground turn east (right) onto Highway 206 and follow it about four miles southeast to Plain. Turn north on Chiwawa River Road (Forest Road 62) and follow it for miles up the river.

Boat ramp: There are several places along Chiwawa River Road to launch a kayak or small raft, the most popular of which is just upstream from Grouse Creek, about 12 miles upstream from Plain. Most boaters run all the way into the Wenatchee to take out, but three bridges across the Chiwawa provide takeouts for shorter trips.

Facilities: Lake Wenatchee State Park is the closest thing to a full-service campground in the area, but it doesn't have any RV hookups. The nearest food, gas, lodging and other facilities is in Leavenworth.

Water sports/restrictions: This is a kayaker's river.

Contact: Wenatchee National Forest, Lake Wenatchee Ranger District, tel. (509) 763-3103; Lake Wenatchee State Park, tel. (509) 763-3101; Washington State Parks and Recreation Commission, tel. (800) 233-0321 (information), tel. (800) 452-5687 (reservations).

20 Fish Lake

Rating: 7

This 500-acre gem in the high country above Lake Wenatchee is best known for its year-round trout and perch fishing, but it's also a beautiful summertime boating destination. One of the prettiest lakes in eastern Washington,

it also happens to be in one of the prettiest settings, a combination that in itself makes the long trip here from western Washington worth the trouble. The downside is the shortage of facilities on and around the lake, and that no doubt keeps lots of folks away. Many make it as far as Lake Wenatchee and call it good enough.

Location: Northeast of Lake Wenatchee; map A3, grid h6.

How to get there: Take U.S. 2 over Stevens Pass or east from Wenatchee and turn north on Highway 207 about 14 miles northwest of Wenatchee. Stay on 207 past the intersection of Highway 209, over the river on the steel bridge, and bear right at the Y; then it's a short distance to the lake on your left.

Boat ramp: There's a boat ramp at each end of the lake. Cascade Hideaway Resort near the west end has a single-lane ramp with a loading float and a small gravel parking area. At the east end is the Cove Resort, with a single-lane gravel ramp and loading float, along with a gravel parking area.

Facilities: The Cove Resort has rental boats and motors, cabins, RV and tent sites, as well as a small store. There's a small cafe with good food on U.S. 2 just west of the Highway 207 intersection. Lake Wenatchee State Park is two miles to the south. Food, gas, lodging, and other facilities are available in Leavenworth to the east.

Water sports/restrictions: All water sports are permitted.

Contact: The Cove Resort, tel. (509) 763-3130; Cascade Hideaway Resort, tel. (509) 763-5104; Washington State Parks and Recreation Commission, tel. (800) 233-0321 (information), tel. (800) 452-5687 (reservations).

21 Lake Wenatchee

Rating: 7

At more than 2,400 acres, it's one of the largest natural lakes in the state, and the woodsy, rural flavor makes it a wonderful place to get away from the hustle and bustle of real life. Everyone from skiers to paddlers will appreciate the scenery that's comprised of snowy peaks and pine-covered hillsides. The kids will appreciate the swimming if you take them later in the summer, after the big lake has had some time to warm. What the kids may not appreciate is that there are no malls, arcades, or other amenities of the kind that today's youngsters have come to know and love. Make them rough it and enjoy the outdoors; it's good for them. Oh well, you tried, so leave them home and enjoy Lake Wenatchee without them.

Location: North of Leavenworth; map A3, grid h6.

How to get there: Drive east from Monroe or west from Leavenworth on U.S. 2 and turn north on Highway 207, which parallels the north side of the lake.

Boat ramp: The lake has three boat ramps. One is at Lake Wenatchee State Park, a single lane with a loading float. The launch fee here is $4 for noncampers, free if you're camping at the park. The second ramp is at Glacier View Campground, which is on the south side of the lake, near the west end. It's a natural ramp with no hard surface but works well for smaller boats. Cougar Inn, on the north side of the lake near the west end, has a one-lane ramp with loading float and room for about two dozen cars and trailers. It charges $5 round-trip for launching.

Facilities: There are about 30 tent sites (no hookups) at Lake Wenatchee State Park, located just off Highway 207 near

the west end of the lake. The park has a large swim beach at the east end of the lake. Glacier View Campground, on the south side of the lake via Forest Road 6607, has 20 campsites. Dirty Face Campground (U.S. Forest Service) has three campsites. Cougar Inn has boat rentals, a swim beach, restaurant, rooms and cabins, campsites, and a picnic area. The nearest restaurant is on U.S. 2, just west of the intersection of U.S. 2 and Highway 207. Other food, gas, lodging, and RV parks are located in Leavenworth.

Water sports/restrictions: All water sports are permitted.

Contact: The Cove Resort, tel. (509) 763-3130; Wenatchee National Forest, Lake Wenatchee Ranger District, tel. (509) 763-3103; Lake Wenatchee State Park, tel. (509) 763-3101; Washington State Parks and Recreation Commission, tel. (800) 233-03212 (information), tel. (800) 452-5687 (reservations); Cougar Inn, tel. (509) 763-3354.

22 Entiat River

Rating: 5

There's more challenging whitewater upstream for skilled paddlers, but the lower 12 miles or so of the Entiat is just right for moderately capable paddlers to test their skills and enjoy the slightly subdued thrills of running Class II water. Best run in May and June, when there's at least 1,000 cubic feet of water per second running through it, the lower Entiat is lots of fun with relatively little danger involved. There is a low dam across the river about halfway between Ardenvoir and the river mouth, but it can negotiated quite easily at normal spring flow. If you aren't sure, it also can be easily portaged. If you have time at the end of your run, drive back up the river about 20 miles above your put-in point and see what you missed by not running the upper canyon stretch of the river. If you're like me, you'll be glad you didn't do it.

Location: Enters Columbia River at Entiat; map A3, grid h8.

How to get there: Take U.S. 97 to the town of Entiat and turn west on Entiat River Road, which follows the river upstream for well over 30 miles.

Boat ramp: There are no ramps, but if you look around near the river mouth at the town of Entiat, you can find a place to carry a kayak from the water. If all else fails, paddle on into the Columbia and turn upstream (left) to reach the city park boat ramp about 300 yards above the mouth of the Entiat. Launching upstream also involves carrying a boat, and the most popular places to do that are around the small community of Ardenvoir.

Facilities: Cottonwood, North Fork, Silver Falls, Lake Creek, and Fox Creek Campgrounds (all U.S. Forest Service facilities) are scattered along the upper half of the Entiat and offer nearly 100 campsites altogether. For people visiting the lower Entiat, there's a city park in town with 31 RV sites, showers, and a trailer dump. Food and gas are also available in Entiat.

Water sports/restrictions: Kayaking, rafting, and fishing are available.

Contact: Wenatchee National Forest, Entiat Ranger District, tel. (509) 784-1511.

23 Icicle Creek (Icicle River)

Rating: 6

I can't hear or think about this little Wenatchee River tributary without remembering the March afternoon many years ago when I took a break from a two-day meeting in Leavenworth to stretch my legs and turned up Icicle Road to take a look. What I remember most is stopping at several places along the road, peering down into the fast-flowing stream, and wondering how far I'd get in my drift boat. Fortunately, I never got brave enough or drunk enough or whatever it might have taken to get up the nerve to carry out my fantasy. Even during spring's high-water periods there isn't enough water between the boulders to get a wide-beamed drift boat through most of the rock gardens I saw that day. Even rafters stay away, and this is almost the sole domain of hard-core, expert kayakers. When I think about it, even being hard-core and expert may not be enough; it might help if you're a little touched in the head.

Even the short and easier run from Snow Creek to the salmon hatchery includes some Class IV rapids and more big boulders than I'd want to deal with on two miles of river. Farther up, the Class V and Class VI water you'll find is enough to make even the most gonzo kayakers cringe. There are many places where if you make a mistake, it will be your last, as the river will pin you in its deadly grasp or roll and bounce the life out of you over hundreds of boulders that range from the size of bowling balls to the size of small houses. Scouting from the road as you drive upstream will reveal some, but not all, of the hazards; so ask around to get the latest information before you go, stop and look wherever possible, and don't be too proud to change your mind if it looks like more than you can handle. Others have been too proud to turn back, and the Icicle has extracted the ultimate price for their bravado.

Location: Southwest of Leavenworth; map A3, grids i4 and i5.

How to get there: Take U.S. 2 to Leavenworth and turn south on East Leavenworth Road or Icicle Road to parallel the lower end of Icicle Creek. Icicle Road (Forest Service Road 7600) continues upstream some 15 miles past the national fish hatchery on the lower end of the creek.

Boat ramp: There are several places to carry a boat to the water, including Ida Creek Campground and along the road at the mouth of Snow Creek.

Facilities: There are seven U.S. Forest Service campgrounds along the creek, all with at least some campsites. Working upstream, Eightmile Campground has 45 sites, Bridge Creek Campground has six, Johnny Creek Campground has 56, Ida Creek Campground has 10, Chatter Creek Campground has 12, Rock Island Campground has 22, and Blackpine Creek Horse Camp has eight. There's also a large private RV park and campground about three miles up Icicle Road. Motels, bed-and-breakfast facilities, gas, food, and other facilities are available nearby in Leavenworth.

Water sports/restrictions: This one's for expert kayakers only.

Contact: Wenatchee National Forest, Leavenworth Ranger District, tel. (509) 782-1413; Icicle River RV Park and Campground, tel. (509) 548-5420.

24 Columbia River (from Rock Island Dam upstream to Chelan Falls)

Rating: 8

This is a fun-in-the-sun place, where water sports are simply a part of life from Memorial Day to Labor Day. And the most popular sports are the high-speed sports. Although the fishing for walleyes, steelhead, and other species can be very good, and although this is a fine place to paddle the rocky shoreline in search of wildlife and interesting sights, powerboating is the big thing here. That's especially true if the powerboat is small and jet-propelled or if it's trailing a rope attached to anyone on some kind of planing device. If you're into skiing, wakeboarding, kneeboarding, or tubing, you'll find a home here. And on those days when the wind comes up, which are fairly common, windsurfing is another good possibility.

Get a few miles north of Wenatchee and the boat traffic thins out quickly except around all the major parks, ramps, and other access points. There are only a couple of towns along the river between Wenatchee and Chelan, so there are many miles of river (reservoir) where you can get away from other boats to ski flat water, paddle in peace, or just find some quiet water to lie back and soak up the sun.

Location: North and south of Wenatchee; map A3, grid i8.

How to get there: Drive east on U.S. 2 or west on Highway 28 to Wenatchee and turn north on U.S. 97 to follow the river upstream. Drive south out of Wenatchee on Highway 28 (east side of the river) or Highway 285 (west side of river) to follow the river downstream.

Boat ramp: There are four boat ramps on the Chelan County (west) side of the Columbia and six on the Douglas County (east) side of the river in this stretch:

- **Riverfront Park:** On the west side of the Columbia, Riverfront Park is at the foot of Orondo Street in downtown Wenatchee and has a two-lane concrete ramp with a loading float and room for about two dozen cars and trailers. Located in a small cove, it's well protected from the river current and wind. Take Wenatchee Avenue to Thurston and turn east on Thurston Street, following it one block. Cross Columbia Avenue, turn left, and go down the hill, taking the first right. Go one block and turn left; then take the next right to the water and the ramp.

- **Wenatchee Confluence State Park:** Just north of Wenatchee on the north bank of the Wenatchee River is Wenatchee Confluence State Park, where there are two wide, asphalt ramps, a large loading float, and lots of paved parking nearby. There's a $4 launch fee at the state park. Take the Highway 285 exit off U.S. 2 in Wenatchee and go south to the second light. Turn left at the light and you're headed toward the river and the park.

- **Entiat Park:** About 15 miles upstream from Wenatchee is the town of Entiat, where the City of Entiat maintains Entiat Park, with a single-lane concrete-plank ramp with a short loading float. There's room to park maybe 20 cars and trailers nearby, providing access to the Columbia but also the mouth of the Entiat River a few hundred yards to the south. The park is visible from the highway on the east side as you pass through town.

- **Chelan Falls Park:** South of Chelan is Chelan Falls Park, a day-use area with a two-lane ramp, two loading floats, lots of parking, and rest rooms. Launching is free at this Chelan County PUD site. To get there from the junction of U.S. 97 and Highway 150, turn south on SR 150 and drive a mile to Chelan Falls; then go left on Chestnut Street, drive a block, go right on First Street, and follow it 200 yards to the park.

- **Rock Island Hydro Park:** On the east side of the river just downstream of East Wenatchee, there's a good concrete ramp with a loading float and about three dozen boat/trailer parking spaces at Douglas County PUD's Rock Island Hydro Park. Take Highway 28 south from Wenatchee toward Quincy and you'll see the park and its boat ramp, two miles out of Wenatchee, on the right.

- **Lincoln Rock State Park:** A few miles upstream from Wenatchee is Lincoln Rock State Park, where there's a three-lane concrete ramp with loading floats for each ramp and lots of parking for cars and trailers. The launch fee is $4 round-trip, with an annual permit available for $40. Campers at the park don't have to pay the launch fee. Get there by taking U.S. 97 north from Wenatchee about five miles to the park entrance on the left.

- **Orondo Park:** Working upstream on U.S. 97, the next ramp is at Orondo Park, maintained by the Port of Douglas County and located near the intersection of Highway 97 and Highway 2. This single-lane ramp has a loading float and nearby moorage floats. There's a $4 launch fee, with a $40 annual permit available.

- **Orondo Ramp:** Three miles upstream is another single-lane rap with a small gravel parking area with room for maybe two cars. You have to watch closely for the gravel road off Highway 97 leading about 100 yards down to the ramp. The ramp isn't marked, but you'll see it if you're paying attention.

- **Doroga State Park:** Right under the huge power line that crosses over the highway and the river about six miles north of the Highway 2 intersection is Doroga State Park. Doroga has a two-lane ramp with floats and room for at least three dozen cars and trailers. The launch fee is $4 round-trip, $40 per year.

- **Beebe Bridge Park:** Located just downstream from where Highway 97 crosses over the Columbia is Beebe Bridge Park, where you'll find one of the best launch ramps on the Columbia. The two-lane concrete ramp is big enough and offers good enough traction to launch boats of almost any size with almost any vehicle, and it has loading floats. It has parking for dozens of cars/trailers, and launching is free. It's maintained by Chelan County PUD.

Facilities: Camping is available at Wenatchee Confluence, Lincoln, and Doroga State Parks. All three have large day-use areas, with roped swim beaches, picnic areas, rest rooms, tennis and basketball courts, covered cooking areas, and other amenities. Short-term moorage is available at Wenatchee's Riverfront Park.

Entiat Park has 50 tent sites and 31 RV sites with power, picnic tables and cooking shelters, and a swim beach. Rock Island Hydro Park has a large, roped swimming area, rest rooms, covered picnic shelters, tennis and basketball courts, a volleyball pit, baseball fields, picnic tables, and lots of grass, not to mention a paved hiking trail along the river. There's small-boat moorage available at Orondo Park ($3.50 per night), plus camping, fuel, and a weekend snack bar during the summer.

Beebe Bridge Park has tent and RV sites ($15 per night), a large swim beach, rest rooms with showers, and tennis and basketball courts. The day-use park at Chelan Falls has a large, roped swim beach with plenty of sun and green lawn, picnic tables, a covered cooking area, and baseball, tennis, volleyball, and basketball facilities. Wenatchee has a wide range of motels, bed-and-breakfasts, restaurants, and other facilities. Personal watercraft and other equipment are available for rent from SSR Sports at Lincoln Rock.

Water sports/restrictions: All water sports are permitted.

Contact: Lincoln Rock State Park, tel. (509) 884-8702; Washington State Parks and Recreation Commission, tel. (800) 233-0321 (information), tel. (800) 452-5687 (reservations); Wenatchee Chamber of Commerce, tel. (800) 572-7753; East Wenatchee Chamber of Commerce, tel. (800) 572-7753; Chelan County Public Utility District, tel. (509) 663-8121; SSR Sports, tel. (800) 308-0367.

25 Wenatchee River

Rating: 9

Take your pick; there's a stretch of this big river that meets your river-running needs and fits your paddling or rowing skill level. The choices include the almost-docile 10-mile run from Cashmere down to the mouth of the river at Wenatchee, the Class II water from Lake Wenatchee down to Highway 2, the 19-mile stretch of Class III rapids from Leavenworth to Monitor that's so popular with the commercial rafting groups, the challenging Class IV run on the Little Wenatchee above the lake, and the nasty, experts-only seven miles of boat-crunching whitewater that is Tumwater Canyon.

Relatively few boaters run the Little Wenatchee, partly because it's a long drive from anywhere, with few good options for launching and takeout, and partly because most folks get sidetracked along the way and opt for one of the other runs down closer to Highway 2. The upper river, accessible via Forest Service Road 6500 above Lake Wenatchee, does offer some serious challenges during the high water of spring. If you're looking for a chance to test yourself on a piece of river that includes boulder drops of significant size, fast, narrow canyons, and other tests of your Class IV paddling skills with little chance of meeting anyone else on the river, it may work for you.

The next section of river, from the Lake Wenatchee outlet down to Tumwater Falls Campground on Highway 2, is much more gentle, consisting mostly of Class I water with a couple of Class II rapids along the way. Like the rest of the river, it's highest and most challenging in the spring, but this stretch of nearly 20 miles provides a pleasant and worthwhile day on the water throughout much of the year. Although the water level is low and you may do a little more bottom bumping in fall, that time of year may provide you with a chance to see red-sided sockeye salmon as they make their way from the Columbia into Lake Wenatchee and beyond.

If you run this entire stretch in a day, get an early start. You can cut it almost in half by lunching or taking out at Plain. Next is the toughest part of the Wenatchee, run only by the big boys who are up to the challenge. As if a low dam across the river and a Class VI drop in the middle of it weren't enough, this entire seven-mile stretch of water from Tumwater Campground down to Leavenworth becomes one long Class V+ during the high flows of spring. Some of the worst parts, including the hole called Exit (take the hint), can be scouted from Highway 2, but you need more than scouting before deciding to run this part of the Wenatchee. It's a gorgeous canyon, but if you decide to run it, you won't have any time to enjoy the scenery.

Below Leavenworth is the most popular stretch of river, awesome during the high flows from May to July, when most of the commercial operations and private boaters like to run it. The full run from Leavenworth down to Monitor covers about 19 miles of river, but taking out at Cashmere cuts about three miles off that distance. Some of this Class III section is very impressive in the spring, with a dozen places where you stand a good chance of getting wet and perhaps half that many spots where you can get separated from your boat in less time than it takes to describe it. Folks have a short distance to get warmed up on this run before the whitewater gets serious. It isn't long before they start the 250-yard-long series of waves called Rock and Roll, with the infamous hole called Devil's Eyeball near its upper end. A short distance downstream there's a dam that should be portaged, and then the fun continues, through rapids like Drunkard's Drop and Snowblind. All these prepare boaters for what many consider the highlight of the trip, the huge hole and curler called Suffocator, guaranteed to soak you and fairly likely to throw you out of the boat if you hit it squarely.

There are a few more good rapids above and just below Cashmere before the river settles down and becomes a mostly Class I cruise on down to Wenatchee. The one Class II rapid you'll encounter on this part of the river is a short distance below Monitor, just around the corner from the county park that separates the river from Highway 2. Canoeists and novice kayakers can easily avoid this because it's in the right-hand channel, and all you have to do is stay to the left and go down that channel instead.

What's that you say, you're not even a river runner? No problem here. The

Wenatchee has as many deep, slow pools as it has rapids, with room for swimming and wading along its edges. This is, however, cool water, and it is a river, not a swimming pool with a lifeguard watching you like a hawk. People who forgot those facts have died for their mistakes. Inner tubing is another possibility, but stick with the stretch of river from Monitor down if you're going tubing. Class III and Class IV rapids have no mercy on people who step into the river with inadequate flotation or inadequate respect for moving water.

Location: Joins the Columbia at Wenatchee; map A3, grid i7.

How to get there: Take U.S. 2 east from Wenatchee and you'll parallel more than 25 miles of the lower Wenatchee River. To reach the middle stretch of the river, turn east off U.S. 2 near Tumwater Campground and drive upriver on River Road. To reach the Little Wenatchee above Lake Wenatchee, turn north off U.S. 2 on Highway 207 and drive up the north side of the lake. About a mile west of the lake's west end, turn south (left) on Forest Road 6500, which runs along the river's north side for about 15 miles.

Boat ramp: Developed boat ramps are located in four places from Leavenworth downstream, and there are several undeveloped spots where paddlers and anglers get their boats to the river:

- **Leavenworth Boat Launch:** The Department of Fish and Wildlife's ramp at Leavenworth is located just east of town, off East Leavenworth Road. It's a one-lane concrete ramp with room for about 40 cars in its gravel parking area. To reach it, drive west on U.S. 2 from Leavenworth about half a mile, cross the Wenatchee River, and turn right on East Leavenworth Road. Go half a mile and turn right on the gravel road that leads about 50 yards to the launch and parking area. A $10 Washington Department of Fish and Wildlife access decal is required to use all public launch areas maintained by the WDFW.

- **Peshastin Boat Ramp:** The Department of Fish and Wildlife's Peshastin ramp is located off School Street, near the east end of town. It's a one-lane natural-surface ramp with parking for about two dozen cars. A $10 Washington Department of Fish and Wildlife access decal is required to use all public launch areas maintained by the WDFW.

- **Riverside Park:** This one-lane concrete ramp is located in Cashmere on Maple Street. The park's large parking area is some distance from the boat launch. To get there, take Cottage Avenue in Cashmere about 200 yards to Maple Street and turn left. Follow Maple two blocks to the park and its boat ramp.

- **Wenatchee Confluence State Park:** Located just upstream from the mouth of the Wenatchee, on the Columbia River, it has a two-lane asphalt ramp, a loading float, and a large paved parking area. There's a $4 launch fee here, with a $40 annual permit from the State Parks and Recreation Commission. The annual permit is good at all state parks for the calendar year.

Those undeveloped launch sites for kayaks, canoes, and other craft small enough to carry are more numerous, including:

- The highway bridge at the small town of Plain

- Tumwater Campground along Highway 2

- Lake Creek Campground on the Little Wenatchee above Lake Wenatchee.

- The Highway 207 bridge near the east end of the lake

- The highway bridge at the small town of Plain

- Tumwater Campground along Highway 2

- Several turn-out spots alongside Highway 2 in Tumwater Canyon (just look for the wide spots)

- The upstream side of the Monitor Bridge (off Sleepy Hollow Road)

- Wenatchee River County Park near Monitor

- Walla Walla Point Park, downstream from the mouth of the Wenatchee on the Columbia

Facilities: There are four U.S. Forest Service campgrounds along the river above the lake, providing a total of 23 campsites among them. Tumwater Campground, on the lower river just off U.S. 2, has 80 campsites, including some that are large enough for trailers and RVs. Lake Wenatchee State Park, with its 30 tent sites, rest rooms, and picnic area, is another good possibility. Four U.S. Forest Service campgrounds are also along Icicle Creek, a Wenatchee River tributary near Leavenworth. The biggest of these is Johnny Creek Campground about 12 miles up the Icicle. There's a KOA campground in Leavenworth and several other RV parks and private campgrounds along the river and Highway 2. Motels, bed-and-breakfast facilities, and other accommodations are numerous in Leavenworth, Cashmere, and Wenatchee. Several commercial rafting companies offer trips on the river, mostly on the Leavenworth-to-Cashmere stretch.

Water sports/restrictions: Rafting, kayaking, fishing, and (in some places) swimming are the best options here.

Contact: Wenatchee National Forest,

Lake Wenatchee Ranger District, tel. (509) 763-3103; Wenatchee National Forest, Leavenworth Ranger District, tel. (509) 782-1413; Lake Wenatchee State Park, tel. (509) 763-3101; Washington State Parks and Recreation Commission, tel. (800) 233-0321 (information), tel. (800) 452-5687 (reservations); Wenatchee Chamber of Commerce, tel. (800) 572-7753; Leavenworth Chamber of Commerce, tel. (509) 548-5807; Tumwater Campground, tel. (800) 280-2267; All Seasons River Inn, Leavenworth, tel. (800) 254-0555; Anderson's River Chalet, Leavenworth, tel. (509) 763-8046; Best Western Icicle Inn, Leavenworth, tel. (800) 558-2438; Icicle River RV Park and Campground, Leavenworth, tel. (509) 548-5420; Pine Village KOA, Leavenworth, tel. (509) 548-7709; River's Edge Lodge, Peshastin, tel. (800) 451-5285; Village Inn Motel, Cashmere, tel. (800) 793-3522; Travel Lodge of Wenatchee, tel. (800) 235-8165; River Recreation, Inc., tel. (800) 464-5899; Downstream River Runners, tel. (360) 805-9899; Alpine Adventures, tel. (800) 926-7238; Wild and Scenic River Tours, tel. (800) 413-6840; All Rivers Adventures, tel. (800) 743-5628; River Riders, Inc., tel. (800) 448-RAFT.

26 Upper Cle Elum River

Rating: 8

The great thing about this clear, darting stream besides the beautiful country it happens to run through is that it has something to offer paddlers of varying skill levels. You really have two choices here depending on your paddling ability and the size of your—uh, depending on how brave you are. The river above Salmon la Sac Campground includes a number of Class III to Class IV+ rapids, including the famous Triple

Falls, where it drops over a series of six- to 10-foot drops in rapid succession. Most of the tricky water can be seen from the road as you're driving up to launch, but a couple are out of sight to drivers and should be scouted carefully as you work your way downriver. The four-mile float from Salmon la Sac down to the head of the lake at Cle Elum River Campground requires much less technical skill and is a good Class II run for intermediate-level paddlers.

Location: Flows into the north end of Lake Cle Elum south of Salmon la Sac; map A3, grid j4

How to get there: Take Interstate 90 to Cle Elum and turn north on Highway 903, staying on it all the way up the east side of Lake Cle Elum and paralleling the river upstream.

Boat ramp: There are no formal ramps, but boaters carry or drag their boats to the river at various places between Tacquala Lake and the upper end of Lake Cle Elum. Good possibilities include the mouths of Scatter Creek, Silver Creek, and little Boulder Creek, as well as Salmon La Sac and Cle Elum River Campgrounds.

Facilities: The U.S. Forest Service campground at Salmon la Sac has over 100 campsites for tents and RVs. The Forest Service's Red Mountain and Cle Elum River Campgrounds also have campsites, water, and rest rooms.

Water sports/restrictions: Kayaking, rafting, and fishing are the main attractions, depending on river flow.

Contact: Wenatchee National Forest, Cle Elum Ranger District, tel. (509) 674-4411; Pacific Water Sports, tel. (206) 246-9385.

27 Cooper Lake

Rating: 6

This 120-acre lake in the hills above Lake Cle Elum is open to year-round fishing, but you won't find any boats on it in the dead of winter unless they're frozen in place by the ice layer that collects on the lake's surface for several months every year. Summertime weather and water conditions are much more boater friendly, and the lake has quite a few visitors during the summer camping and vacation season. Anglers comprise the largest group of boaters by far, but this is a great place for a peaceful paddle early on a summer morning or on a calm, warm evening. The mountain scenery is fabulous, and the lake a deep clear blue. For what it's worth, a few folks also boat the Cooper River, which runs out of the east end of the lake and tumbles about four miles into the Cle Elum River below Salmon la Sac Campground. I say "tumbles" because that's exactly what it does. More like one continuous waterfall than a river, it's a Class V stream where only the expert need bother suiting up. Because of its small size, limited attraction, and potential dangers, I didn't include it as a separate listing.

Location: Northwest of Salmon la Sac; map A3, grid j3.

How to get there: Take Interstate 90 to Cle Elum and turn north on Highway 903. Three miles past the north end of Lake Cle Elum turn west (left) on Forest Road 46 and follow it about five miles to Forest Road 4616; turn north (right) and follow the road along the north side of Cooper Lake.

Boat ramp: There's a launch ramp at the U.S. Forest Service's Owhi Campground on the lake's north shore.

Facilities: Owhi Campground has about 30 campsites. Food, gas, and lodging are available in and around Cle Elum.

Water sports/restrictions: Paddling and fishing are the main attractions. Gas motors are prohibited on the lake.

Contact: Wenatchee National Forest, Cle Elum Ranger District, tel. (509) 674-4411.

28 Keechelus Lake

Rating: 3

If only one out of every 100 cars passing by it on Interstate 90 were pulling a boat to Keechelus, it would be a mighty busy place. But in fact this big impoundment on the upper Yakima River gets very little use by boaters for several reasons. First and foremost, boat ramps are few and far between, and lakeside facilities are all but nonexistent. The lake level also fluctuates greatly from season to season, to the point that the main boat ramp near the west end of the reservoir doesn't reach the water for extended periods. When the water's low, wide expanses of mud and stumps lie between solid ground and the water's edge. The lake is usually full throughout most of the summer, but at nearly 2,500 acres and located just a few hundred feet lower than the nearby ski slopes, it never warms up enough to provide comfortable or even bearable swimming conditions. At least when it's full, it's a pretty bit of scenery for travelers racing in both directions over Snoqualmie Pass. Maybe that's all it will ever be.

Location: Alongside Interstate 90 at Hyak; map A3, grid j2.

How to get there: Take Interstate 90 to Snoqualmie Pass and exit to the south at Hyak, following Forest Road 9070 to the northwest corner of the lake and the boat ramp. To reach the southwest corner of the lake, turn south of Interstate 90 at Crystal Springs.

Boat ramp: The rough boat ramp near the northwest corner of the lake also has rest rooms and a picnic area.

Facilities: The U.S. Forest Service campground at Crystal Springs has about two dozen campsites, some of which are large enough for RVs. Restaurants, motels, gas, and groceries are available at Snoqualmie Summit.

Water sports/restrictions: All water sports are permitted.

Contact: Mount Baker-Snoqualmie National Forest, North Bend Ranger District, tel. (425) 888-1421; Wenatchee National Forest, Cle Elum Ranger District, tel. (509) 674-4411.

LAKE ROOSEVELT

MAP A4

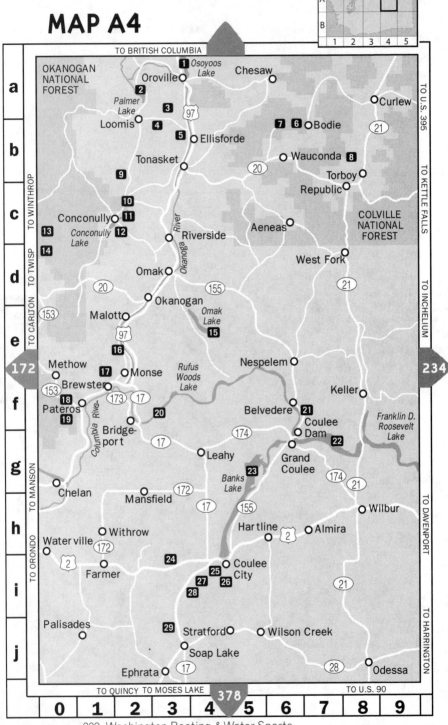

CHAPTER A4

◻1 Osoyoos Lake

Rating: 7

Less than half of this 10-mile-long lake is in Washington, but that's enough to provide lots of boating opportunity. At over 5,700 acres, this is a big lake with plenty to see and do. Unless you happen to live in Oroville or somewhere near, Osoyoos is a long haul, and that's what keeps it from becoming more of a major boating destination. The state park near the south end helps, giving folks from the Evergreen State a place to camp and call home while they visit, but you still know you've done some traveling by the time you make it to the lake, and you're even more sure by the time you get home.

Location: North of Oroville; map A4; grid a3.

How to get there: Take U.S. 97 to Oroville and continue through town along the west side of the lake.

Boat ramp: There's a wide, two-lane ramp with two loading floats at Osoyoos Lake State Park, which is at the south end of the lake. The paved parking lot at the park has room for dozens of cars and trailers. Launch fee at the park is $4 round-trip, with an annual permit available for $40. Nearby is the City of Oroville's Deep Bay Park, which has a single-lane ramp with parking for about 20 cars and trailers.

Facilities: The state park has a large swim beach, 80 tent sites, rest rooms with showers, and picnic tables. The city park also has a swim beach, picnic shelter, picnic tables, and rest rooms. Food, gas, lodging, and other amenities are readily available in Oroville.

Water sports/restrictions: All water sports are permitted.

Contact: Osoyoos Lake State Park, tel. (509) 476-3321; Washington State Parks and Recreation Commission, tel. (800) 233-0321 (information), tel. (800) 452-5687 (reservations).

◻2 Palmer Lake

Rating: 6

This is another eastern Washington lake that suffers from a location problem. If it happened to be somewhere closer to a major trans-state highway, it would probably be a popular boating destination. But since it's several miles west of Highway 2 and out of sight for nearly every visitor coming to this part of Okanogan County, Palmer doesn't have much of a tourist following. Local anglers in search of smallmouth bass are fond of it, and they don't mind that out-of-towners haven't discovered the lake. To them, it's a 2,000-acre farm pond where the fishin's good and the outsiders are all but nonexistent. This big lake in typical Okanogan ranching country is a great place to explore in a canoe or other small boat, and with nearly 10 miles of shoreline, you could explore it for a long time.

Location: Southwest of Oroville; map A4, grid a2.

How to get there: Take U.S. 97 to Ellisforde and turn west over the Okanogan River to County Road 9437, which parallels the west side of the river. Turn south (left) and drive just over a mile to Loomis-Oroville Road (County Road 9425) and turn west (right). Drive past Whitestone and Spectacle Lakes to the town of Loomis and turn right on Stehekin Road. From there it's about five miles to the lake.

Boat ramp: There are gravel boat ramps at the north and south ends of the lake. The Washington Department of Natural

Resources' Palmer Lake Campground at the north end is steep, and loose gravel could cause launching problems. There's room for about two dozen cars and trailers to park there. Palmer Lake Recreation Site, managed by the Bureau of Land Management, has a more gradual grade but is rough. There's room for about 20 cars and trailers in the gravel lot.

Facilities: Lodging is available at Chopaka Lodge and there are RV and tent sites at Sully's Trailer Park and RV, both within easy driving range of the lake. Additional facilities are abundant in Oroville.

Water sports/restrictions: All water sports are permitted.

Contact: Chopaka Lodge, tel. (509) 223-3131; Sully's Trailer Park and RV, tel. (509) 223-2303.

3 Wannacut Lake

Rating: 9

Big, deep, and cool, with pine-covered slopes rising from water's edge to the tops of steep hills hundreds of feet above, Wannacut may best represent the true essence of an Okanogan County lake. The lake looks, feels, even sounds much the way it did decades ago, thanks to its location well off the beaten path and at least in part to boating regulations that prohibit waterskiing and PWC riding on the lake. Such regulations seem to make perfect sense here, as though turning tight circles or cutting a slashing wake on Wannacut's pristine surface would represent some sort of aquatic sacrilege. A higher power just might not appreciate seeing this lake disturbed much. Wannacut covers more than 400 acres and is located in one of the prettiest settings you'll find anywhere. It's on the cool side for swimming until at least July, but very popular with trout anglers in search of fat, carry-over rainbows. It's a wonderful lake to explore in a kayak, canoe, rowboat, or small powerboat.

Location: Southwest of Oroville; map A4, grid a3.

How to get there: Take U.S. 97 to Ellisforde, turn west across the Okanogan River and north (right) on County Road 9437, which parallels the west side of the river. Drive north about eight miles to Blue Lake Road (County Road 4510) and turn west (left). Drive four miles (past Blue Lake) to the T, turn left, and drive about a mile to the lake on the left.

Boat ramp: There are two boat ramps on this popular northern Okanogan County lake. Sun Cove Resort, about halfway down the lake's west side, has a single-lane rock and gravel ramp that's always in very good condition. It has a large loading float. At the south end of the lake is a one-lane concrete-plank ramp managed by the Washington Department of Fish and Wildlife. It has room for about three dozen cars and trailers. A $10 WDFW access decal is required to use the public launch areas maintained by the Washington Department of Fish and Wildlife.

Facilities: Sun Cove Resort has moorage, boat rentals, rest rooms with showers, rental cabins, tent and RV sites, a store, swimming area, and other facilities.

Water sports/restrictions: Waterskiing and PWC riding are prohibited on the lake.

Contact: Sun Cove Resort, tel. (509) 476-2223 (April through October only).

4 Spectacle Lake

Rating: 8

This 315-acre lake in the heart of Okanogan County's sun country is a favorite of many boaters, anglers, swimmers, and water lovers of all kinds. Like several Okanogan County lakes, it has time and day restrictions on some kinds of activities so that everyone can have time and space to do their thing. It seems to work here most of the time, but occasionally one of the thrill-seeking folks has to be persuaded to get off the water and leave room for the more sedate pursuits. Because it warms quickly with the summer sun, this is as great swimming lake.

Location: Northwest of Tonasket; map A4, grid b3.

How to get there: Take U.S. 97 to Ellisforde and turn west, over the Okanogan River, to County Road 9437, which parallels the west side of the river. Turn south (left) and drive just over a mile to Loomis-Oroville Road (County Road 9425) and turn west (right). Drive past Whitestone Lake and continue on to the Spectacle, which is alongside the left side of the road.

Boat ramp: There are no fewer than five places to launch a boat on Spectacle Lake. Spectacle Falls Resort, Rainbow Resort, and Spectacle Lake Resort all have single-lane gravel ramps with loading floats. The Spectacle Falls and Spectacle Lake Resort ramps are for park guests only. Rainbow Falls Resort allows nonguests to use the ramp for $4 round-trip. A single-lane gravel ramp managed by the Department of Wildlife is at the west end of the lake and a WDFW concrete-plank ramp is near the east end. Considerably more parking is available at the latter. A $10 WDFW access decal is required to use the public launch areas maintained by the Washington Department of Fish and Wildlife.

Facilities: Spectacle Falls Resort has rental cabins, RV sites with full hookups, boat rentals, and rest rooms with showers. Rainbow Resort offers moorage, RV sites, rental cabins, boat rentals, and rest rooms with showers. At Spectacle Lake Resort you'll find boat moorage, boat rentals, RV sites, motel rooms, a convenience store, and showers. Food and gas are available in Tonasket several miles to the southeast.

Water sports/restrictions: Waterskiing and PWC riding are allowed only on Monday, Tuesday, Thursday, and Saturday between 10 a.m. and 6 p.m.

Contact: Spectacle Lake Resort, tel. (509) 223-3433 (April 1 through October 31 only); Spectacle Falls Resort, tel. (509) 223-4141 (April through July only); Rainbow Resort, tel. (509) 223-3700.

5 Whitestone Lake

Rating: 6

Although not a popular attraction for visitors, Whitestone is a productive fishing lake for bass and other warm-water species. The road to Spectacle Lake runs right past it, but most people chug on by, hardly noticing the long, skinny lake that parallels the road for nearly two miles. It's also a good destination for paddlers and other small-craft operators looking for something off the beaten path.

Location: Northwest of Tonasket; map A4, grid b3.

How to get there: Take U.S. 97 to Ellisforde and turn west over the Okanogan River to County Road 9437, which parallels the west side of the river. Turn south (left) and drive just over a mile to Loomis-Oroville Road (County Road 9425) and turn west (right). Drive about three miles to the lake, which is alongside the road on the left.

Boat ramp: You'll find a concrete-plank boat ramp (single lane) and toilets at the public access area on the lake. Most of the parking area was paved a few years ago. A $10 WDFW access decal is required to use the public launch areas maintained by the Washington Department of Fish and Wildlife.

Facilities: There are three resorts with virtually everything an angler might need at Spectacle Lake a few miles to the west.

Water sports/restrictions: All water sports are permitted, but anglers and paddlers use it most.

Contact: Spectacle Lake Resort, tel. (509) 223-3433 (April 1 through October 31 only); Spectacle Falls Resort, tel. (509) 223-4141 (April through July only); Rainbow Resort, tel. (509) 223-3700; Cascade Toys and Sports, tel. (509) 826-4148.

6 Beth, Beaver, and Little Beaver Lakes

Rating: 7

You won't find these three small lakes in most fishing or boating guide books, so maybe I'm the only one who thinks they're worthy. They're beautifully quiet bodies of water, and the surrounding pine-covered hills make the whole place wonderfully inviting. Great places to paddling in a canoe or kayak, they're also productive trout-fishing spots early in the summer and again in the fall. During the hot days of July and August, they warm well into the comfort range for swimming.

Location: West of Bodie, Okanogan National Forest; map A4, grid b6.

How to get there: Take U.S. 97 to Tonasket and turn east on Highway 20, following it about 18 miles to Bonaparte Lake Road (County Road 4953). Continue about six miles past Bonaparte Lake to Beaver Lake. Little Beaver Lake is immediately to the east, Beth Lake about a mile and a half to the northwest.

Boat ramp: A concrete-plank ramp on Beth Lake Campground and a gravel ramp at the picnic area on Beaver Lake are available. Boats can be carried or dragged to the water at Little Beaver.

Facilities: The U.S. Forest Service maintains two campgrounds in the area. Beaver Lake Campground has five tent/trailer spaces, while Beth lake Campground has eight sites. Both campgrounds have drinking water and vault toilets. Bonaparte Lake Resort to the south has cabins, RV and tent sites, some groceries, and other amenities.

Water sports/restrictions: Paddling and fishing are permitted here.

Contact: Okanogan National Forest, Tonasket Ranger District, tel. (509) 486-2186; Bonaparte Lake Resort, tel. (509) 486-2828 (April through October only).

7 Bonaparte Lake

Rating: 7

This 160-acre lake in some of Okanogan County's wildest country is a great getaway spot if you don't mind leaving many of the trappings of urban life behind for a while. Its restrictive speed limit and other regulations make it a good bet for anglers and paddlers who want to escape the more fast-paced water sports. The lake's mid-section is deep—over 100 feet in places—so it remains cool and offers good fishing for lake trout and other cool-water species. The water is quite clear, too, so it's a natural for divers looking for new places to explore.

Location: Northwest of Wauconda, Okanogan County; map A4, grid b6.

How to get there: Take U.S. 97 to Tonasket and turn east on Highway 20, following it about 18 miles to County Road 4953 (Bonaparte Lake Road) and signs pointing to Bonaparte Lake. Turn north and drive about six miles to the lake.

Boat ramp: Bonaparte Lake Campground has a single-lane concrete ramp and several paved parking spaces. Bonaparte Lake Resort has a gravel ramp with a loading float and gravel parking area.

Facilities: Bonaparte Lake Resort has a large swimming area, rental boats, moorage, tent and RV sites, cabins, a cafe, a convenience store with snack foods and fishing tackle, and other facilities.

Water sports/restrictions: The lake has a 10 mph speed limit. PWC riding and waterskiing are prohibited.

Contact: Bonaparte Lake Resort, tel. (509) 486-2828 (April through October only); Okanogan National Forest, Tonasket Ranger District, tel. (509) 486-2186.

8 Curlew Lake

Rating: 8

You know a lake is popular if it has four private resorts and a state park on its shores, right? It also has six boat ramps of various quality, but all quite usable, so anyone with a boat of just about any size that can make it to the lake can make it into the lake. Bigger than average at 870 acres, Curlew also is prettier than average with pine trees around much of its perimeter and only light development on its shores. All

kinds of boating, skiing, boarding, tubing, paddling, and fishing activities are popular here, and the lake is big enough to accommodate them all. Still, if you want to visit when things are more on the quiet side, I'd suggest the weeks following Labor Day when trout fishing again becomes the main draw after a couple of months on the back burner. Fall in this part of the state is as good as it gets.

Location: Northeast of Republic, Ferry County; map A4, grid b8.

How to get there: Take Highway 20 or Highway 21 to Republic and continue north on Highway 21, which parallels the east side of the lake. To reach the west side of the lake, turn west (left) on West Curlew Lake Road about six miles north of Republic.

Boat ramp: Tiffany's Resort, Black's Beach Resort, Fisherman's Cove Resort, and Pine Point Resort all have concrete boat ramps with floats. Some of the resorts allow nonguests to use their ramps, some don't. There's a two-lane concrete-plank ramp with floats at Curlew Lake State Park. The park has a $4 launch fee unless you're camping there. There's also an unmarked gravel ramp with a half dozen parking spots at Miyoko Point on the lake's west side.

Facilities: There are swim beaches, moorage, boat rentals, cabins, RV and tent sites, convenience stores, rest rooms with showers, and other amenities at the various resorts. Curlew Lake State Park has 75 tent and RV sites, showers and other facilities.

Water sports/restrictions: All water sports are permitted.

Contact: Curlew Lake State Park, tel. (509) 775-3592 (April through October); Washington State Parks and Recreation Commission, tel. (800) 233-0321 (information), tel. (800) 452-5687 (reservations); Pine Point Resort, tel. (509) 775-3643 (April through October); Tiffany's Resort, tel. (509) 775-3152 (April through October); Black's Beach Resort, tel. (509) 775-3989; Fisherman's Cove, tel. (509) 775-3641.

9 Blue Lake (Sinlahekin Valley)

Rating: 7

Although it's a good-sized lake at 160 acres, its prohibition on gas-powered motors keeps things moving at a slow, quiet pace, just right for fly fishing or peaceful paddling. The Sinlahekin Valley is one of Washington's prettiest places, so you'll find plenty of sights worth seeing as you come and go from the lake as well as when you're there. If you want to do a little fishing, forget the worms and salmon eggs; the lake has special regulations that allow only artificial lures and flies.

Location: Southwest of Tonasket; map A4, grid b2.

How to get there: Take U.S. 97 to Riverside and continue north about 5.5 miles to Pine Creek Road (County Road 9410); turn west and drive about 10 miles to Fish Lake. Turning north just past Fish Lake, you'll find yourself on Sinlahekin Road. Continue about four miles north to Blue Lake.

Boat ramp: There's a Department of Fish and Wildlife access area and boat ramp at the northwest corner of the lake. It's a steep sand-and-gravel ramp, best suited to launching nothing bigger than cartoppers and paddle craft. A $10 WDFW access decal is required to use the public launch areas maintained by the Washington Department of Fish and Wildlife.

Facilities: Although there's not an official campground here, lots of people camp in primitive sites around the lake. The nearest campgrounds and other facilities are in and around Conconully to the south.

Water sports/restrictions: Internal combustion engines are prohibited.

Contact: Liar's Cove Resort, tel. (509) 826-1288 (April through October); Shady Pines Resort, tel. (509) 826-2287 (April through October); Conconully Lake Resort, tel. (509) 826-7408; Conconully State Park, tel. (509) 826-7408; Okanogan National Forest Headquarters, tel. (509) 422-2704.

10 Fish Lake

Rating: 6

The popularity of nearby Conconully Lake and Conconully Reservoir keeps Fish Lake from gaining much of a reputation among anglers and boaters alike, but don't let that stop you from paying a visit. While the two Conconullies have boats and people all over them, Fish Lake might provide a peaceful respite from all the hustle and bustle. Nothing fancy here, just a long, narrow lake where you can fish, paddle, or explore at your own pace.

Location: Northeast of Conconully; map A4, grid c2.

How to get there: Take U.S. 97 to Riverside and continue north about 5.5 miles to Pine Creek Road (County Road 9410); turn west and continue just under 10 miles to the lake.

Boat ramp: The lake has two Department of Fish and Wildlife public access areas with single-lane boat ramps and toilets at each. The one at the north end has a gravel ramp, the southern one a concrete-slab ramp. A $10 WDFW access decal is required to use the public launch areas maintained by the Washington Department of Fish and Wildlife.

Facilities: Some people camp at the northern ramp, but there are no amenities there except the pit toilet. The U.S. Forest Service's Sugar Loaf Campground, with five campsites that have room for small trailers and RVs, is two miles south of the lake on Sinlahekin Road. Facilities at Conconully are about seven miles to the south.

Water sports/restrictions: All water sports are permitted, but fishing and paddling are the main draws.

Contact: Liar's Cove Resort, tel. (509) 826-1288 (April through October); Shady Pines Resort, tel. (509) 826-2287 (April through October); Conconully Lake Resort, tel. (509) 826-7408; Conconully State Park, tel. (509) 826-7408; Washington State Parks and Recreation Commission, tel. (800) 233-0321 (information), tel. (800) 452-5687 (reservations); Okanogan National Forest Headquarters, tel. (509) 422-2704.

🔟 Conconully Lake

Rating: 7

Like the reservoir immediately to the southwest, this long, narrow lake provides excellent fishing and is a favorite of other water recreationists as well. It gets nice and warm here by late June, so there's plenty of opportunity to brown up while you ski, swim, fish, wakeboard, ride PWC, or whatever it is you like to do.

Location: Immediately east of the town of Conconully; map A4, grid c2.

How to get there: From the south, drive north on U.S. 97 to Okanogan and turn north on Highway 215 (Conconully Road), which continues north to the town of Conconully. You'll first pass

Conconully Reservoir. The lake is just northeast of the reservoir. From the north, drive south on U.S. 97 to Riverside and turn west on Riverside Cutoff Road, which joins Conconully Road. Turn south (left) on Conconully Road and follow it to the lake.

Boat ramp: Kootenai Camp, at the north end of the lake, has a two-lane ramp of sand and gravel and a small parking area. At the south end of the lake is Conconully State Park with a two-lane concrete ramp that's a very good one. There's room to park about 30 cars and trailers on the gravel lot. The launching fee at the state park is $4 unless you're camping in the park.

Facilities: Conconully Lake Resort has RV and tent sites, rest rooms and showers, moorage, boat rental, and a small grocery store with fishing tackle. Nearby Conconully State Park has over 80 tent sites, rest rooms, and showers.

Water sports/restrictions: OK, this a little complicated, so bear with me. Skiing and PWC riding are allowed from 9 a.m. to 6 p.m. During July and August the hours are extended to 9 p.m. on Wednesday, Friday and Saturday only. Got it? I'm not sure I do.

Contact: Conconully Lake Resort, tel. (509) 826-0813; Conconully State Park, tel. (509) 826-7408; Washington State Parks and Recreation Commission tel. (800) 233-0321 (information), tel. (800) 452-5687 (reservations).

🔢 Conconully Reservoir

Rating: 7

Whatever you might do on Conconully Lake, you can do the same here. The only difference between the two is the shape, with the lake being long and lean and the reservoir having more of a pyramid shape, somewhat wider at its south end. The lake warms quickly in the summer and provides excellent swimming opportunities. Trout fishing is good here early and late in the day, so go catch a few rainbows before breakfast and then get back out on the water for all the other things there are to do here.

Location: Immediately south of the town of Conconully; map A4, grid c2.

How to get there: From the south, take U.S. 97 to Okanogan and turn north on Highway 215, also called Conconully Road, which eventually runs along the east side of the reservoir. From the north, drive south on U.S. 97 to Riverside and turn west on Riverside Cutoff Road, which joins Conconully Road about six miles west of U.S. 97. Turn right on Conconully Road and follow it to the reservoir.

Boat ramp: Liar's Cove Resort has a one-lane gravel ramp with a loading float, but it's for resort guests only.

Facilities: Liar's Cove Resort and Shady Pines Resort offer a wide range of facilities, including RV sites with hookups, rest rooms and showers, boat ramps, boat rental, and tackle. Conconully State Park has over 80 tent sites, rest rooms with showers, and picnic areas.

Water sports/restrictions: One more time: Skiing and PWC riding are allowed from 9 a.m. to 6 p.m. During July and August the hours are extended to 9 p.m. on Wednesday, Friday and Saturday only.

Contact: Liar's Cove Resort, tel. (509) 826-1288 (April through October); Shady Pines Resort, tel. (509) 826-2287 (April through October); Conconully State Park, tel. (509) 826-7408.

13 Cougar Lake

Rating: 4

Like nearby Davis and Campbell Lakes, this one has a fall and winter fishing season, but other boating activity occurs throughout the year. Paddling and other small-boat sports are the norm since there isn't a boat ramp at the lake, just a place where you can carry or drag small craft to the water. That's OK because this is a small lake by any standard, covering only about 20 acres, and there wouldn't be room for very many activities at the same time anyway. If you're hanging out around Winthrop with time on your hands, an all-day trip to Cougar and the area's two other lakes might be an interesting diversion, but I wouldn't haul a boat halfway across the state just to paddle here.

Location: East of Winthrop; map A4, grid c0.

How to get there: Take Highway 20 to Winthrop and drive north out of town, past Pearrygin Lake to Bear Creek Road. Take Forest Road 100 off Bear Creek Road and follow it to the sharp switchback to the left. A dirt road leads from the switchback down to the lake.

Boat ramp: There's a Department of Fish and Wildlife access area on the lake with a place to slide a boat into the water, but it's not suitable for launching trailer boats. A $10 WDFW access decal is required to use the public launch areas maintained by the Washington Department of Fish and Wildlife.

Facilities: All accommodations are in Winthrop.

Water sports/restrictions: Fishing season runs September through March. Other boating activities are limited by the lack of a trailer boat ramp.

Contact: Okanogan National Forest, Winthrop Ranger District, tel. (509) 996-2266; Pine-Near Trailer Park, tel. (509) 996-2391; Methow Valley KOA Campground, tel. (509) 996-2255; Chewuch Inn, tel. (509) 996-3107.

14 Campbell Lake

Rating: 4

If you just read the above listing for Cougar Lake, you probably don't have to read this one. They're close together, similar in size, similar in boating limitations because of the small launching area, and both have fall-through-winter fishing seasons, which are unusual. Like Cougar and Davis Lakes, this wouldn't be a worthwhile destination for someone 200 miles away, but paddling all three might be fun on a spring weekend.

Location: East of Winthrop; map A4, grid d0.

How to get there: Take Highway 20 to Winthrop and drive southeast on Bear Creek Road from town and past the golf course. Turn east on Lester Road and follow it about three winding miles to the lake.

Boat ramp: The lake has a rough boat launch, managed by the Department of Fish and Wildlife, but it's not suitable for trailer boats.

Facilities: Amenities are available in Winthrop and Twisp.

Water sports/restrictions: Paddling and fishing are the best bets. Fishing season runs from September through March.

Contact: Methow Wildlife Area, tel. (509) 996-2559; Pine-Near Trailer Park, tel. (509) 996-2391; Methow Valley KOA Campground, tel. (509) 996-2255; Chewuch Inn, tel. (509) 996-3107.

15 Omak Lake

Rating: 5

Covering more than 3,200 acres and with a good boat ramp facility, this sprawling lake near the center of Okanogan County might appear to be one of Washington's most underutilized bodies of water when it comes to boating. Lots of room to explore and play, with plenty of summertime sun, would seem to make it a logical boating and water sports playground. And it offers trophy fishing for Lahontan cutthroat trout, some of which grow nearly as long as a man's leg. But the lake isn't in a choice location as far as driving accessibility is concerned, and there's very little in the way of facilities for visiting boaters. Lakeside lodging, restaurant, and other accommodations are nonexistent, and there aren't any swim beaches or other play spots for the kids. I think the Colville Confederated Tribes have a gold mine on their hands and haven't realized it yet. Then again, maybe they like the lake as it is. If you like the idea of having a huge lake pretty much to yourself, enjoy boating open water for the sake of boating, and don't mind working at little to get there, Omak Lake might be well worth investigating. If you're going to fish here, you'll have to be aware of tribal angling regulations and have a tribal fishing permit. A three-day permit is available for $15, a seven-day permit for $20, and a season-long permit for $30. Kids under 16 years of age can fish without a license if they're with a licensed adult. Tribal permits are available in all towns on and around the Colville Reservation.

Location: Southeast of Okanogan; map A4, grid e4.

How to get there: Take U.S. 97 to Omak and turn east on Highway 155, then south on the road through Antoine pass to the lake.

Boat ramp: There's a boat ramp managed by the Colville Indian Tribe near the north end of the lake. It's a good one, three lanes wide, with a gravel parking area large enough for about two dozen cars and trailers.

Facilities: Food, gas, and lodging are available in Omak and Okanogan.

Water sports/restrictions:

Contact: Cascade Toys and Sports, tel. (509) 826-4148; Colville Confederated Tribes, Fish and Wildlife Department, tel. (509) 634-8845.

16 Okanogan River

Rating: 7

If there's such a thing as a Pacific Northwest river that is underutilized by boaters, it just might be the Okanogan. In some ways that's to be expected, but for other reasons it's a little surprising. It's expected because the river doesn't offer much in the way of thrilling rapids and exciting whitewater challenges. The stream's location, a long distance from both Spokane and the population centers of western Washington, certainly doesn't help its popularity either. On the other hand, it has a major highway running beside it virtually its entire length, and off that highway are no fewer than eight developed boat ramps and several accessible gravel bars where small boats could be launched or taken out of the water.

What's more, most of the river bank outside the public access areas is under private ownership, making boat travel the most effective way to explore this large stream that offers excellent fishing for smallmouth bass and other game fish. Although kayaks might first come to mind on a river this size, it's

really big enough for use by drift boaters and rafters throughout much of the year, but most of it is gentle enough to accommodate canoeists. With all the put-in and take-out spots listed above, it shouldn't be difficult to find a float that fits your schedule and your paddling or rowing ability the next time you're looking for something to do for an afternoon in the Okanogan Valley.

Location: Joins the Columbia River east of Brewster; map A4, grid e3.

How to get there: Take U.S. 97 east or Highway 17 north to the confluence of the Okanogan and Columbia and continue north on U.S. 97 to follow the Okanogan upstream.

Boat ramp: Besides several gravel bars and wide spots along Highway 97 where paddle craft and small boats can be carried or dragged to the river, there are eight boat ramps of various quality scattered along the Okanogan between Oroville and the mouth of the river:

- **Highway 97 Bridge:** The uppermost ramp, located along Highway 97 a mile south of Oroville, is a good Department of Fish and Wildlife gravel ramp with plenty of parking. A $10 WDFW access decal is required to use the public launch areas maintained by the Washington Department of Fish and Wildlife.

- **Tonasket Lagoons Park:** The next ramp downstream from Oroville is about 15 highway miles south (18 or 19 river miles) at Tonasket Lagoons Park just south of Tonasket. Maintained by the City of Tonasket, it's a concrete ramp with plenty of room to park about 20 cars and trailers. Take Fourth Street in Tonasket to Railroad Avenue and turn south, following Railroad to the maintenance shop. Turn right on the gravel road at the shop building to the park and ramp.

- **Bonaparte Ramp:** About a mile south of Tonasket is another Department of Fish and Wildlife ramp, marked by a "Public Fishing" sign along Highway 97. A steep bank, moderate current, and some buildup of sand make this more of a hand-carry ramp than a trailer ramp, and parking is limited. A $10 WDFW access decal is required to use the public launch areas maintained by the Washington Department of Fish and Wildlife.

- **Riverside-Crowfoot Ramp:** There's another WDFW ramp in Riverside at the end of Cooper Street. This natural ramp (no surface materials) also gets some deep accumulations of silt at times. It has lots of parking and is marked by a "Public Fishing" sign at the intersection of Highway 97 and Kendall Street (which leads to Cooper). Don't forget the access decal from the WDFW if you're going to use this facility.

- **East-Side Park:** There's a launching spot at East-side Park in Omak, with a gravel ramp and room for several dozen cars and trailers. Located at the east end of the Highway 155 bridge, it is maintained by the City of Omak.

- **Okanogan City Ramp:** The City of Okanogan also maintains a park with a boat ramp, located on Tyee Street. The ramp is concrete and is protected from the river current here by several upstream boulders. The gravel parking area is a little rough but has room for about a dozen cars and trailers. From Second Avenue in Okanogan, go to Tyee Street and turn east, driving two blocks to the city park and its ramp.

- **Monse Bridge:** One of two ramps a short distance apart near Brewster is just downstream of the Monse Bridge. This ramp is smaller and harder to spot than the one farther upstream because there are no signs. Just turn left after crossing the bridge (from Highway 97) and take the first left on an unmarked gravel road.

- **Monse River Road Ramp:** About three-quarters of a mile upstream from the bridge is a ramp that's easier to find. Like the one downstream, it's on the Douglas County (west) side of the river. This upper ramp is a gravel ramp with more parking, maintained by Douglas County PUD. It has room to park at least a dozen cars and trailers. From Brewster, go east on U.S. 97 about three miles and turn left on Monse River Road. Follow the road three-quarters of a mile and look for the ramp on the right.

Facilities: Tonasket Lagoons Park offers several beaches that are popular with swimmers and has picnic tables, covered cooking areas, barbecue grills, and a small concession stand. Omak's East-side Park has campsites with and without hookups, a large play/sports area with ball fields and kids' playground equipment, picnic areas and an RV dump station. There are plenty of motels and RV parks in the major towns along the river—Okanogan, Omak, Tonasket and Oroville. Restaurants, grocery stores, gas stations, tackle shops, and other facilities also are available in all four. Osoyoos Lake State Park is in Oroville at the upper end of the Okanogan.

Water sports/restrictions: Kayaking, rafting, canoeing, fishing, tubing, and powerboating are permitted, depending on what part of the river you visit.

Contact: Cascade Toys and Sports, tel. (509) 826-4148; Darrell's Sporting Goods, tel. (509) 476-2112; Osoyoos Lake State Park, tel. (509) 476-3321; Washington State Parks and Recreation Commission, tel. (800) 233-0321 (information), tel. (800) 452-5687 (reservations).

17 Rat Lake

Rating: 5

I know what you're thinking; what the heck is this guy doing sending us off to a place called Rat Lake? Can't you just picture it, a pleasant spring weekend, slight breeze, and you sailing the crystal-clear waters of Okanogan County, the sole member and commanding officer of the Rat Lake Yacht Club? OK, so maybe it's not such a pretty picture, but the lake is nicer than it sounds. And if you visit it during the spring or summer, there won't be any trollers getting in your way. The lake has a fall-and-winter fishing season. At 60-plus acres, Rat Lake is big enough to explore and enjoy in any kind of craft, and it's a worthwhile side trip if you're holing up in the Brewster area on your way to or from somewhere else. And no, the area isn't infested with rats. It is, however, somewhat infested with rattlers. You know, as in snakes. That's how it got its name. So you're no longer interested? Think of the poisonous reptiles as a very good reason to stay in the boat and not do too much shoreline exploring.

Location: North of Brewster; map A4, grid e1.

How to get there: Take U.S. 97 to Brewster and turn north on Paradise Mill Road. Take Rat Lake Road to the right about three miles north of town and continue another two miles to the lake.

Boat ramp: There's a Department of Fish and Wildlife boat ramp at the south end of the lake. It's a good concrete ramp with plenty of parking in a large gravel lot. A $10 WDFW access decal is required to use the public launch areas maintained by the Washington Department of Fish and Wildlife.

Facilities: Food, gas, lodging, and RV sites are available in Brewster.

Water sports/restrictions: All water sports are permitted.

Contact: Columbia Cove RV Park, tel. (509) 689-2994; Brewster Chamber of Commerce, tel. (509) 689-2517.

18 Methow River

Rating: 9

Maybe it's true of most rivers, but if I had to describe the Methow as simply as possible, I'd say it has something for almost everyone when it comes to water recreation. It has calm water for fishing and peaceful paddling, even swimming and tubing to some degree, yet it also offers some of the most exciting whitewater to be found anywhere in the state. What's more, these various river uses are separated by space and time, so people enjoying one don't often get in the way of people trying to enjoy another. Steelhead anglers, for example, are most active here in the late summer and fall when the river is running fairly low, while most of the paddlers like the river in spring when the flow is high. Swimmers and tubers are most numerous in between, when the summer sun is hottest. All are treated to some of the prettiest country scenery that Okanogan County has to offer.

The most famous part of the Methow among boaters and the stretch that draws the biggest crowds is near the lower end of the river between the little burg of Methow and the mouth of the river at Pateros. Known as Black Canyon, it's a wild ride through Class III and some Class IV holes and rapids, and features some of the biggest waves this side of the Wenatchee. Boat traffic here is heavy from May to early

July, when river volume typically ranges from 4,000 to 10,000 cubic feet. It's not unusual to see one commercial rafting group after another parading through Black Canyon on a warm June weekend. Highlight of the trip—or lowlight if it buries you—is a huge boat eater known affectionately as the Black Hole, but there are several thrilling holes and rapids throughout this run, with ample opportunity to feel for yourself how chilly spring runoff water can be.

Most folks make the shorter trip (16 miles) through Black Canyon, launching at the fishing access spot near the mouth of McFarland Creek, which enters the river from the west side about three miles upstream from Methow. If you're looking for a long day on the water, you might launch instead at Carlton, adding nearly 10 river miles to the trip. The water from Carlton down to McFarland Creek includes a few Class II rapids to give paddlers some warm-up opportunities before getting into the more serious water of Black Canyon. The Carlton-McFarland Creek run, of course, can be enjoyed all by itself if you aren't up to the bigger stuff below. The water is even mellower farther upstream and is popular with canoeists as well as rafters and kayakers.

The 10-mile run from Winthrop down to Twisp is a Class I trip, while the stretch from Twisp to Carlton includes a little Class II water. The biggest inconveniences on both stretches are four weirs across the river. Some of these can be run at certain river levels, but there are decent portage routes around all of them. A second danger on this upper part of the Methow, especially during the high-water months of spring and early summer, are logs and trees that get dislodged from the bank and wash into the river. As on any river, these can be deadly.

Location: Enters Columbia River at Pateros; map A4, grid f1.

How to get there: Take Highway 20 east to Mazama and drive downstream along the river. Near Twisp, turn south on Highway 153 to stay near the Methow. From the south take U.S. 97 to Pateros and turn north on Highway 153.

Boat ramp: There are lots of places to get a boat into the Methow, but far fewer official boat ramps. The main ramp on the river is near its mouth and is used primarily by anglers and some boaters headed for the Columbia. The Pateros Boat Landing ramp is off Warren Avenue in Pateros and consists of a one-lane concrete ramp with a loading float. It has a fairly large paved parking area. Managed by the Pateros Parks and Recreation Department, its maintenance depends partly on donations from boaters who use the ramps. Paddlers are more likely to use lessformal launch sites that are scattered along the river between Winthrop and the river mouth. At Winthrop there's a decent place to launch near the gauging station at the Highway 20 bridge. Downstream, boaters launch and take out at the little city park near the mouth of the Twisp River just west of Highway 20 in Twisp. There's a fishing access at Carlton that serves as a take-out point for boaters making the upstream float and a put-in site for those going to Methow or on through Black Canyon to Pateros. Boaters making a shorter Black Canyon run or chickening out before they get there can launch or take out at another public fishing access, this one along Highway 20 at the mouth of McFarland Creek.

Facilities: Alta Lake State Park, located near the mouth of the river west of Pateros, has tent and RV sites, rest rooms, showers, and picnic areas. Food, gas, and lodging are available in Pateros, Twisp, and Winthrop. Several commercial rafting companies offer trips on the Methow.

Water sports/restrictions: Canoeing, kayaking, rafting, and fishing are the main activities. There's some power-boating in and around the river mouth.

Contact: Pine-Near Trailer Park, tel. (509) 996-2391; Methow Valley KOA Campground, tel. (509) 996-2255; Chewuch Inn, tel. (509) 996-3107; Pateros Motor Inn, tel. (800) 444-1985; Alta Lake State Park, tel. (509) 923-2473; Washington State Parks and Recreation Commission, tel. (800) 233-0321 (information), tel. (800) 452-5687 (reservations). All Rivers Adventures, tel. (800) 743-568; Osprey River Adventures, tel. (800) 997-4116; River Riders, Inc., tel. (800) 448-RAFT; River Recreation, Inc., tel. (800) 290-4500.

19 Alta Lake

Rating: 7

The sun shines a lot here, and when it does, Alta Lake becomes one of Okanogan County's most popular places. It covers more than 180 acres, and during the height of summer almost every one of those acres is being used by someone swimming, skiing, sailing, tubing, boarding, PWC riding, wading, or just sprawling out on an air mattress soaking up the sun. Special regulations limiting the time when skiers and PWC operators can be on the lake help to make life a little more pleasant for paddlers and anglers during the early morning and evening hours. The lake's easy access off nearby Highway 97 adds to its popularity among boaters and other water lovers. Trout fishing can be very good early in the season before the water warms too much.

Location: Southwest of Pateros; map A4, grid f0.

How to get there: Take Highway 97 to Pateros and turn north on Highway 153. Drive two miles to Alta Lake Road, turn west (left) and drive two miles to the lake.

Boat ramp: Alta Lake has two boat ramps, one at Alta Lake State Park and one at Whistlin' Pines Resort. The state park ramp is a two-lane concrete ramp with a loading float. The launch fee is $4 round-trip. An annual permit, good at all state parks, is available for $40. Launching is free if you're a registered park guest. The ramp at Whistlin' Pines is two lanes wide and had a natural surface. It also has a loading ramp and a small gravel parking area. Launching fees here are $2.50 for cartoppers, $3.50 for trailer boats under 16 feet, and $5 for larger boats.

Facilities: Alta Lake State Park has 15 tent sites and over 30 RV sites with full hookups, rest rooms with showers, and picnic tables. It also has a boat ramp. Whistlin' Pines Resort has moorage, 75 tent and RV sites, rental cabins, rest rooms with showers, and a small store with groceries and fishing tackle.

Water sports/restrictions: All water sports are permitted. Water skiing and PWC riding are limited to the hours of 9 a.m. to 6 p.m. during fishing season, which runs from late April through October.

Contact: Alta Lake State Park, tel. (509) 923-2473; Washington State Parks and Recreation Commission, tel. (800) 233-0321 (information), tel. (800) 452-5687 (reservations); Whistlin' Pines Resort, tel. (509) 923-2548.

20 Columbia River (including Upper Lake Entiat, Lake Pateros, and Rufus Woods Lake)

Rating: 7

Although this entire stretch of the once-wild Columbia is controlled by man, it's a part of the big river that is least explored by humans. There's a major highway along many miles of it, but some large areas of its shoreline have little or no road access. The best way to explore much of it, especially that part that lies behind Chief Joseph Dam and is known as Rufus Woods Lake, is by boat. That doesn't mean, however, that boating facilities dot the river every few hundred yards or so. You might be impressed with all the boat ramps and other facilities named earlier in this listing, but when you see them on a map, you realize that river access sites and accommodations for boaters along the river are few and damned far between. The facilities named earlier are spread out over nearly 90 miles of river and reservoirs, so they're sparse when compared to those on many of the state's waters. That doesn't mean, though, that you shouldn't consider this part of the Columbia system a viable boating destination, because it certainly is.

If you like your boating destinations somewhat wild and woolly, this is a great place to spend part of your summer. There are lots of wide-open spaces, both on the land and on the water, so you'll never run out of interesting places to explore. Because it's part of one big series of reservoirs and because the sun shines hot here in the summer, the water's surface is warm by midsummer. So it's a great place to swim, ski, and do the other things that will get you all wet; and it doesn't take long to dry off when you get out, either.

Rufus Woods Lake, the 50-mile-long impoundment behind Chief Joseph Dam, is by far the most removed from large concentrations of human activity. With boat ramps located only at its extreme ends and little shoreline development in between, this is a place where you can spend a day on the water and see few other people even in summer. With two of its three boat ramps located within a few miles of the dam, that's where a bulk of the skiers, wind surfers, and PWC operators spend most of their time.

While some come here for getaway boating, many come for a crack at the reservoir's huge rainbow trout. This is the home of those fat, sexless, triploid rainbows that grow to football shapes and trophy proportions. The state-record rainbow, a whopping 25-pounds, was caught here in January 1998. The lake also has good numbers of kokanee and walleyes.

If you want to explore this stretch of the Columbia right, you'll need time, so don't expect to get the full picture during a long weekend stay. One word of caution, especially if you do much boating downstream from Chief Joseph or Wells dams. Water levels may change dramatically from time to time, throwing some serious curves to boaters who aren't paying attention. Higher flows mean stronger currents and the possibility of debris in the water, so the entire personality of the river can change remarkably. Sand and gravel bars also come and go with the changes in water levels, so channels that are passable one day may leave you aground the next. Making assumptions about water depth can get you in trouble anywhere, and it's especially important to pay attention here.

Location: From Chelan Falls upstream to Grand Coulee Dam; map A4, grid f3.

How to get there: Drive north on U.S. 97 from Chelan Falls to parallel the southern part of this section. Take Highway 155 north from Coulee City or Highway 174 north from Wilbur to Grand Coulee to reach that part of the river directly downstream from Grand Coulee Dam. To reach the other end of this section of the Columbia, drive east from Pateros on U.S. 97 and turn south on Highway 17 near Fort Okanogan.

Boat ramp: There are 11 boat ramps on this stretch of the Columbia and its reservoirs:

- **Beebe Bridge Park:** Located just downstream from where Highway 97 crosses over the Columbia (and slightly west of where this map section begins) is Beebe Bridge Park, where you'll find one of the best launch ramps on the Columbia. The two-lane concrete ramp is big enough and offers good enough traction to launch boats of almost any size with almost any vehicle, and it has loading floats. It has parking for dozens of cars/trailers, and launching is free. It's maintained by Chelan County PUD.

- **Marina Park:** The next ramp on the Douglas County side of the river is at Marina Park just west of Bridgeport off Seventh Street. It's a two-lane ramp with loading floats and is another good one, but parking is much more limited than at Beebe Bridge. To find the ramp, drive west from Bridgeport on Highway 173 just over a mile and go west on Columbia Avenue for three blocks. Turn right on Seventh Street and go one block to the park.

- **Upstream Ramp:** A few miles east of Bridgeport is another ramp, this one at the bottom end of Rufus Woods Lake. Managed by the U.S.

Army Corps of Engineers, it's one-lane concrete ramp with a loading float and room to park about 10 cars and trailers. From Bridgeport cross Highway 17 and go east on Pearl Hill Road two miles, turning left at the sign pointing to the ramp.

- **Chelan Falls Park:** On the Chelan/Okanogan side of the river, the first ramp you encounter driving up Highway 97 is the ramp at Chelan Falls Park. It's a two-lane concrete-plank ramp with loading floats and parking for at least two dozen cars and trailers. Launching is free at this Chelan County PUD facility. From the junction of U.S. 97 and Highway 150, go south one mile on SR 150 to Chelan Falls, then left on Chestnut Street, following it one block. Turn right on First Street and go 200 yards to the park, on the left.

- **Carpenter Island Ramp:** The next ramp upstream, although it's maintained by Douglas County, is on the Chelan County side of the river just below Wells Dam. Launching is free at this single-lane ramp, but when the dam is spilling lots of water, the waves and current sometimes make tricky launching. Driving north from Chelan on U.S. 97, go four miles and stay northward on U.S. 97. Turn right at the Aswell-Wells Dam sign and go half a mile. Turn right at the sign designating Carpenter Island and the public fishing launch sign.

- **Starr Ramp:** Now in Okanogan County, the next ramp is on the right side of Highway 97 about two miles south of Starr (look closely for that one on a map). The single-lane concrete ramp is on an unmarked gravel road about a mile after you cross into Okanogan County from Chelan County.

- **Northeast Pateros Ramp:** This Douglas County PUD facility is a one-lane concrete ramp with a large gravel parking area. Find it by taking

U.S. 97 to Dawson Street and turning south, driving two blocks to Lakeshore. Turn left on Lakeshore and go 500 feet to the ramp on the right. Donations are requested if you use this ramp.

- **Pateros Boat Landing:** This is another one where donations from ramp users help pay for maintenance. The ramp is one lane with a loading float. Off U.S. 97 at Pateros, turn left on N Street, then left again on Warren Avenue. Go a quarter mile and turn left at the boat landing sign.

- **Brewster Park:** The next ramp along Highway 97 is at Brewster, off Seventh Street. Located right next to Columbia Cove Park, it's a good single-lane ramp with loading floats and parking for maybe 20 cars and trailers.

- **Bridgeport State Park:** There's a very good two-lane concrete ramp with loading floats at Bridgeport State Park about two miles above Chief Joseph Dam on Rufus Woods Lake. Launching here costs $4 unless you're a registered guest at the park. An annual launch permit, costing $40, is valid at all state parks. Take Highway 17 out of Bridgeport, cross the river and take the first right past the bridge. Drive 2.5 miles to the park.

- **Elmer City Boat Ramp:** The next ramp upstream on Rufus Woods is clear out at the other end near the town of Elmer City. It has two lanes, one gravel and one concrete, and room for about 30 cars with trailers. Launching is free at this ramp, which is maintained by the Corps of Engineers. Drive north from Grand Coulee Dam on Highway 125 about eight miles; then turn left to Seaton Grove, going 200 yards, then right on the unmarked paved road. Follow that road less than half a mile to the boat ramp at the end of the road.

Facilities: Food, gas, RV parks, and lodging are available in Chelan, Pateros, Brewster, Bridgeport, Coulee Dam, and Grand Coulee. Lake Pateros Motor Inn is right on the river at Pateros and has moorage for guests who arrive by boat. Marina Park near Bridgeport has tent and RV sites, a large swim beach, picnic shelters, and other amenities. Columbia Cove Park in Brewster has RV hookups, picnic shelters, rest rooms with showers, a swim beach, and other amenities. Bridgeport State Park, at the lower end of Rufus Woods Lake, offers about three dozen tent and RV sites. Beebe Bridge Park has tent and RV sites ($15 per night), a large swim beach, rest rooms with showers, and tennis and basketball courts. The day-use park at Chelan Falls has a large, roped swim beach with plenty of sun and green lawn, picnic tables, a covered cooking area, and baseball, tennis, volleyball, and basketball facilities.

Water sports/restrictions:

Contact: Lake Pateros Motor Inn, tel. (800) 444-1985; Coulee Playland Resort, tel. (509) 633-2671; Big Wally's, tel. (509) 632-5504; Bridgeport State Park, tel. (509) 686-7231; Washington State Parks and Recreation Commission, tel. (800) 233-0321 (information), tel. (800) 452-5687 (reservations); Columbia Cove RV Park, tel. (509) 689-2994; Brewster Chamber of Commerce, tel. (509) 689-3589.

21 Buffalo Lake

Rating: 6

Fishermen are probably happy about it, but in some ways it's too bad this lake has a prohibition on skiing and PWC use. At 500 acres it's a huge lake with more than enough room for everyone to do their thing. A lake this big in the middle of eastern Washington's sun country with such restrictive boating regulations seems like a waste of good recreational opportunity. Oh well, guess I'm not in charge.

Anyway, this lake is not only big, but quite deep, so it takes a few weeks of hot weather to get it to the comfortable stage for swimmers and other water lovers. By midsummer, though, it's there and provides fair sport for the folks who show up. Generally, that's not very many people. Outside fishing circles, Buffalo Lake isn't very well known among Washington's boating public.

If you do come here to fish, you need to remember that Buffalo Lake is within the boundaries of the Colville Indian Reservation where a tribal angling permit is required. The cost is $15 for a three-day permit, $20 for a seven-day permit, and $30 for a season permit that's valid from January 1 through December 31. A winter-fishing permit costing $5 is also required for fishing during the lake's special winter season that runs from January 1 to March 15. The permits, as well as tribal angling regulations, are available from some resorts and businesses in Nespelem, Inchelium, Republic, Colville, Kettle Falls, Elmer City, Brewster, Omak, and other towns in and around the Colville Indian Reservation.

Location: Northeast of Coulee Dam, Colville Indian Reservation; map A4, grid f7.

How to get there: Take Highway 155 north from Coulee Dam or south from Nespelem and turn east on Rebecca Lake Road. Drive past Rebecca Lake to Buffalo Lake Road and follow it to the lake.

Boat ramp: The lake has two launch facilities, one at Reynolds' Resort and one at Buffalo Lake Access Campground. The resort has a single-lane gravel ramp with two loading floats and a gravel parking area with room for about 10 cars and trailers. There's a launch fee of $3 to $5, depending on the size of the boat. Launching on a one-lane gravel ramp is free at the campground. It's managed by the Colville Confederated Tribes.

Facilities: Reynolds' Resort has fuel, boat rentals, cabins, and RV and tent sites. There are RV and tent sites and picnic tables at the campground. Other amenities are available to the south in Grand Coulee and Coulee Dam.

Water sports/restrictions: Waterskiing and PWC riding are prohibited.

Contact: Reynolds' Resort, tel. (509) 633-1092; Colville Confederated Tribes, Fish and Wildlife Department, tel. (509) 634-8845.

22 Lower Lake Roosevelt
Rating: 9

From Crescent Bay near Grand Coulee Dam to the Lincoln Mill boat ramp where it makes its sharp turn northward, the bottom end of Lake Roosevelt is a summertime paradise; you can find a place to pursue your favorite activity on, in, under, or around the water. The only thing that keeps it from being an absolute mob scene from Memorial Day to Labor Day each year is its location far from any of the Northwest's major population centers. That remoteness and relative desolation are part of the reason that the lake is such a fantastic boating destination, at least in the hearts and minds of many of its biggest fans, me included.

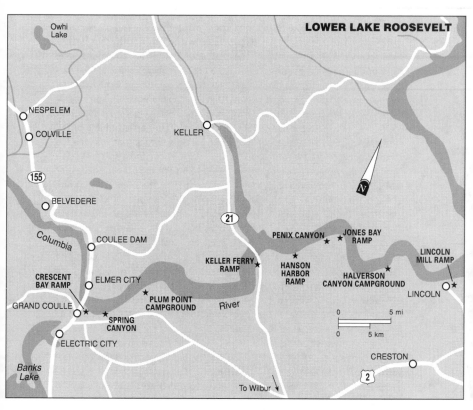

The lake's shoreline isn't and never will be dotted with homes and commercial facilities. Most of the south side is within the Lake Roosevelt National Recreation Area, while the northern shoreline is the south boundary of the Colville Indian Reservation, so development on either side of the water is highly unlikely. Much of the shoreline wouldn't be suitable for development anyway since it is lined with tall rock cliffs and boulder-strewn rock slides, many of them dropping straight off into the depths without even a hint of horizontal beach between land and the water. There are, however, some places where the beach is more gradual and even places where long expanses of sand and gravel are available to beach on, play on, and camp on.

Houseboating is a big deal here, and several concessionaires have rentals that are available for a few days, a week, or longer. Trailering a small boat to the lake and towing it behind the houseboat for skiing, fishing, and exploring is a popular strategy. At night most houseboaters stake their floating homes to a sloping beach somewhere and set up housekeeping. Depending on the size of the craft and how sociable the renter is, a houseboat will accommodate six to 12 people.

Boat camping is another possibility and one that I happen to favor when I visit lower Roosevelt. You can stay at the developed camping parks such as Spring Canyon, Keller Ferry, and Seven

Bays, where you can travel to and from by car and even trailer in and out of the water every day if you choose. These developed road-accessible areas, though, get busy during the summer, so you may have trouble getting a camping spot without a reservation. Or if you're like me, you might have trouble sleeping at night with all the happy camping going on around you.

You can also let your pioneering spirit take you a step further, camping at one of the more primitive camping spots like Plum Point, Goldsmith, Penix Canyon, Halverson Canyon, or Sterling Point. These campsites have places where you can beach or anchor a boat, and most have vault toilets and a picnic table or two. The next step is for the truly adventurous: striking out on your own and camping wherever the urge hits you (and where you can find a flat, semi-soft place to pitch your tent and/or put your sleeping bag). But if you're a tent camper looking for total seclusion, you might be disappointed. Many a camper has found a sheltered bay or sandy beach along the Lake Roosevelt shoreline, unloaded the boat, pitched the tent, cooked dinner, and settled back for a quiet evening of solitude only to have a houseboat round the bend about sunset, nose up to the beach 100 feet away, and commence partying. It happens quite often during the peak of the vacation season, from the July 4 weekend through Labor Day because there simply are too few good camping beaches around the lake.

Skiing, riding PWC riding, tubing, sail-boarding, and swimming all are excellent options here, and so is fishing. There are probably as many species of freshwater fish available in Lake Roosevelt as any other body of water in Washington, including large kokanee, rainbow trout, walleyes, smallmouth bass, whitefish and burbot. While you're at the bottom end of the lake, you probably should check out the reason for its existence: Grand Coulee Dam. Built in the 1930s, it's still considered one of man's greatest construction feats. Tours are available of the big, man-made rock that changed the Columbia River forever. You'll also want to hit the big lawn at the visitor center below the dam at least one evening during your visit to see the world's largest laser light show, which uses the face of the dam as a screen. It includes a little hydroelectric propaganda, but it's still pretty cool. The laser shows kick off the season each year on Memorial Day weekend with a fireworks display and other festivities.

Location: From Grand Coulee Dam up to Lincoln; map A4, grid g7. (See the Lower Lake Roosevelt inset map. Refer also to the Upper Lake Roosevelt inset map in Chapter A5.)

How to get there: Take Highway 155 north from Coulee City, Highways 174 or 21 north from Wilbur, or Highway 25 north from Davenport to reach major access areas on the lower lake.

Boat ramp: There are launch ramps at six locations along this end of Roosevelt, plus three more within a few miles uplake (see Chapter A5). The following boat ramps are listed on either the Lower Lake Roosevelt inset map or the Upper Lake Roosevelt inset map in Chapter A5.

- **National Park Service Ramp/ Crescent Bay:** Just above Grand Coulee Dam on the south side of the lake is the National Park Service ramp at Crescent Bay. There's a $6 launch fee at this single-lane ramp, which has a loading float and parking spaces for several dozen cars and trailers. Get there by driving half a mile north from Grand Coulee on Highway 155 and turning right on the unmarked gravel rod leading to the ramp.

- **Spring Canyon Ramp:** The well-maintained ramp at Spring Canyon Campground three miles east of Grand Coulee has two lanes and three loading floats, with plenty of paved parking. It's managed by the National Park Service as part of the Coulee Dam National Recreation Area, and a $6 launch fee was imposed here and at other Park Service ramps in 1998.

- **Keller Ferry Ramp:** The same $6 fee is charged at Keller Ferry where there's a three-lane paved ramp and large loading float, along with paved parking for dozens of boat and trailers. Get there by taking Highway 174 north from Wilbur and turning right on Highway 21. As you approach the ferry ramp, turn left into the park and boat ramp.

- **Hanson Harbor Ramp:** This launch site is several miles east of Keller Ferry on Hanson Harbor Road, and it has a one-lane ramp with a large paved parking area. A $6 launch fee is charged here as well. Go north from Wilburn on Highway 174, right on Highway 21, then 6.2 miles, almost to mile marker 99. Turn right just before the marker on the unmarked gravel road and go two miles before turning left on Gollehon Road. Drive two miles on Gollehon and turn left on Hanson Road, which leads five miles to the ramp.

- **Jones Bay Ramp:** The next ramp uplake is at Jones Bay Campground, also reached via Hanson Harbor Road. Rather than going to the end of Hanson Harbor Road, veer right at the Y and proceed three miles to Jones Bay. This site has a one-lane paved ramp and loading float. A $6 fee is charged here as well.

- **Lincoln Mill Ramp:** About 14 miles farther up the lake from Jones Bay is the Lincoln Mill ramp, a large, paved, four laner with a loading float and lots of paved parking. Managed by Lincoln County, this excellent ramp has no launch fee. To get there, drive east from Creston on U.S. 2, turn left on Lincoln Road, and go eight miles to the end.

Facilities: There are campgrounds at Crescent Bay, Spring Canyon, Plum Point, Keller Ferry, Penix Canyon, Jones Bay, Halverson Canyon, and Hawk Creek, all of which are on the south side of the lake. Keller Park Campground is along Highway 21 near the upper end of the lake's San Poil Arm. Houseboat rentals are available in Keller Ferry and uplake at Seven Bays Marina (reservations required). Skiffs, larger powerboats, and jet boats also are available for rent, as are skis, knee boards, and other equipment. Fuel docks are available at Crescent Bay and Keller Ferry. Boat-sewage pump-out facilities are available at Spring Canyon and Keller Ferry. There are roped swim beaches at Spring Canyon and Keller Ferry, and Hanson Harbor has a large sandy beach that's adequate for swimming. A full range of services is available at Grand Coulee and Coulee Dam.

Water sports/restrictions: All water sports are permitted.

Contact: Coulee Dam Area chamber of Commerce, tel. (800) COULEE2 or tel. (509) 633-3074; Keller Ferry Marina, tel. (509) 647-5755; Roosevelt Recreational Enterprises, tel. (800) 648-LAKE.

23 Banks Lake

Rating: 8

I said it in *Washington Fishing*, and I'll say it again here: Banks Lake has some-

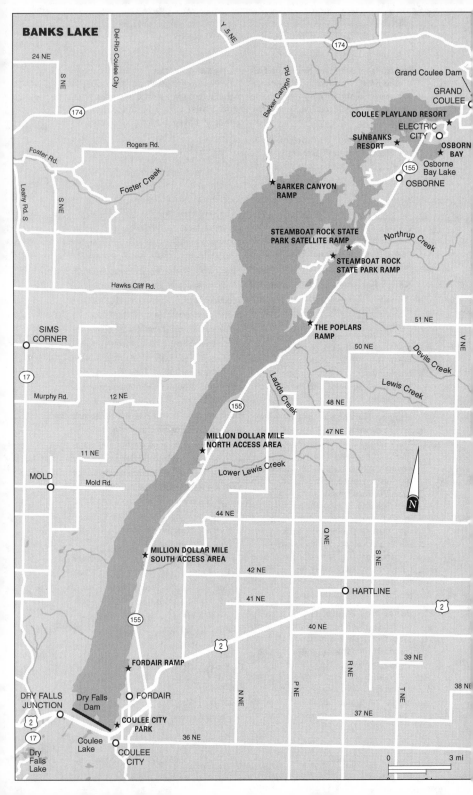

thing to offer everyone who visits it. One of the Columbia Basin's top fishing lakes, it's also one of its best places to water ski, ride PWC, swim, cruise, or do almost anything else involving water. If there's an exception, it might be sailing, because the wind here tends to be an all-or-nothing proposition. You might sit out in the middle of the lake for hours or days waiting for something to happen; then when it does, you wish to hell it hadn't started.

Several years ago, a large group of neighbors got together and made its annual trip to Banks shortly after school let out. The weather was beautiful for the first day and a half, but on the afternoon of the second day the wind started kicking up, and by dinner time I was glad I had devoted the day to hiking and biking instead of boating. As campers throughout Steamboat Rock State Park went about the task of firing up their barbecues and setting out paper plates, it really was beginning to howl. Gaining strength, the summer storm soon began to blow toys and other small items around the park, and then tents began to collapse. A few uninitiated campers had neglected to tie down their temporary homes, so dome tents were soon rolling awkwardly across the lawn. Smart boaters, of course, headed for shelter when the wind started, but at least one aluminum fishing boat was swamped, its occupants left to drift with the wind until things calmed down and someone else came along to pick them up. It all happened quickly and with little or no warning, so it's lucky that no one was hurt or worse. The moral, of course, is that a big lake like this can change personality in a hurry, so be prepared. And if you're in a sailboat, be ready for anything. Most of the

time, though, Banks is a 22-mile-long pussycat, in summer a place where blue skies, warm temperatures, and calm water are the rule.

Much of the boating and water sports activity is centered on the north end of the lake where the state park and various campgrounds and resorts serve as staging areas for folks who scatter in all directions to do their thing. Devil's Punch Bowl, a shallow bay between Steamboat Rock and the east side of the lake, is often the scene of most early-summer activity, since its shallow waters warm faster than the rest of the lake. The lake, by the way, is actually an overflow reservoir holding Columbia River water that's released from nearby Lake Roosevelt and held back by two-mile-wide Dry Falls Dam, down by Coulee City. The Coulee City area is probably the second-busiest part of the lake as folks come and go from the city park boat ramp and the Department of Wildlife ramp a couple of miles to the north.

When it kicks up, wind is the biggest problem for Banks Lake boaters; the second-biggest problem is the fluctuating water level. It's usually rising during the early part of the summer, presenting little problem, but when it begins to drop, it exposes rock piles, reefs, and ledges that can be murder on props and lower units. Contour maps of the lake are available from various sources and are worth the investment. Paying attention to your depthsounder, needless to say, is another good idea.

Location: Between Grand Coulee at the north and Coulee City at the south; map A4, grid g5. (See the Banks Lake inset map.)

How to get there: Take Highway 17 or U.S. 2 to Coulee City and turn north on

Highway 155 to parallel the east side of the lake all the way to Electric City.

Boat ramp: Would you believe 11 launch sites on one lake? All boat ramps are listed on the Banks Lake inset map. Here's the rundown:

- **Coulee City Park:** Working your way up the lake from the dam, you won't have to travel far before you find the ramp at Coulee City's Community Park. Maintained by the city's parks and recreation department, it has four paved lanes and three loading floats. Launching is free. To reach it from the junction of U.S. 2 and Highway 17, drive east on U.S. 2 for two miles and turn north (left) at the east end of Dry Falls Dam. The park and ramp are on your left.

- **Fordair Ramp:** Less than two miles out of Coulee City to the north is the Department of Fish and Wildlife's Fordair access area and one-lane ramp. It has room to park about a half dozen cars and trailers. A $10 WDFW access decal is required to use the public launch areas maintained by the Washington Department of Fish and Wildlife. To reach it from Coulee City, go east on U.S. 2 for one-third mile and turn left on County Road I 8, following it just over half a mile and turning right on Fordair Road. Go one-third mile on Fordair and turn left on J Road NE, following it a mile and a half to the ramp at the end of the road.

- **Million Dollar Mile South Access Area:** Another WDFW ramp is located along Highway 155 about six miles north of Coulee City. It's a one-lane gravel ramp with room for about a dozen cars and trailers and is marked by a "Public Fishing" sign along the highway. A $10 WDFW access decal is required to use the public launch areas maintained by the Washington Department of Fish and Wildlife.

- **Million Dollar Mile North Access Area (Midlake Ramp):** Another sign marks the WDFW ramp along Highway 155 about three miles farther up the lake, known by locals as the midlake ramp. Located on a narrow little canal off the main lake, it can be a tricky place to load and unload a boat in low water, but it has plenty of parking. Don't forget the WDFW access decal.

- **The Poplars Ramp:** There's another Department of Fish and Wildlife ramp at the junction of Highway 155 and the entrance road to Steamboat Rock State Park. It's actually an old roadbed that drops into the lake at the south end of the shallow bay known as Devil's Punch Bowl. An access decal is required here, too. Turn west off Highway 155 at the Steamboat Rock State Park entrance sign and take the first right down the old highway to the water's edge.

- **Steamboat Rock State Park Ramp:** An excellent four-lane ramp just north of the camping areas at Steamboat Rock State Park, this one has a loading float and parking for more than 100 cars and trailers. The park entrance is well marked off Highway 155, eight miles south of Electric City.

- **Steamboat Rock State Park Satellite Ramp:** To the northeast, on the north side of the peninsula that juts off the eastern shore to form the upper boundary of Devil's Punch bowl, is another State Parks ramp, this one not as good as the other. In fact, it's breaking up badly and may not be usable for long unless it gets some radical TLC pretty soon. The fee is $4 fee to use the main park ramp and $3 to use the satellite ramp. Washington State Parks also issues a $40 annual launch fee good at any park ramp. It's marked by a sign along Highway 155 five miles south of Electric City.

- **Barker Canyon Ramp:** The only ramp on the west side of Banks is in Barker Canyon in what would have to be called the lake's northwest corner. You reach this Department of Fish and Wildlife ramp by driving west from Grand Coulee on Highway 174, going about 10 miles to Barker Canyon Road, turning south (left) and driving six miles to the end of the road. A $10 WDFW access decal is required to use the public launch areas maintained by the Washington Department of Fish and Wildlife.

- **Sunbanks Resort:** There's another ramp at Sunbanks Resort near the south entrance to Osborne Bay. This single-lane concrete-plank ramp has a loading float and room for about a dozen cars and trailers to park.

- **Osborne Bay:** This large bay near the north end of Banks also has a Department of Fish and Wildlife ramp near its east end. It's a natural ramp with no surfacing materials, and I wouldn't recommend launching large trailer boats here. You'll need that $10 decal to use this ramp. To reach it, drive south from Electric City on Highway 155 for one mile and turn left at milepost 23. Follow the gravel road just over a mile to its end.

- **Coulee Playland Resort:** This long-time resort near the north end of the lake has a two-lane concrete ramp with three loading floats and nearby moorage. It's right along Highway 155 at the south end of Electric City.

Facilities: Big Wally's, which is right along the highway just north of Coulee City, is a good place to stop for gas, supplies, and information about the lake. A fishing guide service is also available there. The city park in Coulee City also has a nice swim beach, boat moorage, play equipment, and picnic areas. At the north end of the lake is Steamboat Rock State Park, which has a very good swim beach, tent and RV sites (reservations required), boat ramps and floats, rest rooms and showers, and a small store with ice, snacks, and groceries. A little farther north in Electric City are Coulee Playland and the Skydeck Motel, both right on the water. Groceries, restaurants, watering holes, gas stations, and motels are also available in Electric City. The Department of Fish and Wildlife access area at midlake is one of the few WDFW access sites where overnight camping is permitted, but it's not particularly pretty.

Water sports/restrictions: All water sports are permitted.

Contact: Big Wally's, tel. (509) 632-5504; Steamboat Rock State Park, tel. (509) 633-1304; Washington State Parks and Recreation Commission, tel. (800) 233-0321 (information), tel. (800) 452-5687 (reservations); Coulee Playland Resort, tel. (509) 633-2671; Skydeck Motel, tel. (509) 633-0290.

24 Jameson Lake

Rating: 6

One of Washington's top trout lakes, it has suffered from rising and falling water levels in recent years. Those changing water levels also affect boating because they're sometime dramatic enough to flood the public launch ramp and other Jameson facilities. When it's accessible, though, it's over 330 acres of warm-weather boating fun, with the very real possibility of catching a big rainbow trout or two in the bargain. The main problem for most folks is accessibility, since they really have to want to go to Jameson Lake in order to wind up there. It's some distance away from any of eastern Washington's larger towns and away from major highways as well.

Location: Southeast of Mansfield; map A4, grid h3.

How to get there: Take Highway 2 east from Waterville or west from Coulee City and turn north on Jameson Lake Road, following it a little over six miles to the lake. A road leading around the east side of the lake to the north isn't always passable, so a different route may be in order if you want to reach the north end of Jameson by road. Take Highway 172 to Mansfield and drive south from town on Mansfield Road. Just over three miles from town, where Berg Road begins, turn left and follow Wittig Road toward the north end of Jameson Lake.

Boat ramp: Besides the public access area and boat ramp, there are resorts at both ends of the lake that have ramps. A $10 WDFW access decal is required to use the public launch areas maintained by the Washington Department of Fish and Wildlife.

Facilities: Two resorts, Jack's and Jameson Lake, have campsites, moorage, a limited supply of groceries, and other amenities. The nearest towns are Waterville to the west and Coulee City to the east.

Water sports/restrictions: Fishing and paddling are the main attractions.

Contact: Jack's Resort, tel. (509) 683-1095 (April through July 4 and the month of October only); Jameson Lake Resort, tel. (509) 683-1141.

25 Dry Falls Lake

Rating: 7

Dramatic scenery, a wealth of birds and wildlife, and excellent fishing are enough to keep people coming back to this part of the Grand Coulee. Formed by the water and ice that came crash-ing out of Lake Missoula long before even the oldest among us were around, this is an awesome place. Paddle it on a quiet spring evening and you may think that every bird in the Columbia Basin is within earshot. At only 99 acres, Dry Falls goes largely unnoticed among the many lakes in this area with more facilities and easier access. Don't be one who forgets to notice the next time you're in the area.

Location: Southwest of Coulee City; map A4, grid i4.

How to get there: Take Highway 17 south from Dry Falls Junction or north from Soap Lake to the Sun Lakes State Park entrance and turn east into the park. About 1.2 miles off the highway, turn left at the sign pointing to Dry Falls Lake. Continue following signs to the lake for about three miles, passing Rainbow and Perch Lakes on the left. The last mile to Dry Falls is over rough, dirt road where pickups or four-wheel-drive vehicles are recommended.

Boat ramp: There is no boat ramp on the lake, but it's fairly easy to carry a cartopper, canoe, or float tube to the edge of the water.

Facilities: Nearby Sun Lakes State Park has 18 RV sites and 175 tent sites for campers, as well as rest rooms, showers and picnic areas. Food and gas are available in Coulee City, and there's plenty of lodging available to the south in Soap Lake.

Water sports/restrictions: Paddling and fishing are permitted. Motors of all kinds are prohibited.

Contact: Sun Lakes State Park, tel. (509) 632-5583; Washington State Parks and Recreation Commission, tel. (800) 233-0321 (information), tel. (800) 452-5687 (reservations).

26 Deep Lake

Rating: 6

Like nearby Dry Falls Lake, Deep is best known for its trout fishing, but canoeists and kayakers visiting the many waters to the north and south might want to swing by for a visit while they're in the area. It's about 100 acres in size and has lots of birds and wildlife to see and hear. You'll have to carry or drag your boat a short distance to the water, but no big deal. Take a trout rod if you visit during the spring or early summer.

Location: Southwest of Coulee City; map A4, grid i4.

How to get there: Take Highway 17 north from Soap Lake or south from Dry Falls Junction to the Sun Lakes State Park entrance and turn east into the park. After dropping down the hill into the bottom of the Grand Coulee, follow the signs eastward to the Deep Lake.

Boat ramp: There is no boat ramp on the lake, but you can get a cartopper or canoe to the water quite easily.

Facilities: Nearby Sun Lakes State Park has 18 RV sites and 175 tent sites for campers, as well as rest rooms, showers, and picnic areas. Food and gas are available in Coulee City, and there's plenty of lodging available to the south in Soap Lake.

Water sports/restrictions: Paddling and fishing are the main draws. The lake has a 5 mph speed limit and a prohibition on all forms of skiing and other powerboat sports.

Contact: Sun Lakes State Park, tel. (509) 632-5583; Washington State Parks and Recreation Commission, tel. (800) 233-0321 (information), tel. (800) 452-5687 (reservations); Big Wally's, tel. (509) 632-5504.

27 Park Lake

Rating: 8

Since it's one of the Columbia Basin's top trout-fishing lakes, angling is the first priority here in the spring and early summer. That's why it has special prohibitions on skiing in effect early in the season. But once things open up especially after the first of July, Park and nearby Blue Lake come to life for all forms of water sports. It covers almost 350 acres, so there's plenty of room to get away from the swim beaches to ski or operate PWC in open water. Right in the heart of Washington's sunbelt, it's also a great place to work on that tan while you're playing; just don't overdo it as lots of folks do when they first get here. Look around the beach at the state park or one of the resorts early in the summer and it's easy to pick out the western Washingtonians from the east siders. Those from across the Cascades are the bright red ones. They don't call 'em the Sun Lakes for nothing.

Location: Southwest of Coulee City; map A4, grid i4.

How to get there: Drive south from Dry Falls Junction or north from Soap Lake on Highway 17, which parallels the lake's southwestern shoreline. Turn east at the Sun Lakes State Park entrance to reach the resort, state park, and other facilities at the northeast end of the lake.

Boat ramp: The lake has three launch sites. Sun Lakes State Park has a two-lane, asphalt ramp with a loading float and parking for about 20 cars and trailers. There's a $4 launch fee, and a $40 annual permit is available, good at state parks throughout Washington. Laurent's Sun Village Resort has two ramps, one concrete and one gravel, with several loading floats. These gently sloping ramps are in fairly shallow water, so people with larger boats usually go elsewhere. The resort charges a $2 launch fee. There's also a Department of Fish and Wildlife ramp on the lake, marked by a "Public Fishing" sign off Park Lake Road. It's a bit of a stretch calling this a boat ramp, since you can't get a trailer into it, but it's good for launching cartoppers and paddle craft. But the fee's the same as on other WDFW sites; you still need that access decal, which costs $10 (per year) unless you have a fishing and/or hunting license.

Facilities: Sun Lake State Park has a large number of tent sites and a few RV sites with hookups. Sun Village Resort has over 100 RV sites, a big swim beach, store, rental boats, moorage, rest rooms with showers, picnic shelters and tables, a large play field, and other facilities.

Water sports/restrictions: All water sports are permitted, but the lake does have some special regulations that all boaters should be aware of. The lake is off-limits to skiers from opening day of fishing season to until May 20 each year. From May 20 to July 1, skiing is prohibited before 10 a.m. and after 8 p.m. Skiers must follow a counterclockwise pattern and stay out of areas posted or buoyed for swimming or nowake limits.

Contact: Sun Lakes State Park, tel. (509) 632-5583; Sun Lakes Park Resort, tel. (509) 632-5291; Washington State Parks and Recreation Commission, tel. (800) 233-0321 (information), tel. (800) 452-5687 (reservations).

28 Blue Lake

Rating: 8

Even bigger than Park Lake to the north, this 500-acre playground is a favorite of sun seekers from all over the Northwest. Regulations aimed at making life easier for anglers are in effect through June; then Blue Lake really starts hopping. When the water's calm, it's one of the best waterskiing lakes around, and when it gets choppy it's a great place for PWC riders to play. When the wind comes up—which may happen at any time—it even becomes a place where windsurfers can have their fun. Whatever the surface conditions, though, it's a great place to swim and soak up the sun. If you come here in May or June, bring your fishing tackle; like Park Lake, Blue is a prime rainbow trout lake, one of the best in the Columbia Basin.

Location: Southwest of Coulee City; map A4, grid i4.

How to get there: Take Highway 17 north from Soap Lake or south from Dry Falls Junction. The road runs right along the west side of the lake, with side roads at the north and south end leading to resort facilities on the lake.

Boat ramp: Coulee Lodge Resort has a concrete ramp with loading float and room for several dozen cars and trailers. The resort charges a $3 launch fee. Blue Lake Resort has a one-lane gravel ramp with parking for about a dozen cars and trailers and charges a $2 launch fee. The lake also has a Department of Fish and Wildlife access area, with one concrete ramp and one gravel ramp located side by side with a rock barrier between them. There's room for about 30 cars and trailers at the WDFW access area. A $10 WDFW access decal is required to use the public launch areas maintained by the Washington Department of Fish and Wildlife.

Facilities: Coulee Lodge at the north end of the lake has RV sites, a small store, rest rooms and showers, a swim area, moorage dock, boat rentals, and other accommodations. Blue Lake Resort has boat moorage, a swim area, rental cabins, tent and RV sites, a play area, and convenience/tackle store.

Water sports/restrictions: All water sports are permitted, but the lake does have some special regulations that all boaters should be aware of. The lake is off-limits to skiers from opening day of fishing season to until May 20 each year. From May 20 to July 1, skiing is prohibited before 10 a.m. and after 8 p.m. Skiers must follow a counter-clockwise pattern and stay out of areas posted or buoyed for swimming or no-wake limits.

Contact: Coulee Lodge, tel. (509) 632-5565; Blue Lake Resort, tel. (509) 632-5364; Sun Village Resort, tel. (509) 632-5664; Sun Lakes State Park, tel. (509) 632-5583; Washington State Parks and Recreation Commission, tel. (800) 233-0321 (information), tel. (800) 452-5687 (reservations).

29 Lake Lenore

Rating: 7

If you don't mind working just a bit to get your boat on the water, this 1,600-acre lake north of Soap Lake is worth exploring. Four access sites along the highway on the lake's east side provide places to carry or slide a small boat to the water's edge. Other boats you see will likely carry anglers, since this is one of central Washington's premier trophy-trout lakes, with Lahontan cutthroats as large as 10 pounds. Most of the fishing, though, occurs at the north and south ends of the lake, so if you paddle the middle portion, you may have it to yourself. The steep western bank, most of which is lined with basalt cliffs, is the best place to find solitude. Birds and wildlife are abundant, and there are few hazards for paddlers to worry about except the wind. It can build in a hurry and whistle up this canyon to form large whitecaps on Lenore. Always have an escape route and hiding spot in mind if the weather begins to change.

Location: North of Soap Lake; map A4, grid i3.

How to get there: Drive south from Dry Falls Junction or north from Soap Lake on Highway 17, which parallels the east side of the lake.

Boat ramp: There are no formal boat ramps, but there are several public access areas on the east side of the lake where launching a small cartopper or float tube is an easy chore.

Facilities: Resorts and the state park to the north provide RV and tent sites, showers, groceries, tackle, and other necessities. Food, gas, and lodging are available in Soap Lake a few miles to the south.

Water sports/restrictions: Paddling and fishing are it. All but electric motors are prohibited.

Contact: Blue Lake Resort, tel. (509) 632-5364; Coulee Lodge, tel. (509) 632-5565; Sun Lakes State Park, tel. (509) 632-5583; Washington State Parks and Recreation Commission, tel. (800) 233-0321 (information), tel. (800) 452-5687 (reservations).

ELOIKA LAKE

MAP A5

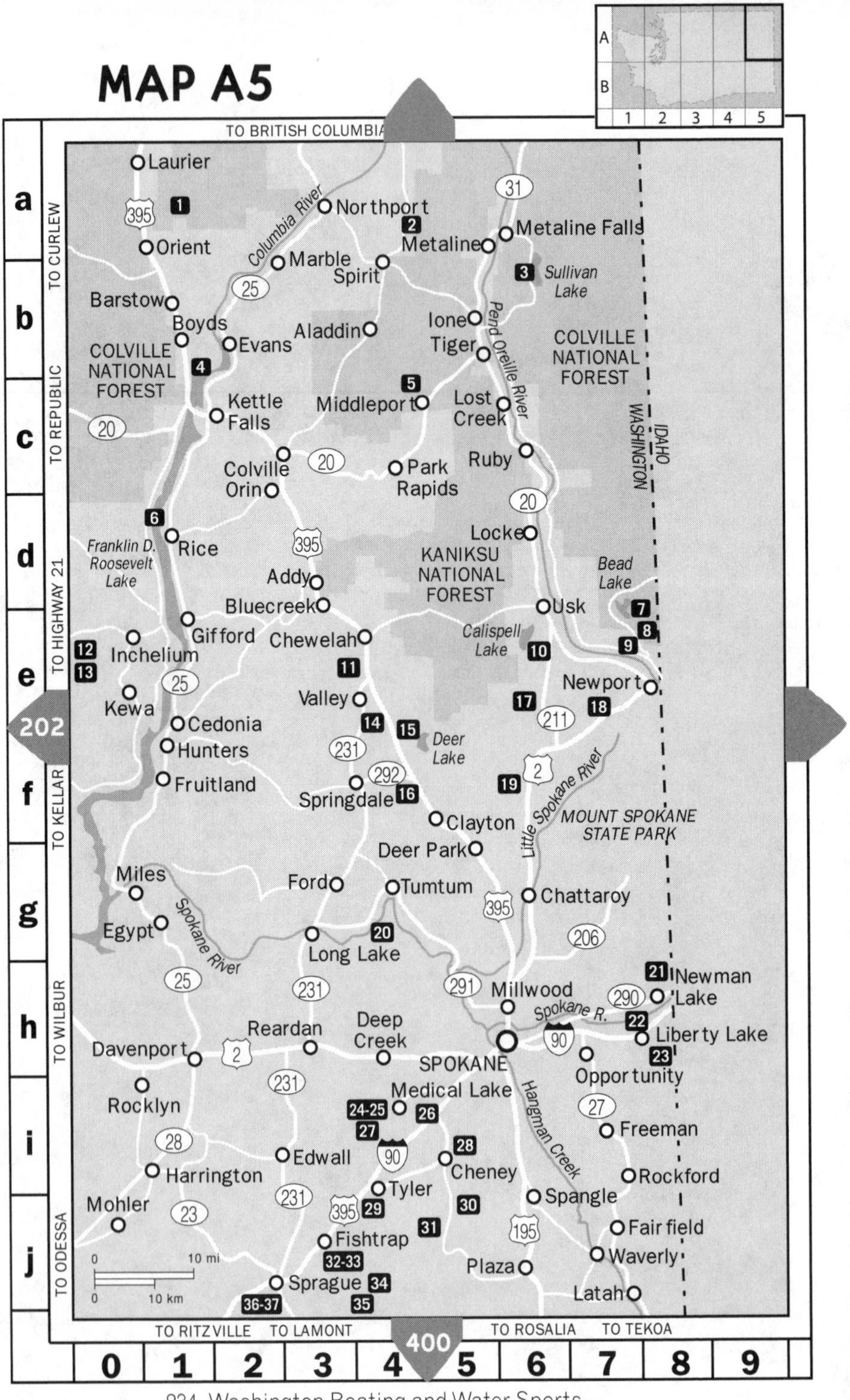

TO BRITISH COLUMBIA

a
Laurier
395 **1**
Orient
Columbia River
Northport **2**
Metaline
31
Metaline Falls
Marble
Spirit
3 Sullivan Lake

b
Barstow
Boyds
25
Evans
Aladdin
Ione
Tiger
COLVILLE NATIONAL FOREST
Pend Oreille River
COLVILLE NATIONAL FOREST
4
Kettle Falls
Middleport **5**
Lost Creek

c
20
Colville
Orin
20
Park Rapids
Ruby
Locke
20
IDAHO WASHINGTON

d
6
Rice
Franklin D. Roosevelt Lake
395
Addy
KANIKSU NATIONAL FOREST
Bead Lake
Bluecreek
Usk
7
8

e
12
13
Inchelium
Gifford
Chewelah
Calispell Lake
10
Newport
9
25
11
17
18
Kewa
Valley
211
202
14 **15**
Deer Lake

f
Cedonia
Hunters
Fruitland
231
292
Springdale **16**
19
2
Little Spokane River
MOUNT SPOKANE STATE PARK
Clayton
Deer Park

g
Miles
Egypt
Spokane River
Ford
Tumtum
395
Chattaroy
206
20
Long Lake

h
25
231
291
Millwood
Spokane R.
21 Newman Lake
290
22
Reardan
Deep Creek
23
Davenport
2
SPOKANE
90
Liberty Lake
231
Medical Lake
Opportunity

i
Rocklyn
24-25
26
27
27
28
Freeman
28
Rockford
Edwall
90
Cheney
Harrington
28
Hangman Creek

j
Mohler
23
395
29
Tyler
30
Spangle
195
Fairfield
Fishtrap
31
Waverly
32-33
34
Sprague
Plaza
Latah
36-37
35
0   10 mi
0   10 km

TO RITZVILLE   TO LAMONT   **400**   TO ROSALIA   TO TEKOA

0 1 2 3 4 5 6 7 8 9

TO CURLEW
TO REPUBLIC
TO HIGHWAY 21
TO KELLAR
TO WILBUR
TO ODESSA

CHAPTER A5

◘ Pierre Lake

Rating: 6

Looking for a place to really get away? Have I got a lake for you! OK, no more sounding like a real estate salesman. If getting away to a smallish lake back in the woods and well off the heavily traveled path sounds like your idea of a good boating time, maybe Pierre is worth considering. Located in Colville National Forest about six miles south of the Canadian border, this 100-acre lake has limited facilities and a rather rough boat ramp that keeps a lot of traffic away. It's a beautiful place to paddle or cast for trout, and the Forest Service campground near its shores usually has empty campsites except on long holiday weekends. You probably wouldn't want to spend a month here unless you're a hermit, but a couple of days would be nice.

Location: Northeast of Orient; map A5, grid a1.

How to get there: Take U.S. 395 to Barstow and turn east onto Barstow-Pierre Lake Road, which soon turns north and leads about 10 miles to the west side of the lake.

Boat ramp: A U.S. Forest Service ramp on the lake's western shore has a gravel service and loading float but drops off quite sharply a short distance from shore. Larger boats might have trouble launching here.

Facilities: There's a U.S. Forest Service campground on the west side of the lake.

Water sports/restrictions: Paddling and fishing are good bets here.

Contact: The Sport Spot, tel. (509) 738-6710 (rings at a home during the winter off-season); Colville National Forest,

Kettle Falls Ranger District, tel. (509) 738-6111.

◙ Deep Lake

Rating: 6

Like Pierre Lake (above), this isn't a place you're likely to stumble across while on your way to or from somewhere else; you have to make a determined effort to find yourself on the shores of this large Stevens County lake. And if you do find yourself there, you'll probably be happy about it. It's a pretty lake in a pretty spot, covering nearly 200 acres in the heart of the Colville National Forest. After you've spent day or two exploring the lake, expand your adventures to include some of the many streams, all of which flow into Deep Creek and eventually into the Columbia River near the town of Northport.

Location: Southeast of Northport, Stevens County; map A5, grid a4.

How to get there: Take U.S. 395 to Colville and turn east on Highway 20. Just east of town turn north at the sign pointing toward Northport (Colville-Aladdin-Northport Road) and follow it to the small town of Spirit. Go east on Deep Lake-Boundary Road and follow it to the east side of the lake.

Boat ramp: The lake has a Department of Fish and Wildlife access area with a boat ramp and toilets. The concrete-plank ramp was in poor shape as of early 1999. Owners of larger boats should take it easy.

Facilities: The nearest facilities are in Northport.

Water sports/restrictions: All water sports are permitted.

Contact:); Colville National Forest, Kettle Falls Ranger District, tel. (509) 738-6111.

3 Sullivan Lake

Rating: 7

The biggest, deepest, and maybe the coldest lake in northeastern Washington has a lot to offer boaters and water enthusiasts of all kinds. Although quite a haul even from Spokane, it's a destination that's well worth the trip. It covers nearly 1,300 acres, thanks to the damming of Harvey Creek in the early 1930s that made an already big natural lake even bigger. Resting in a large basin with steep hills rising above it to the east, it has places that are over 300 feet deep. All that deep water, of course, warms slowly in the summer, so you can turn purple after a short swim even in early July, but folks still like to swim here. I don't happen to be one of them. Skiing, tubing, wake boarding, PWC riding, windsurfing, sailing, cruising, and fishing all are popular at Sullivan. The location of its campgrounds at opposite ends of the lake seems to help keep the middle of the lake open, so there's always plenty of elbow room on the water, even during long holiday weekends. If you have fantasies about caching trophy trout, you might be interested to know that the state-record brown trout, a whopping 22-pounder, was caught here in the '60s.

Location: Southeast of Metaline Falls, Pend Oreille County; map A5, grid b6.

How to get there: Take Highway 20 to the small town of Tiger and turn north on Highway 31. Just south of Ione turn east (right) on Sullivan Lake Road and follow it to the lake.

Boat ramp: There are boat ramps at the north and south ends of the lake. The U.S. Forest Service ramp at the north end is a single-lane concrete ramp with a loading float and parking for over a dozen cars and trailers. It's a good ramp even for larger boats, and it's free. The Forest Service ramp at the south end is similar but has less parking.

Facilities: Campgrounds at both ends of the lake have tent and RV sites, day-use areas with swim beaches, rest rooms, picnic areas, and RV dump stations. Food, gas, motels, trailer parks, and bed-and-breakfast facilities are available in Ione.

Water sports/restrictions: All water sports are permitted.

Contact: Colville National Forest, Newport Ranger District, tel. (509) 447-3129, Ione Chamber of Commerce, tel. (509) 442-3200.

4 Kettle River

Rating: 6

This large but gentle tributary to the Columbia has a lot to offer paddlers and other moving-water enthusiasts. Some lament that it's too bad the Kettle isn't a little closer to home, but if it were, it might lose some of the charm that makes it so attractive in the first place. The real downside here is that access is limited, with private ownership making it impossible to reach the river throughout much of its length. That's fairly typical along a lot of Washington rivers, but here some of the land owners seem even less cordial toward visiting boaters than in other parts of the state. Maybe they're just not used to company. If you aren't sure about shoreline ownership, stay in your boat to avoid possible confrontations. This big river is a good place to paddle or row throughout most of the year, but watch it during peak runoff periods from Memorial Day to the Fourth of July, when it really gets rolling.

Location: Enters north end of Lake Roosevelt north of Kettle Falls; map A5, grid b1.

How to get there: Take U.S. 395 north from Kettle Falls to parallel the west side of the river all the way to the Canadian border.

Boat ramp: Bridges across the river near Laurier and Orient provide good launch possibilities, and there are places along Highway 395 about five miles north of Orient and in a couple of places between Orient and Barstow where it's possible to launch or take out along the highway.

Facilities: Food, gas, and lodging are available in Kettle Falls, with limited facilities available in the several small towns along the river.

Water sports/restrictions: Kayaking, canoeing, rafting, and tubing are good possibilities on most of the river. Some good swimming holes are found on the lower river where it slows to meet the Columbia at the upper end of Lake Roosevelt.

Contact: The Sport Spot, tel. (509) 738-6710 (Rings at a residence during the winter); Colville National Forest, Kettle Falls Ranger District, tel. (509) 738-6111.

5 Little Pend Oreille Chain of Lakes

Rating: 6

Lots of private summer homes and cabins, combined with wide-open regulations that allow almost all boating and water activities, make these beautiful little lakes in the pine forests of Stevens County busy throughout the summer. With only one small, rather rough boat ramp serving the entire chain of lakes, I'm always surprised to see so many boaters, skiers, PWC operators, anglers, and paddlers on these lakes. Some of the lakes are really too small for skiing and full-tilt powerboat-

ing, but those things are going on here, and it can get a little scary at times. It might be a good idea to visit either before the fishing season opens in late April or after the vacation season ends in September.

Location: Northeast of Colville; map A5, grid c5.

How to get there: Drive west from Tiger or east from Colville on Highway 20, which runs right along the north or west shore of most of the Little Pend Oreille lakes.

Boat ramp: The public access area and boat ramp for Heritage, Thomas, Gillette, and Sherry Lakes is located on Gillette Lake at Gillette Campground. (These four lakes, the largest in the chain, are connected.)

Facilities: A private resort on Gillette Lake offers tent and RV sites, boat rentals, fishing docks, and a grocery store. There are also U.S. Forest Service campgrounds on Gillette, Thomas, and Leo lakes.

Water sports/restrictions: All water sports are permitted.

Contact: Beaver Lodge, tel. (509) 684-5657.

6 Upper Lake Roosevelt

Rating: 9

If you're the adventurous type, you've already been here. Its location and vastness make this one of Washington's last frontiers for boaters, right up there with roadless Ross Lake (see section A3). There are also roadless stretches along this part of Lake Roosevelt, particularly the east side of the lake from the Spokane Arm north to Hunters and much of the Spokane Arm itself both above and below Porcupine Bay. If you're looking for places where you can be in a little water world of

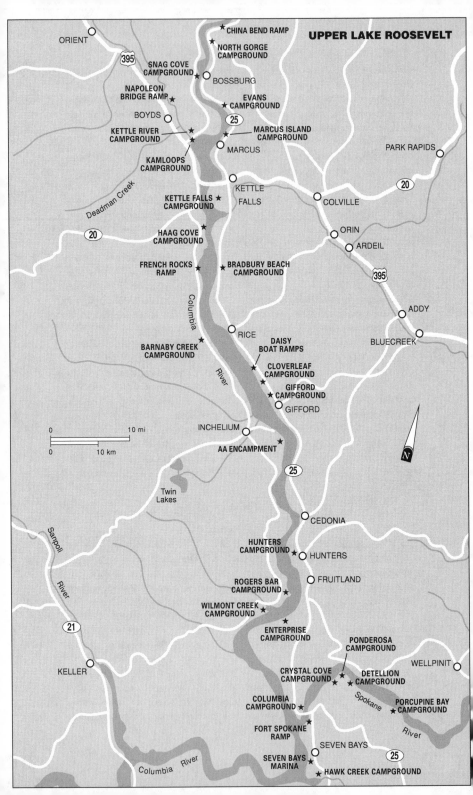

your own, these areas certainly qualify. It's not so much that no one else could possibly be there, but you know that, like you, everyone else around got there by water, so they're fellow adventurers. Although the campgrounds along the lake's shoreline make both boat camping and RV access possible, most of the folks who spend their nights on Roosevelt do so in the comfort of a houseboat.

The houseboat fleet out of Keller Ferry, Seven Bays, and Kettle Falls has done more to popularize Lake Roosevelt and make it a real vacation destination than any other single factor; most people who know anything about the big lake associate it with houseboating. Having your bed, your kitchen, your toys—even your waterslide—with you at all times makes a vacation on the water as easy as it could possibly be, and you can spend the night wherever you can find a beach to hammer in your moorage stakes. Many houseboaters bring their ski boats, fishing boats, or personal watercraft along for daytime play and exploration. The recreational options are virtually unlimited, so you'll see some people fishing, some skiing, some wake-boarding, some PWC riding, some tubing, some swimming, some windsurfing, some scuba diving, and some just bobbing around on inner tubes or air mattresses, soaking up the hot eastern Washington sun. It all works here, and even during the busiest vacation periods of July and August you can usually stake out your own couple hundred acres to do it in solitude. Did I mention that the lake is over 150 miles long and has over 660 miles of shoreline?

You can avoid other humans almost completely by visiting Roosevelt before July or after August, but off-season boating here does have its drawbacks. The lake level is quite low during the winter and early spring, so launching at some ramps can be difficult, and some narrow, protected bays are without water. Lake levels come up in May and June, sometimes at the rate of inches a day, with the lake nearly full by early July. Boaters need to be aware of changing water levels and depths to avoid surprises on this lake where about 99% of the bottom is solid rock. Fall is a great time to visit, but by October the temperatures at night are downright chilly.

Location: From Kettle Falls south to the mouth of the Spokane River; map A5, grid d1. (See the Upper Lake Roosevelt inset map. Refer also to the Lower Lake Roosevelt inset map in Chapter A4.)

How to get there: Take Highway 25 north from Davenport to parallel much of the east side of the lake.

Boat ramp: If my math is right, there are 16 places to launch boats along Lake Roosevelt from where it turns north near Hawk Creek to the upper end of the lake. The following boat ramps are listed on the Upper Lake Roosevelt inset map. Refer also to the Lower Lake Roosevelt inset map in Chapter A4.

• **Hawk Creek Campground:** Starting at the south end, Hawk Creek Campground has a single-lane ramp with a loading float and a small gravel parking area. Water levels are fine for launching here during the summer, but at times when the reservoir is low, such as late fall and spring, this may not be a good bet. Round-trip launch fee at this National Park Service ramp is $6. To reach it, drive north from Davenport on Highway 25 about 22 miles and turn left on Miles-Creston Road, following it seven miles. Turn right at the Hawk Creek Campground sign and go just over a mile to the campground and ramp.

- **Seven Bays Marina:** Three miles north of Hawk Creek is Seven Bays Marina, where there's a good concrete ramp four lanes wide, with lots of room to park cars and boat trailers. Other services also are available at this Colville Indian Tribe facility. Take Highway 25 about 22 miles north from Davenport, turn left on Miles-Creston Road, and drive five miles. Turn right on Seven Bays Road and follow it three miles to the marina.

- **Fort Spokane Ramp:** The next ramp to the north is at Fort Spokane Campground where the Spokane River enters Lake Roosevelt from the east. Fort Spokane has a three-lane concrete ramp with several loading floats. There's a $6 launch fee at this National Park Service ramp 23 miles north of Davenport via Highway 25.

- **Porcupine Bay Campground:** Up the Spokane Arm about 10 miles east of the main lake is the two-lane ramp at Porcupine Bay Campground. It has loading floats and lots of parking. Drive north from Davenport on Highway 25, turning east (right) 12 miles north of town on Porcupine Bay Road. The ramp is at the end of the road five miles off the highway. The launch fee here is $6.

- **Hunters Campground:** Next is the three-lane National Park Service ramp at Hunters Campground, another good one, located in a protected bay about a mile off Highway 25 about 43 miles north of Davenport. This is another Park Service ramp with a $6 launch fee.

- **Gifford Campground:** The Park Service ramp at Gifford Campground is next, a three-lane concrete ramp with several loading floats and room for about two dozen cars and trailers on a paved parking area. It's

25 miles south of Kettle Falls via Highway 25. The launch fee is $6.

- **Daisy Boat Ramps:** There are two more single-lane Park Service ramps near Daisy, about a mile apart along Highway 25. One is 23 miles south of Kettle Falls, the other 24 miles south of Kettle Falls. Its costs $6 to launch at both of them.

- **Bradbury Beach Campground:** Another National Park Service ramp is at Bradbury Beach Campground, about midway between Kettle Falls and the Daisy ramps. The launch fee here also is $6.

- **French Rocks Ramp:** Across the lake from Bradbury Beach is the National Park Service ramp at French Rocks, a one-lane concrete ramp with a loading float. Reach this one by driving north out of Kettle Falls on U.S. 395 and turning west on Highway 20, following it 4.5 miles before turning south (left) on Inchelium-Kettle Falls Road. Go seven miles on Kettle Falls Road and turn left on the unmarked road leading to French Rocks. Even though you have to work hard to find it, you still have to pay the $6 launch fee once you get there.

- **Kettle Falls Campground:** Up the lake farther on the east side is Kettle Falls Campground with its excellent, four-lane concrete ramp and loading floats. Folks don't seem to mind paying the $6 fee to launch at this top-of-the-line ramp as they do some of the others. Get there by driving south of the U.S. 395/Highway 25 intersection half a mile on Highway 25 and turning west (right) on Old Kettle Road. Follow it 2.5 miles and turn left on Kettle Park Road, going another quarter mile to the campground. The site also has a marina, boat rentals, and other facilities.

- **Marcus Island Campground:** The Park Service's Marcus Island Campground is next, with a single-lane concrete-plank ramp and loading floats. Yes, the $6 launch fee applies here, too. The campground and ramp are found by taking U.S. 395 west out of Kettle Falls just half a mile. turning north (right) on Highway 25, and going 5.5 miles to the campground entrance on the left.

- **Evans Campground:** A short distance north is Evans Campground, another National Park Service site with a single-lane ramp and floats. The $6 launch fee applies here. From Kettle Falls go west on U.S. 395 half a mile and turning right on Highway 25. Drive north on Highway 25 just under 10 miles and turn left into the campground.

- **Snag Cove Campground:** The name may give you cause to wonder, but there's a good ramp at Snag Cove Campground, a single-lane concrete ramp and loading float, as well as the usual $6 launch fee. Get there by taking U.S. 395 west then north from Kettle Falls and going right on Newport-Flat Creek Road, following it 7.5 miles to the campground, on the right.

- **Napoleon Bridge Ramp:** Uplake another three miles is Napoleon Bridge, with another single-lane ramp. There are no campers here, and there have been some problems with vandalism, so be careful about investing your $6 launch fee here. If you must, get there by driving north from Kettle Falls on U.S. 395, turning right on Napoleon Road, going one mile, crossing the river, and turning right on Hedland-Napoleon Road.

- **North Gorge Campground:** Next is North Gorge Campground, which has a good concrete ramp two lanes wide, with loading floats. It's 17 miles north of Kettle Falls via Highway 25. The Park Service's $6 launch fee is in effect here, too.

- **China Bend Ramp:** Another National Park Service ramp, one lane wide with loading floats, is located where the river begins to slow at the head end of the reservoir. It has a $6 launch fee, like the others. Get there by driving west from Kettle Falls on U.S. 395 for half a mile, turning right on Highway 25, and following it 20 miles north to the ramp, which is on the left.

- **Crow Butte State Park:** Ten miles downstream (west) is Crow Butte State Park, where there's a three-lane hard-surface ramp with parking for about 50 cars and trailers. The launch fee here is $4 round-trip, with a $40 annual permit available from the State Parks and Recreation Commission. The park is right alongside Highway 14.

All National Park Service ramps have a $6 launch fee, which covers the round-trip in and out of the water.

Facilities: Besides the campgrounds with boat ramps listed above, there are other road-accessible National Park Service campgrounds at (working up-lake from Hawk Creek) Columbia, Pierre, Wilmont Creek, Rogers Bar, AA Encampment (east side of lake), Cloverleaf, Barnaby Creek (east side), Haag Cove (east side), Kamloops, and Kettle River (east side). Boat-in campsites include Ponderosa, Crystal Cove, and Detellion (all on the Spokane Arm); and Enterprise and Barnaby Island (east side). Seven Bays Marina has campsites, a restaurant, convenience store, propane, and moorage. Facilities at Kettle Falls include RV and tent sites, moorage and boat rentals, a large swim area, picnic area, RV dump station, showers, and a convenience store. Houseboats are available for rent at Seven Bays and Kettle Falls, as well as at Keller Ferry down the lake.

Water sports/restrictions: All water sports are permitted.

Contact: Coulee Dam Area Chamber of Commerce, tel. (800) COULEE2 or tel. (509) 633-3074; National Park Service, Kettle Falls District, tel. (509) 738-6831; Seven Bays Marina, tel. (509) 725-1676; Roosevelt Recreational Enterprises, tel. (800) 648-LAKE; Dakota Columbia Houseboat Adventures, tel. (800) 816-2431.

7 Bead Lake

Rating: 3

The good news here is that the lake once again has a public boat ramp. After several years with virtually no boating access, the U.S. Forest Service in 1999 reopened a ramp in Mineral Bay at the lake's south end. The bad news is that it has very limited parking, with room for maybe a half dozen cars and trailers at a time. The rest of the bad news is that this 720-acre lake has no other facilities of any kind, so you'd better show up fully self-contained if you're going to play a while. With steep banks all around it, Bead is a tough place to swim or play around the water's edge. The exceptions are two or three gradual beaches in Mineral Bay and the narrow bays at the lake's northeast corner. Most people come here to fish, and that probably won't change much with re-opening of the boat-launching facilities.

Location: East of Usk, Pend Oreille County; map A5, grid e7.

How to get there: Take U.S. 2 to Newport and across the Pend Oreille River; then take the first left to continue north up the east side of the river on LeClerc Creek Road. A little over three miles from the bridge go right on Bead Lake Road and follow it to the lake.

Boat ramp: There's a U.S. Forest Service boat ramp with limited parking at the south end of the lake.

Facilities: There are no facilities on the lake, but food, gas, lodging, and other amenities are available in Newport a few miles to the south.

Water sports/restrictions: All water sports are permitted, but few are in practice.

Contact: Colville National Forest, Newport Ranger District, tel. (509) 447-3129; Washington Department of Wildlife, Spokane regional office, tel. (509) 456-4082.

8 Marshall Lake

Rating: 6

A great place to fish for cutthroat trout and paddle a canoe or kayak, you won't find much else to do here. This is a fishing lake first and foremost, so paddling without a fly rod in your hand might even draw funny looks from some of the locals. We need peaceful, quiet places for water recreation, and the rules here seem to have taken that option about as far as they can go.

Location: North of Newport, Pend Oreille County; map A5, grid e8.

How to get there: Take U.S. 2 to Newport and cross the Pend Oreille River on the east side of town. Take the first left after crossing the bridge and drive about three miles to Bead Lake Road. Turn right on Bead Lake Road, drive three miles, and turn right on Marshall Lake Road, which leads to the lake.

Boat ramp: There's a WDFW public access area with a boat ramp at the lake's south end. It's a three-lane gravel ramp, suited best to smaller boats. A $10 WDFW access decal is required to use the public launch areas maintained by the Washington Department of Fish and Wildlife.

Facilities: Marshall Lake Resort is located at the south end of the lake, near the boat ramp.

Water sports/restrictions: The lake has a 5 mph speed limit and no-swimming regulation.

Contact: Marshall Lake Resort, tel. (509) 447-4158.

9 Pend Oreille River

Rating: 7

Some map in my head says rivers should flow either west, toward the Pacific Ocean, or south, toward the bottom . . . or something. The Pend Oreille River, though, breaks what I think should be the rules and wanders off toward Canada in an obvious case of misdirection and total confusion. It must be some sort of water-runs-downhill thing. Anyway, along its misguided, 67-mile journey across the northeastern corner of the state from Idaho to British Columbia, it provides a lot of fishing, power-boating, PWC riding, paddling and other water recreation for a large segment of the population from Spokane north.

Quite deep and wide along much of its length, it's also slowed by a couple of dams along the way, so it has much of the character of the Columbia, into which it flows after it crosses out of Washington and into British Columbia. Because of its size and flow, it's quite popular with powerboaters, including anglers who search its waters for largemouth bass, walleyes, and other species. It offers a wide variety of boat camping and paddling trips, many of which would take adventurous boaters through some of the state's prettiest rural countryside. However, I would make such a trip either before or after spring runoff when the Pend Oreille can get wild and woolly in places. Boundary Dam is another contributing factor when it comes to water levels on the river. During summer, drawdown for power generation occurs on a daily basis, especially downstream from the town of Metaline. Close to the dam the water may fluctuate several feet each day.

Location: Flows south from British Columbia through Pend Oreille County and into Idaho at Newport; map A5, grid e8. (See Pend Oreille River inset map.)

How to get there: Take Highway 20 north from Newport to follow the river upstream all the way to the town of Tiger. From Tiger upstream, Highway 31 parallels several miles of the river.

Boat ramp: There are 17 developed boat ramps along the river from Newport to Boundary Dam at the Canadian border: (The following boat ramps are listed on the Pend Oreille River inset map.)

• **Old American Kampground:** Starting at Newport, there's a ramp at the Old American Kampground on Newport Avenue. It's a concrete ramp with a loading float, but you have to be a guest at the campground to use it. To get there, drive north from U.S. 2 in Newport on Newport Avenue about one-quarter mile to the RV park entrance.

• **Pioneer Park:** Next is the U.S. Forest Service ramp at Pioneer Park, off Le Clerc Road on the north side of the river. This two-lane concrete ramp is a little uneven and rough. To get there, drive east on U.S. 2 from Newport and go three-quarters of a mile. Cross the river and turn left on LeClerc Creek Road; go two miles and turn left to the park entrance.

• **Sandy Shores Ramp:** About three miles farther up Le Clerc Creek Road is the Sandy Shores ramp, managed by Pend Oreille County. This is a single-lane concrete ramp with a somewhat rough and eroded approach.

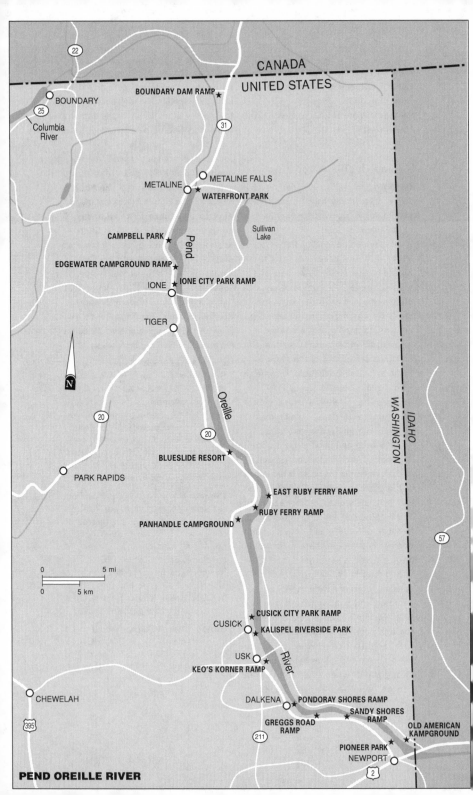

- **Greggs Road Ramp:** Two miles downriver (north) is another county ramp, this one off Greggs Road. It's a single-lane concrete ramp with limited parking. Greggs Road is nine miles up the river from Highway 2 via Le Clerc Creek Road.

- **Pondoray Shores Ramp:** Go two miles farther north on Le Clerc Road and you'll come to Pondoray Shores, where there's a one-lane gravel ramp with a few parking spots nearby. This rough and rutted ramp may be suited only to smaller trailer boats, paddle craft, and cartoppers.

- **Keo's Korner Ramp:** The next ramp to the north is on the west side of the river off Highway 20 at Usk. Known as the Keo's Korner ramp, it's a gravel two laner, with a $1 launch fee payable at the Usk General Store, the site's owner. It has several rough campsites nearby. If you want detailed directions, take Highway 20 north to Usk and turn east (right) on Kings Lake Road. Follow Kings Lake Road half a mile, past the Usk General Store, and turn left, following the gravel road to the river at the bottom of the hill.

- **Kalispel Riverside Park:** The Kalispel Indian Tribe maintains this single-lane concrete ramp on Le Clerc Road (east side of the river) about two miles north of Usk. Beware of dropping your boat-trailer tires off the steep end of the ramp. Take Highway 20 to Usk and turn east on Kings Lake Road, following it a mile to Le Clerc Creek Road. Turn north (left) on LeClerc Creek Road and go 2.5 miles to Kalispel tribal headquarters, turning left and driving another three-quarters of a mile to the ramp.

- **Cusick City Park Ramp:** The city park in Cusick has a concrete ramp with a large loading float and room for about a dozen cars and trailers. To find it, go north on Highway 20 to Cusick and turn right at Calispell Creek Road, following it half a mile to the park.

- **Panhandle Campground:** Midway between Usk and Ione but on the east side of the river is the U.S. Forest Service ramp at Panhandle Campground, where there's a two-lane concrete ramp. This launch site is in rough shape. To find it, turn east off Highway 31 just south of Ione and go half a mile on Sullivan Lake Road. Cross the river and turn south (right) on Le Clerc Creek Road, driving 17 miles to the campground, on the right.

- **Ruby Ferry Ramp:** The next ramp is at Ruby Ferry, on the west side of the river about 15 miles north of the intersection of Highway 2 and Highway 211. This Department of Fish and Wildlife ramp is a fairly steep, one-lane concrete ramp. A $10 WDFW access decal is required to use the public launch areas maintained by the Washington Department of Fish and Wildlife.

- **East Ruby Ferry Ramp:** The old ferry landing on the east side of the river also now serves as a boat ramp. It's a Pend Oreille County ramp with a two-lane natural surface. Larger trailer boats might have trouble getting in and out of the water. Reach it from Highway 31 near Ione by driving east on Sullivan Lake Road, crossing the river and turning south (right) on Le Clerc Creek Road. Drive south 15 miles to the unmarked gravel road that leads 50 yards to the ramp.

- **Blueslide Resort:** Two miles farther downriver (north) on the west side is Blueslide Resort, where there's a one-lane concrete ramp with a loading float. It's operated by the resort, and there's a $5 launch fee, round-trip. It's just off Highway 20 18.5 miles north of the junction of Highway 20 and Highway 211.

- **Ione City Park Ramp:** The next ramp is at Ione City Park, a one-lane concrete ramp with a loading float and lots of parking on a gravel lot. Turn east off Highway 31 at milepost 4 in Ione and drive two blocks to the park and ramp.

- **Edgewater Campground Ramp:** Just north of Ione and across the river is the U.S. Forest Service's Edgewater Campground, where there's a one-lane concrete ramp with limited parking. To find it, turn east off Highway 31 just south of Ione on Sullivan Lake Road, cross the river, and turn north (left) on Box Canyon Road. Drive north two miles to the campground.

- **Campbell Park:** About four miles north of Ione on Highway 31 is Campbell Park, managed by Pend Oreille County PUD. There's a one-lane gravel ramp at the park just above Box Canyon Dam. Camping also is available here.

- **Waterfront Park:** The next ramp downstream is at Waterfront Park, in the town of Metaline. It's a one-lane concrete ramp that's plenty adequate for launching large trailer boats. Reach it by driving north to Metaline on Highway 31 and turning right at the sign designating the park to the right.

- **Boundary Dam Ramp:** The last boat ramp on the Washington stretch of the river is at Boundary Dam Park. Maintained by Seattle City Light (That's right, Seattle), it's a good concrete ramp with a loading float and lots of nearby parking. To get there, drive north from Metaline on Highway 31 and turn left on Boundary Road. Continue 10 miles on Boundary Road and turn right at the Boundary Dam sign, continuing one mile to the campground and boat ramp sign.

Facilities: A few tent and RV sites are available at Pioneer Park, across the river from Newport. Panhandle Campground (Forest Service) has several tent and RV sites, vault toilets, a large picnic area and a fair swim beach. Riverbend Park, near Usk, has tent and RV sites, picnic area, swim beach and other amenities. Blueslide Resort has moorage, RV and tent sites, cabins, rest rooms with showers, motel units, a picnic area, and a small store. The Ione City Park provides river access, swimming, picnic tables, and rest rooms. The U.S. Forest Service campground at Edgewater has tent sites and a picnic area near the water. Pend Oreille County PUD's Campbell Park has tent sites, picnic areas, vault toilets, and a swimming area on the river. Boundary Dam Park, near the Washington/British Columbia border, has campsites, rest rooms, picnic area, and a swim beach.

Contact: Newport Chamber of Commerce, tel. (509) 447-5812; Keo's Korner, tel. (509) 445-1294; Ione Chamber of Commerce, tel. (509) 442-3223; Blueslide Resort, tel. (509) 445-1327; Circle Motel (Metaline), tel. (509) 446-4343; Boundary Dam, tel. (509) 446-3083; Colville National Forest, Newport Ranger District, tel. (509) 447-3129.

10 Davis Lake

Rating: 5

Like other Pend Oreille County lakes of under 200 acres, this one has restrictive regulations that include a no-wake, 5 mph speed limit. That means the bigger boats go elsewhere and paddlers can explore the lake at their leisure. With nearly 150 acres to explore, plan on giving it the better part of a day.

Location: South of Usk, Pend Oreille County; map A5, grid e6.

How to get there: Drive north from Spokane on U.S. 2 and turn left on Highway 211, following it about 10 miles to the lake on the left.

Boat ramp: You'll find a public access area and Washington Department of Fish and Wildlife boat ramp on the lake. The ramp has two gravel lanes and one lane with concrete planking. Parking is limited to about two dozen cars and trailers. A $10 WDFW access decal is required to use the public launch areas maintained by the Washington Department of Fish and Wildlife.

Facilities: The nearest lodging and RV facilities are in Usk to the north.

Water sports/restrictions: The lake has a 5 mph speed limit, so paddling and fishing are the main attractions.

Contact: The Inn at Usk, tel. (509) 445-1526; Keo's Korner, tel. (509) 445-1294.

11 Waitts Lake

Rating: 7

This big lake in the pine country of Stevens County is close enough to Spokane to draw good crowds during the summer vacation season and on long holiday weekends. As popular with skiers and PWC riders as it is with anglers, it gets a little busy at times, but everyone seems to have a good time without any major disagreements. Maybe that's because the lake's 455 acres provide enough room for people to spread out and keep clear of each other.

Location: West of Valley, Stevens County; map A5, grid e3.

How to get there: Take U.S. 395 north from Spokane and turn west at Loon Lake on Highway 292, following it to Springdale. Proceed north from Springdale on Highway 231 to the town of Valley and turn west on Waitts Lake Road, following it about four miles to the lake.

Boat ramp: The lake has boat-launch facilities in four locations. Waitts Lake Resort has a single-lane gravel ramp with a loading float and room for a half dozen cars and trailers. There's a $4 launch fee if you're not a resort guest. Silver Beach Resort also charges $4 round-trip for launching at its one-lane concrete ramp. The ramp has a loading float and room to park about a dozen cars and trailers. Winona Beach Resort has a one-lane gravel ramp with a loading float and large gravel parking area. The Department of Fish and Wildlife ramp on Waitts is a one-lane concrete-plank ramp with a large parking area. A $10 WDFW access decal is required to use the public launch areas maintained by the Washington Department of Fish and Wildlife.

Facilities: Waitts Lake Resort has tent and RV sites, rental boats, cabins, a fishing dock, restaurant, and a small store. It's the only resort on the lake that's open year-round. Silver Beach and Winona Beach Resorts offer moorage, boat rentals, cabins, rest rooms with showers, swimming areas, RV and tent sites, picnic areas, and other amenities.

Water sports/restrictions: All water sports are permitted.

Contact: Silver Beach Resort, tel. (509) 937-2811; Waitts Lake Resort, tel. (509) 937-2400; Winona Beach Resort, tel. (509) 937-2231.

12 North Twin Lake

Rating: 5

The real estate folks are right when they say location is everything. The popularity of this big lake and its twin to the immediate south suffers because they're in a location that most folks can't reach all that easily. In fact, you don't discover North or South Twin while on your way to some other boating destination; Twin Lakes Road goes to Twin Lakes, and you're not likely to be trailering your boat along that road unless you're going to North Twin or South Twin. It's too bad they're so far off the well-traveled path, because they have something to offer power-boaters, paddlers, anglers, PWC riders, and other water enthusiasts. The lakeside resort and the good trout fishing help to draw some folks here from all over Washington, but there are few other amenities to bring people to the lake. North Twin covers about 700 acres, plenty of room for any boating activity you may enjoy. If you're thinking about going there for the first time to fish, remember that Colville fishing permits are required here, and they're available at the resort or from businesses throughout the area. The cost is $15 for three days, $20 for seven days, and $30 for the year.

Location: West of Inchelium, Colville Indian Reservation; map A5, grid e0.

How to get there: Take Highway 20 east from Republic or west from Kettle Falls, turn south at Sherman Creek onto Inchelium-Kettle Falls Road, and follow it to Inchelium. From there go west on Twin Lakes Road and follow it a little over eight miles to the lake.

Boat ramp: There's a single-lane concrete ramp with a loading float at Rainbow Beach Resort.

Facilities: The resort on the north side of the lake offers most of the necessities, including fuel, moorage, boat rentals, rental cabins, a swim area, and small store.

Water sports/restrictions: All water sports are permitted.

Contact: Rainbow Beach Resort, tel. (509) 722-5901.

13 South Twin Lake
Rating: 5

This is the larger twin of the pair, covering more than 900 acres. Again, it's lightly used by boaters compared to other large lakes in more readily accessible parts of the state. There are dirt roads and trails around part of it, but also plenty of places to get away from everyone and enjoy some aquatic real estate you can call your own. Tribal fishing permits—not state licenses—are required here. You'll pay $15 for three days, $20 for seven days, $30 for the season.

Location: Southwest of Inchelium, Colville Indian Reservation; map A5, grid e0.

How to get there: Take Highway 20 east from Republic or west from Kettle Falls, turn south at Sherman Creek onto Inchelium-Kettle Falls Road and follow it to Inchelium. From there go west on Twin Lakes Road and follow it a about eight miles to the road turning south (right) to the lake.

Boat ramp: Hartman's Log Cabin Resort has a gravel ramp reinforced with steel matting and a small loading ramp.

Facilities: The resort near the north end of the lake has boat rentals, moorage, RV sites, cabins, a motel, convenience store, and laundry facilities.

Water sports/restrictions: All water sports are permitted.

Contact: Hartman's Log Cabin Resort, tel. (509) 722-3543 (April through October only).

🔢 Jumpoff Joe Lake

Rating: 6

It only covers about 100 acres, but this pretty lake in southern Stevens County is worth a visit if you're looking for a place to spend the day wetting a line or using your shoulders on a pretty lake in a pretty setting. And, no, I don't really know the meaning of the name, Jumpoff Joe. I've asked around and heard different explanations and choose not to believe any of them. So there.

Location: Southeast of Valley, Stevens County; map A5, grid e4.

How to get there: Take U.S. 395 north from Spokane to Beitey Road and turn east (left). Turn left again on Jumpoff Joe Road and follow it to the east side of the lake.

Boat ramp: You'll find a WDFW access area with a two-lane gravel boat ramp on the lake and a one-lane concrete-plank ramp at Jumpoff Joe Lake Resort. The resort charges $3 round-trip for launching. A $10 WDFW access decal is required to use the public launch areas maintained by the Washington Department of Fish and Wildlife.

Facilities: Jumpoff Joe Resort has tent and RV sites, cabins, boat rentals, moorage, and fishing docks.

Water sports/restrictions: Fishing and paddling are good bets. Waterskiing and PWC operation are prohibited.

Contact: Jumpoff Joe Resort, tel. (509) 937-2133.

🔢 Deer Lake

Rating: 7

Covering more than 1,100 acres, this is a big lake with plenty of room for everybody. It's also cool and deep, with places near the south end showing depths over 70 feet. These conditions are well suited to the cold-water-loving Mackinaw, or lake trout, a trophy that draws many anglers to Deer Lake in spring and early summer. As the water warms in summer and anglers turn their attention from Mackinaw to other species, nonanglers begin to show up in ever-growing numbers, and by early July there's a little bit of everything going on here. A popular ski lake and PWC lake, Deer is also used by sailors, wake-boarders, tubers, and swimmers. The steep drop-offs along the lake's south side and on both sides of the narrow neck of water near the north end are often investigated by divers from throughout the Inland Empire. Although there aren't a lot of boaters' facilities on the lake, it's big enough and offers enough variety to keep people here for weeklong vacations and longer.

Location: Northeast of Loon Lake; map A5, grid f5.

How to get there: Drive north from Spokane on U.S. 395 and turn east (right) on Deer Lake Loop Road, following it about two miles to the lake.

Boat ramp: The single-lane concrete ramp at the Department of Fish and Wildlife's access area and the one-lane ramp at Deer Lake Resort are on the lake's west side. The resort charges $5 for launching, round-trip. $10 WDFW access decal is required to use the public launch areas maintained by the Washington Department of Fish and Wildlife.

Facilities: Deer Lake Resort and Sunrise Resort have boat moorage, picnic tables, a small store, rest rooms and showers, RV sites with full hookups, and other amenities. More facilities are found nearby, along Highway 395.

Water sports/restrictions: All water sports are permitted.

Contact: Deer Lake Resort, tel. (509)

233-2081; Sunrise Point Resort, tel. (509) 233-2342.

16 Loon Lake

Rating: 8

Like nearby Deer Lake, Loon covers more than 1,100 acres and is very clear, deep and cool. The deepest spots are near the rocky southeast corner where the depth reaches more than 100 feet. A great place to cool off in summer, Loon gets some good-sized crowds from the Spokane area when the temperatures rise. All the usual boating and water sports activities happen here, including fishing for kokanee, lake trout, and other species.

Location: At the town of Loon Lake; map 5A, grid f4.

How to get there: Drive north from Spokane on U.S. 395 until you see the lake on the left.

Boat ramp: Besides a public access area on the west side, there are resorts on both sides of the lake, all with boat ramps. The WDFW ramp is a two laner, one gravel and one concrete. It has a large gravel parking area with room for about three dozen cars and trailers. A $10 WDFW access decal is required to use the public launch areas maintained by the Washington Department of Fish and Wildlife. Shore Acres Resort, also on the lake's west side, has a concrete ramp with a loading float and room for about a dozen cars and trailers. Launch fee at the resort is $6, round-trip. Granite Point Park right along Highway 395 on the east side of the lake has a concrete ramp, floats, and parking for about 20 cars and trailers. Besides a $3 entrance fee at the resort, there's a $2 launch fee.

Facilities: Shore Acres has moorage, boat rentals, a large swim area, a small store, rental cabins, RV and tent sites, rest rooms with showers, picnic tables, and other amenities. At Granite Point you'll find moorage, a swim beach, boat rentals, cabins, RV hookups, a cafe, picnic area, and playground area.

Water sports/restrictions: All water sports are permitted.

Contact: Granite Point Park, tel. (509) 233-2100 (April through October only); Shore Acres Resort, tel. (509) 233-2474.

17 Sacheen Lake

Rating: 7

In a pretty county with lots of clear, cool lakes, this clear, cool lake is often overlooked by boaters. It's readily accessible via Highway 211, but lots of folks pass it by on their way to bigger lakes or waters with perhaps more facilities and amenities. That's just fine with the people who have discovered the beauty of this 180-acre gem because they can go about doing their thing without a whole lot of competition.

Location: Near Highway 211, west of Newport; Map A5, grid e6.

How to get there: Take U.S. 2 north from Spokane and turn north (left) on Highway 211. The lake is on the left about four miles off U.S. 2.

Boat ramp: The lake has a single-lane concrete-plank Department of Fish and Wildlife boat ramp. A $10 WDFW access decal is required to use the public launch areas maintained by the Washington Department of Fish and Wildlife.

Facilities: Diamond Lake Resort is a few miles away to the southeast off U.S. 2.

Water sports/restrictions: All water sports are permitted. The lake has a 35 mph speed limit.

Contact: Diamond Lake Resort, tel. (509) 447-4474.

18 Diamond Lake

Rating: 7

This lake right alongside Highway 2 southwest of Newport has almost 760 acres to play on, so folks from as far away as Spokane come here regularly to do just that. Like may of the lakes in this beautiful part of the Evergreen State, the scenery alone makes the trip worthwhile, but Diamond is also a great water destination in its own right. Because of its size, it's a little slow to warm in the summer. Maybe that explains why by the Fourth of July everyone seems to be going full-tilt here as though they're making up for lost time. If you're a paddler and not in that big a hurry, you might take the time to explore the steep bank and the large island on the north side of the lake.

Location: Southwest of Newport; map A5, grid f7.

How to get there: Take U.S. 2 north from Spokane until you pass right by within casting distance of the lake's south side.

Boat ramp: There's a Department of Fish and Wildlife boat ramp on the south side of the lake. A $10 WDFW access decal is required to use the public launch areas maintained by the Washington Department of Fish and Wildlife.

Facilities: Diamond Lake Resort has tent and RV sites, picnic tables, rest rooms, and a small grocery store.

Water sports/restrictions: All water sports are permitted. The lake has a 35 mph speed limit.

Contact: Diamond Lake Resort, tel. (509) 447-4474 (April through Labor Day only).

19 Eloika Lake

Rating: 7

Primarily a fishing lake, especially for trophy-class largemouth bass, this big lake just south of the Spokane-Pend Oreille county line is also something of a natural wildlife preserve, with birds and animals of all kinds abundant in and around it. This is the only place I've ever snagged a muskrat on an artificial lure, for whatever that little tidbit of trivia might possibly be worth. The occasional water-skier finds his or her way onto the lake now and then, but after a couple of dirty looks from bass anglers, they leave before they meet the same fate as that muskrat. Although it covers about 660 acres, it's less than 15 feet deep in its deepest spot, so Eloika warms quickly in the spring.

Location: Northeast of Deer Park; map A5, grid f6.

How to get there: Take U.S. 2 north from Spokane and turn west (left) on Bridges Road or Oregon Road to reach the east side of the lake.

Boat ramp: A Department of Fish and Wildlife boat ramp and a resort ramp are both on the east side of the lake. The WDFW ramp is a one-lane concrete-plank ramp with a large gravel parking area. A $10 WDFW access decal is required to use the public launch areas maintained by the Washington Department of Fish and Wildlife. The ramp at Jerry's Landing Resort just north of the public access is a concrete ramp with a float. There's a $3 launch fee at the resort.

Facilities: Jerry's Landing has RV and tent sites, cabins, boat rentals, moorage, and a small store, as well as a small swim beach with a jungle of water weeds at its outer edges.

Water sports/restrictions: Personal watercraft are prohibited on the lake.

Contact: Jerry's Landing, tel. (509) 292-2337.

20 Long Lake

Rating: 6

This long, narrow impoundment on the Spokane River has everything from fishing to skiing, windsurfing to swimming, so it's fairly popular with Spokane-area residents. The facilities are few and far between on the 20-mile-long reservoir, so most people visit it on a day-use basis rather than staying for long visits.

Location: Spokane River impoundment, west of Spokane; map A5, grid g3.

How to get there: Take Interstate 90 to Sprague and turn north on Highway 231, following it to U.S. 2. Turn east on U.S. 2 and drive about three miles to Reardan; then continue north on Highway 231 all the way to the Spokane River below Long Lake Dam. Cross the river and turn east (right) on Corkscrew Canyon Road. Drive five miles to the gravel road that drops down the hill to the right and leads to the boat ramp.

Boat ramp: A state park with a boat ramp and a resort with a ramp are on the east side near the upper end of the lake. Riverside State Park has a one-lane concrete ramp with a loading float. There's a $3 launch fee at the park, with a $40 annual permit available. Registered park guests don't have to pay the launch fee. Nine Mile Resort has a two-lane concrete ramp with two floats and limited parking. The resort charges $5 to launch most days, $6 on weekends and holidays. Farther down the lake are two more boat ramps, one at a private resort and one at a Department of Natural Resources campground. The resort ramp is a two-lane concrete ramp with a float at Forshee's Resort in Tum Tum. There's a $4 launch fee here. Launches are free at the DNR ramp, a concrete two laner with a loading float. It's located at Long Lake Camp six miles west of the resort.

Facilities: Riverside State Park has over 100 tent sites. Nine Mile Resort has RV sites with hookups and tent sites without, a swim area, picnic tables and picnic shelters, and rest rooms with showers. Forshee's Resort has moorage, picnic tables, and a restaurant and lounge. Long Lake Camp has tent sites, picnic shelters and tables, ski floats, a swim area, and vault toilets.

Water sports/restrictions: All water sports are permitted.

Contact: Riverside State Park, tel. (509) 456-3964; Washington State Parks and Recreation Commission, tel. (800) 233-0321 (information), tel. (800) 452-5687 (reservations); Nine Mile Falls Resort, tel. (509) 468-8422 (Memorial Day through Labor Day only).

21 Newman Lake

Rating: 6

Maybe no one else is talking about it, but I think the introduction of tiger muskies into this 1,200-acre lake a few miles northeast of Spokane was the beginning of the end for swimming and other water recreation on Newman. Think about it: Three- to four-foot-long fish with 16-penny finishing nails for teeth and a taste for flesh lurking in the weeds near every swim beach and boat dock, just waiting for an unsuspecting swimmer to wander into striking range or dangle his feet in the water a little too long. Then—whomp!

—a leg severed at the knee. Okay, maybe I've been reading too much Stephen King. After catching my first tiger muskie right along the edge of a public swim beach at Mayfield Lake several years ago, I just automatically associate the big predatory fish with little kids splashing around in shallow water. Actually, there's never been a documented case of a muskie eating a child, although one did attack an angler's boat on Mayfield a few years back, inflicting major scratches in the craft's finish and breaking off several teeth as it snapped and snarled while the hapless fisherman tried to unhook and release it. I guess it didn't appreciate the nice treatment it was getting.

Tiger muskies were introduced into Newman in an attempt by the State Fish and Wildlife Department to provide a trophy fishery and make a dent in the lake's exploding trash-fish population. The carnivorous fish pose little threat to people, most of whom are bigger than they are, and they added one more option to what was already a healthy menu of watery activities available at Newman Lake. Now, along with swimming, skiing, sailing, boarding, tubing, and PWC riding, visitors to the lake can snorkel around the weed beds, hoping for a face-to-face encounter with one of Washington's newest and largest game fish. Just don't decorate your arm to resemble a small fish and wiggle it enticingly in front of a tiger muskie's nose. That's just asking for trouble.

Location: Northeast of Spokane near the Idaho border; map A5, grid h8.

How to get there: Drive east from Spokane on Highway 290 and turn north (left) on Newman Lake Road.

Boat ramp: There are a Department of Fish and Wildlife ramp and ramps at two private resorts on the lake. The WDFW ramp is a concrete two-laner, but it was in bad shape in the spring of 1999. A $10 WDFW access decal is required to use the public launch areas maintained by the Washington Department of Fish and Wildlife. Sutton Bay Resort's one-lane concrete ramp has a loading float and is a good-quality ramp. There's a $2 launch fee, plus an access fee to the resort's day-use area where the ramp is located. Cherokee Landing Resort also has a one-lane concrete ramp with a float, but there's room for only three or four cars and trailers to park there. The resort charges $3 round-trip for launching.

Facilities: Sutton Bay Resort has boat rentals and moorage, a large (and popular) swim area, cabins, and tent sites. Cherokee Landing's facilities include boat rentals, moorage, campsites, a convenience store, and a fishing dock.

Water sports/restrictions: All water sports are permitted.

Contact: Cherokee Landing Resort, tel. (509) 226-3843; Sutton Bay Resort, tel. (509) 226-3660.

22 Spokane River

Rating: 7

Spokane Falls presents a major obstacle to river runners on this big stream that runs right through the heart of eastern Washington's biggest city. Don't try to run the falls because it's suicidal, not to mention illegal. Now that we have that important public-service message out of the way, let's talk about the parts of the Spokane that you can play on. There are several of them. The upriver portion from the Idaho state line to Upriver Dam at the edge of Spokane's downtown district is popular with almost everyone who likes moving water.

Ranging from flat water immediately above the dam to moderate Class II whitewater in stretches above Plantes Ferry Park, it's a favorite with kayakers and canoeists, and rafters also use it when the river is running at moderate levels. In summer when the river is low and warm, this stretch of river becomes a playground for tubers and other weekend water enthusiasts Several slow spots along this stretch also are popular with swimmers. The three or four miles of river immediately below the falls are quite gentle, providing some good canoe and kayak water, but downstream from Spokane Falls Community College it gets interesting to say the least, with several Class III rapids and even some Class IV tumblers when the river is high. This is serious kayaking and rafting water, but some people don't take it seriously. Perhaps it's unfortunate to have such an inviting stretch of river so close to a college, because this part of the river seems to claim a student every year or two, as the end of finals and the start of warm weather coincide with the high-water period of spring runoff.

Below Nine Mile Falls the river slows to flat water again as it backs up behind Long Lake Dam and a lower dam a few miles downstream. (See Long Lake listing, above.) From there, it's a short distance to the still waters of Lake Roosevelt and the mouth of the Spokane, where powerboating, swimming, walleye fishing, and other reservoir activities are popular.

Location: Flows westerly through Spokane and into the east side of Lake Roosevelt at Fort Spokane; map A5, grid h7.

How to get there: Drive northwest out of Spokane on Highway 291 to reach portions of the river from downtown to the upper end of Long Lake. Drive east from town on Interstate 90 and take roads to the north to reach the section of river between Spokane and the Idaho state line.

Boat ramp: The best-known and most popular put-in/take-out spot on the river is at Plantes Ferry Park, managed by the Spokane County Parks and Recreation Department. Located on Upstream Drive (Wellesley Road), it's a natural-surface ramp where boats can be trailered or hand carried to the river. Upstream is a hand-carry launching spot at the north end of the Harvard Road bridge, and downstream it's possible to hand carry a boat from the water at Upriver Dam. Downstream from Spokane Falls, some paddlers hand carry their boats to the water at the base of the Maple Street bridge, and there's a popular put-in/take-out spot just downstream from the Fort Wright Drive bridge over the river near Fort Spokane Community College. The ramps at Nine Mile Resort and Riverside State Park are on slow-water sections of the Spokane near the upper end of Long Lake. Both are concrete ramps with loading floats.

Facilities: Food, gas, lodging, and other amenities are readily available throughout the area. Riverside State Park has tent and RV sites and other facilities.

Water sports/restrictions: Kayaking, rafting, canoeing, inner-tubing, fishing, and swimming all are popular here. Boaters MUST WEAR Coast Guard-approved life jackets on this river. (Why wouldn't you?)

Contact: Spokane County Parks and Recreation Department, tel. (509) 625-6200; The Outdoor Sportsman, tel. (509) 328-1556; Riverside State Park tel. (509) 456-3964; Washington State Parks and

Recreation Commission, tel. (800) 233-0321 (information), tel. (800) 452-5687 (reservations).

23 Liberty Lake

Rating: 5

Limited public access has always been a problem on this big lake east of Spokane. Most of the shoreline is under private ownership, so visitors are out of luck unless they use the WDFW's access area to get onto the lake. Congestion at the ramp can be a problem, not only with early season anglers but during the summer months when skiers, PWC riders, tubers, and other folks join into the mix. Don't forget to put that access permit on your car if you're going to join them. The lake is large (over 700 acres) but shallow (less than 30 feet deep), so it warms quickly in the summer.

Location: East of Spokane; map A5, grid h8.

How to get there: Take Interstate 90 east from Spokane and turn south at the signs pointing the way to Liberty Lake. The lake is about a mile and a half off the freeway on the left side of the road.

Boat ramp: The Department of Fish and Wildlife ramp on the lake is in tough shape. It's a two-lane concrete ramp with a large, paved parking area and a paved walkway along part of the beach. A $10 WDFW access decal is required to use the public launch areas maintained by the Washington Department of Fish and Wildlife.

Facilities: There are RV parks, lodging, food, and other facilities nearby and throughout the Spokane area.

Water sports/restrictions: All water sports are permitted.

Contact: Washington Department of Fish and Wildlife, Spokane regional office, tel. (509) 456-4082; Sportsmen's Surplus, tel. (509) 467-5970.

24 West Medical Lake

Rating: 6

One of eastern Washington's best trout-fishing lakes, West Medical is also an easy access spot for people wanting to get out and explore a little. The 235-acre lake has a wealth of aquatic vegetation and insect life, so critters of all kinds inhabit the area or come here to feed. Almost totally undeveloped, the shore is a bird-watcher's paradise, with red-winged blackbirds only one of many species available and abundant. The downside here is that the lake is used for irrigation, so water levels may vary significantly from season to season.

Location: West of the town of Medical Lake; map A4, grid i4.

How to get there: Take Interstate 90 east from Sprague or west from Spokane and turn north on Salnave Road (Highway 902). Before getting to the town of Medical Lake, turn west (left) on Fancher Road and drive 0.4 mile to the south end of the lake.

Boat ramp: The Department of Fish and Wildlife ramp at the southwest corner of the lake is one of the biggest and best in the region. It's a four-lane concrete-plank ramp with room for perhaps 100 cars and trailers to park nearby.

Facilities: This is one of relatively few lakes where the public access area includes a paved path to the water for wheelchair access along the beach. West Medical Lake Resort next to the public access area at the lake's south end has RV and tent sites, moorage, boat rentals, rest rooms with showers, and a fishing float.

Water sports/restrictions: Fishing and paddling are the main events here.
Contact: West Medical Lake Resort, tel. (509) 299-3921 (April through September only).

25 Medical Lake

Rating: 6

The same things that make for quality fishing also make for quality paddling on this 150-acre lake on the edge of the town with the same name. The fishing regulations prohibit boat motors of all kinds, so rowing and paddling are the standard means of locomotion. Since the rules also prohibit fishing with anything but artificial lures and flies, the lake doesn't have throngs of hungry meat-fishermen crowding its waters. It's an intimate, quiet place to spend a few hours watching wildlife or just drifting lazily to give body and brain a rest.

Location: West of the town of Medical Lake; map A5, grid i4.

How to get there: Take Interstate 90 east from Sprague or west from Spokane and turn north on Salnave Road (Highway 902). Before getting to the town of Medical Lake, turn west (left) on Fancher Road and then take an immediate right into the public access area of Medical Lake.

Boat ramp: There's a WDFW public access area and boat ramp at the south end of the lake. A $10 WDFW access decal is required to use the public launch areas maintained by the Washington Department of Fish and Wildlife.

Facilities: Food, gas, and lodging are available in the town of Medical Lake.

Water sports/restrictions: Fishing and paddling are permitted.

Contact: West Medical Lake Resort, tel. (509) 299-3921.

26 Silver Lake

Rating: 7

Low water levels sometimes cause problems for folks trying to launch here, especially with larger boats. But that doesn't stop some fairly large crowds from turning out at Silver Lake on a warm summer day. The lake is popular with local swimmers, skiers, PWC riders, and others looking for fun in the sun. At times the anglers of spring are still on the water when the nonanglers of summer arrive, and it can get a little tense then. Mostly, though, everybody at Silver Lake has a good time doing what they like to do. The lake is a big one, covering well over 400 acres.

Location: Southeast of Medical Lake; map A5, grid i4.

How to get there: Take Interstate 90 west from Sprague or east from Spokane and turn north onto Four Lakes Road, following the signs toward the town of Medical Lake. Silver Lake will be on the left about three miles off the freeway.

Boat ramp: The lake has a public access area and a boat ramp, as well as a private resort with boat-launching facilities. The two-lane concrete ramp at the WDFW access area has a large gravel parking area that's seen better days. A $10 WDFW access decal is required to use the public launch areas maintained by the Washington Department of Fish and Wildlife. Picnic Pine Resort has a one-lane concrete ramp with limited parking in a nearby gravel lot. A $2 launch fee is charged at the resort.

Facilities: Picnic Pines Resort has a large swim area, boat moorage, a fishing dock, picnic areas, RV and tent sites, a restaurant, and a small convenience store. Food and gas are available in nearby Medical Lake.

Water sports/restrictions: All water sports are permitted.

Contact: Picnic Pines Resort, tel. (509) 299-3223; Washington Department of Fish and Wildlife, Spokane regional office, tel. (509) 456-4082.

27 Clear Lake

Rating: 7

Although it's 375 acres when full, you can't depend on Clear Lake to be full, thanks to irrigation drawdown. As the pumps do their damage, the water level may drop down beyond the reach of the boat ramps, causing obvious problems for folks trying to get on the water with their bigger boats, PWC, and other vessels that can't be carried or dragged to the water. When there's enough water, though, this is a roomy lake that can accommodate lots of skiers, swimmers, tubers, and PWC riders.

Location: South of Medical Lake; map A5, grid i4.

How to get there: Drive west from Sprague or east from Spokane on Interstate 90 and turn north on Salnave Road, also known as Highway 902. Less than a quarter of a mile from the freeway, turn right on Clear Lake Road and follow it to the east side of the lake.

Boat ramp: A two-lane Department of Fish and Wildlife ramp and single-lane ramps at Rainbow Cove and Mallard Bay Resorts provide good access to the lake. Rainbow Cove has a $4 launch fee; Mallard Bay charges $3 for launching. A $10 WDFW access decal is required to use the public launch areas maintained by the Washington Department of Fish and Wildlife.

Facilities: Rainbow Cove Resort has boat rentals, moorage, RV and tent sites, showers, a cafe, convenience store, picnic area, and small swim beach. Mallard Bay Resort has campsites, cabins, boat rentals, a store, swimming area, picnic area, and showers.

Water sports/restrictions: All water sports are permitted.

Contact: Rainbow Cove Resort, tel. (509) 299-3717, Mallard Bay Resort, tel. (509) 299-3830.

28 Fish Lake

Rating: 6

Mostly a place to go catch eastern brook trout, this 50-acre lake near Cheney is also a good place to spend a few relaxing hours in a canoe, kayak, or small rowboat. The no-motors regulation keeps the noise down and the water's surface smooth. It's a little busy in late April and May when early season anglers turn out in good numbers and again when the daytime swimmers show up in June, but summer evenings and fall afternoons are great here if you want peace and quiet. The lake's shoreline has quite a few homes on it.

Location: Northeast of Cheney; map A5, grid i5.

How to get there: Take Interstate 90 east from Sprague or west from Spokane and exit onto Highway 904 to Cheney. Drive northeast out of Cheney on Cheney-Spokane Road. The lake is on the right about 2.5 miles from Cheney.

Boat ramp: There's a county park with a boat ramp and beach access on the north side of the lake.

Facilities: Food, gas, and lodging are available in Cheney.

Water sports/restrictions: Internal combustion engines are prohibited.

Contact: Spokane County Parks and Recreation Department, tel. (509) 625-6200.

29 Hog Canyon Lake

Rating: 5

Anglers and paddlers aren't very likely to even see each other on this small lake with a beautifully poetic name. Anglers come here during the cold months when the lake's winter fishing season is open, while paddlers aren't likely to show up at least until the ice melts off the lake, usually late February or March. Covering only 50 acres, the lake has no development along its rocky shores, so it has somewhat of a wilderness feeling to it. Guess you could say it's a pretty little lake with an ugly little name. It's very shallow, perhaps 12 feet at its deepest point, so it warms quickly in the summer. That makes for lousy trout survival and is part of the reason that the lake is open to winter fishing only, but it makes for good swimming if the urge should strike you while you're exploring the lake.

Location: Northeast of Sprague; map A5, grid j3.

How to get there: Take Interstate 90 to exit 254 and turn south on Old State Highway, following it a mile to Peterson Road. Go left on Peterson and cross Brown Road, continuing on a mile and a half to the entrance to the access area for Hog Canyon Lake. The rutted dirt road into the access area can be a bit treacherous.

Boat ramp: There's a single-lane gravel ramp with limited parking at the south end of the lake. Trailering a large boat to this launch site isn't recommended. A $10 WDFW access decal is required to use the public launch areas maintained by the Washington Department of Fish and Wildlife.

Facilities: The nearest food, gas, and lodging are in Sprague.

Water sports/restrictions: Fishing and paddling are the best bets.

Contact: Four Seasons Campground, tel. (509) 257-2332 (March through November); Purple Sage Motel, tel. (509) 257-2507.

30 Chapman Lake

Rating: 6

This is really kind of a strange lake. Its north end is wedged into a deep bowl with steep basalt cliffs dropping down to the water's edge. Much of this north end is over 100 feet deep, and there are places where it's more than 160 feet deep. The narrow southern half of the lake, on the other hand, shallows out considerably, and you would do well to find a place deeper than 30 feet throughout this part of Chapman. There's even a long ribbon of marsh and knee-deep water extending several hundred yards from the lake's southern tip. Put all this together and you have a 150-acre lake that's worth exploring in a canoe or small boat. The changing features and personality of the lake from one end to the other makes the trip worthwhile. Anglers like it because they have a trout lake in Chapman's north half, a bass lake in its southern half.

Location: South of Cheney; map A5, grid j5.

How to get there: Drive south from Cheney on Cheney-Spangle Road and turn west (right) on Pine Grove Road. Drive a little over three miles to Cheney-Plaza Road and turn right; continue 1.5 miles and turn right again down the gravel road leading to the south end of the lake.

Boat ramp: There's a single-lane gravel launch ramp with a loading float at Chapman Lake Resort.

Facilities: Chapman Lake Resort has RV and tent sites, boat moorage, a small store, and rest rooms. Food, gas, and lodging are available in Cheney.

Water sports/restrictions: There's a 5 mph speed limit on the lake. Fishing and paddling are the attractions.

Contact: Chapman Lake Resort, tel. (509) 523-2221 (April through October).

31 Badger Lake

Rating: 7

This long, narrow lake in a rocky draw south of Cheney is one of Spokane County's prettiest and in many ways one of its most intriguing. Its bottom contours show a couple of holes nearing or exceeding 100 feet, while other spots along the bottom rise sharply to within a few feet of the surface. Although I don't know any divers who have explored it, I'm sure it offers fascinating possibilities for scuba enthusiasts. I do know from experience that the springtime trout fishing can be excellent here, especially when the mayflies hatch and the rainbows seem willing to commit suicide over anything soft and feathery that's fished along its surface. Fishing Badger also gave me the chance to prowl along its steep, rocky banks, some of the most interesting and beautiful shoreline scenery you'll find anywhere.

Location: South of Cheney; map A5, grid j5.

How to get there: Drive south from Cheney on Mullinix Road and turn east (left) on Dover Road, following it to the west side of the lake.

Boat ramp: There's a Department of Fish and Wildlife access and boat ramp on the lake's north side. It's a two laner with concrete planks and a large parking area. A $10 WDFW access decal is required to use the public launch areas maintained by the Washington Department of Fish and Wildlife.

Facilities: Food, gas, and lodging are available in Cheney.

Water sports/restrictions: All water sports are permitted.

Contact: Washington Department of Wildlife, Spokane regional office, tel. (509) 456-4082.

32 Fishtrap Lake

Rating: 5

If you're looking for boating solitude, DO NOT come to Fishtrap Lake during the last week of April and the first few weeks of May. That's the start of Washington's general fishing season, and this 195-acre Lincoln County lake happens to be one of the Inland Empire's most productive—and therefore most popular—trout-fishing lakes. Things begin to calm by Memorial Day weekend, offering paddlers and small-boat operators a chance to explore this five-mile-long lake in relative peace. The only real sign of human development on the lake's shores are at the north end, where Fishtrap Lake Resort and the public access area are located. The area's abundant birds and wildlife keep the trip interesting as you work your way south, toward the narrowest part of the lake and the small dam that helped to form it. Most of the lake's northern two-thirds is 20 to 25 feet deep; most of its southern one-third is 12 to 18 feet deep. Maybe all that uniformity is why the rainbow trout grow so plump and so stupid here, making Fishtrap a place where you almost have to leave your bait at home to avoid catching a limit here on opening day.

Location: Northeast of Sprague; map A5, grid j3.

How to get there: Take Interstate 90 east from Sprague or west from

Spokane and take the Fishtrap exit to the south. Drive three miles to Scroggie Road and turn east (left) to the north end of the lake.

Boat ramp: There are two boat ramps near the north end of the lake, one maintained by the Department of Fish and Wildlife and the other by Fishtrap Lake Resort. The WDFW ramp has two lanes, one gravel and one concrete-plank construction, both of them in rather tough shape last time I was there. A $10 WDFW access decal is required to use the public launch areas maintained by the Washington Department of Fish and Wildlife. The resort ramp is gravel and one lane, and has a $3 launch fee.

Facilities: Fishtrap Lake Resort has boat rentals and moorage, RV and tent spaces, a fishing dock, small convenience store, and rest rooms with showers.

Water sports/restrictions: Fishing and paddling are good bets here. Waterskiing and PWC riding are prohibited.

Contact: Fishtrap Lake Resort, tel. (509) 235-2284.

33 Amber Lake

Rating: 6

The 115-acre lake south of Cheney looks in some ways like a smaller version of nearby Williams and Badger Lakes, but it doesn't feel the same. Maybe that's because the lake has special fishing and boating rules that make it a quieter, more laid-back place. Gas motors are prohibited, so the loudest sound you may hear is the soft hum of an electric trolling motor or the swish of a fly rod waving in the dry air. It's a nice place to paddle as well as fish and a great destination on a warm, early summer evening or first thing in

the morning on a summer day that's going to be scorcher. If you want to hide from any other boaters who may be on the lake, go up behind the island near the lake's east end.

Location: Southwest of Cheney; map A5, grid j4.

How to get there: From the west, exit Interstate 90 at Sprague and drive east out of town on Old State Highway. Turn south (right) on Martin Road and follow it about 11 miles to Mullinex Road. Turn north (left) on Mullinex and follow it about six miles to Pine Spring Road. Turn west (left) and follow it to the lake. From the east, exit Interstate 90 at Tyler and drive south on Pine Spring Road, staying on it all the way to the lake.

Boat ramp: There's a public access area and boat ramp on the north side of the lake. It's a one-lane ramp with concrete planks and a fairly large gravel parking area.

Facilities: The nearest food, gas, and lodging are in Sprague and Cheney.

Water sports/restrictions: Internal-combustion engines are banned here.

Contact: Four Seasons Campground, tel. (509) 257-2332; Purple Sage Motel, tel. (509) 257-2507.

34 Williams Lake

Rating: 8

Covering more than 300 acres, this is the biggest of several lakes in the immediate area and has the most facilities for boaters, anglers, and other visitors. This is another one where the water level may fluctuate quite a lot, and it sometimes leaves the WDFW ramp high and dry. You might call ahead to be sure of the lake's status before trailering a long distance. Otherwise, Williams offers excellent boating, excellent fishing, and an excellent excuse to just get out on the water.

Location: Southwest of Cheney; map A5, grid j4.

How to get there: Take Martin Road east from Sprague, turn north on Mullinex Road and east on Williams Lake Road to the lake. From Cheney follow Mullinex Road south to Williams Lake Road, turn east (left), and you're there.

Boat ramp: You'll find a public access and boat ramp on the lake, along with two resorts that have boat ramps. The WDFW facility is a two-lane concrete-plank ramp that's a bit chewed-up and a small gravel parking area. A $10 WDFW access decal is required to use the public launch areas maintained by the Washington Department of Fish and Wildlife. The ramp at Klink's Williams Lake Resort is a concrete one laner with a loading float and gravel parking area. The concrete, one-lane ramp at Bunker's Resort and Marina also has a loading float and gravel parking lot. Both resorts charge $3 for round-trip launching.

Facilities: The two resorts have boat rentals, moorage, fishing docks, convenience stores, rest rooms, cabins, and RV sites. Bunker's has a restaurant.

Water sports/restrictions: All water sports are permitted.

Contact: Klink's Williams Lake Resort, tel. (509) 235-2391; Bunker's Resort and Marina, tel. (509) 235-5212 (late April through November only).

35 Downs Lake

Rating: 5

It covers more than 400 acres, but most of it is between five and 10 feet deep, so it warms like a son of a gun in the eastern Washington sun by early June.

Bass fishing and bird-watching are good here, and if you get too warm doing either, take a quick dip. The only problem is that the water here may not provide much relief from the heat.

Location: Southeast of Sprague; map A5, grid j3.

How to get there: Take Interstate 90 to Sprague, exit the freeway, and take Old State Highway east to Martin Road, following it about six miles to the gravel road turning south to the lake.

Boat ramp: There's a gravel boat ramp at Downs Lake Resort.

Facilities: Downs Lake Resort has the basics; the rest is in Cheney.

Water sports/restrictions: Fishing and paddling are the main draws here. Waterskiing and PWC riding are prohibited.

Contact: Downs Lake Resort, tel. (509) 235-2314.

36 Sprague Lake

Rating: 7

Known mostly for its angling pot pourri that includes everything from cutthroat trout to smallmouth bass and walleyes, this big lake right alongside Interstate 90 is also an interesting place to explore in a kayak, canoe, or small powerboat. With almost no development around it, it's a haven for wildlife watchers or anyone else who likes prowling around wild and natural areas. Check out the old cabin on the rock island near the western shore while you're prowling around the islands and bays in that part of the lake. Waterfowl and shore birds abound, and other creatures you might spot run the gamut from turtles to mule deer. You'll see other boaters here, but most of them are concentrating on catching fish and will hardly notice you.

Location: Southwest of Sprague, south side of Interstate 90; map A5, grid j2.

How to get there: Take Interstate 90 to the town of Sprague, hit Main Street and follow it out of town to the southwest. The road parallels the lake for several miles.

Boat ramp: The lake has four boat ramps, two of them at resorts and two along the undeveloped east side of the lake. Sprague Lake Resort at the lake's north end has a one-lane blacktop ramp with a loading float. On the west of the lake, Four Seasons Campground has a good hard-surface ramp with a loading dock. Both resorts charge a launch fee. The two concrete ramps with gravel parking areas on the east side of the lake are self-serve ramps with a can to put money in for their use. Both have rough gravel access and parking areas and nothing for facilities around them.

Facilities: Sprague Lake Resort has RV and tent sites, moorage, a fishing dock, tackle and a few other supplies, rest rooms with showers, and picnic area. Four Seasons Campground has RV and tent sites, cabins, moorage, rental boats, a picnic area, and a store.

Water sports/restrictions: Waterskiing and PWC riding are prohibited.

Contact: Sprague Lake Resort, tel. (509) 257-2864; Four Seasons Campground, tel. (509) 257-2332.

37 Fourth of July Lake

Rating: 4

This is another of those winter-only lakes that's open to fishing only from the first of December through the end of March, so visit it with your canoe or kayak from spring to fall and you'll probably have all 110 acres of it to yourself. It's not the most scenic place in the whole world, but OK for a few hours of paddling and investigating.

Location: South of Sprague; map A5, grid j2.

How to get there: Take Interstate 90 to Sprague and turn south onto Highway 23. Drive a mile and turn west (right) on the gravel and dirt road that begins at the one-mile marker.

Boat ramp: There's a rough Department of Fish and Wildlife boat ramp at the north end of the lake. A $10 WDFW access decal is required to use the public launch areas maintained by the Washington Department of Fish and Wildlife.

Facilities: Food, gas, lodging, and RV facilities are available in and around Sprague.

Water sports/restrictions: Gas engines are prohibited.

Contact: Four Seasons Campground, tel. (509) 257-2332; Purple Sage Motel, tel. (509) 257-2507; Sprague Lake Resort, tel. (509) 257-2864.

MAP B1

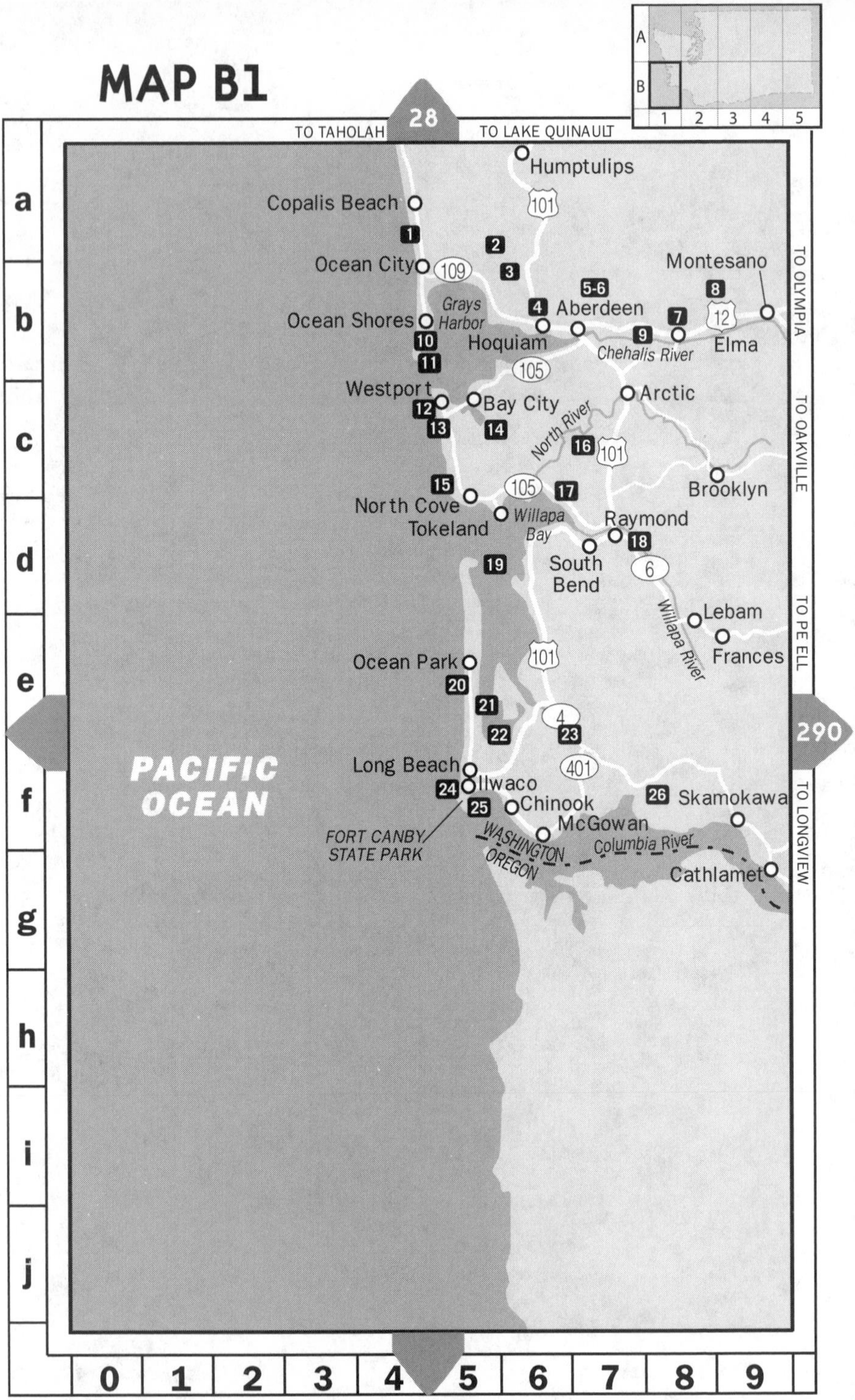
28
TO TAHOLAH
TO LAKE QUINAULT
Humptulips
101
Copalis Beach
1
2
Ocean City
109
3
Montesano
8
5-6
Grays
Harbor
4
Aberdeen
7
12
Ocean Shores
10
9
Hoquiam
Chehalis River
Elma
11
105
Westport
Arctic
Bay City
12
13
14
North River
16
101
Brooklyn
15
105
17
North Cove
Tokeland
Willapa
Bay
Raymond
18
South
Bend
19
6
Lebam
Willapa River
Frances
Ocean Park
101
20
21
4
22
23
290
PACIFIC
OCEAN
Long Beach
401
24
Ilwaco
26
Skamokawa
25
Chinook
McGowan
FORT CANBY
STATE PARK
WASHINGTON
OREGON
Columbia River
Cathlamet
TO OLYMPIA
TO OAKVILLE
TO PE ELL
TO LONGVIEW
a
b
c
d
e
f
g
h
i
j
0
1
2
3
4
5
6
7
8
9
A
B
1
2
3
4
5

CHAPTER B1

◼ North Beach Surf

Rating: 5

Although this section of Pacific Ocean frontage from Ocean Shores north to Moclips includes some of Washington's most beautiful beaches, it's so far off the beaten path that it gets relatively little traffic, either on land or water. A few surfers, mostly those hermit types who like to get away from the crowds, ride some of these beaches. They tend to reach the water via the three state parks in the area, Pacific Beach, Griffiths-Priday, and Ocean City. Because of the light foot and boat traffic here during the fall and winter months, this is a good stretch of Washington's beaches to search for glass floats from Asia; they aren't exactly common, but finding one is well within the realm of possibility during and following a period of stormy weather.

If you're looking for protected water to prowl for a few hours in your canoe or kayak, the best bet is in the protected two miles of estuary at the mouth of the Copalis River. Griffiths-Priday State Park is located between the river and the ocean on a narrow peninsula and provides access to the river for those willing to drag or carry their paddle craft a few yards. On a high tide it's possible to make your way some distance upriver from the park.

Location: From Moclips south to Ocean Shores; map B1, grid a4.

How to get there: Take Highway 109 west from Hoquiam and turn west (left) on any of the public roads leading to the beach.

Boat ramp: There are no boat ramps in this area.

Facilities: Food and gas are available at Copalis Beach, all other amenities at Ocean Shores. Ocean City State Park has tent sites, RV spaces, and rest rooms with showers.

Water sports/restrictions: Surfing, beachcombing, and some paddling are available here; swimming isn't recommended.

Contact: Ocean City State Park, tel. (360) 289-3553; Washington State Parks and Recreation Commission, tel. (800) 233-0321 (information), tel. (800) 452-5687 (reservations); Ocean Shores Chamber of Commerce Visitor Information Center, tel. (800) 762-3224.

◻ Humptulips River

Rating: 7

It wasn't all that many years ago that winter steelhead anglers and tribal gill-net fishermen were the only people spending much time on the Hump, but more and more folks interested in things other than fishing are finding their way to this big gentle river that flows into the north side of Grays Harbor. If you time your visit right, you might find that you have the river pretty much to yourself, no matter what section of it you choose to explore. Time it wrong, though, and you're likely to encounter more boat and bank traffic than you thought possible. The wrong time is during the height of the fall salmon run or the winter steelhead run when the Humptulips hosts hundreds of sport and commercial fishers on any given day. Adding to the complication for boaters during these times is the fact that the tribal folks are fishing with gill nets, which in some areas may stretch across much of the river's surface. Someone in a kayak, canoe, or inner tub would be wise indeed to avoid becoming entangled in one of these nylon sweepers.

If you do float the Humptulips when anglers are on the river, try not to interfere with their efforts. Most salmon and steelhead fishers prefer that boats pass close to their position, not through the middle of the channel or against the far side, because that's probably where they're casting. If you can get by behind them without passing in front of them at all, so much the better.

The potential dangers of getting stuck in a net are most evident on the lower mile or two of the river, but the most interesting challenges posed by the river itself are found on the upper reaches, including the forks where small channels, shallow riffles, boulders, and tight turns will put novice or intermediate paddlers through their paces. You won't find anything more serious than Class II, though, so the challenges aren't particularly dangerous. From U.S. 101 to the ramp at Highway 109 about the only interruptions in an otherwise leisurely float through serene countryside are an occasional large boulder or submerged log, a few sweepers, and several medium-speed chutes.

Location: Flows into Grays Harbor's North Bay northwest of Hoquiam; map B1, grid a6.

How to get there: Take U.S. 101 north from Hoquiam and drive about 22 miles to the middle portion of the river. To reach the lower Humptulips, turn west (left) off U.S. 101 onto the Ocean Beach Road about three miles north of Hoquiam and follow it to the river.

Boat ramp: There are boat ramps of various quality off East Humptulips and McNutt Roads, both of which are upstream from the U.S. 101 bridge. Donkey Creek Road, which heads east off U.S. 101 a few miles north of the highway bridge, winds along and crosses the West Fork Humptulips, offering several places to launch small boats. There are also several launching spots off Copalis Crossing Road, which runs along the west side of the river between U.S. 101 and Copalis Crossing. There's also a good paved ramp at the Highway 109 bridge a mile or so above the mouth of the river. A $10 WDFW access decal is required to use the public launch areas maintained by the Washington Department of Fish and Wildlife.

Facilities: There's a small store and gas station just north of the U.S. 101 bridge over the river, and the Red Rooster Tavern a few miles to the south is a good place to wet your whistle and get a good sandwich too. Lodging and additional facilities are available in Hoquiam and Aberdeen about 25 miles to the south.

Water sports/restrictions: Kayaking, rafting, drift-boating, canoeing, tubing, and swimming are possible here.

Contact: Grays Harbor Chamber of Commerce, tel. (800) 321-1924; Washington Department of Fish and Wildlife, Montesano regional office, tel. (360) 249-4628; White Water Sports, tel. (206) 246-9385.

3 Failor Lake

Rating: 5

At 65 acres Failor Lake isn't very big, but it's a favorite of Grays Harbor County anglers and boaters alike. Its busiest time is on opening day of the statewide general fishing season, but a hot day in July or August also will bring out a good crowd. Although some anglers may not like it if they get delayed, it's OK to launch nonfishing craft here IF your vehicle is adorned with an access decal issued by the

Department of Fish and Wildlife. The decal is free with your fishing or hunting license and costs only $10 for the calendar year if you don't hunt or fish. Wildlife agents will cite you if they find you using these boat ramps and access areas without the decal. If you wait until after the early spring angling crowds and the daytime sun-seekers leave, summer evenings are a great time to explore the Failor shoreline in a canoe, kayak, or even a small rowboat. The undeveloped shoreline may offer glimpses of eagles, ospreys, and other raptors, as well as such mammals as river otter, muskrat, mink, deer, fox, and maybe even a black bear.

Location: North of Hoquiam and west of U.S. 101; map B1, grid a6.

How to get there: Drive north about nine miles from Hoquiam on U.S. 101 and turn west (left) on Failor Lake Road. The lake is about two and a half miles off the highway.

Boat ramp: There's a Department of Fish and Wildlife boat ramp at the lake's public access area. A $10 WDFW access decal is required to use the public launch areas maintained by the WDFW.

Facilities: All other facilities are in Hoquiam and Aberdeen.

Water sports/restrictions: Fishing and paddling are the best bets here.

Contact: Grays Harbor Chamber of Commerce, tel. (800) 321-1924; Washington Department of Fish and Wildlife, Montesano regional office, tel. (360) 249-4628.

4 Hoquiam River

Rating: 6

If you're looking for whitewater, you're in the wrong place. Fact is, the water here hardly moves at all except with the ris-

ing and falling tide. If you make the mistake of trying to float downstream from one of the two launch sites listed above to the boat ramp near the mouth of the Hoquiam during a time when the tide is flooding and there's any kind of a serious south wind, you may have to paddle like crazy just to keep stay even. The moral, of course, is to plan your trip on the Hoquiam so that you use the tide to your advantage. Any good tide table can help you do that. What you'll find here is slow water and a lazy setting, just right for a thoroughly relaxing few hours on the water. The only real human development here, aside from the clear-cutting that happened decades ago, is on the lower mile or so; above that it's natural grass and forestland and lots of birds and wildlife to spot if you're on your toes. You probably won't even see anyone else on the river unless you boat the forks of the Hoquiam during the fall cutthroat trout or salmon season or the winter steelhead fishery.

Location: Enters the east end of Grays Harbor at Hoquiam; map B1, grid b6.

How to get there: Take U.S. 101 north from Hoquiam to parallel the west side of the river. East Hoquiam Road out of Hoquiam parallels the East Fork of the Hoquiam and provides good access.

Boat ramp: There's a boat ramp near the mouth of the Hoquiam off 28th Street in Aberdeen about a quarter mile above the river mouth. A good launch site on the West Fork Hoquiam is found along U.S. 101 on the east side of the highway about a mile and a half north of where the Ocean Beach Highway takes off to the west. A good place to launch on the East Fork Hoquiam is about five miles upstream from the confluence with the West Fork, off East Hoquiam Road.

Facilities: Food, gas, lodging, and tackle are just a few minutes away in Hoquiam and Aberdeen.

Water sports/restrictions: Kayaking and canoeing are the best options here.

Contact: Grays Harbor Chamber of Commerce, tel. (800) 321-1924; Washington Department of Fish and Wildlife, Montesano regional office, tel. (360) 249-4628

5 Wishkah River

Rating: 5

Like most of the streams entering Grays Harbor, the Wishkah is a slow mover, so you won't find anything in the way of rapids or whitewater. Its small size, slow speed, and meandering nature make this a good stream for beginning paddlers. The upper part of this float will take you through some pleasant woodlands and natural areas, but the lower part is ugly, unless you like rust, rotting pilings, and mud (during low tide). Like the Hoquiam (above), you'll want to time this float so that you take advantage of a falling tide; otherwise you'll be paddling upstream as you try to get downstream. The biggest adventure on this trip will come at the end when you have to cross the Chehalis to reach the take-out spot. Be alert for larger powerboats and the possibility of rough water, depending on weather and tides.

Location: Flows into the east end of Grays Harbor at Aberdeen; map B1, grid b7.

How to get there: Take U.S. 12 to Aberdeen and turn north on Wishkah Road.

Boat ramp: You'll find public access and a fairly rough launch for canoes, kayaks, and other small boats about six miles upstream from the river's mouth, off Wishkah Road. The only place to take out at the bottom end is across the Chehalis River from the mouth of the Wishkah at the end of Boone Road in South Aberdeen. Getting to this take-out site by car involves crossing the Chehalis on the U.S. 101 bridge as though you were heading west toward Westport.

Facilities: Food, lodging, gas, tackle, and plenty of watering holes are available in Aberdeen.

Water sports/restrictions: Paddling and limited powerboating are available here.

Contact: Grays Harbor Chamber of Commerce, tel. (800) 321-1924; Washington Department of Fish and Wildlife, Montesano regional office, tel. (360) 249-4628.

6 Lake Aberdeen

Rating: 5

The sand and gravel beach at the city park makes this one of Grays Harbor's popular summertime swimming holes, and the 63-acre lake warms quickly. There isn't room to do a lot of hot-rodding on the lake, so most of the bigger and fast craft go elsewhere to have their fun. It's a short run from Aberdeen and Hoquiam to the park, so canoeists, kayakers, and other paddlers can get here in a short time for a little flat-water relaxation on a calm summer evening.

Location: Northeast of Aberdeen; map B1, grid b7.

How to get there: Driving west on U.S. 12 toward Aberdeen, turn north (right) at the "Fish Hatchery-Aberdeen Lake" sign, which is about a mile west of the new development where the old Central Park drive-in theater used to be.

Boat ramp: There's a city park boat ramp on the east side of the lake, with all other amenities in Aberdeen.

Facilities: The city park has rest rooms and a small picnic area. Food, fuel, lodging, and other facilities are in Aberdeen, a few miles to the west.

Water sports/restrictions: All water sports are permitted.

Contact: Grays Harbor Chamber of Commerce, tel. (800) 321-1924; Washington Department of Fish and Wildlife, Montesano regional office, tel. (360) 249-4628.

7 Wynoochee River

Rating: 7

Unless you were able to drop a kayak over the face of Wynoochee Dam and run the narrow little canyon immediately below it, the Wynoochee is a docile stream with nothing more notable than a couple of rapids that might make Class II. However, this Chehalis River tributary runs though some scenic and very rural country where wildlife is abundant, so it's worth a day's float even if not for the whitewater thrill of it all. It gets lots of boat traffic from steelhead anglers during both the summer and winter seasons, but relatively few kayakers or rafters make the long drive out here from the major Puget Sound population centers. There are, in fact, more exciting streams a lot closer to home. But if you just happen to be passing through southern Grays Harbor County with your boat and have a few hours to kill, there are much worse places to spend the time.

Location: Joins the Chehalis River at Montesano; map B1, grid b8.

How to get there: Take Highway 8/U.S. 12 west from Olympia and turn north

(right) on the Wynoochee Road about a mile and a half past Montesano.

Boat ramp: There are two Department of Fish and Wildlife access areas with boat ramps on the river, both off Wynoochee Valley Road. The lower one is three miles off Highway 8, near the mouth of Black Creek, the second another six miles up the road, where the turn is marked by a public fishing sign. There's also a take-out site on the Chehalis River, just upstream from the mouth of the Wynoochee, and there are a couple of places well upriver on the Wynoochee where it's possible to drag a small raft or kayak over the bank or off the end of logging roads that come close to the river. One such spot is half a mile above the mouth of Schafer Creek. A $10 WDFW access decal is required to use the public launch areas maintained by the Washington Department of Fish and Wildlife.

Facilities: Montesano has food, fuel, and other necessities.

Water sports/restrictions: Drift boating, rafting, kayaking, canoeing and tubing are good options here, with some swimming on the lower river.

Contact: Grays Harbor Chamber of Commerce, tel. (800) 321-1924; Washington Department of Fish and Wildlife, Montesano regional office, tel. (360) 249-4628.

8 Satsop River

Rating: 7

I learned a valuable lesson on the West Fork Satsop one January day back in the mid-'70s. I should add right here that this valuable lesson has been lost on me dozens of times since that January day, but at least I remember it. Anyway, a friend and I decided that we needed to float the West Fork Satsop.

We had heard rumors that it may be home to a few of the large but elusive wild steelhead for which many Olympic Peninsula rivers are famous, and we took it upon ourselves to learn once and for all if the rumors were true. We had to learn for ourselves, you see, because this was, after all, scientific research of the most serious kind. Since we were determined to leave no stone unturned in our quest for the truth, we filled my friend's drift boat with a full day's provisions: all our steelhead tackle and a case of beer. The rumors, it turned out, were true, and we collected evidence in the form of two steelhead weighing 14 and 18 pounds. But we scoured every inch of the West Fork Satsop in our quest for those specimens, and by the time we finished our research it was pitch-black and we weren't within sight of the pickup and boat trailer we had left some 12 hours earlier. What was the lesson I learned from all this? No, it wasn't that you need more than a case of beer if you're going to float the West Fork Satsop. It's that you also need food if you're going to float the West Fork Satsop, because there's more to see and do there than you might expect, and it will take a full day to do it right.

We made our stupid and memorable float from the famed Swinging Bridge down to the confluence of the East and West Forks, and that's still a favorite run of many Satsop boaters. The East Fork run, from Schafer State Park to the confluence, though, is just about as pretty, but a little shorter. Either one is a nice trip for the paddler or rower who doesn't want to worry about any water more serious than easy Class II. The main river from the confluence down to the highway bridge or even farther down to the Chehalis is even easier, except that you may meet more boat traffic in the form of local anglers in search of salmon or steelhead. And speaking of anglers, you might want to avoid the Satsop entirely from the first of October until Christmas, because that's when the coho and chum salmon runs are in, and the river really gets clogged with anglers. The Satsop is one of Washington's top salmon-fishing streams, and it may be impossible to dodge and dart your way through the flying hooks and sinkers without running the risk of serious injury. And heaven help you if you manage to get yourself between a screaming, swearing angler and his hooked fish. They shoot people in this part of the country for a whole lot less.

Location: Joins the Chehalis River west of Elma; map B1, grid b9.

How to get there: Take Highway 8/U.S. 12 west from Olympia to Satsop, which is about four miles west of Elma. Turn north (right) onto East Satsop Road and follow it upriver.

Boat ramp: Favorite put-in sites are at Swinging Bridge Park, about seven miles up the West Fork Satsop from its confluence with the East Fork, and Schafer State Park five miles above the confluence on the East Fork. A flat stretch of gravel bar off West Satsop Road right at the confluence serves as a take-out site for some and a put-in for those who want to float the main Satsop. There's also a good paved ramp on the downstream side of the Highway 8/U.S. 12 bridge (accessible only from the eastbound lanes of the highway) and on the Chehalis River about 400 yards upstream from the mouth of the Satsop off Keys Road. The Department of Fish and Wildlife manages these last two ramps. A $10 WDFW access decal is required to use the public launch areas maintained by the Washington Department of Fish and Wildlife.

Facilities: Schafer State Park, located on the East Fork Satsop, has tent sites and a few spaces with RV hookups and rest rooms. Gas, food, and lodging are available at Elma.

Water sports/restrictions: Drift boating, rafting, kayaking, canoeing, snorkeling, and tubing are popular here. A $10 WDFW access decal is required to use the public launch areas maintained by the Washington Department of Fish and Wildlife.

Contact: Schafer State Park, tel. (360) 482-3852; Washington State Parks and Recreation Commission, tel. (800) 233-0321 (information), tel. (800) 452-5687 (reservations).

9 Lower Chehalis River

Rating: 6

The lower reaches of this major Gray Harbor tributary are influenced by the tides, so it's constantly presenting a different face to visitors. That's a good news-bad news story for boaters. The good news is that the scenery is ever changing, so you never see the same river twice unless you spend a lot of time there. The bad news is that boaters must stay on their toes and adjust to the river's changing moods as its level rises and drops, especially on the lowermost part from the Highway 107 bridge downstream. The entire stretch of the Chehalis within this section is a lazy, slow-moving stream that offers little in the way of dangers except for the occasional sweeper or submerged obstacle that could catch you off guard if you're not paying any attention.

Boaters won't see much in the way of human activity on most of this river, except for the occasional sturgeon angler and during the fall a good number of salmon anglers downstream from the launch at the Highway 107 bridge. You're more likely to see various forms of wildlife than humans at other times of year, as the Chehalis has good populations of ducks and geese, black-tailed deer, Roosevelt elk, coyote, fox, beaver, mink, river otter, and black bear.

One spring afternoon several years ago while a friend and I were anchored about two miles downstream from the Highway 107 ramp, we glanced downriver 100 yards and saw something swimming across the river. We popped free from the anchor and drifted toward it for a closer look, coming to within maybe 30 yards before realizing that it was a bear. I scrambled for my camera, my friend scrambled to start the outboard, and the bear scrambled toward the muddy bank as fast as it could go. When we got about 10 yards from it, the half-grown bruin glared over its shoulder, let out a threatening snarl, and I suddenly had visions of it turning around and trying to climb aboard. I didn't need any photos of an angry bear chewing on my fishing partner, so we backed off and let the rattled bear go about its business without further harassment. Like most of the rest of my photos, my bear shots turned out only so-so, but we had a fun story to tell when we got home that night.

Location: Enters the east end of Grays Harbor at Aberdeen; map B1, grid b7.

How to get there: Take Interstate 5 to Grand Mound and turn west onto U.S. 12, following the river downstream. Or take Highway 8 west from Olympia and either turn south to follow the

Chehalis upstream toward Oakville or continue west to parallel the river downstream to Aberdeen.

Boat ramp: There's a paved boat ramp behind the police/fire station off F Street at Cosmopolis, another off Highway 107 beneath the highway bridge just south of Montesano, one upstream from the mouth of the Satsop River off Keys Road, a fourth one at Porter, and one at Cedarville off Elma Gate Road. A $10 WDFW access decal is required to use the public launch areas maintained by the Washington Department of Fish and Wildlife.

Facilities: Food, gas, lodging, and other amenities are available in Elma, Montesano, Aberdeen, and Hoquiam.

Water sports/restrictions: All water sports are permitted.

Contact: Grays Harbor Chamber of Commerce, tel. (800) 321-1924; Washington Department of Fish and Wildlife, Montesano regional office, tel. (360) 249-4628.

10 Duck Lake

Rating: 6

This 450-acre man-made lake south of Ocean Shores is just about all things to all boaters around the Ocean Shores area who want a little freshwater action. With the Pacific Ocean to the west and Grays Harbor to the east, it's nice that there's this large a body of freshwater in the middle for cruising, sailing, skiing, paddling, and swimming. The lake also offers good fishing for trout and several warmwater species, so take your pick. Although some of the lake is developed, there are still lots of brushy shorelines, channels and large bays to explore with either a paddle or a fishing rod in

your hands. Spring exploration here will provide you with lots of opportunities to spot songbirds, shorebirds, and waterfowl around the lake. After all, it is named Duck Lake.

Location: South of Ocean Shores; map B1, grid b5.

How to get there: Take Highway 109 west from Hoquiam to Highway 115. Turn south (left) and drive through Ocean Shores. Turn left on either Chance A La Mer and drive to the boat ramp near the north end of the lake or continue south to Ocean Lake Way, turn left, and drive to Duck Lake Drive. Turn right and follow Duck Lake Drive to the southern boat ramp.

Boat ramp: The ramp nearer the north end of the lake is suitable for launching trailer boats of good size, while the southern ramp is better for cartoppers and smaller craft.

Facilities: Food, gas, and lodging are available in Ocean Shores.

Water sports/restrictions: All water sports are permitted.

Contact: Ocean City State Park, tel. (360) 289-3553; Washington State Parks and Recreation Commission, tel. (800) 233-0321 (information), tel. (800) 452-5687 (reservations); Ocean Shores Chamber of Commerce Visitor Information Center, tel. (800) 762-3224.

11 Grays Harbor North Entrance

Rating: 6

There aren't many places left in Washington where you can get in a boat of almost any kind, take off in almost any direction you want to go, see miles of mostly unspoiled scenery, and perhaps not see another boat or another person for hours. But if you use your boat to explore the North Bay portion of Grays

Harbor, you'll be in one of those places. Although signs of human encroachment are easy to spot all around, it is just so far away from population centers that you can feel truly alone here while on the water if that's the kind of thing you look for once in a while. That solitude, though, isn't without a price, and part of the price you pay here is unpredictable weather that can put a stop to your adventure before it begins or, even worse, threaten your safety during the middle of your trip. Fog and sudden storms are part of the deal whenever you do your boating on or near the wild and woolly Northwest coast, so pay attention to the weather when planning and executing your trip to this part of the state.

Location: South of Ocean Shores; map B1, grid b4.

How to get there: Take Highway 109 west from Hoquiam to Highway 115, turn south, and drive through Ocean Shores. Bear west on any of the major cross streets to get onto Sand Dune Drive and take it to Ocean Shores Boulevard, which ends at the North Jetty.

Boat ramp: There's a single-lane concrete ramp just inside the harbor's north entrance five miles south of the main Ocean Shores business district. The ramp is open from 7 a.m. to 7 p.m. during the summer and 7 a.m. to 5 p.m. from October to May. It has a $5.50 launch fee. A three-lane ramp with a dock and rest rooms is available on the south side of Grays Harbor in Westport.

Facilities: Westport Marina, across the harbor to the south, has open moorage ($8 per day and up), electrical hookups, boat-sewage pump-out facilities, rest rooms with showers, and a fuel dock, with marine repair, groceries, restaurants, and motels nearby. Food,

gas, lodging, and other amenities are available in Ocean Shores.

Water sports/restrictions: Powerboating, sailing, windsurfing, paddling, wading, and swimming are popular activities. You'll need NOAA nautical chart 18502 for these waters.

Contact: Ocean Shores Marina and RV Park, tel. (800) 742-0414; Ocean Shores Chamber of Commerce Visitor Information Center, tel. (800) 762-3224; Grays Harbor Chamber of Commerce, tel. (800) 321-1924; Port of Grays Harbor/ Westport Marina, tel. (360) 268-9665.

12 Westport Inshore

Rating: 8

Once the sole domain of salmon anglers and the businesses they supported, Westport and the south side of Grays Harbor have diversified over the past two decades, and that diversification has made this a better destination for most water recreationists. Sure, we all miss the virtually unlimited salmon fishing and the bounty it offered, but I remember lots of times when it was nearly impossible to find a parking spot here, let alone get in and out of Westport's only boat ramp in less than an hour. Now there's room for smaller boats in the Westport boat basin, and it's even possible to get around in a paddle craft with at least some assurance of not being swamped or run over by a bigger boat on its way to the fishing grounds. In fact, the boat basin is an interesting place to prowl and explore in a kayak or canoe, and there are lots of places here to drop a crab pot or fish for pile perch and small rockfish around the rock jetties and pilings.

Outside the boat basin (where both the boat ramp and fuel docks are located), there's plenty to see and explore in

Grays Harbor itself. Turn to the west toward the harbor entrance, and you'll pass the half dozen finger jetties that help protect the point. Then it's Half Moon Bay, a long stretch of sandy beach between the finger jetties and the South Jetty beyond. This stretch is popular with surfers, several dozen of whom may gather here on any weekend when conditions are right. The waters of Half Moon Bay also produce lots of tasty Dungeness crab, so red-and-white crab pot buoys may present a small challenge for boaters here when the pot season is open. The end of the South Jetty marks the beginning of the famous Grays Harbor Bar, where many boaters have paid for their mistakes with lost boats and even lost lives. (See details about the bar under the Westport Offshore listing, below.)

One of the big draws to the open middle portion of Grays Harbor is the fall salmon fishery that usually occurs here, the so-called Buoy 13 season (named after the westernmost boundary of the open fishing area). Depending on the size of hatchery runs coming back to the Chehalis River and other Grays Harbor tributaries, this season may provide good fishing for coho, chinooks, or both, and the harbor may be crowded with fishing boats during evening and weekend tides. Keep that in mind if you visit Grays Harbor in the fall.

If you come out of the Westport boat basin and turn right to the south and east, you'll be turning into South Bay, a good place for paddlers to get away from most winds and the worst of the tidal currents. Wildlife of all kinds is abundant here, both along the grassy shores of the mainland and on Grass Island, which lies inside the bay about two miles south of the boat basin. If

you continue south and pass under the Highway 105 bridge at Bay City, you can also explore the maze of waterways in the intricate estuary around Laidlaw Island or even paddle up into the southeast corner of the bay and the mouth of the Elk River.

If you come out of the boat basin on an easterly course, you will be heading toward the mouth of the Johns River and the Johns River Wildlife Area, certainly worth exploring in a small powerboat or paddle boat. Besides lots of waterfowl, shorebirds, raptors, and other flying wildlife, you may see seals, otters, black-tailed deer, and Roosevelt elk. Cutthroat trout fishing can be quite good here in the summer, and it's also the site of some serious combat fishing among boaters for a run of hatchery chinook salmon that has returned in good numbers over the past few years. You might want to avoid those crowds unless you like the idea of hooking and landing a fat 20-pounder to throw on the barbecue at the end of the day.

Boaters time it right might be treated to a good look at the *Lady Washington,* a 112-foot replica of the eighteenth-century square-rigger that explored Northwest waters more than 200 years ago. Launched in 1989 for Washington's centennial celebration, the *Lady* sails regularly from her home port of Aberdeen, sometimes touring Grays Harbor and sometimes sailing to other destinations throughout the Northwest. Used to help teach youngsters the basics of seamanship and teamwork, she also carries up to 60 passengers on scheduled trips.

Location: South entrance to Grays Harbor; map B1, grid c5.

How to get there: Take Highway 105 west from Aberdeen and turn north (right) at the Y as you approach the coast.

Boat ramp: There's a wide, paved, four-lane ramp with floats at the end of Wilson Street, which is on the right as you pass the BP gas station on the way into the Westport dock area.

Facilities: Westport Marina has open moorage ($8 per day and up), electric hookups, boat pump-out facilities, rest rooms with showers, a fuel dock, and drinking water, with boat repair nearby. Public rest rooms, restaurants, grocery stores, lodging, RV parks, gas, diesel, and bait and tackle all are available in and around Westport.

Water sports/restrictions: All water sports are permitted. NOAA nautical chart 18502 is best for these waters.

Contact: Port of Grays Harbor/Westport Marina, tel. (360) 268-9665; Westport/Grayland Chamber of Commerce Visitor Information Center, tel. (800) 345-6223. For nautical charts of this area, contact Captain's Nautical Supply, tel. (206) 283-7242.

13 Westport Offshore

Rating: 8

For more than 20 years, from the late '50s through the late '70s, there was only one good reason to venture out of Westport and head into the open Pacific Ocean: to fish for (and usually catch) salmon. Westport was known as the Salmon Capital of the World, so fishing drove the recreational opportunities and the economy here. Salmon fishing out of Westport still can be excellent, but the limits are smaller and the seasons shorter, so people have come to realize that there's plenty more to do here than fish. The fact is that Westport offers good access to the open ocean off the south central Washington coast, and more and more recreational boaters are using it for just that.

Making the decision to leave Westport and head for the open waters to the west, of course, involves crossing the famous Grays Harbor Bar—or Westport Bar, as it's often called—and that's an adventure that shouldn't be taken lightly. The bar can be a monster when all the water trying to escape Grays Harbor on an ebbing tide meets a strong westerly wind at the narrow, shallow harbor entrance. Swells and even breaking waves of 10 to 15 feet aren't uncommon under those conditions, and it's not a pretty place to be when the bar is in that kind of mood. Wise boaters change their plans if they encounter a snotty bar on their way out in the morning, but where it really gets tough is when boats are trying to come back to port and the bar has kicked up while they were outside. Even though the urge to return home is strong, you may be better off consulting the tide book and waiting the necessary time for the flow to diminish and the water to settle down. Push your luck, your equipment, and your boating skills, and it could be your last trip. Even when the bar is calm, remember your basic nautical training and follow the markers in and out of the Grays Harbor entrance. The waves and currents are constantly moving the bottom sands around, and venturing outside the traffic lanes can get you in trouble.

Once outside the bar, you still have to be alert, especially for commercial crab pots, but you can dodge them while still enjoying the feeling of freedom that comes with being on the open ocean. At this point I could presume to tell you about all the things to see and places to go on the vast Pacific Ocean, but that would make for a mighty thick book. Whether you turn south toward Willapa Bay and the Long Beach Peninsula, turn north past Ocean Shores and head for LaPush, or venture west into the great wide ocean, you're on your own now.

Location: South entrance to Grays Harbor; map B1, grid c5.

How to get there: Take Highway 105 west from Aberdeen and turn north (right) at the Y as you approach the coast.

Boat ramp: There's a wide, paved, four-lane ramp with floats at the end of Wilson Street, which is on the right as you pass the BP gas station on your way into the Westport dock area.

Facilities: Westport Marina has open moorage ($8 per day and up), electric hookups, boat pump-out facilities, rest rooms with showers, a fuel dock, and drinking water, with boat repair nearby. Public rest rooms, restaurants, grocery stores, lodging, RV parks, gas, diesel, and bait and tackle all are available in and around Westport.

Water sports/restrictions: Powerboating and party-boat trips including fishing and whale-watching charters are the main draws here. The best NOAA nautical chart for these waters is chart 18502.

Contact: Port of Grays Harbor/Westport Marina, tel. (360) 268-9665; Westport/Grayland Chamber of Commerce Visitor Information Center, tel. (800) 345-6223. For nautical charts of this area, contact Captain's Nautical Supply, tel. (206) 283-7242.

14 Elk River

Rating: 5

Paddlers making their way from South Bay and Highway 105 will enjoy the es-tuarine scenery and excellent opportunities for wildlife viewing and photography. In the late summer and fall, high tides and heavy rains bring in good numbers of sea-run cutthroat trout, so carry a light spinning rod and a selection of small spinners and spoons along to try your luck.

Location: Flows into Grays Harbor's South Bay near Bay City; map B1, grid c6.

How to get there: Drive southwest out of Aberdeen on Highway 105 and turn east on Johns River Road. Turn south (right) on the gravel road about two miles from the highway and drive about three miles to the Elk River.

Boat ramp: It's possible to put a small boat, kayak, or canoe in the water at the west end of the Highway 105 bridge over South Bay and paddle or motor about three miles to the southeast to find the mouth of the Elk.

Facilities: The nearest food, gas, motels, tackle, and other amenities are in Westport and Aberdeen.

Water sports/restrictions: Kayaking, canoeing, and powerboating in a small craft are possible here.

Contact: Westport/Grayland Chamber of Commerce Visitor Information Center, tel. (800) 345-6223; Grays Harbor Chamber of Commerce, tel. (800) 321-1924; Washington Department of Fish and Wildlife, Montesano regional office, tel. (360) 249-2648.

15 South Beach Surf

Rating: 7

Perhaps Washington's best-known stretch of ocean beach, this is a great place for the whole family, and don't forget the dog. Just as we adults feel the urge to keep walking when we get to the wide-open ocean beaches, kids and dogs feel the urge to do it all at a much faster pace, and that's just fine. Although Southern Californians may think they have a corner on surfing, try telling that to a hardy pack of Northwesterners who seem to get along just fine on these sandy shores that extend from the Grays Harbor entrance to Cape Shoalwater and the north entrance to Willapa Bay.

The surfing here can be excellent, especially for those who like the idea of riding waves onto smooth, safe beaches with no dangerous rocks. Driftwood and other obstacles, though, may be present, so don't let your guard down completely. When the weather's calm and the waves lie down, the surfers go elsewhere, and a few folks take to water beyond the surf line in kayaks. Paddling here provides an interesting perspective on Washington's coastline, one that few people ever get. But remember that even when the water is calm, it may be moving, so don't just throw a boat in and hope your arms take you where you want to go; if you're paddling into the current, you might lose ground and end up touring the coast in the opposite direction you planned.

Location: Coastal beach from Westport south to Cape Shoalwater, northern entrance to Willapa Bay; map B1, grid c5.

How to get there: Take Highway 105 southwest from Aberdeen or northwest from Raymond. Several paved roads heading west off the highway lead to the beach, all of which is public.

Boat ramp: The nearest ramps are in Westport at the end of Wilson Street and in Willapa Bay to the south near Tokeland.

Facilities: Twin Harbors State Park to the north and Grayland Beach State Park to the south have tent spaces, RV hookups, and rest rooms with showers; other facilities are available at Westport and Tokeland.

Water sports/restrictions: Surfing, surf fishing, wading, and beachcombing are the main activities. Digging razor clams can be worthwhile on low tides when the season is open (license required).

Contact: Grayland Beach State Park, tel. (360) 268-9717; Washington State Parks and Recreation Commission, tel. (800) 233-0321 (information), tel. (800) 452-5687 (reservations); Westport/ Grayland Chamber of Commerce Visitor Information Center, tel. (800) 345-6223; Grays Harbor Chamber of Commerce, tel. (800) 321-1924.

16 North River

Rating: 2

Actually more like a deep creek in some places and a slough in others, this river offers a little paddling opportunity that includes some gentle riffles and several places where you'll have to crawl and drag your way over and around downed trees, stumps, and logjams. It doesn't help that the riverbank is steep and slippery in many places, making it hard to get out of the water to avoid problems. The North is probably more work than fun for the average paddler, and chances are that if you should meet up with any of the locals, they won't be particularly happy to see you.

Location: Enters Willapa Bay east of Tokeland; map B1, grid c6.

How to get there: Take U.S. 101 south from Aberdeen or north from Raymond and turn east at Arctic on North River Road to reach the upper river. Turn west off U.S. 101 onto Lund Road and follow it downriver to American Mill Road to explore lower portions of the river. To reach the two miles of river at the mouth, take Highway 105 west from Raymond or south from Aberdeen and turn north near the west end of the highway bridge to the access area and boat ramp.

Boat ramp: There's a good boat ramp at the mouth of the river, right off Highway 105.

Facilities: There are a store and a tavern at Arctic and other facilities available in Raymond and Aberdeen.

Water sports/restrictions: Kayaking and canoeing are possibilities here.

Contact: Washington Department of Fish and Wildlife, Montesano regional office, tel. (360) 249-4628.

17 Smith Creek

Rating: 3

The brush, downed trees, steep banks, and limited access that keep bank anglers to a minimum here also have a negative effect on boating activity on this little Willapa Bay tributary. You can paddle a short distance upstream from the boat ramp off U.S. 101 at the creek mouth, but that's about the only sure thing here. Along most of its length you're at the mercy of the stream's surroundings, and they're tough.

Location: Flows into the north end of Willapa Bay northwest of Raymond; map B1, grid c6.

How to get there: Take U.S. 101 north from Raymond or south from Aberdeen and turn east on Smith Creek Road to reach about 12 miles of the creek between the highway and the small town of Brooklyn. Turn west off U.S. 101 on Dixon Road to reach part of the lower section of the creek. To explore the waters near the creek mouth, drive west

from Raymond on Highway 105 and turn right into the boat ramp and access area just across the Smith Creek bridge.

Boat ramp: The boat ramp at the mouth of the creek is a good one.

Facilities: Other amenities for visiting anglers are available in Raymond.

Water sports/restrictions: Paddling and tubing are possibilities. A $10 WDFW access decal is required to use the public launch areas maintained by the Washington Department of Fish and Wildlife.

Contact: Washington Department of Fish and Wildlife, Montesano regional office, tel. (360) 249-4628.

18 Willapa River

Rating: 7

Known more for its salmon, steelhead, and cutthroat trout fishing, the Willapa is also a worthwhile destination for boaters, especially kayakers and canoeists looking for calm waters and interesting scenery. From the Department of Fish and Wildlife access area at the mouth of Wilson Creek down to the ramp at the west end of South Bend, the lower 10 miles of river is slow and deep, lined in some areas with old pilings and overhanging spruce and cedar trees along much of the stretch. It's not very scenic along the final two or three miles, as the river runs through the town of Raymond and along the edge of South Bend. You may encounter powerboat traffic along this stretch, especially during the fall salmon season, but most of the boats are moving slowly, maybe because of all the stumps and pilings in the river, maybe just because they're fishermen and they don't want to stir up the fish. Whatever the reason, they don't pose much of a threat to paddlers. Some of the commercial boats on the lower three miles of the river may be in a bigger hurry, so give them a wide berth.

The lower Willapa to well above the Wilson Creek ramp is influenced by the tide, but paddlers shouldn't have trouble making progress against it in either direction. If you float the upper stretch of the river, give yourself more time than you think you'll need. While it's only about 17 miles by road from Lebam to Raymond, it's more like a 25-mile trip by river from Lebam to the Wilson Creek ramp, thanks to the Willapa's winding nature. And since there's no fast water, you'll have to keep paddling to stay on the move. It's a long trip, mostly through farm lands and alder flats.

Location: Enters the northeast corner of Willapa Bay near South Bend; map B1, grid d7.

How to get there: Take U.S. 101 to Raymond and turn east on Willapa-Monohan Landing Road at the north end of the highway bridge just north of town to reach some of the lower end of the river. To reach upstream sections of the Willapa, take Highway 6 east from Raymond or west from Chehalis.

Boat ramp: One boat ramp is near the river mouth at the west end of South Bend, and another is at Old Willapa on Willapa-Monohan Landing Road about three miles upstream from the U.S. 101 bridge. It's possible to put a small boat into the river in several places along Highway 6, including the highway bridge over the river near Menlo and upstream from the salmon hatchery between Lebam and Globe. A $10 WDFW access decal is required to use the public launch areas maintained by the Washington Department of Fish and Wildlife.

Facilities: There's a fair selection of restaurants and some lodging available in Raymond and South Bend.

Water sports/restrictions: Paddling, drift boating, tubing, and swimming are possible on the upper Willapa, and powerboating is possible on the lower reaches.

Contact: Raymond Chamber of Commerce Visitor Information Center, tel. (360) 942-5419; Washington Department of Fish and Wildlife, Montesano regional office, tel. (360) 249-4628.

19 Willapa Bay

Rating: 7

Although this is one of the most interesting waterways along the entire Northwest coast, in some ways it's not very boater friendly. Fluctuating tides fill it to the brim and beyond on a flood tide, sometimes covering shoreline facilities with several inches to several feet of saltwater. Then ebb tides can sometimes leave boat ramps not only high and dry but may be hundreds of yards from the water as well.

Boating facilities are sparse, and many of them are oriented toward their commercial fishing clientele, not recreational boaters. And commercial fishing can become an outright hazard for boaters unfortunate enough to be stuck trying to work their way through the maze of nets and traffic in and around the bay during summer and fall fishing seasons. The good news is that none of these things need stop serious boaters from getting out and exploring this fascinating waterway. The uncontrollable forces of nature that keep boaters on their toes also keep Willapa Bay from being heavily developed, so it's greatly unchanged from what it was a quarter century or even a half century

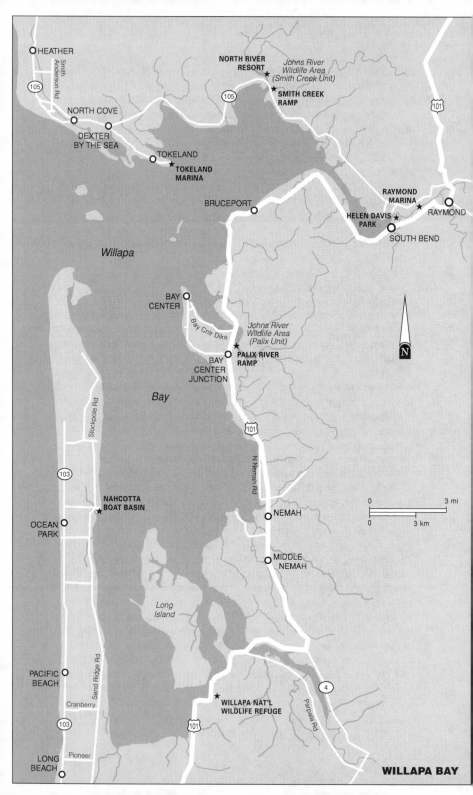

WILLAPA BAY

ago. There are still lots of wild and natural places on the bay, places where you can cruise or paddle for hours at a time without seeing another person or having another boat come within a mile of you.

Prowling around the edges of Willapa Bay early or late in the day is very likely to provide glimpses of black-tailed deer, Roosevelt elk, even black bear. More common sights include harbor seals, bald eagles, osprey, Canada geese, and a wide variety of ducks. In late summer the salmon fishing can be excellent here, and in fall it's a waterfowl hunter's paradise. While development has remained light around the bay, one thing has changed rather dramatically over the past few decades. The marsh weed spartina has taken over much of the bay's shoreline, choking out native plants and destroying natural habitat for many native fish and wildlife species. The stuff came here a decade ago with oyster seed from the East Coast and has spread unchecked over hundreds of shoreline acres.

While you're exploring Willapa Bay, check out the quaint little towns of Tokeland, Bay Center, and Nahcotta, all of which are right on the water and all of which have marinas where you can moor to get out and do some exploring on foot. If you plan ahead with reservations or just get lucky with your timing, you might stay at the historic Tokeland Hotel or have dinner at the Ark in Nahcotta. The hotel is fascinating and the Ark would be a great place to eat if only for the view of the bay, the food's excellent, too. While paddlers might have no trouble, powerboaters need to remember that this is a shallow bay with a maze of channels running through it in every direction. It's easy to suffer the embarrassment of running aground, so don't come here without a chart. The one you want is 18504.

If you have time during the low tide before or after you fish, you might venture across to the east side of the Long Beach Peninsula and the port town of Nahcotta. There you'll find Nahcotta Tidelands Interpretive Center and several acres of public tidelands on Willapa Bay where you can gather oysters and dig clams. That way even if the fishing is slow, you can still return home with enough fresh seafood for a delicious meal.

Location: West of Raymond; map B1, grid d5. (See the Willapa Bay inset map.)

How to get there: The north side of the bay is accessible by Highway 105 from Aberdeen or Raymond, the south end and east side via U.S. 101.

Boat ramp: There are seven ramps and launching facilities on Willapa Bay. These are listed on the Willapa Bay inset map.

- **Tokeland Marina:** Starting at the north end of the bay, there's a one-lane concrete ramp with a loading float at the Port of Willapa Harbor's Tokeland Marina. There's a $6 launch fee. To reach the ramp, take Highway 105 West from Raymond and turn southeast on Tokeland Road. Turn left on Front Lane and go two blocks to the boat ramp.

- **North River Resort:** This resort along Highway 105 maintains a ramp at the mouth of the North River. This one-lane gravel ramp is a good one, and a fee is charged by the resort for its use. Take Highway 105 west from Raymond for just over 10 miles and turn right at the resort sign.

- **Smith Creek Ramp:** Less than half a mile east of North River Resort is the Department of Fish and Wildlife's ramp at the mouth of Smith Creek. This is a single-lane concrete ramp with a fairly large parking area, but boaters have to go under the nearby Highway 105 bridge to reach the bay, and this can be a tight squeeze, even impossible, for larger boats on a high tide.

- **Helen Davis Park:** The WDFW's ramp at Helen Davis Park on the mouth of the Willapa River also provides access to the bay. It's a single-wide concrete ramp that has seen better days. A $10 WDFW access decal is required to use the public launch areas maintained by the Washington Department of Fish and Wildlife. To reach it, go west on U.S. 101 from South Bend about 250 yards to the park.

- **Palix River Ramp:** The WDFW ramp at the mouth of the Palix River near Bay Center also provides access to Willapa Bay. It's a two-lane ramp of concrete planks, with a fairly large gravel parking area. A $10 WDFW access decal is required to use the public launch areas maintained by the Washington Department of Fish and Wildlife. Drive south 15 miles from South Bend on U.S. 101 and cross the Palix River, turning left into the parking area about 200 yards past the bridge.

- **Willapa National Wildlife Refuge:** Several miles south of the Palix Ramp is the one-lane gravel ramp at the Willapa National Wildlife Refuge. It has a small loading float. A $5 launch fee is now charged at this ramp. Drive west from Naselle on Highway 4 about five miles, then west on U.S. 101 about 3.5 miles to the ramp right alongside the highway on the left.

- **Nahcotta Boat Basin:** Around on the west side of the bay, this is the only place a trailered boat can be launched on this side of Willapa Bay.

It's a fixed hoist, managed by the Port of Peninsula, and a fee is charged for launching. Call ahead (360-665-4547) to check on weekend closures during the winter. To find it, take Highway 103 through Ocean Park and turn right on 275th Street, following it to the hoist at the end of the road.

Facilities: The Port of Willapa Harbor's Tokeland Marina has open moorage for 20 cents a foot, rest rooms, boat repair, and groceries nearby. Bay Center Marina also has open moorage at the same 20 cents a foot. The Port's Raymond Marina also charges 20 cents per foot for open moorage, and it also has a hoist, electrical hookups, and drinking water, with boat repair and grocery stores nearby. The Port of Peninsula's Nahcotta Boat Basin has open moorage with variable fees, a launch hoist, drinking water, electrical hookups, boat-sewage pump-out facilities, rest rooms, a fuel dock, and a nearby restaurant.

The little town of Tokeland has a couple of places to stay, including the historic Tokeland Hotel, which has some of the best home cookin' in Pacific County. Bush Pioneer County Park about two miles north of Bay Center has picnic tables and shelters and RV and tent sites. There are also motels, cabins, and RV parks in Raymond and South Bend, which are at the northeast corner of the bay, and along much of the Long Beach Peninsula, which borders most of the bay's west side.

Water sports/restrictions: All water sports are permitted. You'll need NOAA nautical chart 18504 for these waters.

Contact: Tokeland Marina, tel. (360) 267-5417; Bay Center Marina tel. (360) 942-3422; Port of Willapa Bay/Raymond, tel. (360) 942-3422; Long Beach Peninsula Visitor's Bureau, tel. (800) 451-2542; Raymond Chamber of Commerce Visitor Information Center, tel. (360) 942-5419. For nautical charts of this area, contact Captain's Nautical Supply, tel. (206) 283-7242.

20 Long Beach Peninsula Surf

Rating: 6

Most folks Visit this long expanse of gorgeous beach by land, not water, since it's a favorite spot for kite flying, hiking, and other nonmotorized activities. Some surfers from the Portland area come here, but it's a long trip to Long Beach from Washington's major population centers to the north. And during the summer months when most of the crowds Visit the area, the surf is generally calm. Wading and splashing around in the surf is fun, but the water is cold, and most folks don't play long at such games before turning various shades of purple or blue. On particularly calm days it's possible to launch a kayak down at Fort Canby or even drag it to the water's edge along the sandy beach and paddle out through the low surf to work along the beach, but few people take the chance. There's just too much water that's more protected and safer to the south in the Columbia estuary or on the other side of the peninsula inside Willapa Bay.

Location: Leadbetter Point south to Cape Disappointment; map B1, grid e5.

How to get there: Take U.S. 101 west to the small town of Seaview and go north on Highway 103. Several roads to the west lead to the beach.

Boat ramp: The nearest ramp is at Fort Canby State Park at the mouth of the Columbia near the south end of the Long Beach Peninsula.

Facilities: Campgrounds, RV parks, motels, and restaurants in Long Beach and Ocean Park.

Water sports/restrictions: Surfing, beachcombing, some powerboating, swimming, and windsurfing are possible.

Contact: Long Beach Peninsula Visitor's Bureau, tel. (800) 451-2542.

21 Long Beach Peninsula Lakes

Rating: 6

Loomis Lake, at about 170 acres, is the biggest and best known of the Long Beach lakes and probably offers the most in the way of water recreation. It's fairly crowded with trout anglers for a few weeks in late April and May, but as the water warms, the fishermen become scarcer and the lake becomes busy with other kinds of fun. Although it's a big lake, it's also quite shallow, so it warms fast once summer arrives. Black Lake, a 30-acre lake known for its lunker brood stock rainbow trout in the spring and its easy access all year long, lies between Seaview and Ilwaco about three miles south of the other lakes. It is right alongside the road, and there's even a large parking area on the shoulder to get out and look if you don't have time to do anything more. Something else that adds to its attraction is that you can rent a small boat here if you don't have your own with you when you Visit. The boat rental facility is at the south end of the lake, but it's open only during the spring and summer months.

Location: Long Beach Peninsula, from Ocean Park south to Ilwaco; map B1, grid f5.

How to get there: Take U.S. 101 to the extreme southwest corner of Washington and turn north at Seaview on Highway 103.

Boat ramp: There are State Department of Fish and Wildlife access areas with natural-surface boat ramps on Loomis Lake and Island Lake. The Loomis Lake ramp has a loading float. The parking areas in both areas are small, big enough for maybe a half dozen cars and trailers. The other lakes are without formal launch areas, but cartoppers, canoes, and kayaks may be carried to the water at some of them. A $10 WDFW access decal is required to use the public launch areas maintained by the Washington Department of Fish and Wildlife.

Facilities: Food, gas, RV and tent sites, and lodging are readily available on the Long Beach Peninsula. The possibilities for lodging include several very nice bed-and-breakfasts and a couple of large motels. If you're going to be around at dinnertime, make reservations at the 42nd Street Cafe in Seaview (great home-cooked meals and fantastic service) or at the Ark Restaurant in Nahcotta (excellent food and a great view of Willapa Bay).

Water sports/restrictions: Depending on what lake or lakes you Visit, the possibilities include swimming, snorkeling, paddling, rowing, sailing, and powerboating.

Contact: Long Beach Peninsula Visitor's Bureau, tel. (800) 451-2542.

22 Bear River

Rating: 4

This is a small, slow-moving stream that doesn't get much attention from boaters. That makes sense, since it's so close to Willapa Bay, the Columbia River, and other, more important boating destinations. But if you want to prowl around a pretty area on a small stream some day and get away from most every other human being on earth, this one might be worth a day of your time.

Location: Enters south end of Willapa Bay; map B1, grid f6.

How to get there: Take U.S. 101 south from South Bend or take Highway 4 west from Longview to its junction with U.S. 101 and follow it south. The highway crosses over Bear River about six miles northeast of Ilwaco.

Boat ramp: It's possible (but not easy) to drop a canoe or kayak into the lower river at the U.S. 101 bridge and at another point way upstream off Bear River Road, which you reach via Chinook Valley Road from near the Ilwaco Airport.

Facilities: Food, gas, lodging, tackle, and other amenities are available in Ilwaco. Fort Canby State Park is just south of Ilwaco.

Water sports/restrictions: Paddling and tubing are the best bets here.

Contact: Long Beach Peninsula Visitor's Bureau, tel. (800) 451-2542; Fort Canby State Park, tel. (360) 642-3078; Washington State Parks and Recreation Commission, tel. (800) 233-0321 (information), tel. (800) 452-5687 (reservations).

23 Naselle River

Rating: 5

You'll find the Naselle listed in any decent fishing book, thanks to its fairly good salmon, steelhead, and sea-run cutthroat trout fishing, but not in many paddling books. That's because access is limited, it's a long way from almost anywhere in the civilized world, and it's only a so-so river for water sports. But the way I see it, paddling or tubing on a so-so river is better than not paddling or tubing at all, so here it is. Besides, as the famous mountain climber, ol' what's-his-name, so aptly put it: "Because it's there." Class I and Class II rapids are the most exciting water you'll find here, but the Naselle flows through some pretty country, and you might see deer, bear, and elk here. There are lots of birds and smaller critters to see as well. If you happen to be in extreme southwest Washington anyway, why not investigate the Naselle— just because it's there.

Location: Enters the southeast corner of Willapa Bay; map B1, grid e6.

How to get there: Take Highway 4 west from Longview to Naselle or drive south from South Bend on U.S. 101, turn southeast on Highway 4, and drive about six miles to Naselle.

Boat ramp: There's a Department of Fish and Wildlife access area where small boats can be launched just above tidewater off Highway 401 a mile south of Highway 4. It's also possible to launch a kayak or canoe off the side of Naselle Road upstream of the salmon hatchery on the upper Naselle.

Facilities: You'll find food and gas in Naselle, and there's a campground on Highway 4 about three miles east of town. Fort Canby State Park is a few miles to the west.

Water sports/restrictions: Paddling and inner tubing are the best possibilities here.

Contact: Fort Canby State Park, tel. (360) 642-3078; Washington State Parks and Recreation Commission, tel. (800) 233-0321 (information), tel. (800) 452-5687 (reservations).

24 Ilwaco Offshore

Rating: 7

Like Westport to the north, the most difficult part of getting into the Pacific Ocean from Ilwaco lies in pitting your boating skill against a river mouth that has over the years earned the nickname "Graveyard of the Pacific." If it sounds a little ominous, it should. This is one of those places where if you don't respect the water and what it might do to you, you don't have any business being there. The combination of a strong ebbing tide and stiff westerly winds is the most dangerous, but some people pay little attention to the Columbia River Bar until it's too late. The U.S. Coast Guard stays busy here during the fishing and boating season, rescuing or recovering the bodies of boaters who didn't take the bar seriously. It might be nasty on the bar even when the water immediately upriver and immediately outside on the ocean are relatively calm. Good boaters have lost it all here, so don't take chances.

Once you get across the Columbia Bar, the choice is yours. Most Washington boaters go north to get a look at the Long Beach Peninsula that they could never get from shore. Some cruise on north to Willapa Bay, Grays Harbor or points north along the ruggedly beautiful north coast of Washington. To the south lies a shoreline that's just as beautiful, the Oregon coast.

Location: Outside the mouth of the Columbia River southwest of Ilwaco; map B1, grid f5.

How to get there: Take U.S. 101 south from Raymond or Highway 4 west from Kelso.

Boat ramp: The best boat ramp in the area is the two-lane blacktop ramp at

Fort Canby State Park near the mouth of the Columbia some two miles southwest of Ilwaco. The launch fee is $4 round-trip, and an annual launch permit is available for $40 from Washington State Parks.

Facilities: Fort Canby State Park, one of the state's largest campgrounds, is just south of town.

Water sports/restrictions: All water sports are permitted, but some require lots of common sense. NOAA nautical chart 18521 is a must for these waters.

Contact: Fort Canby State Park, tel. (360) 642-3078; Washington State Parks and Recreation Commission, tel. (800) 233-0321 (information), tel. (800) 452-5687 (reservations). For nautical charts of this area, contact Captain's Nautical Supply, tel. (206) 283-7242.

25 Columbia River Estuary

Rating: 7

The waters immediately outside Ilwaco on the Washington side of the Columbia River mouth are known, at least to some, as Baker Bay, and it's an area that sees a lot of boating activity pretty much on a year-round basis. Much of the boat traffic is comprised of anglers, since this is still one of Washington's best salmon and sturgeon fishing areas. The famous Buoy 10 salmon fishery near the mouth of the Columbia has been one of the Northwest's most popular since it began in the mid-'80s. Sturgeon fishing is popular not only with private-boat anglers and bank fishermen, but also with anglers who charter bigger boats out of Ilwaco and other ports to pursue these big, prehistoric bottom-dwellers.

When the wind is blowing strong here, a few hardy windsurfers take to the lower Columbia, and when it's extremely calm—which isn't very often—a few early morning water-skiers might be spotted. These wide-open waters are also popular with the growing population of PWC riders. Sailing vessels are fairly rare, thanks to the many shoals and sandbars on the lower Columbia. Upriver from Ilwaco, paddling is becoming more popular all the time, and a trip along the shoreline in a kayak or canoe is very likely to provide glimpses of harbor seals, a wide range of waterfowl and shorebirds, fox, coyote, otter, beaver, black-tailed deer, elk, and maybe even a black bear.

Location: Mouth of Columbia River near Ilwaco; map B1, grid f5.

How to get there: Take U.S. 101 south from Raymond or Highway 4 west from Kelso.

Boat ramp: There's a two-lane boat ramp with lots of parking at Fort Canby State Park near the mouth of the Columbia about two miles southwest of Ilwaco. The launch fee is $4, and an annual permit is available from Washington State Parks for $40.

Facilities: The Port of Ilwaco's marina has open moorage for $9 to $17.50 per boat, a hoist, water and electricity to the dock, rest rooms with showers, boat-sewage pump-out facilities, fuel docks, boat repair, groceries, and restaurants. The Port of Wahkiakum's Skamokawa Vista Park has water and electrical hookups for RVs, rest rooms, and showers; Fort Canby State Park has RV and tent sites, rest rooms with showers, and other amenities. There's also a store with food, beverages, and bait and tackle in the park. Restaurants, motels, gas stations, and watering holes are easy to find in Ilwaco and to the north in Long Beach. Several charter companies work out of Ilwaco. If you want to explore the estuary in a paddle craft but would like to learn more about it as you go, or if you need to rent a paddle craft to do it on your own, Skamokawa Paddle Center can reserve you a spot on one of their kayaks or paddle tours or rent you the kayak or canoe you need. It also operates a nine-unit bed-and-breakfast at its facility in the little town of Skamokawa.

Water sports/restrictions: All water sports are permitted. NOAA nautical chart 18521 is a must for boating this area.

Contact: Port of Ilwaco, tel. (360) 642-3143; Skamokawa Vista Park, tel. (360) 795-8605; Fort Canby State Park, tel. (360) 642-3078; Washington State Parks and Recreation Commission, tel. (800) 233-0321 (information), tel. (800) 452-5687 (reservations); Dave's Shell, tel. (360) 642-2320; Skamokawa Paddle Center, tel. (800) 920-2777. For nautical charts of this area, contact Captain's Nautical Supply, tel. (206) 283-7242.

26 Grays River

Rating: 5

If you paddle from the confluence of the West Fork and South Fork Grays, you'll find a little moving water as the river makes its way around low gravel islands and through a series of twists, turns and gentle riffles. Soon after you pass beneath the Highway 4 bridge, though, the river begins to slow, the banks become more steep and more thickly covered with blackberry and other brush, and the river starts to slow into the virtual slough it will be over much of its length. A high point of boating this river is passing beneath Washington's only covered bridge, which spans the Grays just off Highway 4 about two miles northeast of Rosburg.

Below the bridge you soon encounter tidewater, so if you plan to float on toward the river mouth it would be easier if the tide is ebbing. This is a gentle enough stream that it's not absolutely necessary for you to be paddling with the tide, but it's a little easier on the arms and back that way. Grays Bay, the large estuary area off the river mouth, is also worth investigating if you have time and the weather is cooperative. A strong southerly will make things a lot tougher for you to boat in this area.

Location: Enters the lower Columbia River west of Skamokawa; map B1, grid f8.

How to get there: Take Highway 4 west from Cathlamet or east from Naselle. Take Loop Road south off the highway (midway between the little town of Grays River and the highway bridge over the river) to reach much of the middle portion of the river or turn south on Highway 403 near Rosburg to reach the lower river.

Boat ramp: There's an access area with a rough boat ramp just south of Rosburg, about 4.5 miles above the mouth of the river. Possibilities for dragging a small boat to the river include a couple of gravel bars near the road along Highway 4 some eight miles above the river mouth and near the confluence of the West and South Forks off Fossil Road.

Facilities: Ilwaco, the nearest town of any size, is about 20 miles to the southeast and offers food, gas, and lodging. Some distance to the west is Fort Canby State Park, which has tent and RV sites, rest rooms with showers, and a small store.

Water sports/restrictions: Kayaking, canoeing, rafting, and tubing are good bets here.

Contact: Skamokawa Paddle Center, tel. (800) 920-2777; Fort Canby State Park, tel. (360) 642-3078; Washington State Parks and Recreation Commission, tel. (800) 233-0321 (information), tel. (800) 452-5687 (reservations).

PADDLERS PATROL THE SHORE OF DEEP LAKE, JUST SOUTH OF OLYMPIA

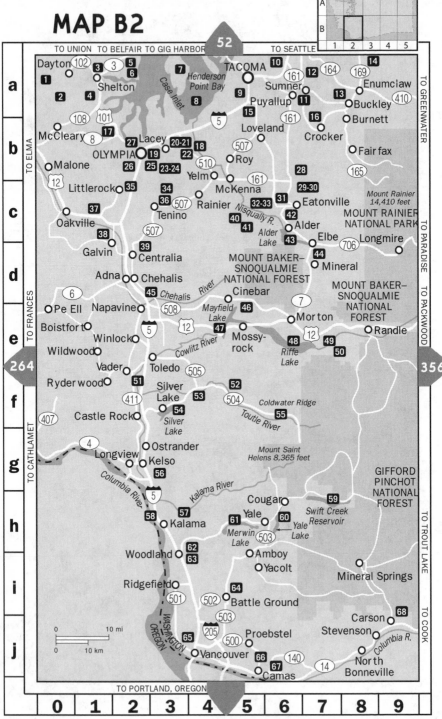

MAP B2

52

a

Dayton 102
3
3
5
6
7
Henderson Point Bay
TACOMA 10
12 164
169
14
1
Shelton
4
8
9
Sumner
161
Enumclaw
2
Puyallup
11
13
410
15
Buckley
Burnett

b

108 101
McCleary
8
17
Lacey
20-21
18
Loveland
16
Crocker
Fair fax
OLYMPIA
27
19
22
165
Malone
26
25
23-24
510
507
Roy
28
12
Littlerock
35
Yelm
161
29-30
Mount Rainier 14,410 feet
34
McKenna
31

c

37
36
507
Rainier
32-33
Eatonville
42
MOUNT RAINIER NATIONAL PARK
Oakville
Tenino
40
41
Alder
Longmire
38
507
Nisqually R.
43
Elbe
706
Galvin
39
Alder Lake
44

d

Centralia
MOUNT BAKER–SNOQUALMIE NATIONAL FOREST
Mineral
Adna
Chehalis
Cinebar
MOUNT BAKER–SNOQUALMIE NATIONAL FOREST
45
Chehalis River
Mayfield Lake
46
7
Pe Ell
Napavine
508
Morton
Randle

e

Boistfort
12
47
Winlock
5
Cowlitz River
Mossyrock
48
12
49
Wildwood
Riffe Lake
50
Vader
Toledo
505
Ryderwood
51
Silver Lake
52

f

411
53
Coldwater Ridge
Castle Rock
54
Silver Lake
55
Toutle River

g

4
Ostrander
Mount Saint Helens 8,365 feet
GIFFORD PINCHOT NATIONAL FOREST
Longview
Kelso
56
Columbia River
Kalama River

h

Cougar
59
57
Yale
60
Swift Creek Reservoir
58
Kalama
61
Yale Lake
Merwin Lake
503
Woodland
62
63
Amboy
Yacolt
Mineral Springs

i

Ridgefield
64
501
502
Battle Ground
503
Carson
68

j

205
Stevenson
65
500
Proebstel
Columbia R.
Vancouver
66
67
140
North Bonneville
Camas
14

0   10 mi
0   10 km

WASHINGTON
OREGON

TO GREENWATER
TO PARADISE
TO PACKWOOD
TO TROUT LAKE
TO COOK
TO ELMA
TO FRANCES
TO CATHLAMET

264
356

A
B
1 2 3 4 5

CHAPTER B2

1 Lake Nahwatzel

Rating: 7

Covering some 270 acres, this is a large lake with a lot to offer boaters and water enthusiasts of all kinds. Perhaps what keeps it from becoming a mob scene on a hot summer weekend is that there are several other large lakes within easier driving range of folks in Shelton and Olympia. Perhaps the single-lane gravel boat ramp with limited parking also keeps visitor numbers low. Those who do make it all the way out to Nahwatzel, though, usually find it to their liking and keep coming back.

Location: Northwest of Shelton; map B2, grid a0.

How to get there: Take U.S. 101 to Shelton and turn west on Shelton-Matlock Road, following it about 11 miles to the lake, which is on the north (right) side of the road.

Boat ramp: There's a single-lane Department of Fish and Wildlife boat ramp on the south side of the lake. A $10 WDFW access decal is required to use the public launch area maintained by the Washington Department of Fish and Wildlife.

Facilities: Lake Nahwatzel Resort has two cabins and a trailer for rent, RV sites, restaurant, and bar. Other facilities are in Shelton.

Water sports/restrictions: All water sports are permitted. Mason County boating regulations include a 6 mph speed limit within 100 feet of any swimmer, within 150 feet of any shoreline or nonmotorized vessel, and within 300 feet of any public boat ramp; an 8 mph speed limit on freshwater lakes from a half hour after sunset to a half hour before sunrise; and a 50 mph speed limit during daylight hours on all waters unless otherwise posted. Water-skiers must stay at least 300 feet from the shoreline on salt water and at least 150 feet from the shoreline on fresh water. All ski/tow traffic must go in a counterclockwise direction.

Contact: Lake Nahwatzel Resort, tel. (360) 426-3823 (April through September only).

2 Lost Lake

Rating: 6

This 120-acre lake west of Shelton is almost two lakes in one, so if you don't like one part of it, you can go to the other and be on a new body of water without having to load your boat back onto the trailer. The north half of the lake is cooler because it's much deeper, with places over 60 feet deep. A narrow neck of water connects it to the southern half, which has a maximum depth of about 30 feet and features two islands, one quite large. The access area and boat ramp are on the northern half of the lake. Oh yes, don't get lost on your way to the lake.

Location: Southwest of Shelton; map B2, grid a0.

How to get there: Take U.S. 101 to Shelton and exit onto Highway 3, following it two miles into town. Turn west (left) onto Lost Lake Road and follow it 10 miles to the sign pointing to the lake. Turn right at the sign and drive about a mile to the lake.

Boat ramp: A boat ramp and rest rooms are available at the access area. A $10 WDFW access decal is required to use the public launch area maintained by the Washington Department of Fish and Wildlife.

Facilities: Food, gas, and lodging are available in Shelton.

Water sports/restrictions: All water

sports are permitted. Mason County boating regulations include a 6 mph speed limit within 100 feet of any swimmer, within 150 feet of any shoreline or nonmotorized vessel, and within 300 feet of any public boat ramp; an 8 mph speed limit on freshwater lakes from a half hour after sunset to a half hour before sunrise; and a 50 mph speed limit during daylight hours on all waters unless otherwise posted. Water-skiers must stay at least 300 feet from the shoreline on salt water and at least 150 feet from the shoreline on fresh water. All ski/tow traffic must go in a counter-clockwise direction.

Contact: Verle's Sport Center, tel. (360) 426-0933.

3 Island Lake

Rating: 7

I think it's time we take the bull by the horns and start renaming some of these Washington lakes. I mean, after all, how many "Island Lakes" do we really need? Just because a lake happens to have an island in the middle of it shouldn't automatically make it "Island Lake," should it? Let's get a little creative here. There, I've vented and now I feel better. OK, it's true that this Island Lake does really have an island, and the large shoal extending north from the island is perhaps the best place for the public to swim here. This is a popular boating lake, but the gravel parking lot at the public access area is somewhat rutted, not very big, and sort of on a hillside, so it gets crowded with only a few vehicles and boat trailers. Most of the lake's north end is developed with homes, docks, and private beaches, but the southern half still has a fair amount of wild shoreline and lots of birds and wildlife to see. Paddlers will probably prefer to turn right

out of the access area to explore the large coves at the southwest and southeast corners of the lake, thereby avoiding most of the motorized traffic that tends to circle the island and stick to the more open waters at the north end and east side of the lake.

Location: North of Shelton; map B2, grid a1.

How to get there: Follow U.S. 101 north about two miles past Shelton and turn east on Shelton Springs Road, also known as the Dayton Cutoff. Drive just over half a mile on Shelton Spring Road and turn left on Island Lake Drive, following it 0.4 mile to the Public Fishing sign on the right.

Boat ramp: A Department of Fish and Wildlife boat ramp is located on the west end of the lake. A $10 WDFW access decal is required to use the public launch area maintained by the Washington Department of Fish and Wildlife.

Facilities: Groceries and gasoline are available at the intersection of U.S. 101 and Shelton Springs Road. All other amenities are available in Shelton.

Water sports/restrictions: All water sports are permitted. Mason County boating regulations include a 6 mph speed limit within 100 feet of any swimmer, within 150 feet of any shoreline or nonmotorized vessel, and within 300 feet of any public boat ramp; an 8 mph speed limit on freshwater lakes from a half hour after sunset to a half hour before sunrise; and a 50 mph speed limit during daylight hours on all waters unless otherwise posted. Water-skiers must stay at least 300 feet from the shoreline on salt water and at least 150 feet from the shoreline on fresh water. All ski/tow traffic must go in a counter-clockwise direction.

Contact: Verle's Sport Center, tel. (360) 426-0933.

4 Lake Isabella

Rating: 6

Because it's fairly shallow, this 200-acre lake southwest of Shelton warms quickly in the spring and early summer, so it's a favorite of water enthusiasts from all over southern Mason County. Waterskiing and PWC riding are popular here during the summer, but the paddler or angler in search of a quiet place to play usually can find somewhere near the shoreline to get away from the fast movers.

Location: South of Shelton; map B2, grid a1.

How to get there: Turn west off U.S. 101 to Delight Park Road just south of Shelton (the Golden Pheasant Tavern is the landmark to look for) and watch for the public access to the lake on the right.

Boat ramp: There's a public access area with a boat ramp on the south side of the lake. A $10 WDFW access decal is required to use the public launch area maintained by the Washington Department of Fish and Wildlife.

Facilities: Other amenities are available in Shelton and Olympia.

Water sports/restrictions: All water sports are permitted. Mason County boating regulations include a 6 mph speed limit within 100 feet of any swimmer, within 150 feet of any shoreline or nonmotorized vessel, and within 300 feet of any public boat ramp; an 8 mph speed limit on freshwater lakes from a half hour after sunset to a half hour before sunrise; and a 50 mph speed limit during daylight hours on all waters unless otherwise posted. Water-skiers must stay at least 300 feet from the shoreline on salt water and at least 150 feet from the shoreline on fresh water. All ski/tow traffic must go in a counter-clockwise direction.

Contact: Verle's Sport Center, tel. (360) 426-0933.

5 Spencer Lake

Rating: 7

Every time I think about this popular 230-acre lake northeast of Shelton, two things come to mind, One is excellent trout fishing; the other is a scene I witnessed at the lake's public boat ramp one Fourth of July a few years ago.

On that cool Independence Day afternoon, I pulled into the access area to see if anyone happened to be fishing. There were only a couple of boat trailers in the lot, but an elderly man had his car backed into the launch ramp and was trying to load his boat onto the trailer. He was having a devil of a time, not so much because he didn't know what he was doing, but because a couple of kids were zooming around on personal watercraft only a few yards away, and their wakes were drenching the old man and knocking his boat on and off the trailer so that he couldn't get it positioned squarely. I don't think the kids were trying to screw the guy up, but they were oblivious to the havoc they were creating. Besides their total lack of courtesy, they were operating their PWC illegally, zooming around within 20 or 30 feet of shore and right in front of the boat ramp. They also were tearing up a big bed of lily pads and other shallow-water vegetation, and who knows what may have happened to any waterfowl and other wildlife that may have been around before these two yahoos showed up. Through a series of easily understood hand signals—mostly just one—I suggested the kids leave, and then I helped the guy finish loading his boat, all the time hoping for the Mason County Sheriff's marine patrol to come along in time to see what was happening. They didn't show, but if they had I'm sure it would have been ticketsville for the two PWC jockeys, and rightly so.

I like to think that what I saw that afternoon was a rare example of over-zealous youthful exuberance and stupidity on Spencer, but I don't know. It gets to be a busy place on a summer weekend, and I'm sure that PWC are common here all summer. The county has very specific boating regulations in effect (see restrictions below), but some people are ignorant of them or just don't give a damn. It's up to the rest of us to remind them that if they act like a bunch of jackasses out there they're fouling things up for all boaters. That's my sermon for the day. Just drop a dollar on the plate when it passes by.

Location: Northeast of Shelton; map B2, grid a2.

How to get there: Take Highway 3 northeast from Shelton about 10 miles and turn east (right) on Pickering Road, then right on Spencer Lake Road.

Boat ramp: A public access area and a one-lane boat ramp with a small loading float are on the west side of the lake. Spencer Lake Resort has a two-lane ramp, one with concrete planks and the other all-gravel. The resort launch has a large gravel parking area with room for dozens of cars and trailers. A $10 WDFW access decal is required to use the public launch area maintained by the Washington Department of Fish and Wildlife.

Facilities: There's a small restaurant at the resort right along Pickering Road. Other facilities are in Shelton.

Water sports/restrictions: All water sports are permitted. Mason County boating regulations include a 6 mph speed limit within 100 feet of any swimmer, within 150 feet of any shoreline or nonmotorized vessel, and within 300 feet of any public boat ramp; an 8 mph speed limit on freshwater lakes from a half hour after sunset to a half hour before sunrise; and a 50 mph speed limit during daylight hours on all waters unless otherwise posted. Water-skiers must stay at least 300 feet from the shoreline on salt water and at least 150 feet from the shoreline on fresh water. All ski/tow traffic must go in a counterclockwise direction.

Contact: Verle's Sport Center, tel. (360) 426-0933; Spencer Lake Resort, tel. (360) 426-2505.

6 Phillips Lake

Rating: 7

Boating activities tend to be a lot calmer here compared to nearby Spencer Lake. This is more of a paddler's and angler's lake, although waterskiing and other activities certainly are popular here. At about 110 acres, it just doesn't seem to get noticed as much by boaters. It's usually peaceful and quiet, with lots of room to get away in a paddle craft even if others are using the lake.

Location: Northeast of Shelton; map B2, grid a2.

How to get there: Take Highway 3 northeast from Shelton about 10 miles and turn east (right) on Pickering Road. Drive about two miles (past Spencer Lake), turn south (right) on Phillips Lake Loop, and follow it about a mile to the lake.

Boat ramp: A Department of Fish and Wildlife boat ramp and access area are on the lake. A $10 WDFW access decal is required to use the public launch area maintained by the Washington Department of Fish and Wildlife.

Facilities: Food, gas, tackle, and lodging are available in Shelton.

Water sports/restrictions: All water sports are permitted. Mason County boating regulations include a 6 mph speed limit within 100 feet of any swimmer, within 150 feet of any shoreline or nonmotorized vessel, and within 300 feet of any public boat ramp; an 8 mph speed limit on freshwater lakes from a half hour after sunset to a half hour before sunrise; and a 50 mph speed limit during daylight hours on all waters unless otherwise posted. Water-skiers must stay at least 300 feet from the shoreline on salt water and at least 150 feet from the shoreline on fresh water. All ski/tow traffic must go in a counterclockwise direction.

Contact: Verle's Sport Center, tel. (360) 426-0933.

7 Bay Lake

Rating: 6

Anglers flock to this lake in huge numbers early in the spring, most of them in search of trout that are stocked here by the thousands. As the weather warms in May and June, this large, shallow lake warms quickly, and the trout anglers soon give way to other boaters. The access area here has one of the biggest parking lots of any western Washington lakes, so there's plenty of room for boat trailers of all kinds. Likewise, the lake covers well over 100 acres, so there's plenty of room on the water as well.

Location: Longbranch Peninsula; map B2, grid a3.

How to get there: Take Highway 302 southwest from Purdy to Lakebay. Cross the bridge, drive up the hill about 100 yards, and turn left at the sign pointing to Penrose Point State Park. Wind up and over the hill and turn right at the T intersection. The lake's public access area is on the right, about half a mile from the T.

Boat ramp: The large gravel access area managed by the Department of Fish and Wildlife has a boat ramp and rest rooms. A $10 WDFW access decal is required to use the public launch area maintained by the Washington Department of Fish and Wildlife.

Facilities: The state park has tent sites for camping.

Water sports/restrictions: All water sports are permitted.

Contact: Washington State Parks and Recreation Commission, tel. (800) 233-0321 (information), tel. (800) 452-5687 (reservations).

8 South Puget Sound

Rating: 10

This is the last wild and woolly part of Puget Sound, where in many areas the homes are few and far between and where a boater can get out on the water and feel a real sense of exploration and pioneer spirit. It's not all that way, of course, but you don't have to get very far away from the bigger cities of Tacoma and Olympia to feel that you're away from the rat race. In fact, with places like Point Defiance Park and Priest Point Park nearby, Tacoma and Olympia have forested hillsides and undeveloped shoreline right alongside their busiest waterways. Get a few minutes farther away and it gets more laid back in a hurry. That close link between the natural places and the populated places is part of the charm of southern Puget Sound. You don't have to go far to get away from it all, and even when you are away from it all, the facilities and amenities are within easy range.

The intricacies of the waterways themselves are part of the reason for this best-of-all-worlds quality. From Tacoma south, Puget Sound spreads out in all directions, with inlets, peninsulas, islands, bays, and channels going every which way. Look at a chart or map of the area and it's easy to see that you can round a bend in any of 100 places and be in an entirely different water world from the one you just left. In fact, without a good chart, you can get lost here in a hurry, especially if you decide to set out to see some territory. Each of the area's major bays and inlets is worth exploring for at least a day in a powerboat or several days in a canoe or kayak. Divers could spend several days in each, since these waters include some of Puget Sound's most fascinating underwater possibilities.

Tacoma's Commencement Bay, of course, is the most urban and the most industrialized, but it has a broad range of attractions, from the port area around the mouth of the Puyallup River (watch out for the shallow bar off the river mouth) and the great views of the city skyline to waterfront eateries and Point Defiance Pak. Across the water to the northwest is Gig Harbor, where many of the shops, restaurants, and other businesses are within a couple blocks of the water. Although fairly deep in midchannel, the harbor entrance is one of the narrowest in Puget Sound. Once inside you'll find a place that's obviously water oriented, with pleasure boats and commercial fishing vessels by the hundreds.

After experiencing laid-back Gig Harbor, you owe it to yourself to experience the wilds of the Tacoma Narrows. If you pass through the narrows when the tide is running, you'll be impressed with the water's speed and the backwaters that form behind the huge piers helping to hold the world's largest suspension bridge in place. Go there at slack tide and you can wet a line or dive the sunken skeleton of the first Narrows Bridge, now home to some of Puget Sound's biggest octopus, lingcod, and other saltwater bottom-dwellers. And before I forget to mention it, there's another fascinating dive spot at the southwest corner of Vashon Island north of the narrows. It's called Point Dalco, and at its eastern edge is a steep wall that offers great possibilities for experienced divers on a slack tide.

If you're looking for a dive that's a little less challenging, head northwest from Dalco, across the south end of Colvos Passage, to Sunrise Beach. This is another slack-water dive featuring a rock wall with lots of wolf eel, octopus, rockfish, and some lingcod, and it's within reach of both boat and shore divers. One more popular dive spot to consider is Titlow Beach, south of the Narrows Bridge on the Tacoma (east) side. There's an old ferry dock at this site, as well as sunken barges and other attractions, and it all can be reached from shore. Diving and bottomfishing are also worthwhile about four miles south of the bridge at Toliva Shoal, which is marked with a bell off the entrance to Carr Inlet.

To the northwest, Hale Passage and Wollochet Bay are beautiful waterways, or go up the west side of Fox Island to the upper end of Carr Inlet and Purdy. If you go in the fall, watch for coho salmon jumping and splashing off the mouth of Minter Creek, where a state salmon hatchery is located. As you start into Carr, watch for all the seals on Gertrude Island, but don't get too close. That big island on the south side of Gertrude is McNeil Island, and they get a little nervous when boats come too close to the beach. McNeil is home to a prison facility, and you wouldn't want to give any of the island's residents (inmates) any ideas.

Farther south, don't be surprised if you encounter clusters of fishing boats concentrated around Anderson Island's Lyle Point, Devil's Head at the south end of the Longbranch Peninsula, or Johnson Point at the east entrance to Henderson Inlet. These are some of the Olympia area's top salmon-fishing spots, especially for chinook, so give the fishing boats room to do their thing or slow down, break out the rods, and join them for a few hours. Turn south as you round Johnson Point and you'll drop into Henderson Inlet, the first of a half dozen narrow waterways that give the south end of Puget Sound that spiderweb appearance you see on a map or chart. One point of interest in Henderson is the old crane that sits atop a rotting dock at Chapman Bay. This was once the terminus of the Chehalis-Western rail line, where logs were unloaded from flatcars and rafted up for the trip to the Port of Olympia, Puget Sound mills, and other destinations. The old log booms and floats are now haul-out platforms for hundreds of harbor seals. Much of the inlet's south end is lightly developed and a great place for seeing a wide variety of wildlife.

Just south of Chapman Bay and the old log dump is Woodard Bay, where paddlers like to launch off Woodard Bay Road and make their way out into Henderson for a few hours. Turn west out of Henderson Inlet into Dana Passage and you'll soon come to Boston Harbor, a laid-back little moorage that's the recreational and social center of this waterfront community. The little lighthouse at Dofflemyer Point, with the harbor in the background, is a photographer's dream just before sunset on a clear evening. Head south from Boston Harbor and you're in Budd Inlet, which leads right into downtown Olympia. Priest Point Park is on the port side just before you reach town. There are several restau-rants on the waterfront with guest moorage, and Percival Landing provides mooring virtually in the heart of the city. (Can you tell I like it here?)

To the west and northwest are Eld and Totten inlets, both long, winding fingers of water that end in rich estuaries and productive salmon streams. Off the west side of Totten is Little Skookum Inlet, with its narrow, canyonlike entrance. If you want to visit Shelton from Puget Sound, you have to make your way through seven-mile-long Hammersley Inlet, another skinny channel with high banks on both sides. When the tide is running, this narrow channel becomes a saltwater river, so pay attention to the currents and time your trip for slack tides if you're concerned. Also be on the lookout for tugs with large log rafts in tow.

As you make your way up Pickering Passage, take the time to turn into Jarrell Cove, even if it's just for a few minutes. This state park at the north end of Hartstene Island is one of the prettiest places in the Pacific Northwest. Case Inlet narrows and shallows as it runs north toward the ultimate end of Puget Sound, but on a moderate tide you can make it all the way up to Allyn and the neat little public dock and park there. Just north of Allyn, near the mouth of Coulter Creek, the sound comes to an end, and if you took off overland from that point in a northwesterly direction, you'd come to the end of Hood Canal only two miles away.

Location: Marine waters from Tacoma's Commencement Bay south to Olympia and Shelton, west to Allyn; map B2, grid a4.

How to get there: Primary access to the water around Tacoma and Gig Harbor is via Highway 16, Highway 163, and roads and streets off those two highways.

Highway access between Tacoma and Olympia is off roads leading west from Interstate 5. U.S. 101 and roads leading east from it provide access to the waters between Olympia and Shelton. Highway 3 is the main link between Shelton and Allyn and is the main access route to the water between those towns.

Boat ramp: There are 29 boat ramps and hoists along the shoreline of southern Puget Sound:

- **Ole & Charlie's Marina:** The northernmost launch site in this section is the hoist at Ole & Charlie's Marina off Marine View Drive near the northeast corner of Commencement Bay. Round-trip launch fees here go from $15 up. To reach it from Interstate 5, take Exit 137 and go north on 54th Avenue East, then right on Marine View Drive, following it 3.5 miles to the marina.

- **Totem Marina:** Located on the south side of Commencement Bay, this facility has a pair of hoists and two loading floats. One-way use of the slings begins at $7 for boats 19 feet and under. The facilities are located off Schuster Parkway at Fourth Street. To get there, drive northbound on Highway 705 and turn north on Schuster Parkway, following it to the first stoplight, which is Fourth Street. Turn right on Fourth Street and go half a mile to the marina on the left.

- **Asarco Boat Ramp:** There's a one-lane gravel ramp at the old Asarco plant off the end of Ruston Way. A good ramp for smaller boats, it has parking for about 100 cars and trailers. Take the Tacoma City Center exit off Interstate 5 and take Highway 705 to Schuster Parkway. Schuster becomes Ruston Way; stay on it until you come to the ramp on the right just past a string of restaurants and other waterfront businesses.

- **Point Defiance Waterfront Ramp:** Located next to the Vashon Island ferry terminal off the end of Pearl Street, it's one of the Puget Sound area's busiest launch facilities. This site has a three-lane concrete ramp with loading floats and parking for over 100 cars and trailers in three nearby locations. To find it, take Highway 16 west from Tacoma and take the Pearl Street exit, following Pearl north to Point Defiance Park. Drop down the hill to the right at the stoplight near the park entrance, and stay to the right as you approach the ferry landing.

- **Narrows Marina:** Around the corner to the south of Point Defiance just south of the Narrows Bridge is Narrows Marina, where there's a one-lane concrete ramp with parking for about a dozen cars on a nearby gravel lot. This is a steep ramp that sometimes gets a little tough for two-wheel-drive vehicles to use, but it's well protected from the weather by moorage floats and buildings surrounding it. It has a $6 launch fee during the week, $10 on weekends. To find it, take Highway 16 to the 19th Street exit and go west on 19th Street over the hill to the end. The boat ramp is to the right at the end of the road.

- **Gig Harbor Ramp:** Across Puget Sound from Point Defiance is Gig Harbor, where there's a single-lane concrete ramp across the harbor from the city's main business district. Take Highway 16 across the Narrows Bridge to the first Gig Harbor exit and go north to Harbor View Drive. Turn right off Harbor View Drive onto Verhhardson Street, then right again on Randall Drive, following it to the ramp at the end of the street.

- **Wollochet Bay Ramp:** South of Gig Harbor through the Narrows and Hale Passage is Wollochet Bay, where there are a couple of ramps, each with limited parking nearby. The first one, at the end of 10th Street via Point Fosdick Drive, is a good concrete ramp with room to park half a dozen cars and trailers.

- **Wollochet No. 2 Ramp:** The second ramp has even more limited parking, and the nearby landowners aren't crazy about folks who park in their way. Get there by taking Highway 16 across the Narrows Bridge and taking the Wollochet Drive exit. Go west for 5.5 miles and turn left on 37th Street NW. The ramp is at the end of 37th Street. Both Wollochet ramps are maintained by Pierce County.

- **Fox Island:** There's another Pierce County ramp on Fox Island just north of the bridge. It's a single-lane concrete ramp that's seen better days, and the small parking area is also showing signs of slipping into Hale Passage. If you want to use it, take Highway 16 over the Narrows Bridge and exit to Wollochet Drive NW. Go 4.3 miles and turn right on 40th Street NW, following it 1.4 miles to 70th Avenue. Turn left on 70th Avenue and cross the bridge; then turn right into the launch ramp.

- **Horsehead Bay Ramp:** Around Green Point from the north end of Fox Island is Horsehead Bay, where there's a one-lane, asphalt ramp maintained by Pierce County. The No Trespassing signs could make you feel just a little unwanted here, but it's OK as long as you don't tie up to the private floats near the ramp. Get there by taking Highway 16 to Wollochet Drive NW and following it 4.8 miles west. Turn west again on 40th Street NW and drive 4.5 miles. Bear west again on 36th Street NW and follow it two miles to the ramp at the end of the street.

- **Steilacoom Boat Ramp:** On the west side of Puget Sound is Steilacoom, where there's a boat launch maintained by Steilacoom Parks. It's one of a kind, and not the ramp to use if you're looking to practice backing a boat trailer into the water for the very first time. The ramp runs under railroad tracks, so you have to back a boat between the pilings of the rail

overpass. It's kind of a tight squeeze, but it also has a little turn in it to keep you on your toes. As if all this weren't enough, you have to pay a small fee to launch here. Treat yourself by taking Interstate 5 to the Steilacoom exit and going west on Rainier Street. Turn south on Union Avenue and go 100 yards to Commercial Street, turning right and going 100 feet to the parking area just north of the McNeil Island ferry terminal.

- **Swantown Ramp:** The ramp closest to downtown Olympia is the two-lane concrete ramp at Swantown Marina, formerly east Bay Marina, operated by the Port of Olympia. The ramp has a long loading float and a parking area for 50 cars and trailers that overflows every nice weekend during the summer. It's located on Marina Drive off East Bay Road. There's a $5 launch fee here. To get there, take the Port of Olympia exit off Interstate 5 at Olympia and follow Plumb Street to Fourth Avenue, where it becomes East Bay Drive. Go one block past Fourth Avenue and turn left on Marina Drive, following the signs one mile to the ramp, which is at the far end of the marina complex.

- **Boston Harbor Ramp:** East Bay Road eventually becomes Boston Harbor Road, and if you follow it about seven miles out of town to the north you'll come to 73rd. Turn left and drive two blocks to Boston Harbor Marina, where there's a one-lane concrete ramp with a gravel parking area for two dozen cars and trailers. This is a free ramp maintained by Thurston County Parks, but if you try to use it in the fall and winter you may have to wait for Squaxin tribal fishermen to off-load their fish and shellfish onto trucks in the middle of the ramp.

- **Budinich Ramp:** Off Johnson Point Road to the northeast of Olympia is the Budinich ramp, a private ramp where the public may launch for a small fee. It's located at the end of 86th Avenue, which turns left off Johnson Point Road to Henderson Inlet.

- **Zittel's Marina:** Near Johnson Point is Zittel's Marina with a newly renovated concrete ramp and a fixed hoist and a loading float serving both. Reach it by driving north on Johnson Point Road to 92nd Avenue NE and turning right.

- **Puget Marina:** Southeast of Zittel's is Puget Marina, which has a one-lane concrete ramp and loading float. It's located off Marvin Road via Exit 111 from Interstate 5.

- **Luhr's Beach Ramp:** Near the mouth of the Nisqually River northeast of Olympia is the Department of Fish and Wildlife's ramp at Luhr's Beach. This single-lane concrete ramp has nearby parking for about a dozen cars and trailers. Be careful to follow the creek channel north out of the ramp or you'll soon be aground on a moderate to low tide. To get there, take Exit 114 off Interstate 5 and drive west on Martin Way for a mile to Meridian Road, turning north and following Meridian Road for 2.7 miles. Turn east on 46th Avenue NE and follow it a quarter of a mile to D'Milluhr Drive, following it to the end.

- **Young's Cove Ramp:** Northwest of Olympia off Gravelly Beach Loop from U.S. 101 is another private ramp where the public can launch for a small fee. It's a single-lane concrete ramp with a somewhat rickety loading float and limited parking alongside the private driveway. The ramp is in Young's Cove, which opens to the west side of Eld Inlet.

- **Arcadia Ramp:** Between the entrance to Totten Inlet and Hammersley Inlet is Arcadia Point, where there's a Squaxin Indian Tribe ramp. It's two lanes wide and concrete, with parking for about two dozen cars and trailers up the hill about 100 yards. To

reach it, drive north from Olympia on U.S. 101 for 15 miles and turn east (right) on Lynch Road, following it just under 10 miles to the ramp.

- **Port of Shelton Ramp:** Follow Hammersley Inlet west into Shelton to find the Port of Shelton ramp on the north end of town along Highway 3. It has a one-lane gravel ramp with parking for about 20 cars and trailers. Drive north from Shelton on Highway 3 one-quarter of a mile and turn right just past the railroad bridge.

- **Shorecrest Park Ramp:** Go north from Shelton up Oakland Bay to find this one, a Mason County Parks and Recreation Department facility with a one-lane concrete ramp with limited parking. It's on Shorecrest Park Way off Highway 3, about six miles north of Shelton.

- **Latimer's Landing:** Continue north on Highway 3 about 12 miles north of Shelton and turn right on Pickering Road to reach the ramp at Latimer's Landing. Located at the west end of the Hartstene Island bridge, it's one-lane wide and had a loading float. Parking on a gravel lot is nearby. Wind and running tides can cause some problems for people launching and retrieving their boats here. Launching is free at this Mason County Parks and Recreation Department ramp.

- **Fair Harbor Boat Ramp:** Located near Grapeview off Highway 3, this site has a two-lane concrete ramp with a loading float and parking for about 20 cars and trailers. Take Highway 3 north from Shelton or south from Belfair and turn east on Grapeview Road; drive four miles and turn left on Grapeview Loop Road. Follow the loop half a mile to the ramp.

- **Allyn Waterfront Park:** Three miles north of the Grapeview ramp on Highway 3 is the little town of Allyn, where there's a good, two-lane launch ramp with a loading float and parking for about 20 cars and trailers. This free launch is managed by the Port of Allyn.

- **Vaughn Bay Ramp:** The Key Peninsula between Case Inlet and Carr Inlet has boat ramps on both its west and east shores. On the west (Case Inlet) side, the northernmost ramp is in Vaughn Bay off Hall Road. This Pierce County ramp has a single lane with a concrete surface and parking for only a few cars and trailers. Drive west from Purdy on Highway 302 about 8.5 miles and turn south on Wright-Bliss Road. Go 3.2 miles and turn west on Hall Road, following it just over a mile to the ramp at the end of the road.

- **Joemma Beach State Park:** Farther south is the Washington State Parks ramp at Joemma Beach (formerly the Department of Natural Resources' Robert F. Kennedy Park). This one-lane concrete ramp also has a loading float. There's a $3 launch fee. To get there from Purdy, go west on Highway 302 five miles to the Key Peninsula Highway and turn south (left). Drive 10 miles and turn right on Whiteman Road, going 1.2 miles before turning right on Bay Road. Less than a mile down Bay Road you'll come to the park and ramp.

- **Longbranch Ramp:** Around the corner on the Carr Inlet side is the Longbranch Ramp, also a Pierce County facility. The one-lane concrete ramp is located at the end of 72nd Street two miles south of Longbranch.

- **Lakebay Marina:** Three miles north of Longbranch is the ramp at Lakebay Marina, a one-lane concrete ramp with gravel parking lot for about five cars and trailers. You can launch a trailer boat here for $5, a cartopper for $3. To find it, go south from Key Center on the Key Peninsula Highway one mile past the town of Home. Turn left on Cornwall Road and drive half a mile to Lorenz Road, turning right to the ramp.

- **Home Boat Ramp:** A mile farther north is the ramp at Home. It's a one-lane concrete ramp with a gravel parking area for about a dozen cars and trailers. Drive from Key Center to Home on Highway 302, turning left just before you cross the bridge on A Street. Drive half a mile on A Street to the ramp.

Facilities: In Gig Harbor, Arabella's Landing has open moorage, electricity and water to the docks, rest rooms with showers, and boat-sewage pump-out facilities. Peninsula Yacht Basin has open moorage, power and water at the docks, and rest rooms with showers. Jerisich Park has over 400 feet of dock space, a nearby park with rest rooms, and a boat-sewage pump-out facility.

In Tacoma, Chinook Landing Marina on the north side of Commencement Bay has open moorage, power and water to the docks, a small grocery store, rest rooms with showers, and boat-sewage pump-out facilities. Crow's Nest Marina has open moorage, electricity and water to the docks, a boat lift, rest rooms with showers, and sewage pump-out facilities. Ole & Charlie's Marina has covered moorage with electricity and water, a small grocery store, fishing tackle, and rest rooms. Pick's Cove Marine Center has open and covered moorage, electricity and water to the docks, a boat lift, rest rooms with showers, sewage pump-out and laundry facilities. Totem Marina has open and covered moorage, electricity and water to the docks, a small grocery store, a boat lift, laundry facilities, rest rooms and showers, boat-sewage pump-out facilities, and restaurants right alongside it.

At Point Defiance Boathouse Marina you'll find open moorage, rental boats, groceries, fuel docks, rest rooms, boat-sewage pump-out facilities, and a restaurant. Breakwater Marina has open and covered moorage, power and water to the docks, rental boats, sewage pump-out facilities, rest rooms with showers, and fuel docks. Narrows Marina has fuel docks, fishing tackle, boat hardware and boat-sewage pump-out facilities. Steilacoom Marina has open moorage, power and water to the docks, a grocery store, and a boat-sewage dump station. Lakebay Marina offers electricity to the docks, open moorage, rest rooms, and fuel docks. Fair Harbor Marina has fuel docks, open moorage, power to the docks, boat repairs and boat haul-out, and a grocery store.

In Olympia, Zittel's Marina has open moorage, fuel docks, bait and tackle, boat rentals, power and water to the floats, and rest rooms. Boston Harbor Marina has open moorage, fuel docks, groceries, rental boats and rest rooms. Swantown Marina has open moorage, rest rooms with showers, pump-out and dump station for boat sewage, and the newest haul-out facility in Puget Sound. West Bay Marina has fuel docks, boat repairs, haul-out facilities, boat sewage facilities, and a restaurant that has changed owners and names many times but keeps hanging in there. Percival Landing in downtown Olympia has lots of open moorage, power to the docks, pump-out facilities, and easy access to many restaurants and watering holes.

Several state marine parks in southern Puget Sound offer boating facilities. Kopachuck State Park on the east side of Carr Inlet has a couple of moorage buoys but no moorage floats. Like many marine parks, it's a part of the Cascadia Marine Trail system, where paddlers can find a place to pitch their tents as they prowl south Puget Sound. Kopachuck also has an underwater park (diving reef) just offshore. Tiny Cutts Island is just north of Kopachuck. It's accessible by boat only and has nine moorage buoys. Penrose Point State Park is located in Mayo Cove on the west side of Carr Inlet. It has over 300 feet of moorage floats, eight moorage buoys, and boat-sewage dump facilities. On the north side of Anderson Island is Eagle Island, another marine park with moorage buoys only.

Around the end of the Longbranch Peninsula on the east side of Case Inlet, Joemma Beach, also a state park, has 500 feet of moorage on its float and five nearby moorage buoys. It also has a ramp and primitive campsites. Farther up Case Inlet on the west side is McMicken Island, another state marine park. It has five moorage buoys but no other facilities. At the north end of Hartstene Island is Jarrell Cove State Park, where there's nearly 800 feet of moorage space on its float, as well as 14 moorage buoys. On the hill overlooking the cove are several tent and RV sites. Jarrell Cove also has boat-sewage pump-out and dump facilities, and is part of the Cascadia Marine Trail system. To the south on the mainland between the mouth of the Nisqually and Johnson Point is Tolmie State Park, with five moorage buoys and an underwater park for divers. The newest state park in the area is Hope Island, located between Squaxin Island and the entrance to Totten Inlet. It has only one moorage buoy.

Water sports/restrictions: All water sports are permitted. NOAA chart 18448 covers the entire south Puget Sound area.

Contact: Arabella's Landing, tel. (253) 851-1793; Peninsula Yacht Basin, tel. (253) 858-2250; Jerisich Park, tel. (253) 851-8136; Chinook Landing Marina, tel. (253) 627-7676; Port of Tacoma, City Marina, tel.

(253) 572-2524; Breakwater Marina, tel. (253) 752-6663; Point Defiance Boathouse Marina, tel. (253) 591-5325; Totem Marina, tel. (253) 272-4404; Narrows Marina, tel. (253) 564-4222; Pick's Cove Marine Center, tel. (253) 572-3625; Steilacoom Marina, tel. (253) 582-2600; Lakebay Marina, tel. (253) 884-3350; Longbranch Marina, tel. (253) 884-5137 (VHF ch.16); Zittel's Marina, tel. (360) 459-1950; Boston Harbor Marina, tel. (360) 357-5670; Swantown Marina, tel. (360) 786-1400; West Bay Marina, tel. (360) 943-2022; Percival Landing Park, tel. (360) 753-8382; Fair Harbor Marina, tel. (360) 426-4028; For nautical charts of this area, contact Captain's Nautical Supply, tel. (206) 283-7242.

🖢 American Lake

Rating: 8

One of Pierce County's largest lakes, it covers over 1,100 acres and provides water recreation of all kinds for folks around the Tacoma-south Pierce County area. You'd think there'd be plenty of elbow room on a lake that large, but its urban location and nearness to the military bases at Fort Lewis and McChord Air Force Base help to make this a very well-known and popular body of water. About the only thing helping to keep the crowds away is that the lake is, believe it or not, difficult to find if you haven't driven to it before. Most people figure it out eventually, so the crowds just seem to keep getting bigger as the years pass. Because it's a Class A lake by Pierce County standards, it has liberal regulations as far as speed limits go. In fact, along with sprawling Lake Tapps, this is one of only two Pierce County lakes where registered race boats may be tested at certain times of the week (Saturday and Wednesday from March through November). If you're a paddler

or other small-boat operator who doesn't want to be anywhere around when the big fast boys are on the water, you might consider limiting your range to the cove at the south end of the lake, commonly known as Little American Lake. It has a no-wake, 5 mph speed limit in effect at all times.

Location: Southwest of Tacoma; map B2, grid a5.

How to get there: Take Exit 122 off Interstate 5 and go west across the tracks on Berkley Street; go right at the T and drive four blocks to Bill's Boat House, on the left.

Boat ramp: The lake has two boat ramps, one at the north end and the other along the southeast side. The northern ramp is a three-lane concrete job with a loading float and some 80 parking spaces, managed by the City of Lakewood. The southern ramp is managed by the Department of Fish and Wildlife and is a two laner with about 50 parking spaces. Due to past problems with partiers, alcohol is prohibited at the WDFW boat ramp. A $10 WDFW access decal is required to use the public launch area maintained by the Washington Department of Fish and Wildlife.

Facilities: The City of Lakewood manages a park at the lake's north end, with a large swim beach, picnic areas, rest rooms, and kids' playground equipment. Bill's Boathouse, once a hub of activity for anglers and boaters, is now the home of the American Lake Rowing Club. The club has kayak rentals and lakeside cabin rentals.

Water sports/restrictions: All water sports are permitted. As on all Pierce County waters, PWC riders must be at least 16 years old unless there's a parent or guardian onboard with them. County regulations also dictate a 5 mph speed limit within 200 feet of shore, 300 feet of any boat launch, and 100 feet of any other vessel, swimmer, or dock. So-called Little American Lake, which is the part of the lake south of the narrow neck of water at the south end of the lake, has a 5 mph speed limit at all times.

Contact: Bill's Boat House, tel. (253) 588-2594.

10 Five Mile Lake

Rating: 6

The King County park has a good swim beach and plenty of room for lounging around in the sun, but if you want to put a boat in Five Mile you'll have to resort to back power to get it there. The swimming area has docks and other equipment for variety, so you can add cannon balls and belly flops to your swimming activities if you feel like it. The lake's location right alongside Military Road makes for easy access from all over south King and northern Pierce Counties, so keep it in mind when some of the bigger, more well-known lakes get crowded on a hot summer day.

Location: Southeast of Federal Way; map b2, grid a6.

How to get there: Take Military Road south from South 320th in Federal Way. Lake is on the west side of Military, about three miles south of 320th.

Boat ramp: The lake has no boat ramp.

Facilities: A King County park is near the south end of the lake.

Water sports/restrictions: Swimming, fishing, and paddling are the main attractions here.

Contact: King County Parks and Recreation Department, tel. (206) 870-6527.

11 Puyallup River

Rating: 7

OK, the first thing I have to do is confess that I'm one of relatively few people who have wrapped a boat around a rock on the slow-moving Class I and II Puyallup. It's not something I'm proud of, but I thought I'd say it here so that someone else who happened to be there doesn't go blabbing it around before I get a chance to give my version of the story. In my defense I should say that it happened a long time ago, the first time I was ever on the oars of a drift boat, so I was inexperienced to say the least. Still, the mishap was avoidable, and in looking back I can't believe I did it.

It seems a friend just got a new fiberglass boat of which he was justifiably proud, so he took another friend and me on a spring float down the Puyallup from Orting to the confluence of the White River near Sumner. About halfway through the trip he asked if I wanted to row, and since I knew of nothing in the way of major rapids or obstacles on the section of river to come, I thought I would have no trouble. And I didn't, at least not for the first half mile or so. But as we approached a large boulder on one side of the river, I wanted to be sure to give it plenty of room, so I hugged the inside of the curve on the other side to be sure of missing it by as great a distance as possible. There was quite a back current on the inside of the curve, and I slid the boat into that back current right up against the far bank as we passed the boulder. A few yards downstream of the rock, I dropped the oars and reached behind me for a sandwich in the cooler on the floor of the boat. Getting the sandwich took several seconds, and by the time I looked up I was once again upstream of the big rock, and the main river current was about to grab the boat's stern.

Sure enough, the current took hold, causing the boat to spin about 100 degrees, and we were suddenly headed downstream again, only this time we were sideways to the current and bearing down on the boulder fast. By the time I grabbed the right oar, we were on the rock, taking it directly in the middle of the boat on the left side. The boat tried to slide up the side of the rock, and when it did we took about 50 gallons of water over the right gunwale. The entire left side caved in, then sprang back to its original shape, shooting us back off the rock and allowing in more water. Then the boat slipped off the rock toward the middle of the river. In a couple of seconds we were in the clear, but the water was ankle deep in the bottom of the boat.

If we had been in an aluminum or wooden boat, there's no doubt in my mind that it would have collapsed under the strain, and we would all have gone to the bottom with it. But the glass boat took its lumps and prevailed, saving us all from a thorough drenching and maybe a lot worse. I figure all the guff I still take over the event is better than what might have happened. Unmerciful ribbing beats drowning.

Anyway, if you're not a total dipstick as I was that day long ago, you should be able to run the entire accessible length of the Puyallup without any danger. There's nothing more serious than perhaps Class II+ water anywhere from above Orting all the way to the mouth of the White, and from there it just gets slower, wider, and more mellow. The upper portion, from the Orville Road bridge to the mouth of the Carbon, is the most fun, but virtually the whole river is wedged between high, man-made dikes that give the experience an artificial feeling. The prettiest stretch is alongside the High Cedars Golf Course downstream from Orting, where high, forested cliffs border the west side of the river for about half a mile.

Location: Enters Commencement Bay at Tacoma; map B2, grid a6.

How to get there: Take the Puyallup exit off Interstate 5 near the north end of Tacoma to reach the lower Puyallup, which is paralleled by the River Road on the south and North Levee Road on the north. To reach upper portions of the river, take Highway 410 to Sumner or follow Pioneer Avenue east out of Puyallup to Highway 162 (the Sumner-Orting Highway). Side roads to the east off Highway 162 provide river access at Alderton, McMillan, and other places along the way toward Orting. McCutcheon Road runs along the east side of the river from Sumner to McMillan.

Boat ramp: There are two official Department of Wildlife access areas on the river where boats can be launched, and lots of other places near Orting, McMillan and Sumner where it's possible to get a small boat in the water if you know exactly how to go about it. The official spots are at Alderton, where 96th Avenue East crosses the river, and at the Weiss Access off 115th Street East. A couple of the best freelance launch sites are four miles southeast of Orting off Orville Road just downstream from where Orville Road crosses the river and below the Calistoga Avenue bridge between Orting and the Soldiers' Home south of town.

Facilities: The towns of Puyallup and Sumner have everything you need.

Water sports/restrictions: Kayaking, drift boating, rafting, tubing, and canoeing are all possible on this river if you know what you're doing.

Contact: Pacific Water Sports, tel. (206) 246-9385.

12 Lake Tapps

Rating: 8

Six miles long, over three miles wide, and with 50 miles of shoreline, it's by far the largest lake in Pierce County, and on any warm summer weekend it can also be the craziest. Some people will not go boating on this sprawling reservoir on the hill between Bonney Lake and Auburn because they don't think it's safe. Safety, of course, is a relative thing, and what I consider safe someone else might consider unsafe. The fact is that Lake Tapps is considered by many to be western Washington's ultimate aquatic playground. It's also a fact that several boaters have been killed in boating accidents since development around the lake took off in the early '60s, so you decide. One thing's for sure, though–this is Pierce County's largest freshwater playground, and there's a lot of room to play here when the lake is full. Water-skiers have considered the wide-open lake their own for decades, and in recent years other tow sports have gained great popularity; kneeboarding and wakeboarding both are very big here. This is also a place where some of those guys with severe testosterone poisoning go to see what their muscle boats will do, and God help you if you happen to be somewhere between where they are and where they're going. It's kind of like sitting in a Soap Box Derby car halfway down a runway at Sea-Tac Airport, hoping that the next 737 lifts off before it reaches you, and knowing that you're dog meat if it doesn't. Try not to get yourself in that position at Lake Tapps, because these guys ain't airline pilots. I'd rather take my chances with the personal watercraft that sometimes cover the surface of the lake like so many blowflies on a summer day; at least my boat is bigger than most of them. There, I guess I've complained about everyone now, so I'll move on.

One more very important thing you need to know about Lake Tapps is that it isn't there most of the year. I know that sounds strange, but before you accuse me of snorting bilge fumes, let me explain. This is a reservoir built to provide water for a power-generating plant over the hill to the west. For most of the year that's where its water goes, through a big pipe to turn a turbine, so it's a huge lake bed of mud and stumps with a river running through the middle of it on its way to that big pipe. The water is held back and the lake allowed to fill only for about three months each year, from Memorial Day to Labor Day. The folks around here squeeze a lot of recreational activity into those three months, knowing that skiing and muscle-boating are impossible on that big stump bed the rest of the year. It's been going on that way here for decades, but the 1999 announcement by Puget Sound Energy that its power-generating operation here is getting less profitable and that it might discontinue it and let the lake drain permanently really got folks riled up. At the time of this writing the dispute hasn't yet been resolved, but stay tuned. As for me, I hope they iron things out and keep the lake full every summer because I would like to see those muscle boats stay at Tapps.

Location: Northeast of Sumner; map A2, grid a7.

How to get there: Take Highway 410 east from Sumner and turn north on the Sumner-Tapps Highway.

Boat ramp: There are boat ramps near the northeast and northwest corners of the lake. The northern ramp is a three-lane concrete ramp managed by Pierce County Parks. It has two loading floats and a large paved parking area. The other is a two-lane ramp at Allen Yorke Park, managed by the town of Bonney Lake. It's a two-land concrete ramp with lots of parking and is adjacent to a large swim beach and picnic area.

Facilities: Allen Yorke Park, located off Bonney Lake Boulevard about a mile and a half northeast of the town of Bonney Lake, has a large swim beach, picnic tables, playground equipment, rest rooms, and a small snack bar. Food, gas, lodging, and other amenities are available nearby along Highway 410.

Water sports/restrictions: All water sports are permitted. Tapps is classified by Pierce County standards a Class A lake, which means almost anything goes except that a 5 mph speed limit is in effect between sunset and sunrise. As on all Pierce County waters, personal watercraft riders must be at least 16 years old unless there's a parent or guardian onboard with them. County regulations also dictate a 5 mph speed limit with 200 feet of shore, 300 feet of any boat launch, and 100 feet of any other vessel, swimmer or dock. There also are a number of speed limit restrictions in and around Lake Ridge Cove, aimed primarily at providing safe waterskiing conditions.

Contact: Pierce County Parks and Recreation Department, tel. (253) 798-4176; Auburn Sports and Marine, tel. (206) 833-1440.

13 White River

Rating: 6

This midsized stream, which flows off the northeast corner of Mount Rainier to eventually join the Puyallup River at the town of Sumner, has gone through some considerable changes since the first white man appeared in the Puget Sound region. The White, which is commonly called the Stuck River along its lower reaches, originally was a tributary to the Green River, but somebody decided long ago that it would be cool to divert it elsewhere, so a short stretch of canal was dug and the White became a tributary to the Puyallup. As if that weren't enough manipulation of a perfectly good river, a dam was built on its upper reaches near the small community of Greenwater. In 1911 a diversion dam was constructed at the town of Buckley, and about half of the White was sent through a half dozen miles of canals and pipes to flood four existing lakes and form sprawling Lake Tapps. Water tumbles from the lower end of the lake over the hillside through a huge pipe and into a turbine at Dieringer, about midway between Sumner and Auburn, to rejoin the new White River channel that was dug to carry it toward its confluence with the Puyallup.

Though all that human progress was the beginning of the end for the river's once-thriving salmon and steelhead fisheries, it only affected would-be boaters some 90 years later with the creation of certain obstacles that must be avoided for boaters to enjoy a pleasant day of river running. A trip over Mud Mountain Dam, of course, would be a real bummer, and if you chose to go down the wrong half of the stream at Buckley, you'd eventually end up on Lake Tapps, paddling flat water instead of moving water. We don't even want to talk about the end of that exhilarating run through the pipe and into the turbine at Dieringer.

Most of the folks who boat the White make one of two runs, each of them pretty much all-day trips of about a dozen miles or so. The upper run begins either in the main White or the West Fork White off Forest Service Road 74 above the town of Greenwater and ends at Bridge

Camp between Greenwater and Enumclaw. Except during times of extreme snowmelt and runoff such as during the wild spring and early summer of 1999, this run consists mostly of Class II and some Class III water, but large Douglas fir and hemlock trees have been known to drop into or across the river and present unwanted surprises for boaters, so don't take anything for granted.

The most popular lower run is from Buckley to the southeast corner of Auburn, a stretch of river that roughly parallels Highway 164 throughout much of its length. Again, this is mostly Class II water, with a fairly steady, gentle drop and little in the way of dangers for paddlers of intermediate skill or better. If you want a very easy float through slow water, you can paddle from Auburn to the mouth of the White near Sumner, but the steep bank and high, man-made dike along most of this stretch make a boring trip.

Location: Joins the Puyallup River near Sumner; map B2, grid a7.

How to get there: Take Highway 164 or several city streets south from Auburn to the lower river. Follow Highway 410 east from Enumclaw to reach the upper White.

Boat ramp: Rough put-in/take out points are off Forest Service Road 74 above Greenwater, at Bridge Camp between Greenwater and Enumclaw, near the old Marion Grange in Buckley, along gravel bars off various roads and city streets in southeast Auburn, and at the confluence of the White and Puyallup rivers at Sumner.

Facilities: Food, gas, tackle, and lodging are available in Auburn and Sumner.

Water sports/restrictions: Kayaking and fishing are the main attractions. Rafting is a possibility during higher water on the upper river and at all times on the lower river. Canoeing is best suited to the extreme lower river below Auburn.

Contact: Auburn Sports and Marine, tel. (206) 833-1440.

14 Deep Lake

Rating: 7

It provides a lot of aquatic recreation for a little lake (39 acres) well off the main traffic flow in eastern King County. A good part of its popularity is that Deep Lake has a well-kept state park on its southern shore, complete with a very nice swim beach and plenty of lawn for picnics and other lakeside activities. A good fishing lake, Deep would no doubt be even more popular if it has a better-developed boat ramp.

Location: Northeast of Enumclaw; map B2, grid a8.

How to get there: Take Kanaskat Road north from Enumclaw and watch for the Nolte State Park sign on the left.

Boat ramp: There's a narrow boat ramp on the east end of the lake.

Facilities: The state park has a great gravel swim beach, lots of lawn, picnic tables, and a small pier, but no overnight camping.

Water sports/restrictions: Swimming, paddling, and fishing are the primary water sports here.

Contact: Nolte State Park, tel. (360) 825-4646; Washington State Parks and Recreation Commission, tel. (800) 233-0321 (information).

15 Spanaway Lake

Rating: 7

This 260-acre lake is a hub of aquatic activity in the Tacoma/Pierce County area, offering something for everyone who likes to play on, in, or around the water.

The no-wake zone around the entire north end of the lake, including the large island that has a bridge going to it from the mainland, is a haven for paddlers and folks who rent small rowboats at the park, while the southern three-quarters of the lake is pretty much wide-open space where there's plenty of room for PWC riding, kneeboarding, skiing and other fast-boat sports. The shallow coves at the extreme south end and southwest corner of the lake are, like the north end, places where paddlers and other calm-water boaters can escape most of the bigger, faster craft.

Location: In Spanaway, Pierce County; map B2, grid a5.

How to get there: Take Interstate 5 to Highway 512 and turn east. Turn south on Highway 7 and drive south about three miles to Military Road; turn west (right), go one-quarter mile to Breezeman Boulevard, and turn south (left) into the park entrance.

Boat ramp: The county park has a boat ramp, free fishing pier, swim beach, rowboat rentals, and cooking facilities for picnickers.

Facilities: Lodging, and other facilities are available nearby.

Water sports/restrictions: All water sports are permitted. The lake has a 40 mph speed limit and a prohibition on waterskiing around Enchanted Island and the north end of the lake. No boat longer than 22 feet is allowed to use the boat launch without a permit issued by the Pierce County Sheriff's Department. As on all Pierce County waters, PWC riders must be at least 16 years old unless there's a parent or guardian onboard with them. County regulations also dictate a 5 mph speed limit with 200 feet of shore, 300 feet of any boat launch, and 100 feet of any vessel, swimmer, or dock.

Contact: Spanaway Park Boat House, tel. (253) 531-0555; Pierce County Parks and Recreation Department, tel. (253) 798-4176.

16 Carbon River

Rating: 7

Except for two vivid memories from my childhood, it would be easy to say that the Carbon is pretty much a soft touch for river runners. The first is a memory of my dad, a volunteer fireman, coming home from a call one rainy Saturday afternoon around Christmas and telling my mom that he and his cohorts had tried in vain to save the life of a young man who had been pulled from the Carbon after his small raft had capsized during a steelhead-fishing trip. The man and his fishing partner had gone into the river when their raft hit a submerged rock, caught in the current for a few seconds, and filled with ice-cold water. Only the fishing partner lived to fish again.

My second reality check on the Carbon's potential danger came on the last day of my junior year in high school. It was a warm June afternoon, so about 20 of us, including a young teacher, hauled inner tubes of various sizes and various levels of flotation up to a gravel bar near the Highway 162 bridge and launched a school's-out-celebration float that would take us about three miles downstream to another gravel bar near the high school track and football field in Orting.

About halfway through the trip we rounded a fairly sharp bend and found ourselves being swept toward a cluster of alder trees that had uprooted on the bank and fallen into the river, spanning about three-quarters of the stream's width. The first two or three guys were hugging the left bank as they rounded the corner, so they cleared the treetops by several feet. Unfortunately, I rounded the curve near the right bank, and I couldn't back-paddle anywhere near fast enough to avoid the tangle of limbs and tree trunks that filled the water before me. I hit the mess feetfirst, hoping to kick off with my legs and shove myself away from the trees, but when I hit the obstacle, I went over backwards, my inner tube shooting into the air and the strong current pinning me against the trees. Luckily, I was facing downstream, so I could grab a big limb in each hand to pull myself up. The current forced me under at least twice, but after several frightening seconds I got a shot of adrenaline that allowed me to push off and lift myself most of the way out of the water. I sort of rolled over the top of the mess and back into the river on the downstream side. I don't remember where or when I caught up with my inner tube, but I do remember that by the time I climbed back into it, I had a couple of dandy puncture wounds in my chest and stomach and a deep scratch that extended from the middle of my sternum to below my navel.

Without a life jacket among us, it's very fortunate that all 20 of us lived to finish that trip down the Carbon. Still, the lower stretch of the Carbon, from 177th Street down to the confluence of the Carbon and the Puyallup, is a gentle and friendly river for kayakers and rafters, one that's easily runnable except during extremely high water and during the low-water period of late summer when you may have to spend some time dragging over the riffles in a couple of places. It's quite rural, and the scenery includes some impressive hillsides that drop several hundred feet to the river's edge in places behind Orting. The upper Carbon, on the other hand, is for experienced and knowledgeable kayakers only, and even then I'd recommend it only to those whose insurance premiums are paid up. It's Class V and even Class VI water up in that canyon, with few places to escape should you decide to change your mind in the middle of it all. Even with its dangers, I'll take my chances on the lower Carbon, thank you.

Location: Joins the Puyallup River northwest of Orting, Pierce County; map B2, grid a7.

How to get there: Take Highway 162 (the Sumner-Orting Highway) south from Sumner toward the town of Orting. Watch for the gated gravel road to the left about one-quarter mile south of the concrete bridge and another about two miles farther up the road. In Orting, turn left on Bridge Street and follow it to the river to fish the middle stretch of the Carbon.

Boat ramp: There are no formal boat ramps, but it's possible to drop a boat over the bank at 177th Street East and just upstream from the Highway 162 bridge, as well as at couple of places along the gravel road that parallels the river immediately behind the town of Orting.

Facilities: Food and gas are available in Orting.

Water sports/restrictions: Kayaks, rafts, and inner tubes all are used on various stretches of the river.

Contact: Pacific Water Sports, tel. (206) 246-9385.

17 Summit Lake

Rating: 8

This 500-acre lake off Highway 8 is one of the south Puget Sound region's biggest and one of its most popular with water recreationists of all kinds. It's too bad there's not a large resort of some kind here so the public could have better access to some of the best swimming water in western Washington. Boating access is better, thanks to the wide boat ramp and large parking area at the Department of Wildlife's access area on the south side of the lake. Summit is a beautiful lake, with forested hills rising into the sky all around it, and clear, clean water that seems to call everyone to come in and enjoy. Many of the homes around its shores are year-round residences, but there are also dozens of vacation and weekend cabins, too, and they all come to life on holiday weekends. The waterskiing is fantastic here on a summer morning, before most of the other water lovers crank up their engines. This is also a popular PWC lake. Because it lies in a deep basin among the hills, Summit Lake boasts some of the greatest depths of any Thurston County lake. Some places near its center are 100 feet deep, and the lake's clear water makes those depths an inviting place for scuba divers to explore.

Location: West of Olympia; map B2, grid b1.

How to get there: Take Highway 8 west from Olympia about 12 miles to the Summit Lake Road, turn north and follow Summit Lake Road about a mile and a half to the lake.

Boat ramp: A large, paved boat ramp and access area is located near the southwest corner of the lake. A $10 WDFW access decal is required to use the public launch area maintained by the Washington Department of Fish and Wildlife.

Facilities: All other amenities are in Olympia.

Water sports/restrictions: All water sports are permitted. The lake has a 5 mph speed limit in effect during the first 30 days of the general fishing season, which begins in late April. After that 30-day period, a 5 mph speed limit is in effect from sunset until 11 a.m.

Contact: Olympia/Thurston County Chamber of Commerce Visitor Information Center, tel. (360) 357-3362; Tumwater Sports, tel. (360) 352-5161.

18 Nisqually River

Rating: 7

The five-mile stretch of the Nisqually immediately below LaGrande Dam has gotten a lot of publicity in the past few years as kayakers have fought to make recreational boating access a part of Tacoma Power's federal licensing agreement for the next 40 years. The Federal Energy Regulatory Commission in 1998 ordered Tacoma Power to provide boaters with a special wintertime spill during each of three straight years to test whether boating in the steep canyon below the dam could and should be a recognized use of the Nisqually's water, so we won't know for awhile how that might turn out. What we do know is that the canyon stretch of the Nisqually opened up for the three-year trial is a dangerous piece of river, one that only the best of the best might want to consider running. Class V drops and steep canyon walls that offer little chance of escape, not to mention all the work involved in roping boats down to the river for the start of the run, make this a place where only the serious technical boater need apply. Still, we all can dream.

More realistic for most of us are sections of the river downstream from the canyon, beginning at Mashel Prairie, where canyon boaters end their dangerous run. The float from Mashel Prairie down to McKenna is a Class II run under normal water conditions, and provides over a dozen miles of rural scenery and generally boater-friendly water with moderate rock gardens the main challenges. Oh yes, there is one other challenge in the form of a low-head dam across the river about halfway through the run; it must be portaged. From McKenna down to the Yelm hydro facility or the military bridge (tank crossing) below Yelm, the lower stretch of river is more challenging and contains a couple of Class III chutes and one tight corner where the river narrows to only a few yards as it makes a 90-degree left turn. I've run the whole thing in a 16-foot drift boat on several occasions without mishap, so experienced paddlers will have little trouble with even the most difficult spots along this run.

It's also possible to float downstream from the military bridge to the public access just above the highway bridge near Interstate 5, a nice float through several miles of Class I and Class II water. I wouldn't recommend this run in the fall, though, unless you're a salmon angler. Fall and early winter is when the lower Nisqually gets packed with fishermen in search of chinook and chum salmon. Some pools are so crowded with anglers that it might be difficult making it through with several battle scars from flying hooks and sinkers.

Location: Enters Puget Sound between Tacoma and Olympia; map B2, grid b4.

How to get there: Take Interstate 5 to the Old Nisqually exit and follow Pacific Avenue south two miles to Reservation Road. Turn left on Reservation Road, left again on Highway 510 (Olympia-Yelm Highway), which roughly parallels the south side of the river to the town of Yelm. At Yelm, Highway 510 intersects Highway 507, which continues on north, crossing the Nisqually at the small town of McKenna.

Boat ramp: A gravel road leading downriver from the north end of the McKenna bridge runs out onto a gravel bar that serves as a take-out point for boaters coming down from the Mashel Prairie access and a put-in for boaters going downriver to the tank crossing or the Yelm hydro plant.

Facilities: Groceries, gas, and tackle are available in Yelm, lodging nearby in Olympia.

Water sports/restrictions: Kayaking, rafting, drift boating, and tubing are popular here.

Contact: Pacific Water Sports, tel. (206) 246-9385.

19 Chambers Lake

Rating: 5

This is another of those looking-glass-shaped lakes, with a main part at each end and a narrow, shallow canal connecting the two. The larger north end of Chambers covers about 70 acres and has the access area and boat ramp at its north end. The lower part of the lake is just over 10 acres in size. Both are shallow, with maximum depths of about 10 feet and many places where the water is only three to six feet deep. The weedy lake with a shoreline that's still undeveloped is a natural for bass fishing, and that's what most visitors come here to do. But paddlers shouldn't overlook Chambers, because it's usually a quiet place, with lots of opportunity for viewing birds and wildlife of various kinds. A newly developed bike trail is immediately east of the lake in case you want to double your recreational activities while you're in the neighborhood.

Location: Southwest side of Lacey; map B2, grid b3.

How to get there: Take the Sleater-Kinney Road South exit off Interstate 5 at Lacey and drive south to 14th Avenue SE; turn west (right) and drive about half a mile to the public access area on the left.

Boat ramp: There's a boat ramp at the access area. A $10 Washington Department of Fish and Wildlife access decal is required to use the public launch area maintained by the WDFW.

Facilities: Food, gas, lodging, and other amenities are available nearby in Lacey.

Water sports/restrictions: The lake is best suited to paddling and fishing. It has a 5 mph speed limit.

Contact: Tumwater Sports, tel. (360) 352-5161.

20 Hicks Lake

Rating: 7

Fairly large and quite deep by Puget Sound standards, this 170-acre lake south of Lacey warms slowly, but once it does, it becomes a hot spot for local water lovers. The limited size of the public access area and its relative remoteness help to keep the number of visitors in check, but Hicks still gets busy during the summer. If you studied the Thurston County boating regulations, you might think that Hicks has a 5 mph speed limit and other restrictions like most of the county's lakes, but it's under the jurisdiction of the City of Lacey, so speed rules are pretty much no-holds-barred. PWC zip around, skiers cruise along the water, and most folks are hurrying along at a good clip. Better follow the counterclockwise traffic pattern and other standard rules of the road, however, because the Lacey Police Department's marine patrol does a good job of keeping tabs here.

Location: In Lacey; map B2, grid b3.

How to get there: Take the Pacific Avenue exit off Interstate 5 at Lacey and

drive east to Carpenter Road; turn right and follow Carpenter about two miles to Shady Lane. Turn right, drive to the T at Lilac Street, turn left, go a block and a half, and turn left again on Hicks Lake Road. The boat ramp and access area are about one-quarter of a mile down Hicks Lake Road, on the left.

Boat ramp: There's a single-lane boat ramp with limited parking and about 100 feet of gravel beach on the west side of the lake, maintained by the Department of Fish and Wildlife. It's closed and its gate locked during the off-season from late fall to early spring. A $10 WDFW access decal is required to use the public launch area maintained by the Washington Department of Fish and Wildlife.

Facilities: Food, gas, lodging, and other facilities are available in nearby Lacey.

Water sports/restrictions: All water sports are permitted.

Contact: Sports Warehouse, tel. (360) 491-1346.

21 Long Lake

Rating: 7

This 300-acre lake, which is really two lakes connected by a narrow channel, offers plenty of room for skiers, PWC riders and other speed-lovers to get out and stretch their legs, but its no-wake restricted areas are great for paddlers, anglers, tubers and others who want to bob along at a slower pace. The boat ramp on the lake's west side has enough room in its parking lot for lots of cars, and it gets full during the early part of fishing season and whenever a stretch of warm weather sends Thurston County folks flocking to the water.

Location: East side of Lacey; map B2, grid b3.

How to get there: Take the Pacific Avenue exit off Interstate 5 at Lacey, go east on Pacific to Carpenter Road, turn right an follow Carpenter about three miles to the south end of the Thurston County Fairgrounds. Turn left on Boat Launch Road just past the fairgrounds and follow it 200 yards down to the lake.

Boat ramp: There's a large Department of Fish and Wildlife access area with boat ramp and outhouses on the west side of the lake.

Facilities: Food, gas, lodging, and other amenities are available in Lacey.

Water sports/restrictions: All water sports are permitted. The lake has a 5 mph speed limit for the first 30 days of the general fishing season, which begins in late April. That speed limit remains in effect all year in the big cove between the public boat ramp and Holmes Island, at the northern tip of the lake, and in the narrow canal connecting the north and south portions of the lake.

Contact: Sports Warehouse, tel. (360) 491-1346.

22 Lake St. Clair

Rating: 6

This 240-acre lake is spread out all over the place, with narrow channels winding around peninsulas and small islands that seem to take up a large chunk of northern Thurston County. You might think this intricate maze of waterways would have restrictive speed limits and other restrictions, but nooooo. In fact, the 5 mph speed limit in effect on most county lakes doesn't apply to the southern part of this lake at all, not even during the first 30 days of the general fishing season. That might be because this lake happens to be open to year-round fishing, but who am I to guess about things like that. Anyway, if you like the idea of pretending that you're a drug-runner being chased through the

shallow waterways of the Everglades in a muscle boat or some other nonsense, you can go play your games at Lake St. Clair. If you're a more down-to-earth type, you can simply ski or board or ride PWC here to your heart's content, at least on the part of the lake south of the public boat ramp. North of there the 5 mph rule is in effect year-round. That's a good place to fish, paddle, or otherwise avoid drug-running muscle-boaters.

Location: Southeast of Lacey, grid b3.

How to get there: Take Highway 510 southeast from Lacey or northwest from Yelm and turn east on the Yelm Highway. Several roads and streets going north of the Yelm Highway, beginning a mile and a half from SR 510, lead to the lake.

Boat ramp: There's a two-lane Department of Fish and Wildlife boat ramp on the lake. A $10 WDFW access decal is required to use the public launch area maintained by the Washington Department of Fish and Wildlife.

Facilities: Food, gas, lodging, and other needs can be met in Lacey.

Water sports/restrictions: All water sports are permitted.

Contact: Sports Warehouse, tel. (360) 491-1346.

23 Pattison (Patterson) Lake

Rating: 7

If you like to get out on the water early for a chance at hooking a big bass or fat rainbow trout, this is a good place to visit. If you like to throw your kayak or canoe onto the rack atop your car and take it some place where you can paddle until dark to enjoy the sights and sounds of the early evening, this is a good place to visit. If you like to ski, run your PWC, wake-board or just go like hell in a boat, this ISN'T a good place to visit. Thurston County's no-wake speed limit is in effect here, so powerboaters have to go elsewhere, leaving Pattison to those who enjoy the more serene boating pleasures.

Location: South of Lacey; map B2, grid b3.

How to get there: Drive south out of Lacey on Ruddell Road and turn east (left) on Mullen Road. Turn south (right) on Carpenter Road and watch for the brown sign pointing to the public access.

Boat ramp: There's a Department of Fish and Wildlife access area with boat ramp on the east side of the lake. A $10 WDFW access decal is required to use the public launch area maintained by the Washington Department of Fish and Wildlife.

Facilities: Food, gas, lodging, and other amenities can be found in nearby Lacey or Olympia.

Water sports/restrictions: The lake has a 5 mph speed limit, which makes fishing, paddling and other slow-speed sports the big draws here.

Contact: Sports Warehouse, tel. (360) 491-1346; Olympia/Thurston County Chamber of Commerce, Visitor Information Center, tel. (360) 357-3362.

24 Ward Lake

Rating: 5

This 65-acre Thurston County lake sits in a steep basin, so it's surprisingly deep, with some places in excess of 70 feet. That means it warms a little slowly in the summer. That hasn't kept evening partiers from visiting the public access area for a summertime swim in past years, but such activity has been reduced since the Department of Wildlife started posting warning a few years ago that the access area would be closed if the shenanigans continued. Luckily,

most folks come here to fish, so the lake usually is a peaceful place where locals can enjoy the water for a few hours. The 5 mph speed limit that affects most lakes in the county is in effect here, so you won't see any skiers, PWC riders, or other speed-boat enthusiasts.

Location: East of Tumwater; map B4, grid b3.

How to get there: Take Interstate 5 to Tumwater and exit at the Olympia Brewery. Drive east on Custer Way to the four-way blinking light and turn sough (right) on Cleveland Avenue, which becomes the Yelm Highway. Turn north (left) on Boulevard Road, drive seven blocks to 42nd Way SE, turn left and drive about three blocks to the lake.

Boat ramp: A boat ramp and access area are on the east side of the lake. A $10 WDFW access decal is required to use the public launch area maintained by the Washington Department of Fish and Wildlife.

Facilities: All other facilities are in Tumwater.

Water sports/restrictions: paddling and fishing are the main draws. The lake has a 5 mph speed limit.

Contact: Tumwater Sports, tel. (360) 352-5161.

25 Deschutes River

Rating: 7

I've always enjoyed virtually anything that had the words "after work" associated with them, so a few years ago when a couple of friends suggested that we kayak the Deschutes River from Pioneer Park down to the Olympia Brewery after work the next day, I was all for it. It turned out to be a couple of the most pleasant hours I've ever spent on a Northwest stream, not just because after work started about an hour and a half early that day, but because a warm fall afternoon on the Deschutes is one of life's little bright spots. The river was low—not surprising considering it was late September or very early October—but there was enough water between our butts and the bottom to avoid having to get out and drag the boats except in one spot where a fallen tree spanned the river completely. We passed over several dozen chinook salmon that were spawning within a few days of spawning on gravel beds along the way, and on a couple of occasions smaller fish, probably sea-run cutthroat trout, shot out of the depths with a flash of olive-gold and raced off for better cover. As we passed through the Tumwater Valley Golf Course, one member of our threesome spent several minutes out of his kayak, stooping to collect about two dozen golf balls from the knee-deep water, souvenirs of a great afternoon on the river, he said. As we were taking the kayaks out of the water about 6:30 that evening, we encountered the third person we had met along the entire stretch. Like the other two, he was a salmon angler.

In retrospect, there wasn't anything special about what happened on the Deschutes that afternoon. It's what *didn't* happen that made it such a great trip. We didn't see many people, we didn't see much sign of human encroachment along the river, and we didn't have to travel more than 10 minutes from the State Capitol and busy Interstate 5 to find such a boater-friendly stretch of river. There aren't many rivers so close to a western Washington city that offer such a natural feeling to anyone willing to launch a boat in its bubbling waters. We ran the lowest of three possible sections that offer good boating opportunities on the Deschutes, the others being from the Military Road bridge down to the park we used as a put-in and the upstream run from Vail Loop Road down to Military Road. All three runs are on smallish Class I and Class II water, with quite a few sharp turns, submerged stumps, and trees in the river, and in some spots sweepers and brush hanging over or into the river. The uppermost run features a few boulder gardens. Whichever portion of the Deschutes you paddle, though, you'll probably appreciate the gentle nature of this little river and the rural countryside through which it runs.

Location: Flows into Capitol Lake at Olympia; map B2, grid b3.

How to get there: Exit Interstate 5 at the Olympia Brewery in Tumwater and take Custer Avenue to Capitol Way. Turn south (right) and turn left at the first light, which is E Street, to reach a part of the lower river near the Olympia Brewery. Follow Capitol Way south to Henderson and turn left to reach another worthwhile section of the Deschutes. Continue south on Capitol Way (which becomes Pacific Highway SE) to Waldrick Road and turn east (left) to reach several miles of the Deschutes near Offut Lake. To reach portions of the Deschutes farther upstream, drive east from Tenino about three miles on Highway 507 and turn north (left) on Military Road. Drive two miles to the bridge crossing over the river. Parking is limited here to only a couple of cars.

Boat ramp: It's possible to launch a kayak, canoe or small raft at the Military Road bridge, at Pioneer Park near the Henderson Street bridge, just downstream from the E Street bridge or at Deschutes Falls Park just above the falls.

Facilities: Food, gas, lodging, and tackle are available in Tumwater.

Water sports/restrictions: Kayaking,

canoeing, tubing, and fishing are popular here.

Contact: Tumwater Sports, tel. (360) 352-5161; Pacific Water Sports, tel. (206) 246-9385; Olympia/Thurston County Chamber of Commerce, Visitor Information Center, tel. (360) 357-3362.

26 Black Lake

Rating: 8

The Olympia area's biggest lake is also its busiest when it comes to boating activity. They do it all here, from PWC riding to fly fishing, paddling to waterskiing, and on a warm summer weekend they may well be doing it all at the same time. It gets a little hectic here at times, so if you're looking for a peaceful place to paddle, join the anglers who come to the lake at the break of dawn or early in spring, before everyone else converges on this 570-acre boater's haven. Unlike most Thurston County lakes, Black isn't affected by a 5 mph speed limit, except of course around docks, swimmers, other boats and near the shore. There's usually enough room for everyone to stay out of everyone else's way, but sometimes it gets a little close. To best avoid the main flow of boat traffic for fishing or paddling, go to the north end of the lake, where several markers warn boaters to stay clear of the old pilings and stumps that jut out of the water all over the place. Don't be surprised to see several cars parked along the road by those pilings, because bank anglers like to cast here, near the lake's northern outlet.

Location: Southwest of Olympia; map B2, grid b2.

How to get there: Take the Black Lake Boulevard exit off U.S. 101 in west Olympia and drive about two miles to the lake. Turn left on Black Lake-Belmore Road near the north end of the lake, bear right at the fire station and drive about two miles to 66th Avenue, turn right and follow it to the public access area and boat ramp near the south end of the lake.

Boat ramp: There's a two-lane boat ramp at the access area. A $10 WDFW access decal is required to use the public launch area maintained by the Washington Department of Fish and Wildlife.

Facilities: Columbus Park, on the west side of the lake off Black Lake Boulevard, has RV and tent sites, picnic areas and a very good swim beach. A store with gas pumps is located at the intersection of Black Lake-Belmore and Dent Roads, on the east side of the lake. Nearby Olympia has a full line of restaurants, motels, RV parks, marine supply stores and other facilities.

Water sports/restrictions: All water sports are permitted.

Contact: Columbus Park, tel. (360) 786-9460; Olympia/Thurston County Chamber of Commerce, Visitor Information Center, tel. (360) 357-3362.

27 Capitol Lake

Rating: 5

Except during the fall salmon fishing season, it's fairly rare to see even a single boat on Capitol Lake. Part of the problem is that many people don't know there's a boat ramp at the upper end of the lake, a ramp that's well-hidden unless you happen to stumble onto it while prowling around the north end of the park that's located where the Deschutes river slows and widens into Capitol Lake. You can't see the ramp from Interstate 5, because the freeway is directly over the top of it. A 5 mph speed limit and a fair amount of floating debris from the river help keep powerboat traffic off the lake, and paddlers tend to ignore it at least in part because of the freeway noise that's inescapable when you're on the lake. As for anglers, they're only around from about the middle of August until early October, when runs of chinook salmon pass through the lake on their way into the Deschutes; the rest of the year fishing in Capitol Lake is pretty much stinko. Still, I think this is a nice place to row or paddle on a warm spring evening, and the lake offers a perspective on the State Capitol and a corner of downtown Olympia that you can't get anywhere else. Wildlife viewing is quite good, too, with everything from red-wing blackbirds and Canada geese to raccoons, red fox, coyotes and black-tail deer living around the lake's shoreline.

Location: Southwest Olympia; map B2, grid b2.

How to get there: Take exit 103 off Interstate 5 and follow Deschutes Parkway about three-quarters of a mile to Tumwater Historical Park, on the right. To reach the lower part of the lake, continue past the park and under the freeway on Deschutes Parkway.

Boat ramp: You'll find a boat ramp and public fishing dock at the upper end of the lake, almost directly under the Interstate 5 bridge., and it's possible to drag or carry small boats to the water at Marathon Park, on the south side of the lake.

Facilities: At the northwest corner of the lake is an Olympia city park with a decent swim beach but lots of waterfowl crap to keep it from being totally inviting to everyone. Marathon Park, on the lake's south side, is similarly overrun with waterfowl, mostly Canada geese. Pioneer Park, at the upper (east) end is the nicest of the bunch, with a large lawn, play equipment and covered picnic areas. Again, though, watch for goose sign. Food, lodging, and other amenities are available in Olympia and Tumwater. Falls Terrace Restaurant, with good food and one of the best views anywhere, is half a mile south of the lake, overlooking Tumwater Falls.

Water sports/restrictions: The lake has a five mph speed limit. Paddling and fishing are the main attractions. The speed limit, though, is apparently lifted when limited race boats and various skiing and wake-boarding competitions are held on the west end of the lake.

Contact: Olympia/Thurston County Chamber of Commerce, Visitor Information Center, tel. (360) 357-3362; Tumwater Sports, tel. (360) 352-5161.

28 Tanwax Lake

Rating: 6

Far enough away from the major population centers to feel very rural, Tanwax is like one of those places you may have gone for a two-week vacation when you were a kid. But with a good road running out of Tacoma nearly to its shores, it's an easy place to go for a Saturday outing or even on one of those summer evenings when you decide to leave work two hours early. At about 170 acres, Tanwax is big enough for exploration but small enough that you can get off the water and headed home quickly when the day is done. And the fishing's good here, too.

Location: North of Eatonville; map B2, grid b6.

How to get there: Take Highway 161 south from Puyallup and turn left on Tanwax Drive to reach the resort on the north side. Pass Tanwax Drive and take the next left to reach the public boat ramp near the south end of the lake.

Boat ramp: The Department of Fish and Wildlife's access area has a large gravel parking area and a boat ramp that's adequate for launching smaller boats. A $10 WDFW access decal is required to use the public launch area maintained by the Washington Department of Fish and Wildlife.

Facilities: Rainbow Resort has a swim beach, fishing dock and other amenities.

Water sports/restrictions: All water sports are permitted. The lake has a 40 mph speed limit during daylight hours and 5 mph from sunset to sunrise.

Contact: Rainbow Resort, tel. (360) 879-5115.

29 Clear Lake

Rating: 7

Washington has lots of Clear Lakes, but this one is probably the clearest of the Clears, a place that really lives up to its name. I did a lot of swimming here as a kid, and I can testify to the fact that the visibility in its cool waters is a good as it was 40 years ago.

Location: North of Eatonville; map B2, grid c6.

How to get there: Drive south from Puyallup 15 miles on Highway 161 and watch for the lake on your left.

Boat ramp: There's a public access area with boat ramp and rest rooms at the northwest corner of the lake. A $10 WDFW access decal is required to use the public launch area maintained by the Washington Department of Fish and Wildlife.

Facilities: There used to be a private resort at the south end of the lake, but it's no more. The nearest food, gas, and other facilities are a few miles away in Eatonville.

Water sports/restrictions: All water sports are permitted. The lake has a 40 mph speed limit during daylight hours and 5 mph from sunset to sunrise. No

boat longer than 22 feet is allowed on the lake without a permit issued by the Pierce County Sheriff's Department.

Contact: Ohop Valley Grocery, tel. (360) 847-2141.

30 Ohop Lake

Rating: 7

If you're going to do any skiing, boarding, tubing, PWC riding or other fast-water sports here, you'd better have a watch, because if you're timing isn't right, you're out of luck. Ohop has some of the most specific boating regulations of any lake in Washington, and they've been in effect for years. There's an 8 mph speed limit in effect on the lake throughout most of the day, except during the middle of the day, from 11 to 3:30. The county's 40 mph limit kicks in then, giving those with a need for speed a chance to do their thing. Then it's back to slower speeds, and all the bass anglers, paddlers and others who like calm water can go back out to enjoy the peace and quiet. While very specific, the regulations here seem to work, giving everyone an opportunity to enjoy the lake without anyone fouling up anyone else's fun. The regulations are posted at the public access area, so newcomers here can't use ignorance as an excuse.

Location: North of Eatonville; map B2, grid c6.

How to get there: Take Highway 161 south from Puyallup and turn left on Orville Road or take Orville Road south from Kapowsin to reach the lake.

Boat ramp: A large public access area, a boat ramp, and rest rooms are near the south end of the lake. A $10 WDFW access decal is required to use the public launch area maintained by the Washington Department of Fish and Wildlife.

Facilities: The nearest food, gas, and

lodging are available in Eatonville, two miles to the south.

Water sports/restrictions: All water sports are permitted. The lake has an 8 mph speed limit, except from 11 a.m. to 3:30 p.m., when a 40 mph limit is in effect.

Contact: Ohop Valley Grocery, tel. (360) 847-2141.

31 Rapjohn Lake

Rating: 6

If you're looking for a quiet place to get away for an hour's paddle or a little evening bass fishing, this might work very well for you. The lake's small size, only 56 acres, keeps most of the big, fast boats away, and the lake is far enough away from all the major population centers to keep the number of visitors to a minimum. I should note, though, that Pierce County does rate this a Class C lake, which means it's legal to operate a boat at up to 35 miles per hour during daylight hours. That's a heck of a lot faster than I'd want to go here, but I guess I'm never in a big hurry when I'm on the water. It is a popular fishing lake, so spring and early summer are a little busy, but there are lots of other good fishing lakes within a few miles, so the pressure is only moderate. The biggest source of excitement around here in recent years has been the squabble between fall duck hunters and area residents who for some reason prefer waking up to the sound of their alarm clocks rather than the roar of 12-gauges. Unless you visit Rapjohn early on a fall morning, you can avoid that one, too, and usually enjoy a peaceful time on the water.

Location: Northwest of Eatonville; map B2, grid c6.

How to get there: Take Highway 7 south from Spanaway. Exactly two miles south of the Highway 702 (352nd Avenue East) intersection, turn east (left) on the narrow road that leads to the lake.

Boat ramp: There's a Department of Wildlife public access and boat ramp on the west side of the lake. A $10 WDFW access decal is required to use the public launch area maintained by the Washington Department of Fish and Wildlife.

Facilities: The nearest food, gas, lodging, and other amenities are in Eatonville, about six miles to the southeast.

Water sports/restrictions: All water sports are permitted, but there isn't any place here for public swimming. Fishing is the main attraction.

Contact: The Ultimate Fisherman, tel. (253) 845-1202; Tacoma-Pierce County Visitor and Convention Bureau, tel. (800) 272-2662.

32 Silver Lake

Rating: 7

This 138-acre lake in southern Pierce County has about as much to offer water lovers as any body of fresh water in the Puget Sound region. People fish, swim, ski, wake-board, ride PWC, and do about everything else here that you might think of to do on or in the water. With a maximum depth of about 20 feet, it warms quickly in the summer, offering comfortable swimming and splashing throughout the vacation season. Perhaps the only things that keep if from being mobbed from Memorial Day to Labor Day are the fact that it's some distance from all major cities and its proximity to several other lakes that offer their own attraction to swimmers, anglers and boaters.

Location: Northwest of Eatonville; map B2, grid c6.

How to get there: Take Highway 7 south from Spanaway and watch for the Silver Lake Resort sign 3 miles south of the Highway 702 (352nd Avenue East) intersection. Turn west (right) to the lake.

Boat ramp: There's a boat ramp at Henley's Silver Lake Resort. It has a $2 launch fee.

Facilities: Henley's Silver Lake Resort has rental boats, a 250-foot dock that's used mostly for fishing, cabins, tent and RV spaces.

Water sports/restrictions: All water sports are permitted.

Contact: Henley's Silver Lake Resort, tel. (360) 832-3580.

33 Harts Lake

Rating: 7

At 109 acres, this south Pierce County lake is just barely a Class B lake, according to county boating standards, which means that during the day it has a 40 mph speed limit. I can't picture myself—or anyone else, for that matter—going 40 here, but if you like to fast in fairly tight circles, I guess this is a place to do that. Anyway, this is a pretty lake located in one of the few remaining rural areas of the south Puget Sound region, with a little something to offer every kind of water enthusiast. With 50-foot depths in the middle, it's somewhat deeper than most western Washington lakes, so it even offers interesting opportunities for divers. If you do happen to dive here, you may notice that this almost perfectly round lake is as uniform beneath the surface as it is above, with a bottom that drops very uniformly and evenly from the shoreline to the center of the lake. Paddlers who visit Harts Lake might try venturing into Little Harts, which is linked to the southeast side of the big lake by a 500-foot canal.

The smaller lake covers about 10 acres and has a maximum depth of 10 feet.

Location: Southwest of McKenna; map B2, grid c5.

How to get there: Drive east out of McKenna on Highway 702, turn south on Harts Lake Road and follow it about 4 miles to the lake, which is on the right.

Boat ramp: There's a public access area and boat ramp on the lake, managed by the Department of Fish and Wildlife. It's a single-lane gravel ramp with a fairly large gravel parking area and pit toilets. A $10 WDFW access decal is required to use the public launch area maintained by the Washington Department of Fish and Wildlife.

Facilities: There's a resort on the lake with a small swim beach, picnic area, and a small store.

Water sports/restrictions: All water sports are permitted. The lake has a 5 mph speed limit from sunset to sunrise.

Contact: Harts Lake Resort, tel. (360) 458-3477.

34 Offut Lake

Rating: 6

This 192-acre lake between Olympia and Tenino has maintained its rural flavor, thanks in part to the fact that its shoreline is still only lightly developed. Check out the tops of nearby fir trees and you're likely to spot a bald eagle, osprey or red-tailed hawk, and there are lots of waterfowl in the weedy area around the east end of the lake. Fishing is good here, and so is paddling around the edge of the lake looking at the sights and listening to the sounds. Take a fishing rod along if you want; Offut has some big bass and husky rainbow trout. If you quit fishing early, stop by Wolf Haven on your way out. This wildlife park is home to wolves from all over North America, and the small entrance fee is money well spent for what you'll see and learn about these fascinating animals. The road to the resort on the south side of the lake runs right by the entrance to the wolf facility.

Location: Southeast of Tumwater; map B2, grid c3.

How to get there: to reach the public access and boat launch on the north side of the lake, take Pacific Highway SE south from Tumwater and turn left (east) onto Waldrick Road about four miles south of the airport. Watch for the brown Public Access sign about a mile and a half down Waldrick Road and turn right. Continue south past Waldrick Road about a mile and a half and turn left (east) on Offut Lake Road to reach Offut Lake Resort, which is on the south side of the lake.

Boat ramp: Drive south from Olympia on Capitol Boulevard, which becomes Olympia-Tenino Road, and turn east (left) on Waldrick road, following it just over a mile to Walona Street and turning right to the ramp.

Facilities: Offut Lake Resort has a fishing dock, rowboat, paddleboat and outboard rentals, groceries, rental cabins, an RV park and tent sites. Although it doesn't have a roped swim area, visitors do swim from the beach at the resort. Unfortunately, the restaurant that was a Thurston County favorite for many years has closed. The nearest food and gas are in Tenino, with complete facilities in Olympia.

Water sports/restrictions: Paddling and fishing are the main draws here, with some swimming. The standard Thurston County speed limit of 5 miles per hour is in effect here.

Contact: Offut Lake Resort, tel. (360) 264-2438; Olympia/Thurston County Chamber of Commerce, Visitor Information Center, tel. (360) 357-3362.

35 Deep Lake

Rating: 7

A word of advice to divers: Don't grab your tanks and mask to go running off and explore the depths of this misnamed Thurston County lake until you read this entire listing. If you do, you'll probably be disappointed. Truth is, Deep Lake really doesn't have any depths to explore, because it isn't really deep at all. It should be named Moderately Shallow Lake, or if that doesn't seem to roll off you tongue smoothly enough, how about Undeep Lake? Whatever you call it, this lake with a maximum depth of under 20 feet is a handy getaway spot for folks around the Olympia-Lacey-Tumwater area, thanks in great part to the state park land that surrounds its north and west sides. The large, roped swim beach at Millersylvania State Park is a popular play spot all summer, both for folks camping at the park and locals using it for the day. The nearby boat launch won't accommodate large trailer boats, but that's OK since the lake has a 5 mph speed limit anyway. The ramp works fine for small cartoppers, canoes, kayaks and other craft that can be carried a few feet to the water, and it has a large parking area with room for dozens of cars. Most of the lake's shoreline is undeveloped, with lots of aquatic vegetation and wildlife, so it's a great place for an evening paddle. If you visit in the spring, take a fishing rod along, because Deep Lake offers very good trout fishing from the season opener in late April until after Memorial Day.

Location: South of Tumwater; map B2, grid b2.

How to get there: Take Interstate 5 to the 93rd Avenue exit south of Tumwater and drive east on 93rd to Tilley Road. Turn south (right) on Tilley and drive about three miles to the lake, on the right.

Boat ramp: Millersylvania State Park has a boat ramp and short fishing dock, tent and RV spaces and picnic shelters.

Facilities: Millersylvania State Park, on the north side of the lake, has a large swim beach, boat ramp, fishing/moorage float, picnic areas, picnic shelters, tent and RV sites.

Water sports/restrictions: Paddling, swimming and fishing are permitted. The lake has a 5 mph speed limit.

Contact: Millersylvania State Park, tel. (360) 753-1519; Washington State Parks and Recreation Commission, tel. (800) 233-0321 (information), tel. (800) 542-5687 (reservations); Olympia/Thurston County Chamber of Commerce, Visitor Information Center, tel. (360) 357-3362.

36 McIntosh Lake

Rating: 7

There's some development on the north side and west end of the lake, and a state highway along much of its south side, but this 93-acre lake between Tenino and Rainier has managed to maintain its peaceful, rural personality over the years. The Department of Wildlife's boat ramp on the north side offer the only official public access to the lake, but lots of people get to the water along the highway on south side, where several foot paths lead to the water. Some of the locals launch small boats and even swim in these areas, but I would be extremely cautious about going barefoot here; some of the visitors are slobs, and there are too many broken bottles and discarded fish hooks for safe swimming and wading.

Location: Northeast of Tenino; map B2, grid c3.

How to get there: Take Interstate 5 to Grand Mound and exit east onto Pacific Highway SE and follow it about eight miles to Tenino and the junction of Highway 507. Continue east on SR 507 about four miles to Military Road and turn left (north). Follow Military Road about a mile and a half to the boat ramp, on the right. If you continue on SR 507 past Military Road, you'll pass along the south side of the lake.

Boat ramp: There's a public access area with boat ramp and rest rooms on the north side of the lake. A $10 WDFW access decal is required to use the public launch area maintained by the Washington Department of Fish and Wildlife.

Facilities: Food and gas are available nearby in Tenino, and lodging and other amenities are in the Olympia area a few miles to the north.

Water sports/restrictions: There's a 5 mph speed limit on the lake. Fishing and paddling are the main attractions.

Contact: Jayhawks, sporting goods department, tel. (360) 458-5707.

37 Black River

Rating: 7

A few minutes on the Black River and there's a very good chance you'll find yourself singing, "Summertime, and the livin' is easy . . . ." Many people who fish or float the Black say that it looks as though it belongs in the Deep South, not the Pacific Northwest, and it's a valid description. This is one of the slowest, gentlest streams in Washington, with lots of vegetation along and in some places hanging over the water. It's a favorite of people who like fishing or wild flowers in the spring, bird-watching and wildlife viewing in the summer, even duck hunting in the fall. Located along the edge of Capitol State Forest, the river's shoreline is only lightly developed, giving it a very rural—even isolated —personality, even though it flows only

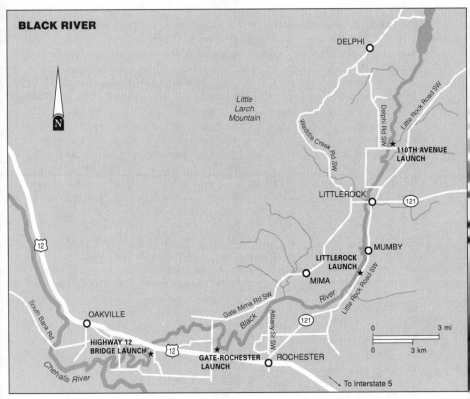

BLACK RIVER

Little Larch Mountain

DELPHI

110TH AVENUE LAUNCH

LITTLEROCK

121

MUMBY

LITTLEROCK LAUNCH

MIMA

OAKVILLE

HIGHWAY 12 BRIDGE LAUNCH

GATE-ROCHESTER LAUNCH

ROCHESTER

To Interstate 5

Black River

0   3 mi
0   3 km

a few minutes from busy Interstate 5 and the Olympia area. A good selection of put-in and take-out spots between its origin at Black Lake and its confluence with the Chehalis River near Oakville offers several trip options, but the river is pretty much the same along its entire distance, very docile and boater friendly. Its overall distance is about 30 miles. I know I'll be sorry for painting such an attractive picture of one of my favorite paddling places and seeing more folks on the river, but this is one of those places that should be shared.

Location: Flows from Black Lake into the Chehalis River near Oakville; map B2, grid c1. (See the Black River inset map.)

How to get there: Take U.S. 12 west of Interstate 5 at Grand Mound and turn north on Highway 121 (Littlerock Road) at Rochester to go upriver or continue west on U.S. 12 through Rochester to where the highway crosses the lower river.

Boat ramp: The Black River has four small, single-lane boat launches, which are listed on the Black River inset map.

- **110th Avenue Launch:** Located about a mile and a half north of Littlerock.

- **Littlerock Launch:** Located two miles south of Littlerock (off Highway 121).

- **Gate-Rochester Launch:** Located two miles west of Rochester (off Moon Road).

- **Highway 12 Bridge Launch:** Located a little over four miles west of Rochester (on the south side of the Highway 12 bridge.)

One of the Littlerock ramps and the one at Rochester are managed by the Washington Department of Fish and Wildlife. A $10 WDFW access decal is required to use the public launch area maintained by the Washington Department of Fish and Wildlife.

Facilities: At least one commercial outfitter, Black River Canoe & Kayaking Trips, runs Black River trips. Food, gas, and lodging are available in and around Rochester.

Water sports/restrictions: Paddling, tubing, and fishing are the attractions here.

Contact: Black River Canoe & Kayaking Trips, tel. (360) 273-6369 (March to October); Pacific Water Sports, tel. (206) 246-9385; Tumwater Sports, tel. (360) 352-5161.

38 Upper Chehalis River

Rating: 7

This big river, which eventually empties into the east end of Grays Harbor near Aberdeen, goes through a lot of changes along its length. If you need proof, just drive up Highway 6 between Adna and Pe Ell, turn north off the highway into Rainbow Falls State Park, and look down at the river as you cross over the bridge leading into the park. Memorize that scene. Then drive back down Highway 6 to Interstate 5, take the Highway 12 exit north of Centralia, and head toward Oakville on Highway 12. Check out the Chehalis near Oakville and you'll probably have trouble believing that it's the same river you saw about an hour earlier. It's big, it's wide, and it's slow, and the whole personality of the stream and its surroundings are different.

All those changes in river mood would be evident from the water as you made your way down the Chehalis, too, but few people get to see it all. Access to this upper portion of the river is quite limited, so relatively few boaters ever spend time on it. There are places to carry or drag a small boat or paddle craft to the river at Pe Ell, Rainbow Falls, and Adna, but from there downstream the river runs almost exclusively through private farmlands where access is a problem unless you happen to know one of the land owners. The next practical put-in/take-out spot is down below Oakville at the Cedarville launch area. If you can get onto the Chehalis, you'll enjoy the rural atmosphere and the easy going nature of the river. You aren't likely to encounter a whole lot of people, but dairy cows are a common sight.

If you want whitewater, the Chehalis has that, too, although most of the world may be unaware of it. In fact, there are couple of canyons upstream from Pe Ell that offer Class III and even Class IV challenges, especially after a couple days of heavy rain brings the flow up. That's the condition that most river runners prefer for making this run. Most notable of the places to get a thrill is shown on most maps as Fisk Falls, a Class V rapids that will test you but not hurt you if you scout it from the rocky ledge on the left side of the river a short distance above the drop.

Location: From Oakville upstream to the forks south of Pe Ell; map B2, grid c1.

How to get there: Take Interstate 5 to Grand Mound, drive west on U.S. 12 and turn south on Albany Street to Independence Road to reach some of the river between Grand Mound and Oakville. Roads of Old Highway 99 between Grand Mound and Chehalis, including Prather Road and Cooks Hill Road, provide some river access. Take Highway 6 west of Interstate 5 at Chehalis to reach over 20 miles of the river from Chehalis upstream to Pe Ell. Upstream (south) from Pe Ell, Weyerhaeuser logging roads roughly parallel the river to the forks and beyond.

Boat ramp: There's a boat ramp off Elma Gate Road at Cedarville, and there are rough drag-in spots or bridge crossings near the confluence of the forks, at Pe Ell, Adna, and Rainbow Falls State Park. A $10 WDFW access decal is required to use the public launch area maintained by the Washington Department of Fish and Wildlife.

Facilities: Rainbow Falls State Park has tent sites and rest rooms. Food, gas, lodging, tackle, and other amenities are available in Centralia and Chehalis.

Water sports/restrictions: Kayaks, rafts, canoes, drift boats, and inner tubes can be used here, but access limits their use.

Contact: Pacific Water Sports, tel. (206) 246-9385; Sunbirds Shopping Center, sporting goods department, tel. (360) 748-3337. Washington State Parks and Recreation Commission, tel. (800) 233-0321 (information), tel. (800) 452-5687 (reservations).

39 Skookumchuck River

Rating: 6

Information on this little river appears in few, if any, paddling publications, probably because it's a hassle to reach and is mainly the stomping grounds of winter steelheaders and summertime trout anglers. It is, however, a scenic and gentle little stream with plenty to offer paddlers in search of a mellow run. Its calm nature also makes this a good spot for tubing, but be on the alert for sweepers and other woody debris that might collect in the river after a heavy rain or windstorm. Skookumchuck Dam, just upstream from the gate that bars public access past the wide turnaround that marks the start of this run, keeps the river flow in check and water levels fairly steady, but you will find tougher going by the end of summer and into early fall. This is a good run in winter, but by February the number of steelhead anglers grows considerably, and the upper part of this run might become a little dangerous due to flying hooks and sinkers.

Location: Flows into the Chehalis River at Centralia; map B2, grid c2.

How to get there: Take Highway 507 north from Centralia or south from Tenino to 184th Avenue SE and turn east. It's a 7.7-mile drive from the highway to Skookumchuck Dam and the end of the road. You'll cross the river twice along the way, once at 2.2 miles and again at 5.7 miles.

Boat ramp: It's possible to drag a kayak or canoe over the bank at the end of the road, and with a little sweat and bushwhacking, you can take out at either of the downstream bridges.

Facilities: Groceries and gas are available in Bucoda and Tenino; all other facilities are in Centralia.

Water sports/restrictions: Paddling, inner tubing, and fishing are the primary activities.

Contact: Sunbirds Shopping Center, sporting goods department, tel. (360) 748-3337.

40 Lawrence Lake

Rating: 7

Very large but not very deep, Lawrence warms quickly in the summer to provide a 300-acre playground for Thurston County swimmers and boaters. It's also a popular fishing lake. Much of the big-boat activity occurs on the main part of

the lake, off to the north and east of the public access area, while paddlers of various kinds might feel a little more comfortable on the somewhat protected smaller section of the lake to the southwest. Wherever you go, though, this is a fun place on a warm summer weekend.
Location: Southeast of Yelm; map B2, grid c5.

How to get there: Take Bald Hills Road southeast off Highway 507 at a place called Five Corners about a mile southeast of Yelm. Follow the road southward until you come to a three-way fork (about a mile after you pass 138th Avenue SE), and go west (right). Drive half a mile to the Lawrence Lake Road and turn south (left). Drive another mile and you'll see the lake on the right.

Boat ramp: There's an access area with boat ramp and rest rooms on the lake, but it's closed annually from the end of October until the middle of April. A $10 WDFW access decal is required to use the public launch area maintained by the Washington Department of Fish and Wildlife.

Facilities: The town of Yelm offers the nearest food, gas, and lodging.

Water sports/restrictions: All water sports are permitted. The lake has a 5 mph speed limit in effect during the first 30 days of the general fishing season, which begins in late April.

Contact: Tumwater Sports, tel. (360) 352-5161.

get out for a closer look at this 170-acre lake in rural eastern Thurston County. Since it's one of the best trout lakes in the region, it's easy to understand the big crowds. Other activities take a distant back seat to fishing, but Clear is worth the trip if you're looking for a calm and quiet place to flex your paddling muscles during the summer or early fall.
Location: West of LaGrande, eastern Thurston County; map A2, grid c5.

How to get there: Turn southeast on Black Hills Road from Highway 507 at Five Corners a mile southeast of Yelm. Follow Black Hills Road just under 10 miles to the south end of the lake, on the left.

Boat ramp: There's a Department of Fish and Wildlife boat ramp on the north side of the lake. It's a two-lane ramp with concrete planks that were in good shape in the spring of 1999. The nearby parking lot has room for perhaps 100 cars with boat trailers. A $10 WDFW access decal is required to use the public launch area maintained by the Washington Department of Fish and Wildlife.

Facilities: Food, gas, and lodging are available in Yelm and Olympia.

Water sports/restrictions: There's a 5 mph speed limit on the lake, so it's best suited to fishing and paddling.

Contact: Washington Department of Fish and Wildlife, Montesano regional office, tel. (360) 249-4628; Olympia/Thurston County Chamber of Commerce Visitor Information Center, tel. (360) 357-3362.

41 Clear Lake

Rating: 6

The biggest day of the year here is the fourth Saturday in April, opening day of the general fishing season. The lake and its access area stay crowded for a few weeks after that, but then things calm down and there's room for nonanglers to

42 Mashel River

Rating: 6

If you're driving south out of Eatonville on Highway 161 and notice the little stream rumbling beneath the bridge just out of town, you probably wouldn't consider it a very interesting boating destination, but explore the Mashel a little further and you might change your mind. During the fall floods and spring runoff periods, and sometimes after a good rain at other times of the year, the Mashel can be an interesting and challenging run. It can, in fact, be downright dangerous, thanks to the fact that any high water might bring new logs, stumps, and trees down the river and deposit them in the most inconvenient places. At several places along the river, steep canyon walls make it tough to avoid the hazards when an entire tree decides to lodge itself in a place where it spans the entire river. Its small size, tight turns, and abundant boulder gardens make the Mashel best suited to smaller, more maneuverable kayaks than any other craft, especially from the Highway 7 bridge upstream.

Location: Joins Nisqually River southwest of Eatonville; map B2, grid c6.

How to get there: Take Highway 161 to Eatonville. Logging roads leading east from town provide access to the upper river. Highway 161 itself parallels part of river to the west of Eatonville.

Boat ramp: There's a rough launching spot at the eastern end of Eatonville from the Center Street bridge, another off the old railroad bridge on the Number 7000 logging road, a third just downstream from the Highway 161 bridge, another at the Highway 7 bridge, and a fifth near the confluence of the Mashel and Nisqually rivers at Mashel Prairie.

Facilities: Food, gas, and lodging are available in and around Eatonville.

Water sports/restrictions: Kayaking is the best option on this small river. It's safe for tubing below the Highway 7 bridge.

Contact: Pacific Water Sports, tel. (206) 246-9385.

43 Alder Lake

Rating: 7

The first word of advice you should have concerning Alder Lake is that it's actually a reservoir created when the upper reaches of the Nisqually were backed up by Alder Dam several decades ago, and its water levels fluctuate dramatically depending how much water is being spilled over the dam. In the winter and early spring the lake is usually quite low in anticipation of spring and early summer runoff that will fill it by the middle of July. If you visit the lake when the water is low, you'll likely find a lot more mud flats and stumps than places to pursue your favorite boating activities. In other words, Alder is a summertime boating place, and from the time school's out through Labor Day weekend it sees quite a lot of recreational activity. It's still a good idea to think about the stumps and other woody debris in the lake, especially if you explore shoreline areas or any of the many shoals along its south side. Old fir and cedar stumps are tough on shear pins, lower units, and other relatively important parts of your boat's motor. They also can be dangerous to your health, so get to know the lake before you go all out, especially when the water is rising during spring and in fall when it begins to drop.

Location: Southeast of LaGrande, southeast corner of Thurston County; map B2, grid c6.

How to get there: Take Highway 7 south from Spanaway or north from Morton. The lake is on the south side of the road.

Boat ramp: Alder Park near the north end of the lake has a two-lane boat ramp. You'll also find a public boat ramp and access area on the northeast side just off the highway, and another off Pleasant Valley Road on the south side. A $10 Washington Department of Fish and

Wildlife access decal is required to use the public launch area maintained by the WDFW.

Facilities: Alder Park has tent and RV spaces, picnic tables, showers and rest rooms, a moorage float, and a small grocery store. The nearest food, gas, lodging, and other facilities are in Eatonville, Elbe and Morton.

Water sports/restrictions: All water sports are permitted. Swimming or boating within 200 feet of any log boom is prohibited.

Contact: Alder Park Store, tel. (360) 569-8824.

44 Mineral Lake

Rating: 8

Long known as one of western Washington's top trout-fishing lakes, Mineral is also a play spot for folks from all over Lewis County. One of the most interesting things about Mineral is that it's managed in a way that keeps conflicts among various recreational user groups to a minimum. Just to be sure that the PWC riders don't bother the anglers and the slow-trollers don't get in the way of the skiers, there's a no-wake speed limit on half the lake, so that anglers can stay on their half of Mineral without having to worry about the wakes of the speed-boaters. The county swim beach, the only one of its kind managed by Lewis County Parks, is an added attraction and hosts some large crowds on summer weekends and holidays.

Location: At the town of Mineral, Lewis County; map B2, grid d7.

How to get there: Take U.S. 12 east from Interstate 5 to Morton and turn north on Highway 7, following it about 13 miles to Mineral Road. From there it's a two-mile drive to the town of Mineral and Mineral Lake.

Boat ramp: A public boat ramp and a resort are on the lake. A $10 WDFW access decal is required to use the public launch area maintained by the Washington Department of Fish and Wildlife.

Facilities: There's a Lewis County park with a swim beach on the west side of the lake. Mineral Lake Resort offers boat rentals, cabins and RV sites (no tent sites), a large fishing dock, tackle and snacks. A small market in town sells groceries.

Water sports/restrictions: All water sports are permitted. There's an 8 mph speed limit on roughly half the lake, but the other half is open to skiing and other speed sports.

Contact: Mineral Lake Resort, tel. (360) 492-5367 (April through September).

45 Newaukum River

Rating: 4

Say its name around river runners and most will respond, "The New-what?" Due to its size, location, and somewhat limited access, it's no wonder this small stream south of Chehalis doesn't have much of a reputation among boaters. It probably should be called Newaukum Creek rather than the Newaukum River, but I didn't get to vote on that one. It almost dries up by the time the fall rains come, but in spring and early summer it offers Class I and Class II water that can offer a fun ride that will get you damp if you aren't careful. Still not sure? The next time you drive down Interstate 5 on your way to Portland or points south, slow down a little in the right lane as you cross the first bridge after leaving Chehalis. That's the Newaukum, and what you see from the freeway is a good example of what you'll get if you decide to float this little Chehalis River tributary.

Location: Joins the Chehalis River northwest of Chehalis; map B2, grid d3.

How to get there: Take Centralia-Alpha Road southeast from Centralia and turn on North Fork Road (left to go upstream on the North Fork Newaukum, right to go downstream). To reach the South Fork Newaukum, take Interstate 5 south from Chehalis and turn east on Highway 508, which parallels much of the river. To reach the lower Newaukum, turn south off Interstate 5 on Rush Road, then west on Newaukum Valley Road.

Boat ramp: There are no formal boat ramps on the river, but several spots along North Fork Road and Newaukum Valley Road offer the possibility of dragging or carrying a small boat to the water.

Facilities: Food, gas, and lodging are available in Centralia and Chehalis.

Water sports/restrictions: Paddling and tubing are possibilities.

Contact: Sunbirds Shopping Center, sporting goods department, tel. (360) 748-3337.

46 Tilton River

Rating: 7

Once known for its trophy winter steelhead, the Tilton now is best known for summertime trout fishing and paddling, with local kids doing their share of tubing and swimming from Morton downstream. This mostly Class II river gets a little wild and woolly about four miles west of Morton where the North Fork Tilton meets the main river, doubling its size and adding some exciting waves right at the confluence. Once you pass this short Class III stretch, things calm down again and stay fairly gentle all the way to what is now the mouth of the river at Mayfield Lake.

Location: Flows into the north arm of Mayfield Lake; map B2, grid e5.

How to get there: Take U.S. 12 to Morton, turn north on Highway 7 and west on Highway 508 to follow the river downstream.

Boat ramp: It's easy to launch a kayak or small raft at the city park off Main Street in Morton. The Highway 508 bridge at the little nontown of Bremer can be a take-out spot on that run or a launch site for a float downstream into Mayfield Lake, where you can take out at Ike Kinswa State Park.

Facilities: Ike Kinswa State Park is located where the Tilton flows into Mayfield Lake and has both tent and RV sites, rest rooms with showers, and other amenities. Food, gas, lodging, and tackle are available in Morton.

Water sports/restrictions: Kayaking, canoeing, tubing, swimming, and fishing are the main draws.

Contact: Ike Kinswa State Park, tel. (360) 983-3402; Washington State Parks and Recreation Commission, tel. (800) 233-0321 (information), tel. (800) 452-5687 (reservations).

47 Mayfield Lake

Rating: 8

This 13-mile-long reservoir, an impoundment behind Mayfield Dam on the Cowlitz River, has something for every water enthusiast within the boundaries of its 33-mile shoreline. It's a little slow to warm in the summer, thanks to the fact that the water entering its upper end comes out the bottom of Mossyrock Dam, where it emerges from the chilly depths of Riffe Lake. But once it does warm, usually by the middle of June, it quickly becomes one of Lewis County's most popular play spots. With several good swim beaches, it's as popular with young families as it is with daredevil

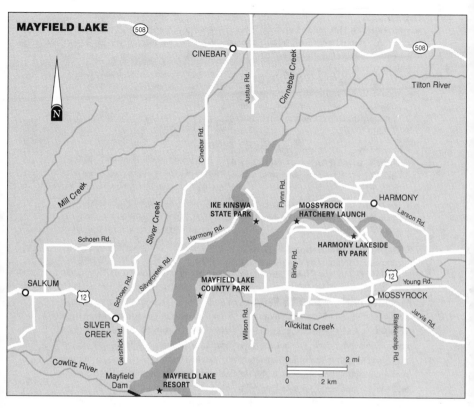

MAYFIELD LAKE

wakeboarders or hotdog skiers who scatter all over the lake's vast surface during the warmer months. Anglers also like it here, thanks in part to the fact that Mayfield is one of few places in the Northwest where they can catch trophy-size tiger muskies, which may grow to four feet in length. If you're a spooky swimmer, you may not want to hear this, but I caught my first tiger muskie from the weeds at the north end of the Mayfield Lake County Park swim area, where it no doubt had spent the day lying in wait for an unsuspecting youngster to venture into striking range. Or maybe not. Anyway, whether you visit Mayfield for an afternoon swim at the county park or spend your entire vacation at the state park on the north side or the resort

near the east end, Mayfield is a place where you can find something new to do on, in, under, or around the water the whole time you're there.

Location: West of Mossyrock, Lewis County; map B2, grid e5. (See the Mayfield Lake inset map.)

How to get there: Take U.S. 12 east from Interstate 5 about 17 miles to the lake. Turn north (left) at Silver Creek to reach Ike Kinswa State Park on the north side of the lake, or cross over the lake on U.S. 12 and go just over a mile to Mayfield Lake County Park on the left.

Boat ramp: The following boat ramps are listed on the Mayfield Lake inset map.

• **Ike Kinswa State Park:** The state park has a hard-surfaced boat ramp.

- **Mossyrock Hatchery Launch:** This rough Department of Fish and Wildlife launch is located at the upper end of the lake, near the Mossyrock Hatchery. A $10 WDFW access decal is required to use the public launch area maintained by the Washington Department of Fish and Wildlife.

- **Harmony Lakeside RV Park:** There's a third ramp at Harmony Lakeside RV Park near the upper end of the lake.

- **Mayfield Lake County Park:** This is an excellent ramp with a moorage float.

- **Mayfield Lake Resort:** This boat ramp is located on the Winston Creek Arm on the lake's south shore near the dam.

Facilities: Ike Kinswa State Park has about 100 tent and RV sites, 40 of them with water and electricity, rest rooms, and a nice swim beach. The county park offers 54 campsites (no utility hookups), rest rooms with showers, picnic shelter and tables, uncovered picnic tables, a large roped swim beach, and playground toys. Snacks and beverages are available at the small store next to the turnoff to the county park, with everything else available in Mossyrock four miles east. Near the east end of the lake on the south side, Harmony Lakeside RV Park has camping facilities, a swim area (that's over a rather steep bank), picnic tables, and boat rentals. Mayfield Lake Resort, on the Winston Creek Arm near the south end of the lake, has trailer hookups, rest rooms, showers, and other camping amenities.

Water sports/restrictions: All water sports are permitted.

Contact: Ike Kinswa State Park, tel. (360) 983-3402; Washington State Parks and Recreation Commission, tel. (800) 233-0321 (information), tel. (800) 452-5687 (reservations); Harmony Lakeside RV Park, tel. (360) 985-2357; Mayfield Lake County Park, tel. (360) 985-2364; (May through September only); Mayfield Lake Resort, tel. (360) 985-2003.

48 Riffe Lake

Rating: 7

Like Mayfield Lake immediately downstream, Riffe is here because the Cowlitz River was dammed by Tacoma Power some 40 years ago. The resulting reservoir is some 16 miles long and offers about 12,000 surface acres for swimming, cruising, sailing, skiing, paddling, fishing, and just about anything else you may want to do on the water. The lake is deep and a little cold, but that doesn't seem to bother the folks who come here to have a good time and get away from the everyday routine. Riffe Lake has a sort of anything-goes feeling to it, and folks here sometimes forget or ignore county safe-boating regulations that include no-wake rules within 200 feet of any shore, dock, or public swimming area. Everywhere you go there are people pushing the envelope, but Riffe seems to have more envelope-pushers than other places, maybe because it's located out in the wilds of eastern Lewis County, where lots of folks will tell you they aren't particularly interested in rules and regulations.

Whether you launch at the east end of the lake or the west end, try to plan enough time during your visit to go all the way uplake or down. There aren't many places in western Washington where you can travel some 16 miles on one body of fresh water and see so little human development along the shore. It gives you the feeling that there still are wide-open spaces in the Evergreen State. Chances are the only other people you'll see are other boaters. Be careful, though of floating debris, which is fairly common on the lake's surface. Be aware also of changing weather if you decide to travel the full length of the lake. The wind can kick up in a hurry here, and you probably know how nasty it can get when the wind gets funneled between steep hills and has 16 miles of open water to gain momentum.

Swimming occurs at many locations around the lake's steep shoreline, but for my money the best swimming is at the two Tacoma Power parks, Mossyrock and Taidnapam, located at opposite ends of the long lake. To swim at either place, you'll have to pay a $3 day-use fee or be a registered camper in the parks' excellent campgrounds.

Location: East of Mossyrock, Lewis County; map B2, grid e6.

How to get there: Take U.S. 12 east from Interstate 5 about 23 miles to Mossyrock, turn south (right) into town, and go east (left) on Aljune Road, which leads to Tacoma Public Utilities' Mossyrock Park campground and boat ramps near the dam. To reach the upper lake, continue on U.S. 12 about five miles past Morton and turn south (right) on Kosmos Road. Bear right to reach the northeast corner of the lake or turn left and drive about four miles on Champion Haul Road to the entrance of the Tacoma Public Utilities' Taidnapam Park near where the Cowlitz River enters the lake. Several primitive camping spots along the lake's south shoreline also are popular with boaters who don't mind roughing it a little.

Boat ramp: There are boat ramps at Mossyrock Park, Taidnapam Park, and the Kosmos access area near the northeast corner of the lake. A $10 WDFW access decal is required to use the public launch area maintained by the Washington Department of Fish and Wildlife.

Facilities: Mossyrock Park at the lower end of the lake has RV hookups, tent sites, boat ramps, and rest rooms with showers, as does Taidnapam Park at the upper end. Both parks have a day-use fee of $3 per person. Groceries, restaurants, gas, and lodging are available in Mossyrock and Morton.

Water sports/restrictions: All water sports are permitted.

Contact: Mossyrock Park, tel. (360) 983-3900; Taidnapam Park, tel. (360) 497-7707.

49 Lake Scanewa

Rating: 6

The uppermost and youngest of the Cowlitz River reservoirs, this one filled in 1994 with the completion of Cowlitz Falls Dam. Its young age and relatively secluded location make Scanewa (pronounced Scan-EE-wah), one of Washington's least-used boating destinations, at least for now. But that's likely to change when word gets out about how pretty it is up in this eastern corner of Lewis County and how good the trout fishing can be here throughout the summer and early fall. Because the word hasn't gotten out yet, this is still a good place to paddle in relative solitude without much worry about bigger, badder boats coming by too close and turning your flat-water trip into something else. There's a good swim beach at the park, but the chilly waters of the Cowlitz River don't warm very quickly up here in the higher country, and I don't think I'd try getting wet here until at least the middle of July or maybe the first of August. Kids, however, who don't seem to have nearly as many nerve endings in their bodies, might like it just fine a lot earlier.

Location: Southeast of Glenoma, Lewis County; map B2, grid e7.

How to get there: Drive east from

Interstate 5 on U.S. 12 and turn south at mile marker 111 on Savio Road. Turn south again on Kiona Road, which eventually becomes Peters Road, and follow it to the campground and the reservoir, on the right.

Boat ramp: The campground/park has a boat ramp.

Facilities: Lewis County Public Utility District operates a campground and a day-use park on the reservoir. The campground, which is closed in winter, offers tent and RV sites, rest rooms, and showers. Food, gas, and lodging are available in Randle.

Water sports/restrictions: All water sports are permitted.

Contact: The Lake Scanewa concessionaire, tel. (360) 497-7175; Lewis County PUD, tel. (360) 497-5351.

50 Cispus River

Rating: 6

If you like the idea of running a medium-small river with lots of Class II and Class III rapids and boulder drops, plenty of forest scenery, and relatively little chance of encountering other boaters along the way, the Cispus should be added to your boating to-do list. You'll have to do some driving to get there unless you happen to be heading up Highway 12 toward White Pass with your kayak on top anyway, but the trip is worth the effort, because this is a fun river to run.

There aren't many places to get bored as you wind your way through continuously interesting water. In fact, it might get downright scary if you visit right after a new stump, log, or entire tree gets deposited in or across the river, which happens here from time to time. The ringside view of Tower Rock is enough to make the run worthwhile if you choose the stretch of river from the Forest Service Road 28 bridge down to the river mouth on Lake Scanewa. If you put in upstream and float down to the Road 28 bridge, you may not have time for scenery because the Cispus gets right up and scoots through much of this stretch. A terrific spring/early summer float when river flows are high, the Cispus is also worthwhile later in the year, although you may have to get out and drag now and then as the flow edges down toward 1,000 cfs, which it will in a normal water year.

Location: Enters Lake Scanewa south of Randle, Lewis County; map B2, grid e8.

How to get there: Take U.S. 12 east from Morton to Randle and turn south (right) on Highway 131. Drive one mile and turn east (left) on Cispus Road/Forest Service Road 23; follow it about 10 miles to Forest Service Road 28. Turn south (right) on 28 and drive a quarter mile to the bridge over the Cispus.

Boat ramp: You can launch a kayak near the Forest Service Road 28 bridge for a run on the lower 16 miles of the Cispus, and this spot also serves as a take-out point for boaters running upper portions of the river. Tower Rock and Iron Creek campgrounds, between the Road 28 bridge and the confluence of the Cispus and Cowlitz, also are good put-in/take-out spots. Just upstream of the mouth of the Cispus on the south side of Lake Scanewa, there's a good take-out place off Forest Service Road 25.

Facilities: Both Tower Rock and Iron Creek campgrounds have tent and RV sites (with a camping fee), rest rooms, picnic areas, and drinking water. At least one paddling company, Alpine Adventures, offers guided trips on the Cispus.

Water sports/restrictions: Kayaking, rafting, and fishing are options here.

Contact: Pacific Water Sports, tel. (206)

246-9385; Alpine Adventures, tel. (800) 926-7238; Gifford-Pinchot National Forest, Randle Ranger Station, tel. (360) 497-1100.

51 Cowlitz River

Rating: 7

If it weren't for the fact that about 90% of the boating activity here has something to do with fishing for salmon and steelhead, I wouldn't even attempt to address the water sports activities on this big river in one listing in one boating book. But since most people *do* come here to fish and since I tell about the river's three big reservoirs in their own listings, I think I can tell what you need to know about the Cowlitz without devoting an entire book to the river. In fact, the fishing has gotten so poor here in recent years that maybe I could include the angling opportunities and still do it in a few paragraphs.

First you should understand that this is one of western Washington's most impressive rivers in terms of size. The Clear Fork of the Cowlitz has its beginning near the Pacific Crest Trail in the Goat Rocks Wilderness and flows nearly 20 miles before meeting first the Ohanapecosh and then the Muddy Fork of the Cowlitz, both of which originate along the southeastern flank of Mount Rainier. The river already is a large one by the time it makes its way out of the mountains and reaches the small town of Packwood. And from there it continues to grow, picking up additional water from the Cispus, the Tilton, the Toutle, and the Coweeman Rivers, along with dozens of smaller streams, before it finally joins the Columbia just south of Longview and Kelso. Only the Snake and the Willamette are larger than the Cowlitz among Columbia River tributaries. The lower river, down around Longview and Kelso, is big water where if you know what you're doing, you can use a big prop-driven boat without any

FISHING ON THE COWLITZ RIVER

problems. Folks who don't know what they're doing, of course, shouldn't be taking their boats out of the front yard, but that's another story.

Anyway, the Toutle River joins the Cowlitz a short distance upstream from the town of Castle Rock, and by that point the Cowlitz becomes the realm of the jet-powered river boat, most of these jet sleds operated by salmon and steelhead anglers. Although few paddlers use it, this stretch of the Cowlitz is surprisingly swift and provides a great ride for rafters, canoeists, and kayakers. It gets even better farther upstream past the boat ramp at Interstate 5 and on up to Massey Bar, where there's another popular ramp that's used mostly by anglers.

Even more heavily fished is the stretch above Massey Bar, which includes the famous fishing waters around the Cowlitz Trout Hatchery and farther upriver to the Cowlitz Salmon Hatchery. There are boat ramps at both locations, and the entire stretch offers interesting but relatively safe paddling water. Again, fishing is numero uno here, so expect company in the form of jet boats and some McKenzie-style drift boats. When the fishing is good, you'll notice a dramatic increase in boat traffic, and early morning paddling might not be a good idea during those times. You could get run over.

The upper reaches of the Cowlitz above new (1994) Cowlitz Falls Dam and Lake Scanewa receives considerably less fishing pressure and runs through rural, forested, even mountainous scenery that helps to make it a great paddling destination. Access is a bit of a problem, though, and the fact that this part of the river is well up Highway 12 toward White Pass makes it a considerable trip for most Washingtonians. The solitude and a chance to get away from other people are part of the attraction for many, so the upper Cowlitz might just be what you semi-hermit types are looking for.

Although swimming and snorkeling are definite possibilities along the entire river, keep in mind that the current of this big river is almost always stronger than it looks, certainly strong enough to get you in trouble in a hurry. Don't treat it like a big lake and you'll probably be just fine, but remember that it's bigger and stronger than you are, and it can also be faster.

Location: Flows into the Columbia River near Kelso; map B2, grid f2.

How to get there: Interstate 5 parallels the east side of the river from Kelso upstream to Toledo. The most popular stretch of river, however, is upstream between Toledo and state salmon hatchery. To reach this area, take U.S. 12 east from Interstate 5, turning south (right) on Tucker Road, left at the Y onto Classe Road, left on Spencer Road, and right onto the road leading past the state trout hatchery and to the river. To reach the salmon hatchery farther upstream, continue about four miles farther on U.S. 12 to Salkum and turn right at the Salmon Hatchery sign.

Boat ramp: There are boat ramps at the trout and salmon hatcheries. A $10 WDFW access decal is required to use the public launch area maintained by the Washington Department of Fish and Wildlife.

Facilities: Barrier Dam Campground, a short distance north of the salmon hatchery on the lower river, has RV spaces. Grocery stores and gas stations are located nearby, most of them along Highway 12. Visitors to the upper river will find limited food, gas, and lodging in Packwood and Randle. On the lower Cowlitz, all amenities are available in Castle Rock, Longview, and Kelso.

Water sports/restrictions: Salmon and steelhead fishing, cruising, paddling, and swimming are the main attractions, depending on what part of the river you're using.

Contact: Pacific Water Sports, tel. (206) 246-9385; Barrier Dam Campground, tel. (360) 985-2495.

52 Green River

Rating: 6

Perhaps the best thing about the Green as far as river runners and anglers are concerned is that it escaped damage during the spectacular and devastating eruption of nearby Mount St. Helens. While the North Fork Toutle, into which the Green runs, suffered serious long-term damage from the volcanic blast, the Green was at the outer edge of the blast zone and came through the whole thing looking almost exactly as it did prior to the May 1980 eruption. So if you ever visited the Green on a summer steelhead fishing trip or a weekend paddle 20 years ago, you'll still recognize it today, except that some of the landscape has been changed by the logging that goes on constantly in this part of the state.

Boaters and steelhead anglers face similar challenges on the Green, in that they both have to battle the rocky river constantly if they hope to be successful. At times it seems that the Green is one big rock garden, with only the number and placement of the boulders distinguishing one section of river from those immediately above and immediately below. The most notable exception is the stretch of canyon about halfway through the lower 12 miles of river, where there are a couple of serious ledges churning up Class III+ waves during moderate to high flows. The rest of this run you simply have to stay on your toes and keep paddling almost constantly to avoid banging from boulder to boulder to boulder to . . . .

Location: Joins the Toutle River near Kid Valley; map B2, grid f4.

How to get there: Turn east off Interstate 5 at Castle Rock onto Highway 504 and drive 26 miles to 19-Mile Camp. Turn north (left) onto Weyerhaeuser's 1000 Road and follow it east to 2500 Road, which parallels much of the upper Green.

Boat ramp: There are several places to launch a kayak, including the second bridge as you drive up the river. A takeout site near the gauging station on the lower end of the Green is the logical choice.

Facilities: The small town of Toutle has limited amenities, but Castle Rock has a complete line of restaurants, motels, stores, gas stations, and other facilities for boaters.

Water sports/restrictions: Kayaking and fishing are the main draws.

Contact: Pacific Water Sports, tel. (206) 246-9385.

53 Toutle River

Rating: 7

Unlike its tributary, the Green River, the Toutle was badly mauled by the 1980 eruption of Mount St. Helens. You may recall that famous TV footage showing a wall of mud surging down a river bed, mowing down ash-laden fir and cedar trees as it went. Well, that was the Toutle, and it never looked the same after the eruption as it looked before. The North Fork Toutle and the main stem were especially hard hit, but the South Fork suffered damage as well.

While the eruption's effects on fish and wildlife have been well-documented, less is said and written about what the changes in the river meant to boaters. The bottom line is that the eruption made the Toutle somewhat more difficult to run. Once a stable river running through a rock and gravel river bed, it now runs through a bed of fine volcanic ash, and that ash is constantly being washed out and re-deposited somewhere else, causing constant change in the river itself. Visit the Toutle during or right after a hard rain and you'll quickly see that the shoreline mud never settles or goes away, it just moves. Even though the river has had some 20 years to cleanse itself, it will take many more decades to get the job done.

Luckily, some parts of the river were relatively unchanged by the volcano, most notably the famous Hollywood Gorge stretch above the Tower Bridge. The rocky canyon walls and large holes continue to thrill boaters just as they did 20 years ago, only now there are more folks running it than there were before the eruption. Above and below Hollywood most of the river is fairly easy Class II water, and the most interesting part of the run is gazing in awe at the riverscape and witnessing the evidence of what happened on that spring morning back in 1980. It can give you a healthy respect for Mother Nature's brute strength.

Location: Flows into the Cowlitz River north of Castle Rock; map B2, grid f4.

How to get there: Turn east off Interstate 5 onto Highway 504, which parallels much of the North Fork Toutle. Turn north (left) on Tower Road while driving up Highway 504, and it's a two-mile drive to the Tower Bridge. Weyerhaeuser's 4100 Road from the town of Toutle parallels the South Fork.

Boat ramp: You can launch just below the Tower Bridge to run the lower main Toutle or use the site as a take-out point for a run that will take you through Hollywood Gorge.

Facilities: Seaquest State Park, located right on Highway 504 near Silver Lake, has a limited number of tent and RV sites, rest rooms with showers, and an RV sewage dump. There are also two private resorts on Silver Lake right alongside the highway. Other than those facilities, the nearest food, gas, and lodging are in Castle Rock.

Water sports/restrictions: Kayaking, rafting and fishing are the main activities.

Contact: Seaquest State Park, tel. (360) 274-8633; Washington State Parks and Recreation Commission, tel. (800) 233-0321 (information), tel. (800) 452-5687 (reservations); Pacific Water Sports, tel. (206) 246-9385.

54 Silver Lake

Rating: 8

Perhaps best known for its largemouth bass fishing, this big, shallow lake is also a great place for nonanglers to go and do their thing. When I say big, I'm not kidding. At last report it covered something like 3,000 acres, which would be considered a sea in several small countries. And I know that a 3,000-acre lake is big enough to get lost on, because I've done it. More accurately, I could say that my friend Jeff Boyer got lost, and I just happened to be with him; yeah, I like the sound of that a lot better.

We were bass fishing the big lake on a cold November day, and a thick fog set in at dusk, while we fished the south side of the lake. One minute we could see across the lake, we turned our backs on open water to make a few more casts, and when we turned back everything looked the same—gray. Darkness rolled in quickly, and just like that we were somewhere on the lake and couldn't see anyone or anything else. Since it was so late in the season, there was no activity on or near the water, so it did no good to listen for something that might lead us in the right direction. Rather than heading across the lake in what we *thought* might be the right direction, Jeff decided that we would follow the shoreline in a direction that would eventually get us back to the boat ramp. After maybe 15 minutes that seemed like two hours, we spotted a light, and sure enough, we were back to where we had launched early that morning. It was a little spooky, but I learned a couple of valuable lessons. I learned that it's not a good idea to fish with Jeff Boyer in November, because he wants to fish until it's dark, and I learned to pack extra food when I go fishing, just in case I get stuck on the water longer than I planned.

Anyway, Silver Lake has lots of weedy, brushy shoreline that's perfect for bass fishing and just about as good for wildlife watching from a kayak or canoe. It also has a lot of wide-open water where there's room for the faster set to ski, slide, skip, skitter, and splash their way along the water's surface. You powerboaters need to be aware of the many potential prop wallopers that lie beneath the lake's surface. It has its share of submerged reefs, boulders, stumps, logs, and other little goodies that will ruin your day should you find them the hard way. Most are near the shore or around the three big islands, but there are others that are less obvious and in less convenient places. Ask around, or better yet, travel at no-wake speed on parts of the lake where you're not sure about the potential dangers.

This 3,000-acre lake is only a few feet deep, and it got even shallower during the summer of 1999 when the old dam that for decades has stabilized the water level began to fall apart. By late summer, boating activity had come to a virtual halt. Things were expected to be well back to normal by the spring of 2000 with the completion of repairs to the dam, but it might be a good idea to call ahead before towing your boat any distance to this big lake.

Location: East of Castle Rock; map B2, grid f3.

How to get there: Take Highway 504 east off Interstate 5 at Castle Rock and drive five miles to the lake on the right (south) side of the highway.

Boat ramp: A Department of Fish and Wildlife boat ramp on the lake is a new, paved one that's a heck of a lot better than the rundown mess that people were using until recently. A $10 WDFW access decal is required to use the public launch area maintained by the Washington Department of Fish and Wildlife. Other ramps are at Streeter's Resort ($2.50 launch fee) and at Silver Lake Resort ($4 launch fee for nonresort guests, $2 for those staying at the resort). All three launches have loading floats.

Facilities: There are three private resorts on or near the lake, two of them just off Highway 504. Streeter's Resort has RV sites, rest rooms with showers, boat rentals, a café, and store. Silver Lake Resort has moorage, boat rentals, a store, rental cabins, picnic area, play equipment, RV sites, and rest rooms with showers. There's also a state park with limited tent and RV spaces right across the highway.

Water sports/restrictions: All water sports are permitted.

Contact: Silver Lake Resort, tel. (360) 274-6141; Streeter's Resort, tel. (360) 274-6112; Seaquest State Park, tel. (360) 274-8633; Washington State Parks and Recreation Commission, tel. (800) 233-

0321 (information), tel. (800) 452-5687 (reservations); Cowlitz County Parks and Recreation Department, tel. (360) 577-3030.

55 Coldwater Lake

Rating: 7

The most fascinating reason to visit this lake near the northwest side of Mount St. Helens is that it didn't exist before the mountain's violent eruption on May 18, 1980, when millions of tons of mud and debris created a natural dam that blocked the flow of Coldwater Creek and created the 700-acre lake. It gives me sort of a spooky feeling when I look up from the water in any direction and see signs of the detestation, but it's also uplifting, as I see plants and trees and wildlife of all kinds once again flourishing. I usually visit the lake to try my hand at catching its large rainbow and cutthroat trout, but it's worth the trip just to paddle uplake from the boat ramp and take in the sights. The whole thing can make you feel insignificant, and you probably won't get away without thinking what it might have been like to be there on that fateful morning when the top of the mountain came off and buried the landscape you're in. The clear, ice blue water of the lake helps intensify the mood, because it allows you to look down into the water at the skeletons of fir and hemlock trees that were snapped like matchsticks or blown out of the ground by the blast.

The downside of paddling Coldwater Lake is that the mountain winds can come barreling down on you in a hurry. Keep an eye on changing weather. Also be warned that you can't just climb out of the boat any old place and tromp around to check things out. Foot traffic is limited only to the trail, and you can be fined for wandering even a few steps from it. Leave enough time at the end of your day on the lake to visit the Coldwater Ridge Visitor Center, which is at the edge of the hill overlooking the lake. And be sure to keep your eye out for the area's many elk herds as you drive along Spirit Lake Highway.

Location: Northwest of Mount St. Helens; map B2, grid f6.

How to get there: Take Interstate 5 to the town of Castle Rock and turn east on Highway 504, following it about 45 miles to the Coldwater Ridge Visitor Center and down the hill to the lake.

Boat ramp: Boat ramp and rest rooms are located at the southeast end of the lake.

Facilities: The nearest stores several miles west on Highway 504.

Water sports/restrictions: Paddling and fishing are the main activities here. Gas-powered motors aren't allowed on the lake, but electric trolling motors are. The U.S. Forest Service charges a $3 per day access fee here.

Contact: Mount St. Helens National Volcanic Monument Headquarters, U.S. Forest Service, tel. (360) 274-2131.

56 Coweeman River

Rating: 5

Limited access along the lower few miles of this Cowlitz river tributary keeps many people from discovering what it has to offer. They pass by on Interstate 5, prowl around the lower river for a while, find mostly private property and high-bank river frontage, and give up. But if you take the time to drive east several miles on Rose Valley Road, you'll find that the little Coweeman has something to offer. It's not a thrilling river, but it does have some skinny spots that will make you work a little, and it's a pleasant place to spend a day. If you run it during the winter, you'll probably meet a number of local steelhead anglers, most of whom are bank fishing along the side of the road. They aren't very used to seeing boats on the river, so excuse their wary looks in your direction. Be cordial and give them room to do their thing.

Location: Enters Cowlitz River south of Kelso; map B2, grid g3.

How to get there: Take Rose Valley Road off Interstate 5 about four miles south of Kelso and follow it northeast to the river.

Boat ramp: There are no developed boat ramps on the river, but turnouts along Rose Valley Road provide places to drop a small boat into the river in several places along its length.

Facilities: Food, gas, lodging, tackle, and other amenities are available in Longview and Kelso.

Water sports/restrictions: Kayaking, drift boating, and fishing are the main activities.

Contact: Bob's Merchandise, tel. (360) 425-3870.

57 Kalama River

Rating: 8

As one who has done both, I can tell you that there are very easy ways to boat the Kalama, and there are some very difficult ways; it all depends on what kind of boat you're using and what part of the river you want to explore.

The hardest I ever worked to get a boat in the river was an April morning when two friends and I decided to fish the stretch of canyon between the river's two fish hatcheries. Our boat was an 18-foot fiberglass drift boat that weighed a few hundred pounds as we slid it off its trailer, but it gained weight in a hurry once we tipped it off the shoulder of the road and started down to the river 150 feet below. With all three of us digging in our heels and hanging on for dear life, the slick-bottomed boat did a virtual free-fall, stern-first, toward the river, bouncing off trees and leaving piles of its finish on rocks along the way. One by one, we lost our grip on the rope to the boat's bow ring, and with fishing tackle bouncing out of it, the boat made the final 30 feet of the trip on its own. The steep bank flattened out a little at the edge of the river, so the boat hit the water at a 45-degree angle, still traveling fast. Launching itself with a huge splash, it continued halfway across the Kalama before one of us caught up with the rope and applied the brakes. Kayakers and rafters still use the steep slide at the guardrail gap where my friends and I almost gave our lives several years ago, but I sure wouldn't recommend it for drift boats.

We usually choose the river's more civilized launch sites, and thanks at least in part to the Kalama's popularity among salmon and steelhead anglers, it has several of them along its lower reaches. Most of the rough launches farther upstream are limited in their usefulness for launching bigger craft but get quite a lot of use from paddlers. Those upper reaches of the Kalama above the second fish hatchery include enticing stretches of Class III water and a couple of hot Class IV rapids. What's that? Falls and Leader Rapids. This upper part of the river gets pretty skinny during the summer, so most paddlers prefer to run it during the rainy season from late fall to spring.

The lower Kalama, below the lower fish hatchery, is gentle, user-friendly water that can be floated in most any river craft and is sometimes used by local kids for summertime tubing, swimming, and general cooling-off, much to the chagrin of some steelhead anglers. Serious fishermen usually are off the water during the summer months long before the boaters and tubers show up, because they know the spooky summer steelhead don't bite well when the sun is on the water. If you do encounter anglers along any of the river, though, be sure to give them plenty of room and stay off the water they're trying to fish.

Location: Joins Kalama River north of Kalama; map B2, grid h3.

How to get there: Take Interstate 5 to the Kalama River Road, about two and a half miles north of Kalama, and follow it east, up the north side of the river.

Boat ramp: There are seven developed boat ramps on the Kalama, as well as several other commonly used rough launches where boats of various kinds may be launched, depending on how hard you want to work at it. A $10 WDFW access decal is required to use the public launch area maintained by the Washington Department of Fish and Wildlife.

Facilities: Tackle, snacks, and lots of fishing talk are available at Pritchard's Western Angler on the Kalama River Road; other facilities are in Kalama and Kelso.

Water sports/restrictions: Kayaking, canoeing, rafting, drift boating, tubing, and fishing are popular upstream from Interstate 5; powerboating occurs between Interstate 5 and the mouth of the Kalama.

Contact: Pacific Water Sports, tel. (206) 246-9385; Pritchard's Western Angler, tel. (360) 673-4690.

58 Lower Columbia River

Rating: 8

If you're looking for a spot to do some boating in the wide-open spaces, have I got a place for you. The lower Columbia is BIG water with a range of personalities that runs the gamut from estuary near Cathlamet to the churning whitewater below Bonneville Dam during the high water of spring runoff. There are places on this part of the Columbia where you can go from 80 feet of water to aground on a sand bar quicker that I can describe it here. Some parts of the river along this stretch are nearly two miles wide, while in several places it narrows to a few hundred feet.

Lowland fields and flood plain border it in some places, rock walls rise straight from the edge of the river to the heavens in others. And as if hundreds of miles of riverbank along its northern and southern shores weren't enough for boaters to explore, islands of all sizes scattered here and there add hundreds more to the mix.

This is a fascinating waterway that offers limitless opportunities for boating and water sports of all kinds. I happen to like the lower end of this big river best, probably because all my life I've lived for each new flood tide, eagerly waiting to see if a new run of salmon, steelhead, or sea-run trout comes in with the rising water. The river down around Cathlamet is influenced by the rising and falling tide, so it's a waterway that's constantly changing, always giving boaters something new and different to look at. A powerboater could spend hours exploring just the 12-mile shoreline of Puget Island, a tour that would probably keep a paddler busy all day. If you want to stay closer to the mainland side of the river, take some time to moor in Cathlamet to check out the Wahkiakum County Historical Museum, or if it's a warm day, motor up to County Line Park for a swim or a picnic in the shade.

If you continue upstream past where Highway 4 parts company with the north shore of the river at the little town of Stella, you'll find lightly developed river frontage for the next several miles along the Washington side. After you boat past the industrialized waterfront along the southwest side of Longview, you have the option of turning north into the mouth of the Cowlitz River, which you can follow upstream for some distance if you want. Or you can continue a little farther upstream and take the five-mile detour around Cottonwood Island through Carrolls Channel. The sandy beach at the southwest corner of Cottonwood Island is a popular spot with boaters, some of whom stop to play in the warm shallow water and catch a few rays for the afternoon, others who call it a weekend destination and pitch their tents near the edge of the water.

A dozen miles upriver you'll see St. Helens, Oregon, to starboard, the mouth of the Lewis River to port. If you hug the Oregon side, you can pass along the west side of 16-mile-long Sauvie Island, through Multnomah Channel, and into the main channel of the lower Willamette River, which you can follow three miles back to the Columbia or continue on up the Willamette to Portland and beyond. If you stay on the Washington side of Sauvie Island up at St. Helens, your options include following the main river channel south toward Vancouver, taking a side trip around Bachelor Island near Ridgefield, or taking Lake River past Ridgefield and continuing south to see some of the Ridgefield National Wildlife Refuge and the lowlands beyond. Staying in the main river channel will take you

past the swim beach and picnic area at Caterpillar Island Park.

From there the river turns in a more easterly direction again. You'll pass Vancouver (with some good waterfront restaurants) and soon come to Marine County Park and Winter County Park, both with good swim beaches and picnic facilities. From there it's under the Highway 205 bridge, past five-mile-long Government Island, Lady Island (through Camas Slough on the north side or the main river channel on the south side), the towns of Camas and Washougal, the swim beach and other facilities at Cottonwood Park, and then Reed Island with its undeveloped Washington State Parks property where you can swim, sun, even camp near the sandy beach. At this point canyon walls close in on both sides of the river, and the points of interest quickly change from the man-made variety to those created by more impressive forces. Bridal Veil Falls, Multnomah Falls, and others cascade off the rocky bluffs along the Oregon side of the river; then equally impressive Beacon Rock looms from the edge of the water on the Washington side. If you feel particularly energetic, you can tie up temporarily to the State Parks float and hike or bike to the base of the rock, where a trail will (eventually) take you to the top for a view that will knock your socks off. From Beacon Rock it's through the narrow channel below Bonneville and the dam itself. Upstream from the dam there's another narrow channel at Bridge of the Gods, and suddenly the river widens. Upstream another two miles is Stevenson, then Carson and the mouth of the Wind River.

If a lot of this sounds like something you might want to see from the water, but you have the misfortune of being boatless, there are some easy remedies for your problem. Several cruise lines offer trips up and down this stretch of the Columbia and beyond. The most fascinating option might be a trip aboard the sternwheeler *Columbia Gorge,* which makes short trips out of Cascade Locks on the Oregon side of the river near Bonneville Dam. Other possibilities include paddlewheel trips of three, four, five, and seven days on the 165-passenger *Queen of the West.* Other companies offer trips lasting anywhere from all day to all week, most of them originating in Portland.

Location: From Cathlamet upstream to the mouth of the Wind River; map B2, grid h3.

How to get there: Take Interstate 5 to Longview and drive west on Highway 4 to reach the Cathlamet-to-Longview stretch of river. Continue south on Interstate 5 to reach the portion of the river between Longview and Vancouver. Drive east from Vancouver on Highway 44 to reach that part of the Columbia between Vancouver and Bonneville Dam.

Boat ramp: There are 17 launch sites on this section of the Columbia River:

- **Elochoman Slough Marina:** Working upstream from Cathlamet, the first ramp is at Elochoman Slough Marina at the end of Second Street on the south side of town. This is a Port of Wahkiakum facility with a $3 launch fee for its two-lane concrete ramp with loading floats. It's a good ramp with a lot of paved parking nearby.

- **Abernathy Creek Ramp:** Next is the Department of Fish and Wildlife ramp about 400 feet up Abernathy Creek, 10 miles west of Longview on Highway 4. This single-lane concrete ramp is a good one, but there's virtually no parking except along the entrance road and there's no sign to tip off drivers along Highway 4.

- **Willow Grove Beach:** The park along the Columbia about four miles west of Highway 432 (Mount Solo Road) and eight miles west of Longview, has a natural-surface ramp that is sometimes plagued by loose sand. It's best for smaller boats pulled by four-wheel-drive vehicles. To find it, go west from Longview on Highway 4 and turn south (left) on Highway 432. Go just under a mile on Highway 432 and turn right on Willow Grove Road, following it four miles to the park and ramp.

- **Coal Creek Ramp:** Coal Creek Slough is just west of Longview, off Highway 4 at milepost 55. There you'll find a Department of Fish and Wildlife ramp wide enough for launching one boat at a time, with parking for about a dozen cars and trailers.

- **Weyerhaeuser Ramp:** Located behind the Weyerhaeuser pulp mill in Longview, this two-lane concrete ramp has a loading float and lots of parking. It's the most popular ramp among local boaters. To find it, take Exit 36 off Interstate 5 and go west on Highway 432, then south on Highway 433. Turn west (right) on Industrial Way and follow it 1.7 miles before turning left at Weyerhaeuser's pulp mill gate. Go 100 feet and veer right on the unmarked paved road, following it to the ramp.

- **Gerhart Gardens Ramp:** The next ramp upstream is actually on the lower Cowlitz River, but provides access into the Columbia from Kelso. Located at Gerhart Gardens Park just north of the Highway 432 bridge over the Cowlitz, it's a three-lane concrete ramp with parking for about three dozen cars and trailers.

- **Kalama River Ramps:** There are two Washington Department of Fish and Wildlife ramps on the lower Kalama River that also provide Columbia River access. Located just west of the Interstate 5 bridge over the Kalama (via Exit 32), these ramps are both one laners, one with a gravel surface and one with concrete planks. The gravel ramp has a small parking area; the second site has ample parking for a couple dozen cars and trailers.

- **Port of Kalama Ramp:** This one is just upstream from the mouth of the Kalama and accessible off Interstate 5 via Exit 30. This two-lane ramp has a hard surface and two loading floats, with room for lots of cars and trailers in the nearby gravel parking area. Boaters who use the ramp are asked to donate toward its upkeep.

- **Dike Road Ramp:** This ramp is at the mouth of the Lewis River. It's a natural-surface ramp where the bottom sometimes falls out. In other words, launch here with a four-wheel-drive vehicle. To find it, drive south from Woodland on South Perkins Road and go half a mile to Whalens Road, turning right and going 1.5 miles. Turn left on Dike Road and go half a mile before turning right on the spur road leading to the ramp.

- **Shillapoo Ramp:** The Department of Fish and Wildlife's Shillapoo Wildlife Area offers the next boat ramp upstream of Woodland. It's located northwest of Vancouver off Highway 501 and has a single-lane concrete-plank ramp.

- **Marine Park Ramp:** The next ramp is at Marine County Park, just east of Vancouver on Marine Park Drive. It's a good, hard-surface, four-lane ramp with loading floats and is managed by the Clark County Parks and Recreation Department. Drive east from Vancouver on Highway 14 and take the first exit right to Columbia Shores Boulevard. Follow it as it turns east and go one mile on what becomes Columbia Parkway. Turn right on Marine Park Drive and you're headed for the ramp.

- **Port of Camas/Washougal:** This ramp is at Camas-Washougal Marina. This four-lane, asphalt ramp with several loading floats is perhaps the premier launch facility on the lower Columbia. The launch fee is $4 round-trip. It's located at the Front Street stoplight on Highway 14 a mile and a half west of Washougal.

- **Beacon Rock State Park:** Thirty-five miles east of Vancouver is Beacon Rock State Park with a two-lane ramp and large float inside a protected side channel off the main river. The launch fee here is $4, which is included in the camping fee if you're registered at the park. From Vancouver, go east 35 miles on Highway 14 and turn right at the Woodward Creek Bridge, following Moorage Road to the ramp.

- **Fort Cascades Ramp:** Launching is free at the Fort Cascades Ramp, just downstream from Bonneville Dam. This two-lane ramp has a loading float and is located in a back eddy that's out of the current except during spring high water. Turn off Highway 14 on Dam Access Road, go to the stop sign, and turn right again. Drive 1.3 miles to the ramp sign on the left.

- **Stevenson Ramp:** There's a single-lane concrete ramp at the town of Stevenson five miles upstream from Bonneville Dam. To find it, turn south off Highway 14 onto Russell Street and go two blocks to Cascade Avenue, turning left and following Cascade to the ramp.

- **Old Hatchery Ramp:** At the mouth of the Wind River is a good, two-lane concrete ramp on Old Hatchery Road, which is left off Highway 14 exactly 50 miles east of Vancouver. It has parking for about 20 cars and trailers, with additional parking along the road shoulder. Watch out for the submerged log in the water just out from the ramp; it has a marker on it that often gets torn off.

- **Home Valley County Park:** Just east of the Wind River mouth, this park has no formal boat ramp, but it's a popular launch site for windsurfers, who carry their boards about 50 yards from the parking lot to the river. A $10 WDFW access decal is required to use the public launch area maintained by the Washington Department of Fish and Wildlife.

Facilities: Elochoman Marina has open moorage ($4 to $10 per boat, depending on size), electrical hookups, boat-sewage pump-out, fuel dock, rest rooms with showers. Boat repair, grocery stores and restaurants are nearby. Kalama Marina has both open and covered moorage at $5 to $7 per boat, electrical hookups and water at the docks, boat-sewage pump-out facilities, and fuel docks. Groceries and motels are available nearby. Camas-Washougal Marina has open and covered moorage for $6 to $10, water and electricity to the docks, boat-sewage pump-out facilities, rest rooms with showers, fuel docks, boat repair, and groceries.

Beacon Rock State Park has about 30 standard tent sites (no hookups), picnic areas, cooking shelters, and rest rooms with showers. Skamania Inn is the newest and biggest motel/conference center of its kind along the lower Columbia. It has a restaurant and also contains a U.S. Forest Service interpretive center with lots of information about the Columbia River Gorge. Home Valley County Park has campsites for $6.50 a night, $2 for each extra vehicle. There are several motels in Vancouver and others in Longview, Kelso, Kalama, Camas, Washougal, and Stevenson.

Water sports/restrictions: All water sports are permitted.

Contact: Clark County Parks and Recreation Department, tel. (360) 696-8171; Skamania County Chamber of Commerce, tel. (800) 989-9178; Columbia River Gorge Visitor Association (Dalles, Oregon, Chamber of Commerce), tel. (800) 984-6743; Skamania Lodge tel. (800) 221-7117; Washington Department of Fish and Wildlife, Vancouver regional office, tel. (360) 906-6702. Sternwheeler Columbia Gorge, tel. (541) 374-8427 (June through September only); Queen of the West, tel. (800) 434-1232; Alaska Sightseeing/Cruise West, tel. (800) 426-7702; Great River Cruises & Tours, tel. (800) 720-0012.

59 Swift Creek Reservoir

Rating: 6

The many bays and creeks along its shoreline make this an interesting place to explore in a small boat, just as its wide-open 4,500 surface acres make it a worthwhile destination for folks who do their boating in larger craft. Whatever your location, you're going to have to do some driving to get here, since the lower (west) end of the reservoir is something like three dozen miles off the interstate. But most of the journey here is a scenic and interesting drive up the Lewis River Valley, so give yourself plenty of time and just enjoy it. Like Yale Reservoir downstream, Swift Creek's water clarity suffers from mud and ash that flows off the south flank of Mount St. Helens with every good rain and throughout spring runoff, so gray-brown water is a very good possibility. And that snow water running off St. Helens also contributes to the lake's below-average water temperatures. If you're coming here to do anything that might get you wet, bring your Neoprene.

Location: East of Cougar, western Skamania County; map B2, grid h7.

How to get there: Take Interstate 5 to Woodland, turn east on Highway 503 and drive 35 miles to where the highway becomes Road 91013. Continue on this road several miles to parallel the north side of the lake.

Boat ramp: There's a public access area and boat ramp near the upper (east) end of the reservoir at Swift Forest Camp. It's a two-lane concrete ramp, but because it's at the upper end of the reservoir, it collects deposits of silt and wood debris. There's a huge gravel parking area nearby. Cartoppers and paddle craft may be launched at several locations along the highway on the north side of the lake.

Facilities: Swift Forest Camp has RV and tent sites, picnic tables, a swim beach, rest rooms, and playground equipment near the lake. Lone Fir, near Cougar, is the next-nearest campground, with both tent and RV sites.

Water sports/restrictions: All water sports are permitted.

Contact: Pacific Power and Light Company, tel. (360) 225-8191; Cougar Store, tel. (360) 238-5228; Lone Fir, tel. (360) 258-5210; Jack's, tel. (360) 231-4276. Call Pacific Power and Light Company, tel. (800) 547-1501 for information on water levels in the reservoir.

60 Yale Lake (Reservoir)

Rating: 6

Located between Merwin and Swift Creek, this one is the smallest of the three, but not by much. It covers about 3,800 acres. While the smallest of the Lewis River reservoirs, it has the most to offer boaters when it comes to facilities, with boat ramps and campgrounds along its entire length. Paddling, skiing, cruising, sailing, diving, fishing, and virtually all other water sports are possible here, but having gone for a dip here one warm June afternoon several years ago, I can tell you that it's a little on the cool side and not my idea of the perfect place to swim early in the summer.

Besides its chilly temperatures, the water also can sometimes be a little cloudy; OK, it can be downright dirty, which doesn't do much for its popularity as a swimming spot. The dirty water—a result of the goings-on at Mount St. Helens some 20 years ago—also can make it difficult for boaters to spot floating logs, limbs, and other debris, so be on the lookout if you choose to speed along the surface of Yale Reservoir when the water is off-color. Like the other two reservoirs in this chain, it gets a lot of floating debris deposited in it during the runoff period of spring, and much of it stays on the water throughout the early summer.

Location: Northeast of Woodland; map B2, grid h6.

How to get there: Take Interstate 5 to Woodland, turn east on Highway 503, and drive about 25 miles to the lake on the right.

Boat ramp: The reservoir has four boat ramps, all managed by Pacific Power and Light Company and all with a $5 launch fee. Saddle Dam Recreation Area, near the west end, has a two-lane concrete ramp with loading floats. Reach it by driving 23 miles east from Woodland on Highway 503 and turning right at Jack's, where 503 splits (and remains 503 both ways.). Follow Highway 503/Lewis River Road south for three miles, turning left on Frasier Road and following it a mile and a half to the park and boat ramp. Yale Park Recreation Area, 28 miles east of Woodland on Highway 503, has a four-lane concrete ramp with three floats and a large gravel parking lot.

Next is Cougar Camp, 31 miles east of Woodland on Highway 503, with a three-lane concrete ramp, loading float, and room for several dozen cars and trailers in its gravel parking lot. Near the upper end of the reservoir, off Sherman Road some 33 miles east of Woodland via Highway 503, is Beaver Bay Recreation Area, which has a one-lane concrete ramp and loading float. Although it's a good ramp, protected by concrete planks on the nearby banks, its location near the upper end of the reservoir makes it susceptible to collecting floating debris from the river. Watch for logs and limbs in the water in and around the ramp.

Facilities: Saddle Dam Recreation Area, Yale Park Recreation Area, Cougar Camp, and Beaver Bay Recreation Area all have swim beaches, picnic tables, rest rooms/changing areas, and grassy areas for sunning or sitting in the shade. Saddle Dam, Cougar Camp, and Beaver Bay also have tent and RV sites, showers, and other amenities for campers. Food, groceries, and tackle are available at Yale Lake Country Store and the Cougar Store, both near the lake. If you need a place to camp, Lone Fir in Cougar has tent and RV spaces.

Water sports/restrictions: All water sports are permitted.

Contact: Pacific Power and Light Company, tel. (360) 225-8191; Cougar Store, tel. (360) 238-5228; Lone Fir, tel. (360) 258-5210; Jack's, tel. (360) 231-4276. Call (800) 547-1501 for information on water levels in the reservoir.

61 Merwin Lake (Reservoir)

Rating: 6

This is the lowermost of the three big Lewis River reservoirs, and therefore the one within easiest reach of boaters heading here via Interstate 5 and Highway 503. And with over 4,000 surface acres, there's plenty of room for boaters to explore once they get here. Although it's still not a quick and easy

trip off the freeway, especially for folks trailering a boat along somewhat winding and hilly Highway 503, Merwin gets plenty of visitors during the summer months. The Pacific Power and Light parks at Speelyai and Cresap Bay have sun-tanned bodies lying all over them on a warm day, and the boat ramps get busy, too.

Activity at both parks did taper off somewhat during the summer of 1999, thanks to a fee increase. It now costs $8 per car to enter the parks, and there's an additional launch fee of $5. The I'll-go-somewhere-else response to these fee increases probably will be short-term, as they usually are, so look for some big crowds again by the summer of 2000. If you do decide to trailer or haul a boat to Merwin, keep an eye on the weather; this is big water located in a deep river valley, and the wind can come blasting down in a hurry. With hiding places fairly few and far between, you don't want to get caught by the wind.

Location: Northeast of Woodland; map B2, grid h5.

How to get there: Take Interstate 5 to Woodland, turn east on Highway 503, and drive about 12 miles to the lake, on the right.

Boat ramp: There are three boat ramps on the reservoir, all of them managed by Pacific Power and Light Company:

- **Merwin Ramp:** This ramp at the west (lower) end of the lake is a rather rough and primitive one, consisting of a natural surface with a lot of large rocks that make trailering difficult. This ramp might best be used for launching paddle craft and other small boats rather than trailer boats. To reach it, drive nine miles east from Woodland on Highway 503 and turn right on Merwin Village Road, then right again on Merwin Hatchery. Drive to its end.

- **Speelyai Bay Park:** Marked by a sign on the right-hand side of Highway 503 about 21 miles east of Woodland, this park has a recently refurbished two-lane concrete ramp with two loading floats. It's in Speelyai Bay, which is well-protected from the wind and the chop of speeding boats out on the main reservoir. Obey the no-wake signs here until you're well clear of the bay, and stay to the west side of the bay entrance to avoid the rocky reef on the east side.

- **Cresap Bay Recreation Area:** About two miles uplake from Speelyai, this is a new Pacific Power and Light facility with a good three-lane concrete ramp and two loading floats. This ramp sometimes has lots of floating wood around it from the river entering the reservoir nearby, especially in the spring and early summer. Reach it by driving 23 miles east from Woodland on Highway 503 and turning south at Jack's onto Highway 503/Lewis River Road (yes, it's Highway 503 in both directions now). Go three miles south on Highway 503/Lewis River Road and turn right at the sign pointing to the park. As at Speelyai, respect the no-wake rules until you're past the buoy line.

Launching isn't cheap at Speelyai or Cresap Bay, thanks to an $8 entrance fee to the park and an additional $5 launch fee. Both ramps and parks are very nice, but for $13 they should probably wash and wax your car for you while you're out on the water.

Facilities: Speelyai Bay Park and Cresap Bay Recreation Area both have large, sand-and-gravel swim beaches, rest room/changing facilities, picnic tables, fishing docks, and loading floats for boaters. Cresap Bay also has boat moorage and a large camping area with tent and RV spaces and an RV dump station. Gas and groceries are available from small stores along the highway.

Water sports/restrictions: All water sports are permitted. No-wake rules are in effect in the two main access areas along the north side of the lake and in the canyon area at the upper (east) end. These no-wake regulations are strictly enforced by Clark and Cowlitz County marine enforcement officers.

Contact: Pacific Power and Light Company, tel. (360) 225-8191; Jack's, tel. (360) 231-4276. Call Pacific Power and Light Company, tel. (800) 547-1501 for information on water levels in the reservoir.

62 North Fork Lewis River

Rating: 7

Paddlers use the upper North Fork quite frequently, even though it's a long way off the main thoroughfares. Most trips start from a rough launch just below the lower falls at Cussed Hollow, some 12 miles upstream from the head of Swift Creek Reservoir, but it's possible to cut that distance in half by launching near the mouth of Rush Creek. If you start higher up, you'll have a chance to run a couple of Class IV rapids, while the lower half of the run consists mostly of Class II water with a couple of Class III challenges thrown in. It's all a good ride.

The North Fork Lewis emerges from the bottom Merwin Reservoir somewhat larger and a lot slower than it enters the upper end of Swift Creek Reservoir, and downstream of Merwin it's a much more docile and easy-going stream. This lower part of the Lewis is primarily the realm of salmon and steelhead anglers, but there's plenty of room for inner-tubing and semi-casual paddling as well. It's not like the whole river is one big frog pond, especially when it's running high during spring runoff, but you won't have to make as many quick decisions as you do in the frothy water above the reservoirs. The main obstacles on the lower Lewis are likely to be other people in bigger, badder boats. Watch out for them, and make sure they see you.

Location: Joins the Columbia River south of Woodland; map B2, grid h4.

How to get there: Take Interstate 5 to Woodland and drive east on Highway 503 to reach the north side of the river or east on County Road 16 to reach the south side.

Boat ramp: Boat ramps on the south side of the river include a rough one (four-wheel-drive only) at the end of Haapa Road and the popular launch farther upstream at Cedar Creek. There are rough launches for paddlers above Swift Creek Reservoir off Forest Service Road 90. A $10 WDFW access decal is required to use the public launch area maintained by the Washington Department of Fish and Wildlife. On the north side of the river there's a launch near the mouth off Dike Road that gets a lot of use from anglers fishing the extreme lower river. Above Woodland on the north side of the river are the Island ramp (about three miles upstream from town) and the rough launch at the golf course, both of which are accessible off Highway 503.

Facilities: You'll find plenty of restaurants, gas stations, and motel accommodations in Woodland, and there are also campgrounds, RV parks, campgrounds, and restaurants here and there along upstream reservoirs.

Water sports/restrictions: Paddling, drift boating, powerboating, tubing, and swimming all are options at various places along this big river.

Contact: Jack's, tel. (360) 231-4276; Pacific Power and Light Company, tel. (800) 547-1501, for information on river flows.

63 East Fork Lewis River

Rating: 7

Ask a serious angler about this river and he'll probably tell you it's the place that produced the state-record winter steelhead back in 1980. Ask a serious paddler about it, and he (or she) is likely to grow a big grin and start talking about Class IV whitewater and getting up the nerve to run a full-blown waterfall. The East Fork of the Lewis River is, in some ways, all things to all river lovers, a stream with a great reputation among those who do the kinds of things people come to a river to do. From its beginnings in the high country of the Gifford Pinchot National Forest just over a ridge from where the Washougal River gets its start, the East Fork tumbles and rumbles its way toward its eventual rendezvous with the bigger North Fork Lewis a few miles southeast of Woodland. On its way it cascades over five official falls and several other drops that more than qualify as falls in the hearts and minds of paddlers who have dropped over them or portaged around them, depending on their bravery and river-running skills.

There are several runs along this river, all of them relatively short four- to six-mile jaunts laid out between the various falls that could cause any range of damage to paddler and paddle craft. Some boaters go as far upstream as the Green Fork, making the run from there down to Sunset Falls. Another run that includes a taste of two streams involves launching in Rock Creek and taking out above Moulton Falls on the East Fork. These and other short runs on the East Fork will take you through a lot of Class III to Class VI+ water. If you want it take it easier, you'll want to confine your efforts to the lower part of the river from Lewisville Park down to LaCenter. This stretch includes a lot of Class II water and is often run by steelhead anglers in drift boats and rafts.

Location: Meets the North Lewis three miles south of Woodland; Map B2, grid i4.

How to get there: Take the LaCenter exit off Interstate 5 south of Woodland and drive east on County Road 42 to County Road 48. Continue east on County Road 48 to N.E. 82nd Avenue and turn south (right). Drive about two miles to the Daybreak Bridge section of the river. To reach areas farther upstream, turn east off N.E. 82nd Avenue onto N.E. 299th Street, which intersects Highway 503. Turn south on 503 and drive about two miles to reach Lewisville County Park. Turn north on Highway 503 and east (right) on Lucia Falls Road to reach several miles of good fishing water farther upstream.

Boat ramp: Ramps can be found at Lewisville County Park, at Daybreak Bridge County Park, and near the mouth of the river at Paradise Point State Park. There are also places to drag or carry a kayak or raft to or from the river near the mouth of the Green Fork, at the Sunset Falls day-use park, and at Moulton Falls County Park.

Facilities: The state park has about 80 campsites, rest rooms with showers, RV pump-out facilities, and other amenities.

Water sports/restrictions: Kayaking, rafting, and fishing are the main activities. No boating is allowed on or below Lucia Falls.

Contact: Pacific Water Sports, tel. (206) 246-9385; Paradise Point State Park, tel. (360) 263-2350; Washington State Parks and Recreation Commission, tel. (800) 233-0321 (information), tel. (800) 452-5687 (reservations).

64 Battle Ground Lake

Rating: 6

Located well off the main traffic flow and covering only 30 acres, this isn't one of the first places that comes to mind when most folks think about prime places for boating and related water sports. But this little lake northeast of the town of Battle Ground offers excellent swimming, fishing, and paddling opportunities, and there's a cozy little state park on its shores with enough room for about 30 tents and RVs. Don't come here to ski, ride your PWC, or skim across the lake in your drag boat, though, because gas engines aren't allowed here.

Location: Northeast of the town of Battle Ground; map B2, grid i5.

How to get there: Drive east off Interstate 5 on Highway 502 to Battle Ground, then north on Heisson Road about three miles to the lake.

Boat ramp: There's a single-lane concrete boat ramp at Battle Ground State Park. The launch fee is $3 round-trip, and a $40 annual permit is available that allows launching at all state park ramps.

Facilities: Battle Ground Lake State Park has about three dozen tent sites, rest rooms, and picnic areas, as well as a swim beach. Food and gas are available in the town of Battle Ground, and there's at least one bed-and-breakfast in town.

Water sports/restrictions: Paddling, swimming, and fishing are permitted here. Internal combustion engines are prohibited on the lake.

Contact: Battle Ground Lake State Park, tel. (360) 687-4621; Washington State Parks and Recreation Commission, tel. (800) 233-0432 (information), tel. (800) 542-5687 (reservations).

65 Vancouver Lake

Rating: 5

At over 2,800 acres, it's one of the biggest lakes in southwestern Washington, but you'd be hard-pressed to find a place deeper than seven feet, so it's also one of the shallowest lakes in southwest Washington. Put the two together and you just might come to the conclusion that this is a popular swimming/playing lake. If you came to that conclusion, you'd be right. This big, shallow lake warms quickly with a few days of warm weather, making it a popular early-summer play spot for Vancouver-area folks who want to get wet. The only problem is that it continues to warm as summer progresses, and gets *very* warm by August or so. Its water starts to turn color as it warms, and swimming begins to look a little less inviting. So I guess you use this as the place to swim in the early summer; then you go looking for more appetizing water holes. It has a county swim beach with easy access. And you won't have trouble with speedboaters if you come here to swim, paddle, or fish for the several species of warm-water fish that inhabit the lake. A no-wake speed limit keeps the big fast boats away.

Location: Northwest of Vancouver; map B2, grid j4.

How to get there: Take Interstate 5 to Vancouver and take the Fourth Plain Boulevard exit. Drive west on Fourth Plain a mile and a half to Fruit Valley Road and turn north (right). Drive a half mile to LaFrambois Road and turn west (left). Drive 1.7 miles on LaFrambois Road to the lake's public access.

Boat ramp: There's a Department of Fish and Wildlife boat ramp near the south end of the lake. A $10 WDFW access decal is required to use the public launch area maintained by the Washington Department of Fish and Wildlife.

Facilities: A county park and swim beach are on the west side of the lake. Food, gas, lodging, and other amenities are available in Vancouver.

Water sports/restrictions: Swimming, paddling, fishing, and waterfowl hunting are the main attractions. The lake has a no-wake speed-limit regulation. No boating is allowed within 200 feet of the public swim beach.

Contact: Clark County Parks and Recreation Department, tel. (360) 696-8171; Washington Department of Fish and Wildlife, Vancouver regional office, tel. (360) 906-6702.

66 Lacamas Lake

Rating: 6

This 300-acre lake north of Camas is quite shallow, so it warms very quickly with the spring sun. Limited access and lots of shoreline weeds, though, restrict its potential as a water-sports capital. Most of the folks who come here do so to fish for bass, brown trout, and other trophies, but there is a fair amount of PWC riding, kneeboarding, and skiing here during the summer. Since facilities are limited, local residents do most of the playing here.

Location: North of Camas; map B2, grid j5.

How to get there: Take Interstate 205 to Highway 14 and drive east to Camas. Take Everett Road north out of Camas and turn west (left) on Leadbetter Road. It's about a mile to the lake on the left.

Boat ramp: There's a public boat ramp on the northeast side of the lake. A $10 WDFW access decal is required to use the public launch area maintained by the Washington Department of Fish and Wildlife.

Facilities: Restaurants, tackle, gas, and other facilities are available in nearby Camas and Washougal.

Water sports/restrictions: All water sports are permitted, but there's a 10 mph speed limit on the lake during the first 15 days of the general fishing season, which begins in late April. Buoy lines near the east and west ends of the lake designate slow/no-wake restrictions in those areas.

Contact: Camas Sports Center, tel. (360) 834-4462.

67 Washougal River

Rating: 7

Portland-area whitewater enthusiasts tend to be more familiar with this energetic little southwest Washington stream than most of us Evergreen Staters are, thanks to its location within easy driving distance of the Portland area. But wherever you happen to live, if you love serious whitewater sport, the kind that includes bouncing off boulders, dodging through fast-water chutes, and flying over falls of various heights and danger levels, you probably already know about the Washougal. Just as any angler worth his salt has heard about the Washougal's reputation for fighting steelhead, most any dedicated whitewater paddler can tell you about the challenges of this fast-moving river.

Depending on what section of the Washougal you run and how much it's rained in the days prior to your trip, about the gentlest run you could hope for would be comprised of solid Class II water with a sprinkling of Class III boulder gardens. Other stretches include hefty servings of Class III and Class IV rapids. And then there's the challenging stuff. The upper reaches of the Washougal above, say, the mouth of Dougal Creek include Class V water that should be scouted by even the most polished of expert paddlers. Almost every run you may want to take features at least one falls or other major obstacle that should be portaged. In other words, this is a river runner's river, where the novice probably shouldn't venture except maybe to watch and learn. The good news is that much of the river can be scouted from the road that parallels most of its length, and there are decent portage routes around most of the toughest water, including falls. The toughest single run here is the upper main river above Dougan Creek, but the entire Washougal is challenging enough to demand respect.

Location: Joins the Columbia River at Camas; map B2, grid j6.

How to get there: Take Highway 14 to Washougal and turn north on Highway 140, which parallels the main river for about 10 miles. Take Skye Road north off Highway 140 and turn east (right) on Washougal River Road to follow the main river upstream, or turn north off Highway 140 on North Fork Road and drive past the Skamania Hatchery, to reach the West Fork Washougal.

Boat ramp: A couple of more or less formal boat launches and several public access spots that serve as rough launch sites can be found along Route 140.

Facilities: Food, gas, lodging, tackle, and other facilities are available in Camas and Washougal.

Water sports/restrictions: Kayaking, rafting, fishing, some tubing, and swimming occur here.

Contact: Pacific Water Sports, tel. (206) 246-9385; Camas Sport Center, tel. (360) 834-4462.

68 Wind River

Rating: 7

This beautiful river that runs much of its length between beautiful canyon walls is a spectacular whitewater stream that doesn't get the publicity or the attention from the river-running community that it deserves. The upper Wind above the high bridge that crosses it about five miles from the Columbia includes a lot of Class III water and even a couple of Class IV spots that will make any boater work for his or her safe passage. A few hardy kayakers even tackle the lower Wind from the high bridge to the mouth, but if you're thinking about it, be advised that Shipherd Falls presents an unrunnable obstacle that must be portaged. If you do choose to float this lower portion of the river, there's a special reward in store, a hot-spring pool right alongside the river. Remember, this is the land of Carson Hot Springs, where warm water bubbles out of the ground in several locations.

Location: Enters the Columbia River at Carson; map B2, grid i9.

How to get there: Take Highway 14 along the Columbia River to Carson and turn north on Wind River Road to reach the upper river. To fish lower portions of the Wind, drive east past Carson and turn left at the bridge crossing over the river mouth.

Boat ramp: There's a Department of Fish and Wildlife boat ramp at the mouth of the river. Kayaks or small rafts can be launched off the road at the high bridge and upstream off Hemlock Road near the hamlet of Stabler. A $10 WDFW access decal is required to use the public launch area maintained by the Washington Department of Fish and Wildlife.

Facilities: Carson Hot Springs is a funky old place with a hotel, campground, restaurant, and hot mineral springs. There are restaurants, gas stations, and other accommodations throughout the area, including huge Skamania Lodge a few miles west in Stevenson.

Water sports/restrictions: Kayaking and fishing are the main draws, but some rafters use the upper river.

Contact: Pacific Water Sports, tel. (206) 246-9385; Camas Sport Center, tel. (360) 427-8267; Carson Hot Springs, tel. (509) 427-8292.

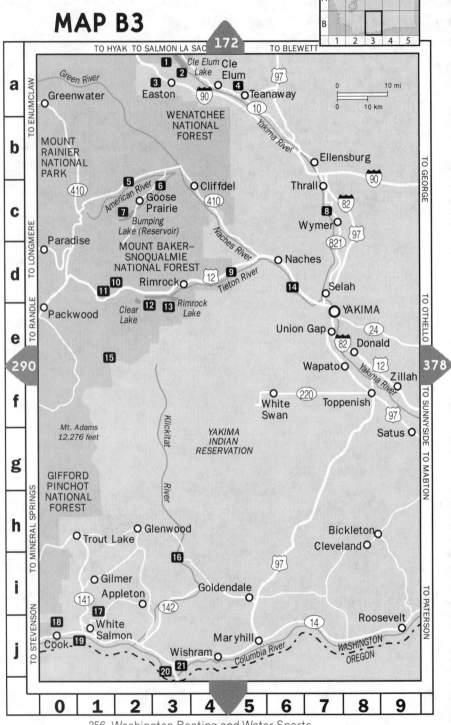

MAP B3

TO HYAK   TO SALMON LA SAC   TO BLEWETT

a

Green River

Greenwater

TO ENUMCLAW

Cle Elum Lake

Cle Elum

■ 1

■ 2

■ 3 Easton

90

4 Teanaway

97

10

WENATCHEE NATIONAL FOREST

Yakima River

0   10 mi
0   10 km

b

MOUNT RAINIER NATIONAL PARK

Ellensburg

90

TO GEORGE

c

410

American River

5 ■   6 ■

7 ■

Goose Prairie

Bumping Lake (Reservoir)

Cliffdel

410

Thrall

8 ■

82

Wymer

97

TO LONGMERE

Paradise

d

MOUNT BAKER–SNOQUALMIE NATIONAL FOREST

Naches River

12   9 ■

Tieton River

Naches

821

Selah

TO RANDLE

11 ■ 10 ■

Rimrock

14 ■

YAKIMA

e

Packwood

Clear Lake

12 ■ 13 ■

Rimrock Lake

Union Gap

82

Donald

24

290

15 ■

Wapato

378

TO OTHELLO

Zillah

Yakima River

12

f

White Swan

220

Toppenish

97

Satus

TO SUNNYSIDE

g

Mt. Adams 12,276 feet

KlickitatRiver

YAKIMA INDIAN RESERVATION

TO MABTON

TO MINERAL SPRINGS

GIFFORD PINCHOT NATIONAL FOREST

h

Trout Lake

Glenwood

Bickleton

Cleveland

i

Gilmer

Appleton

141

16 ■

142

Goldendale

97

Roosevelt

TO PATERSON

j

TO STEVENSON

18 ■

17 ■

White Salmon

Cook 19 ■

20 ■ 21 ■

Wishram

Maryhill

14

Columbia River

WASHINGTON
OREGON

| 0 | 1 | 2 | 3 | 4 | 5 | 6 | 7 | 8 | 9 |

CHAPTER B3

1 Kachess Lake

Rating: 4

Like Lake Keechelus to the west and Lake Cle Elum to east, this big impoundment on the upper Yakima River system would get a lot more use by boaters if a few things were different. Some people have trouble getting excited about the place because of its location in the high country along the east slope of the Cascades, its almost total lack of facilities, fishing that can be described as fair at best, and fluctuating water levels that keep everyone guess about whether they can even launch a boat when they get there. If you decide to spend a day cruising, fishing, sailing, or paddling on Kachess, especially if you do it outside the summer camping season, you may find that you have much of the 4,500-acre lake to yourself. Paddlers might enjoying a day-long trip around the perimeter of the lake's north end, known to most as Little Kachess Lake. The restrictive speed limit north of the campground well keeps most motorboaters out and provides smooth water on this scenic part of the reservoir. Scenic, that is, when the lake is at or near full-pool. And what's with these names and their pronunciation, anyway? This one is pronounced Ka-CHEES, with a long "e" at the end, even though it looks like KA-chess. But nearby Keechelus is pronounced KEH-chellus, as though it has a single "e" in its first syllable. Who taught these lake namers how to spell?

Location: North of Easton, Kittitas County; map B3, grid a3.

How to get there: Drive east from Snoqualmie Summit or west from Cle Elum on Interstate 90. Turn north at Crystal Springs onto Forest Road 49 to reach the upper end of the lake's west side. Forest Road 4828, which is accessible off Forest Road 49 or by turning north off the freeway near Lake Easton, provides access to the southern portion of the lake's west side. To reach the east side of the lake, turn north off Interstate 90 near Lake Easton onto Forest Road 4818.

Boat ramp: There are two boat ramps at Kachess Campground, near the upper end of the lake. One is a two-lane concrete ramp at the south end of the camping area; the other a single-lane gravel ramp at the north end. All are fairly good ramps, and there's a $2 launch fee to use them. These ramps may become high and dry by late summer, thanks to drawdown for irrigation.

Facilities: The U.S. Forest Service's Kachess Campground, located at the northwest corner of the lake, has nearly 200 tent and RV sites, rest rooms, and a boat ramp. Crystal Springs Campground, three miles from the lake along Interstate 90, has about two dozen tent and trailer sites.

Water sports/restrictions: All water sports are permitted. North of the campground there's a 10 mph speed limit on the part of the lake known as Little Kachess Lake. Irrigation drawdown causes severe fluctuations in the water level.

Contact: Wenatchee National Forest, Cle Elum Ranger District, tel. (509) 674-4411.

2 Lake Cle Elum

Rating: 4

The best advice for anyone heading to Lake Cle Elum might be "Enjoy it while you can." The three campgrounds make this a popular vacation destination, but about the time the weather really starts getting nice, the lake begins to disappear. Like the two reservoirs to the west, this one was built to hold water for irrigation in the valleys below, and irrigation season corresponds with vacation boating season. When people are ready to hit the water, much of the water is gone. Launching larger boats becomes difficult to impossible by August, and the lake doesn't begin refilling until the fall rains. If you visit the lake when it's at full-pool early in the year, you'll find almost 5,000 acres of water to fish, paddle, sail, ski, and cruise on. It's a pretty place when it has water.

Location: Northeast of Easton, Kittitas County; map B3, grid a3.

How to get there: take Interstate 90 to Cle Elum and turn north on Highway 903, following it through Roslyn and up the east side of the lake.

Boat ramp: There are boat ramps at Wish Poosh, Morgan Creek, and Dry Creek. The Morgan Creek and Dry Creek ramps are single-lane gravel sites. The Wish Poosh ramp is the biggest and best of the bunch, and the only one I'd recommend for launching larger trailer boats. It's a four-lane concrete-plank ramp with about three dozen parking spaces on a paved lot. Now the bad news: by midsummer these ramps are completely out of the water and pretty much unusable due to drastic drawdown of the reservoir for irrigation.

Facilities: Wish Poosh Campground (U.S. Forest Service) has about 40 campsites. The other two are more primitive, with limited camping space and few facilities. Food, gas, and lodging are available in and around Cle Elum.

Water sports/restrictions: All water sports are permitted. Water levels fluctuate due to irrigation drawdown.

Contact: Wenatchee National Forest, Cle Elum Ranger District, tel. (509) 674-4411.

3 Lake Easton

Rating: 6

Located high in the eastern foothills of the Cascade Mountains, this 235-acre lake stays chilly well into the summer, but that doesn't stop folks from coming here in good numbers to enjoy what it has to offer. The swim beach at Lake Easton State Park is one of Kittitas County's most popular summertime gathering spots, not only with campers visiting the park, but with residents from Cle Elum and surrounding communities as well. Fishing, sailing, skiing, wakeboarding, PWC riding, paddling, and most other water sports also have their share of representatives here as well.

Location: Northwest of Easton, Kittitas County; map B3, grid a3.

How to get there: Take Interstate 90 to Easton and follow the signs to Lake Easton State Park.

Boat ramp: There's a good concrete ramp at Lake Easton State Park. It has a large loading float and paved parking area. The launch fee is $3 unless you're camping in the park. A $40 annual launch permit is available from the State Parks and Recreation Commission.

Facilities: Lake Easton State Park has nearly 100 tent sites and over 40 RV sites with hookups, as well as a large swim beach and play area, canoe and paddleboat rentals, rest rooms, showers, and a roomy boat ramp. There's also a private RV park nearby.

Water sports/restrictions: All water sports are permitted. Irrigation drawdown causes water level fluctuations.

Contact: Lake Easton State Park, tel. (509) 656-2230; Washington State Parks and Recreation Commission, tel. (800) 233-0321 (information), tel. (800) 452-5687 (reservations); RV Town, tel. (509) 656-2360.

4 Teanaway River

Rating: 5

Lots of people see and pass over this little Yakima River tributary as they scoot along Highway 970 between Cle Elum and Blewitt Pass, but very few stop to see what the river has to offer. A major reason for this oversight, no doubt, is that the part of the river they see is running through private ranchland and alongside what look like vacation cabins hugging the river bank. First impressions say, "Private Property: Keep Out." Those impressions are true, to some extent, but there are places where you can reach the river, and when you do, you'll find that it offers some surprisingly good paddling opportunities.

The best access points are off Teanaway Road, which turns north off Highway 970 about four miles east of its intersection with Highway 10 southeast of Cle Elum. You can launch near the start of Teanaway Road off East Masterson Road, or continue about seven miles to where the road crosses over the river and launch there. Either way, you'll find a pretty little river with several Class II rapids and enough personality to keep you interested. The main obstacles are large boulders and the possibility of trees and stumps washed downstream by previous periods of high water. The Teanaway is generally a good run throughout the spring, but gets a little skinny by midsummer. Because much of it does flow through private property, stay in the river and to the best of your ability, in your boat.

Location: Joins the Yakima River southeast of Cle Elum; map B3, grid a5.

How to get there: Take Interstate 90 about two miles east from Cle Elum and turn north on Highway 970, which parallels the lower Teanaway and crosses it about three miles above the river mouth.

0.7 mile past the bridge crossing the river, turn north (left) on Teanaway Road, which parallels the river for several miles and has spurs running up the West, Middle, and East Forks of the Teanaway.

Boat ramp: It's possible to carry a boat to or from the river at the bridge about seven miles up Teanaway Road, at East Masterson Road near the intersection of Teanaway Road and Highway 970, and at the Highway 10 bridge over the river near its mouth.

Facilities: Food, gas, and lodging are available in Cle Elum.

Water sports/restrictions: Kayaking is possible above Highway 970. Canoes and rafts can be used at some water levels on the lower portions of the river.

Contact: Washington Department of Wildlife, Yakima regional office, tel. (509) 575-2740.

5 American River

Rating: 6

Once a favorite of trout anglers who came here to catch hatchery rainbows stocked throughout the summer, the American is now more of a paddler's river than an angler's river. That's partly because trout aren't planted here any more and partly because more and more paddlers are turning up on Washington's rivers every season. The American isn't a big river, but it has maneuvering room enough for a good kayaker, skilled rafter, or daring canoeist to get through unscathed during spring runoff from April through June and maybe into July in a wet year. Some of the upper parts of the river contain Class III+ and even some Class IV water at certain levels, so this is no place to take your first-ever run. The possibility of pine trees and other obstacles in the river adds some potential danger here. Highway 410 runs right beside the river along much of its length, providing opportunities to scout ahead before making the commitment to go.

Location: Joins the Bumping River northwest of Cliffdel, then flows into the Naches.; map B3, grid c2.

How to get there: Take Highway 410 east from Greenwater or west from Cliffdel. The highway parallels the river most of the way from Lodge Pole Campground on the west to American Forks Campground and its confluence with Bumping River on the east, a distance of 12 miles.

Boat ramp: The best places to drag or carry a boat to the water are at Pleasant Valley, Hells Crossing, and American Forks Campgrounds.

Facilities: The U.S. Forest Service's Lodge Pole, Pleasant Valley, Hells Crossing, Pine Needle, American Forks, and Little Naches Campgrounds all have campsites, and they're all on or near the river.

Water sports/restrictions: Kayaking and rafting are good bets; canoes are a possibility on the lower part of the river.

Contact: Wenatchee National Forest, Naches Ranger District, tel. (509) 653-2205.

6 Bumping River

Rating: 6

Like the American River that joins it at American Forks, the Bumping is a pretty little mountain stream flowing through some pleasant, pine-clad surroundings. A little more gradual and tame than the American, the Bumping might be a river where intermediate kayakers feel comfortable. It's a smaller river, running maybe 600 to 700 cfm during spring runoff, but like the American, it can become jammed with fallen trees and other obstacles that make life miserable

for the unskilled or inattentive paddler. The road paralleling it most of its distance offers many viewpoints where the river can be scouted. If you were to make the run all the way from Bumping Lake Campground to American Forks Campground, you'd cover about 10 miles, all of it Class II water.

Location: Joins the Naches River northwest of Cliffdel; map B3, grid c3.

How to get there: Take Highway 410 (Chinook Pass Highway) to Bumping Lake Road (Forest Road 18) and turn south. The road runs alongside the river all the way from the highway to the east end of Bumping Lake. To reach the upper river, take Forest Road 174 south along the east side of Bumping Lake, and follow it to the end; then take the trail that continues upriver.

Boat ramp: It's possible to launch or take out at any of the half dozen campgrounds along the river.

Facilities: U.S. Forest Service campgrounds at Little Naches, American Forks, Cedar Springs, Soda Springs, Cougar Flat, Bumping Crossing, and Bumping Dam all have campsites and other facilities.

Water sports/restrictions: Kayaking is the best bet here; the river is small for rafts and other wide craft.

Contact: Wenatchee National Forest, Naches Ranger District, tel. (509) 653-2205.

7 Bumping Lake (Reservoir)

Rating: 7

Although it's a man-made reservoir resulting from a dam on the Bumping River, this large impoundment in some ways has the feel of a pristine, high-country lake. Covering some 1,300 acres at full-pool, it offers plenty of room for kokanee anglers, paddlers, sailors, skiers, wake-boarders, and others who trailer the rather substantial distance along Highway 410 and Bumping Lake Road to reach the lake. The water level drops throughout the summer, though, and by September the boat ramps may be out of the water and the reservoir only about half the size it was in May or June.

Location: Southwest of Goose Prairie, Yakima County; map B3, grid c2.

How to get there: Take Highway 410 to Bumping Lake Road (Forest Road 18) and turn south. Follow Bumping Lake Road about 11 miles to the east end of the lake.

Boat ramp: The lake has two boat ramps, one at Bumping Lake Marina and one at Bumping Lake Public Boat Landing. The marina ramp has a concrete surface and a loading float. The ramp at the public access is also concrete, but has no float.

Facilities: Bumping Lake Marina has boat rentals, moorage, RV and tent sites, picnic tables and cooking shelters, a convenience store, and a large swim beach. Campsites and beach access also are available at Bumping Lake Campground and Bumping Dam Campground, both located near the northeast end of the lake.

Water sports/restrictions: All water sports are permitted. Water level is determined by irrigation needs.

Contact: Wenatchee National Forest, Naches Ranger District, tel. (509) 653-2205

8 Upper Yakima River

Rating: 9

I'm not sure that my words can do justice to this beautiful river and all the recreation it provides to river lovers from all over the Pacific Northwest. The river itself is gorgeous yet gentle; the land through which it runs ranges from green and cool to rocky and harsh; the weather can be brutally cold in winter, brutally hot in summer, and beautifully pleasant in spring and fall.

The Yakima is Washington's best trout stream, a favorite of paddlers, and one of eastern Washington's top aquatic party spots. There are occasional confrontations among these divergent groups, but they tend to be more philosophical than physical. These confrontations usually stem from differences of opinion on three subjects: blocking access areas, disturbing good trout water, and littering. If you need further explanation, there's a good chance that you're part of the problem.

The closest thing to whitewater on the Yakima is on the upper part, upstream from Ellensburg, where some Class II waves form as the river passes over a few rocky ledges and large gravel bars. On the extreme upper reaches, above the mouth of the Teanaway, boats could encounter downed trees, brush, and other obstacles during or after high water, so scouting is advised on this stretch. From Ellensburg downstream to Roza Dam the river is Class I. The high-water period on this stretch occurs during the summer, and then the main thing boaters have to be aware of is fast river flows and strong currents, with some danger from sweepers along the river bank. When the river is running high, it's easy to miss some of take-out points, so be on your toes. Summertime winds can also cause interesting complications, especially on the slower stretches. It's not unusual for boaters to find themselves moving upstream rather than down on a windy summer afternoon.

Another danger on the river, although it shouldn't be, is Roza Dam. Yeah, I know, you can see and hear it, and there are signs suggesting that taking a boat, inner tube, or other floating device over a dam—even a low dam—isn't a good idea, but some people give it a shot every now and then. Most of them have the blood-alcohol content of aviation fuel, and, even though that gives them the courage to challenge the dam, it doesn't give them the protection to survive it.

Location: Easton downstream to Yakima; map B3, grid c7.

How to get there: To reach the stretch of river between Cle Elum and Ellensburg from the west, take Interstate 90 to Cle Elum and exit onto Highway 907 as though you were headed for Blewett Pass. But instead of going left at the Y a few miles off the freeway, go right onto Highway 10, which parallels the river for several miles. Anglers headed west should follow Interstate 90 to a few miles west of Ellensburg and exit north onto U.S. 97, then turn west (left) onto Highway 10 to go downstream along the river. To reach the canyon portion of the river, drive south from Ellensburg on Highway 821, or drive north from Yakima on Interstate 82 and exit onto Highway 821 about five miles out of town.

Boat ramp: There are 11 places to launch or retrieve a boat along the upper Yakima:

- **East Nelson Ramp:** The uppermost possibility for launching a kayak or raft is at the Department of Fish and Wildlife's access area off East Nelson Siding Road, about seven miles west of Cle Elum. Get there by taking Interstate 90 to East Nelson Siding Road and paralleling the freeway back toward the east to the ramp. A $10 WDFW access decal is required to use the public launch areas maintained by the Washington Department of Fish and Wildlife.

- **Three Bridges Access:** Another WDFW access spot, known locally as Three Bridges, offers another launching possibility above Cle Elum. You won't get a trailer boat in the water here, but it's possible to hand carry paddle craft to the river.

- **Teanaway River Mouth:** About five miles east of Cle Elum, on Highway 10 just east of its intersection with Highway 970, is a Department of Fish and Wildlife access area and boat ramp near the mouth of the Teanaway River.

- **River Raft Rentals:** A fairly popular and easy take-out area is at the River Raft Rentals property on the north side of the river on Highway 10 between Ellensburg and Cle Elum. A small fee is charged to use the RRR ramp on the left side of the river.

- **Gladmar Park Access:** Some boaters—most of them trout fishermen—launch at Gladmar Park to the north of Exit 101 off Interstate 90 and float down to the Ellensburg KOA Campground. Check at the KOA office about parking and accessing the river here.

- **Ringer Loop Ramp:** Next is one of the most heavily used launch sites on the river, the Department of Fish and Wildlife's ramp off Ringer Loop. Ringer Loop is four miles south of Ellensburg on Highway 821, best known as the Yakima Canyon Road. This launch site has a paved ramp, a large gravel parking area, and a pit toilet. A $10 WDFW access decal is required to use the public launch areas maintained by the Washington Department of Fish and Wildlife.

- **Mile 22.5 Access:** Downstream about three miles is a rough launch/takeout spot with limited parking, just off the road between mile marker 21 and mile marker 22.

- **Umtanum Recreation Area:** This fee access spot is just north of mile

16 off Canyon Road. A mile farther downstream is Riverview Campground, where you can launch or take out for a fee. A shuttle service is available.

- **Squaw Creek Access:** Between mile 12 and mile 13 along Canyon Road is the Bureau of Land Management's Squaw Creek Recreation Site. This newly developed site has a paved boat ramp, picnic tables, tent sites, and pit toilets. There's a seven-day camping limit, and the camping fee is only $2 per night.

- **Mile 10 Access Site:** Near river mile 10 is a rough ramp/take-out area with a long stretch of bank access.

- **Roza Recreation Site:** The next launch/take-out spot is the Bureau of Land Management's Roza Recreation Site, marked with a large sign and easy to see from the road. It has a wide blacktop ramp, a large, paved parking area, pit toilets, and campsites for $2 per night, with a seven-day limit.

Facilities: At least two companies, River Raft Rentals and Richie's River Rentals, offer rental rafts, kayaks, and other equipment for Yakima River trips. As for food, gas, lodging, tackle, and other amenities, you'll find everything you need in Easton, Cle Elum, Ellensburg, and Yakima.

Water sports/restrictions: Powerboats of all kinds are prohibited upstream from the launch ramp at Roza Recreation Site. Rafts, drift boats, kayaks, canoes, and inner tubes all see lots of use from this point upstream. Fishing regulations for trout are catch-and-release only.

Contact: Richie's River Rentals, tel. (509) 453-2112; River Raft Rentals tel. (509) 964-2145; Gary's Fly Shoppe/ Yakima River Outfitters, tel. (509) 457-3474; Chinook Sporting Goods, tel. (509) 452-8205; Cascade Toys and Sports, tel. (509) 965-4423.

9 Tieton River

Rating: 7

For nearly 48 weeks of the year, the 20-mile stretch of the Tieton River from Rimrock Dam to its confluence with the Naches River is little more than part of the dramatic scenery along Highway 12. I would even bet that most of the folks who drive alongside the river on their way up or down this stretch of the White Pass Highway couldn't name the stream that bubbles and churns within spitting distance of the road. It's a river that goes all but unnoticed. But in late September when the gates at Rimrock open to spill irrigation water down the river channel, a floodgate of visitors to the river also opens, and the otherwise obscure Tieton becomes for several weeks one of the most popular whitewater rivers in the Pacific Northwest. Especially on weekends a steady stream of kayaks and rafts fills the river, and in some places traffic jams of boats develop on the water while cars and buses meet the same fate in parking areas and wide spots along the highway.

Why all the commotion? Because when it's running at 1,500 or 2,000 cubic feet per second, as it does for about one month out of the year, the Tieton is as close to a perfect whitewater river as there is. The water from Rimrock to Windy Point Campground is an almost constant string of Class II and Class III rapids from the start of the run to the end, with little chance to catch your breath and few places to pull over and think. It's a gas! If you like whitewater, you're in luck; if you like solitude, come back in November.

The water from Windy Point Campground down to the Naches is a little more gentle than the upstream portion of this run, but still offers plenty of Class II water to keep you whooping and hollering most of the way through. The most serious dangers on the Tieton, besides being crushed in a back-up of fellow paddlers, is the riverwide weir about two miles below Willows Campground, which should be portaged on the left, and the possibility of logs, limbs, and other debris in or hanging over the river. If you aren't sure where any such obstacles have developed, be sure to ask around before entering the river; there should be plenty of people to ask.

Location: Joins the Naches River northwest of Naches; map B3, grid d5.

How to get there: Take U.S. 12 east from White Pass or west from Naches to parallel the river between Rimrock Lake and the U.S. 12-Highway 410 junction.

Boat ramp: Paddlers launch and take out at several locations along the river, including the Tieton River Access Area, Hause Creek, Riverbend, Wild Rose, Willows, and Windy Point Campgrounds.

Facilities: The five U.S. Forest Service campgrounds along the river between the dam and the mouth of the river, listed above, are easily accessible from U.S. 12 and offer several dozen primitive campsites. There are stores, restaurants, motels, and cabins along U.S. 12 on the north shore of Rimrock Lake. Several commercial rafting companies offer Tieton River trips.

Water sports/restrictions: Kayaking and rafting are the main attractions.

Contact: Wenatchee National Forest, Naches Ranger District, tel. (509) 653-2205; Getaway Sports, tel. (509) 672-2239; River Riders, Inc., tel. (800) 448-RAFT; All Rivers Adventures, tel. (800) 743-5628; Wild and Scenic River Tours, tel. (800) 413-6840; River Recreation, Inc., tel. (800) 464-5899.

10 Dog Lake

Rating: 7

This is the lake you catch a glimpse of to the left after you top the White Pass summit on U.S. 12 and start the winding descent toward Rimrock Lake. There it is, a beautiful, clear lake with the rocky cliffs and broken rock lining its east side and a patch of small pine and fir trees enclosing the rest of its shoreline. If it's always looked inviting but you've never bothered to stop, here's your invitation. Dog Lake covers only about 60 acres, but it has a welcoming campground and a boat ramp that allows launching of smaller boats. There aren't many subalpine lakes in Washington with an access road and boat ramp, so take advantage of the rare opportunities that Dog Lake affords. If it weren't for the highway noise, you might think you were in boaters' heaven.

Location: East of White Pass Summit; map B3, grid d2.

How to get there: Take U.S. 12 (White Pass Highway) to White Pass and turn north off the road just east of the summit. The lake is within sight of the highway on the north side.

Boat ramp: There's a rough boat ramp at Dog Lake Campground, but it's suitable for launching cartoppers, paddle craft, and small trailer boats.

Facilities: Dog Lake Campground (U.S. Forest Service) has about 10 campsites, Food, gas, and lodging are available nearby to the east.

Water sports/restrictions: Fishing and paddling are the best bets.

Contact: Wenatchee National Forest, Naches Ranger District, tel. (509) 653-2205.

11 Leech Lake

Rating: 5

You'd think the smaller body of water adjacent to a place like Dog Lake would be called Flea Lake, wouldn't you? Well, they apparently didn't think of that, so went with a name equally disgusting, Leech Lake. Although it doesn't sound inviting, it's really a gem. At only 41 acres, the clear, cold lake near the summit of White Pass won't keep you busy for long, but if you're looking for a place to stop for the night on your way to or from eastern Washington on a warm summer evening and you have your canoe or kayak along, consider staying here. If the campground is full, motel units are available right across the highway at White Pass Ski Area. Take a fly rod along if you decide to paddle or row the lake's perimeter; besides beautiful scenery, the lake offers good fishing for large brook trout. Regulations allow fly fishing only.

Location: Near White Pass Summit; map B3, grid d2.

How to get there: Take U.S. 12 (White Pass Highway) to the top of White Pass, where the lake is located immediately north of the highway.

Boat ramp: There is a rough boat ramp, suitable for canoes, kayaks, and small rowboats near the campground that hugs the lakeshore.

Facilities: There are Forest Service campgrounds on and near the lake, with food, gas, and lodging available on the highway nearby.

Water sports/restrictions: All motors are prohibited on the lake.

Contact: Wenatchee National Forest, Naches Ranger District, tel. (509) 653-2205.

12 Clear Lake

Rating: 8

If the bigger water and faster pace at Rimrock Lake get to be too much for you, there's Clear Lake, just to the west. Life is slower and usually quieter here, thanks to a restrictive speed limit that keeps the skiers, PWC riders, and other thrill riders away. This 265-acre lakes is best known for its rainbow and occasional brown trout, but it's also a wonderful place for an early-morning or evening paddle around forested shorelines with great vistas of snow-capped hills and mountains. Like Rimrock, Clear is actually a reservoir, so some fluctuations can occur in its water levels. Usually, though, it remains fairly stable. Due to its popularity among anglers and summer vacationers, the boat ramp can become congested, especially first thing in the morning and during the last hour of daylight in the evening.

Location: East of White Pass Summit, at west end of Rimrock Lake; map B3, grid d2.

How to get there: Take U.S. 12 to the east end of Rimrock Lake and turn south on Forest Service Road 12. A Y near the bottom of the hill will take you to the east or west side of the lake.

Boat ramp: There's a Forest Service boat ramp near the southeast corner of the lake, with a natural-surface ramp where trailer boats can be launched and room off to the side for launching cartoppers and paddle craft. The launch fee here is $5 round-trip.

Facilities: There are U.S. Forest Service campgrounds on the north and south sides of the lake with more than 60 campsites. The camping fee is $5 per night.

Water sports/restrictions: The lake has a 5 mph speed limit. Fishing and paddling are the main attractions.

Contact: Wenatchee National Forest, Naches Ranger District, tel. (509) 653-2205.

13 Rimrock Lake (Reservoir)

Rating: 7

Boaters here have to deal with the same problem that anglers have complained about for years, the problem of a reservoir that's here one month, gone the next. It's not quite that bad, but Rimrock's fate is determined by irrigation needs in the Yakima Valley below. The lake is nearly drained every fall, which provides lots of thrills for paddlers on the Tieton River downstream from Rimrock Dam, but makes Rimrock Lake less and less appealing with each passing day. By November the lake may become more of a pond or, more accurately, a river passing through a big lake bed. That's what this was before the dam was built on the Tieton in the first place, so I guess boaters have to accept the good with the bad. The irrigators giveth and the irrigators taketh away.

When it's full or nearly full, Rimrock provides a complete menu of aquatic recreation activities and is a favorite of boaters in the Yakima/Naches area. The 2,500-acre impoundment is big enough to offer wide-open spaces for skiers, sailors, and others who want room to maneuver, while the protected coves and bays are interesting places for paddlers and small-boat anglers to explore. Be advised, though, that the wind can howl here, sometimes putting a stop to virtually all boating activities for hours or even days at a time. But when it's calm and sunny, as it often is, the backdrop of high mountains and blue skies help to make this a very pleasant place to be in a boat or at the water's edge.

Location: South side of White Pass Highway between White Pass Summit and Rimrock; map B3, grid d3.

How to get there: Take U.S. 12 east from White Pass or west from Naches. The highway parallels the north shore of the reservoir for several miles. Turn south on Forest Service Road 12 at either end of Rimrock to reach the south side.

Boat ramp: There are two U.S. Forest Service ramps and three private resorts on the lake. All have launching fees of $5 round-trip except the privately owned Cove Resort. Silver Beach Resort is the farthest uplake, located a mile so from the west end of the lake along Highway 12. It has a one-lane gravel ramp with a loading float and limited parking on a gravel lot. The next ramp to the east is at Rimrock Campground and Landing, a two-lane gravel ramp with room to park about two dozen cars and trailers. Farther east is Twelve West Resort, where the one-lane gravel ramp with a loading float is protected from the wind and waves by a breakwater.

The easternmost ramp along Highway 12 is at Cove Resort. It's a single-lane gravel ramp with two loading floats. Because of the steep ramp and rough surface, the resort staff use a tractor to launch and retrieve boats, and they charge $6 each way. At the southeast corner of the lake is Peninsula Boat Launch, which is reached by turning off Highway 12 onto Tieton Reservoir Road just west of Hause Creek Campground. The Peninsula ramp is the biggest and best on the lake, with four hard-surfaced lanes and parking for about 25 cars and trailers. The main drawback here is that the ramp is exposed to wind, sometimes causing problems for boaters launching or loading their boats. The wind also deposits quite a lot of debris on and around the ramp.

Facilities: Silver Beach Resort has moorage, a large swim beach, rental cabins, and motel rooms, a store, restaurant and playground. Twelve West Resort has some visitor moorage, RV sites and a restaurant. The Cove Resort offers moorage, RV and tent sites, a restaurant, and a small bait and tackle shop. There are several U.S. Forest Service campground options around and near the lake. Some have $5 per night fees; the more primitive sites are free.

Water sports/restrictions: All water sports are permitted. Fluctuating water levels due to irrigation drawdown are a problem.

Contact: Trout Lodge, tel. (509) 672-2211; Silver Beach Resort, tel. (509) 672-2500; Twelve West Resort. tel. (509) 672-2460; The Cove Resort, tel. (509) 672-2470; Wenatchee National Forest, Naches Ranger District, tel. (509) 653-2205; Getaway Sports, tel. (509) 672-2239.

14 Naches River

Rating: 7

Most of the boating activity on this Yakima River tributary takes place above the confluence of the Tieton where Highway 410 and U.S. 12 part company. This 25-mile stretch of river contains no water that requires super technical paddling skills, but it moves along well enough to provide an exciting and fun ride. The toughest rapids—and the part of the river that most people like most—is at Horseshoe Bend, which is visible right along Highway 410, just under three miles above the take-out place at the Highway 12 bridge. A weir stretches across the river about midway between Horseshoe Bend and the take out point, but it can be portaged or lined on river-right. Except for these two spots, the upper Naches is a consistent Class II river.

Location: Joins the Yakima River at Yakima; map B3, grid d6.

How to get there: Drive east on U.S. 12 from Yakima to parallel the lower Naches. Turn north on Highway 410 to continue upriver.

Boat ramp: Boats can be carried or dragged to the water at Sawmill Flat, Cliffdel, and Cottonwood Campgrounds. Most boaters take out at the Highway 12 bridge where the Tieton River enters the Naches.

Facilities: Besides several U.S. Forest Service campgrounds along the upper river—Little Naches, Halfway Flat, Sawmill Flat, Cliffdel, and Cottonwood— there are also private resorts and RV parks near the river on Highway 410. Other facilities may be found in Naches and Yakima.

Water sports/restrictions: Kayaking, rafting, and fishing are the main attractions.

Contact: Squaw Rock Resort and RV Park, tel. (509) 658-2926; Eagle Rock Campground, tel. (509) 658-2905; Whistlin' Jack Lodge, tel. (509) 658-2433; Wenatchee National Forest, Naches Ranger District, tel. (509) 653-2205.

15 Walloped Lake

Rating: 6

Its large size and high elevation make Walloped unusual. You don't find many 380-acre lakes at nearly 4,000 feet, but that's what you have here. Besides being unusually large for a high-country lake, it's also unusually deep, with spots over 200 feet. It's way off the beaten path, but most of the folks who come here to fish, camp, canoe, hike, ride horses, or just kick back and relax seem to think the trip is well worth the effort. The lake has special fishing regulations, so check the angling pamphlet before deciding what tackle to bring along. Unlike most lakes with such fishing rules, though, Walloped does not have a prohibition on motors; it's probably considered too big a lake to be caught on without some mechanical power. I would disagree, arguing that being caught on Walloped with nothing more than a paddle would be a good thing, not a bad thing.

Location: Southeast of Packwood, southeast corner of Lewis County; map B3, grid e1.

How to get there: Take U.S. 12 to about three miles west of Packwood and turn east on Forest Service Road 21, staying on it about 15 miles to Forest Service Road 2160. Turn east there and follow Road 2160 about four miles to the north side of the lake.

Boat ramp: There's a two-lane concrete-plank ramp at Walloped Lake Campground.

Facilities: The U.S. Forest Service campground on the north side of the lake has several primitive campsites and pit toilets. Food, gas, lodging, and other facilities are in Packwood.

Water sports/restrictions: Fishing and paddling are the primary activities.

Contact: Gifford Pinchot National Forest, Packwood Ranger District, tel. (360) 494-5515.

16 Klickitat River

Rating: 7

Having made the mistake of being there once during the Memorial Day weekend, I think it's fair to say that the majority of people who have run the Klickitat in the past 10 years have done so during that three-day weekend in late May. I didn't even have a boat but was just making a side trip up the river while on the way to somewhere else. I couldn't believe the crowds I encountered, both at the launch sites and at a couple of overlook spots along the highway. It was as though every commercial whitewater rafting company in the Northwest had pulled up stakes and moved to south central Washington for the weekend. Having spent time on the Klickitat only during the summer and early fall when it was unusual to see more than one other boat and maybe three or four bank fishermen on the river, I was amazed at this holiday mob.

The reason for the crowds, I quickly determined, was the river level. During May and early June, when snowmelt in the mountains to the north and west is at its peak, the Klickitat runs at about three times the volume that I had become used to during my late-summer fishing trips. None of the Memorial Day river runners was here to fish; they were here for whitewater fun, and everyone seemed to be having his or her share. Much of the upper half of the river seemed to be one big Class III rapid, with an occasional Class II rest spot, so to speak, mixed in for variety. Except for the possibility of logs in the river, there's no water more severe than Class III on the river during this period, but neither is there very much water any more docile than Class III. The other notable danger for boaters is the rock weir extending most of the way across the river a mile or so upstream from the Klickitat Springs boat ramp. Some kayakers run it, but you'll want to scout it from the highway as you pass by on your way upriver.

While late May usually marks the peak of commercial rafting activity on the Klickitat, it's certainly not the only time of year to float this fantastically beautiful stream. Flowing between steep, basalt canyon walls with relatively little human development except for the nearby highways, it's a river where you can hardly wait to turn the next corner, knowing that the scenery lying ahead will be at least as gorgeous as what you've just passed. During summer and fall, when most of the boaters on the river are anglers, the Klickitat is a gentle stream, mostly Class I and Class II water where there's always room to get around the tough spots and plenty of eddies to pull over and catch your breath before dropping into the next chute or rapids.

If you run the lower river downstream from the town of Klickitat, you'll find two Class III+ drops that discourage most anglers in their drift boats from using this stretch of the river. If you decide to make this lower run, don't overlook the fact that you CANNOT go through to the boat ramp at the mouth of the river. There's a canyon about a mile upstream from the river mouth that narrows to about four feet, with just enough drop and several little turns in it to keep you from having any idea what lies ahead if you were to plunge into its upper end.

Location: Joins the Columbia at the town of Lyle; map B3, grid i3.

How to get there: Take Highway 14 to the town of Lyle and turn north on Highway 142, which follows the river upstream for nearly 20 miles. Continue up Highway 142 a few more miles and turn north at the sign pointing to Glenwood to follow the river several miles more.

Boat ramp: The three official boat ramps on the Klickitat are all Washington Department of Fish and Wildlife facilities along the river, one Highway 142 and two on Glenwood Road. Two concrete-plank ramps are located within a mile of each other near the Klickitat River bridge on Glenwood Road. Both are located at the end of gravel roads leading to the left off the main road, one

about half a mile before the bridge, one just beyond the bridge. The lowermost WDFW ramp is at Klickitat Springs, just over two miles east of Klickitat on Highway 142. This is also a concrete-plank ramp, but, like the other two, it has taken a beating from the river over the years and is in rather poor condition. A $10 WDFW access decal is required to use the public launch areas maintained by the Washington Department of Fish and Wildlife. A fourth ramp, known as the Lyle ramp and located at the mouth of the river on the south side of Highway 14, is used primarily by Indian gill-netters and recreational fishermen in powerboats who fish the lower Klickitat and the Columbia off the Klickitat's mouth. Besides the formal boat-launch sites, there are a few places to launch or take out kayaks and other small boats at wide spots along the highway. One is near the gauging station about midway between the river mouth and the town of Klickitat, another just downstream from Klickitat. If you explore a little, you can find five or six such places.

Facilities: Primitive camping areas are scattered along the river. There are several places along the highway where boats can be launched and where bank-fishing access is available. Groceries are available in Klickitat, more complete facilities to the east in Goldendale. Several whitewater outfitters and a few fishing guides work various parts of the river.

Water sports/restrictions: Kayaking, rafting, canoeing, inner tubing, and fishing for salmon and steelhead are the main attractions.

Contact: Klickitat Wildlife Recreation Area, tel. (509) 773-4459; All Rivers Adventures, tel. (800) 743-5628; River Recreation, Inc., tel. (800) 464-5899; Phil's White Water Adventures, tel. (800) 366-

2004; Garrett's Guide Service, tel. (509) 493-3242; Shade Tree Inn, tel. (509) 364-3471.

17 White Salmon River

Rating: 6

Unless you're a hardcore river runner, you might consider much of the White Salmon more trouble than it's worth. Reaching the water for a run above BZ Corners calls for roping your boat up or down near-vertical hillsides, where it may take almost as long (and a lot more sweat) getting in and out of the water than it takes to make the run downstream. What's more, some of the drops along the upper White Salmon are also nearly vertical, meaning that this is not just a thrilling river but a very challenging, even dangerous, one that's suited only to the most experienced whitewater paddlers. We're talking drops of six to 30 feet here, some of which should be run only by the best of the best. However, as a fatal accident in 1996 demonstrated, even the top paddlers in the world can get into trouble here. Except for the 12-foot drop at Husum Falls, the lower eight miles of the White Salmon from BZ Corners to Northwestern Lake is the gentlest, but even this section contains lots of Class III waters at summertime flow levels. The White Salmon, by the way, is a good summer river for serious kayakers and rafters because it maintains a fairly high flow through much of the warm season, after many Washington rivers have become too low.

Location: Joins the Columbia River just west of the town of White Salmon; map B3, grid i1.

How to get there: Take Highway 14 to the town of White Salmon and turn north on Highway 141 to parallel the river upstream. Several side roads in and around White Salmon provide access to some good fishing water on the lower reaches of the river.

Boat ramp: There's a put-in/take-out spot on private property on the north side of BZ Corners, marked by a sign along Highway 141. The public access area on Northwestern Lake serves as a take-out spot at the lower end of the river system. Farther upriver it's possible to line a kayak over the bank at the west end of the Green Truss Bridge, a local landmark that's familiar to anglers and kayakers. It's also possible to line kayaks into the river near bridges farther upriver, including the bridge on Warner Road.

Facilities: Food, gas, and lodging are readily available in White Salmon. For those who aren't on a diet, stay in the Inn of the White Salmon and enjoy a fantastic breakfast along with a comfortable bed in one of Washington's more interesting old hotel/bed and breakfast facilities. Several rafting companies offer trips on the White Salmon.

Water sports/restrictions: The upper White Salmon is for kayakers only; the lower portion may be run in rafts.

Contact: Phil's White Water Adventures, tel. (800) 366-2004; River Recreation, Inc., tel. (800) 464-5899; River Riders, Inc., tel. (800) 448-RAFT; All Rivers Adventures, tel. (800) 743-5628; Inn of the White Salmon, tel. (509) 493-2335.

18 Little White Salmon River/Drano Lake

Rating: 4

First, let me make one thing very clear: I have done some boating on Drano Lake, but HAVE NEVER and WILL NEVER do any boating on the Little White Salmon River above the lake. The reason for my closed-mindedness is simple; I want to stay alive. The Little White Salmon is a steep, rocky Class V and Class VI river that should be attempted only by expert whitewater paddlers, and then it helps if they're expert paddlers with a bit of a death wish. The river is so nasty, so tough, and with so many obstacles that it could take you all day to make a four- or five-mile run; you'd be out of the boat as much as you'd be in it. Drano Lake, the name given to the backwater where the Little White Salmon meets the Columbia, has some interesting rocky bluffs and forested hillsides along its northern and western flank, and would be a decent place to spend a few hours prospecting in a canoe or small boat. Mostly, though, it's a place where salmon and steelhead anglers congregate in large numbers during the height of the various runs (and when there's an open season on those runs).

Location: Joins the Columbia east of Cook; map B3, grid j0.

How to get there: Take Highway 14 east from Carson or west from White Salmon to the tiny burg of Cook. Drano Lake and the mouth of the Little White Salmon are right along the highway about a mile east of Cook. To reach upriver areas, turn north at Cook and bear north on Cook-Underwood Road, then Willard Road, and finally Oklahoma Road (Forest Service Road 18), which runs almost to the head of the river.

Boat ramp: There's a Skamania County Parks and Recreation Department boat ramp at Drano Lake on the north side of Highway 14. It's a single-lane concrete ramp in good condition, with a large parking area alongside it. Bridges on Willard Road and Cook-Underwood Road offer possibilities for roping or dragging a boat to the river for white-water trips.

Facilities: Moss Creek and Oklahoma Campgrounds (U.S. Forest Service) have both tent and trailer sites, while Big Cedar County Park has tent sites only. Food, gas, and lodging are available in Carson and White Salmon.

Water sports/restrictions: Fishing, paddling, and other small-boat activities are popular in Drano Lake; kayaking on the Little White Salmon is for experts only, with Class V and Class VI water.

Contact: Gifford Pinchot National Forest, Mount Adams Ranger District, tel. (509) 395-2501.

🔟 Northwestern Lake (Reservoir)

Rating: 5

A dam built near the lower end of the White Salmon created this 97-acre lake three miles northwest of White Salmon. It provides good trout fishing at times, but it's not an important boating destination. The public access/boat ramp is the only facility on the lake, and there's nothing particularly exciting it or the scenery around it. Unless you're eager to get out on the water and the wind is blowing up four-foot whitecaps on the Columbia, there's not much reason to visit here.

Location: An impoundment on the White Salmon River, northwest of White Salmon; map B3, grid j1.

How to get there: Take Highway 14 to the town of White Salmon and turn north on Highway 141. About 3.5 miles north of town turn west (left) onto Lakeview Road and follow it around the north end and down the west side of the lake.

Boat ramp: There's a single-lane concrete ramp with a loading float and room to park about two dozen cars and trailers at Northwestern Park on the west side of the lake. When the reservoir is drawn down, this ramps is sometimes left high and dry, suitable only for car-toppers and paddle craft.

Facilities: Everything you may need is available in the town of White Salmon.

Water sports/restrictions: Fishing and small-boat exploration are the main activities.

Contact: Miller's Sports, tel. (509) 493-2233; Inn of the White Salmon, tel. (509) 493-2335.

20 Columbia River (from the mouth of the Wind River to Lake Umatilla)

Rating: 8

Now you're in the world-famous Columbia River Gorge, commonly proclaimed the windsurfing capital of the world. If your idea of a good time involves scooting along the surface of the water at breakneck speed with nothing but a board under your feet, a life jacket strapped tightly to your upper body, and a smile on your face, you've probably already spent considerable time here.

This 135-mile stretch of water, which includes two huge Columbia reservoirs and the better part of a third, is a paradise for sailboarders, some of whom converge on the place whenever they get the word that the wind is up, and some of whom seem to spend every spare moment of their lives here, surfing when it's blowing and resting when it's not. They usually don't have to rest very long between long spells of surfing.

Although the wind is something that most of us consider unpredictable at best, its effects in the Gorge and on its surfing conditions are very well-known to the surfing fraternity. They know where the strongest winds and biggest swells are likely to form, and they tend to sort themselves out according to how their skills and strengths match the wind and water conditions. Horsethief Lake, for example, is protected from the strongest wind and biggest waves, so it's generally recognized as a beginner's spot.

Much of the water near the west end of the Gorge, in places like Stevenson, Home Valley, Drano Lake, and White Salmon, are considered intermediate surfing water by windsurfing standards. An exception is the narrow stretch of river west of White Salmon, off the Spring Creek National Fish Hatchery and the beach known by surfers as Swell City. "Swell" in this case is a noun, not an adjective; the swells build here to very impressive proportions. This part of the Columbia is classified as expert water, where the surfers scream across the bouncy water and many of them spend as much time in the air as they spend on the river's surface In places like this, novices should stay on the beach with the rest of us and watch the real pros do their thing.

Expert-class water becomes more common as you work your way up through the Gorge. At a stretch of Washington State Parks property known as Doug's Beach upstream from the little town of Lyle, the experts get crankin' again, putting on a great show for drivers along Highway 14 and boaters trying to miss the boards as they fight their way upstream or downstream along the river. The section of river above and below Maryhill State Park is another expert stretch, as is much of the water farther upstream toward Roosevelt and on up to McNary Dam. If you're looking for warm weather and truly big water with lots of room to roam on your board, this is heaven. Besides the several wind-surfing access points and facilities on the Washington side of the river, there are many more on the Oregon side.

Good windsurfing water, needless to say, isn't particularly good cruising, skiing, paddling, or fishing water, so folks who pursue these other, less physically demanding water sports tend to hang out on the river at different times and concentrate more of their efforts in areas of the Gorge other than the parts the surfers like. The Gorge has plenty to offer other boaters, but a willingness to wait out the wind or change plans according to the weather simply must be part of your routine.

Besides the big river itself and the dramatic cliffs and steep, rolling hillsides that contain it, this stretch of the Columbia provides a wealth of fantastic scenery and interesting things to do. The possibilities include passing through the locks at Bonneville, The Dalles, and John Day Dams, and depending on the time of the year, watching salmon, steelhead, shad and other species passing through the fish ladders and counting stations at those dams. If you're trailering your boat or have your bikes onboard, side trips off the river to places like the Maryhill Museum, the Stonehenge replica, Carson Hot Springs, the petroglyphs at Horsethief State Park or any of a hundred other fun spots are within reach of the river bank. Fishing is another likely possibility along much of this stretch. Depending on the time of year and where you are in the Gorge, the fishing prospects may include steelhead, chinook salmon, walleyes, smallmouth bass, sturgeon, shad, and more.

Location: From Bonneville Pool at the mouth of the Wind River upstream to Roosevelt on Lake Umatilla; map B3, grid j3.

How to get there: From the west take Highway 14 east from Camas to parallel the north side of the Columbia. From the east take Interstate 82 south from the Tri Cities and turn west on Highway 14 to follow the Columbia downstream.

Boat ramp: Home Valley Waterfront Park, managed by Skamania County, doesn't have a boat ramp, but it's a popular launch site with windsurfers. They have to carry their boards about 50 yards from the parking lot to the river. There's a Skamania County Parks and Recreation Department ramp on Drano Lake at the mouth of the Little White Salmon River. It's a one-lane concrete-plank launch with room for about three dozen cars and trailers on a gravel lot. That's usually plenty of parking room, unless there's a hot salmon fishery going on, when the place gets packed with anglers. It's also used by windsurfers, some of whom stay on the protected waters of the lake. A popular launch site among windsurfers is at a place called Swell City, about two miles west of White Salmon. There's a small day-use fee for launching boards here.

Just east of Swell City is the Spring Creek National Fish Hatchery and a stretch of rocky beach just east of it that's very popular with windsurfers. Bingen Marina has a one-lane asphalt ramp and loading float, along with parking for about three dozen cars and trailers. Windsurfers use the nearby grassy slope and beach to rig and launch their boards. Launching here is free for all craft. The Lyle boat ramp is located near the mouth of the Klickitat River and is a one-lane hard-surface ramp with limited parking near the ramp entrance. Two miles east is Doug's Beach, a stretch of Washington State Parks property where you can't launch a boat, but you can launch a board if you're up to it. Six miles east of Lyle is the natural-surface ramp at Dallesport. Use this one only for launching cartoppers or if you're desperate to get your trailer boat in the water. It's rough, rocky, and requires backing a trailer about 100 yards to the ramp.

Life gets easier farther upriver at the ramp immediately above the Dalles Dam. This launch site has one hard-surface ramp and one gravel ramp, with a loading float between them, and a large, gravel parking lot. Horsethief Lake State Park has a two-lane ramp, one with concrete planks and the other gravel. There's a $3 launch fee here. This ramp is used by both boaters and windsurfers. Avery Park, about four miles upriver from Horsethief Lake, also is popular with windsurfers as well as boaters. Boarders use the grassy bank and beach for launching, while boaters have a one-lane hard-surface ramp. There's parking here for about 40 cars and trailers. It's a free ramp operated by the U.S. Army Corps of Engineers. Maryhill State Park has a two-lane hard-surface ramp with loading floats. Located near the junction of Highway 14 and U.S. 97 coming down the hill from Goldendale, it gets a lot of use throughout much of the year. The launch fee here is $4 unless you're a registered park guest. An annual launch permit is available from the State Parks and Recreation Commission for $40.

Next is the Corps of Engineers ramp just above John Day Dam on Lake Umatilla. It's a one-lane paved ramp with a loading float and room for about two dozen cars and trailers. Another Corps of Engineers ramp is located at the mouth of Rock Creek, 12 miles upstream from John Day Dam. It's a one-lane paved ramp with parking for about 25 cars and trailers, used mostly by bass and walleye anglers. Sunday Cove, about six miles west of Roosevelt, has a poorly maintained Corps of Engineers ramp. This hard-surface ramp is one lane wide and has a small loading float. Roosevelt Park has a good, two-lane, hard-surface ramp with two loading floats. Protected by a small cove off the main river, it's popular with boaters and windsurfers. Launching is free at this Corp of Engineers park. A $10 WDFW access decal is required to use the public launch areas maintained by the Washington Department of Fish and Wildlife.

Facilities: The Port of Klickitat's Bingen Marina has open moorage (free), water and electricity to the docks, rest rooms at the marina, and showers nearby. Fuel docks, restaurants, and grocery stores also are nearby. Horsethief State Park has a dozen tent sites, rest rooms, and showers. Maryhill State Park has over 50 tent/RV sites with water, electric, and sewer hookups, as well as about 35 tent sites with no hookups. Skamania Inn is just west of the mapped area (see section B2) and is the newest and biggest motel/conference center of its kind along the lower Columbia. It has a restaurant and also contains a U.S. Forest Service Interpretive Center with lots of information about the Columbia River Gorge. Home Valley Marine Park has RV and tent sites for $6.50 a night, plus $2 for each additional vehicle. Also on the river at Home Valley is Home Valley RV Park. The Sojourner Motel at Home Valley is a handy stop for people on the river. Inn of the White Salmon in the town of White Salmon is a bed and breakfast that provides a step back into the history of the Columbia Gorge.

Water sports/restrictions: All water sports are permitted.

Contact: Bingen Marina, tel. (509) 493-1655; Columbia Gorge Windsurfing Association, tel. (541) 386-9225 (Oregon number); Klickitat County Tourism, tel. (800) 785-1718; Skamania County Chamber of Commerce, tel. (800) 989-9178; Columbia River Gorge visitor

Association, tel. (800) 984-6743; Skamania Lodge tel. (800) 221-7117; Home Valley RV Park, tel. (509) 427-5300; Skamania County Parks, tel. (509) 427-9478; Inn of the White Salmon, tel. (509) 493-2335; Horsethief Lake State Park, tel. (509) 767-1159; Maryhill State Park, tel. (509) 773-5007; Washington State Parks and Recreation Commission, tel. (800) 233-0321 (information), tel. (800) 452-5687 (reservations).

21 Horsethief Lake

Rating: 4

Really more of a 90-acre Columbia River backwater than a true lake, Horsethief's restrictions make it a quiet place to paddle a canoe or kayak while checking out an interesting part of Washington's history. Near the lake are examples of Indian petroglyphs. Fishing is fair on the lake for a variety of species. The area is used by windsurfers to some extent, mostly those who aren't ready to attack (or be attacked by) the stronger winds and more demanding conditions out on the more exposed sections of the river. **Location:** East of The Dalles Dam, along the Columbia River; map B3, grid j3.

How to get there: Drive east from Lyle on Highway 14. The lake is on the south side of the highway about three miles east of the intersection with U.S. 197.

Boat ramp: Horsethief Lake State Park offers a two-lane boat ramp and lots of shore access. One of the launch lanes is concrete, the other gravel. There's parking for about 25 cars and trailers near the launch area. State Parks charges $3 to launch, and there's an annual launching permit available for $40 from the State Parks and Recreation Commission.

Facilities: Horsethief State Park has a dozen standard tent sites for campers. Camping is also available at Maryhill State Park, about 16 miles to the east. Food, gas, lodging, and other amenities are available across the Columbia River in The Dalles, Oregon.

Water sports/restrictions: The lake has a 5 mph speed limit. Swimming is prohibited.

Contact: Horsethief Lake State Park, tel. (509) 767-1159; Washington State Parks and Recreation Commission, tel. (800) 233-0321 (information), tel. (800) 452-5687 (reservations).

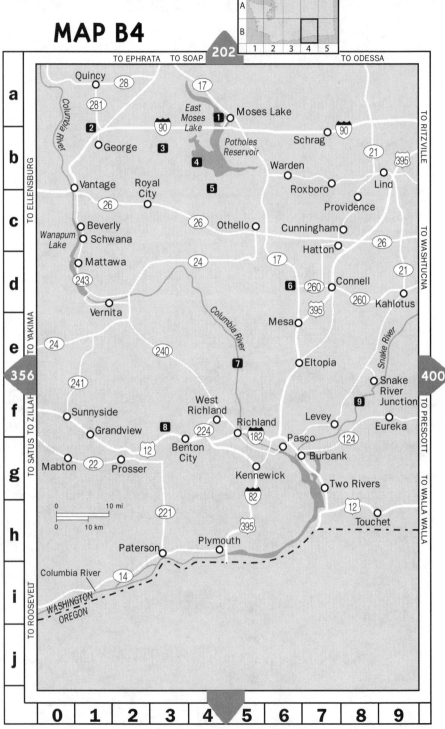

MAP B4

CHAPTER B4

1 Moses Lake

Rating: 10

Although it covers some 6,800 acres, this long, narrow lake is very shallow, and because it's located in the heart of eastern Washington's sun country, it warms quickly in the summer sun. That warmth and easy access via Interstate 90 and Highway 17 make Moses Lake a favorite boating, skiing, fishing, and swimming destination for both locals and visitors from all over the Pacific Northwest. This is a fun place to be in the summer, although on weekends and holidays it gets hectic, maybe even a little crazy. Regulations aimed at keeping people from wrapping themselves around the Interstate 90 bridge pilings or other boats near the bridge are sometimes ignored, leading to some close calls and screamed obscenities. Luckily, most of the speed demons stay on the main lake north of the freeway, leaving room for anglers and paddlers to explore the south end in relative peace and quiet. One of the best things about this lake is that there is room for everyone and things to interest virtually every water enthusiast. Paddlers and anglers enjoy prowling around Marsh, Goat, Gaileys, and Crest Islands as well as the several protected coves located around the lake's shoreline. Most of the lake's boat ramps are located at or near good swim beaches, picnic areas, and other lakefront facili-

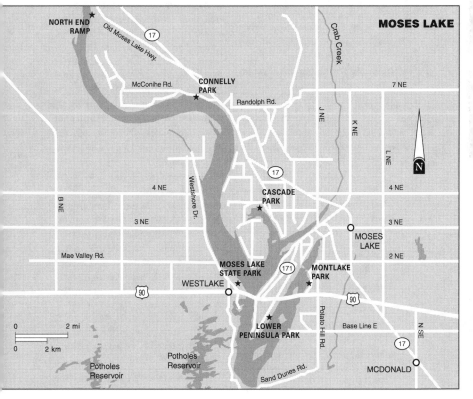

ties, so everyone in the family can do their thing from a central starting point.

How to get there: Take Interstate 90 to Moses Lake. Take the Wapato Drive or Broadway exits (between the two freeway bridges) to reach the south end of the lake, or follow the signs to the state park just west of the first bridge. To reach upper portions of the lake, exit north on Highway 17 and follow it up the east side of the lake.

Boat ramp: There are six boat ramps on the lake, most of them very good facilities. The following boat ramps are listed on the Moses Lake inset map.

- **North End Ramp:** The North End Ramp is off Old Moses Lake Highway, about a mile from the inlet at the north end of the lake. Reach it by taking Highway 17 north about eight miles from town, turning west (left) onto Old Moses Lake Highway and driving four miles to a gravel road that leads left to the ramp.

- **Connelly Park:** Working downlake from there, Connelly Park is on the east side of the lake, off Highway 17 at McConihe Road. It's a two-lane concrete ramp with a loading float and large, paved parking area. It's maintained by the Moses Lake Irrigation District, and launching is free.

- **Cascade Park:** The next ramp as you move south is at Cascade Park, which is near the north end of Lewis Horn off Valley Road near the fair grounds. Launching is also free at this Moses Lake Parks and Recreation Department ramp, a two-lane concrete site with loading floats.

- **Moses Lake State Park:** The two-lane concrete ramp at Moses Lake State Park is on the north side of Interstate 90 at West Shore Road. There's a $3 launch fee at this ramp.

- **Montlake Park:** On the east side of Pelican Horn off Division Street and Linden Avenue, Montlake Park has a two-lane concrete ramp with loading floats. This is another free ramp managed by the Moses Lake Parks and Recreation Department.

- **Lower Peninsula Park:** Farther south on Pelican Horn's west side (off Peninsula Drive) is Lower Peninsula Park, with two concrete launching lanes at its ramp. This is another city ramp where launching is free.

Location: Immediately west of the town of Moses Lake; map B4, grid a4. (See Moses Lake inset map.)

Facilities: Connelly Park, Cascade Park, Peninsula Park, Montlake Park, Neppel Park, and Moses Lake State Park all have public swim beaches. McCosh Park, located at the north end of Pelican Horn off Dogwood Street, has water slides, a swim beach, a tube slide, picnic area, children's playground, concession area, and other facilities. Rental boats, canoes, pedal boats, and PWC are available for rent from Cascade Water Rentals, located at Cascade Marina near Cascade Park. Hallmark Inn & Resort is located right on the lake, with docks, kayak rentals, and other lake-oriented facilities. Moses Lake has a wide array of possibilities for lodging, food and other amenities.

Water sports/restrictions: All water sports are permitted.

Contact: Cascade Park Campground, tel. (509) 766-9240; Sun Crest Resort, tel. (509) 765-0355; Big Sun Resort, tel. (509) 765-8294 (March to November only); Lakeshore Resort, tel. (509) 765-9201; Hallmark Inn & Resort, tel. (509) 765-9211; Cascade Water Rentals, tel. (509) 766-7075 (spring to fall only).

2 Quincy Wildlife Area Lakes

Rating: 5

Most of these relatively small deep lakes

are known for their excellent trout fishing, but they also offer good possibilities for the paddler or other small-boat operator who wants to get away for a pleasant trip on some of the Columbia Basin's pleasant waters. Most of these lakes are frozen in winter, then somewhat crowded with anglers in the spring, but you can always find room to explore one or more of them without running into very much congestion. Fall is an excellent time to visit these lakes because fishing is closed then, so you're likely to have the birds, wildlife, and pleasant autumn weather all to yourself. If size is important, Evergreen Reservoir is the largest of the lot, covering about 235 acres. A distant second is Burke Lake at about 75 acres.

Location: Northwest of George; map B4, grid b1.

How to get there: Take Interstate 90 to George and take Highway 281 north to Road 5 NW. Turn west (left), drive to White Trail Road, and turn left again. Stan Coffin Lake is the first lake on the left, followed by Quincy, then Burke, and then Evergreen Reservoir. Closed roads (hike-in only) to the west lead to Ancient and Dusty lakes.

Boat ramp: There's a single-lane concrete-plank ramp at the Department of Fish and Wildlife access area on Stan Coffin Lake, and a similar facility on Quincy Lake. Burke Lake has three ramps on it. The one at its west end is a gravel one laner; the one at its southwest corner and the one on its east side are one-lane concrete ramps. All are WDFW sites. Evergreen Reservoir also has three ramps, located at its northwest and southwest corners and near the east end. The northwest and east-end ramps are concrete, the southwest one a gravel ramp. A $10 Washington Department of Fish and Wildlife access

decal is required to use the public launch areas maintained by the WDFW.

Facilities: The nearest food, gas, and lodging are in George and to the north in Quincy.

Water sports/restrictions: Fishing and paddling are the main attractions.

Contact: Trinidad Trading Post, tel. (509) 787-3083; Village Inn Motel & RV Park, tel. (509) 787-3515; Shady Tree RV Park, tel. (509) 785-2851.

🔳 Winchester Wasteway

Rating: 5

First, an explanation of terms so that you don't think a trip to Winchester Wasteway is an adventure in sewage travel. "Waste" in this context is the irrigation water running through the channel, water that's wasted because it isn't soaking into a field somewhere upstream. Now that you're perhaps more interested in putting your boat in this wasteway, you should know that it begins in the irrigated fields between Quincy and Ephrata and winds its way southeasterly, eventually joining into the west side of Potholes Reservoir north of Potholes State Park. It offers good fishing in the spring and summer, waterfowl hunting opportunities in the fall, and an excellent, meandering paddle through some of Washington's most wildlife-rich country throughout much of the year.

One good paddle trip is from Winchester Wildlife Area near Interstate 90 down to Dodson Road, where there's ample parking and a good place to get small boats into and out of the water. The float from Dodson Road down to Potholes Reservoir is another good one, but requires an open-water paddle of about three miles at the end of the trip in order to reach the take-out site at the state park. You can avoid this leg of the trip by taking out at Road C SW about a mile west of the reservoir. The wasteway isn't without obstacles for paddlers. They come in the form of waterfalls and culverts, all of which can be portaged quite easily. More difficult to avoid are the dead ends in the channel itself that you'll encounter now and then as the wasteway winds and twists its way through sand dunes before it finally opens up into the reservoir. If you float the wasteway in midsummer, trees and brush overhanging the channel can also lead you astray from time to time.

Because the wasteway flows through public land along much of its course, it's possible to turn a float trip into a camping trip if you wish. There are no facilities along the way, so you'll have to be fully self-contained, but chances are you'll have your chosen campsite all to yourself except for the ample wildlife that will no doubt be nearby to serenade you to sleep.

Location: Flows into the west side of Potholes Reservoir; map B4, grid b3.

How to get there: To reach the wasteway north of Interstate 90, take the Interstate to the Dodson Road exit and leave the freeway to the north. Immediately turn west on the northern frontage road and follow it three miles to the west side of the wasteway. To reach southern parts of Winchester Wasteway, turn south off Interstate 90 onto Dodson Road and follow it 3.5 miles to the water. From there you can continue south to Road 7 SW, turn left, then left again on O'Sullivan Dam Road, and a third left on Road C SE to the water. The wasteway is also accessible by boat from the northwest corner of Potholes Reservoir.

Boat ramp: The best places to get a boat in the water are at Winchester Wildlife Area just north of Interstate 90, at Dodson Road, and off the end of Road C SE near the west end of Potholes Reservoir.

Facilities: Food, gas, and lodging are available in George. Potholes State Park is a few miles to the southeast, as is Mar-Don Resort. Both are on the west side of Potholes Reservoir.

Water sports/restrictions: Paddling, fishing, and hunting are the main attractions.

Contact: Potholes State Park, tel. (509) 765-7271; Washington State Parks and Recreation Commission, tel. (800) 233-0321 (information), tel. (800) 452-5687 (reservations); MarDon Resort, tel. (509) 346-2651.

◪ Potholes Reservoir

Rating: 7

Sometimes called O'Sullivan Reservoir because it was formed by the construction of O'Sullivan Dam across Crab Creek in the late '40s as part of the Columbia Basin Reclamation Project, this sprawling impoundment is one of the Basin's foremost spots for water recreation. Depending on the time of year, it ranges in size from 10,000 acres in the fall to 30,000 acres in the spring, which means that for at least part of the year it's the biggest lake in Grant County, acing out 25,000-acre Banks Lake. Although their shapes and physical appearance are quite different, they are similar in the amount and variety of fun they provide. Like Banks, Potholes is a haven to anglers, skiers, PWC riders, paddlers, sailors, boat-campers, swimmers, tubers, even divers. In some ways, though, Potholes is a much more interesting—even intriguing—destination for boaters and other water lovers, thanks in great part to that maze of sand islands and channels known to most as the Dunes.

Fly over the reservoir or look at an aerial photo of it, and you'll be fascinated by the Dunes. Depending on the water level, the area is a landscape of rolling sand hills cut by miles of narrow waterways or a vast body of water dotted with hundreds of sand islands. The fact that they change constantly at the whim of the water and the wind is both part of the Dunes' attraction and part of the frustration they cause for boaters. Just when you think you know your way around them, they change. There are hundreds of stories of people who have become mixed-up—not lost, mind you—in the Dunes over the years, some of whom didn't find their way out on the same day they went in. That may be OK if you happen to be boat camping, but if you're on a day trip, it can be embarrassing, perhaps even a tad dangerous.

Besides the possibility of getting lost, the Dunes present another potential danger for boaters: other boaters. Some people don't seem to understand that there just might be others around while they're in there, so they speed through the narrow channels, around sand hills where visibility is only a few yards, forcing other boaters up into the sand, nearly wiping out swimmers, anglers, and campers along their reckless route, and generally endangering their lives and the lives of anyone else who has the misfortune of being in the Dunes on that particular day. The advent of personal watercraft has increased the number of such bozos in the Dunes to the point that some longtime Potholes anglers avoid the area during the summer months. Such recklessness is, of course, illegal, but perhaps there haven't been quite enough citations issued here to get that point across. Justice does prevail now and then when one of these goofballs gets stranded on the sand himself, but it's usually someone else who pays the price instead of the culprits.

Despite these daredevils, the Dunes are still a phenomenal boating destination and are a must-see for anyone who goes to Potholes. Whether you're visiting them for the day or planning an extended day with a tent and all your toys, be sure to take along lots of drinking water. You dry out quickly in this part of the state on a warm summer day. The more open waters of the reservoir's southern two-thirds also have plenty to offer visiting boaters. Gradual sand beaches, especially along the west side, offer great swimming possibilities, and the rocky islands and submerged boulders near the south end of the reservoir are fascinating places to explore. The fishing is excellent around all those rocks, which also draw a few divers to the area. Be careful when boating along this rocky end of the lake; more than one lower unit has been destroyed here. If you care, the biggest island, located about three-quarters of a mile out from the face of the rock dam, is Goose Island.

Location: Southwest of Moses Lake; map B4, grid b4.

How to get there: From the southwest take Highway 26 east from Vantage and turn north on Highway 262, following it to the southwest corner of the reservoir. From the southeast take Highway 26 to Othello, turn north on Highway 17, then west on Highway 262. From the north take Interstate 90 to Moses Lake and turn south on Highway 17. Drive just two miles to M Road SE and turn south (right). Follow M Road to Highway 262 and turn west (right) to the south end of Potholes.

Boat ramp: There are several boat ramps on the reservoir and on Lind Coulee, which joins the reservoir at its southeast corner. Potholes State Park near the southwest corner of the reservoir has a paved ramp with loading floats. The launch fee here is $4, or you can buy an annual launch permit, good at all parks, for $40. Just south of the park is the Department of Fish and Wildlife's Glen Williams launch site, with two concrete ramp lanes and lots of parking. Near the west end of the dam at the southwest corner of the reservoir is MarDon Resort's single-lane concrete ramp. There are two ramps near the mouth of Lind Coulee, one on the south side off Highway 262 and one on the north side off Road K5 SE. Both are one-lane gravel ramps. A $10 Washington Department of Fish and Wildlife access decal is required to use the public launch areas maintained by the WDFW.

Facilities: MarDon Resort is a full-service facility with a cafe, bar, grocery, and tackle store, a huge fishing dock, boat ramp, RV and tent sites, cabins, car and boat gas, and other amenities. Potholes State Park, two miles north of the resort, has about a dozen tent sites and over 60 RV sites with hookups, rest rooms, showers, and a boat ramp. Food, gas, and lodging are also available to the south in Othello and to the north in Moses Lake.

Water sports/restrictions: All water sports are permitted.

Contact: Potholes State Park, tel. (509) 765-7271; Washington State Parks and Recreation Commission, tel. (800) 233-0321 (information), tel. (800) 452-5687 (reservations); MarDon Resort, tel. (509) 346-2651.

5 Potholes Area Seep Lakes

Rating: 6

As I mentioned in *Washington Fishing,* it would have been very easy and perhaps appropriate to devote one listing to each of the lakes in this chain, or at least to all the major ones. But that would have added three to four dozen listings and a great amount of detail to wade through for anyone planning to visit this recreation-rich part of the state. It might also have limited the focus for would-be visitors, who might have picked out one or two lakes to visit when they should keep their minds open to exploring as much of this country as they have time for.

What I've found over the years is that when I set out to fish or explore one or two lakes in this chain, I invariable wind up spending time at others. Sometimes I don't even make it to the lake I originally planned to visit. Even on such occasions when I changed my plans drastically, I've never been disappointed. That's the long way of explaining that I lumped them all under one listing for your own good.

These lakes have a common origin in that none of them existed before the construction of O'Sullivan Dam, which backed up Crab Creek to form Potholes Reservoir and forced water through underground fissures that opened into coulees and potholes to become the so-called "Seep Lakes." Beyond that shared lineage, though, each lake is at least somewhat different from the others. They range in size from only a few yards across to more than 180 acres; fishing regulations and fish species availability are different from one lake to the next; boating regulations vary from lake to lake; the things you can see and do cover a wide range of possibilities, depending on what lake or lakes you visit and what time of year you show up.

I don't think there is a bad time of year to visit, but most boaters would agree that their activities are limited from December to March when the lakes all have a layer of ice on their surfaces. A good deal of ice fishing takes place here on the year-round angling lakes, and spring is also a great time to visit with a fishing rod. Every lake in this chain is a good place to paddle, but many kayakers and canoeists prefer the lakes where they don't have to compete with the motorboaters, such as the Hampton Lakes and all the small lakes between Upper Hampton and Soda, which have no-motor regulations. Hutchinson and Shiner lakes are also popular with paddlers, since they're closed to the use gas motors and are connected by a narrow channel so that allows for morning-long paddle around several miles of shoreline.

Whatever lake or lakes you explore, you're almost certain to see a wide variety of birds and wildlife. This is, after all, a national wildlife refuge, and there are ducks, geese, songbirds, and small mammals almost everywhere you look.

Location: Southeast of Potholes Reservoir; map B4, grid b4.

How to get there: From the north take Highway 26 from Vantage or Highway 17 from Moses Lake to Highway 262 and take any of several gravel or dirt roads to the south from the south end of Potholes Reservoir to reach various lakes in the chain. From the south take Highway 26 to Othello and turn north on McManamon Road.

Boat ramp: Soda Lake, one of the biggest in the chain, has a two-lane gravel ramp at the campground near its northwest corner and a three-lane gravel ramp near the dam at its south end. Another of the larger lakes, Upper Goose, also has two ramps. There's a single-lane concrete ramp near its north end and a single-lane gravel ramp near the south end. Warden Lake, another of the chain's largest, has a two-lane gravel ramp near its north end. Between Soda and Warden Lakes is Susan Lake, which has a two-lane natural ramp that becomes rough and muddy after heavy use in the spring. Lower Goose Lake has a one-lane gravel-and-rock ramp that also gets a little rugged in the spring. Long Lake, another of the larger lakes in the group, has a one-lane gravel ramp.

Nearby is good-sized Canal Lake, which has one of the best ramps of the bunch, a concrete-plank two laner with a fairly large, partly paved parking area. Between Long and Canal is Heart Lake, which has a single-lane concrete-plank ramp. South Teal Lake has a one-lane gravel ramp that has seen much better days. There's a natural-surface ramp at Herman Lake that's adequate for launching small trailer boats and cartoppers; a ramp of similar quality is at nearby Lyle Lake. To the west, Halfmoon Lake also has a natural-surface ramp that works for cartoppers and paddle craft. Another small ramp with a natural surface is located near the west end of Hutchinson Lake. Boaters also use this ramp to reach Shiner Lake, which is connected to Hutchinson by a shallow channel.

Access roads running through the chain offer the possibility for carrying small boats to many other lakes, depending on your energy and enthusiasm. Some lakes require a pack or drag of only a few yards, while others are nearly a mile from the nearest road or parking area.

Facilities: MarDon Resort is a full-service facility with a cafe, bar, grocery, and tackle store, a huge fishing dock, boat ramp, RV and tent sites, cabins, car and boat gas, and other amenities. Potholes

State Park, two miles north of the resort, has about a dozen tent sites and over 60 RV sites with hookups, rest rooms, showers, and a boat ramp. Food, gas, and lodging are also available to the south in Othello.

Water sports/restrictions: Swimming is prohibited in all lakes within the Columbia National Wildlife Refuge, which includes virtually all the Seep Lakes. All motors are prohibited on some lakes, gaspowered motors prohibited on others, and there are no motor restrictions on still others. Fishing season is year-round on about half of the lakes, March through July or March through September on the others. Pick up a copy of the latest refuge regulations when you enter the area.

Contact: Potholes State Park, tel. (509) 765-7271; MarDon Resort, tel. (509) 346-2651; Columbia National Wildlife Refuge, tel. (509) 488-2668.

6 Scooteney Reservoir

Rating: 5

I have to admit that the first time I really noticed Scooteney Reservoir, while I was passing by it along Highway 17 on my way to the Tri-Cities, I wasn't impressed. Of course, it was the dead of winter, the wind was blowing about 20 miles an hour, and the reservoir was covered with several inches of ice and snow. I muttered something like "What a desolate place," or maybe even "What a hell hole." The next time I ventured past Scooteney was late spring, there was some greenery around the lake, and several boats were out on the water. No, I didn't say, "What a beautiful lake," but I think I did admit, "Maybe this isn't so bad." Having grown up on the green, tree-covered west side of the Cascades, I don't think I could ever view Scooteney as God's gift to boaters, thanks to rather

boring landscape surrounding it. But when it comes to water sports, it has enough going for it to draw folks from all over this part of southeastern Washington. Formed by the damming of Potholes Canal in the '50s, this 900-acre impoundment has a maximum depth of about 30 feet, so it warms quickly in the summer and is well populated with swimmers, skiers, and other fun lovers by the Fourth of July. The county park at its south end is the center of activity. Although a fair bet for spring bass fishing, most of the angling activity at Scooteney occurs in the winter when anglers converge on it to catch yellow perch through the ice. Don't bother bringing your boat along for that one.

Location: Southeast of Othello; map B4, grid d6.

How to get there: Take Highway 26 to Othello and turn south on Highway 17. Turn south (right) on Schoolaney Road and east (left) on Horseshoe Road to reach the west side of the reservoir. Continue past Schoolaney Road about three miles and take either of the next two right-hand turns off the highway to reach the reservoir's east side.

Boat ramp: A very good three-lane concrete ramp with a loading float is at Scooteney Park, managed by Franklin County. The ramp also has a large, partly paved parking lot with room for at least 75 cars and trailers.

Facilities: Scooteney Park has a swim beach, picnic area with barbecue grates, RV and tent sites, and an RV dump station.

Water sports/restrictions: All water sports are permitted.

Contact: Sportsman RV, tel. (509) 488-3424; Greater Othello Chamber of Commerce/Visitor Information Center, tel. (800) 684-2556.

7 Columbia River (between Rock Island Dam and Roosevelt)

Rating: 8

I always think about this stretch of the Columbia as being the all-or-nothing part of the river. Most of the boating activity centers on certain places and certain times of the year, and if you go somewhere else or visit at other times, you may have what seems like miles of river all to yourself. Since there are places along this stretch where the river is nearly a mile wide, you can be alone on a fairly short stretch and literally have miles—square miles, anyway—that are all yours.

One of the busiest parts of the river, especially in summer, is the few miles upstream and downstream from Crescent Bar, about five miles southwest of Quincy. This is one of the key summer play spots for folks around Wenatchee, Quincy, and Ephrata, but its warm water and blue skies also hold a strong attraction for folks from as far away as Seattle and Spokane. You begin feeling more like having a good time the minute you break over the crest of the hill off Highway 28 and start the long descent down toward the edge of the river where the boat ramp and other facilities are located. By the time you cross the short bridge connecting the bar itself to the mainland, you're ready for action. Well, at least that's the way I feel, and I don't think I'm alone.

Crescent Bar is near the top end of the backwater from Wanapum Dam, known, oddly enough, as Wanapum Pool. The lower one-third of the pool is another place that gets quite a lot of boating, swimming, and skiing activity. That's partly because Interstate 90 runs right over the river about five miles above Wanapum Dam, providing access to much of the free world; partly because there's a state park midway between the dam and the interstate; partly because Vantage—the closest thing to a town in the immediate vicinity—has boat ramps, gas stations, campgrounds, and other amenities for boaters; and partly because this is one of the widest parts of the river, with plenty of room to play. So the lower end of Wanpum Pool becomes busy on a warm summer weekend, especially a weekend when someone like Rod Stewart, the Moody Blues, or Bonnie Raitt is entertaining at The Gorge, which sits atop the east bank of the river about midway up Wanapum Pool. In fact, there are places on the river where, they say, the music sounds nearly as good as it does up on the hill where folks are packed in like cordwood after paying $30 to $50 each to get in.

With the exception of a short period in the fall, the next 65 miles of river, from Wanapum Dam down to North Richland, gets relatively light use. This section includes Priest Rapids Reservoir and the Hanford Reach, the longest free-flowing section of this heavily dammed river. The Hanford Reach is a boater's paradise as long as the boater likes real rivers, wildlife, and light boating traffic. Paddlers and anglers are especially fond of the Reach mostly because the majority of other recreationists are somewhere else.

This section of river gave up Washington's state-record smallmouth bass several years ago, and it still provides excellent steelhead and salmon fishing at certain times of year. And that brings us to that short period in the fall I mentioned earlier, the time when this part of the river does get busy. The fall chinook run here provides some of the best salmon fishing still available on the Columbia, so for a while in October the boat traffic gets thick in some places, especially around the Vernita Bridge, where many of the anglers launch. With the very real possibility of catching a salmon 40 pounds or larger, why wouldn't they come here in droves?

Like any other free-flowing river, the Hanford Reach has its dangers. Places like Coyote Rapids, five miles downstream from the bridge at Vernita, can eat you alive if you aren't paying attention. Another danger here is getting caught on the beach at the Hanford Nuclear Reservation. Let's just say they'd rather you didn't trespass. After all, every boater's a Commie spy, right? The river gets very busy again at about the Richland city limits, and stays that way past the mouth of the Snake River a couple of miles southeast of Pasco.

The people in the Tri-Cities love their water, and the Columbia is where most of them go to play and cool off. Look closely at the list of boat ramps, waterfront parks, campgrounds, and other facilities that are along this stretch of the river and you'll understand the importance of the Columbia and the recreation it provides to the people of Richland, Pasco, and Kennewick. Some parts of the river are busy every day in the summer and whenever there's a warm, calm Saturday or Sunday throughout much of the year. A few miles below the mouth of the Snake, the boating crowds begin to thin out again, at least where Washington boaters are concerned. The folks from Umatilla and Hermiston, Oregon, turn out in good numbers to play on Lake Wallula (above McNary Dam) and Lake Umatilla (below McNary).

The last hurrah for Washingtonians is around Crow Butte State Park, nearly 30 river miles downstream from McNary Dam. Water activities are big here, which should come as no big surprise when you realize that Crow Butte is on an island in the middle of the river. The summer temperatures here are hot and the water is warm, so Crow Butte is a favorite of everyone from swimmers to windsurfers, wakeboarders to PWC riders.

Location: From Rock Island Dam downstream to Roosevelt; map B4, grid e4.

How to get there: Highway 28 between Wenatchee and Quincy provides access to the east side of the river between Wenatchee and Crescent Bar. To reach the east side of the river downstream from Vantage, turn south off Interstate 90 on Highway 243. Turn south on Highway 24 at Vernita to reach the popular stretch of river around the Vernita Bridge. Turn south off Highway 24 onto Seagull Road and then west on Road 170 to reach the popular steelhead-fishing stretch of river at Ringold. Roads out of Richland and Pasco provide access to the stretch of the Columbia between Ringold and the Tri-Cities. The best access here is via the South Columbia River Road, which runs up the east side of the river from Pasco. Access on the east side of the Columbia from the Tri-Cities to Wallula is via U.S. 12. to reach the stretch of river between McNary Dam and John Day Dam, take Highway 14 east from Wishram or west from U.S. 395.

Boat ramp: There are 34 boat ramps on this stretch of the Columbia River:

- **Rock Island Hydro Park:** Working downstream from Rock Island Dam, the first ramp is at Rock Island Hydro Park, about two miles south of East Wenatchee on Highway 28. Managed by the Chelan County Public Utilities District, it's a one-lane ramp wide enough to allow two boats at a time if they were friends in a hurry to get on or off the water (and both knew how to back a trailer).

- **Crescent Bar Ramp:** Next is the Grant County PUD's ramp at Crescent Bar off Highway 28 about six miles west of Quincy. This two-lane concrete ramp has loading floats and gets a lot of use during the summer months. There's a $7 daily fee for parking here, $15 for overnight parking, with a $50 annual permit available.

- **Sunland Estates:** Downstream a few miles from Crescent Bar is the Department of Fish and Wildlife's ramp at Sunland Estates. This is a one-lane concrete-plank ramp with nearby parking for about 35 cars and trailers. To get there, drive east from Vantage on Interstate 90 to Exit 143, turning north on Silica Road and following it six miles. Turn left on Sunland Road and drive three miles to the sign on the left pointing to the public access area and ramp.

- **Ginko State Park:** The next ramp is on the Kittitas County (west) side of the river, at Ginko State Park. It's a one-lane hard-surface ramp with limited parking nearby. There's a $4 launch fee here. Take the Vantage exit off Interstate 90 and drive north one mile on the main drag through town. Turn right on the unmarked paved road at the state park boundary, and follow it one mile down the hill to the ramp.

- **Vantage Ramp:** About a mile farther downstream on the Kittitas County side of the river is the Wanapum/Vantage boat ramp, right alongside Interstate 90 at the west end of the Vantage Bridge. This concrete ramp has a launch float and room for over 50 cars and trailers in the paved parking lot. It's a little strange in that it has a two-lane ramp by the float and a third one about 50 feet away from the others. Launching is free at this Kittitas County facility.

- **Wanapum State Park:** On the same side of the river about three miles downstream is the two-lane concrete-plank ramp at Wanapum State Park. It has a loading float and lots of parking, and the launch fee is $4 unless you're a registered park guest. Reach it by taking the Vantage exit off Interstate 90 and turning south on Wanapum Road. The park is three miles off the interstate.

- **Getty's Cove:** Also on the west side of the river a short distance past the state park is Getty's Cove Resort, which has a one-lane paved boat ramp. A launch fee is charged here. Although the river is on the left as you approach via Wanapum Road from the freeway, the resort and its ramp are on the right, at the edge of a narrow cove extending several hundred feet off the main river.

- **Upstream Wanapum Dam Ramp:** This ramp is on the Grant County (east) side of the river, just upstream from Wanapum Dam, off Highway 243. Managed by the Grant County Public Utility District, it's a single-lane concrete ramp with a loading float and parking for about a dozen cars and trailers. Get there by taking Interstate 90 to the Yakima/Pullman exit at the east end of the Vantage Bridge and going south on Highway 26 for just over one mile to Highway 243. Follow Highway 243 about four miles and turn right at Wanapum Dam. Take an immediate right and you're there.

- **Downstream Wanapum Dam Ramp:** Just downstream from Wanapum Dam on the Grant County side is another county PUD ramp, this one a one-lane concrete ramp with a large gravel parking area. Follow the directions to the upstream ramp, but continue past the dam and turn right at the tour center.

- **Buckshot Ranch Boat Ramp:** Located about four miles north of Priest Rapids Dam, this is another Grant County PUD launch. It's at the

Buckshot Ranch site and has two lanes, both concrete-ramp construction, with a large gravel parking area. Drive south on Highway 243 two miles from Mattawa Junction and turn right at the public fishing sign onto Road 26 SW. Go one mile to a second sign and follow the gravel road three-quarters of a mile to the ramp.

- **Desert Aire Ramp:** Two miles south of Buckshot Ranch, off Desert Aire Road, is yet another Grant County PUD ramp, this one with two concrete lanes and a loading float. There's a $3 launch fee here.

- **Vernita Bridge Ramp:** Nine miles downstream from Priest Rapids Dam is the Highway 24 bridge at Vernita, where the Department of Fish and Wildlife has a natural-surface ramp about four lanes wide and a gravel parking area with room for about 50 cars and trailers. Although it's rather rough and primitive, this ramp gets a lot of use during the fall chinook salmon fishing season. Drive west from the junction of Highway 243 and Highway 24 and turn left at the public fishing sign, following the rough gravel road east back toward the bridge.

- **White Bluffs Ramp:** The next ramp downstream is the WDFW ramp at White Bluffs in Franklin County (east side of the river) about 18 miles downstream from Vernita. It's a very good two-lane concrete ramp at the site of the old White Bluffs Ferry Terminal. Take Wahluke Road off Highway 24 and drive south four miles to the power lines; then turn right and drive just under two miles on the gravel road to the ramp.

- **Wahluke Ramp:** Also on the Franklin County side of the river is the one-lane gravel ramp at the Department of Wildlife's Wahluke Wildlife Area, 11 miles northwest of Pasco via Taylor Flats and Ringold

Spring Roads. Steelhead and salmon anglers use this one quite extensively.

- **Ringold Springs Ramp:** The WDFW's ramp at Ringold Springs is another gravel one laner that's used mostly by anglers. To reach it from Pasco, drive north on Taylor Flats Road 18 miles and turn west (left) onto Ringold Road, following it three miles. Turn left onto Ringold Springs Road and go just under a mile to Ringold River Road. The road turns to gravel at this intersection, but go straight through to the ramp.

- **Grove's Park:** It's about 14 miles downstream to the next ramp, this one on the Benton County (west) side of the river off George Washington Way at Groves Park in Richland. This Richland Parks and Recreation Department launch is good, with a four-lane concrete ramp, loading float, and spaces for about 50 cars and trailers. To reach it, turn off George Washington Way in Richland onto Snyder Road and go east three-quarters of a mile to its end. The boat ramp is on the right.

- **Howard Amon Park:** Three miles south of Groves Park, also off George Washington Way, is the Richland Parks and Recreation Department's Howard Amon Park, which has two sets of boat ramps, one at the north end of the park and one at the south. Between the two they provide five lanes of concrete-surface ramps, with loading floats available at the northern site. There's room to park perhaps 100 cars and trailers near the two ramps.

- **Columbia Point Ramp:** Another mile south on George Washington Way is Columbia Point, a Richland Parks and Recreation facility with a four-lane concrete ramp, three floats and parking for about 150 cars and trailers. To get there, take the George Washington Way exit off U.S. 12 in Richland and go north about 300 yards to Adams Street. Turn right on Adams and follow it to the park, on the left at the end of the street.

- **Wye Park Ramp:** Richland's Wye Park has a two-lane concrete ramp and loading float. It's on Columbia Drive, north of Highway 240. To get there, take the Edison Street exit off Highway 240 and go north to Columbia Drive. Turn left on Columbia and follow it to the park, on the right.

- **Chiawana Park:** On the Franklin County side of the Columbia is Chiawana Park. Reached via Court Street and Road 88 west from Pasco, this park has a two-lane concrete ramp and loading float, with parking for about 30 cars and trailers. Go west from Pasco on Court Street and turn south on Road 88 to the park. At the park entrance turn left and follow the paved road to the ramp.

- **Columbia Park West Ramp:** On the west side of the river the next ramp is at Columbia Park West, a Richland Parks and Recreation facility with a two-lane concrete ramp, loading floats, and parking for about 100 cars and trailers. To reach it from Kennewick, drive west on Highway 240 for two miles to the Edison Street exit and turn right on Edison. Turn left on Columbia Drive and go 1.2 miles, then right on the unmarked road leading to the ramp.

- **Columbia Park Ramp:** This park, a Kennewick Parks and Recreation Department site, offers a huge boat-launching facility. Located just off Highway 240 at Edison Street, it has an eight-lane concrete ramp, loading floats, and a gravel parking area with room for over 100 cars and trailers.

- **Road 54 Ramp:** Across the river in Pasco is the U.S. Army Corps of Engineers ramp off Sylvester Street and Road 54. It's a two-lane concrete ramp with a gravel parking area that holds 30 cars and trailers. It's seen better days but is still very usable.

Take U.S. 12 to Pasco and get off at the blue bridge to go west on Sylvester Street. Follow Sylvester for two miles and turn south on Road 54. The ramp is 100 yards down Road 54, on the left.

- **Pasco Boat Basin:** Near the east end of Pasco off Fourth Avenue is the Pasco Boat Basin and its four-lane concrete ramp. This is a Corps of Engineers site with a loading float and room to park about 20 cars and trailers. Drive south from Pasco on Highway 397 and turn south onto Fourth Avenue, following it two blocks to the ramp at the end of the street.

- **Metz Marina:** Back on the Benton County side of the river is the Port of Kennewick's Metz Marina, where there are a four-lane concrete boat ramp, loading floats, and room to park about three dozen cars and trailers. A hoist is also located nearby. Take Columbia Drive east off U.S. 395 and turn left on Washington Street, going half a mile to the marina on the right.

- **Sacajawea State Park:** On the north side of the Snake River mouth is Sacajawea State Park, with a two-lane concrete ramp and loading floats located in a protected cove. The launch fee here is $4, with a yearly permit available for $40. Drive east on U.S. 12 from Pasco for seven miles and turn right just before crossing the bridge over the Snake River.

- **Hood Park/Hood Park boat Basin:** Two Corps of Engineers ramps on the south shore of the Snake River also provide access to Lake Wallula and the Columbia. Hood Park has three lanes of concrete ramps and two loading floats, and the nearby Hood Park Boat Basin has a one-lane concrete ramp and one loading float. Cross the Snake River eastbound on U.S. 12 and turn left on

Ice Harbor Drive, turning left again almost immediately at the park entrance.

• **Two Rivers Park:** Straight across the Columbia from the mouth of the Snake is the two-lane concrete ramp at Benton County's Two Rivers Park. From Highway 397 in Kennewick, turn east on Hedges Road and drive just over a mile to Finley Road, turning north (left) and following Finley half a mile to the park entrance on the right.

• **McNary Wildlife Refuge:** Near the southwest corner of McNary Island on the east side of the Columbia is the U.S. Fish and Wildlife Service boat ramp that serves the McNary National Wildlife Refuge. It's a one-lane concrete-plank ramp in a shallow cove, where the water level sometimes drops below the end of the ramp. It's accessible via gravel roads leading west off U.S. 12 about eight miles south of Pasco.

• **Madame Dorian Park:** About 15 miles south of Pasco is Madame Dorian Park, in the large bay where the Walla Walla River enters the Columbia from the east. The Army Corps of Engineers ramp here is a one-lane gravel ramp with a gravel parking area that holds about two dozen cars and trailers. Drive east from Pasco on U.S. 12 for 16 miles and turn left on North Shore Road, taking an immediate right into the park.

• **North McNary Ramp:** It's more than 20 miles downstream to the next ramp on the Washington side of the river just east of McNary Dam. The Army Corps of Engineers North McNary ramp has a single concrete lane and parking for about 80 cars and trailers. To find it, drive east from the junction of Highway 14 and U.S. 395 toward the McNary fish ladder viewing area and turn left toward the boat ramp.

• **Plymouth Park:** Just downstream from McNary Dam is another Corp of Engineers ramp at Plymouth Park. It's a wide, two-lane concrete ramp with loading floats and parking for about 20 cars and trailers. Take Plymouth Road south of Highway 14 and drive a mile. Turn west (right) on Christie Road and watch for the boat ramp sign to the left.

• **Paterson Ramp:** About 12 miles west is the Paterson access on the Umatilla National Wildlife Refuge. The U.S. Fish and Wildlife Service ramp here is a natural-surface, gently sloping gravel bar with room to park along the beach nearby. There's nothing here in the way of facilities. Take Highway 14 to Paterson and turn south on Kent Road, following it three-quarters of a mile to its end.

• **Crow Butte State Park:** Ten miles downstream (west) is Crow Butte State Park, where there's a three-lane hard-surface ramp with parking for about 50 cars and trailers. The launch fee here is $4 round-trip, with a $40 annual permit available from the State Parks and Recreation Commission. The park is right alongside Highway 14.

If you use any of the Washington Department of Fish and Wildlife ramps up-river, remember that a $10 Washington Department of Fish and Wildlife access decal is required to use the public launch areas maintained by the WDFW.

Facilities: Rock Island Hydro Park, south of East Wenatchee, has a large, roped swim area, rest rooms, a covered picnic shelter, picnic tables, tennis and basketball courts, baseball fields, a volleyball pit, access to a paved hiking trail along the river, and lots of open grassy space near the river. Crescent Bar Resort and the area around it has moorage, boat and PWC rentals, RV and tent sites with hookups, motel units, a swim beach, and other facilities. Wanapum State Park near Vantage has 50 RV and tent sites with water, electricity and sewer hookups, picnic tables, rest rooms with showers. There's a large, gravel swim beach, rest rooms/dressing rooms and picnic tables in the day-use area.

Getty's Cove Resort, above Wanapum Dam, has RV and tent sites, rest rooms with showers, a small store, PWC rentals, and is open from spring to fall only. Like other overnight facilities throughout this area, it's packed on weekends when there's a concert at The Gorge. Groves Park and Howard Amon Park near Richland both have large swim beaches and picnic areas near the river. Columbia Point Park has moorage, a swim beach, picnic areas, barbecue grills, play equipment and other amenities. There's a swim beach a play area, picnic tables, and other facilities at Wye Park, too.

Columbia Park West in Richland has moorage, picnic spots, a swim beach, and PWC and pontoon boat rentals. Columbia Park in Kennewick has tent and RV campsites, a large, roped swim beach, picnic areas, trails, basketball and tennis courts, rest rooms with showers, an RV dump station, and even a golf course. The Port of Kennewick's Metz Marina has covered and open moorage ($12 for boats 25 feet and under, $16 for boats over 25 feet), a hoist, water and electricity to the docks, boat-sewage pump-out facilities, rest rooms, fuel docks, boat repair, and nearby groceries and lodging. At the Pasco Boat Basin you'll find swim beaches at the adjacent park, moorage, boat repair, fuel docks, and other services.

Sacajawea State Park is a day-use park with a swim beach, picnic tables, barbecue pits, and rest rooms. There's a roped swim beach at Plymouth Park, as well as campsites, picnic tables, barbecue pits, showers, and an RV dump station. At Crow Butte State Park you'll find 50 campsites with water, electricity and sewage hookups, rest rooms with showers, a roped swim beach, and picnic areas.

Water sports/restrictions: All water sports are permitted.

Contact: Crescent Bar Resort, tel. (509) 787-1511; Malibu Rentals (Crescent Bar), tel. (509) 884-7658; Vantage KOA, tel. (509) 856-2230; Desert Aire Motel, tel. (509) 932-4300; Richland Parks and Recreation Department, tel. (509) 942-7529; Metz Marina, tel. (509) 582-8709; Sacajawea State Park (no overnight camping), tel. (509) 545-2361; Crow Butte State Park, tel. (509) 875-2644; Washington State Parks and Recreation Commission, tel. (800) 233-0321 (information), tel. (800) 452-5687 (reservations).

8 Lower Yakima River

Rating: 7

A friend who spends as much time as possible fishing and playing on the rivers of the Pacific Northwest once told me that he thought the Yakima River from the town of Yakima downstream was just about as boring as that part of the river above town was fun and exciting. Now that's quite a generalization, and I don't totally agree with it. Part of the reason for his devalued view of the lower Yakima, I'm sure, is that he's a trout angler and doesn't have much use for any species of fish except trout. I can't argue that Washington's best stream trout fishing is on the upper portions of the Yakima and that the lower part of the river is better known for its smallmouth bass, channel catfish, and other so-called warm-water game fish.

But different doesn't necessarily mean better or worse, and I don't think the lower half of the Yakima River is boring once you learn a little about it.

Many of the gentle riffles and runs along Interstate 82 from Selah Gap to Granger are lined with shady woodlands that shelter it from the sight of nearby farms and croplands and the sound of traffic on the busy highways that parallel it for most of this stretch. The river slows and most of the trees disappear a few miles downstream from Granger, but there's still nothing boring about it; it's just bigger, slower water. The 15-mile stretch of the river between Granger and Mabton, where it's farthest away from the busy interstate to the north, is a long series of oxbows, giving it the feeling of a lazy, southern river, except the vegetation and wildlife along the river is very different and the air much drier. It's a much bigger river when it joins Interstate 82 again near Prosser, but it still has plenty of character, and several gravel bars, boulder patches, and basalt ledges between Prosser and Benton City provide not only good paddling water, but some of the Yakima's best opportunities to catch a large smallmouth bass or two.

From Benton City the river turns north and runs about a dozen miles toward the big corner known as the Horn, where Horn Rapids Dam slows its progress as it turns southeasterly again and heads down the final leg of its journey toward the Columbia, which it joins just south of Richland. Far from boring, the lower half of the Yakima offers boaters perhaps their best opportunity to see the many faces of a Northwest River, one that offers everything: lively paddling and tubing water; slow, warm swimming water; boulder gardens and gravel bars for catching smallmouth bass from a drift boat; and deep, slow channels where a powerboat operator can anchor and cast for catfish. There's nothing boring about a stream that offers all these options.

Location: Flows southeasterly from Yakima into the Columbia south of Richland; map B4, grid f3.

How to get there: Drive east from Yakima or west from Prosser on Interstate 82 or Highway 22 to reach the upper half of this stretch of the Yakima. Interstate 82 parallels the river between Prosser and Benton City. From there downstream access is off Highway 225 out of Benton City and Highway 240 from Richland.

Boat ramp:

- **Harlan Landing:** Starting just north of Yakima, the first launch site on the river is the single-lane concrete ramp at Harlan Landing on the east side of the river at the mouth of the Naches. Take Rest Haven Road off Interstate 82 to reach it.

- **Sarg Hubbard Landing:** Small boats can be hand carried to the west bank of the river at Sarg Hubbard Landing, which is just south of Terrace Heights Drive and east of Interstate 82 in Yakima.

- **Robertson Landing:** North of Highway 24 near Yakima Meadows Racetrack is Robertson Landing, where it's easy to get boats into the river from the east bank.

- **Century Landing:** Also on the east side of the river, near the Interstate 82 bridge at Union Gap, Century Landing has a one-lane concrete ramp.

- **WDFW Ramp #1:** There's another one-lane concrete ramp just south of Union Gap off Mellis Road, this one maintained by the Washington Department of Fish and Wildlife. A $10 Washington Department of Fish and Wildlife access decal is required to use the public launch areas maintained by the WDFW.

- **WDFW Ramp #2:** Next is the natural-surface WDFW ramp off Interstate 82 at the Parker exit a few miles south of Union Gap.

- **WDFW Ramp #3:** Another one-lane concrete ramp managed by WDFW is located on Zillah Road in Zillah at the south end of town.

- **WDFW Ramp#4:** The next ramp is about 14 river miles downstream southwest of Sunnyside. This Department of Wildlife ramp located off South Emerald Road is a one laner with a natural surface that sometimes gets muddy and difficult to use.

- **Sulfur Creek Ramp:** Five miles downstream is the Bureau of Reclamation's Sulfur Creek ramp, located at the end of Midvale Road between Sunnyside and Mabton. This is a steep, rough launch that requires dragging or carrying boats over the bank to the river.

- **Gannon Launch:** Another mile and a half downstream is the Gannon launch site, a one-lane gravel ramp managed by WDFW where trailer boats can be launched. Turn south on Midvale Road in Sunnyside, left on Alexander Road and right on Highway 241, following it about four miles to the river and the ramp.

- **Riverfront Park:** This two-lane concrete ramp in Prosser is managed by the Prosser Parks and Recreation Department.

- **WDFW Ramp #5:** From Prosser it's more than 15 river miles down to the next ramp, a Department of Fish and Wildlife site at Benton City. This natural-surface ramp is in an area of fairly fast current and is best used for hand launching smaller boats. A $10 Washington Department of Fish and Wildlife access decal is required to use the public launch areas maintained by the WDFW.

- **Horn Rapids Ramp:** From Benton City the Yakima turns sharply to the north, running in that direction for about 10 miles before twisting back to the southeast toward Richland. Near that bend in the river is Horn Rapids, site of a two-lane concrete-plank ramp managed by Benton County's Parks and Recreation Department. This is one of the best ramps on the river, and the last one on the Yakima itself.

The lower end of the river is best reached from Tri-Cities-area boat ramps on the Columbia. (See previous listing for Columbia River ramp locations.)

Facilities: Perhaps the best-known facility along the river is the Yakima Greenway Trail in Yakima, one of eastern Washington's best riverside trails for hiking, running, biking, skating, and other recreation. Several parks and playgrounds are scattered along the 10-mile trail throughout Yakima. Picnic areas along the river include those at Harlan Landing, Sarg Hubbard Park, Sherman Park, Robertson Landing, Century Landing, Riverfront Park in Prosser, and Horn Rapids Park. The Yakima KOA campground and Yakima Sportsman State Park both are located near the river. Food, gas, and lodging are available in Yakima, Granger, Sunnyside, Grandview, Prosser, and the Tri-Cities.

Water sports/restrictions: Swimming, rafting, inner tubing, drift boating, fishing, and paddling are popular between Yakima and Prosser; power-boating is more feasible from Prosser downstream.

Contact: Yakima Chamber of Commerce, tel. (509) 248-2021; Chinook Sporting Goods, tel. (509) 452-8205; Yakima Greenway Foundation, tel. (509) 453-8280; Yakima KOA, tel. (509) 248-5882; Yakima Sportsman State Park, tel. (509) 575-2774; Washington State Parks and Recreation

Commission, tel. (800) 233-0321 (information), tel. (800) 452-5687 (reservations); Sunnyside Wildlife Area, tel. (509) 837-7644.

9 Lower Snake River (from the mouth up to Lower Monumental Dam)

Rating: 8

If you're looking for big water and warm weather (at least in the summer), this may be your ultimate boating destination. Although the lower Snake River dams have made life miserable—even impossible—for the river's salmon runs, they created a series of deep, slow reservoirs where swimmers, sailors, tubers, wake-boarders, PWC riders, wind surfers, bass anglers, paddlers, and other water recreations have a great time from early spring through Labor Day and beyond. Corps of Engineers parks and boat ramps along this stretch of river are staging areas for most activities, but it's also possible to load a boat and head upstream or down to destinations at least somewhat away from the crowds. Summertime temperatures in this part of the state often reach well into the 90s, providing ample excuse for getting into the water. While heat stroke is a possibility, a greater danger to boaters are the winds that can come roaring through these canyons with little warning and reach dangerous strength in a matter of minutes. Pay attention to avoid finding yourself in a tough situation, and always have a hiding spot in mind should you be caught a long way from the nearest boat ramp.

Location: Joins the Columbia River southeast of Pasco; map B4, grid g7.

How to get there: Drive east from the Tri-Cities on Highway 124 to reach the lower end of the river. Upstream sections of the river are accessible from the town of Kahlotus by driving south on Highway 260 or Highway 261.

Boat ramp: Upstream from the river mouth on the Walla Walla County (south) side of the river, the first ramp is at the Hood Park Boat Basin, almost under the Highway 12 bridge about a mile from where the Snake joins the Columbia. This U.S. Army Corps of Engineers launch is a single-lane ramp with a loading float. Unless they've done some grading since the last two times I was there, the road to this ramp has about a million chuck holes and bumps; take it easy. Just upstream is the main boat ramp at Hood Park, a three-lane concrete-plank ramp with several loading floats and lots of parking. This is a very good ramp, and suitable for boats of almost any size. About nine miles upstream, above Ice Harbor Dam, is Charbonneau Park, where there's a four-lane concrete ramp with loading floats and lots of parking. It gets lots of use but is protected by a rock jetty and can be used in virtually all water and weather conditions. Seven miles upstream on Lake Sacajawea is Fishhook Park, with its two-lane concrete boat ramp. Ten years ago this was one of the best ramps on the Snake, but it has seen lots of use and is beginning to show its age. Still, you can launch most boats here, and there's plenty of room to park. The next ramp on the south side of the river is some distance upstream, at Matthew, just two miles below Lower Monumental Dam. Like the others mentioned so far, this is a Corps of Engineers facility, with a one-lane concrete ramp, loading float, and parking for about 30 cars and trailers. This steep ramp is protected from wind and rough water by a pair of rock jetties, one upstream and one downstream.

Back to the mouth of the Snake on the Franklin County (north) side, the first ramp is at Sacajawea State Park, located right at the point of land where the Snake meets the Columbia. This two-lane concrete ramp has loading floats and is located in a calm bay where river currents and wind have minimal influence. There's a $4 launch fee here, with a $40 annual permit available from State Parks and Recreation Commission headquarters. Next is the Corps of Engineers ramp just above Ice Harbor Dam, a two-lane concrete ramp with a loading float and lots of room to park in a large gravel lot. Three miles upstream is Levey Park, a Corps of Engineers site with a single-lane concrete-plank ramp and loading float. This park and its boat ramp are closed in the winter. Three miles downstream from Lower Monu-mental Dam is Windust Park, with a less-than-inviting name but a decent two-lane boat ramp. One lane is gravel, the other concrete. There are no loading floats at this Corps of Engineers ramp.

Facilities: There are good swim beaches at Hood Park, Charbonneau Park, Fish-hook Park, Sacajawea State Park, Levey Park, and Windust Park. RV and tent sites for campers are available at Char-bonneau Park, Fishhook Park, Saca-jawea State Park and Windust Park. Food, gas, lodging, marinas, and other facilities are available in Kennewick, Pasco, and Richland.

Contact: Sacajawea State Park, tel. (509) 545-2361; Washington State Parks and Recreation Commission, tel. (800) 233-0321 (information), tel. (800) 452-5687 (reservations); Tri-Cities Visitor and Convention Bureau, tel. (800) 254-5824.

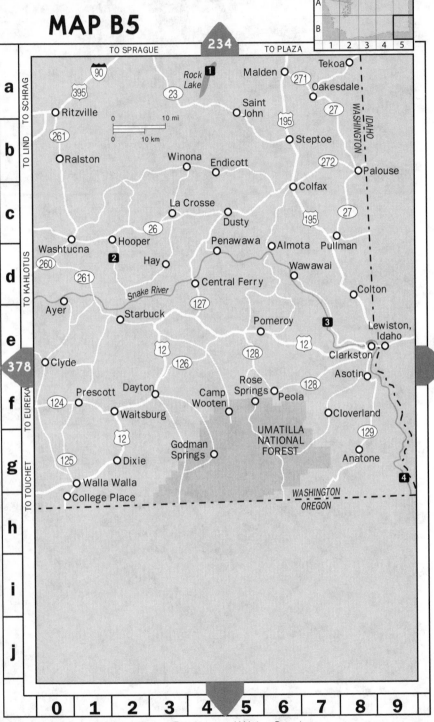

MAP B5

CHAPTER B5

🔳 Rock Lake

Rating: 5

Look around Whitman County for the biggest body of water not directly connected to the Snake River and you'll find Rock Lake every time. At well over 2,100 acres, it's not only the biggest natural lake in Whitman County but the biggest natural lake in all of arid southeastern Washington. You might think that as such it would draw people in by the thousands, but no. Besides being the area's biggest lake, it's also one of the area's most out-of-the-way lakes, located about six miles northwest of St. John and a couple miles north of lightly traveled Highway 23. Not so many people trailer their boats all the way to Rock Lake when the alternative is the sprawling Snake River and its huge impoundments to the south. Another strike against it is that during the summer, when people are looking for clean, cool water to play in and around, Rock Lake becomes dirty, thanks to irrigation runoff that makes its way into the lake from small streams draining many of the region's agricultural lands.

Seven miles long and only a few hundred feet wide, Rock Lake is bordered on both sides by high rock cliffs, an interesting and somewhat eerie setting once you find yourself there. Although much of the lake is very deep, it also has some shallow spots in places you might not expect to find them. The result of not knowing where you're going and what's under you can cost you a shear pin, a lower unit, or your entire boat, so pay attention.

I mentioned some things about Rock Lake in *Washington Fishing* that may be worth mentioning again here. Some of the locals and regular visitors to the lake say that it's haunted by the ghosts of Indians who used to camp near its south end. Others may tell you that a train once derailed and plunged to the bottom of the deep lake, and that sometimes you can still hear the sound of the moaning engine or the wail of its steam whistle rising from the depths. Still another story is that the lake has some kind of resident monster that may decide to have a visiting swimmer or angler for breakfast now and then. I'm not worried about that one, but the wind does catch me off guard here once in a while. This isn't a good place to be caught at the upper end of the canyon when a southerly starts whistling up the lake. Be alert to changing weather and head south for the boat ramp at the first sign of a building breeze.

Location: Northwest of St. John; map B5, grid a4.

How to get there: Take Highway 23 south from Sprague or west from St. John to Ewan and turn north on Rock Lake Road, which leads about three miles to the lake.

Boat ramp: There's a one-lane gravel ramp with a parking area large enough for about 30 cars and trailers at the south end of the lake. It's managed by the State Department of Fish and Wildlife. A $10 Washington Department of Fish and Wildlife access decal is required to use the public launch areas maintained by the WDFW.

Facilities: Food and gas are available in St. John. For lodging you'll have to go to Cheney or Sprague.

Water sports/restrictions: All water sports are permitted.

Contact: Four Seasons Campground, tel. (509) 257-2332; Purple Sage Motel, tel. (509) 257-2507; Sprague Lake Resort, tel. (509) 257-2864; Washington Department of Fish and Wildlife, Spokane regional office, tel. (509) 456-4082.

2 Palouse River

Rating: 6

Although certainly not one of its biggest in terms of volume, the Palouse is one of the Northwest's longest. Its main stem and its north and south forks meander across about 125 miles of southeast Washington real estate from where it enters the state to where it flows into the Snake at Lyons Ferry. Paddlers can enjoy much of the river's length, provided they do it when the opportunity presents itself. Most of it would be a bumpy, bangy, achy-breaky trip during summer, fall, or winter; but for a few weeks in early spring when snowmelt raises the river to about twice its normal flow, paddlers can float much of the Palouse, including the North Fork from the town of Palouse downstream to Colfax without too much fear of banging bottom or spending much time dragging instead of paddling. The river is a fairly gentle one along most of its length, ranging from Class I to Class II water, but there are a couple of notable exceptions. Some of the river from Hooper downstream to Palouse Falls is Class IV whitewater, and should be run only by expert paddlers. And then there's Palouse Falls itself, a spectacular cascade nearly 200 feet tall. It's possible to launch a kayak or canoe at Lyons Ferry and paddle upstream about six miles to the pool at the base of the falls during moderate spring flows. Knowing how impressive the falls is from the safety of the viewing area at Palouse Falls State Park, even during autumn, it must be something else when you're looking at it from near the bottom when the river flow is in the 1,000 cfs range. It's on my to-do list.

Location: Joins the Snake River at Lyons Ferry, Columbia-Walla Walla county line; map B5, grid d2.

How to get there: Take Highway 260 east from Connell and turn south on Highway 261 to reach the lower Palouse and Palouse Falls. The best access to upper portions of the river is provided by the Endicott Road, which is reached by driving west from Colfax about four miles on Highway 26 and turning north on Endicott Road.

Boat ramp: There are places to carry a canoe or kayak to the river off Main Street in Palouse, off Brown Road near Elberton, off Highway 26 just west of Colfax, off Endicott-St. John Road north of Endicott, off Endicott West at Winona, and off Highway 26 and adjoining side roads both east and west of Hooper. There's a two-lane concrete ramp at Lyon's Ferry State Park where the Palouse River joins the Snake. Launching at the park costs $4 round-trip, with a $40 annual permit available from the State Parks and Recreation Commission.

Facilities: Lyons Ferry State Park and Palouse Falls State Park both have tent sites, restrooms, showers, picnic areas, and other amenities. Food, gas, and lodging are available in Colfax.

Water sports/restrictions: Kayaking and canoeing are possible above Palouse Falls; paddling, swimming, waterskiing, and powerboating are options at the mouth of the river.

Contact: Lyons Ferry State Park tel. (509) 646-3252; Palouse Falls State Park, tel. (509) 549-3551; Washington State Parks and Recreation Commission, tel. (800) 233-0321 (information), tel. (800) 452-5687 (reservations); Tiffany's River Inn, tel. (509) 397-3208.

3 Upper Snake River

Rating: 8

This largest tributary to the Columbia offers a wealth of boating and water recreation opportunities. As you can tell from the long list of boat ramps and facilities, there are many places and many ways to get at the Snake and enjoy what it has to offer. Locals flock to some of the more accessible parts of the river on weekends and during the evening hours of summer, but thanks to its location in lightly populated southeastern Washington, much of this huge river is uncrowded, even underutilized throughout much of the year.

If you camp on or near it for a week or two during the summer, you'll be surprised at how much elbow room you have, especially if you're used to spending time on Puget Sound, Lake Washington, and some of the other busy waterways around the Seattle/Tacoma /Everett area. The long, narrow reservoirs of the Snake seem abandoned by comparison, except right around the big state parks and major marinas. You get a little bit of everything if you spend some time investigating this section of the Snake. Much of it is more like one big, continuous lake, thanks to Lower Monumental, Little Goose, and Lower Granite Dams, which back up much of the river between Clarkston and Kahlotus. Here you'll find all the room you could ever want to cruise, sail, paddle, ski, fish, swim, board, tube, dive, ride a PWC, or whatever it is you like to do on the water.

As anywhere on big open water, the main thing to be careful of is the wind, which can turn the normally placid reservoirs into miles of three-foot whitecaps in a matter of minutes. Extreme heat can also be a problem in summer, especially for those of us from the milder western side of the state who are used to getting a cooling rain every few days or so.

South of Clarkston the river gains speed as you move upstream toward world-famous Hells Canyon, and there's no doubt about the change in its personality as you work your way along this stretch of the Washington-Idaho border. Although there are still lots of places to ski, sail, swim, and do all the other things that are popular downstream, moving-water activities begin to prevail. Now you're getting into river-running country, where flat-bottom, aluminum sleds equipped with powerful jet pumps become a lot more common than tradiational, V-bottom craft with props. Steelhead fishing, whitewater paddling, rafting, hunting (in fall), and river touring are the big draws up here, as the steep canyon walls close in on the river even tighter than they did a few miles downstream.

Above Heller Bar and the mouth of the Grande Ronde, the river becomes a place where you had better know what you're doing or be with someone who does; that rule applies whether you're running upstream in a powerboat or paddling downstream in a kayak or raft. As you work your way up toward Hells Canyon, the Snake gets to be more and more a strong, fast river with little mercy for boaters who don't show it appropriate respect. Luckily, there are lots of professional rafting and powerboat outfitters who can take you beyond where your own capabilities fall short, some of them offering day trips into the canyon and others providing multiday adventures that include camping or staying in comfortable lodges along the river.

Location: From Lower Monumental Dam to the Oregon border; map B5, grid e7.

How to get there: Parts of the river are accessible by taking Highway 127 south from the small town of Dusty or north from the even smaller town of Dodge. Highway 261 crosses the river near Lyons Ferry and the mouth of the Palouse River. Highway 263 runs south from Kahlotus to parallel the river beginning at Lower Monumental Dam. Drive west from Pullman on Highway 194 to Almota and that part of the river immediately downstream from Lower Granite Dam. The most accessible part of the Snake in Washington is that section from Clarkston downstream to Wawawai, where the Wawawai River Road parallels the east side of the river for more than 20 miles. Take the Snake River Road south out of Clarkston to drive along the Snake's west bank all the way to the mouth of the Grande Ronde.

Boat ramp: There are 25 boat ramps on this section of the Snake River:

- **Devil's Bench Ramp:** Working upstream from Lower Monumental Dam, there's a U.S. Army Corps of Engineers launch site on the Franklin County (north) side of the river (which is Lake Herbert G. West at this point) at Devil's Bench, just upstream from the dam. It's a two-lane concrete ramp with a loading float and parking for at least 100 cars and trailers. It's reached by turning southeast off Devil's Canyon Road just north of the dam.

- **Ayer Boat Basin:** On the south side of the river about nine miles upstream from the dam is Ayer Boat Basin and a two-lane Corps of Engineers ramp. It's a concrete ramp, good for launching any size boat, and has a loading float. Get there by driving north from Walla Walla on Highway 125 and turning west (left) on Highway 124. Go seven miles and turn right on Ayer Road, following it 25 miles to the boat basin and ramp.

- **Lyons Ferry State Park:** Several miles upstream where the Palouse River enters the Snake from the north is Lyons Ferry State Park, with its two-lane concrete ramp and loading float. The launch fee is $4 here, with an annual permit available for $40 (good at all state parks). The park and its ramp are closed from November 1 through March 31. Drive south from Washtucna on Highway 260/261 about six miles and hang left on Highway 261, following it 12 miles to the park entrance.

- **Lyons Ferry Marina:** This Port of Columbia-operated marina on the south side of the river has a one-lane concrete-plank ramp with a loading dock and parking for several dozen cars and trailers. It has a $4 round-trip launch fee. Take Highway 26 west from Othello to Wahtucna and go south on Highway 260/261 for seven miles, bearing left on Highway 261. Drive 15 miles to Lyons Ferry Road, turn right, and then take another quick right to the marina.

- **Tucannon River Ramp:** Still on the south side of the Snake, at the mouth of the Tucannon River there's another Corps of Engineers ramp used mostly by paddlers and anglers. It's doubtful that a trailer boat can reach the water here, but it's useful for launching kayaks, canoes, and cartop fishing boats. This ramp is actually in the Tucannon, requiring a short trip downstream to reach the Snake. The ramp is alongside Highway 261 three miles northwest of Starbuck.

- **Texas Rapids Recreation Area:** The next ramp is also on the south side of the Snake about four miles downstream from Little Goose Dam at a spot called Texas Rapids. This Corps of Engineers ramp is a concrete single lane, with parking for about 30 cars and trailers. This ramp has a rock jetty near it to protect against wind and water action. Get there by going west from Starbuck on Highway 261 about a mile and turning right on Little Goose Dam Road, following it five miles to the ramp.

• **Riparia Ramp:** The next ramp, located at Riparia on the north side of the river, is a single-lane concrete ramp managed by the Corps of Engineers. As of spring 1999 large deposits of sand and gravel had clogged this ramp to the point that large trailer boats could no longer use it. Take Highway 26 east from Washtucna about 15 miles to Rock Springs Road and turn right. Rock Springs Road changes names a time or two, but stay with it for 15 miles, turning right just beyond the railroad trestle.

• **Little Goose Landing:** The next ramp is a short distance above Little Goose Dam on the south side of the river (now Lake Bryan). It's another Corps of Engineers ramp, one-lane with a loading float and parking for about two dozen cars and trailers. Drive west from Starbuck on Highway 261 about a mile and turn right on Little Goose Dam Road, following it 10 miles to the dam. At the south end of the dam continue east another mile to the ramp.

• **Central Ferry State Park:** The four-lane concrete ramp at Central Ferry State Park is one of the best launch sites on the river. It's on the north side of the Snake off Highway 127. This ramp has loading floats and lots of paved parking, but be careful when trailering a large boat down the ramps here; some of the concrete slabs are buckled and widely spaced. This ramp has a $4 launch fee and an additional fee for overnight parking of cars and trailers.

• **Port of Garfield Ramp:** Upstream and across the river from Central Ferry is a Port of Garfield ramp. In a large bay on the west side of Highway 127, this one-lane concrete ramp has a waterlogged loading float and parking for about 20 cars and trailers.

• **Willow Landing:** Next on the south side of the river is Willow Landing, a Corps of Engineers site with a one-lane concrete ramp and loading float, located in a small cove that offers protection from wind and water action. This is a fairly good ramp, but it sometimes collects sand and gravel that hinders launching larger boats. Drive east from Dayton on U.S. 12 about 22 miles and turn left on Highway 127, following it 9.2 miles. Turn right on Lower Deadman Road and follow it two miles to Hastings Hill Road. Turn left and go five miles to Willows Bar and the ramp.

• **Lambi Creek Campground:** The next ramp is about 15 miles upstream on the south side at Lambi Creek Campground. It's a narrow, concrete ramp that's been falling apart for some time. I wouldn't launch a large boat here unless I thought it was disposable. If you insist, though, drive west from Pullman on Highway 194 to Lower Granite Dam, cross the river, and turn right on Almota Ferry Road, following it four miles to the right turn into the campground.

• **Illia Landing:** The single-lane concrete ramp at Illia Landing just upstream from Lambi Creek is in somewhat better shape. This Corps of Engineers ramp has a loading float and is protected from the wind by a concrete breakwater.

• **Boyer Park:** Next is the Port of Whitman County's Boyer Park on the north side of the river about two miles downstream from Lower Granite Dam. This is a very good, three-lane concrete ramp with loading floats and a fair amount of parking. A marina, campground, restaurant, moorage, and other facilities also are available here. It's just off Highway 194 about 20 miles west of Pullman.

• **Offield Landing:** The next two ramps are a short distance upstream from

Lower Granite Dam, one on either side of the river (Lower Granite Lake). Offield Landing, on the south (Garfield County) side of the river has a one-lane concrete ramp with a float and parking for about a dozen cars and trailers. Drive south from Colfax on Almota Road for about 20 miles to Lower Granite Dam, cross the river, and turn left. Drive one mile before turning left into the ramp area.

- **Wawawai Landing:** On the other side of the river is Wawawai Landing, where the one-lane concrete ramp and loading float are well protected by a concrete breakwater. Drive west from Pullman on Wawawai-Pullman Road about 12 miles and turn right on Wawawai Grad Road, following it six miles to the bottom of the canyon and the ramp. Both Offield and Wawawai are Corps of Engineers facilities.

- **Blyton Landing:** Next is the single-lane concrete-plank ramp at Blyton Landing on the north side of the river. This ramp has a float and is protected by rock breakwaters on both sides. Get there by driving west from Pullman on Wawawai-Pullman Road 12 miles and turning right on Wawawai Grade Road. Go six miles to Wawawai River Road and follow it 12 miles to milepost 22, turning right into the ramp.

- **Nisqually John Landing:** Four miles upstream is the single-lane concrete ramp at Nisqually John Landing. Naturally protected from the elements by its location at the entrance to Nisqually John Canyon, this ramp tends to collect some debris that may sometimes hinder launching. It's a Corps of Engineers ramp. Follow the directions to Blyton Landing but drive to milepost 28.3 to reach Nisqually John.

- **Chief Timothy State Park:** Next is Chief Timothy State Park, located on a large island where U.S. 12 meets the river about 10 miles west of Clarkston. The park has a four-lane concrete ramp with a couple of loading floats and a parking lot for about 40 cars and trailers. Launching here costs $4 round-trip, with a $40 annual permit available from State Parks.

- **Hells Canyon Marina:** This facility at the northwest edge of Clarkston has a good, two-lane concrete ramp and large loading float. Take Highway 128 (15th Street) north from U.S. 12 at the west end of Clarkston and turn left just before crossing Red Wolf Bridge.

- **Greenbelt Ramp:** Managed by the Corps of Engineers, this two-lane concrete ramp has a loading float and lots of paved parking for cars and trailers. There's a $2 round trip launch fee. Follow Bridge Street to the east end of Clarkston and turn left on Fifth Street. Drive one block on Fifth and turn right on Fair Street, following it to the park.

- **Swallows Park:** At the south end of Clarkston is Swallows Park, with a very good four-lane concrete ramp and several loading floats. Maintained by the Corps of Engineers, this is another site where a $2 launch fee is charged. To find it, drive south out of Clarkston on Highway 129 about two miles, and you'll see the park and ramp on the left.

- **Chief Looking Glass Park:** Three miles farther upstream (south) at the town of Asotin is Chief Looking Glass Park, managed by the Asotin Parks and Recreation Department. This is a good ramp, with two concrete lanes and a loading float, with lots of paved parking. Highway 129 out of Clarkston goes right past it.

- **Asotin Slough Ramp:** About a mile upstream is the Corps of Engineers' Asotin Slough Ramp, a one-lane ramp that sometimes gets large accumulations of silt to foul things up for boaters. It's just off Second Street in Asotin.

- **Heller Bar:** It's about 20 miles upstream to the next ramp, the two-lane concrete-plank ramp at Heller Bar near the mouth of the Grande Ronde River. There's parking for about 50 cars and trailers at this site, which is managed by the Bureau of Land Management. Get there by driving south from Asotin on Snake River Road about 22 miles.

Facilities: The Port of Columbia's Lyons Ferry Marina has both open and covered moorage, electrical hookups, boat-sewage pump-out facilities, a fuel dock, showers, boat repair, groceries, and a restaurant. Lyons Ferry State Park at the confluence of the Palouse and Snake Rivers, has 49 campsites, restrooms, showers, and a good swim beach. Central Ferry State Park just off Highway 127 has 60 tent and RV sites with electrical and water hookups, showers, picnic areas, boat-sewage pump-out facilities and a swim beach. Boyer Park and Marina has open moorage ($5 minimum moorage fee), boat-sewage pump-out facilities, showers, a fuel dock, grocery store, restaurant, RV sites, picnic shelters and tables, motel rooms, and a large swim beach. Chief Timothy State Park, off U.S. 12 west of Clarkston, has 33 tent sites and 31 RV sites with hookups, restrooms and showers, boat-sewage pump-out facilities, along with a long expanse of swim beach and river frontage. It even has some RV sites on the south side with their own moorage docks. Hells Canyon Marina has open moorage ($5 daily minimum), sewage pump-out facilities, electrical hookup, fuel dock, boat repair, a grocery store, and a restaurant. There are large swim beaches at Swallows Park in Clarkston and Chief Looking Glass Park in Asotin. It's OK to camp at Heller Bar for a maximum of two weeks; fuel and a restaurant are also available at Heller. Food, gas, lodging, river outfitters, and other facilities are available in Clarkston. Beamer's Hells Canyon Tours & Excursions has been running trips into hells Canyon for decades.

Water sports/restrictions: All water sports are permitted.

Contact: Lyons Ferry Marina, tel. (509) 399-2001; Boyer Marina, tel. (509) 397-3208; Hells Canyon Marina/Resort, tel. (509) 758-6963; Lyons Ferry State Park, tel. (509) 646-3252; Central Ferry State Park, tel. (509) 549-3551; Chief Timothy State Park, tel. (509) 758-9580; Washington State Parks and Recreation Commission, tel. (800) 233-0321 (information), tel. (800) 452-5687 (reservations); Beamer's Hells Canyon Tours & Excursions, tel. (800) 522-6966; U.S. Army Corps of Engineers, Walla Walla District, tel. (509) 527-7424, Clarkston District, tel. (509) 751-0240.

4 Grande Ronde River

Rating: 7

This extremely pretty river in some of Washington's most dramatic and scenic country requires considerable effort to boat. It's not so much that it's a tough boating river, but much of it is roadless, so you have to do your homework and your roadwork if you want to explore it. The stretch west (upstream) from the Highway 129 bridge offers the best bank access via Grande Ronde River Road, which parallels its north shore. Some boaters float this stretch by launching in Troy, Oregon, and paddling down to one of the boat ramps near the bridge. You have to work harder to float the stretch downstream from Highway 129. It's nearly 20 miles from the bridge to the mouth of the river at Heller Bar, with no good options for taking out before you reach that destination. Much of it is Class II water, but at a spot known as the

Narrows, where the Grande Ronde is constricted between rock walls only a few feet wide, things get very interesting. The waves and haystacks here are of Class III proportion, Class IV when the river is running high.

The Narrows is about five miles upstream from the take-out site, discouraging a lot of folks from even attempting this run. Also discouraging are the logistics of spotting vehicles for this trip. Unless you have good friends at Heller Bar, plan on launching at the Highway 129 bridge, driving north about 30 miles to Asotin or nearly as far on Montgomery Ridge Road to the Snake, then south again, up the Snake to the mouth of the Grande Ronde. Any way you cut it, it's nearly two hours each way. Those who make the trip, however, soon forget about the long drive, because floating the Grande Ronde is like being on a miniature version of Oregon's Deschutes or maybe even a mini-Hells Canyon with gentler water. The canyon walls are spectacular, wildlife is abundant, and the river is sparkling clean and cool. Although you might meet other people who are on the river for the sake of just being there, you're more likely to encounter anglers here, as this is a popular steelhead-fishing spot. In the fall, some hunters take to the river to pursue mule deer, chukar partridge, and other game.

Location: Joins the Snake River near the southeastern corner of the state; map B5, grid h9.

How to get there: Take Highway 129 south from Clarkston. The highway crosses the river about three miles from the Oregon border, and Grande Ronde Road parallels the north side of the river for several miles west of the bridge. To reach the lower few miles of the river, drive south out of Clarkston on Highway 129 to Asotin; then follow the Snake River Road along the Snake to the mouth of the Grande Ronde.

Boat ramp: The only ramp for the lower end of the Grande Ronde is at Heller Bar, near where the river flows into the Snake. This two-lane concrete ramp operated by the Bureau of Land Management has a large parking area. There are two ramps near the south end of the Highway 129 bridge over the Grande Ronde. On the upstream (west) side is a single-lane gravel ramp managed by the Department of Fish and Wildlife. On the east side of the road is another gravel ramp, located at a State Department of Transportation gravel pit. Both ramps are rough and best suited to launching small trailer boats or cartoppers. A $10 Washington Department of Fish and Wildlife access decal is required to use the public launch areas maintained by the WDFW.

Facilities: Fields Spring State Park a few miles north of the river on Highway 129 has a limited number of tent sites. There's a river-accessible restaurant at Heller Bar near the mouth of the Grande Ronde. Camping is allowed for a maximum of 14 days at the BLM access area and boat ramp at Heller Bar.

Water sports/restrictions: Fishing and paddling are the main attractions

Contact: Fields Spring State Park, tel. (509) 256-3332; Washington State Parks and Recreation Commission, tel. (800) 233-0321 (information), tel. (800) 452-5687 (reservations); Washington Department of Fish and Wildlife, Spokane regional office, tel. (509) 456-4082.

INDEX

BOAT AND ADVENTURE TRAVEL OUTFITTERS

COUNTY AND CITY PARKS

LAWS AND REGULATIONS

STATE PARKS

ABOUT THE AUTHOR

A lifelong Northwesterner, Terry Rudnick has explored the waterways and woods of the Evergreen State since he was old enough to find his way around. He has been writing about fishing, hunting, boating, camping, bird dogs, and other outdoor subjects since 1971, and his feature articles, columns, and photos have appeared in more than 30 magazines and newspapers. His seminars and slide shows on fishing and other outdoor activities also are in demand, and he has been a featured speaker at over 40 sports and boating trade shows throughout the West. He also speaks regularly to fishing, boating, and civic organizations. His dozens of writing and photography awards include National Conservationist of the Year in Communications (1990) from Trout Unlimited.

Rudnick is also the author of *Washington Fishing*, now in its third edition, and co-author of *How to Catch Trophy Halibut*.

FOGHORN ⚓ OUTDOORS

Founded in 1985, Foghorn Press has quickly become one of the country's premier publishers of outdoor recreation guidebooks. Foghorn Press books are available throughout the United States in bookstores and some outdoor retailers.

101 Great Hikes of the San Francisco Bay Area, 1st ed.	1-57354-068-4	$15.95
Alaska Fishing, 2nd ed.	0-935701-51-6	$20.95
America's Wilderness, 1st ed.	0-935701-47-8	$19.95
Arizona and New Mexico Camping, 3rd ed.	1-57354-044-7	$18.95
Atlanta Dog Lover's Companion, 1st ed.	1-57354-008-0	$17.95
Baja Camping, 3rd ed.	1-57354-069-2	$14.95
Bay Area Dog Lover's Companion, 3rd ed.	1-57354-039-0	$17.95
Boston Dog Lover's Companion, 2nd ed.	1-57354-074-9	$17.95
California Beaches, 2nd ed.	1-57354-060-9	$19.95
California Camping, 11th ed.	1-57354-053-6	$20.95
California Dog Lover's Companion, 3rd ed.	1-57354-046-3	$20.95
California Fishing, 5th ed.	1-57354-052-8	$20.95
California Golf, 9th ed.	1-57354-091-9	$24.95
California Hiking, 4th ed.	1-57354-056-0	$20.95
California Recreational Lakes and Rivers, 2nd ed.	1-57354-065-x	$19.95
California Waterfalls, 2nd ed.	1-57354-070-6	$17.95
California Wildlife: The Complete Guide, 1st ed.	1-57354-087-0	$16.95
Camper's Companion, 3rd ed.	1-57354-000-5	$15.95
Colorado Camping, 2nd ed.	1-57354-085-4	$18.95
Day-Hiking California's National Parks, 1st ed.	1-57354-055-2	$18.95
Easy Biking in Northern California, 2nd ed.	1-57354-061-7	$12.95
Easy Camping in Northern California, 2nd ed.	1-57354-064-1	$12.95
Easy Camping in Southern California, 1st ed.	1-57354-004-8	$12.95
Easy Hiking in Northern California, 2nd ed.	1-57354-062-5	$12.95
Easy Hiking in Southern California, 1st ed.	1-57354-006-4	$12.95
Florida Beaches, 1st ed.	1-57354-054-4	$19.95
Florida Camping, 1st ed.	1-57354-018-8	$20.95
Florida Dog Lover's Companion, 2nd ed.	1-57354-042-0	$20.95
Montana, Wyoming and Idaho Camping, 1st ed.	1-57354-086-2	$18.95
New England Camping, 2nd ed.	1-57354-058-7	$19.95
New England Hiking, 2nd ed.	1-57354-057-9	$18.95
Outdoor Getaway Guide: Southern CA, 1st ed.	1-57354-011-0	$14.95
Pacific Northwest Camping, 7th ed.	1-57354-080-3	$19.95
Pacific Northwest Hiking, 3rd ed.	1-57354-059-5	$20.95
Seattle Dog Lover's Companion, 1st ed.	1-57354-002-1	$17.95
Tahoe, 2nd ed.	1-57354-024-2	$20.95
Texas Dog Lover's Companion, 1st ed.	1-57354-045-5	$20.95
Texas Handbook, 4th ed.	1-56691-112-5	$18.95
Tom Stienstra's Outdoor Getaway Guide: No. CA, 3rd ed.	1-57354-038-2	$18.95
Utah and Nevada Camping, 1st ed.	1-57354-012-9	$18.95
Utah Hiking, 1st ed.	1-57354-043-9	$15.95
Washington Boating and Water Sports, 1st ed.	1-57354-071-4	$19.95
Washington Fishing, 3rd ed.	1-57354-084-6	$18.95
Washington, DC-Baltimore Dog Lover's Companion, 1st ed.	1-57354-041-2	$17.95

For more information, call 1-800-FOGHORN
email: info@travelmatters.com
or write to: Avalon Travel Publishing, Foghorn Outdoors
5855 Beaudry St., Emeryville, CA 94608

CHAPTER REFERENCE MAPS

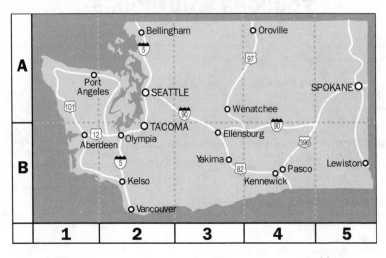